SOCIAL ETHICS

Morality and Social Policy

SEVENTH EDITION

Thomas A. Mappes

Frostburg State University

Jane S. Zembaty

University of Dayton

Boston   Burr Ridge, IL   Dubuque, IA   Madison, WI   New York
San Francisco   St. Louis   Bangkok   Bogotá   Caracas   Kuala Lumpur
Lisbon   London   Madrid   Mexico City   Milan   Montreal   New Delhi
Santiago   Seoul   Singapore   Sydney   Taipei   Toronto

Higher Education

SOCIAL ETHICS: MORALITY AND SOCIAL POLICY, SEVENTH EDITION

Published by McGraw-Hill, an imprint of The McGraw-Hill Companies, Inc., 1221 Avenue of the Americas, New York, NY 10020. Copyright © 2007, 2002, 1997, 1992, 1987, 1982, 1977 by the McGraw-Hill Companies, Inc. All rights reserved. No part of this publication may be reproduced or distributed in any form or by any means, or stored in a database or retrieval system, without the prior written consent of The McGraw-Hill Companies, Inc., including, but not limited to, in any network or other electronic storage or transmission, or broadcast for distance learning.

This book is printed on acid-free paper.

2 3 4 5 6 7 8 9 0 QPF/QPF 0 9 8 7 6

ISBN-13: 978-0-07-312545-9
ISBN-10: 0-07-312545-8

Editor in Chief: *Emily Barrosse*
Publisher: *Lyn Uhl*
Senior Sponsoring Editor: *Jon-David Hague*
Development Editor: *Nadia Bidwell, Barking Dog Editorial*
Project Manager: *Melanie Field, Strawberry Field Publishing*
Manuscript Editor: *Jennifer Gordon*
Interior Designer: *Brad Greene*
Senior Production Supervisor: *Tandra Jorgensen*

Cover: *Paul Klee, Architectur m. d. Fenster, 1919, 157.* Architecture with window, oil and pen on paper on wooden panel. 50 × 41.5 cm. © Zentrum Paul Klee, Bern

This book was set in 10.5/12 Times by ITC, India, and printed on 45# New Era Matte by Quebecor World, Fairfield.

Library of Congress Cataloging-in-Publication Data

Mappes, Thomas A.
  Social ethics: morality and social policy / Thomas A. Mappes, Jane S. Zembaty.—7th ed.
    p. cm.
  Includes bibliographical references.
  ISBN 0-07-312545-8
  1. Social class. 2. United States—Social policy. 3. United States—Moral conditions. I. Title.
  Sports sciences. I. Title

HM665.M27   2007
170—dc21   2006045643

www.mhhe.com

About the Authors

Thomas A. Mappes, Professor of Philosophy at Frostburg State University, is the coeditor (with David DeGrazia) of *Biomedical Ethics* (McGraw-Hill, 6th ed., 2006). He is the author of several articles, including "Persistent Vegetative State, Prospective Thinking, and Advance Directives" and (with Jane S. Zembaty) "Patient Choices, Family Interests, and Physician Obligations."

Jane S. Zembaty, Professor Emerita of Philosophy at the University of Dayton, continues to work in social ethics. She coedited the first three editions of *Biomedical Ethics,* and her published work includes articles on Greek philosophy, such as "Plato's *Republic* and Greek Morality on Lying" and "Aristotle on Lying."

*To Vera Mappes—whose presence always
makes the world a kinder and better place*

To Kay, Casey, and Terry—lifelong friends

Contents

PART TWO: LIBERTY ISSUES

CHAPTER 6   DRUG CONTROL AND ADDICTION   272

CHAPTER 7   TERRORISM, HUMAN RIGHTS, AND CIVIL LIBERTIES   316

PART THREE: JUSTICE ISSUES

CHAPTER 8   SOCIAL AND ECONOMIC JUSTICE   371

CHAPTER 9   WORLD HUNGER AND POVERTY   430

PART FOUR: PLANETARY ISSUES

CHAPTER 10   ANIMALS   478

CHAPTER 11   THE ENVIRONMENT   521

Preface

Is physician-assisted suicide a morally defensible practice? Is the death penalty a morally acceptable type of punishment? Is society justified in enacting laws that limit the access of consenting adults to pornographic materials? Is society justified in enacting laws that prohibit the sale and use of drugs such as marijuana and cocaine? Do more affluent individuals and countries have a moral obligation to eliminate starvation and malnutrition among the needy? Is the interest of human beings in eating meat sufficient to justify the way in which we raise and slaughter animals?

The answers we give to such moral questions and the social policies we adopt in keeping with our answers will directly affect our lives. It is not surprising, therefore, that discussions of these and other contemporary moral issues often involve rhetorical arguments whose intent is to elicit highly emotional, unreflective responses. This book is designed to provide material that will encourage reflective and critical examination of some contemporary moral problems. To achieve this end, we have developed chapters that bring the central issues into clear focus, while allowing the supporting arguments for widely diverse positions to be presented by those who embrace them. We have also tried to provide readings that are free of unnecessary technical jargon and yet introduce serious moral argumentation.

NEW TO THE SEVENTH EDITION

In this seventh edition, we have introduced one entirely new chapter, "Terrorism, Human Rights, and Civil Liberties," designed to address a topic of compelling contemporary importance. We have also transformed the former sexual morality chapter into a chapter entitled "Sex and Marriage," allowing us to combine four new selections on the topic of same-sex marriage with previously included material on the topic of sexual morality. In the world hunger and poverty chapter, we have added four new selections. One focuses attention on the realities of extreme poverty and international responses to it. The other three are dedicated to a consideration of a previously unexplored topic: the ethical issues associated with the existence of international sweatshops.

There are no structural changes in the other chapters, but we have added a number of important new readings. The abortion chapter includes two new selections— one presenting a somewhat distinctive moderate approach that also reflects a feminist consciousness and the other offering an analysis of the United States Supreme Court decision on "partial-birth abortion" in *Stenberg v. Carhart* (2000). The death penalty chapter includes a new selection offering an analysis of procedural arguments against the death penalty. The chapter on pornography and hate speech now includes a legal opinion from a 1995 case in which the Stanford hate-speech code was found to be unconstitutional. The drug chapter contains a new selection defending the legitimacy of paternalistic restrictions, and the social and economic justice chapter now includes a selection that emphasizes the importance of gender equity and calls for a new vision of the welfare state.

ORGANIZATION OF THIS TEXT

The various chapters of *Social Ethics* have always fallen into certain natural groupings, but in this seventh edition we have highlighted these natural groupings by displaying the chapters within the framework of an overall part structure. Chapters 1 through 3 fall unambiguously into the category of "Life-and-Death Issues," now identified as Part One of the book. Chapters 4 through 7 are organized under the heading "Liberty Issues." Chapters 5 and 6 fall neatly into place under this Part Two heading. The issues under examination in Chapters 4 and 7, however, cannot be completely assimilated to the category of liberty issues. In Chapter 4, the discussion of same-sex marriage can easily be understood as focusing on a liberty issue— whether same-sex couples should be free to marry—whereas the same is not true of the discussion of sexual morality. In Chapter 7, the discussion of civil liberties associated with the effort to combat terrorism clearly raises liberty issues whereas the earlier discussion in that chapter of the morality of terrorism does not have such an overt liberty-issue dimension. Chapters 8 and 9 naturally fall under the Part Three heading "Justice Issues," the former chapter focusing on matters of justice internal to a society and the latter chapter focusing on the dimension of international justice. Chapters 10 and 11, where concern is focused on animals and the environment, naturally fall under the Part Four heading "Planetary Issues." Although these part headings now make clear how the various chapters fall into certain natural groupings, it remains true, as always, that each individual chapter can be approached as a self-contained entity.

PEDAGOGICAL FEATURES

We are confident that *teachability* will continue to be the most salient characteristic of *Social Ethics*. Various editorial features employed in earlier editions to enhance teachability have been retained in the seventh. An introduction to each chapter both sets the ethical issues and scans the various positions together with their supporting argumentation. Every selection is prefaced by a short statement of some of the key points or arguments to be found in the selection. Every selection is followed by questions whose purpose is to elicit further critical analysis and discussion. Finally, each chapter concludes with a short annotated bibliography designed to guide the reader in further research.

LEGAL OPINIONS

In order to emphasize the connection of contemporary moral problems with matters of social policy, we have liberally incorporated relevant legal opinions. We have taken substantial editorial license by deleting almost all of the numerous citations that usually attend legal writing in order to render the legal opinions maximally readable to the nonlegal eye. Those interested in further legal research can check the appropriate credit lines for the necessary bibliographical data to locate the cases in their original form. We should also note that, where appropriate, both in legal cases and in other readings, we have renumbered footnotes.

ACKNOWLEDGMENTS

We wish to thank Frostburg State University and the University of Dayton for their ongoing support of this project. In particular, we wish to thank the reference librarians and other helpful library personnel at our two universities. We are indebted, of course, to all those whose work is reprinted in these pages. We are also indebted to Joy Kroeger-Mappes, Marilyn Fischer, and Mark Wicclair for their valuable suggestions and advice over many editions of this book; to Jean-Marie Makang, Skott Brill, Frank Fleckenstein, Gene Gall, and David DeGrazia, who have also furnished us with valuable counsel; and to the following reviewers who have provided us with very useful reactions and suggestions: Luis Cabrera, Arizona State University; David Hildebrand, University of Colorado; Regina Hobaugh, Holy Family University; Ed Sherline, University of Wyoming; Bonnie Tilson, Durham Technical Community College.

We are especially grateful to Nadia Bidwell at Barking Dog Editorial and Jon-David Hague and Lisa Pinto at McGraw-Hill for their consistent responsiveness to our needs and concerns. Finally, we must express our thanks to Shelley Dress and Linda McKinley for their valuable help with manuscript preparation and to Brandy Ritchie and Molly Ness for their very capable assistance in proofreading. We are also very grateful to Jennifer Gordon for her exemplary work as copy editor and to Melanie Field at Strawberry Field Publishing for so capably guiding this edition through the production process.

Thomas A. Mappes
Jane S. Zembaty

CHAPTER 1

Abortion

The primary concern in this chapter is the issue of the ethical (moral) acceptability of abortion. Some attention is also given to the social-policy aspects of abortion, especially in conjunction with decisions made by the United States Supreme Court.

ABORTION: THE ETHICAL ISSUE

Discussions of the ethical acceptability of abortion often take for granted (1) an awareness of the various reasons that may be given for having an abortion and (2) a basic acquaintance with the biological development of a human fetus.

1 Reasons for Abortion

Why would a woman have an abortion? The following catalog, not meant to provide an exhaustive survey, is sufficient to indicate that there is a wide range of potential reasons.

   a. In certain extreme cases, if the fetus is allowed to develop normally and come to term, the pregnant woman herself will die.
   b. In other cases it is not the woman's life but her health, physical or mental, that will be severely endangered if the pregnancy is allowed to continue.
   c. There are also cases in which the pregnancy will probably, or surely, produce a severely impaired child.
   d. There are others in which the pregnancy is the result of rape or incest.[1]
   e. There are instances in which the pregnant woman is unmarried, and there will be the social stigma of illegitimacy.
   f. There are other instances in which having a child, or having another child, will be an unbearable financial burden.

---

[1]The expression *therapeutic abortion* suggests abortion for medical reasons. Accordingly, abortions corresponding to reasons (a), (b), and (c) are usually said to be therapeutic. More problematically, abortions corresponding to reason (d) have often been identified as therapeutic. Because pregnancies resulting from rape or incest are typically traumatic, perhaps it is presumed that such pregnancies are a threat to mental health. Alternatively, perhaps calling such an abortion "therapeutic" is just a way of indicating that it is thought to be justifiable.

g. Certainly common, and perhaps most common of all, are those instances in which having a child will interfere with the happiness of the woman, the joint happiness of the couple, of even the joint happiness of a family unit that already includes children. There are almost endless possibilities in this final category. The woman may desire a professional career. A couple may be content and happy together and feel their relationship would be damaged by the intrusion of a child. Parents may have older children and not feel up to raising another child, and so forth.

2   The Biological Development of a Human Fetus

During the course of a human pregnancy, in the nine-month period from conception to birth, the entity resulting from conception undergoes a continual process of change and development. *Conception* takes place when a male germ cell (the spermatozoon) combines with a female germ cell (the ovum), resulting in a single cell (the single cell zygote), which embodies the full genetic code, twenty-three pairs of chromosomes. The single-cell zygote—also commonly identified as a newly formed *embryo*—soon begins a process of cellular division. While continuing to grow and beginning to take shape, the embryo moves through the fallopian tube and then undergoes gradual *implantation* at the uterine wall. The process of implantation is complete about eight to ten days after conception. The embryonic period continues until the end of the eighth week, and it is during this period—subsequent to implantation—that organ systems and other recognizably human characteristics begin to undergo noticeable development; in particular, rudimentary electrical activity in the brain may be detectable as early as the end of the sixth week. From the end of the eighth week until birth, the developing entity is formally designated a fetus. (The term *fetus,* however, is commonly used as a general term to designate the developing entity, whatever its stage of development.) Two other points in the development of the fetus are especially noteworthy as relevant to discussions of abortion, but these points are usually identified by reference to gestational age as calculated not from conception but from the first day of the woman's last menstrual period. Accordingly, somewhere around the sixteenth to the eighteenth week there usually occurs *quickening,* the point at which the woman begins to feel the movements of the fetus. And somewhere around the twenty-second week, *viability* becomes a realistic possibility. Viability is the point at which the fetus is capable of surviving outside the womb.

With the facts of fetal development in clear view, it may be helpful to describe the various abortion procedures. First-trimester abortions were at one time performed by *dilation and curettage* (D&C), but that procedure was essentially replaced in the 1970s by *vacuum aspiration,* often referred to as "suction abortion." D&C involves the stretching (dilation) of the cervix and the scraping (curettage) of the inner walls of the uterus. In vacuum aspiration, the fetus is sucked out of the uterus by means of a tube connected to a suction pump. Although standard vacuum aspiration cannot effectively be performed prior to about two months after a pregnant woman's last period, a related technique—*manual vacuum aspiration* (MVA)—now provides the possibility of much earlier surgical abortion. In MVA, ultrasound is used to locate the tiny (smaller than a pea) gestational sac, which is then removed with a handheld vacuum syringe. The use of RU-486, a chemical method for the termination of early pregnancies, is discussed later in this introduction.

Abortions beyond the first trimester require procedures such as *dilation and evacuation* (D&E), *induction techniques,* or *hysterotomy.* In D&E, which is the procedure most commonly used for second-trimester abortions, a forceps is used to dismember the fetus within the uterus; the fetal remains are then withdrawn through the cervix. In one notable induction technique, a saline solution injected into the amniotic cavity induces labor, thereby expelling the fetus. Another important induction technique uses prostaglandins (hormonelike substances) to induce labor. Hysterotomy—in essence, a miniature cesarean section—is a major surgical procedure and is not commonly used in the United States.

A brief discussion of fetal development, together with a cursory survey of various reasons for abortion, has prepared the way for a formulation of the ethical issue of abortion in its broadest terms. *Up to what point of fetal development, if any, and for what reasons, if any, is abortion ethically acceptable?* Some hold that abortion is *never* ethically acceptable, or at most that it is acceptable only when necessary to save the life of the pregnant woman. This view is frequently termed the *conservative* view on abortion. Others hold that abortion is *always* ethically acceptable—at any point of fetal development and for any of the standard reasons. This view is frequently termed the *liberal* view on abortion. Still others are anxious to defend perspectives that are termed *moderate* views, holding that abortion is ethically acceptable up to a certain point of fetal development *and/or* holding that some reasons provide a sufficient justification for abortion, whereas others do not.

THE CONSERVATIVE VIEW AND THE LIBERAL VIEW

The *moral status* of the fetus has been a pivotal issue in discussions of the ethical acceptability of abortion. To say that the fetus has full moral status is to say that it is entitled to the same degree of moral consideration deserved by more fully developed human beings, such as the writer and the reader of these words. Assigning full moral status to the fetus entails, in particular, that the fetus has a right to life that must be taken as seriously as the right to life of any other human being. On the other hand, to say that the fetus has no significant moral status is to say that it has no rights worth mentioning. In particular, it does not possess a significant right to life. Conservatives typically claim that the fetus has full moral status, and liberals typically claim that the fetus has no significant moral status. (Some moderates argue that the fetus has a subsidiary or *partial* moral status.) Since the fetus has no significant moral status, the liberal is prone to argue, it has no more right to life than a piece of tissue, such as an appendix, and an abortion is no more morally objectionable than an appendectomy. Since the fetus has full moral status, the conservative is prone to argue, its right to life must be respected with the utmost seriousness, and an abortion, except perhaps to save the life of a pregnant woman, is as morally objectionable as any other murder.

Discussions of the moral status of the fetus often refer directly to the biological development of the fetus and pose the question: At what point in the continuous development of the fetus does a human life exist? In the context of such discussions, *human* implies full moral status, *nonhuman* implies no significant moral status, and any notion of partial moral status is systematically excluded. To distinguish the human from the nonhuman, to "draw the line," and to do so in a nonarbitrary way, is the central matter of concern. A conservative on abortion typically holds that the line must be drawn at conception. Usually the conservative argues that conception is the only point at which the line can be nonarbitrarily drawn. Against attempts to draw the line at points such as implantation, quickening, viability, and birth, considerations of continuity in the development of the fetus are pressed. The conservative argues that a line cannot be drawn securely anywhere along the path of fetal development. It is said that the line will inescapably slide back to the point of conception in order to find objective support—by reference to the fact that the full genetic code is present subsequent to conception, whereas it is not present prior to conception.

With regard to drawing the line, a liberal typically contends that the fetus remains nonhuman even in its most advanced stages of development. The liberal, of course, does not mean to deny that a fetus is biologically a human fetus. Rather, the claim is that the fetus is not human in any morally significant sense—that is, the fetus has no significant moral status. This point is often made in terms of the concept of personhood. Mary Anne Warren, who defends the liberal view on abortion in one of this chapter's selections, argues that the fetus is not a person. She also contends that the fetus bears so little resemblance to a person that it cannot be said to have a significant right to life. It is important to notice, as Warren analyzes the concept of personhood, that even a newborn baby is not a person. This conclusion, as might be expected, prompts Warren to a consideration of the moral justifiability of infanticide, an issue closely related to the problem of abortion.

Although the conservative view on abortion is most commonly predicated on the straightforward contention that the fetus is a person from conception, there are at least two other lines of argument that have been advanced in its defense. One conservative, advancing what might be labeled "the presumption argument," writes:

> In being willing to kill the embryo, we accept responsibility for killing what we must admit *may* be a person. There is some reason to believe it is—namely the *fact* that it is a living, human individual and the inconclusiveness of arguments that try to exclude it from the protected circle of personhood.
> *To be willing to kill what for all we know could be a person is to be willing to kill it if it is a person.* And since we cannot absolutely settle if it is a person except by a metaphysical postulate, for all practical purposes we must hold that to be willing to kill the embryo is to be willing to kill a person.[2]

In accordance with this line of argument, although it may not be possible to show conclusively that the fetus is a person from conception, we must presume that it is. Another line of argument that has been advanced by some conservatives emphasizes the potential rather than the actual personhood of the fetus. Even if the fetus is not a person, it is said, there can be no doubt that it is a potential person. Accordingly,

[2]Germain Grisez, *Abortion: The Myths, the Realities, and the Arguments* (New York: Corpus Books, 1970), p. 306.

by virtue of its potential personhood, the fetus must be accorded a right to life. Warren, in response to this line of argument, argues that the potential personhood of the fetus provides no basis for the claim that it has a significant right to life.

The Roman Catholic church is a very prominent proponent of the conservative view on abortion. In this chapter's first reading, Pope John Paul II gives voice to the Catholic tradition on the issue of abortion. In another reading in this chapter, Don Marquis argues for a very conservative view on abortion, but he does not argue for what is commonly referred to as "the" conservative view on abortion. Whereas the standard conservative (such as John Paul II) is committed to a "sanctity-of-life" viewpoint, according to which the lives of all biologically human beings (assuming their moral innocence) are considered immune from attack, Marquis bases his opposition to abortion on a distinctive theory about the wrongness of killing. Although Marquis claims that there is a strong moral presumption against abortion, and although he clearly believes that the vast majority of abortions are seriously immoral, he is not committed to the standard conservative contention that the only possible exception is the case in which abortion is necessary to save the life of the pregnant woman.

MODERATE VIEWS

The conservative and liberal views, as explicated, constitute two extreme poles on the spectrum of ethical views on abortion. Each of the extreme views is marked by a formal simplicity. The conservative proclaims abortion to be immoral, irrespective of the stage of fetal development and irrespective of alleged justifying reasons. The one exception, admitted by some conservatives, is the case in which abortion is necessary to save the life of the pregnant woman. The liberal proclaims abortion to be morally acceptable, irrespective of the stage of fetal development.[3] Moreover, there is no need to draw distinctions between those reasons that are sufficient to justify abortion and those that are not. No justification is needed. The moderate, in vivid contrast to both the conservative and the liberal, is unwilling either to condemn or to condone abortion in sweeping terms. Some abortions are morally justifiable; some are morally objectionable. In some moderate views, the stage of fetal development is a relevant factor in assessing the moral acceptability of abortion. In other moderate views, the alleged justifying reason is a relevant factor in assessing the moral acceptability of abortion. In still other moderate views, both the stage of fetal development and the alleged justifying reason are relevant factors in assessing the moral acceptability of abortion.

Moderate views have been developed in accordance with the following, clearly identifiable strategies.

---

[3]In considering the liberal contention that abortions are morally acceptable irrespective of the stage of fetal development, we should take note of an ambiguity in the concept of abortion. Does *abortion* refer merely to the termination of a pregnancy in the sense of detaching the fetus from the pregnant woman, or does *abortion* entail the death of the fetus as well? Whereas the abortion of a *previable* fetus entails its death, the "abortion" of a *viable* fetus—at least, by means of hysterotomy (a miniature cesarean section)—does not entail the death of the fetus and would seem to be tantamount to the birth of a baby. With regard to the "abortion" of a *viable* fetus, liberals can defend the woman's right to detach the fetus from her body without contending that the woman has the right to insist on the death of the child.

1 Moderation of the Conservative View

One strategy for generating a moderate view presumes the typical conservative contention that the fetus is a person (i.e., has full moral status) from conception. What is denied, however, is that we must conclude to the moral impermissibility of abortion in *all* or nearly all cases. In a widely discussed article reprinted in this chapter, Judith Jarvis Thomson attempts to moderate the conservative view in just this way. For Thomson, even if it is presumed that the fetus is a person from conception, abortion is morally justified in a significant range of cases.

2 Moderation of the Liberal View

A second strategy for generating a moderate view presumes the liberal contention that the fetus has no significant moral status, even in the latest stages of pregnancy. What is denied, however, is that we must conclude to the moral permissibility of abortion in *all* cases. It might be said, in accordance with this line of thought, that abortion, even though it does not violate the rights of the fetus (which is presumed to have no rights), remains ethically problematic to the extent that negative social consequences flow from its practice. Such an argument seems especially forceful in the later stages of pregnancy, when the fetus increasingly resembles a newborn infant. It is argued that very late abortions have a brutalizing effect on those involved and, in various ways, lead to the breakdown of attitudes associated with respect for human life. Thus, the conclusion is that very late abortions cannot be morally justified in the absence of very weighty reasons.

3 Moderation in Drawing the Line

A third strategy for generating a moderate view—in fact, a whole range of moderate views—is associated with drawing-the-line discussions. Whereas the conservative typically draws the line between human (full moral status) and nonhuman (negligible moral status) at conception and the liberal typically draws that same line at birth (or even somewhat later), a moderate view may be generated by drawing the line somewhere between these two extremes. For example, one might draw the line at implantation, at the point where brain activity begins, at quickening, at viability, and so forth.[4] Whereas drawing the line at implantation would tend to generate a rather "conservative" moderate view, drawing the line at viability would tend to generate a rather "liberal" moderate view. Wherever the line is drawn, it is the burden of

---

[4]L. W. Sumner argues that the line should be drawn at the point at which the fetus becomes sentient—that is, capable of feeling pleasure and pain. "It is likely that a fetus is unable to feel pleasure or pain at the beginning of the second trimester and likely that it is able to do so at the end of that trimester. If this is so, then the threshold of sentience, and thus also the threshold of moral standing, occurs sometime during the second trimester." L. W. Sumner, "Abortion," in Donald VanDeVeer and Tom Regan, eds. *Health Care Ethics: An Introduction* (Philadelphia: Temple University Press, 1987), p. 179. Jeff McMahan also considers the problem of determining the onset of consciousness/sentience in the developing fetus. "Most neurologists accept that the earliest point at which consciousness is possible is around the twentieth week of pregnancy. . . . It is, however, unlikely that consciousness becomes possible until at least another month—that is, until around the sixth month." Jeff McMahan, *The Ethics of Killing* (New York: Oxford University Press, 2002), p. 267.

any such moderate view to show that the point specified is a nonarbitrary one. Once such a point has been specified, however, it might be argued that abortion is ethically acceptable before that point and ethically unacceptable after that point. Of course, further stipulations may be added in accordance with strategies (1) and (2).

4   Moderation in the Assignment of Moral Status

A fourth strategy for generating a moderate view is dependent upon assigning the fetus some sort of *partial moral status*.[5] It would seem that anyone who defends a moderate view based on the concept of partial moral status must first of all face the problem of explicating the nature of such partial moral status. Second, and closely related, is the problem of showing how the interests of those with partial moral status (or perhaps the claims that can be made on their behalf) are to be weighed against the interests and rights of those who have full moral status. In one of the readings in this chapter, Margaret Olivia Little presents a unique, nuanced discussion of the morality of abortion. Her overall analysis is calculated to be responsive to the particular identities, commitments, and personal ideals of individual women who face abortion decisions, but the point of departure for her analysis can be understood as the claim that the fetus has some sort of partial moral status.

FEMINISM AND ABORTION

Inasmuch as Little's analysis pays particular attention to the moral experience of women facing abortion decisions, it may properly be understood as incorporating a distinctively *feminist* component. Since feminist perspectives will also be introduced in several other chapters of this book, there is good reason at this point to say something—by way of introduction—about feminism in general and feminist ethics in particular.

Although feminism is a school of thought (and a political movement) whose complexities defy any easy explication, it is probably fair to say that feminists are committed to the following set of claims: (1) traditional society is patriarchal—that is, male dominated; (2) many of the institutions of contemporary society—in various ways and to various degrees—continue to advantage men at the expense of women; (3) traditional values and thought patterns typically express a male point of view, often submerging or distorting the experience of women; (4) many of these traditional values and thought patterns continue to exercise influence in contemporary society. A feminist also typically argues that the resulting state of affairs is fundamentally unjust, that women must be liberated from it, and that society must be extensively restructured (reformed, revolutionized), although there is a wide range of opinion within feminism about what exactly needs to be done.

When ethical analysis proceeds from a feminist point of view, there is a commitment to take seriously the moral experience of women and a consistent effort to eliminate any traces of male bias in ethical thinking. Among other things, taking

---

[5]Daniel Callahan embraces this approach in *Abortion: Law, Choice and Morality* (New York: Macmillan, 1970), chap. 14, pp. 493–501.

seriously the moral experience of women involves insistence on the importance of *relationships* and the responsibilities to which relationships give rise. In accordance with the moral experience of women, feminists tend to view human beings as fundamentally connected and interdependent rather than radically independent individuals, as more traditional (male) paradigms might suggest. Feminist ethics is also deeply committed to the overriding moral importance of ending oppression in general and the oppression of women in particular. (A suggested analysis of the concept of oppression is presented by Iris M. Young in Chapter 8.) In feminist ethics, when a particular institution or social practice is being morally evaluated, it is always important to determine if that institution or practice has any systematic connection with the oppression of women. Indeed, in the context of the abortion debate, feminists often argue that political opposition to abortion is a reflection of patriarchy and is systematically connected with other forms of patriarchal oppression.[6]

ABORTION AND SOCIAL POLICY

In the United States, the Supreme Court's decision in *Roe v. Wade* (1973) has been the focal point of the social-policy debate over abortion. This case had the effect, for all practical purposes, of legalizing "abortion on request." The Court held that it is unconstitutional for a state to have laws prohibiting the abortion of a previable fetus. According to the *Roe* Court, a woman has a constitutionally guaranteed right to terminate a pregnancy (prior to viability), although a state, for reasons related to maternal health, may restrict the manner and circumstances in which abortions are performed subsequent to the end of the first trimester. The reasoning underlying the Court's holding in *Roe* can be found in the majority opinion reprinted in this chapter.

Since the action of the Court in *Roe* had the practical effect of establishing a woman's legal right to choose whether or not to abort, it was enthusiastically received by "right-to-choose" forces. On the other hand, "right-to-life" forces, committed to the conservative view on the morality of abortion, vehemently denounced the Court for "legalizing murder." In response to *Roe,* right-to-life forces adopted a number of political strategies, several of which are discussed in this introduction.

Right-to-life forces originally worked for the enactment of a constitutional amendment directly overruling *Roe*. The proposed "human life amendment"— declaring the personhood of the fetus—was calculated to achieve the legal prohibition of abortion, allowing an exception only for abortions necessary to save the life of a pregnant woman. Right-to-life support also emerged for the idea of a constitutional amendment allowing Congress and/or each state to decide whether to restrict abortion. (If this sort of amendment were enacted, it would undoubtedly have the

---

[6]See, for example, Susan Sherwin, *No Longer Patient: Feminist Ethics and Health Care* (Philadelphia: Temple University Press, 1992), Chapter 5. Sherwin is especially critical of the role of conservative religious institutions in the social-policy debate over abortion in the United States and Canada. Thus, in part, her views provide an interesting counterpoint to the views of John Paul II. Sherwin also defends the right of pregnant women to make abortion decisions by constructing a feminist account of the moral status of the fetus.

effect of prohibiting abortion, or at least severely restricting it, in a number of states.) Right-to-choose forces reacted in strong opposition to these proposed constitutional amendments. In their view, any effort to achieve the legal prohibition of abortion represents an illicit attempt by one group (conservatives on abortion) to impose their moral views on those who have different views.

In 1980, right-to-life forces were notably successful in working toward a more limited political aim: the cutoff of Medicaid funding for abortion. Medicaid is a social program designed to provide public funds to pay for the medical care of impoverished people. At issue in *Harris v. McRae,* decided by the Supreme Court in 1980, was the constitutionality of the so-called Hyde amendment, legislation that had passed Congress with vigorous right-to-life support. The Hyde amendment, in the version considered by the Court, restricted federal Medicaid funding to (1) cases in which the pregnant woman's life is endangered and (2) cases of rape and incest. The Court, in a five-to-four decision, upheld the constitutionality of the Hyde amendment. According to the Court, a woman's right to an abortion does not entail *the right to have society fund the abortion.* However, if there is no constitutional obstacle to the cutoff of Medicaid funding for abortion, it must still be asked whether society's refusal to fund the abortions of poor women is an ethically sound social policy. Considerations of social justice are often pressed by those who argue that it is not.

With the decision of the Supreme Court in *Webster v. Reproductive Health Services* (1989), right-to-life forces celebrated a dramatic victory. Two crucial provisions of a Missouri statue were upheld. One provision bans the use of *public* facilities and *public* employees in the performance of abortions. Another requires physicians to perform tests to determine the viability of any fetus believed to be twenty weeks or older. From the perspective of right-to-life forces, the Court's holding in *Webster* represented the first benefits of a long-term strategy to undermine *Roe v. Wade* by controlling (through the political process) the appointment of new Supreme Court justices. More important than the actual holding of the case was the fact that the Court had apparently indicated its willingness to abandon *Roe.* In *Planned Parenthood of Southeastern Pennsylvania v. Casey, Governor of Pennsylvania* (1992), however, the Court once again reflected ongoing changes in its membership and reaffirmed the "essential holding" of *Roe.*

The emergence of RU-486 (mifepristone), a drug developed in France, has further complicated the social-policy debate over abortion in the United States. RU-486 can be taken as an "abortion pill" and, in combination with a second drug taken to induce contractions, effectively terminates early pregnancies.[7] Throughout the 1990s, right-to-choose forces emphasized the importance of access to this very private, nonsurgical form of abortion and worked to make RU-486 legally available in the United States. The drug first became legally available to pregnant women in the United States in September 2000, under a protocol approved by the Food and Drug Administration. Of course, right-to-life forces bitterly oppose the legal availability

---

[7]RU-486 is not to be confused with the "morning after" pill. RU-486 dislodges an embryo already implanted in the uterus; the "morning after" pill prevents implantation (although it may also prevent ovulation and fertilization).

of RU-486. They refer to the drug as a "human pesticide" and denounce its use as "chemical warfare on the unborn."

Another dimension of the social-policy debate over abortion in the United States involves the use of a rare, late-term abortion procedure identified medically as either *intact dilation and extraction* (intact D&X) or just *dilation and extraction* (D&X). Opponents of the procedure commonly refer to it as "partial-birth abortion." Intact D&X, which is sometimes used for late second-trimester abortions, as well as for third-trimester abortions, can be understood as a variation on the D&E procedure discussed earlier. In its most notable form, intact D&X involves the partial, feet-first delivery of the fetus, followed by extraction of the brain in order to collapse the skull, so that the head can then pass through the cervix. Whereas standard D&E results in a dismembered fetus, intact D&X results in an "intact" fetus. The history of legislative efforts to ban "partial-birth abortion" is already very complex, as is the history of constitutional challenges to such bans. In *Stenberg v. Carhart* (2000), the United States Supreme Court struck down Nebraska's ban on "partial-birth abortion." At the time this case was decided, similar bans existed in about thirty states. Subsequently, Congress passed the Partial Birth Abortion Ban Act of 2003. As of this writing (spring 2006), the federal ban has been found unconstitutional by district court judges in San Francisco, New York, and Lincoln, Nebraska. Further, the Nebraska district-court ruling has been upheld by the Eighth Circuit Court of Appeals, and the case *(Gonzales v. Carhart)* is expected to be heard by the Supreme Court in fall 2006. In one of this chapter's readings, George J. Annas provides a rich account of the constitutional issues in *Stenberg* as they played out in the Supreme Court decision. The analytic framework embraced by the five-to-four majority in *Stenberg* seems to entail that the Partial Birth Abortion Ban Act of 2003 is unconstitutional, but the changing constituency of the Supreme Court introduces a significant element of uncertainty— on this particular issue and on all abortion-related issues.

Thomas A. Mappes

The Unspeakable Crime of Abortion

Pope John Paul II

Insisting that we must "call things by their proper name," Pope John Paul II identifies abortion as the *murder* of an innocent and defenseless human being. He considers some of the reasons ordinarily given to justify abortion and concludes that such reasons are never sufficient to justify the deliberate killing of an innocent human being. He then identifies several groups of people and claims that these

From *Evangelium Vitae,* encyclical letter of John Paul II, March 25, 1995. Reprinted with permission. © Libreria Editrice Vaticana, 00120 Città del Vaticano.

groups, in various ways, share in the moral guilt associated with the practice of abortion. In the end, John Paul II argues that *from the moment of conception* a human being is a person or, at any rate, must be respected and treated as a person.

Among all the crimes which can be committed against life, procured abortion has characteristics making it particularly serious and deplorable. The Second Vatican Council defines abortion, together with infanticide, as an "unspeakable crime."[1]

But today, in many people's consciences, the perception of its gravity has become progressively obscured. The acceptance of abortion in the popular mind, in behaviour and even in law itself, is a telling sign of an extremely dangerous crisis of the moral sense, which is becoming more and more incapable of distinguishing between good and evil, even when the fundamental right to life is at stake. Given such a grave situation, we need now more than ever to have the courage to look the truth in the eye and to *call things by their proper name,* without yielding to convenient compromises or to the temptation of self-deception. In this regard the reproach of the Prophet is extremely straightforward: "Woe to those who call evil good and good evil, who put darkness for light and light for darkness" (*Is* 5:20). Especially in the case of abortion there is a widespread use of ambiguous terminology, such as "interruption of pregnancy," which tends to hide abortion's true nature and to attenuate its seriousness in public opinion. Perhaps this linguistic phenomenon is itself a symptom of an uneasiness of conscience. But no word has the power to change the reality of things: procured abortion is *the deliberate and direct killing, by whatever means it is carried out, of a human being in the initial phase of his or her existence, extending from conception to birth.*

The moral gravity of procured abortion is apparent in all its truth if we recognize that we are dealing with murder and, in particular, when we consider the specific elements involved. The one eliminated is a human being at the very beginning of life. No one more absolutely *innocent* could be imagined. In no way could this human being ever be considered an aggressor, much less an unjust aggressor! He or she is *weak,* defenseless, even to the point of lacking that minimal form of defence consisting in the poignant power of a newborn baby's cries and tears. The unborn child is *totally entrusted* to the protection and care of the woman carrying him or her in the womb. And yet sometimes it is precisely the mother herself who makes the decision and asks for the child to be eliminated, and who then goes about having it done.

It is true that the decision to have an abortion is often tragic and painful for the mother, insofar as the decision to rid herself of the fruit of conception is not made for purely selfish reasons or out of convenience, but out of a desire to protect certain important values such as her own health or a decent standard of living for the other members of the family. Sometimes it is feared that the child to be born would live in such conditions that it would be better if the birth did not take place. Nevertheless, these reasons and others like them, however serious and tragic, *can never justify the deliberate killing of an innocent human being.*

As well as the mother, there are often other people too who decide upon the death of the child in the womb. In the first place, the father of the child may be to blame, not only when he directly pressures the woman to have an abortion, but also when he indirectly encourages such a decision on her part by leaving her alone to face the problems of pregnancy:[2] in this way the family is thus mortally wounded and profaned in its nature as a community of love and in its vocation to be the "sanctuary of life." Nor can one overlook the pressures which sometimes come from the wider family circle and from friends. Sometimes the woman is subjected to such strong pressure that she feels psychologically forced to have an abortion: certainly in this case moral responsibility lies particularly with those who have directly or indirectly obliged her to have an abortion. Doctors and nurses are also responsible, when they place at the service of death skills which were acquired for promoting life.

But responsibility likewise falls on the legislators who have promoted and approved abortion laws, and, to the extent that they have a say in the matter, on the administrators of the health-care centres where abortions are performed. A general and no less serious responsibility lies with those who have encouraged the spread of an attitude of sexual permissiveness and a lack of esteem for motherhood, and with those who should have ensured—but did not—effective family and social policies in support of families, especially larger families and those with particular financial and educational needs. Finally, one cannot overlook the network of complicity which reaches out to include international institutions, foundations and associations which systematically campaign for the legalization and spread of abortion in the world. In this sense abortion goes beyond the responsibility of individuals and beyond the harm done to them, and takes on a distinctly social dimension. It is a most serious *wound* inflicted on society and its culture by the very people who ought to be society's promoters and defenders. As I wrote in my *Letter to Families,* "we are facing an immense threat to life: not only to the life of individuals but also to that of civilization itself."[3] We are facing what can be called a *"structure of sin" which opposes human life not yet born.*

Some people try to justify abortion by claiming that the result of conception, at least up to a certain number of days, cannot yet be considered a personal human life. But in fact, "from the time that the ovum is fertilized, a life is begun which is neither that of the father nor the mother; it is rather the life of a new human being with his own growth. It would never be made human if it were not human already. This has always been clear, and . . . modern genetic science offers clear confirmation. It has demonstrated that from the first instant there is established the programme of what this living being will be: a person, this individual person with his characteristic aspects already well determined. Right from fertilization the adventure of a human life begins, and each of its capacities requires time—a rather lengthy time—to find its place and to be in a position to act."[4] Even if the presence of a spiritual soul cannot be ascertained by empirical data, the results themselves of scientific research on the human embryo provide "a valuable indication for discerning by the use of reason a personal presence at the moment of the first appearance of a human life: how could a human individual not be a human person?"[5]

Furthermore, what is at stake is so important that, from the standpoint of moral obligation, the mere probability that a human person is involved would suffice to justify an absolutely clear prohibition of any intervention aimed at killing a human embryo. Precisely for this reason, over and above all scientific debates and those philosophical affirmations to which the Magisterium has not expressly committed itself, the Church has always taught and continues to teach that the result of human procreation, from the first moment of its existence, must be guaranteed that unconditional respect which is morally due to the human being in his or her totality and unity as body and spirit: *"The human being is to be respected and treated as a person from the moment of conception;* and therefore from that same moment his rights as a person must be recognized, among which in the first place is the inviolable right of every innocent human being to life."[6] . . .

NOTES

1 Pastoral Constitution on the Church in the Modern World *Gaudium et Spes,* 51: "Abortus necnon infanticidium nefanda sunt crimina."

2 Cf. John Paul II, Apostolic Letter *Mulieris Dignitatem* (15 August 1988), 14: *AAS* 80 (1988), 1686.

3 No. 21: *AAS* 86 (1994), 920.

4 Congregation for the Doctrine of the Faith, *Declaration on Procured Abortion* (18 November 1974), Nos. 12–13: *AAS* 66 (1974), 738.

5 Congregation for the Doctrine of the Faith, Instruction on Respect for Human Life in Its Origin and on the Dignity of Procreation *Donum Vitae* (22 February 1987), I, No. 1: *AAS* 80 (1988), 78–79.

6 *Ibid., loc. cit.,* 79.

QUESTIONS

1 John Paul II emphasizes that we must "call things by their proper name." Is abortion *murder*?

2 Is the fetus a *person* from the moment of conception? If not, at what point does a developing human being become a person?

On the Moral and Legal Status of Abortion

Mary Anne Warren

Warren, defending the liberal view on abortion, promptly distinguishes two senses of the term *human:* (1) One is human *in the genetic sense* when one is a member of the biological species *Homo sapiens.* (2) One is human *in the moral sense* when one is a full-fledged member of the moral community. Warren attacks

Reprinted with the permission on the author and the publisher from *The Monist,* vol. 57, no.1 (January 1973). "Postscript on Infanticide" reprinted with permission of the author from Richard Wasserstrom, ed., *Today's Moral Problems* (New York: Macmillan, 1975).

the presupposition underlying the standard conservative argument against abortion—that the fetus is human in the moral sense. She contends that the moral community, the set of beings with full and equal moral rights, consists of all and only people (persons). (Thus, she takes the concept of personhood to be equivalent to the concept of humanity in the moral sense.) After analyzing the concept of a person, she concludes that there is no stage of fetal development at which a fetus resembles a person enough to have a significant right to life. She also argues that the fetus's *potential* for being a person does not provide a basis for the claim that it has a significant right to life. It follows, in her view, that a woman's right to obtain an abortion is absolute. Abortion is morally justified at any stage of fetal development, and no legal restrictions should be placed on a woman's right to abort. In a concluding postscript, Warren briefly assesses the moral justifiability of infanticide.

The question which we must answer in order to produce a satisfactory solution to the problem of the moral status of abortion is this: How are we to define the moral community, the set of beings with full and equal moral rights, such that we can decide whether a human fetus is a member of this community or not? What sort of entity, exactly, has the inalienable rights to life, liberty, and the pursuit of happiness? Jefferson attributed these rights to all *men,* and it may or may not be fair to suggest that he intended to attribute them *only* to men. Perhaps he ought to have attributed them to all human beings. If so, then we arrive, first, at [John] Noonan's problem of defining what makes a being human, and, second, at the equally vital question which Noonan does not consider, namely, What reason is there for identifying the moral community with the set of all human beings, in whatever way we have chosen to define that term?

1   ON THE DEFINITION OF "HUMAN"

One reason why this vital second question is so frequently overlooked in the debate over the moral status of abortion is that the term "human" has two distinct, but not often distinguished, senses. This fact results in a slide of meaning, which serves to conceal the fallaciousness of the traditional argument that since (1) it is wrong to kill innocent human beings, and (2) fetuses are innocent human beings, then (3) it is wrong to kill fetuses. For if "human" is used in the same sense in both (1) and (2) then, whichever of the two senses is meant, one of these premises is question-begging. And if it is used in two different senses then of course the conclusion doesn't follow.

Thus, (1) is a self-evident moral truth,[1] and avoids begging the question about abortion, only if "human being" is used to mean something like "a full-fledged member of the moral community." (It may or may not also be meant to refer exclusively to members of the species *Homo sapiens.*) We may call this the *moral* sense of "human." It is not to be confused with what we will call the *genetic* sense, i.e., the sense in which *any* member of the species is a human being, and no member of any other species could be. If (1) is acceptable only if the moral sense is intended, (2) is non-question-begging only if what is intended is the genetic sense.

In "Deciding Who Is Human," Noonan argues for the classification of fetuses with human beings by pointing to the presence of the full genetic code, and the potential capacity for rational thought.[2] It is clear that what he needs to show, for his version of the traditional argument to be valid, is that fetuses are human in the moral sense, the sense in which it is analytically true that all human beings have full moral rights. But, in the absence of any argument showing that whatever is genetically human is also morally human, and he gives none, nothing more than genetic humanity can be demonstrated by the presence of the human genetic code. And, as we will see, the *potential* capacity for rational thought can at most show that an entity has the potential for *becoming* human in the moral sense.

2 DEFINING THE MORAL COMMUNITY

Can it be established that genetic humanity is sufficient for moral humanity? I think that there are very good reasons for not defining the moral community in this way. I would like to suggest an alternative way of defining the moral community, which I will argue for only to the extent of explaining why it is, or should be, self-evident. The suggestion is simply that the moral community consists of all and only *people,* rather than all and only human beings;[3] and probably the best way of demonstrating its self-evidence is by considering the concept of personhood, to see what sorts of entity are and are not persons, and what the decision that a being is or is not a person implies about its moral rights.

What characteristics entitle an entity to be considered a person? This is obviously not the place to attempt a complete analysis of the concept of personhood, but we do not need such a fully adequate analysis just to determine whether and why a fetus is or isn't a person. All we need is a rough and approximate list of the most basic criteria of personhood, and some idea of which, or how many, of these an entity must satisfy in order to properly be considered a person.

In searching for such criteria, it is useful to look beyond the set of people with whom we are acquainted, and ask how we would decide whether a totally alien being was a person or not. (For we have no right to assume that genetic humanity is necessary for personhood.) Imagine a space traveler who lands on an unknown planet and encounters a race of beings utterly unlike any he has ever seen or heard of. If he wants to be sure of behaving morally toward these beings, he has to somehow decide whether they are people, and hence have full moral rights, or whether they are the sort of thing which he need not feel guilty about treating as, for example, a source of food.

How should he go about making this decision? If he has some anthropological background, he might look for such things as religion, art, and the manufacturing of tools, weapons, or shelters, since these factors have been used to distinguish our human from our prehuman ancestors, in what seems to be closer to the moral than the genetic sense of "human." And no doubt he would be right to consider the presence of such factors as good evidence that the alien beings were people, and morally human. It would, however, be overly anthropocentric of him to take the absence of these things as adequate evidence that they were not, since we can imagine people who have progressed beyond, or evolved without ever developing, these cultural characteristics.

I suggest that the traits which are most central to the concept of personhood, or humanity in the moral sense, are, very roughly, the following:

1 consciousness (of objects and events external and/or internal to the being), and in particular the capacity to feel pain;

2 reasoning (the *developed* capacity to solve new and relatively complex problems);

3 self-motivated activity (activity which is relatively independent of either genetic or direct external control);

4 the capacity to communicate, by whatever means, messages of an indefinite variety of types, that is, not just with an indefinite number of possible contents, but on indefinitely many possible topics;

5 the presence of self-concepts, and self-awareness, either individual or racial, or both.

Admittedly, there are apt to be a great many problems involved in formulating precise definitions of these criteria, let alone in developing universally valid behavioral criteria for deciding when they apply. But I will assume that both we and our explorer know approximately what (1)–(5) mean, and that he is also able to determine whether or not they apply. How, then, should he use his findings to decide whether or not the alien beings are people? We needn't suppose that an entity must have *all* of these attributes to be properly considered a person; (1) and (2) alone may well be sufficient for personhood, and quite probably (1)–(3) are sufficient. Neither do we need to insist that any one of these criteria is *necessary* for personhood, although once again (1) and (2) look like fairly good candidates for necessary conditions, as does (3), if "activity" is construed so as to include the activity of reasoning.

All we need to claim, to demonstrate that a fetus is not a person, is that any being which satisfies *none* of (1)–(5) is certainly not a person. I consider this claim to be so obvious that I think anyone who denied it, and claimed that a being which satisfied none of (1)–(5) was a person all the same, would thereby demonstrate that he had no notion at all of what a person is—perhaps because he had confused the concept of a person with that of genetic humanity. If the opponents of abortion were to deny the appropriateness of these five criteria, I do not know what further arguments would convince them. We would probably have to admit that our conceptual schemes were indeed irreconcilably different, and that our dispute could not be settled objectively.

I do not expect this to happen, however, since I think that the concept of a person is one which is very nearly universal (to people), and that it is common to both proabortionists and antiabortionists, even though neither group has fully realized the relevance of this concept to the resolution of their dispute. Furthermore, I think that on reflection even the antiabortionists ought to agree not only that (1)–(5) are central to the concept of personhood, but also that it is a part of this concept that all and only people have full moral rights. The concept of a person is in part a moral concept; once we have admitted that *x* is a person we have recognized, even if we have not agreed to respect, *x*'s right to be treated as a member of the moral community. It is true that the claim that *x is a human being* is more commonly voiced as part of an appeal to treat x decently than is the claim that x is a person, but this is either because "human being" is here used in the sense which implies person-hood, or because the genetic and moral senses of "human" have been confused.

Now if (1)–(5) are indeed the primary criteria of personhood, then it is clear that genetic humanity is neither necessary nor sufficient for establishing that an entity is a person. Some human beings are not people, and there may well be people who are not human beings. A man or woman whose consciousness has been perma-nently obliterated but who remains alive is a human being which is no longer a per-son; defective human beings, with no appreciable mental capacity, are not and presumably never will be people; and a fetus is a human being which is not yet a person, and which therefore cannot coherently be said to have full moral rights. Citizens of the next century should be prepared to recognize highly advanced, self-aware robots or computers, should such be developed, and intelligent inhabitants of other worlds, should such be found, as people in the fullest sense, and to respect their moral rights. But to ascribe full moral rights to an entity which is not a person is as absurd as to ascribe moral obligations and responsibilities to such an entity.

3   FETAL DEVELOPMENT AND THE RIGHT TO LIFE

Two problems arise in the application of these suggestions for the definition of the moral community to the determination of the precise moral status of a human fetus. Given that the paradigm example of a person is a normal adult human being, then (1) How like this paradigm, in particular how far advanced since conception, does a human being need to be before it begins to have a right to life by virtue, not of being fully a person as of yet, but of being *like* a person? and (2) To what extent, if any, does the fact that a fetus has the *potential* for becoming a person endow it with some of the same rights? Each of these questions requires some comment.

In answering the first question, we need not attempt a detailed consideration of the moral rights of organisms which are not developed enough, aware enough, intelligent enough, etc., to be considered people, but which resemble people in some respects. It does seem reasonable to suggest that the more like a person, in the relevant respects, a being is, the stronger is the case for regarding it as having a right to life, and indeed the stronger its right to life is. Thus we ought to take seriously the suggestion that, insofar as "the human individual develops biologically in a con-tinuous fashion . . . the rights of a human person might develop in the same way."[4] But we must keep in mind that the attributes which are relevant in determining whether or not an entity is enough like a person to be regarded as having some of the same moral rights are no different from those which are relevant to determining whether or not it is fully a person—i.e., are no different from (1)–(5)—and that being genetically human, or having recognizably human facial and other physical features, or detectable brain activity, or the capacity to survive outside the uterus, are simply not among these relevant attributes.

Thus it is clear that even though a seven- or eight-month fetus has features which make it apt to arouse in us almost the same powerful protective instinct as is com-monly aroused by a small infant, nevertheless it is not significantly more person-like than is a very small embryo. It is *somewhat* more personlike; it can apparently feel and respond to pain, and it may even have a rudimentary form of conscious-ness, insofar as its brain is quite active. Nevertheless, it seems safe to say that it is not fully conscious, in the way that an infant of a few months is, and that it cannot reason, or communicate messages of indefinitely many sorts, does not engage in self-motivated activity, and has no self-awareness. Thus, in the *relevant* respects, a fetus, even a fully developed one, is considerably less personlike than is the aver-age mature mammal, indeed the average fish. And I think that a rational person must conclude that if the right to life of a fetus is to be based upon its resemblance to a person, then it cannot be said to have any more right to life than, let us say, a newborn guppy (which also seems to be capable of feeling pain), and that a right of that magnitude could never override a woman's right to obtain an abortion, at any stage of her pregnancy.

There may, of course, be other arguments in favor of placing legal limits upon the stage of pregnancy in which an abortion may be performed. Given the relative safety of the new techniques of artificially inducing labor during the third trimester, the danger to the woman's life or health is no longer such an argument. Neither is the fact that people tend to respond to the thought of abortion in the later stages of pregnancy with emotional repulsion, since mere emotional responses cannot take the place of moral reasoning in determining what ought to be permit-ted. Nor, finally, is the frequently heard argument that legalizing abortion, espe-cially late in the pregnancy, may erode the level of respect for human life, leading, perhaps, to an increase in unjustified euthanasia and other crimes. For this threat, if it is a threat, can be better met by educating people to the kinds of moral dis-tinctions which we are making here than by limiting access to abortion (which limitation may, in its disregard for the rights of women, be just as damaging to the level of respect for human rights).

Thus, since the fact that even a fully developed fetus is not personlike enough to have any significant right to life on the basis of its personlikeness shows that no legal restrictions upon the stage of pregnancy in which an abortion may be per-formed can be justified on the grounds that we should protect the rights of the older fetus, and since there is no other apparent justification for such restrictions, we may conclude that they are entirely unjustified. Whether or not it would be *indecent* (whatever that means) for a woman in her seventh month to obtain an abortion just to avoid having to postpone a trip to Europe, it would not, in itself, be *immoral,* and therefore it ought to be permitted.

4   POTENTIAL PERSONHOOD AND THE RIGHT TO LIFE

We have seen that a fetus does not resemble a person in any way which can sup-port the claim that it has even some of the same rights. But what about its *potential,* the fact that if nurtured and allowed to develop naturally it will very probably become a person? Doesn't that alone give it at least some right to life? It is hard to deny that the fact that an entity is a potential person is a strong prima facie reason for not destroying it; but we need not conclude from this that a poten-tial person has a right to life, by virtue of that potential. It may be that our feeling that it is better, other things being equal, not to destroy a potential person is better explained by the fact that potential people are still (felt to be) an invaluable resource, not to be lightly squandered. Surely, if every speck of dust were a potential person, we would be much less apt to conclude that every potential person has a right to become actual.

Still, we do not need to insist that a potential person has no right to life whatever. There may well be something immoral, and not just imprudent, about wantonly destroying potential people, when doing so isn't necessary to protect anyone's rights. But even if a potential person does have some prima facie right to life, such a right could not possibly outweigh the right of a woman to obtain an abortion, since the rights of any actual person invariably outweigh those of any potential person, whenever the two conflict. Since this may not be immediately obvious in the case of a human fetus, let us look at another case.

Suppose that our space explorer falls into the hands of an alien culture, whose scientists decide to create a few hundred thousand or more human beings, by breaking his body into its component cells, and using these to create fully developed human beings, with, of course, his genetic code. We may imagine that each of these newly created men will have all of the original man's abilities, skills, knowledge, and so on, and also have an individual self-concept, in short that each of them will be a bona fide (though hardly unique) person. Imagine that the whole project will take only seconds, and that its chances of success are extremely high, and that our explorer knows all of this, and also knows that these people will be treated fairly. I maintain that in such a situation he would have every right to escape if he could, and thus to deprive all of these potential people of their potential lives; for his right to life outweighs all of theirs together, in spite of the fact that they are all genetically human, all innocent, and all have a very high probability of becoming people very soon, if only he refrains from acting.

Indeed, I think he would have a right to escape even if it were not his life which the alien scientists planned to take, but only a year of his freedom, or, indeed, only a day. Nor would he be obligated to stay if he had gotten captured (thus bringing all these people-potentials into existence) because of his own carelessness, or even if he had done so deliberately, knowing the consequences. Regardless of how he got captured, he is not morally obligated to remain in captivity for *any* period of time for the sake of permitting any number of potential people to come into actuality, so great is the margin by which one actual person's right to liberty outweighs whatever right to life even a hundred thousand potential people have. And it seems reasonable to conclude that the rights of a woman will outweigh by a similar margin whatever right to life a fetus may have by virtue of its potential personhood.

Thus, neither a fetus's resemblance to a person, nor its potential for becoming a person provides any basis whatever for the claim that it has any significant right to life. Consequently, a woman's right to protect her health, happiness, freedom, and even her life,[5] by terminating an unwanted pregnancy, will always override whatever right to life it may be appropriate to ascribe to a fetus, even a fully developed one. And thus, in the absence of any overwhelming social need for every possible child, the laws which restrict the right to obtain an abortion, or limit the period of pregnancy during which an abortion may be performed, are a wholly unjustified violation of a woman's most basic moral and constitutional rights.[6]

POSTSCRIPT ON INFANTICIDE

Since the publication of this article, many people have written to point out that my argument appears to justify not only abortion, but infanticide as well. For a new-born infant is not significantly more personlike than an advanced fetus, and consequently it would seem that if the destruction of the latter is permissible so too must be that of the former. Inasmuch as most people, regardless of how they feel about the morality of abortion, consider infanticide a form of murder, this might appear to represent a serious flaw in my argument.

Now, if I am right in holding that it is only people who have a full-fledged right to life, and who can be murdered, and if the criteria of personhood are as I have described them, then it obviously follows that killing a newborn infant isn't murder. It does *not* follow, however, that infanticide is permissible, for two reasons. In the first place, it would be wrong, at least in this country and in this period of history, and other things being equal, to kill a newborn infant, because even if its parents do not want it and would not suffer from its destruction, there are other people who would like to have it, and would, in all probability, be deprived of a great deal of pleasure by its destruction. Thus, infanticide is wrong for reasons analogous to those which make it wrong to wantonly destroy natural resources, or great works of art.

Secondly, most people, at least in this country, value infants and would much prefer that they be preserved, even if foster parents are not immediately available. Most of us would rather be taxed to support orphanages than allow unwanted infants to be destroyed. So long as there are people who want an infant preserved, and who are willing and able to provide the means of caring for it, under reasonably humane conditions, it is *ceteris paribus,* wrong to destroy it.

But, it might be replied, if this argument shows that infanticide is wrong, at least at this time and in this country, doesn't it also show that abortion is wrong? After all, many people value fetuses, are disturbed by their destruction, and would much prefer that they be preserved, even at some cost to themselves. Furthermore, as a potential source of pleasure to some foster family, a fetus is just as valuable as an infant. There is, however, a crucial difference between the two cases: so long as the fetus is unborn, its preservation, contrary to the wishes of the pregnant woman, violates her rights to freedom, happiness, and self-determination. Her rights override the rights of those who would like the fetus preserved, just as if someone's life or limb is threatened by a wild animal, his right to protect himself by destroying the animal overrides the rights of those who would prefer that the animal not be harmed.

The minute the infant is born, however, its preservation no longer violates any of its mother's rights, even if she wants it destroyed, because she is free to put it up for adoption. Consequently, while the moment of birth does not mark any sharp discontinuity in the degree to which an infant possesses the right to life, it does mark the end of its mother's right to determine its fate. Indeed, if abortion could be performed without killing the fetus, she would never possess the right to have the fetus destroyed, for the same reasons that she has no right to have an infant destroyed.

On the other hand, it follows from my argument that when an unwanted or defective infant is born into a society which cannot afford and/or is not willing to care for it, then its destruction is permissible. This conclusion will, no doubt, strike many people as heartless and immoral; but remember that the very existence of people who feel this way, and who are willing and able to provide care for unwanted infants, is reason enough to conclude that they should be preserved.

NOTES

1 Of course, the principle that it is (always) wrong to kill innocent human beings is in need of many other modifications, e.g., that it may be permissible to do so to save a greater number of other innocent human beings, but we may safely ignore these complications here.

2 John Noonan, "Deciding Who Is Human," *Natural Law Forum,* 13 (1968), 135.

3 From here on, we will use "human" to mean genetically human, since the moral sense seems closely connected to, and perhaps derived from, the assumption that genetic humanity is sufficient for membership in the moral community.

4 Thomas L. Hayes, "A Biological View," *Commonweal,* 85 (March 17, 1967), 677–78; quoted by Daniel Callahan, in *Abortion: Law, Choice and Morality* (London: Macmillan & Co., 1970).

5 That is, insofar as the death rate, for the woman, is higher for childbirth than for early abortion.

6 My thanks to the following people, who were kind enough to read and criticize an earlier version of this paper: Herbert Gold, Gene Glass, Anne Lauterbach, Judith Thomson, Mary Mothersill, and Timothy Binkley.

QUESTIONS

1 Would you endorse Warren's analysis of the concept of personhood?

2 Does the fetus, even if it is not an *actual* person, have a significant right to life on the grounds that it is a *potential* person?

3 Is a newborn infant a person? In any case, are there any circumstances in which infanticide would be morally permissible?

Why Abortion Is Immoral

Don Marquis

Marquis argues that abortion, with rare exceptions, is seriously immoral. He bases this conclusion on a theory that he presents and defends about the wrongness of killing. In his view, killing another adult human being is wrong precisely because the victim is deprived of all the value—"activities, projects, experiences, and enjoyments"—of his or her future. Since abortion deprives a typical fetus of a "future like ours," he contends, the moral presumption against abortion is as strong as the presumption against killing another adult human being.

Reprinted, as slightly modified by the author, with permission of the author and the publisher from the *Journal of Philosophy,* vol. 86 (April 1989).

The view that abortion is, with rare exceptions, seriously immoral has received little support in the recent philosophical literature. No doubt most philosophers affiliated with secular institutions of higher education believe that the anti-abortion position is either a symptom of irrational religious dogma or a conclusion generated by seriously confused philosophical argument. The purpose of this essay is to undermine this general belief. This essay sets out an argument that purports to show, as well as any argument in ethics can show, that abortion is, except possibly in rare cases, seriously immoral, that it is in the same moral category as killing an innocent adult human being.

This argument is based on a major assumption: If fetuses are in the same category as adult human beings with respect to the moral value of their lives, then the *presumption* that any particular abortion is immoral is exceedingly strong. Such a presumption could be overridden only by considerations more compelling than a woman's right to privacy. The defense of this assumption is beyond the scope of this essay.[1]

Furthermore, this essay will neglect a discussion of whether there are any such compelling considerations and what they are. Plainly there are strong candidates: abortion before implantation, abortion when the life of a woman is threatened by a pregnancy or abortion after rape. The casuistry of these hard cases will not be explored in this essay. The purpose of this essay is to develop a general argument for the claim that, subject to the assumption above, the overwhelming majority of deliberate abortions are seriously immoral. . . .

. . . A necessary condition of resolving the abortion controversy is a . . . theoretical account of the wrongness of killing. After all, if we merely believe, but do not understand, why killing adult human beings such as ourselves is wrong, how could we conceivably show that abortion is either immoral or permissible? . . .

In order to develop such an account, we can start from the following unproblematic assumption concerning our own case: it is wrong to kill *us*. Why is it wrong? Some answers can be easily eliminated. It might be said that what makes killing us wrong is that a killing brutalizes the one who kills. But the brutalization consists of being inured to the performance of an act that is hideously immoral; hence, the brutalization does not explain the immorality. It might be said that what makes killing us wrong is the great loss others would experience due to our absence. Although such hubris is understandable, such an explanation does not account for the wrongness of killing hermits, or those whose lives are relatively independent and whose friends find it easy to make new friends.

A more obvious answer is better. What primarily makes killing wrong is neither its effect on the murderer nor its effect on the victim's friends and relatives, but its effect on the victim. The loss of one's life is one of the greatest losses one can suffer. The loss of one's life deprives one of all the experiences, activities, projects, and enjoyments that would otherwise have constituted one's future. Therefore, killing someone is wrong, primarily because the killing inflicts (one of) the greatest possible losses on the victim. To describe this as the loss of life can be misleading, however. The change in my biological state does not by itself make killing me wrong. The effect of the loss of my biological life is the loss to me of all those activities, projects, experiences, and enjoyments which would otherwise have constituted my future personal life. These activities, projects, experiences, and enjoyments are either valuable for their own sakes or are means to something else that is valuable for its own sake. Some parts of my future are not valued by me now, but will come to be valued by me as I grow older and as my values and capacities change. When I am killed, I am deprived both of what I now value which would have been part of my future personal life, but also what I would come to value. Therefore, when I die, I am deprived of all of the value of my future. Inflicting this loss on me is ultimately what makes killing me wrong. This being the case, it would seem that what makes killing *any* adult human being prima facie seriously wrong is the loss of his or her future.[2]

How should this rudimentary theory of the wrongness of killing be evaluated? It cannot be faulted for deriving an 'ought' from an 'is', for it does not. The analysis assumes that killing me (or you, reader) is prima facie seriously wrong. The point of the analysis is to establish which natural property ultimately explains the wrongness of the killing, given that it is wrong. A natural property will ultimately explain the wrongness of killing, only if (1) the explanation fits with our intuitions about the matter and (2) there is no other natural property that provides the basis for a better explanation of the wrongness of killing. This analysis rests on the intuition that what makes killing a particular human or animal wrong is what it does to that particular human or animal. What makes killing wrong is some natural effect or other of the killing. Some would deny this. For instance, a divine-command theorist in ethics would deny it. Surely this denial is, however, one of those features of divine-command theory which renders it so implausible.

The claim that what makes killing wrong is the loss of the victim's future is directly supported by two considerations. In the first place, this theory explains why we regard killing as one of the worst of crimes. Killing is especially wrong, because it deprives the victim of more than perhaps any other crime. In the second place, people with AIDS or cancer who know they are dying believe, of course, that dying is a very bad thing for them. They believe that the loss of a future to them that they would otherwise have experienced is what makes their premature death a very bad thing for them. A better theory of the wrongness of killing would require a different natural property associated with killing which better fits with the attitudes of the dying. What could it be?

The view that what makes killing wrong is the loss to the victim of the value of the victim's future gains additional support when some of its implications are examined. In the first place, it is incompatible with the view that it is wrong to kill only beings who are biologically human. It is possible that there exists a different species from another planet whose members have a future like ours. Since having a future like that is what makes killing someone wrong, this theory entails that it would be wrong to kill members of such a species. Hence, this theory is opposed to the claim that only life that is biologically human has great moral worth, a claim which many anti-abortionists have seemed to adopt. This opposition, which this theory has in common with personhood theories, seems to be a merit of the theory.

In the second place, the claim that the loss of one's future is the wrong-making feature of one's being killed entails the possibility that the futures of some actual nonhuman mammals on our own planet are sufficiently like ours that it is seriously wrong to kill them also. Whether some animals do have the same right to life as human beings depends on adding to the account of the wrongness of killing some additional account of just what it is about my future or the futures of other adult human beings which makes it wrong to kill us. No such additional account will be offered in this essay. Undoubtedly, the provision of such an account would be a very difficult matter. Undoubtedly, any such account would be quite controversial. Hence, it surely should not reflect badly on this sketch of an elementary theory of the wrongness of killing that it is indeterminate with respect to some very difficult issues regarding animal rights.

In the third place, the claim that the loss of one's future is the wrong-making feature of one's being killed does not entail, as sanctity of human life theories do, that active euthanasia is wrong. Persons who are severely and incurably ill, who face a future of pain and despair, and who wish to die will not have suffered a loss if they are killed. It is, strictly speaking, the value of a human's future which makes killing wrong in this theory. This being so, killing does not necessarily wrong some persons who are sick and dying. Of course, there may be other reasons for a prohibition of active euthanasia, but that is another matter. Sanctity-of-human-life theories seem to hold that active euthanasia is seriously wrong even in an individual case where there seems to be good reason for it independently of public policy considerations. This consequence is most implausible, and it is a plus for the claim that the loss of a future of value is what makes killing wrong that it does not share this consequence.

In the fourth place, the account of the wrongness of killing defended in this essay does straightforwardly entail that it is prima facie seriously wrong to kill children and infants, for we do presume that they have futures of value. Since we do believe that it is wrong to kill defenseless little babies, it is important that a theory of the wrongness of killing easily account for this. Personhood theories of the wrongness of killing, on the other hand, cannot straightforwardly account for the wrongness of killing infants and young children. Hence, such theories must add special ad hoc accounts of the wrongness of killing the young. The plausibility of such ad hoc theories seems to be a function of how desperately one wants such theories to work. The claim that the primary wrong-making feature of a killing is the loss to the victim of the value of its future accounts for the wrongness of killing young children and infants directly; it makes the wrongness of such acts as obvious as we actually think it is. This is a further merit of this theory. Accordingly, it seems that this value of a future-like-ours theory of the wrongness of killing shares strengths of both sanctity-of-life and personhood accounts while avoiding weaknesses of both. In addition, it meshes with a central intuition concerning what makes killing wrong.

The claim that the primary wrong-making feature of a killing is the loss to the victim of the value of its future has obvious consequences for the ethics of abortion. The future of a standard fetus includes a set of experiences, projects, activities, and such which are identical with the futures of adult human beings and are identical with the futures of young children. Since the reason that is sufficient to explain why it is wrong to kill human beings after the time of birth is a reason that also applies to fetuses, it follows that abortion is prima facie seriously morally wrong.

This argument does not rely on the invalid inference that, since it is wrong to kill persons, it is wrong to kill potential persons also. The category that is morally central to this analysis is the category of having a valuable future like ours; it is not the category of personhood. The argument to the conclusion that abortion is prima facie seriously morally wrong proceeded independently of the notion of person or potential person or any equivalent. Someone may wish to start with this analysis in terms of the value of a human future, conclude that abortion is, except perhaps in rare circumstances, seriously morally wrong, infer that fetuses have the right to life, and then call fetuses "persons" as a result of their having the right to life. Clearly, in this case, the category of person is being used to state the *conclusion* of the analysis rather than to generate the *argument* of the analysis.

The structure of this anti-abortion argument can be both illuminated and defended by comparing it to what appears to be the best argument for the wrongness of the wanton infliction of pain on animals. This latter argument is based on the assumption that it is prima facie wrong to inflict pain on me (or you, reader). What is the natural property associated with the infliction of pain which makes such infliction wrong? The obvious answer seems to be that the infliction of pain causes suffering and that suffering is a misfortune. The suffering caused by the infliction of pain is what makes the wanton infliction of pain on me wrong. The wanton infliction of pain on other adult humans causes suffering. The wanton infliction of pain on animals causes suffering. Since causing suffering is what makes the wanton infliction of pain wrong and since the wanton infliction of pain on animals causes suffering, it follows that the wanton infliction of pain on animals is wrong.

This argument for the wrongness of the wanton infliction of pain on animals shares a number of structural features with the argument for the serious prima facie wrongness of abortion. Both arguments start with an obvious assumption concerning what it is wrong to do to me (or you, reader). Both then look for the characteristic or the consequence of the wrong action which makes the action wrong. Both recognize that the wrong-making feature of these immoral actions is a property of actions sometimes directed at individuals other than postnatal human beings. If the structure of the argument for the wrongness of the wanton infliction of pain on animals is sound, then the structure of the argument for the prima facie serious wrongness of abortion is also sound, for the structure of the two arguments is the same. The structure common to both is the key to the explanation of how the wrongness of abortion can be demonstrated without recourse to the category of person. In neither argument is that category crucial. . . .

Of course, this value of a future-like-ours argument, if sound, shows only that abortion is prima facie wrong, not that it is wrong in any and all circumstances. Since the loss of the future to a standard fetus, if killed, is, however, at least as great a loss as the loss of the future to a standard adult human being who is killed, abortion, like ordinary killing, could be justified only by the most compelling reasons. The loss of one's life is almost the greatest misfortune that can happen to one. Presumably abortion could be justified in some circumstances, only if the loss consequent on failing to abort would be at least as great. Accordingly, morally permissible abortions will be rare indeed unless, perhaps, they occur so early in pregnancy that a fetus is not yet definitely an individual. Hence, this argument should be taken as showing that abortion is presumptively very seriously wrong, where the presumption is very strong—as strong as the presumption that killing another adult human being is wrong. . . .

In this essay, it has been argued that the correct ethic of the wrongness of killing can be extended to fetal life and used to show that there is a strong presumption that any abortion is morally impermissible. If the ethic of killing adopted here entails, however, that contraception is also seriously immoral, then there would appear to be a difficulty with the analysis of this essay.

But this analysis does not entail that contraception is wrong. Of course, contraception prevents the actualization of a possible future of value. Hence, it follows from the claim that futures of value should be maximized that contraception is prima facie immoral. This obligation to maximize does not exist, however; furthermore, nothing in the ethics of killing in this paper entails that it does. The ethics of killing in this essay would entail that contraception is wrong only if something were denied a human future of value by contraception. Nothing at all is denied such a future by contraception, however.

Candidates for a subject of harm by contraception fall into four categories: (1) some sperm or other, (2) some ovum or other, (3) a sperm and an ovum separately, and (4) a sperm and an ovum together. Assigning the harm to some sperm is utterly arbitrary, for no reason can be given for making a sperm the subject of harm rather than an ovum. Assigning the harm to some ovum is utterly arbitrary, for no reason can be given for making an ovum the subject of harm rather than a sperm. One might attempt to avoid these problems by insisting that contraception deprives both the sperm and the ovum separately of a valuable future like ours. On this alternative, too many futures are lost. Contraception was supposed to be wrong, because it deprived us of one future of value, not two. One might attempt to avoid this problem by holding that contraception deprives the combination of sperm and ovum of a valuable future like ours. But here the definite article misleads. At the time of contraception, there are hundreds of millions of sperm, one (released) ovum and millions of possible combinations of all of these. There is no actual combination at all. Is the subject of the loss to be a merely possible combination? Which one? This alternative does not yield an actual subject of harm either. Accordingly, the immorality of contraception is not entailed by the loss of a future-like-ours argument simply because there is no nonarbitrarily identifiable subject of the loss in the case of contraception. . . .

The purpose of this essay has been to set out an argument for the serious presumptive wrongness of abortion subject to the assumption that the moral permissibility of abortion stands or falls on the moral status of the fetus. Since a fetus possesses a property, the possession of which in adult human beings is sufficient to make killing an adult human being wrong, abortion is wrong. This way of dealing with the problem of abortion seems superior to other approaches to the ethics of abortion, because it rests on an ethics of killing which is close to self-evident, because the crucial morally relevant property clearly applies to fetuses, and because the argument avoids the usual equivocations on 'human life', 'human being', or 'person'. The argument rests neither on religious claims nor on Papal dogma. It is not subject to the objection of "speciesism." Its soundness is compatible with the moral permissibility of euthanasia and contraception. It deals with our intuitions concerning young children.

Finally, this analysis can be viewed as resolving a standard problem—indeed, *the* standard problem—concerning the ethics of abortion. Clearly, it is wrong to kill adult human beings. Clearly, it is not wrong to end the life of some arbitrarily chosen single human cell. Fetuses seem to be like arbitrarily chosen human cells in some respects and like adult humans in other respects. The problem of the ethics of abortion is the problem of determining the fetal property that settles this moral controversy. The thesis of this essay is that the problem of the ethics of abortion, so understood, is solvable.

NOTES

1 Judith Jarvis Thomson has rejected this assumption in a famous essay, "A Defense of Abortion," *Philosophy and Public Affairs* 1, #1 (1971), 47–66.
2 I have been most influenced on this matter by Jonathan Glover, *Causing Death and Saving Lives* (New York: Penguin, 1977), ch. 3; and Robert Young, "What Is So Wrong with Killing People?" *Philosophy*, LIV, 210 (1979): 515–528.

QUESTIONS

1 If the wrongness of killing derives from the fact that the victim is deprived of the value of his or her future, does it follow that it is less wrong to kill someone fifty years old than it is to kill someone twenty years old? If so, does this implication suggest that there is some deficiency in Marquis's theory about the wrongness of killing?
2 Does Marquis provide a satisfactory response to the possible objection that his theory about the wrongness of killing implies that contraception is morally wrong?
3 If Marquis's basic approach is accepted, which abortions could still be considered morally justified?

A Defense of Abortion[1]

Judith Jarvis Thomson

In an effort to moderate the conservative view, Thomson argues that the standard conservative claim about the moral impermissibility of abortion cannot be sustained even if (for the sake of argument) it is presumed that the fetus is a person from conception. Her central point is that the moral impermissibility of abortion does not follow simply from the admission that the fetus (as a person) has a right to life. In her view, the right to life is to be understood as the right not to be killed

Philosophy and Public Affairs, vol. 1, no. 1 (1971), pp. 47–50, 54–66. © 1971 by Princeton University Press. Reprinted by permission of Blackwell Publishing Ltd.

unjustly and does not entail the right to use another person's body. In cases where the pregnant woman has not extended to the fetus the right to use her body, most prominently in the case of rape, Thomson holds that abortion is not unjust killing and, thus, does not violate the fetus's right to life. Thomson acknowledges that there may be cases in which the fetus (presumed to be a person) has a right to the use of the pregnant woman's body and, thus, some cases where abortion would be unjust killing. She proceeds to distinguish between the moral demands of justice and the moral demands of decency. In some cases, she maintains, an abortion does no injustice (to the fetus) yet may be subject to moral criticism on the grounds that minimal standards of moral decency are transgressed.

Most opposition to abortion relies on the premise that the fetus is a human being, a person, from the moment of conception. The premise is argued for, but, as I think, not well. Take, for example, the most common argument. We are asked to notice that the development of a human being from conception through birth into child-hood is continuous; then it is said that to draw a line, to choose a point in this devel-opment and say "before this point the thing is not a person, after this point it is a person" is to make an arbitrary choice, a choice for which in the nature of things no good reason can be given. It is concluded that the fetus is, or anyway that we had better say it is, a person from the moment of conception. But this conclusion does not follow. Similar things might be said about the development of an acorn into an oak tree, and it does not follow that acorns are oak trees, or that we had better say they are. Arguments of this form are sometimes called "slippery slope arguments"—the phrase is perhaps self-explanatory—and it is dismaying that opponents of abor-tion rely on them so heavily and uncritically.

I am inclined to agree, however, that the prospects for "drawing a line" in the development of the fetus look dim. I am inclined to think also that we shall probably have to agree that the fetus has already become a human person well before birth. Indeed, it comes as a surprise when one first learns how early in its life it begins to acquire human characteristics. By the tenth week, for example, it already has a face, arms and legs, fingers and toes; it has internal organs, and brain activity is detectable.[2] On the other hand, I think that the premise is false, that the fetus is not a person from the moment of conception. A newly fertilized ovum, a newly implanted clump of cells, is no more a person than an acorn is an oak tree. But I shall not discuss any of this. For it seems to me to be of great interest to ask what happens if, for the sake of argument, we allow the premise. How, precisely, are we supposed to get from there to the conclusion that abortion is morally impermissible? Opponents of abortion com-monly spend most of their time establishing that the fetus is a person, and hardly any time explaining the step from there to the impermissibility of abortion. Perhaps they think the step too simple and obvious to require much comment. Or perhaps instead they are simply being economical in argument. Many of those who defend abortion rely on the premise that the fetus is not a person, but only a bit of tissue that will become a person at birth; and why pay out more arguments than you have to? Whatever the explanation, I suggest that the step they take is neither easy nor obvi-ous, that it calls for closer examination than it is commonly given, and that when we do give it this closer examination we shall feel inclined to reject it.

I propose, then, that we grant that the fetus is a person from the moment of conception. How does the argument go from here? Something like this, I take it. Every person has a right to life. So the fetus has a right to life. No doubt the mother has a right to decide what shall happen in and to her body; everyone would grant that. But surely a person's right to life is stronger and more stringent than the mother's right to decide what happens in and to her body, and so outweighs it. So the fetus may not be killed; an abortion may not be performed.

It sounds plausible. But now let me ask you to imagine this. You wake up in the morning and find yourself back to back in bed with an unconscious violinist. A famous unconscious violinist. He has been found to have a fatal kidney ailment, and the Society of Music Lovers has canvassed all the available medical records and found that you alone have the right blood type to help. They have therefore kidnapped you, and last night the violinist's circulatory system was plugged into yours, so that your kidneys can be used to extract poisons from his blood as well as your own. The director of the hospital now tells you, "Look, we're sorry the Society of Music Lovers did this to you—we would never have permitted it if we had known. But still, they did it, and the violinist now is plugged into you. To unplug you would be to kill him. But never mind, it's only for nine months. By then he will have recovered from his ailment, and can safely be unplugged from you." Is it morally incumbent on you to accede to this situation? No doubt it would be very nice of you if you did, a great kindness. But do you *have* to accede to it? What if it were not nine months, but nine years? Or longer still? What if the director of the hospital says, "Tough luck, I agree, but you've now got to stay in bed, with the violinist plugged into you, for the rest of your life. Because remember this. All persons have a right to life, and violinists are persons. Granted you have a right to decide what happens in and to your body, but a person's right to life outweighs your right to decide what happens in and to your body. So you cannot ever be unplugged from him." I imagine you would regard this as outrageous, which suggests that something really is wrong with that plausible-sounding argument I mentioned a moment ago.

In this case, of course, you were kidnapped; you didn't volunteer for the operation that plugged the violinist into your kidneys. Can those who oppose abortion on the ground I mentioned make an exception for a pregnancy due to rape? Certainly. They can say that persons have a right to life only if they didn't come into existence because of rape; or they can say that all persons have a right to life, but that some have less of a right to life than others, in particular, that those who came into existence because of rape have less. But these statements have a rather unpleasant sound. Surely the question of whether you have a right to life at all, or how much of it you have, shouldn't turn on the question of whether or not you are the product of a rape. And in fact the people who oppose abortion on the ground I mentioned do not make this distinction, and hence do not make an exception in case of rape.

Nor do they make an exception for a case in which the mother has to spend the nine months of her pregnancy in bed. They would agree that would be a great pity, and hard on the mother; but all the same, all persons have a right to life, the fetus is a person, and so on. I suspect, in fact, that they would not make an exception for a case in which, miraculously enough, the pregnancy went on for nine years, or even the rest of the mother's life.

Some won't even make an exception for a case in which continuation of the pregnancy is likely to shorten the mother's life; they regard abortion as impermissible even to save the mother's life. Such cases are nowadays very rare, and many opponents of abortion do not accept this extreme view. . . .

[1] Where the mother's life is not at stake, the argument I mentioned at the outset seems to have a much stronger pull. "Everyone has a right to life, so the unborn person has a right to life." And isn't the child's right to life weightier than anything other than the mother's own right to life, which she might put forward as ground for an abortion?

This argument treats the right to life as if it were unproblematic. It is not, and this seems to me to be precisely the source of the mistake.

For we should now, at long last, ask what it comes to, to have a right to life. In some views having a right to life includes having a right to be given at least the bare minimum one needs for continued life. But suppose that what in fact *is* the bare minimum a man needs for continued life is something he has no right at all to be given? If I am sick unto death, and the only thing that will save my life is the touch of Henry Fonda's cool hand on my fevered brow, then all the same, I have no right to be given the touch of Henry Fonda's cool hand on my fevered brow. It would be frightfully nice of him to fly in from the West Coast to provide it. It would be less nice, though no doubt well meant, if my friends flew out to the West Coast and carried Henry Fonda back with them. But I have no right at all against anybody that he should do this for me. Or again, to return to the story I told earlier, the fact that for continued life that violinist needs the continued use of your kidneys does not establish that he has a right to be given the continued use of your kidneys. He certainly has no right against you that *you* should give him continued use of your kidneys. For nobody has any right to use your kidneys unless you give him such a right; and nobody has the right against you that you shall give him this right—if you do allow him to go on using your kidneys, this is a kindness on your part, and not something he can claim from you as his due. Nor has he any right against anybody else that *they* should give him continued use of your kidneys. Certainly he had no right against the Society of Music Lovers that they should plug him into you in the first place. And if you now start to unplug yourself, having learned that you will otherwise have to spend nine years in bed with him, there is nobody in the world who must try to prevent you, in order to see to it that he is given something he has a right to be given.

Some people are rather stricter about the right to life. In their view, it does not include the right to be given anything, but amounts to, and only to, the right not to be killed by anybody. But here a related difficulty arises. If everybody is to refrain from killing that violinist, then everybody must refrain from doing a great many different sorts of things. Everybody must refrain from slitting his throat, everybody must refrain from shooting him—and everybody must refrain from unplugging you from him. But does he have a right against everybody that they shall refrain from unplugging you from him? To refrain from doing this is to allow him to continue to use your kidneys. It could be argued that he has a right against us that *we* should allow him to continue to use your kidneys. That is, while he had no right against us that we should give him the use of your kidneys, it might be argued that he anyway has a right against us that we shall not now intervene and deprive him of the use of your kidneys. I shall come back to third-party interventions later. But certainly the violinist has no right against you that *you* shall allow him to continue to use your kidneys. As I said, if you do allow him to use them, it is a kindness on your part, and not something you owe him.

The difficulty I point to here is not peculiar to the right to life. It reappears in connection with all the other natural rights; and it is something which an adequate account of rights must deal with. For present purposes it is enough just to draw attention to it. But I would stress that I am not arguing that people do not have a right to life—quite to the contrary, it seems to me that the primary control we must place on the acceptability of an account of rights is that it should turn out in that account to be a truth that all persons have a right to life. I am arguing only that having a right to life does not guarantee having either a right to be given the use of or a right to be allowed continued use of another person's body—even if one needs it for life itself. So the right to life will not serve the opponents of abortion in the very simple and clear way in which they seem to have thought it would.

[2] There is another way to bring out the difficulty. In the most ordinary sort of case, to deprive someone of what he has a right to is to treat him unjustly. Suppose a boy and his small brother are jointly given a box of chocolates for Christmas. If the older boy takes the box and refuses to give his brother any of the chocolates, he is unjust to him, for the brother has been given a right to half of them. But suppose that, having learned that otherwise it means nine years in bed with that violinist, you unplug yourself from him. You surely are not being unjust to him, for you gave him no right to use your kidneys, and no one else can have given him any such right. But we have to notice that in unplugging yourself, you are killing him; and violinists, like everybody else, have a right to life, and thus in the view we were considering just now, the right not to be killed. So here you do what he supposedly has a right you shall not do, but you do not act unjustly to him in doing it.

The emendation which may be made at this point is this: the right to life consists not in the right not to be killed, but rather in the right not to be killed unjustly. This runs a risk of circularity, but never mind: it would enable us to square the fact that the violinist has a right to life with the fact that you do not act unjustly toward him in unplugging yourself, thereby killing him. For if you do not kill him unjustly, you do not violate his right to life, and so it is no wonder you do him no injustice.

But if this emendation is accepted, the gap in the argument against abortion stares us plainly in the face: it is by no means enough to show that the fetus is a person, and to remind us that all persons have a right to life—we need to be shown also that killing the fetus violates its right to life, i.e., that abortion is unjust killing. And is it?

I suppose we may take it as a datum that in a case of pregnancy due to rape the mother has not given the unborn person a right to the use of her body for food and shelter. Indeed, in what pregnancy could it be supposed that the mother has given the unborn person such a right? It is not as if there were unborn persons drifting about the world, to whom a woman who wants a child says "I invite you in."

But it might be argued that there are other ways one can have acquired a right to the use of another person's body than by having been invited to use it by that person. Suppose a woman voluntarily indulges in intercourse, knowing of the chance it will issue in pregnancy, and then she does become pregnant; is she not in part responsible for the presence, in fact the very existence, of the unborn person inside her? No doubt she did not invite it in. But doesn't her partial responsibility for its being there itself give it a right to the use of her body?[3] If so, then her aborting it would be more like the boy's taking away the chocolates, and less like your unplugging yourself from the violinist—doing so would be depriving it of what it does have a right to, and thus would be doing it an injustice.

And then, too, it might be asked whether or not she can kill it even to save her own life: If she voluntarily called it into existence, how can she now kill it, even in self-defense?

The first thing to be said about this is that it is something new. Opponents of abortion have been so concerned to make out the independence of the fetus, in order to establish that it has a right to life, just as its mother does, that they have tended to overlook the possible support they might gain from making out that the fetus is *dependent* on the mother, in order to establish that she has a special kind of responsibility for it, a responsibility that gives it rights against her which are not possessed by any independent person—such as an ailing violinist who is a stranger to her.

On the other hand, this argument would give the unborn person a right to its mother's body only if her pregnancy resulted from a voluntary act, undertaken in full knowledge of the chance a pregnancy might result from it. It would leave out entirely the unborn person whose existence is due to rape. Pending the availability of some further argument, then, we would be left with the conclusion that unborn persons whose existence is due to rape have no right to the use of their mothers' bodies, and thus that aborting them is not depriving them of anything they have a right to and hence is not unjust killing.

And we should also notice that it is not at all plain that this argument really does go even as far as it purports to. For there are cases and cases, and the details make a difference. If the room is stuffy, and I therefore open a window to air it, and a burglar climbs in, it would be absurd to say, "Ah, now he can stay, she's given him a right to the use of her house—for she is partially responsible for his presence there, having voluntarily done what enabled him to get in, in full knowledge that there are such things as burglars, and that burglars burgle." It would be still more absurd to say this if I had had bars installed outside my windows, precisely to prevent burglars from getting in, and a burglar got in only because of a defect in the bars. It remains equally absurd if we imagine it is not a burglar who climbs in, but an innocent person who blunders or falls in. Again, suppose it were like this: people-seeds drift about in the air like pollen, and if you open your windows, one may drift in and take root in your carpets or upholstery. You don't want children, so you fix up your windows with fine mesh screens, the very best you can buy. As can happen, however, and on very, very rare occasions does happen, one of the screens is defective; and a seed drifts in and takes root. Does the person-plant who now develops have a right to the use of your house? Surely not—despite the fact that you voluntarily opened your windows, you knowingly kept carpets and upholstered furniture, and you knew that screens were sometimes defective. Someone may argue that you are responsible for its rooting, that it does have a right to your house, because after all you *could* have lived out your life with bare floors and furniture, or with sealed windows and doors. But this won't do—for by the same token anyone can avoid a pregnancy due to rape by having a hysterectomy, or anyway by never leaving home without a (reliable!) army.

It seems to me that the argument we are looking at can establish at most that there are *some* cases in which the unborn person has a right to the use of its mother's body, and therefore *some* cases in which abortion is unjust killing. There is room for much discussion and argument as to precisely which, if any. But I think we should sidestep this issue and leave it open, for at any rate the argument certainly does not establish that all abortion is unjust killing.

[3] There is room for yet another argument here, however. We surely must all grant that there may be cases in which it would be morally indecent to detach a person from your body at the cost of his life. Suppose you learn that what the violinist needs is not nine years of your life, but only one hour: all you need do to save his life is to spend one hour in that bed with him. Suppose also that letting him use your kidneys for that one hour would not affect your health in the slightest. Admittedly you were kidnapped. Admittedly you did not give anyone permission to plug him into you. Nevertheless it seems to me plain you *ought* to allow him to use your kidneys for that hour—it would be indecent to refuse.

Again, suppose pregnancy lasted only an hour, and constituted no threat to life or health. And suppose that a woman becomes pregnant as a result of rape. Admittedly she did not voluntarily do anything to bring about the existence of a child. Admittedly she did nothing at all which would give the unborn person a right to the use of her body. All the same it might well be said, as in the newly emended violinist story, that she *ought* to allow it to remain for that hour—that it would be indecent in her to refuse.

Now some people are inclined to use the term "right" in such a way that it follows from the fact that you ought to allow a person to use your body for the hour he needs, that he has a right to use your body for the hour he needs, even though he has not been given that right by any person or act. They may say that it follows also that if you refuse, you act unjustly toward him. This use of the term is perhaps so common that it cannot be called wrong; nevertheless it seems to me to be an unfortunate loosening of what we would do better to keep a tight rein on. Suppose that box of chocolates I mentioned earlier had not been given to both boys jointly, but was given only to the older boy. There he sits, stolidly eating his way through the box, his small brother watching enviously. Here we are likely to say "You ought not to be so mean. You ought to give your brother some of those chocolates." My own view is that it just does not follow from the truth of this that the brother has any right to any of the chocolates. If the boy refuses to give his brother any, he is greedy, stingy, callous—but not unjust. I suppose that the people I have in mind will say it does follow that the brother has a right to some of the chocolates, and thus that the boy does act unjustly if he refuses to give his brother any. But the effect of saying this is to obscure what we should keep distinct, namely the difference between the boy's refusal in this case and the boy's refusal in the earlier case, in which the box was given to both boys jointly, and in which the small brother thus had what was from any point of view clear title to half.

A further objection to so using the term "right" that from the fact that A ought to do a thing for B, it follows that B has a right against A that A do it for him, is that it is going to make the question of whether or not a man has a right to a thing turn on how easy it is to provide him with it; and this seems not merely unfortunate, but morally unacceptable. Take the case of Henry Fonda again. I said earlier that I had no right to the touch of his cool hand on my fevered brow, even though I needed it to save my life. I said it would be frightfully nice of him to fly in from the West Coast to provide me with it, but that I had no right against him that he should do so. But suppose he isn't on the West Coast. Suppose he has only to walk across the room, place a hand briefly on my brow—and lo, my life is saved. Then surely he ought to do it, it would be indecent to refuse. Is it to be said "Ah, well, it follows that in this case she has a right to the touch of his hand on her brow, and so it would be an injustice in him to refuse"? So that I have a right to it when it is easy for him to provide it, though no right when it's hard? It's rather a shocking idea that anyone's rights should fade away and disappear as it gets harder and harder to accord them to him.

So my own view is that even though you ought to let the violinist use your kidneys for the one hour he needs, we should not conclude that he has a right to do so—we would say that if you refuse, you are, like the boy who owns all the chocolates and will give none away, self-centered and callous, indecent in fact, but not unjust. And similarly, that even supposing a case in which a woman pregnant due to rape ought to allow the unborn person to use her body for the hour he needs, we should not conclude that he has a right to do so; we should conclude that she is self-centered, callous, indecent, but not unjust, if she refuses. The complaints are no less grave; they are just different. However, there is no need to insist on this point. If anyone does wish to deduce "he has a right" from "you ought," then all the same he must surely grant that there are cases in which it is not morally required of you that you allow that violinist to use your kidneys, and in which he does not have a right to use them, and in which you do not do him an injustice if you refuse. And so also for mother and unborn child. Except in such cases as the unborn person has a right to demand it—and we were leaving open the possibility that there may be such cases—nobody is morally *required* to make large sacrifices, of health, of all other interests and concerns, of all other duties and commitments, for nine years, or even for nine months, in order to keep another person alive.

[4] We have in fact to distinguish between two kinds of Samaritan: the Good Samaritan and what we might call the Minimally Decent Samaritan. The story of the Good Samaritan, you will remember, goes like this:

> A certain man went down from Jerusalem to Jericho, and fell among thieves, which stripped him of his raiment, and wounded him, and departed, leaving him half dead.
>
> And by chance there came down a certain priest that way; and when he saw him, he passed by on the other side.
>
> And likewise a Levite, when he was at the place, came and looked on him, and passed by on the other side.
>
> But a certain Samaritan, as he journeyed, came where he was; and when he saw him he had compassion on him.

And went to him, and bound up his wounds, pouring in oil and wine, and set him on his own beast, and brought him to an inn, and took care of him.

And on the morrow, when he departed, he took out two pence, and gave them to the host, and said unto him, "Take care of him; and whatsoever thou spendest more, when I come again, I will repay thee."

(Luke 10:30–35)

The Good Samaritan went out of his way, at some cost to himself, to help one in need of it. We are not told what the options were, that is, whether or not the priest and the Levite could have helped by doing less than the Good Samaritan did, but assuming they could have, then the fact they did nothing at all shows they were not even Minimally Decent Samaritans, not because they were not Samaritans, but because they were not even minimally decent.

These things are a matter of degree, of course, but there is a difference, and it comes out perhaps most clearly in the story of Kitty Genovese, who, as you will remember, was murdered while thirty-eight people watched or listened, and did nothing at all to help her. A Good Samaritan would have rushed out to give direct assistance against the murderer. Or perhaps we had better allow that it would have been a Splendid Samaritan who did this, on the ground that it would have involved a risk of death for himself. But the thirty-eight not only did not do this, they did not even trouble to pick up a phone to call the police. Minimally Decent Samaritanism would call for doing at least that, and their not having done it was monstrous.

After telling the story of the Good Samaritan, Jesus said "Go, and do thou likewise." Perhaps he meant that we are morally required to act as the Good Samaritan did. Perhaps he was urging people to do more than is morally required of them. At all events it seems plain that it was not morally required of any of the thirty-eight that he rush out to give direct assistance at the risk of his own life, and that it is not morally required of anyone that he give long stretches of his life—nine years or nine months—to sustaining the life of a person who has no special right (we were leaving open the possibility of this) to demand it.

Indeed, with one rather striking class of exceptions, no one in any country in the world is *legally* required to do anywhere near as much as this for anyone else. The class of exceptions is obvious. My main concern here is not the state of the law in respect to abortion, but it is worth drawing attention to the fact that in no state in this country is any man compelled by law to be even a Minimally Decent Samaritan to any person; there is no law under which charges could be brought against the thirty-eight who stood by while Kitty Genovese died. By contrast, in most states in this country women are compelled by law to be not merely Minimally Decent Samaritans, but Good Samaritans to unborn persons inside them. This doesn't by itself settle anything one way or the other, because it may well be argued that there should be laws in this country—as there are in many European countries—compelling at least Minimally Decent Samaritanism.[4] But it does show that there is a gross injustice in the existing state of the law. And it shows also that the groups currently working against liberalization of abortion laws, in fact working toward having it declared unconstitutional for a state to permit abortion, had better start working for the adoption of Good Samaritan laws generally, or earn the charge that they are acting in bad faith.

I should think, myself, that Minimally Decent Samaritan laws would be one thing, Good Samaritan laws quite another, and in fact highly improper. But we are not here concerned with the law. What we should ask is not whether anybody should be compelled by law to be a Good Samaritan, but whether we must accede to a situation in which somebody is being compelled—by nature, perhaps—to be a Good Samaritan. We have, in other words, to look now at third-party interventions. I have been arguing that no person is morally required to make large sacrifices to sustain the life of another who has no right to demand them, and this even where the sacrifices do not include life itself; we are not morally required to be Good Samaritans or anyway Very Good Samaritans to one another. But what if a man cannot extricate himself from such a situation? What if he appeals to us to extricate him? It seems to me plain that there are cases in which we can, cases in which a Good Samaritan would extricate him. There you are, you were kidnapped, and nine years in bed with that violinist lie ahead of you. You have your own life to lead. You are sorry, but you simply cannot see giving up so much of your life to the sustaining of his. You cannot extricate yourself, and ask us to do so. I should have thought that—in light of his having no right to the use of your body—it was obvious that we do not have to accede to your being forced to give up so much. We can do what you ask. There is no injustice to the violinist in our doing so.

[5] Following the lead of the opponents of abortion, I have throughout been speaking of the fetus merely as a person, and what I have been asking is whether or not the argument we began with, which proceeds only from the fetus' being a person, really does establish its conclusion. I have argued that it does not.

But of course there are arguments and arguments, and it may be said that I have simply fastened on the wrong one. It may be said that what is important is not merely the fact that the fetus is a person, but that it is a person for whom the woman has a special kind of responsibility issuing from the fact that she is its mother. And it might be argued that all my analogies are therefore irrelevant—for you do not have that special kind of responsibility for that violinist, Henry Fonda does not have that special kind of responsibility for me. And our attention might be drawn to the fact that men and women both *are* compelled by law to provide support for their children.

I have in effect dealt (briefly) with this argument in section [2] above; but a (still briefer) recapitulation now may be in order. Surely we do not have any such "special responsibility" for a person unless we have assumed it, explicitly or implicitly. If a set of parents do not try to prevent pregnancy, do not obtain an abortion, and then at the time of birth of the child do not put it out for adoption, but rather take it home with them, then they have assumed responsibility for it, they have given it rights, and they cannot *now* withdraw support from it at the cost of its life because they now find it difficult to go on providing for it. But if they have taken all reasonable precautions against having a child, they do not simply by virtue of their biological relationship to the child who comes into existence have a special responsibility for it. They may wish to assume responsibility for it, or they may not wish to. And I am suggesting that if assuming responsibility for it would require large sacrifices, then they may refuse. A Good Samaritan would not refuse—or anyway, a Splendid Samaritan, if the sacrifices that had to be made were enormous. But then so would a Good Samaritan assume responsibility for that violinist; so would Henry Fonda, if he is a Good Samaritan, fly in from the West Coast and assume responsibility for me.

[6] My argument will be found unsatisfactory on two counts by many of those who want to regard abortion as morally permissible. First, while I do argue that abortion is not impermissible, I do not argue that it is always permissible. There may well be cases in which carrying the child to term requires only Minimally Decent Samaritanism of the mother, and this is a standard we must not fall below. I am inclined to think it a merit of my account precisely that it does *not* give a general yes or a general no. It allows for and supports our sense that, for example, a sick and desperately frightened fourteen-year-old schoolgirl, pregnant due to rape, may *of course* choose abortion, and that any law which rules this out is an insane law. And it also allows for and supports our sense that in other cases resort to abortion is even positively indecent. It would be indecent in the woman to request an abortion, and indecent in a doctor to perform it, if she is in her seventh month, and wants the abortion just to avoid the nuisance of postponing a trip abroad. The very fact that the arguments I have been drawing attention to treat all cases of abortion, or even all cases of abortion in which the mother's life is not at stake, as morally on a par ought to have made them suspect at the outset.

Secondly, while I am arguing for the permissibility of abortion in some cases, I am not arguing for the right to secure the death of the unborn child. It is easy to confuse these two things in that up to a certain point in the life of the fetus it is not able to survive outside the mother's body; hence removing it from her body guarantees its death. But they are importantly different. I have argued that you are not morally required to spend nine months in bed, sustaining the life of that violinist; but to say this is by no means to say that if, when you unplug yourself, there is a miracle and he survives, you then have a right to turn round and slit his throat. You may detach yourself even if this costs him his life; you have no right to be guaranteed his death, by some other means, if unplugging yourself does not kill him. There are some people who will feel dissatisfied by this feature of my argument. A woman may be utterly devastated by the thought of a child, a bit of herself, put out for adoption and never seen or heard of again. She may therefore want not merely that the child be detached from her, but more, that it die. Some opponents of abortion are inclined to regard this as beneath contempt—thereby showing insensitivity to what is surely a powerful source of despair. All the same, I agree that the desire for the child's death is not one which anybody may gratify, should it turn out to be possible to detach the child alive.

At this place, however, it should be remembered that we have only been pretending throughout that the fetus is a human being from the moment of conception. A very early abortion is surely not the killing of a person, and so is not dealt with by anything I have said here.

NOTES

1 I am very much indebted to James Thomson for discussion, criticism, and many helpful suggestions.

2 Daniel Callahan, *Abortion: Law, Choice and Morality* (New York, 1970), p. 373. This book gives a fascinating survey of the available information on abortion. The Jewish

tradition is surveyed in David M. Feldman, *Birth Control in Jewish Law* (New York, 1968), Part 5, the Catholic tradition in John T. Noonan, Jr., "An Almost Absolute Value in History," in *The Morality of Abortion,* ed. John T. Noonan, Jr. (Cambridge, Mass., 1970).

3 The need for a discussion of this argument was brought home to me by members of the Society for Ethical and Legal Philosophy, to whom this paper was originally presented.

4 For a discussion of the difficulties involved, and a survey of the European experience with such laws, see *The Good Samaritan and the Law,* ed. James M. Ratcliffe (New York, 1966).

QUESTIONS

1 To what extent, if at all, does Thomson succeed in her effort to moderate the conservative view on abortion?

2 Does Thomson provide a defensible account of the right to life?

3 Thomson's overall analysis culminates in a moderate view on abortion, but does her moderate view incline more in a conservative direction or more in a liberal direction?

The Morality of Abortion

Margaret Olivia Little

Little argues that abortion is a morally weighty matter even if we put aside the claim that the fetus is a person. In her view, "burgeoning human life" matters morally; it has some degree of value (moral status) and, thus, to that extent is worthy of respect. From this general starting point, Little explores the morality of abortion, paying special attention to two themes—motherhood and respect for creation—that often play a role in the thinking of women struggling with a decision to continue or end pregnancy. She explains how each of these themes adds a layer of complexity to a woman's decision to continue or end pregnancy, and she ultimately argues that personal decisions about the morality of abortion depend in part on the unique way in which individual women construct their fundamental identities, commitments, and personal ideals.

. . . Just as we cannot assume that abortion is monstrous if fetuses are persons, so too we cannot assume that abortion is empty of moral import if they are not. Given all the ink that has been spilt on arbitrating the question of fetal personhood, one might be forgiven for having thought so: on some accounts, decisions about whether to continue or end a pregnancy really are, from a moral point of view, just like decisions about whether to cut one's hair.

Reprinted with permission of the publisher from *A Companion to Applied Ethics* (2003), edited by R. G. Frey and Christopher Heath Wellman, pp. 319–324. © 2003 by Blackwell Publishing Ltd.

But as Ronald Dworkin (1993) has urged, to think abortion morally weighty does not require supposition that the fetus is a person, or even a creature with interests in continued life. Destruction of a Da Vinci painting, he points out, is not bad *for the painting*—the painting has no interests. Instead, it is regrettable because of the deep value it has. So, too, one of the reasons we might regard abortion as morally weighty does not have to do with its being bad *for the fetus*—a setback to its interests—for it may not satisfy the criteria of having interests. Abortion may be weighty, instead, because there is something precious and significant about germinating human life that deserves our deep respect. This, as Dworkin puts it, locates issues of abortion in a different neighborhood of our moral commitments: namely, the accommodation we owe to things of value. That an organism is a potential person may not make it a claims-bearer, but it does mean it has a kind of stature that is worthy of respect.

This intuition, dismissed by some as mere sentimentality, is, I think, both important and broadly held. Very few people regard abortion as the moral equivalent of contraception. Most think a society better morally—not just by public health measures—if it regards abortion as a back-up to failed contraception rather than as routine birth control. Reasons adequate for contraception do not translate transparently as reasons adequate for abortion. Indeed, there is a telling shift in presumption: for most people, it takes no reason at all to justify contracepting; it takes *some* reason to justify ending a pregnancy. That a human life has now begun matters morally.

Burgeoning human life, we might put it, is *respect-worthy*. This is why we care not just whether, but how, abortion is done—while crass jokes are made or with solemnity—and why we care how the fetal remains are treated. It is why the thought of someone aborting for genuinely trivial reasons—to fit into a favorite party dress, say—makes us morally queasy. Perhaps, most basically, it is why the thought of someone aborting with casual indifference fills us with misgiving. Abortion involves loss. Not just loss of the hope that various parties might have invested, but loss of something valuable in its own right. To respect something is to appreciate fully the value it has and the claims it presents to us; someone who aborts but never gives it a second thought has not exhibited genuine appreciation of the value and moral status of that which is now gone.

But if many share the intuition that early human life has a value deserving of respect, there is considerable disagreement about what that respect looks like. There is considerable conflict, that is, over what accommodation we owe to burgeoning human life. In part, of course, this is due to disagreement over the *degree* of value such life should be accorded: those for whom it is thoroughly modest will have very different views on issues, from abortion to stem-cell research, from those for whom it is transcendent. But this is only part of the story. Obscured by analogies to Da Vinci paintings, some of the most important sources of conflict, especially for the vast middle rank of moderates, ride atop rough agreement on "degree" of fetal value. If we listen to women's own struggles about when it is morally decent to end pregnancy, what we hear are themes about *motherhood* and *respect for creation*. These themes are enormously complex, I want to argue, for they enter stories on both sides of the ledger: for some women, as reasons to continue pregnancy, and for others, as reasons to end it. Let me start with motherhood.

For many women who contemplate abortion, the desire to end pregnancy is not, or not centrally, a desire to avoid the nine months of pregnancy; it is to avoid what lies on the far side of those months—namely, motherhood. If gestation were simply a matter of rendering, say, somewhat risky assistance to help a burgeoning human life they have come across—if they could somehow render that assistance without thereby adding a member to their family—the decision faced would be a far different one. But gestation does not just allow cells to become a person; it turns one into a mother.

One of the most common reasons women give for wanting to abort is that they do not want to become a mother—now, ever, again, with this partner, or no reliable partner, with these few resources, or these many that are now, after so many years of mothering, slated finally to another cause (Hursthouse, 1987: ch. 8.4). Nor does adoption represent a universal solution. To give up a child would be for some a life-long trauma; others occupy fortunate circumstances that would, by their own lights, make it unjustified to give over a child for others to rear. Or again—and most frequently—she does not want to raise a child just now but knows that if she *does* carry the pregnancy to term, she will not *want* to give up the child for adoption. Gestation, she knows, is likely to reshape her heart and soul, transforming her into a mother emotionally, not just officially; and it is precisely that transformation she does not want to undergo. It is because continuing pregnancy brings with it this new identity and, likely, relationship, then, that many feel it legitimate to decline.

But pregnancy's connection to motherhood also enters the phenomenology of abortion in just the opposite direction. For some women, that it would be her child is precisely why she feels she must continue the pregnancy, even if motherhood is not what she desired. To be pregnant is to have one's potential child knocking at one's door: to abort is to turn one's back on it, a decision, many women say, that would haunt them forever. On this view, the desire to avoid motherhood, so compelling as a reason to use contraception, is uneasy grounds to abort: for once an embryo is on the scene, it is not about rejecting motherhood, it is about rejecting one's *child*. Not literally, of course, since there is no child yet extant to stand as the object of rejection. But the stance one should take to pregnancy, sought or not, is one of *acceptance:* when a potential family member is knocking at the door, one should move over, make room, and welcome her in.

These two intuitive stances represent just profoundly different ways of *gestalting* the situation of ending pregnancy. On the first view, abortion is closer to contraception: hardly equivalent, because it means the demise of something of value. But the desire to avoid the enterprise and identity of motherhood is an understandable and honorable basis for deciding to end a pregnancy. Given that there is no child yet on the scene, one does not owe special openness to the relationship that stands at the end of pregnancy's trajectory. On the second view, abortion is closer to exiting a parental relationship: hardly equivalent, for one of the key relata is not yet fully present. But one's decision about whether to continue the pregnancy already feels specially constrained; that one would be related to the resulting person exerts now some moral force. It would take especially grave reasons to refuse assistance here, for the norms of parenthood already have toehold. Assessing the moral status of abortion, it turns out, then, is not just about assessing the contours of generic respect owed to burgeoning human life, it is about assessing the salience of *impending relationship*. And this is an issue that functions in different ways for different women—and, sometimes, in one and the same woman.

In my own view, until the fetus is a person, we should recognize a moral prerogative to decline parenthood and end the pregnancy. Not because motherhood is necessarily a burden (though it can be), but because it so thoroughly changes what we might call one's fundamental *practical identity*. The enterprise of mothering restructures the self—changing the shape of one's heart, the primary commitments by which one lives one's life, the terms by which one judges one's life a success or a failure. If the enterprise is eschewed and one decides to give the child over to another, the identity of mother still changes the normative facts that are true of one, as there is now someone by whom one does well or poorly (see Ross, 1982). And either way—whether one rears the child or lets it go—to continue a pregnancy means that a piece of one's heart, as the saying goes, will forever walk outside one's body. As profound as the respect we should have for burgeoning human life, we should acknowledge moral prerogatives over identity-constituting commitments and enterprises as profound as motherhood.

Whether one agrees with this view or not, there is at any rate another layer of the moral story here. If women find themselves with different ways of *gestalting* the prospective relationship involved in pregnancy, it is in part because they have different identities, commitments, and ideals that such a prospect intersects with, commitments which, while permissibly idiosyncratic, are morally authoritative for *them*. If one woman feels already duty-bound by the norms of parenthood to nurture this creature, for example, it may be for the very good reason that, in an important personal sense, she already *is* its mother. She finds herself (perhaps to her surprise) with a maternal commitment to this creature. But taking on the identity of mother toward something just *is* to take on certain imperatives about its well-being as categorical. Her job is thus clear: it is to help this creature reach its fullest potential. For another woman, on the other hand, the identity of mother is yet to be taken on; it is tried on, perhaps accepted, but perhaps declined—in which case respect is owed, but love is saved, or confirmed, for others—other relationships, other projects, other passions.

And, again, if one woman feels she owes a stance of welcome to burgeoning human life that comes her way, it may be, not because she thinks such a stance authoritative for all, but because of the virtues around which her practical identity is now oriented: receptivity to life's agenda, for instance, or responsiveness to that which is most vulnerable. For another woman, the virtues to be exercised may tug in just the other direction: loyalty to treasured life plans, a commitment that it be she, not the chances of biology, that should determine her life's course, bolstering self-direction after a life too long ruled by serendipity and fate.

Deciding when it is morally decent to end a pregnancy, it turns out, is an admixture of settling impersonally or universally authoritative moral requirements, and of discovering and arbitrating—sometimes after agonizing deliberation, sometimes in a decision no less deep for its immediacy—one's own commitments, identity, and defining virtues.

A similarly complex story appears when we turn to the second theme. Another thread that appears in many women's stories in the face of unsought pregnancy is respect for the weighty responsibility involved in creating human life. Once again, it is a theme that pulls and tugs in different directions.

In its most familiar direction, it shows up in many stories of why an unsought pregnancy is continued. Many people believe that one's responsibility to nurture new life is importantly amplified if one is responsible for bringing about its existence in the first place. Just what it takes to count as responsible here is a point on which individuals diverge (whether voluntary intercourse with contraception is different from intercourse without use of birth control, and again from intentionally deciding to become pregnant at the IVF clinic). But triggering the relevant standard of responsibility for creation, it is felt, brings with it a heightened responsibility to nurture: it is disrespectful to create human life only to allow it to wither. Put more rigorously, one who is responsible for bringing about a creature that has intrinsic value in virtue of its potential to become a person has a special responsibility to enable it to reach that end state.

But the idea of respect for creation is also, if less frequently acknowledged, sometimes the reason why women are moved to *end* pregnancies. As Barbara Katz Rothman (1989) puts it, decisions to abort often represent, not a decision to destroy, but a refusal to create. Many people have deeply felt convictions about the circumstances under which they feel it right for them to bring a child into the world. Can it be brought into a decent world, an intact family, a society that can minimally respect its agency? These considerations may persist even after conception has taken place; for while the *embryo* has already been created, a person has not. Some women decide to abort, that is, not because they do not *want* the resulting child—indeed, they may yearn for nothing more, and desperately wish that their circumstances were otherwise—but because they do not think bringing a child into the world is the right thing for them to do.

These are abortions marked by moral language. A woman wants to abort because she knows she could not give up a child for adoption but feels she could not give the child the sort of life, or be the sort of parent, she thinks a child *deserves;* a woman who would have to give up the child thinks it would be *unfair* to bring a child into existence already burdened by rejection, however well grounded its reasons; a woman living in a country marked by poverty and gender apartheid wants to abort because she decides it would be *wrong* for her to bear a daughter whose life, like hers, would be filled with so much injustice and hardship.

Some have thought that such decisions betray a simple fallacy: unless the child's life were literally going to be worse than non-existence, how can one abort out of concern for the future child? But the worry here is not that one would be imposing a *harm* on the child by bringing it into existence (as though children who are in the situations mentioned have lives that are not worth living). The claim is that bringing about a person's life in these circumstances would do violence to her ideals of creating and parenthood. She does not want to bring into existence a daughter she cannot love and care for, she does not want to bring into existence a person whose life will be marked by disrespect or rejection.

Nor does the claim imply judgment on women who *do* continue pregnancies in similar circumstances—as though there were here an obligation to abort. For the norms in question, once again, need not be impersonally authoritative moral claims. Like ideals of good parenting, they mark out considerations all should be sensitive to, perhaps, but equally reasonable people may adhere to different variations and weightings. Still, they are normative for those who do have them; far from expressing mere matters of taste, the ideals one does accept carry an important kind of categoricity, issuing imperatives whose authority is not reducible to mere desire. These are, at root, issue about *integrity,* and the importance of maintaining integrity over one's participation in this enterprise precisely because it is so normatively weighty.

What is usually emphasized in the morality of abortion is the ethics of destruction, but there is a balancing ethics of creation. And for many people, conflict about abortion is a conflict *within* that ethics. On the one hand, we now have on hand an entity that has a measure of sanctity: that it has begun is reason to help it continue, perhaps especially if one has had a role in its procreation, which is why even early abortion is not normatively equivalent to contraception. On the other hand, not to end a pregnancy *is* to do something else, namely, to continue creating a person, and, for some women, pregnancy strikes in circumstances in which they cannot countenance that enterprise. For some, the sanctity of developing human life will be strong enough to tip the balance toward continuing the pregnancy; for others, their norms of respectful creation will hold sway. For those who believe that the norms governing creation of a person are mild relative to the normative telos of embryonic life, being a responsible creator means continuing to gestate, and doing the best one can to bring about the conditions under which that creation will be more respectful. For others, though, the normativity of fetal telos is mild and their standards of respectful creation high, and the lesson goes in just the other direction: it is a sign of respect not to continue creating when certain background conditions, such as a loving family or adequate resources, are not in place.

However one thinks these issues settle out, they will not be resolved by austere contemplation of the value of human life. They require wrestling with the rich meanings of creation, responsibility, and kinship. And these issues, I have suggested, are just as much issues about one's integrity as they are about what is impersonally obligatory. On many treatments of abortion, considerations about whether or not to continue a pregnancy are exhausted by preferences, on the one hand, and universally authoritative moral demands, on the other; but some of the most important terrain lies in between.

REFERENCES

Dworkin, R. (1993) *Life's Dominion: An Argument About Abortion, Euthanasia, and Individual Freedom.* New York: Alfred A. Knopf.

Hursthouse, R. (1987) *Beginning Lives.* Oxford: Open University Press.

Ross, S. L. (1982) Abortion and the death of the fetus. *Philosophy and Public Affairs,* 11:232–45.

Rothman, B. K. (1989) *Recreating Motherhood: Ideology and Technology in a Patriarchal Society.* New York: Norton.

QUESTIONS

1 Do you agree with Little that the morality of individual abortion decisions properly depends—at least to some extent—on the fundamental identities, commitments, and personal ideals of the women who face such decisions?
2 Can you think of some concrete situations in which considerations related to motherhood and/or respect for creation might incline a woman to abortion? Can you think of some concrete situations in which considerations related to motherhood and/or respect for creation might incline a woman against abortion?

Majority Opinion in *Roe v. Wade*

Justice Harry A. Blackmun

In this case, a pregnant single woman, suing under the fictitious name of Jane Roe, challenged the constitutionality of the existing Texas criminal abortion law. According to the Texas Penal Code, the performance of an abortion, except to save the life of the pregnant woman, constituted a crime punishable by a prison sentence of two to five years. At the time this case was finally resolved by the United States Supreme Court, abortion legislation varied widely from state to state. Some states, principally New York, had already legalized abortion on demand. Most other states, however, had legalized various forms of therapeutic abortion but had retained some measure of restrictive abortion legislation.

Justice Blackmun, writing an opinion concurred in by six other justices, argues that a woman's decision to terminate a pregnancy is encompassed by a *right to privacy*—but only up to a certain point in the development of the fetus. As the right to privacy is not an absolute right, it must yield at some point to the state's legitimate interests. Justice Blackmun contends that the state has a legitimate interest in protecting the health of the pregnant woman and that this interest becomes compelling at approximately the end of the first trimester in the development of the fetus. He also contends that the state has a legitimate interest in protecting potential life and that this interest becomes compelling at the point of viability.

It is . . . apparent that at common law, at the time of the adoption of our Constitution, and throughout the major portion of the 19th century, abortion was viewed with less disfavor than under most American statutes currently in effect. Phrasing it another way, a woman enjoyed a substantially broader right to terminate a pregnancy than she does in most States today. At least with respect to the early stage of pregnancy, and very possibly without such a limitation, the opportunity to make this choice was present in this country well into the 19th century. Even later, the law continued for some time to treat less punitively an abortion procured in early pregnancy. . . .

United States Supreme Court. 410 U.S. 113 (1973).

Three reasons have been advanced to explain historically the enactment of criminal abortion laws in the 19th century and to justify their continued existence.

It has been argued occasionally that these laws were the product of a Victorian social concern to discourage illicit sexual conduct. Texas, however, does not advance this justification in the present case, and it appears that no court or commentator has taken the argument seriously. . . .

A second reason is concerned with abortion as a medical procedure. When most criminal abortion laws were first enacted, the procedure was a hazardous one for the woman. This was particularly true prior to the development of antisepsis. Antiseptic techniques, of course, were based on discoveries by Lister, Pasteur, and others first announced in 1867, but were not generally accepted and employed until about the turn of the century. Abortion mortality was high. Even after 1900, and perhaps until as late as the development of antibiotics in the 1940's, standard modern techniques such as dilatation and curettage were not nearly so safe as they are today. Thus it has been argued that a State's real concern in enacting a criminal abortion law was to protect the pregnant woman, that is, to restrain her from submitting to a procedure that placed her life in serious jeopardy.

Modern medical techniques have altered this situation. Appellants and various *amici* refer to medical data indicating that abortion in early pregnancy, that is, prior to the end of first trimester, although not without its risk, is now relatively safe. Mortality rates for women undergoing early abortions, where the procedure is legal, appear to be as low as or lower than the rates for normal childbirth. Consequently, any interest of the State in protecting the woman from an inherently hazardous procedure, except when it would be equally dangerous for her to forgo it, has largely disappeared. Of course, important state interests in the area of health and medical standards do remain. The State has a legitimate interest in seeing to it that abortion, like any other medical procedure, is performed under circumstances that insure maximum safety for the patient. This interest obviously extends at least to the performing physician and his staff, to the facilities involved, to the availability of after-care, and to adequate provision for any complication or emergency that might arise. The prevalence of high mortality rates at illegal "abortion mills" strengthens, rather than weakens, the State's interest in regulating the conditions under which abortions are performed. Moreover, the risk to the woman increases as her pregnancy continues. Thus the State retains a definite interest in protecting the woman's own health and safety when an abortion is performed at a late stage of pregnancy.

The third reason is the State's interest—some phrase it in terms of duty—in protecting prenatal life. Some of the argument for this justification rests on the theory that a new human life is present from the moment of conception. The State's interest and general obligation to protect life then extends, it is argued, to prenatal life. Only when the life of the pregnant mother herself is at stake, balanced against the life she carries within her, should the interest of the embryo or fetus not prevail. Logically, of course, a legitimate state interest in this area need not stand or fall on acceptance of the belief that life begins at conception or at some other point prior to live birth. In assessing the State's interest, recognition may be given to the less rigid claim that as long as at least *potential* life is involved, the State may assert interests beyond the protection of the pregnant woman alone.

Parties challenging state abortion laws have sharply disputed in some courts the contention that a purpose of these laws, when enacted, was to protect prenatal life. Pointing to the absence of legislative history to support the contention, they claim that most state laws were designed solely to protect the woman. Because medical advances have lessened this concern, at least with respect to abortion in early pregnancy, they argue that with respect to such abortions the laws can no longer be justified by any state interest. There is some scholarly support for this view of original purpose. The few state courts called upon to interpret their laws in the late 19th and early 20th centuries did focus on the State's interest in protecting the woman's health rather than in preserving the embryo and fetus. . . .

The Constitution does not explicitly mention any right of privacy. In a line of decisions, however, going back perhaps as far as *Union Pacific R. Co. v. Botsford* (1891), the Court has recognized that a right of personal privacy, or a guarantee of certain areas or zones of privacy, does exist under the Constitution. In varying contexts the Court or individual Justices have indeed found at least the roots of that right in the First Amendment, . . . in the Fourth and Fifth Amendments . . . in the penumbras of the Bill of Rights . . . in the Ninth Amendment . . . or in the concept of liberty guaranteed by the first section of the Fourteenth Amendment. . . . These decisions make it clear that only personal rights that can be deemed "fundamental" or "implicit in the concept of ordered liberty," . . . are included in this guarantee of personal privacy. They also make it clear that the right has some extension to activities relating to marriage, . . . procreation, . . . contraception, . . . family relationships, . . . and child rearing and education. . . .

This right of privacy, whether it be founded in the Fourteenth Amendment's concept of personal liberty and restrictions upon state action, as we feel it is, or, as the District Court determined, in the Ninth Amendment's reservation of rights to the people, is broad enough to encompass a woman's decision whether or not to terminate her pregnancy. . . .

. . . [A]ppellants and some *amici* argue that the woman's right is absolute and that she is entitled to terminate her pregnancy at whatever time, in whatever way, and for whatever reason she alone chooses. With this we do not agree. Appellants' arguments that Texas either has no valid interest at all in regulating the abortion decision, or no interest strong enough to support any limitation upon the woman's sole determination, is unpersuasive. The Court's decisions recognizing a right of privacy also acknowledge that some state regulation in areas protected by that right is appropriate. As noted above, a state may properly assert important interests in safe-guarding health, in maintaining medical standards, and in protecting potential life. At some point in pregnancy, these respective interests become sufficiently compelling to sustain regulation of the factors that govern the abortion decision. The privacy right involved, therefore, cannot be said to be absolute. . . .

We therefore conclude that the right of personal privacy includes the abortion decision, but that this right is not unqualified and must be considered against important state interests in regulation.

We note that those federal and state courts that have recently considered abortion law challenges have reached the same conclusion. . . .

Although the results are divided, most of these courts have agreed that the right of privacy, however based, is broad enough to cover the abortion decision; that the right, nonetheless, is not absolute and is subject to some limitations; and that at some point the state interests as to protection of health, medical standards, and prenatal life, become dominant. We agree with this approach. . . .

The appellee and certain *amici* argue that the fetus is a "person" within the language and meaning of the Fourteenth Amendment. In support of this they outline at length and in detail the well-known facts of fetal development. If this suggestion of personhood is established, the appellant's case, of course, collapses, for the fetus' right to life is then guaranteed specifically by the Amendment. The appellant conceded as much on reargument. On the other hand, the appellee conceded on reargument that no case could be cited that holds that a fetus is a person within the meaning of the Fourteenth Amendment. . . .

All this, together with our observation, *supra,* that throughout the major portion of the 19th century prevailing legal abortion practices were far freer than they are today, persuades us that the word "person," as used in the Fourteenth Amendment, does not include the unborn. . . . Indeed, our decision in *United States v. Vuitch* (1971) inferentially is to the same effect, for we there would not have indulged in statutory interpretation favorable to abortion in specified circumstances if the necessary consequence was the termination of life entitled to Fourteenth Amendment protection.

. . . As we have intimated above, it is reasonable and appropriate for a State to decide that at some point in time another interest, that of health of the mother or that of potential human life, becomes significantly involved. The woman's privacy is no longer sole and any right of privacy she possesses must be measured accordingly.

Texas urges that, apart from the Fourteenth Amendment, life begins at conception and is present throughout pregnancy, and that, therefore, the State has a compelling interest in protecting that life from and after conception. We need not resolve the difficult question of when life begins. When those trained in the respective disciplines of medicine, philosophy, and theology are unable to arrive at any consensus, the judiciary, at this point in the development of man's knowledge, is not in a position to speculate as to the answer.

It should be sufficient to note briefly the wide divergence of thinking on this most sensitive and difficult question. There has always been strong support for the view that life does not begin until live birth. This was the belief of the Stoics. It appears to be the predominant, though not the unanimous, attitude of the Jewish faith. It may be taken to represent also the position of a large segment of the Protestant community, insofar as that can be ascertained; organized groups that have taken a formal position on the abortion issue have generally regarded abortion as a matter for the conscience of the individual and her family. As we have noted, the common law found greater significance in quickening. Physicians and their scientific colleagues have regarded that event with less interest and have tended to focus either upon conception or upon live birth or upon the interim point at which the fetus becomes "viable," that is, potentially able to live outside the mother's womb, albeit with artificial aid. Viability is usually placed at about seven months (28 weeks) but may occur earlier, even at 24 weeks. . . .

In areas other than criminal abortion the law has been reluctant to endorse any theory that life, as we recognize it, begins before live birth or to accord legal rights to the unborn except in narrowly defined situations and except when the rights are contingent upon live birth. . . . In short, the unborn have never been recognized in the law as persons in the whole sense.

In view of all this, we do not agree that, by adopting one theory of life, Texas may override the rights of the pregnant woman that are at stake. We repeat, however, that the State does have an important and legitimate interest in preserving and protecting the health of the pregnant woman, whether she be a resident of the State or a non-resident who seeks medical consultation and treatment there, and that it has still *another* important and legitimate interest in protecting the potentiality of human life. These interests are separate and distinct. Each grows in substantiality as the woman approaches term and, at a point during pregnancy, each becomes "compelling."

With respect to the State's important and legitimate interest in the health of the mother, the "compelling" point, in the light of present medical knowledge, is at approximately the end of the first trimester. This is so because of the now established medical fact . . . that until the end of the first trimester mortality in abortion is less than mortality in normal childbirth. It follows that, from and after this point, a State may regulate the abortion procedure to the extent that the regulation reasonably relates to the preservation and protection of maternal health. Examples of permissible state regulation in this area are requirements as to the qualifications of the person who is to perform the abortion; as to the licensure of that person; as to the facility in which the procedure is to be performed, that is, whether it must be a hospital or may be a clinic or some other place of less-than-hospital status; as to the licensing of the facility; and the like.

This means, on the other hand, that, for the period of pregnancy prior to this "compelling" point, the attending physician, in consultation with his patient, is free to determine, without regulation by the State, that in his medical judgment the patient's pregnancy should be terminated. If that decision is reached, the judgment may be effectuated by an abortion free of interference by the State.

With respect to the State's important and legitimate interest in potential life, the "compelling" point is at viability. This is so because the fetus then presumably has the capability of meaningful life outside the mother's womb. State regulation protective of fetal life after viability thus has both logical and biological justifications. If the State is interested in protecting fetal life after viability, it may go so far as to proscribe abortion during that period except when it is necessary to preserve the life or health of the mother. . . .

To summarize and repeat:

1 A state criminal abortion statute of the current Texas type, that excepts from criminality only a *life saving* procedure on behalf of the mother, without regard to pregnancy stage and without recognition of the other interests involved, is violative of the Due Process Clause of the Fourteenth Amendment.

(a) For the stage prior to approximately the end of the first trimester, the abortion decision and its effectuation must be left to the medical judgment of the pregnant woman's attending physician.

(b) For the stage subsequent to approximately the end of the first trimester, the State, in promoting its interest in the health of the mother, may, if it chooses, regulate the abortion procedure in ways that are reasonably related to maternal health.

(c) For the stage subsequent to viability the State, in promoting its interest in the potentiality of human life, may, if it chooses, regulate, and even proscribe, abortion except where it is necessary, in appropriate medical judgment, for the preservation of the life or health of the mother.

2 The State may define the term "physician," as it has been employed [here], to mean only a physician currently licensed by the State, and may proscribe any abortion by a person who is not a physician as so defined.

. . . The decision leaves the State free to place increasing restrictions on abortion as the period of pregnancy lengthens, so long as those restrictions are tailored to the recognized state interests. The decision vindicates the right of the physician to administer medical treatment according to his professional judgment up to the points where important state interests provide compelling justifications for intervention. Up to those points the abortion decision in all its aspects is inherently, and primarily, a medical decision, and basic responsibility for it must rest with the physician. If an individual practitioner abuses the privilege of exercising proper medical judgment, the usual remedies, judicial and intraprofessional, are available. . . .

QUESTIONS

1 Justice Blackmun contends that the state's legitimate interest in protecting the health of the mother becomes *compelling* at the end of the first trimester. Does the Court's choice of this particular point as "compelling" have any substantial justification, or is the choice fundamentally arbitrary?

2 Justice Blackmun contends that the state's legitimate interest in protecting potential life becomes *compelling* at the point of viability. Does the Court's choice of this particular point as "compelling" have any substantial justification, or is the choice fundamentally arbitrary?

3 Justice Blackmun *explicitly* disavows entering into philosophical speculation on the problem of the beginning of human life. To what extent could it be said that he *implicitly* takes a philosophical position on this problem?

"Partial-Birth Abortion" and the Supreme Court

George J. Annas

Annas reviews and interprets the issues at stake in the case of *Stenberg v. Carhart,* a case decided by the U.S. Supreme Court in 2000. In *Stenberg,* decided by a five-to-four majority, the Court declared unconstitutional a Nebraska law banning "partial-birth abortion" except when necessary to save the life of a pregnant

Adapted with permission of the publisher from *The New England Journal of Medicine,* vol. 344 (January 11, 2001), pp. 152–156. Copyright © 2001 Massachusetts Medical Society. All rights reserved.

woman. Annas identifies the two major constitutional issues raised by the case, explains Justice Breyer's reasoning in the majority opinion, and provides a brief survey of the various concurring and dissenting opinions.

Abortion has long been, and remains, the most politicized medical procedure in the United States. It has been the subject of more state and federal legislation than all other medical procedures combined. The U.S. Supreme Court, which almost never hears cases about medical procedures, has regularly heard cases over the past 25 years concerning the constitutionality of various state laws designed to limit abortion. Thus, it was only a matter of time before the Court would hear a case on the constitutionality of laws restricting so-called partial-birth abortion.[1] When the Court heard a challenge to Nebraska's law, statutes relating to partial-birth abortion had been enacted in 30 states, and two bills banning such abortions had been passed by Congress. All the appeals courts except one, the Seventh Circuit Court of Appeals, had found these laws unconstitutional, and the opinion of that court rested on an extremely narrow interpretation of the law.[2]

The controversies surrounding partial-birth abortion are over how to describe the procedure and whether physicians ever need to use it to protect the health of a pregnant woman. The Supreme Court confronted these issues in the case of *Stenberg* v. *Carhart* last summer [2000].[3]

THE NEBRASKA PARTIAL-BIRTH ABORTION LAW

The Nebraska law provides that "no partial birth abortion shall be performed in this state, unless such procedure is necessary to save the life of the mother whose life is endangered by a physical disorder, physical illness, or physical injury, including a life-endangering physical condition caused by or arising from the pregnancy itself."[4] Like the federal acts twice passed by Congress and vetoed by President Bill Clinton, the Nebraska law defined partial-birth abortion as "an abortion in which the person performing the abortion partially delivers vaginally a living unborn child before killing the unborn child and completing the delivery." The law further defines the phrase "partially delivers vaginally a living unborn child before killing the unborn child" to mean "deliberately and intentionally delivering into the vagina a living unborn child, or a substantial portion thereof, for the purpose of performing a procedure that the person performing such procedure knows will kill the unborn child and does kill the unborn child."[4] Violation of the law is a felony that carries a prison term of up to 20 years, a fine of up to $25,000, and automatic revocation of a medical license.

Dr. Leroy Carhart, a Nebraska physician who performs abortions, sued in federal court to have the law declared unconstitutional. U.S. District Court judge Richard G. Kopf reviewed abortion procedures in detail, using a drawing of female pelvic anatomy as an attachment to his opinion, before holding that the statute was unconstitutional because it endangered women's lives and health and was void for vagueness because physicians could not know what conduct it proscribed.[5] The Court of Appeals for the Eighth Circuit affirmed the District Court ruling.[6] By a five-to-four vote, the Supreme Court ruled on June 28, 2000, that the Nebraska law and all other laws banning partial-birth abortion are unconstitutional.

THE MAJORITY DECISION

The opinion of the Court was written by Justice Stephen Breyer, one of only two current justices (the other is Ruth Bader Ginsburg) who had not previously expressed an opinion in a major decision about abortion. The opinion is best understood as a direct application to the Nebraska law of the principles articulated in the 1973 decision in *Roe* v. *Wade*[7] and the 1992 decision in *Planned Parenthood of Southeastern Pennsylvania* v. *Casey*.[8] In *Roe* the Court held that because a woman's right to privacy is "fundamental," states must demonstrate a "compelling interest" in order to restrict abortion, and they are unable to demonstrate such an interest before the time when the fetus becomes viable. Moreover, *Roe* made it clear that the state could not favor the life of the fetus over the life or health of the pregnant woman. The Court in *Casey* affirmed the core holding of *Roe,* that states cannot outlaw abortion before the time of fetal viability and can do so thereafter only if the woman's life and health are protected. States were permitted, however, to regulate abortions so long as any restriction did not impose an "undue burden" on the pregnant woman's liberty interest in terminating her pregnancy.

The Nebraska ban applies throughout pregnancy and has no exception to preserve a woman's health. Under *Roe* and *Casey,* the state of Nebraska had to demonstrate that the state had at least a legitimate interest in outlawing partial-birth abortions and that doing so would not place an undue burden on women. Because it is a criminal statute, the legislature had to be very clear about what exactly the statute prohibited. In order to determine exactly what was and was not prohibited, Justice Breyer, like the trial court judge, devoted nearly the entirety of his opinion to describing various abortion procedures and comparing them with the language of the Nebraska law.

HOW ABORTIONS ARE PERFORMED

Justice Breyer introduced his descriptions of abortion procedures by stating that they may seem "clinically cold or callous to some, perhaps horrifying to others," but that he saw no other way "to acquaint the reader with the technical distinctions among different abortion methods and related factual matters, upon which the outcome of this case depends." Breyer noted, among other facts, that 90 percent of abortions in the United States are performed before 12 weeks of gestation, and almost all the rest are performed between 12 and 24 weeks. Almost all second-trimester abortions are performed by means of dilation and evacuation, with variations depending on the stage of gestation. Breyer quoted a report from the American Medical Association (AMA) as saying that at 13 to 15 weeks of gestation, "D&E [dilation and evacuation] is similar to vacuum aspiration except that the cervix must be dilated more widely because surgical instruments are used to remove larger pieces of tissue." After 15 weeks, the AMA report continues, because of the increased size of the fetus and the rigidity of its bones, "dismemberment or other destructive procedures are more likely to be required . . . to remove fetal and placental tissue." And after 20 weeks, "some physicians use intrafetal potassium chloride or digoxin to induce fetal demise . . . to facilitate evacuation."[3]

Breyer then made a series of observations and factual conclusions that determined the outcome of the case. He found, first, that the various dilation-and-evacuation procedures have in common the dilation of the cervix, the removal of at least some fetal tissue with the use of surgical instruments, and (after the 15th week) the potential need for dismemberment of the fetus. When dismemberment does occur, it typically occurs "as the doctor pulls a portion of the fetus through the cervix into the birth canal." Breyer noted that a variation of dilation and evacuation, which the physicians who testified at the trial referred to as "intact D&E" or dilation and extraction, is used at 16 weeks at the earliest, when vacuum aspiration is ineffective and the fetal skull is too large to pass through the cervix. Dilation and extraction may proceed in two ways: if the fetus presents head first, the physician collapses the skull and then extracts the intact fetus through the cervix; if there is a breech presentation, the physician pulls the fetal body through the cervix, then collapses the skull, and then extracts the fetus.[3]

On the basis of information from medical textbooks and the position taken by the American College of Obstetricians and Gynecologists,[9] Breyer concluded that "intact D&E and D&X [dilation and extraction] are sufficiently similar for us [the Court] to use the terms interchangeably." There are no accurate statistics available on the number of dilation-and-extraction abortions performed in the United States, and Breyer cited estimates ranging from 640 to 5000 cases per year. He found that such abortions are performed for a variety of reasons, including reducing the danger caused by the passage of sharp bone fragments through the cervix, minimizing the number of surgical instruments used (and thereby decreasing the likelihood of uterine perforation), reducing the likelihood of infection, and helping to ensure the removal of all fetal tissue. Dilation and extraction is also the preferred method for fetuses with hydrocephaly and anomalies incompatible with fetal survival.[3]

All this was much more detail about a medical procedure than had ever appeared before in a Supreme Court opinion. The factual conclusions, however, were necessary to answering the two major constitutional questions posed by Nebraska's ban: Must a law prohibiting the use of a medical procedure for abortion contain an exception to protect the health of the pregnant woman as defined in *Roe*? And does the Nebraska law "unduly burden" a woman's right to choose to terminate her pregnancy as defined in *Casey*? Justice Breyer's answer to both of these questions was yes.

WOMEN'S HEALTH

Justice Breyer recited the rule, as stated in *Roe* v. *Wade,* that a state may outlaw abortion after the fetus is viable in order to promote its interest in protecting potential human life, "except where it is necessary, in appropriate medical judgment, for the preservation of the life or health of the mother." Breyer logically concluded that if *Roe* requires an exception for the mother's health after fetal viability, it must require one before viability, when the state has less of an interest in protecting fetal life.

Would the ban in fact adversely affect the health of pregnant women who want to terminate their pregnancies? Breyer concluded that it would, on the basis of the belief of "significant medical authority" that "in some circumstances, D&X would be the safest procedure." Breyer found especially persuasive the brief to the Court in which the American College of Obstetricians and Gynecologists stated specifically that dilation and extraction "may be the best or most appropriate procedure in a particular circumstance to save the life or preserve the health of a woman."[3,9] Nebraska relied on a contrary statement of the AMA that "there does not appear to be any identified situation in which intact D&X is the only appropriate procedure to induce abortion."[3]

Breyer rejected the argument that the word "necessary," as used in the opinion *Planned Parenthood* v. *Casey*—"necessary, in appropriate medical judgment, for the preservation of the life or health of the mother"[8]—means an "absolute necessity" or requires "absolute proof." He concluded that the words "'appropriate medical judgment' must embody the judicial need to tolerate responsible differences of medical opinion." Breyer, who has special expertise in administrative law and risk assessment, went on to say that "the division of medical opinion about the matter at most means uncertainty, a factor that signals the presence of risk, not its absence." He concluded that "where substantial medical authority supports the proposition that banning a particular abortion procedure could endanger women's health, *Casey* requires the statute to include a health exception when the procedure is 'necessary, in appropriate medical judgment, for the preservation of the life or health of the mother.'"[3]

DISTINGUISHING BETWEEN DILATION AND EXTRACTION AND DILATION AND EVACUATION

The second constitutional issue was whether the statute imposed an "undue burden" on a woman's liberty to terminate her pregnancy before the fetus was viable. The answer to this question depended on whether the statute was precisely written so as to apply only to the rare dilation-and-extraction procedures and not to the more routine dilation-and-evacuation procedures as well. On the basis of the statute's descriptions of the procedure, Breyer concluded that its language "does not track the medical differences between D&E and D&X."

Breyer stated that it would have been a simple matter for the state legislature to provide an exception for dilation-and-evacuation procedures, but given the medical material he quoted in his opinion, it is difficult to see how this could be effectively done. The attorney general of Nebraska, for example, argued unpersuasively that the two procedures were actually distinguished by the words "substantial portion" of the fetus, which the attorney general interpreted as meaning "the child up to the head" and thus not including "a fetal arm or leg or anything less than the entire fetal body." Because of the vagueness of the statute, Justice Breyer concluded that the statute threatened physicians who would otherwise perform dilation-and-evacuation procedures, but who would not now perform them because they would "fear prosecution, conviction, and imprisonment." This results in placing "an undue burden on a woman's right to make an abortion decision."

THE CONCURRING OPINIONS

Justices John Paul Stevens, Sandra Day O'Connor, and Ruth Bader Ginsburg each wrote brief concurring opinions. Stevens emphasized that the extent of the rhetoric surrounding abortion often obscures the fact that, during the past 27 years, the core holding of *Roe* v. *Wade* "has been endorsed by all but 4 of the 17 justices who have addressed the issue." He also argued (persuasively, I think) that "the notion that either of these two equally gruesome procedures [dilation and extraction and dilation and evacuation after 15 weeks] performed at this late stage of gestation is more akin to infanticide than the other, or that the State furthers any legitimate interest by banning one but not the other, is simply irrational." Justice O'Connor agreed with Breyer but added that she thought "a ban on partial-birth abortion that only proscribed the D&X method of abortion and that included an exception to preserve the life and health of the mother would be constitutional." Justice Ginsburg emphasized that the Nebraska law would "not save any fetus from destruction" nor "protect the lives or health of pregnant women" and that therefore the state had no legitimate interest in enacting it.[3] She also cited Chief Judge Richard Posner, who had made this point in an extremely cogent dissent to the opinion of the Seventh Circuit Court. "These statutes," wrote Posner, "are not concerned with saving fetuses . . . [or] with protecting the health of women. . . . They are concerned with making a statement in an ongoing war for public opinion. . . . The statement is that fetal life is more important than women's health."[2]

THE DISSENTING OPINIONS

There are four dissenting opinions, the two major ones written by Justices Anthony Kennedy and Clarence Thomas; Chief Justice William Rehnquist joined both of them, and Justice Antonin Scalia joined the Thomas dissent. Justice Kennedy objected to the majority's use of medical textbooks and terminology to describe abortion procedures, arguing that this technical language "views the procedures from the perspective of the abortionist, rather than from the perspective of a society shocked when confronted with a new method of ending human life . . . [and] may obscure matters for persons not trained in medical terminology." He did not refer to physicians as physicians, instead calling them "abortionists," and proceeded to describe the dilation-and-extraction procedure in lay terms. His version included such descriptions as the following: "with only the head of the fetus remaining in utero, the abortionist tears open the skull [using] . . . a pair of scissors."[3] Kennedy concluded that permitting an exception to preserve the health of the woman would be the equivalent of forbidding Nebraska to ban partial-birth abortion. In his words "A ban which depends on 'the appropriate medical judgment' of Dr. Carhart is no ban at all."[3]

Kennedy's central argument was that under *Casey,* states "have an interest in forbidding medical procedures which, in the State's reasonable determination, might cause the medical profession or society as a whole to become insensitive, even disdainful, to life, including life in the human fetus." But this argument could apply to all abortions, and it is not, in fact, what *Casey* held. Moreover, he argued that it is irrelevant that the majority of the justices cannot see the difference between dilation and evacuation and dilation and extraction. "The issue is not whether members of the judiciary can see a difference between the two procedures," Kennedy wrote. "It is whether Nebraska can." Regardless of whether physicians can distinguish between legal and illegal medical procedures, Kennedy argued that the state of Nebraska has a "right to declare a moral difference" between two medical procedures.

Kennedy also believes that there is a real difference, arguing, for instance, that "D&X perverts the natural birth process to a greater degree than D&E, commandeering the live birth process until the skull is pierced;" that the fetus is "killed outside of the womb;" and that dilation and extraction bears a "stronger resemblance to infanticide." Finding that the state has a legitimate interest in outlawing this abortion procedure, Kennedy then argued that the Court has no medical expertise sufficient to second-guess the Nebraska legislature on its determination that abortion by dilation and extraction is no safer than other methods of abortion and is therefore never medically necessary. In this view, outlawing dilation-and-extraction abortions (which Kennedy believes are the only type affected by the statute) would deprive no woman of access to a safe abortion, and thus cannot, under the terms set forth by *Casey,* place an undue burden on the pregnant woman.

Justice Thomas, like Kennedy, was upset by Breyer's "sanitized" medical descriptions, noting that since *Roe,* "this Court has never described the various methods of aborting a second- or third-trimester fetus." Thomas also argued that the statute's plain language can and should be interpreted as including only abortions by dilation and extraction, and not by dilation and evacuation. To the argument that "partial-birth abortion" is not a medical term, he replied simply and accurately, "There is, of course, no requirement that a legislature use terminology accepted by the medical community." Thomas disagreed that the state cannot second-guess physicians who believe use of a particular abortion method is necessary to preserve a woman's health. He argued that the majority opinion "eviscerates *Casey's* undue burden standard and imposes unfettered abortion on demand." In his view, the resolution of differences among physicians regarding the safety of abortion procedures should be left to the state legislatures.[3] The dissenters, in short, do not believe that physicians can be trusted to make good-faith decisions about the health of their patients. . . .

MEDICINE AND ABORTION

A deeper discussion of the availability of safe abortions to protect women's lives and liberty may be too much to ask of the Supreme Court. Maybe, in the debate over abortion, we are all past the point at which facts and logic matter. As the decision in *Stenberg* underlines, the law can determine whether abortions are permitted, but only physicians—with their patients—can determine how they may be performed safely. Ultimately, the central question regarding abortion remains who should make the decision: the state or women and their physicians together. The answer of the Supreme Court, as articulated in *Roe* v. *Wade* and its companion case, *Doe* v. *Bolton,*[10] and now strongly reinforced in *Stenberg,* is that the decision belongs to the woman and her physician together. In this respect, the Court has been remarkably consistent in all the abortion cases it has heard.

REFERENCES

1 Annas G. J. Partial-birth abortion, Congress, and the Constitution. N. Engl J Med 1998; 339:279–83.
2 *The Hope Clinic v. Ryan,* 195 F.3d 857 (7th Cir. 1999) (Posner J, dissenting).
3 *Stenberg v. Carhart,* 530 U.S. 914 (2000).
4 Neb. Rev. Stat. Ann. sec. 28–328(1) (Supp. 1999).
5 *Carhart v. Stenberg,* 11 F. Supp.2d 1099 (Neb. 1998).
6 *Stenberg v. Carhart,* 192 F.3d 1142 (1999).
7 *Roe v. Wade,* 410 U.S. 113 (1973).
8 *Planned Parenthood of Southeastern Pennsylvania v. Casey,* 502 U.S. 1056 (1992).
9 Brief for American College of Obstetricians and Gynecologists et al. as Amici Curiae, 21–22.
10 *Doe v. Bolton,* 410 U.S. 179 (1973).

QUESTIONS

1 It there a morally significant distinction between the dilation and extraction procedure and the more common dilation and evacuation procedure?
2 Are you inclined to favor a ban on "partial-birth abortion"? Could such a ban be formulated in a way that would avoid the constitutional problems identified in *Stenberg*?

SUGGESTED ADDITIONAL READINGS FOR CHAPTER 1

BOLTON, MARTHA BRANDT: "Responsible Women and Abortion Decisions." In Onora O'Neill and William Ruddick, eds., *Having Children: Philosophical and Legal Reflections on Parenthood.* New York: Oxford University Press, 1979, pp. 40–51. In defending a moderate view on the morality of abortion, Bolton emphasizes the importance of contextual features in the life of a pregnant woman. She argues that the decision to bear a child must fit into a woman's life and make sense in terms of her responsibilities to her family and to the larger society.

BOONIN, DAVID: *A Defense of Abortion.* Cambridge: Cambridge University Press, 2003. Boonin contends (1) that the fetus does not acquire a right to life until the onset of organized cortical brain activity, which on his reading of the evidence occurs sometime between the twenty-fifth and thirty-second week; and (2) that, even if the fetus had a right to life as early as conception, it would not follow from that fact that most abortions are morally impermissible.

BRODY, BARUCH: "On the Humanity of the Foetus." In Robert L. Perkins, ed. *Abortion: Pro and Con.* Cambridge, Mass.: Schenkman, 1974, pp. 69–90. Brody critically examines various proposals for "drawing the line" on the humanity of the fetus, ultimately suggesting that the most defensible view would draw the line at the point where fetal brain activity begins.

DWYER, SUSAN, and JOEL FEINBERG, eds.: *The Problem of Abortion,* 3d ed. Belmont, Calif.: Wadsworth, 1997. This useful anthology features a wide range of articles on the moral justifiability of abortion. It also includes a very extensive bibliography.

ENGELHARDT, H. TRISTRAM, JR.: "The Ontology of Abortion." *Ethics,* vol. 84, April 1974, pp. 217–234. Engelhardt focuses attention on the issue of "whether or to what extent the fetus is a person." He argues that, strictly speaking, a human person is not present until the later stages of infancy. However, he finds the point of viability significant in that, with viability, an infant can play the social role of "child" and thus be treated "as if it were a person."

ENGLISH, JANE: "Abortion and the Concept of a Person." *Canadian Journal of Philosophy,* vol. 5, October 1975, pp. 233–243. English advances one line of argument calculated to moderate the conservative view on the morality of abortion and another line of argument calculated to moderate the liberal view.

LANGERAK, EDWARD A.: "Abortion: Listening to the Middle." *Hastings Center Report,* vol. 9, October 1979, pp. 24–28. Langerak suggests a theoretical framework for a moderate view that incorporates two "widely shared beliefs": (1) that there is something about the fetus *itself* that makes abortion morally problematic and (2) that late abortions are significantly more problematic than early abortions.

NOONAN, JOHN T., JR.: "An Almost Absolute Value in History." In John T. Noonan, Jr., ed., *The Morality of Abortion: Legal and Historical Perspectives.* Cambridge, Mass.: Harvard University Press, 1970, pp. 51–59. In this well-known statement of the conservative view on the morality of abortion, Noonan argues that conception is the only objectively based and nonarbitrary point at which to "draw the line" between the nonhuman and the human.

POJMAN, LOUIS P., and FRANCIS J. BECKWITH, eds.: *The Abortion Controversy: 25 Years After Roe v. Wade: A Reader,* 2d ed. Belmont, Calif: Wadsworth, 1998. The articles in this long anthology are organized under eight headings, including "Evaluations of *Roe v. Wade,*" "Personhood Arguments on Abortion," and "Feminist Arguments on Abortion."

STONE, JIM: "Why Potentiality Matters." *Canadian Journal of Philosophy,* vol. 17, December 1987, pp. 815–830. Stone argues that a fetal right to life can be effectively grounded in the fact that a fetus is *potentially* an adult human being.

TONG, ROSEMARIE: *Feminist Approaches to Bioethics: Theoretical Reflections and Practical Applications.* Boulder, Colo.: Westview Press, 1997. In Chapter 6 of this book, Tong contrasts feminist and nonfeminist perspectives on abortion. She also distinguishes among various feminist approaches.

CHAPTER 2

Euthanasia and Physician-Assisted Suicide

The mercy killing of patients by physicians, whether called "active euthanasia" (as it is here) or simply "euthanasia," is a topic of long-standing controversy. Can active euthanasia—especially in response to the request of a competent patient—be morally justified? Should it be legalized? Parallel questions can be raised about physician-assisted suicide, a closely related topic that has also generated intense discussion. This chapter is designed to deal with ethical and social-policy questions about active euthanasia and physician-assisted suicide.

EUTHANASIA: SOME IMPORTANT DISTINCTIONS

There is both a narrow and a broad sense of *euthanasia,* and the difference between the two is best understood by reference to the categories of killing and allowing to die, although the distinction between killing and allowing to die is itself a controversial one. Understood in the narrow sense, the category of euthanasia is limited to mercy *killing*. Thus, if a physician believes a terminally ill patient is better off dead and for that reason (mercifully) administers a lethal dose of a drug to the patient, this act is a paradigm of euthanasia. On the other hand, if a physician *allows a patient to die* (e.g., by withholding or withdrawing a respirator), this does not count as euthanasia. Although the narrow sense of *euthanasia* is becoming increasingly common, many writers still use the word in the broad sense. Understood in the broad sense, the category of euthanasia encompasses both killing and allowing to die (on grounds of mercy). Of course, the underlying assumption in conceptualizing the withholding or withdrawing of treatment under the heading of euthanasia is that the physician withholds or withdraws life-sustaining treatment (mercifully) for the precise purpose of bringing about the patient's death. Those who employ the broad sense of *euthanasia* typically distinguish between *active* euthanasia (i.e., killing) and *passive* euthanasia (i.e., allowing to die).

One other distinction is of central importance in discussions of euthanasia. *Voluntary* euthanasia proceeds in response to the (informed) request of a competent patient. *Nonvoluntary* euthanasia involves an individual who is incompetent to give consent. The possibility of nonvoluntary euthanasia might arise with regard to adults who have for any number of reasons (e.g., Alzheimer's disease) lost their decision-making capacity, and it might arise with regard to newborn infants, children, and severely retarded adults. Both voluntary and nonvoluntary euthanasia may be further distinguished from *involuntary* euthanasia, which entails acting against the will or, at any rate, without the permission of a competent person. It is important to note, however, that some writers use the phrase *involuntary euthanasia* in referring to what has been identified here as *nonvoluntary euthanasia*.

If the voluntary/nonvoluntary distinction is combined with the active/passive distinction, four types of euthanasia can be distinguished: (1) voluntary active euthanasia, (2) nonvoluntary active euthanasia, (3) voluntary passive euthanasia, and (4) nonvoluntary passive euthanasia. Contemporary debate, however, focuses on the moral legitimacy of active euthanasia, especially voluntary active euthanasia. There is far less controversy about the moral legitimacy of passive euthanasia, whether voluntary or nonvoluntary. At any rate, the idea that it can be morally appropriate to withhold or withdraw life-sustaining treatment is firmly established, at least in the United States. This is not to say, of course, that there are no issues related to the specific conditions that must be satisfied in order for the withholding or withdrawing of life-sustaining treatment to be morally appropriate. In particular, there are areas of controversy related to withholding or withdrawing life-sustaining treatment from incompetent patients in various categories (e.g., severely impaired newborn infants).

ADVANCE DIRECTIVES

Depending on a patient's particular circumstances, life-sustaining treatment can take a variety of forms—for example, mechanical respiration, cardiopulmonary resuscitation, kidney dialysis, surgery, antibiotics, and artificial nutrition and hydration. The ordinary presumption is that a competent adult has both a moral and a legal right to refuse any medical treatment, including life-sustaining treatment. However, the rigors of incurable illness and the dying process frequently deprive previously competent patients of their decision-making capacity. How can a person best ensure that his or her personal wishes with regard to life-sustaining treatment (in various possible circumstances) will be honored even if decision-making capacity is lost? Although communication of one's attitudes and preferences to one's physician, family, and friends surely provides some measure of protection, it is frequently asserted that the most effective protection comes through the formation of *advance directives*.

There are two basic types of advance directives, and each has legal status in almost all, if not all, of the states. In executing an *instructional* directive, a person specifies instructions about his or her care in the event that decision-making capacity is lost. Such a directive, especially when it deals specifically with a person's wishes regarding life-sustaining treatment in various possible circumstances, is commonly called a *living will*. In executing a *proxy* directive, a person specifies a substitute decision maker to make health-care decisions for him or her in the event that decision-making capacity is lost. The legal mechanism for executing a proxy directive is often called a *durable power of attorney for health care*. Since purging ambiguities from even the most explicit written directives is difficult, as is foreseeing all the contingencies that might give rise to a need for treatment decisions, many commentators recommend the execution of a durable power of attorney for health care even if a person has already executed a living will.

THE MORALITY OF ACTIVE EUTHANASIA

James Rachels argues in this chapter for the moral legitimacy of active euthanasia. One of his central claims is that there is no morally significant distinction between killing and allowing to die. Daniel Callahan, by way of contrast, defends the coherence and moral importance of the distinction between killing and allowing to die. Callahan is opposed to active euthanasia and argues that killing patients is incompatible with the role of the physician in society. In his view, the power of the physician must be used "only to cure or comfort, never to kill." Dan W. Brock, in turn, rejects the idea that active euthanasia is incompatible with the fundamental professional commitments of a physician. Furthermore, in stating a case for the moral legitimacy of voluntary active euthanasia, Brock appeals to the centrality of two fundamental values—individual autonomy (self-determination) and individual well-being.

Those, like Rachels, who argue for the moral legitimacy of active euthanasia usually emphasize considerations of humaneness. When the intent of argument (as in the case of Brock) is to provide a defense of *voluntary* active euthanasia, the humanitarian appeal is typically conjoined with an appeal to the primacy of individual autonomy. Thus, the overall case for the moral legitimacy of voluntary active euthanasia incorporates two basic arguments: (1) It is cruel and inhumane to refuse the plea of a terminally ill person for his or her life to be mercifully ended in order to avoid future suffering and/or indignity. (2) Individual choice should be respected to the extent that it does not result in harm to others. Since no one is harmed—at least in typical cases—by terminally ill patients' undergoing active euthanasia, a decision to have one's life ended in this fashion should be respected.

Those who argue against the moral legitimacy of active euthanasia typically rest their case on one or all of the following claims: (1) Killing an innocent person is intrinsically wrong. (2) Killing is incompatible with the professional responsibilities of the physician. (3) Any systematic acceptance of active euthanasia would lead to detrimental social consequences (e.g., via a lessening of respect for human life). This third line of argument is the one that is typically most emphasized in discussions concerning the legalization of active euthanasia.

PHYSICIAN-ASSISTED SUICIDE

Any discussion of physician-assisted suicide is likely to bring to mind questions about the morality and rationality of suicide itself—questions that cannot be fully addressed in this chapter.[1] Suicide, according to a more or less standard definition, is the intentional termination of one's own life. Under what conditions, if any, is suicide morally acceptable? Classical literature on the morality of suicide provides a number of sources who issue a strong moral condemnation of suicide. The traditional arguments against suicide include religiously based arguments as well as arguments that are philosophical in character. Saint Thomas Aquinas (1225–1274), for example, argues that suicide is to be condemned not only because it violates our duty to God but also because it violates the natural law, and, moreover, because it injures the community. A contrasting point of view has a more contemporary ring but is not without support in the classical literature: Suicide is morally acceptable to the extent that it does no substantial damage to the interests of other individuals.

Closely associated with the issue of the morality of suicide is the issue of the rationality of suicide. Clearly, many suicides are irrational, the product of disordered thinking. But it is sometimes asserted that a suicidal intention is necessarily irrational and thus a symptom of mental illness and incompetence. In other words, it is impossible for a *competent* adult to have a suicidal intention. Although this point seems to be built into some psychiatric theories, many philosophers—and, today, many psychiatrists as well—consider it an implausible contention. Consider, in particular, the case of a terminally ill patient experiencing intense suffering with no realistic prospect of relief. If it is correct to say that such a person is better off dead, then it is hard to deny that suicide could be a rational choice. Of course, none of this is meant to deny the distorting effects that depression can exercise over human judgment.

Arguments for and against the moral legitimacy of physician-assisted suicide largely parallel the standard arguments for and against the moral legitimacy of voluntary active euthanasia, and one might wonder if there is a morally significant difference between these two practices. Physician-assisted suicide typically involves a physician in one or both of the following roles: (1) providing *information* to a patient about how to commit suicide in an effective manner and (2) providing the *means* necessary for an effective suicide (most commonly, by writing a prescription for a lethal amount of medication). Other modes of physician assistance in suicide might include providing moral support for the patient's decision, "supervising" the actual suicide, and helping the patient carry out the necessary physical actions. For example, a very frail patient might need a certain amount of physical assistance just to take pills.

In both physician-assisted suicide and voluntary active euthanasia, a physician plays an active role in bringing about the death of a patient. However, at face value, there is a difference between the two: In voluntary active euthanasia it is the physician

---

[1] For one avenue into the philosophical literature on suicide, see M. Pabst Battin and David J. Mayo, eds., *Suicide: The Philosophical Issues* (New York: St. Martin's Press, 1980). This valuable collection of articles includes material on the concept of suicide, the morality of suicide, and the rationality of suicide.

who ultimately kills the patient, whereas in physician-assisted suicide it is the patient who ultimately kills himself or herself, albeit with the assistance of the physician. It is a controversial issue whether this difference in terms of ultimate causal agency can serve as a basis for the claim that there is a morally significant difference between physician-assisted suicide and voluntary active euthanasia.

An important development in the public debate over physician-assisted suicide took place in 1997, when the United States Supreme Court unanimously upheld the constitutionality of state statutes prohibiting physician assistance in suicide. In *Washington v. Glucksberg,* the Court rejected the claim that the Due Process Clause of the Fourteenth Amendment encompasses a fundamental right to physician-assisted suicide. In the companion case *Vacco v. Quill,* the Court rejected the claim that the Equal Protection Clause of the Fourteenth Amendment is violated by a state prohibiting physician-assisted suicide while at the same time permitting the withdrawal of life-sustaining treatment. In resolving this second case, the Court explicitly committed itself to the legitimacy and importance of drawing a distinction between assisting suicide and withdrawing life-sustaining treatment.

Each of the physician-assisted suicide cases was decided by a nine-to-zero vote, but the Court is not nearly so unified on the construction of the underlying issues as these unanimous votes might suggest. The Court's underlying fragmentation of viewpoint is reflected in a host of concurring opinions generated by the cases. Chief Justice William H. Rehnquist wrote the "Opinion of the Court" in each of the cases, but only four other justices actually concurred in these opinions, and one of these four, Justice Sandra Day O'Connor, also crafted a concurring opinion. The opinion of Chief Justice Rehnquist in *Washington v. Glucksberg* is reprinted in this chapter, as is the concurring opinion of Justice O'Connor.

ACTIVE EUTHANASIA, PHYSICIAN-ASSISTED SUICIDE, AND SOCIAL POLICY

Should active euthanasia be legalized? If so, in what form or forms and with what safeguards? Although active euthanasia is presently illegal in all fifty states and the District of Columbia, proposals for its legalization have been recurrently advanced. Most commonly, these proposals call for the legalization of *voluntary* active euthanasia.

There are some who consider active euthanasia in any form intrinsically immoral (sometimes on overtly religious grounds) and, for this reason, oppose the legalization of voluntary active euthanasia. Others are opposed to legalization because of their conviction that physicians in particular should not kill. Still others, such as Stephen G. Potts in this chapter, do not necessarily object to individual acts of voluntary active euthanasia but still stand opposed to any social policy that would permit its practice. The concern here is with the adverse social consequences of legalization. In this vein, it is alleged that vulnerable persons would be subject to abuse, that a disincentive for the availability of supportive services for the dying would be created, and that public trust and confidence in physicians would be undermined. Another consequentialist concern is embodied in a frequently made "slippery slope" argument: The legalization of voluntary active euthanasia would lead us down a slippery slope to the legalization of nonvoluntary (and perhaps involuntary) euthanasia. Those who support the legalization of voluntary active euthanasia recognize that some unfortunate consequences may result from legalization. However, they typically seek to establish that potential dangers are either overstated or can be minimized with appropriate safeguards.

Although arguments advanced against the legalization of physician-assisted suicide largely parallel those advanced against the legalization of voluntary active euthanasia, it is frequently argued that there is far less risk of abuse involved in the legalization of physician-assisted suicide. This point of view is embraced by David T. Watts and Timothy Howell in one of this chapter's readings. These two physicians recommend the legalization of physician-assisted suicide, although they do not favor allowing a physician to "supervise" or directly aid a patient in committing suicide. They would restrict physicians to providing information about suicide and writing prescriptions for a lethal amount of medication. According to another point of view, since terminally ill patients are already free to refuse nutrition and hydration, and thereby bring about death, there is no compelling need to legalize physician-assisted suicide (or voluntary active euthanasia).[2] Franklin G. Miller and Diane E. Meier give voice to this point of view in an article included in this chapter.

The Oregon Model

One concrete model for the legalization of physician-assisted suicide has emerged in Oregon. In November 1994, voters in Oregon approved by a margin of 51 to 49 percent a ballot initiative known as the Oregon Death with Dignity Act. This law survived constitutional challenges and ultimately went into effect on October 27, 1997; it also survived a second referendum in November 1997 in which Oregon voters opposed repeal by a margin of 60 to 40 percent. The law permits Oregon physicians to prescribe lethal drugs for Oregon adult residents who are terminally ill and who want to end their own lives. In order for a patient to be eligible for such assistance, the attending physician must determine that the patient has a terminal disease—a diagnosis entailing that the patient is expected to die within six months—and a consulting physician must confirm this diagnosis. The following requirements are also stipulated. (1) The patient must make an initial oral request, reiterate the oral request after fifteen days have passed, and also submit a written request, supported by two witnesses. (2) Before writing the prescription, the attending physician must wait at least fifteen days after the patient's initial request and at least forty-eight hours after the written request. (3) The attending physician must fully inform the patient about the diagnosis, prognosis, and feasible alternatives—including comfort care, hospice care, and pain control. (4) Both the attending physician and the consulting physician must certify that the patient is "capable" (i.e., has decision-making capacity), is acting voluntarily, and has made an informed

---

[2]A related argument identifies the availability of *terminal sedation* as a reason why it is not necessary to legalize physician-assisted suicide. The idea of terminal sedation naturally arises in those (presumably) few cases in which the severe pain or suffering of a terminally ill patient is resistant to established palliative techniques and cannot be alleviated except by *sedation into unconsciousness* until death occurs.

choice. (5) If either physician believes that the patient's judgment might be impaired (e.g., by depression), the patient must be referred for counseling. The Oregon law allows the attending physician and others to be present when the patient takes the lethal dose.

The Oregon Department of Human Services is charged with the responsibility of reporting annually on the practice of physician-assisted suicide in Oregon.[3] In 2004, thirty-seven patients in Oregon used physician-assisted suicide to end their lives, accounting for about one of every 800 Oregon deaths that year. In the seven-year period subsequent to legalization, 1998–2004, a total of 208 Oregonians used physician-assisted suicide to end their lives. With the United States Supreme Court ruling in *Gonzales v. Oregon* (2006), the practice of physician-assisted suicide in Oregon survived another legal challenge. The Bush administration had contended that physicians in Oregon who prescribe lethal drugs for the purpose of assisting suicide are in violation of the Controlled Substances Act, but the Court rejected this claim and upheld the Oregon law.

Consider, for a moment, some of the issues that might arise in specifying appropriate limits for the practice of physician-assisted suicide and/or voluntary active euthanasia. Would we want to restrict availability to patients who are terminally ill (according to some definition), to patients who are experiencing unbearable suffering (according to some definition), or to patients who are *both* terminally ill and experiencing unbearable suffering?[4] And if voluntary active euthanasia is at issue, would we want to insist that a patient be competent at the time he or she undergoes active euthanasia, or would we also want to allow for the possibility of active euthanasia in accordance with an advance directive?

Voluntary active euthanasia is a well-established practice in the Netherlands. One of the interesting aspects of the Dutch system is its requirement that active euthanasia be available only if the patient is experiencing unbearable suffering (with no prospect of improvement), but there is no requirement that the patient be terminally ill. Another interesting feature of the Dutch system is its explicit acceptance of an advance-directive principle. That is, active euthanasia may be provided for patients who have become incompetent but who had clearly expressed their request for active euthanasia in a written declaration while competent.

The Dutch Model

Both voluntary active euthanasia (VAE) and physician-assisted suicide (PAS) have been openly available to patients in the Netherlands for many years. For example, a government-sponsored study reported that in 1990 there were 2,300 cases of VAE and 400 cases of PAS, accounting for about 3 percent of overall mortality that year. And yet, until more recently, these practices were not strictly legal. Rather, the

---

[3]These annual reports are available on the Oregon Department of Human Services home page (www.dhs.state.or.us/publichealth/chs/pas/pas.cfm).

[4]For an argument to restrict availability (at least at the present time) to those who are terminally ill, see Martin Gunderson and David J. Mayo, "Restricting Physician-Assisted Death to the Terminally Ill," *Hastings Center Report,* vol. 30, November-December 2000, pp. 17–23.

operational understanding was that Dutch physicians would be immune from prosecution as long as they adhered to a set of guidelines worked out by agreement of the medical and legal communities. In 2002, however, the year in which the Dutch Termination of Life on Request and Assisted Suicide Act (TLRASA) went into effect, VAE and PAS were formally legalized in the Netherlands.

The TLRASA stipulates that any physician who properly conforms to "due care criteria" in the provision of VAE/PAS and promptly reports to a regional review committee any case in which VAE or PAS has been provided will be immune from prosecution. Further, in order to comply with the due care criteria, the TLRASA specifies that the physician must:

(a) be satisfied that the patient has made a voluntary and carefully considered request;

(b) be satisfied that the patient's suffering was unbearable, and that there was no prospect of improvement;

(c) have informed the patient about his situation and his prospects;

(d) have come to the conclusion, together with the patient, that there is no reasonable alternative in light of the patient's situation;

(e) have consulted at least one other, independent physician, who must have seen the patient and given a written opinion on the due care criteria referred to in (a) to (d) above; and (f) have terminated the patient's life or provided assistance with suicide with due medical care and attention.

A regional review committee is charged with the responsibility of reviewing each reported case of VAE/PAS in order to determine if physician actions have properly conformed to the due care criteria.

The TLRASA explicitly allows for the possibility of active euthanasia in accordance with an advance-directive principle. That is, in essence, active euthanasia may be provided for a presently incompetent patient who, while competent, made a written declaration requesting that his or her life be terminated under specified circumstances. The TLRASA further allows for the possibility of VAE/PAS in the case of a minor who is at least twelve years old and "is deemed to be capable of making a reasonable appraisal of his own interests." Requests from sixteen- and seventeen-year-olds can be complied with but only on the condition of *consultation* with parents (or guardian), although parental/guardian approval is not required. Requests from twelve- to fifteen-year-olds can also be complied with but only on the condition of parental/guardian *consent*.

Several questions naturally arise. Does the Dutch system provide a morally sound framework for the practice of active euthanasia and physician-assisted suicide? In particular, are the TLRASA provisions related to minors morally sound? Does the Dutch system incorporate adequate safeguards against abuse? Should active euthanasia be legalized in the United States along the lines of the Dutch model? As would be expected, opponents of legalization in the United States typically advance numerous criticisms of the Dutch system, but even many proponents of legalization in the United States are somewhat wary of the Dutch model, believing that it does not incorporate adequate safeguards against abuse—or, at any rate, that it would not provide adequate safeguards within the framework of American society.

Thomas A. Mappes

Active and Passive Euthanasia

James Rachels

In this classic article, Rachels identifies the "conventional doctrine" on the morality of euthanasia as the doctrine that allows passive euthanasia but does not allow active euthanasia. He then argues that the conventional doctrine may be challenged for four reasons. First, active euthanasia is in many cases more humane than passive euthanasia. Second, the conventional doctrine leads to decisions concerning life and death on irrelevant grounds. Third, the doctrine rests on a distinction between killing and letting die that itself has no moral importance. Fourth, the most common argument in favor of the doctrine is invalid.

The distinction between active and passive euthanasia is thought to be crucial for medical ethics. The idea is that it is permissible, at least in some cases, to withhold treatment and allow a patient to die, but it is never permissible to take any direct action designed to kill the patient. This doctrine seems to be accepted by most doctors, and it is endorsed in a statement adopted by the House of Delegates of the American Medical Association on December 4, 1973:

> The intentional termination of the life of one human being by another—mercy killing—is contrary to that for which the medical profession stands and is contrary to the policy of the American Medical Association.
>
> The cessation of the employment of extraordinary means to prolong the life of the body when there is irrefutable evidence that biological death is imminent is the decision of the patient and/or his immediate family. The advice and judgment of the physician should be freely available to the patient and/or his immediate family.

However, a strong case can be made against this doctrine. In what follows, I will set out some of the relevant arguments, and urge doctors to reconsider their views on this matter.

To begin with a familiar type of situation, a patient who is dying of incurable cancer of the throat is in terrible pain, which can no longer be satisfactorily alleviated. He is certain to die within a few days, even if present treatment is continued, but he does not want to go on living for those days since the pain is unbearable. So he asks the doctor for an end to it, and his family joins in the request.

Suppose the doctor agrees to withhold treatment, as the conventional doctrine says he may. The justification for his doing so is that the patient is in terrible agony, and since he is going to die anyway, it would be wrong to prolong his suffering needlessly. But now notice this. If one simply withholds treatment, it may take the patient longer to die, and so he may suffer more than he would if more direct action were taken and a lethal injection given. This fact provides strong reason for thinking that, once the initial decision not to prolong his agony has been made, active euthanasia is actually preferable to passive euthanasia, rather than the reverse. To

Reprinted with permission from *The New England Journal of Medicine*, vol. 292, no. 2 (January 9, 1975), pp. 78–80.

say otherwise is to endorse the option that leads to more suffering rather than less, and is contrary to the humanitarian impulse that prompts the decision not to pro-long his life in the first place.

Part of my point is that the process of being "allowed to die" can be relatively slow and painful, whereas being given a lethal injection is relatively quick and painless. Let me give a different sort of example. In the United States about one in 600 babies is born with Down's syndrome. Most of these babies are otherwise healthy—that is, with only the usual pediatric care, they will proceed to an other-wise normal infancy. Some, however, are born with congenital defects such as intestinal obstructions that require operations if they are to live. Sometimes, the parents and the doctor will decide not to operate, and let the infant die. Anthony Shaw describes what happens then:

> . . . When surgery is denied [the doctor] must try to keep the infant from suffering while natural forces sap the baby's life away. As a surgeon whose natural inclination is to use the scalpel to fight off death, standing by and watching a salvageable baby die is the most emotionally exhausting experience I know. It is easy at a conference, in a theoretical dis-cussion, to decide that such infants should be allowed to die. It is altogether different to stand by in the nursery and watch as dehydration and infection wither a tiny being over hours and days. This is a terrible ordeal for me and the hospital staff—much more so than for the parents who never set foot in the nursery.[1]

I can understand why some people are opposed to all euthanasia, and insist that such infants must be allowed to live. I think I can also understand why other peo-ple favor destroying these babies quickly and painlessly. But why should anyone favor letting "dehydration and infection wither a tiny being over hours and days"? The doctrine that says that a baby may be allowed to dehydrate and wither, but may not be given an injection that would end its life without suffering, seems so patently cruel as to require no further refutation. The strong language is not intended to offend, but only to put the point in the clearest possible way.

My second argument is that the conventional doctrine leads to decisions con-cerning life and death made on irrelevant grounds.

Consider again the case of the infants with Down's syndrome who need opera-tions for congenital defects unrelated to the syndrome to live. Sometimes, there is no operation, and the baby dies, but when there is no such defect, the baby lives on. Now, an operation such as that to remove an intestinal obstruction is not prohibi-tively difficult. The reason why such operations are not performed in these cases is, clearly, that the child has Down's syndrome and the parents and doctor judge that because of that fact it is better for the child to die.

But notice that this situation is absurd, no matter what view one takes of the lives and potentials of such babies. If the life of such an infant is worth preserving, what does it matter if it needs a simple operation? Or, if one thinks it better that such a baby should not live on, what difference does it make that it happens to have an unobstructed intestinal tract? In either case, the matter of life and death is being decided on irrelevant grounds. It is the Down's syndrome, and not the intestines, that is the issue. The matter should be decided, if at all, on that basis, and not be allowed to depend on the essentially irrelevant question of whether the intestinal tract is blocked.

What makes this situation possible, of course, is the idea that when there is an intestinal blockage, one can "let the baby die," but when there is no such defect there is nothing that can be done, for one must not "kill" it. The fact that this idea leads to such results as deciding life or death on irrelevant grounds is another good reason why the doctrine should be rejected.

One reason why so many people think that there is an important moral difference between active and passive euthanasia is that they think killing someone is morally worse than letting someone die. But is it? Is killing, in itself, worse than letting die? To investigate this issue, two cases may be considered that are exactly alike except that one involves killing whereas the other involves letting someone die. Then, it can be asked whether this difference makes any difference to the moral assessments. It is important that the cases be exactly alike, except for this one difference, since otherwise one cannot be confident that it is this difference and not some other that accounts for any variation in the assessments of the two cases. So, let us consider this pair of cases:

In the first, Smith stands to gain a large inheritance if anything should happen to his six-year-old cousin. One evening while the child is taking his bath, Smith sneaks into the bathroom and drowns the child, and then arranges things so that it will look like an accident.

In the second, Jones also stands to gain if anything should happen to his six-year-old cousin. Like Smith, Jones sneaks in planning to drown the child in his bath. However, just as he enters the bathroom Jones sees the child slip and hit his head, and fall face down in the water. Jones is delighted; he stands by, ready to push the child's head back under if it is necessary, but it is not necessary. With only a little thrashing about the child drowns all by himself, "accidentally," as Jones watches and does nothing.

Now Smith killed the child, whereas Jones "merely" let the child die. That is the only difference between them. Did either man behave better, from a moral point of view? If the difference between killing and letting die were in itself a morally important matter, one should say that Jones's behavior was less reprehensible than Smith's. But does one really want to say that? I think not. In the first place, both men acted from the same motive, personal gain, and both had exactly the same end in view when they acted. It may be inferred from Smith's conduct that he is a bad man, although that judgment may be withdrawn or modified if certain further facts are learned about him— for example, that he is mentally deranged. But would not the very same thing be inferred about Jones from his conduct? And would not the same further considerations also be relevant to any modification of this judgment? Moreover, suppose Jones pleaded, in his own defense, "After all, I didn't do anything except just stand there and watch the child drown. I didn't kill him; I only let him die." Again, if letting die were in itself less bad than killing, this defense should have at least some weight. But it does not. Such a "defense" can only be regarded as a grotesque perversion of moral reasoning. Morally speaking, it is no defense at all.

Now, it may be pointed out, quite properly, that the cases of euthanasia with which doctors are concerned are not like this at all. They do not involve personal gain or the destruction of normally healthy children. Doctors are concerned only with cases in which the patient's life is of no further use to him, or in which the patient's life has become or will soon become a terrible burden. However, the point is the same in these cases: the bare difference between killing and letting die does not, in itself, make a moral difference. If a doctor lets a patient die, for humane reasons, he is in the same moral position as if he had given the patient a lethal injection for humane reasons. If his decision was wrong—if, for example, the patient's illness was in fact curable—the decision would be equally regrettable no matter which method was used to carry it out. And if the doctor's decision was the right one, the method used is not in itself important.

The AMA policy statement isolates the crucial issue very well; the crucial issue is "the intentional termination of the life of one human being by another." But after identifying this issue, and forbidding "mercy killing," the statement goes on to deny that the cessation of treatment is the intentional termination of a life. This is where the mistake comes in, for what is the cessation of treatment, in these circumstances, if it is not "the intentional termination of the life of one human being by another?" Of course, it is exactly that, and if it were not, there would be no point to it.

Many people will find this judgment hard to accept. One reason, I think, is that it is very easy to conflate the question of whether killing is, in itself, worse than letting die, with the very different question of whether most actual cases of killing are more reprehensible than most actual cases of letting die. Most actual cases of killing are clearly terrible (think, for example, of all the murders reported in the newspapers), and one hears of such cases every day. On the other hand, one hardly ever hears of a case of letting die, except for the actions of doctors who are motivated by humanitarian reasons. So one learns to think of killing in a much worse light than of letting die. But this does not mean that there is something about killing that makes it in itself worse than letting die, for it is not the bare difference between killing and letting die that makes the difference in these cases. Rather, the other factors—the murderer's motive of personal gain, for example, contrasted with the doctor's humanitarian motivation—account for different reactions to the different cases.

I have argued that killing is not in itself any worse than letting die; if my contention is right, it follows that active euthanasia is not any worse than passive euthanasia. What arguments can be given on the other side? The most common, I believe, is the following:

"The important difference between active and passive euthanasia is that, in passive euthanasia, the doctor does not do anything to bring about the patient's death. The doctor does nothing, and the patient dies of whatever ills already afflict him. In active euthanasia, however, the doctor does something to bring about the patient's death: he kills him. The doctor who gives the patient with cancer a lethal injection has himself caused his patient's death; whereas if he merely ceases treatment, the cancer is the cause of the death."

A number of points need to be made here. The first is that it is not exactly correct to say that in passive euthanasia the doctor does nothing, for he does do one thing that is very important: he lets the patient die. "Letting someone die" is certainly different, in some respects, from other types of action—mainly in that it is a kind of action that one may perform by way of not performing certain other actions.

For example, one may let a patient die by way of not giving medication, just as one may insult someone by way of not shaking his hand. But for any purpose of moral assessment, it is a type of action nonetheless. The decision to let a patient die is subject to moral appraisal in the same way that a decision to kill him would be subject to moral appraisal: it may be assessed as wise or unwise, compassionate or sadistic, right or wrong. If a doctor deliberately let a patient die who was suffering from a routinely curable illness, the doctor would certainly be to blame for what he had done, just as he would be to blame if he had needlessly killed the patient. Charges against him would then be appropriate. If so, it would be no defense at all for him to insist that he didn't "do anything." He would have done something very serious indeed, for he let his patient die.

Fixing the cause of death may be very important from a legal point of view, for it may determine whether criminal charges are brought against the doctor. But I do not think that this notion can be used to show a moral difference between active and passive euthanasia. The reason why it is considered bad to be the cause of someone's death is that death is regarded as a great evil—and so it is. However, if it has been decided that euthanasia—even passive euthanasia—is desirable in a given case, it has also been decided that in this instance death is no greater an evil than the patient's continued existence. And if this is true, the usual reason for not wanting to be the cause of someone's death simply does not apply.

Finally, doctors may think that all of this is only of academic interest—the sort of thing that philosophers may worry about but that has no practical bearing on their own work. After all, doctors must be concerned about the legal consequences of what they do, and active euthanasia is clearly forbidden by the law. But even so, doctors should also be concerned with the fact that the law is forcing upon them a moral doctrine that may well be indefensible, and has a considerable effect on their practices. Of course, most doctors are not now in the position of being coerced in this matter, for they do not regard themselves as merely going along with what the law requires. Rather, in statements such as the AMA policy statement that I have quoted, they are endorsing this doctrine as a central point of medical ethics. In that statement, active euthanasia is condemned not merely as illegal but as "contrary to that for which the medical profession stands," whereas passive euthanasia is approved. However, the preceding considerations suggest that there is really no moral difference between the two, considered in themselves (there may be important moral differences in some cases in their *consequences,* but, as I pointed out, these differences may make active euthanasia, and not passive euthanasia, the morally preferable option). So, whereas doctors may have to discriminate between active and passive euthanasia to satisfy the law, they should not do any more than that. In particular, they should not give the distinction any added authority and weight by writing it into official statements of medical ethics.

NOTE

1 A. Shaw: "Doctor, Do We Have a Choice?" *The New York Times Magazine,* Jan. 30, 1972, p. 54.

QUESTIONS

1 Can the conventional doctrine on active and passive euthanasia be defended against Rachels's arguments?
2 Rachels seems to argue for the moral legitimacy of active euthanasia in general, not the moral legitimacy of *voluntary* active euthanasia in particular. Is nonvoluntary active euthanasia ever morally justified?
3 Can you imagine medical circumstances in which you would be better off dead? If so, would you welcome the possibility of active euthanasia, or only passive euthanasia? Do your religious beliefs play any role in your thinking on this issue?

Killing and Allowing to Die

Daniel Callahan

Callahan maintains that there is a valid distinction between killing and allowing to die, and he defends the distinction by reference to three overlapping perspectives—metaphysical, moral, and medical. In terms of a metaphysical perspective, Callahan emphasizes that the external world is distinct from the self and has its own causal dynamism. In terms of a moral perspective, he emphasizes the difference between *physical causality* and *moral culpability*. In conjunction with a medical perspective, he insists that killing patients is incompatible with the role of the physician in society.

. . . No valid distinction, many now argue, can be made between killing and allowing to die, or between an act of commission and one of omission. The standard distinction being challenged rests on the commonplace observation that lives can come to an end as the result of: (a) the direct action of another who becomes the cause of death (as in shooting a person), and (b) the result of impersonal forces where no human agent has acted (death by lightning, or by disease). The purpose of the distinction has been to separate those deaths caused by human action, and those caused by nonhuman events. It is, as a distinction, meant to say something about human beings and their relationship to the world. It is a way of articulating the difference between those actions for which human beings can be held rightly responsible, or blamed, and those of which they are innocent. At issue is the difference between physical causality, the realm of impersonal events, and moral culpability, the realm of human responsibility.

The challenges encompass two points. The first is that people can become equally dead by our omissions as well as our commissions. We can refrain from

Reprinted with permission of the author and the publisher from *Hastings Center Report,* vol. 19 (January/February 1989), Special Supplement, pp. 5–6. © The Hastings Center.

saving them when it is possible to do so, and they will be just as dead as if we shot them. It is our decision itself that is the reason for their death, not necessarily how we effectuate that decision. That fact establishes the basis of the second point: if we *intend* their death, it can be brought about as well by omitted acts as by those we commit. The crucial moral point is not how they die, but our intention about their death. We can, then, be responsible for the death of another by intending that they die and accomplish that end by standing aside and allowing them to die.

Despite these criticisms—resting upon ambiguities that can readily be acknowledged—the distinction between killing and allowing to die remains, I contend, perfectly valid. It not only has a logical validity but, no less importantly, a social validity whose place must be central in moral judgments. As a way of putting the distinction into perspective, I want to suggest that it is best understood as expressing three different, though overlapping, perspectives on nature and human action. I will call them the metaphysical, the moral, and the medical perspectives.

Metaphysical   The first and most fundamental premise of the distinction between killing and allowing to die is that there is a sharp difference between the self and the external world. Unlike the childish fantasy that the world is nothing more than a projection of the self, or the neurotic person's fear that he or she is responsible for everything that goes wrong, the distinction is meant to uphold a simple notion: there is a world external to the self that has its own, and independent, causal dynamism. The mistake behind a conflation of killing and allowing to die is to assume that the self has become master of everything within and outside of the self. It is as if the conceit that modern man might ultimately control nature has been internalized: that, if the self might be able to influence nature by its actions, then the self and nature must be one.

Of course that is a fantasy. The fact that we can intervene in nature, and cure or control many diseases, does not erase the difference between the self and the external world. It is as "out there" as ever, even if more under our sway. That sway, however great, is always limited. We can cure disease, but not always the chronic illness that comes with the cure. We can forestall death with modern medicine, but death always wins in the long run because of the innate limitations of the body, inherently and stubbornly beyond final human control. And we can distinguish between a diseased body and an aging body, but in the end if we wait long enough they always become one and the same body. To attempt to deny the distinction between killing and allowing to die is, then, mistakenly to impute more power to human action than it actually has and to accept the conceit that nature has now fallen wholly within the realm of human control. Not so.

Moral   At the center of the distinction between killing and allowing to die is the difference between physical causality and moral culpability. To bring the life of another to an end by an injection kills the other directly; our action is the physical cause of the death. To allow someone to die from a disease we cannot cure (and that we did not cause) is to permit the disease to act as the cause of death. The notion of physical causality in both cases rests on the difference between human agency and the action of external nature. The ambiguity arises precisely because we can be morally culpable for killing someone (if we have no moral right to do so, as we would in self-defense) and no less culpable for allowing someone to die (if we have both the possibility and the obligation of keeping that person alive). Thus there are cases where, morally speaking, it makes no difference whether we killed or allowed to die; we are equally responsible. In those instances, the lines of physical causality and moral culpability happen to cross. Yet the fact that they can cross in some cases in no way shows that they are always, or even usually, one and the same. We can normally find the difference in all but the most obscure cases. We should not, then, use the ambiguity of such cases to do away altogether with the distinction between killing and allowing to die. The ambiguity may obscure, but does not erase, the line between the two.

There is one group of ambiguous cases that is especially troublesome. Even if we grant the ordinary validity between killing and allowing to die, what about those cases that combine (a) an illness that renders a patient unable to carry out an ordinary biological function (to breathe or eat on his own, for example), and (b) our turning off a respirator or removing an artificial feeding tube? On the level of physical causality, have we killed the patient or allowed him to die? In one sense, it is our action that shortens his life, and yet in another sense his underlying disease brings his life to an end. I believe it reasonable to say that, since his life was being sustained by artificial means (respirator or feeding tube) made necessary because of the fact that he had an incapacitating disease, his disease is the ultimate reality behind his death. But for its reality, there would be no need for artificial sustenance in the first place and no moral issue at all. To lose sight of the paramount reality of the disease is to lose sight of the difference between our selves and the outer world.

I quickly add, and underscore, a moral point: the person who, without good moral reason, turns off a respirator or pulls a feeding tube, can be morally culpable; that the patient has been allowed to die of his underlying condition does not morally excuse him. The moral question is whether we are obliged to continue treating a life that is being artifically sustained. To cease treatment may or may not be morally acceptable; but it should be understood, in either case, that the physical cause of death was the underlying disease.

Medical   An important social purpose of the distinction between killing and allowing to die has been that of protecting the historical role of the physician as one who tries to cure or comfort patients rather than to kill patients. Physicians have been given special knowledge about the body, knowledge that can be used to kill or to cure. They are also given great privileges in making use of that knowledge. It is thus all the more important that physicians' social role and power be, and be seen to be, a limited power. It may be used only to cure or comfort, never to kill. They have not been given, nor should they be given, the power to use their knowledge and skills to bring life to an end. It would open the way for powerful misuse and, no less importantly, represent an intrinsic violation of what it has meant to be a physician.

Yet if it is possible for physicians to misuse their knowledge and power to kill people directly, are they thereby required to use that same knowledge always to keep people alive, always to resist a disease that can itself kill the patient? The traditional answer has been: not necessarily. For the physician's ultimate obligation is to the welfare of the patient, and excessive treatment can be as detrimental to that welfare as inadequate treatment. Put another way, the obligation to resist the lethal power of disease is limited—it ceases when the patient is unwilling to have it resisted, or where the resistance no longer serves the patient's welfare. Behind this moral premise is the recognition that disease (of some kind) ultimately triumphs and that death is both inevitable sooner or later and not, in any case, always the greatest human evil. To demand of the physician that he always struggle against disease, as if it was in his power always to conquer it, would be to fall into the same metaphysical trap mentioned above: that of assuming that no distinction can be drawn between natural and human agency.

A final word. I suggested [in an earlier discussion] that the most potent motive for active euthanasia and assisted suicide stems from a dread of the power of medicine. That power then seems to take on a drive of its own regardless of the welfare or wishes of patients. No one can easily say no—not physicians, not patients, not families. My guess is that happens because too many have already come to believe that it is their choice, and their choice alone, which brings about death; and they do not want to exercise that kind of authority. The solution is not to erase the distinction between killing and allowing to die, but to underscore its validity and importance. We can bring disease as a cause of death back into the care of the dying.

QUESTIONS

1 Is there a valid distinction between killing and allowing to die?
2 Do you agree with Callahan that the power of the physician must be used "only to cure or comfort, never to kill"?

Voluntary Active Euthanasia

Dan W. Brock

In this excerpt from a much longer article, Brock argues that two fundamental ethical values support the ethical permissibility of voluntary active euthanasia. These values are individual self-determination (autonomy) and individual well-being, the same two values that support the consensus view that patients have a right to make decisions about life-sustaining treatment. Brock also argues that allowing physicians to perform euthanasia is not incompatible with the "moral center" of medicine.

Reprinted with permission of the author and the publisher from *Hastings Center Report,* vol. 22 (March/April 1992), pp. 11, 16. © The Hastings Center.

. . . The central ethical argument for [voluntary active] euthanasia is familiar. It is that the very same two fundamental ethical values supporting the consensus on patient's rights to decide about life-sustaining treatment also support the ethical permissibility of euthanasia. These values are individual self-determination or autonomy and individual well-being. By self-determination as it bears on euthanasia, I mean people's interest in making important decisions about their lives for themselves according to their own values or conceptions of a good life, and in being left free to act on those decisions. Self-determination is valuable because it permits people to form and live in accordance with their own conception of a good life, at least within the bounds of justice and consistent with others doing so as well. In exercising self-determination people take responsibility for their lives and for the kinds of persons they become. A central aspect of human dignity lies in people's capacity to direct their lives in this way. The value of exercising self-determination presupposes some minimum of decision-making capacities or competence, which thus limits the scope of euthanasia supported by self-determination; it cannot justifiably be administered, for example, in cases of serious dementia or treatable clinical depression.

Does the value of individual self-determination extend to the time and manner of one's death? Most people are very concerned about the nature of the last stage of their lives. This reflects not just a fear of experiencing substantial suffering when dying, but also a desire to retain dignity and control during this last period of life. Death is today increasingly preceded by a long period of significant physical and mental decline, due in part to the technological interventions of modern medicine. Many people adjust to these disabilities and find meaning and value in new activities and ways. Others find the impairments and burdens in the last stage of their lives at some point sufficiently great to make life no longer worth living. For many patients near death, maintaining the quality of one's life, avoiding great suffering, maintaining one's dignity, and insuring that others remember us as we wish them to become of paramount importance and outweigh merely extending one's life. But there is no single, objectively correct answer for everyone as to when, if at all, one's life becomes all things considered a burden and unwanted. If self-determination is a fundamental value, then the great variability among people on this question makes it especially important that individuals control the manner, circumstances, and timing of their dying and death.

The other main value that supports euthanasia is individual well-being. It might seem that individual well-being conflicts with a person's self-determination when the person requests euthanasia. Life itself is commonly taken to be a central good for persons, often valued for its own sake, as well as necessary for pursuit of all other goods within a life. But when a competent patient decides to forgo all further life-sustaining treatment then the patient, either explicitly or implicitly, commonly decides that the best life possible for him or her with treatment is of sufficiently poor quality that it is worse than no further life at all. Life is no longer considered a benefit by the patient, but has now become a burden. The same judgment underlies a request for euthanasia: continued life is seen by the patient as no longer a benefit, but now a burden. Especially in the often severely compromised and debilitated states of many critically ill or dying patients, there is no objective standard, but only the competent patient's judgment of whether continued life is no longer a benefit.

Of course, sometimes there are conditions, such as clinical depression, that call into question whether the patient has made a competent choice, either to forgo life-sustaining treatment or to seek euthanasia, and then the patient's choice need not be evidence that continued life is no longer a benefit for him or her. Just as with decisions about treatment, a determination of incompetence can warrant not honoring the patient's choice; in the case of treatment, we then transfer decisional authority to a surrogate, though in the case of voluntary active euthanasia a determination that the patient is incompetent means that choice is not possible.

The value or right of self-determination does not entitle patients to compel physicians to act contrary to their own moral or professional values. Physicians are moral and professional agents whose own self-determination or integrity should be respected as well. If performing euthanasia became legally permissible, but conflicted with a particular physician's reasonable understanding of his or her moral or professional responsibilities, the care of a patient who requested euthanasia should be transferred to another. . . .

. . . Permitting physicians to perform euthanasia, it is said, would be incompatible with their fundamental moral and professional commitment as healers to care for patients and to protect life. Moreover, if euthanasia by physicians became common, patients would come to fear that a medication was intended not to treat or care, but instead to kill, and would thus lose trust in their physicians. This position was forcefully stated in a paper by Willard Gaylin and his colleagues:

> The very soul of medicine is on trial. . . . This issue touches medicine at its moral center; if this moral center collapses, if physicians become killers or are even licensed to kill, the profession—and, therewith, each physician—will never again be worthy of trust and respect as healer and comforter and protector of life in all its frailty.

These authors go on to make clear that, while they oppose permitting anyone to perform euthanasia, their special concern is with physicians doing so:

> We call on fellow physicians to say that they will not deliberately kill. We must also say to each of our fellow physicians that we will not tolerate killing of patients and that we shall take disciplinary action against doctors who kill. And we must say to the broader community that if it insists on tolerating or legalizing active euthanasia, it will have to find nonphysicians to do its killing.[1]

If permitting physicians to kill would undermine the very "moral center" of medicine, then almost certainly physicians should not be permitted to perform euthanasia. But how persuasive is this claim? Patients should not fear, as a consequence of permitting *voluntary* active euthanasia, that their physicians will substitute a lethal injection for what patients want and believe is part of their care. If active euthanasia is restricted to cases in which it is truly voluntary, then no patient should fear getting it unless she or he has voluntarily requested it. (The fear that we might in time also come to accept nonvoluntary, or even involuntary, active euthanasia is a slippery slope worry I address [in a later section].) Patients' trust of their physicians could be increased, not eroded, by knowledge that physicians will provide aid in dying when patients seek it.

Might Gaylin and his colleagues nevertheless be correct in their claim that the moral center of medicine would collapse if physicians were to become killers? This question raises what at the deepest level should be the guiding aims of medicine, a question that obviously cannot be fully explored here. But I do want to say enough to indicate the direction that I believe an appropriate response to this challenge should take. In spelling out above what I called the positive argument for voluntary active euthanasia, I suggested that two principal values—respecting patients' self-determination and promoting their well-being—underlie the consensus that competent patients, or the surrogates of incompetent patients, are entitled to refuse any life-sustaining treatment and to choose from among available alternative treatments. It is the commitment to these two values in guiding physicians' actions as healers, comforters, and protectors of their patients' lives that should be at the "moral center" of medicine, and these two values support physicians' administering euthanasia when their patients make competent requests for it.

What should not be at that moral center is a commitment to preserving patients' lives as such, without regard to whether those patients want their lives preserved or judge their preservation a benefit to them. . . .

REFERENCE

1 Willard Gaylin, Leon R. Kass, Edmund D. Pellegrino, and Mark Siegler, "Doctors Must Not Kill," *JAMA* 259 (1988): 2139–40.

QUESTIONS

1 Are considerations of self-determination and individual well-being sufficient to establish the moral legitimacy of voluntary active euthanasia?
2 Is the provision of voluntary active euthanasia by physicians "incompatible with their fundamental moral and professional commitment as healers"? If voluntary active euthanasia were legalized, would patients lose trust in physicians?

Objections to the Institutionalisation of Euthanasia

Stephen G. Potts

Potts argues against any scheme that would institutionalize—that is, legalize— (voluntary active) euthanasia. He identifies and briefly discusses a wide range of risks posed by legalization, and he insists that the burden of proof falls on the proponents of legalization. Potts endorses the "right to die" but insists that this right does not entail the right to receive assistance in suicide or the right to be killed.

Reprinted with permission of the publisher from Stephen G. Potts, "Looking for the Exit Door: Killing and Caring in Modern Medicine," *Houston Law Review,* vol. 25 (1988), pp. 504–509, 510–511.

[I am opposed] to any attempt to institutionalise euthanasia . . . because the risks of such institutionalisation are so grave as to outweigh the very real suffering of those who might benefit from it.

RISKS OF INSTITUTIONALISATION

Among the potential effects of a legalised practice of euthanasia are the following:

1 Reduced Pressure to Improve Curative or Symptomatic Treatment   If euthanasia had been legal forty years ago, it is quite possible that there would be no hospice movement today. The improvement in terminal care is a direct result of attempts made to minimise suffering. If that suffering had been extinguished by extinguishing the patients who bore it, then we may never have known the advances in the control of pain, nausea, breathlessness and other terminal symptoms that the last twenty years have seen.

Some diseases that were terminal a few decades ago are now routinely cured by newly developed treatments. Earlier acceptance of euthanasia might well have undercut the urgency of the research efforts which led to the discovery of those treatments. If we accept euthanasia now, we may well delay by decades the discovery of effective treatments for those diseases that are now terminal.

2 Abandonment of Hope   Every doctor can tell stories of patients expected to die within days who surprise everyone with their extraordinary recoveries. Every doctor has experienced the wonderful embarrassment of being proven wrong in their pessimistic prognosis. To make euthanasia a legitimate option as soon as the prognosis is pessimistic enough is to reduce the probability of such extraordinary recoveries from low to zero.

3 Increased Fear of Hospitals and Doctors   Despite all the efforts at health education, it seems there will always be a transference of the patient's fear of illness from the illness to the doctors and hospitals who treat it. This fear is still very real and leads to large numbers of late presentations of illnesses that might have been cured if only the patients had sought help earlier. To institutionalise euthanasia, however carefully, would undoubtedly magnify all the latent fear of doctors and hospitals harbored by the public. The inevitable result would be a rise in late presentations and, therefore, preventable deaths.

4 Difficulties of Oversight and Regulation   [Proposals to legalise euthanasia typically] list sets of precautions designed to prevent abuses. They acknowledge that such abuses are a possibility. I am far from convinced that the precautions are sufficient to prevent either those abuses that have been foreseen or those that may arise after passage of the law. The history of legal "loopholes" is not a cheering one: Abuses might arise when the patient is wealthy and an inheritance is at stake, when the doctor has made mistakes in diagnosis and treatment and hopes to avoid detection, when insurance coverage for treatment costs is about to expire, and in a host of other circumstances.

5   Pressure on the Patient   [Proposals to legalise euthanasia typically] seek to limit the influence of the patient's family on the decision, again acknowledging the risks posed by such influence. Families have all kinds of subtle ways, conscious and unconscious, of putting pressure on a patient to request euthanasia and relieve them of the financial and social burden of care. Many patients already feel guilty for imposing burdens on those who care for them, even when the families are happy to bear that burden. To provide an avenue for the discharge of that guilt in a request for euthanasia is to risk putting to death a great many patients who do not wish to die.

6   Conflict with Aims of Medicine   The pro-euthanasia movement cheerfully hands the dirty work of the actual killing to the doctors who, by and large, neither seek nor welcome the responsibility. There is little examination of the psychological stresses imposed on those whose training and professional outlook are geared to the saving of lives by asking them to start taking lives on a regular basis. Euthanasia advocates seem very confident that doctors can be relied on to make the enormous efforts sometimes necessary to save some lives, while at the same time assenting to requests to take other lives. Such confidence reflects, perhaps, a high opinion of doctors' psychic robustness, but it is a confidence seriously undermined by the shocking rates of depression, suicide, alcoholism, drug addiction, and marital discord consistently recorded among this group.

7   Dangers of Societal Acceptance   It must never be forgotten that doctors, nurses, and hospital administrators have personal lives, homes, and families, or that they are something more than just doctors, nurses, or hospital administrators. They are *citizens* and a significant part of the society around them. I am very worried about what the institutionalisation of euthanasia will do to society, in general, and, particularly, how much it will further erode our attachment to the sixth commandment. ["Thou shalt not kill."] How will we regard murderers? What will we say to the terrorist who justifies killing as a means to his political end when we ourselves justify killing as a means to a humanitarian end? I do not know and I daresay the euthanasia advocates do not either, but I worry about it and they appear not to. They need to justify their complacency.

8   The Slippery Slope   How long after acceptance of voluntary euthanasia will we hear the calls for nonvoluntary euthanasia? There are thousands of comatose or demented patients sustained by little more than good nursing care. They are an enormous financial and social burden. How soon will the advocates of euthanasia be arguing that we should "assist them in dying"—for, after all, they won't mind, will they?

How soon after *that* will we hear the calls for involuntary euthanasia, the disposal of the burdensome, the unproductive, the polluters of the gene pool? We must never forget the way the Nazi euthanasia programme made this progression in a few short years. "Oh, but they were barbarians," you say, and so they were, but not at the outset.

If developments in terminal care can be represented by a progression from the CURE mode of medical care to the CARE mode, enacting voluntary euthanasia legislation would permit a further progression to the KILL mode. The slippery slope argument represents the fear that, if this step is taken, then it will be difficult to avoid a further progression to the CULL mode, as illustrated:

CURE   The central aim of medicine
CARE   The central aim of terminal care once patients are beyond cure
KILL   The aim of the proponents of euthanasia for those patients beyond cure and not helped by care
CULL   The feared result of weakening the prohibition on euthanasia

I do not know how easy these moves will be to resist once voluntary euthanasia is accepted, but I have seen little evidence that the modern euthanasia advocates care about resisting them or even worry that they might be possible.

9   Costs and Benefits   Perhaps the most disturbing risk of all is posed by the growing concern over medical costs. Euthanasia is, after all, a very cheap service. The cost of a dose of barbiturates and curare and the few hours in a hospital bed that it takes them to act is minute compared to the massive bills incurred by many patients in the last weeks and months of their lives. Already in Britain, there is a serious underprovision of expensive therapies like renal dialysis and intensive care, with the result that many otherwise preventable deaths occur. Legalising euthanasia would save substantial financial resources which could be diverted to more "useful" treatments. These economic concerns already exert pressure to accept euthanasia, and, if accepted, they will inevitably tend to enlarge the category of patients for whom euthanasia is permitted.

Each of these objections could, and should, be expanded and pressed harder. I do not propose to do so now, for it is sufficient for my purposes to list them as *risks*, not inevitabilities. Several elements go into our judgment of the severity of a risk: the *probability* that the harm in question will arise (the odds), the *severity* of the harm in question (the stakes), and the ease with which the harm in question can be corrected (the *reversibility*). The institutionalisation of euthanasia is such a radical departure from anything that has gone before in Western society that we simply cannot judge the probability of any or all of the listed consequences. Nor can we rule any of them out. There must, however, be agreement that the severity of each of the harms listed is enough to give serious cause for concern, and the severity of all the harms together is enough to horrify. Furthermore, many of the potential harms seem likely to prove very difficult, if not impossible, to reverse by reinstituting a ban on euthanasia.

WEIGHING THE RISKS

For all these reasons, the burden of proof *must* lie with those who would have us gamble by legalising euthanasia. They should demonstrate beyond reasonable doubt that the dangers listed will not arise, just as chemical companies proposing to introduce a new drug are required to demonstrate that it is safe as well as beneficial.

Thus far, the proponents of euthanasia have relied exclusively on the compassion they arouse with tales of torment mercifully cut short by death, and have made little or no attempt to shoulder the burden of proving that legalising euthanasia is safe. Until they make such an attempt and carry it off successfully, their proposed legislation must be rejected outright.

THE RIGHT TO DIE AND THE DUTY TO KILL

The nature of my arguments should have made it clear by now that I object, not so much to individual acts of euthanasia, but to institutionalising it as a practice. All the pro-euthanasia arguments turn on the individual case of the patient in pain, suffering at the center of an intolerable existence. They exert powerful calls on our compassion, and appeal to our pity; therefore, we assent too readily when it is claimed that such patients have a "*right to die*" as an escape from torment. So long as the right to die means no more than the right to refuse life-prolonging treatment and the right to rational suicide, I agree. The advocates of euthanasia want to go much further than this though. They want to extend the right to die to encompass the right to receive assistance in suicide and, beyond that, the right to be killed. Here, the focus shifts from the patient to the agent, and from the killed to the killer; but, the argument begins to break down because our compassion does not extend this far.

If it is true that there is a right to be assisted in suicide or a right to be killed, then it follows that someone, somewhere, has a *duty* to provide the assistance or to do the killing. When we look at the proposed legislation, it is very clear upon whom the advocates of euthanasia would place this duty: the doctor. It would be the doctor's job to provide the pills and the doctor's job to give the lethal injection. The regulation of euthanasia is meant to prevent anyone, other than the doctor, from doing it. Such regulation would ensure that the doctor does it with the proper precautions and consultations, and would give the doctor security from legal sanctions for doing it. The emotive appeal of euthanasia is undeniably powerful, but it lasts only so long as we can avoid thinking about who has to do the killing, and where, and when, and how. Proposals to institutionalise euthanasia force us to think hard about these things, and the chill that their contemplation generates is deep enough to freeze any proponent's ardor. . . .

[One final objection to the institutionalisation of euthanasia] relates to another set out above (#5. Pressure on the patient). The objection turns on the concern that many requests for euthanasia will not be truly voluntary because of pressure on the patient or the patient's fear of becoming a burden. There is a significant risk that legalising voluntary euthanasia out of respect for the *right* to die will generate many requests for euthanasia out of a perceived *duty* to die. . . .

QUESTIONS

1 Does Potts provide a compelling case against the legalization of voluntary active euthanasia?

2 Should voluntary active euthanasia be legalized? If so, what procedures and safeguards should be introduced to govern the practice?

Assisted Suicide Is Not Voluntary Active Euthanasia

David T. Watts and Timothy Howell

Watts and Howell argue that it is important to distinguish between voluntary active euthanasia and physician-assisted suicide and to distinguish among three types of assisted suicide: (1) providing information, (2) providing the means (typically, by writing a prescription for a lethal amount of medication), and (3) supervising or directly aiding. Although they believe that the legalization of voluntary active euthanasia would have severe adverse consequences, and thus endorse many of the standard arguments against voluntary active euthanasia, they find the same arguments to be substantially weaker when directed against assisted suicide. In their view, physician-assisted suicide should be legalized. However, they argue that physicians should be limited to indirect participation in a patient's suicide—that is, the provision of information or means; physicians should not be permitted to supervise or directly aid a patient in committing suicide.

. . . [Ongoing] developments highlight some of the confusion emerging from discussions of voluntary active euthanasia (V.A.E.) and assisted suicide. A significant source of confusion has been the tendency to join these concepts or even to consider them synonymous. For example, the AGS Position Statement on V.A.E. and a recent article by Teno and Lynn in the *Journal of the American Geriatrics Society* both reject easing restrictions on V.A.E. and assisted suicide while making arguments *only* against euthanasia.[1,2] The National Hospice Organization also opposes euthanasia and assisted suicide, but it, too, appears to blur the distinction between them in stating that "euthanasia encompasses . . . in some settings, physician-assisted suicide."[3] Others appear to use the terms euthanasia and assisted suicide synonymously in arguing against both.

In contrast, the AMA Ethics and Health Policy Counsel argues against physician-assisted suicide and distinguishes this from euthanasia.[4] The AMA Council on Ethical and Judicial Affairs also acknowledges there is "an ethically relevant distinction between euthanasia and assisted suicide that makes assisted suicide a more attractive option." Yet it then goes on to assert that "the ethical concerns about physician-assisted suicide are similar to those of euthanasia since both are essentially interventions intended to cause death."[5]

In order to weigh and appreciate the merits of the different arguments for and against V.A.E. and physician-assisted suicide, it is critical that appropriate distinctions be made. For example, we believe the arguments made in the references cited above and by others[6,7] against euthanasia are telling. However, we find that these same arguments are substantially weaker when used against assisted suicide. And while we agree with the AMA Council on Ethical and Judicial Affairs that

Reprinted with permission of Blackwell Publishing Ltd. from *Journal of the American Geriatrics Society,* vol. 40 (October 1992), pp. 1043–1046.

an ethically relevant distinction exists between euthanasia and assisted suicide, we think it is important to distinguish further between different forms of assisted suicide. Only by doing so can we begin to sort out some of the apparent confusion in attitudes toward these issues. We caution our readers that the literature on this topic, while growing, remains preliminary, with little empirical research yet completed. Our arguments, however, are philosophical in nature and do not ultimately stand or fall on empirical data.

DEFINITIONS

Voluntary active euthanasia: Administration of medications or other interventions intended to cause death at a patient's request.

Assisted suicide: Provision of information, means, or direct assistance by which a patient may take his or her own life. Assisted suicide involves several possible levels of assistance: *providing information,* for example, may mean providing toxicological information or describing techniques by which someone may commit suicide; *providing the means* can involve written prescriptions for lethal amounts of medication; *supervising or directly aiding* includes inserting an intravenous line and instructing on starting a lethal infusion.

These levels of assistance have very different implications. Providing only information or means allows individuals to retain the greatest degree of control in choosing the time and mode of their deaths. Physician participation is only indirect. This type of limited assistance is exemplified by the widely reported case of Dr. Timothy Quill, who prescribed a lethal quantity of barbiturates at the request of one of his patients who had leukemia.[8] By contrast, supervising or directly aiding is the type of physician involvement characterizing the case of Dr. Jack Kevorkian and Janet Adkins. Adkins was a 54-year-old woman with a diagnosis of Alzheimer-type dementia who sought Kevorkian's assistance in ending her life. Dr. Kevorkian inserted an intravenous catheter and instructed Mrs. Adkins on activating a lethal infusion of potassium following barbiturate sedation, a process personally monitored by Kevorkian. This form of assisted suicide carries significant potential for physician influence or control of the process, and from it there is only a relatively short step to physician initiation (i.e., active euthanasia). We therefore reject physician-supervised suicide for the arguments commonly made against V.A.E., namely, that legalization would have serious adverse consequences, including potential abuse of vulnerable persons, mistrust of physicians, and diminished availability of supportive services for the dying.[2,3,5–7] We find each of these arguments, however, insufficient when applied to more limited forms of physician-assisted suicide (i.e., providing information or means).

WILL ASSISTED SUICIDE LEAD TO ABUSE OF VULNERABLE PERSONS?

A major concern is that some patients will request euthanasia or assisted suicide out of convenience to others.[2,4] It is certainly possible that a patient's desire to avoid being a burden could lead to such a request. With euthanasia, there is danger that a patient's request might find too ready acceptance. With assisted suicide, however, the ultimate decision, and the ultimate action, are the patient's, not the physician's. This places an important check and balance on physician initiation or patient acquiescence in euthanasia. As the AMA Council on Ethical and Judicial Affairs acknowledges, a greater level of patient autonomy is afforded by physician-assisted suicide than by euthanasia.[5]

Culturally or socially mediated requests for assisted suicide would remain a significant concern. Patients might also request aid in suicide out of fear, pain, ambivalence, or depression. The requirement that patients commit the ultimate act themselves cannot alone provide a sufficient safeguard. It would be incumbent on physicians to determine, insofar as possible, that requests for assisted suicide were not unduly influenced and that reversible conditions were optimally treated. As to how physicians might respond to such requests, data from the Netherlands indicate that about 75% of euthanasia requests in that country are refused.[9] It is our impression that most requests for assisted suicide, therefore, appear to represent opportunities for improved symptom control. We believe most serious requests would likely come from patients experiencing distressing symptoms of terminal illness.[10] By opening the door for counseling or treatment of reversible conditions, requests for assisted suicide might actually lead to averting some suicides which would have otherwise occurred.

Another concern regarding euthanasia is that it could come to be accepted without valid consent and that such a practice would more likely affect the frail and impoverished. The Remmelink Commission's investigation of euthanasia in the Netherlands appeared to justify such concerns in estimating that Dutch physicians may have performed 1,000 acts of involuntary euthanasia involving incompetent individuals.[11] But while euthanasia opens up the possibility of invalid consent, with assisted suicide consent is integral to the process. Because the choice of action clearly rests with the individual, there is substantially less likelihood for the abuse of assisted suicide as a societal vehicle for cost containment. And there is little basis for assuming that requests for assisted suicide would come primarily from frail and impoverished persons. Prolonged debilitation inherent in many illnesses is familiar to an increasing number of patients, family members, and health professionals. Such illnesses represent a greater financial threat to the middle- and upper-middle class, since the poor and disenfranchised have less to spend down to indigency. Thus, we suspect requests for assisted suicide might actually be more common from the educated, affluent, and outspoken.

Patients diagnosed with terminal or debilitating conditions are often vulnerable. We agree that such patients might request assisted suicide out of fear of pain, suffering, or isolation, and that too ready acceptance of such requests could be disastrous. Yet, we believe that patients' interests can be safeguarded by requirements for persistent, competent requests as well as thorough assessments for conditions, such as clinical depression, which could be reversed, treated, or ameliorated. Foley recently outlined an approach to the suicidal cancer patient.[12] We share her view that many such patients' requests to terminate life are altered by the availability of expert, continuing hospice services. We concur with Foley and others in calling for the wider availability of such services,[1,2] so that requests for assisted suicide arising from pain, depression, or other distressing symptoms can be reduced to a minimum.

WOULD ASSISTED SUICIDE UNDERMINE TRUST BETWEEN PATIENTS AND PHYSICIANS?

The cardinal distinction between V.A.E. and assisted suicide is that V.A.E. is killing by physicians, while suicide is self-killing. Prohibiting both euthanasia and physician-supervised suicide (i.e., with direct physician involvement) should diminish worries that patients might have about physicians wrongly administering lethal medicine. At present, physician-patient trust is compromised by widespread concern that physicians try too hard to keep dying patients alive. The very strength of the physician-patient relationship has been cited as a justification for physician involvement in assisted suicide.[13]

A number of ethicists have expressed concern that both euthanasia and assisted suicide, if legalized, would have a negative impact on the way society perceives the role of physicians.[2,4,6,7] Limited forms of assisted suicide, however, have been viewed more positively.[14] Public and professional attitudes appear to be evolving on this issue. A 1990 Gallup poll found that 66% of respondents believed someone in great pain, with "no hope of improvement," had the moral right to commit suicide; in 1975 the figure was 41%.[15] A panel of distinguished physicians has stated that it is not immoral for a physician to assist in the rational suicide of a terminally ill person.[16] The recent publication of a book on techniques of committing or assisting suicide evoked wide interest and significant support for the right of people to take control of their dying.[17] For a significant segment of society, physician involvement in assisted suicide may be welcomed, not feared. Furthermore, while relatively few might be likely to seek assistance with suicide if stricken with a debilitating illness, a substantial number might take solace knowing they could request such assistance.

There is another argument raised against V.A.E. that we believe also falters when used to object to assisted suicide. It has been maintained that prohibiting euthanasia forces physicians to focus on the humane care of dying patients, including meticulous attention to their symptoms.[2,10] This argument implies that physicians find it easier to relieve the suffering of dying patients by ending their lives rather than attempting the difficult task of palliating their symptoms. But for some patients, the suffering may not be amenable to even the most expert palliation. Even in such instances, some argue that limited forms of assisted suicide should be prohibited on the grounds that not to forbid them would open the door for more generalized, less stringent applications of assisted suicide.

To us, this "slippery slope" argument seems to imply that the moral integrity of the medical profession must be maintained, even if at the cost of prolonged, unnecessary suffering by at least some dying patients. We believe such a posture is itself inhumane and not acceptable. It contradicts a fundamental principle that is an essential ingredient of physician-patient trust: that patient comfort should be a primary goal of the physician in the face of incurable illness. Furthermore, by allowing limited physician involvement in assisted suicide, physicians can respect both the principle of caring that guides them and the patients for whom caring alone is insufficient. We concede that there is another alternative: terminally ill patients who cannot avoid pain while awake may be given continuous anesthetic levels of medication.[2] But this is exactly the sort of dying process we believe many in our society want to avoid.

WILL ASSISTED SUICIDE AND EUTHANASIA WEAKEN SOCIETAL RESOLVE TO INCREASE RESOURCES ALLOCATED TO CARE OF THE DYING?

This argument assumes that V.A.E. and assisted suicide would both be widely practiced, and that their very availability would decrease tangible concern for those not choosing euthanasia or suicide. However, euthanasia is rarely requested even by terminal cancer patients.[2] In the Netherlands, euthanasia accounts for less than 2% of all deaths.[9] These data suggest that even if assisted suicide were available to those with intractable pain or distressing terminal conditions, it would likely be an option chosen by relatively few. With assisted suicide limited to relatively few cases, this argument collapses. For with only a few requesting assisted suicide, the vast number of patients with debilitating illnesses would be undiminished, and their numbers should remain sufficient to motivate societal concern for their needs. Furthermore, to withhold assisted suicide from the few making serious, valid requests would be to subordinate needlessly the interests of these few to those of the many. Compounding their tragedy would be the fact that these individuals could not even benefit from any increase in therapeutic resources prompted by their suffering, insofar as their conditions are, by definition, not able to be ameliorated.

CONCLUSION

We have argued that assisted suicide and voluntary active euthanasia are different and that each has differing implications for medical practice and society. Further discussion should consider the merits and disadvantages of each, a process enhanced by contrasting them. We have further argued that different forms of assisted suicide can be distinguished both clinically and philosophically. Although some may argue that all forms of assisted suicide are fundamentally the same, we believe the differences can be contrasted as starkly as a written prescription and a suicide machine.

We do not advocate ready acceptance of requests for suicide, nor do we wish to romanticize the concept of rational suicide.[18] In some situations, however, where severe debilitating illness cannot be reversed, suicide may represent a rational choice. If this is the case, then physician assistance could make the process more humane. Along with other geriatricians, we often face dilemmas involving the management of chronic illnesses in late life. We believe we can best serve our patients, and preserve their trust, by respecting their desire for autonomy, dignity, and quality, not only of life, but of dying.

REFERENCES

1 AGS Public Policy Committee. Voluntary active euthanasia. J Am Geriatr Soc 1991;39:826.
2 Teno J, Lynn J. Voluntary active euthanasia: The individual case and public policy. J Am Geriatr Soc 1991;39:827–830.
3 National Hospice Organization. Statement of the National Hospice Organization Opposing the Legalization of Euthanasia and Assisted Suicide. Arlington, VA: National Hospice Organization, 1991.

4 Orentlicher D. Physician participation in assisted suicide. JAMA 1989;262:1844–1845.

5 AMA. Report of the Council on Ethical and Judicial Affairs: Decisions Near the End of Life. Chicago, IL: American Medical Association, 1991.

6 Singer PA. Should doctors kill patients? Can Med Assoc J 1988;138:1000–1001.

7 Singer PA, Siegler M. Euthanasia—a critique. N Engl J Med 1990;322:1881–1883.

8 Quill TE. Death and dignity: A case of individualized decision making. N Engl J Med 1991;324:691–694.

9 Van der Maas PJ, Van Delden JJM, Pijnenborg L, Looman CWN. Euthanasia and other medical decisions concerning the end of life. Lancet 1991;338:669–674.

10 Palmore EB. Arguments for assisted suicide (letter). Gerontologist 1991;31:854.

11 Karel R. Undertreatment of pain, depression needs to be addressed before euthanasia made legal in U.S. Psychiatric News, December 20, 1991, pp. 5, 13, 23.

12 Foley KM. The relationship of pain and symptom management to patient requests for physician-assisted suicide. J Pain Symptom Manag 1991;6:289–297.

13 Jecker NS. Giving death a hand. When the dying and the doctor stand in a special relationship. J Am Geriatr Soc 1991;39:831–835.

14 American College of Physicians. ACP to DA, Grand Jury: Dr. Quill acted "humanely." ACP Observer, September, 1991, p. 5.

15 Ames K, Wilson L, Sawhill R et al. Last rights. Newsweek August 26, 1991, pp. 40–41.

16 Wanzer SH, Federman DD, Adelstein SJ et al. The physician's responsibility toward hopelessly ill patients: A second look. N Engl J Med 1989;320:844–849.

17 Humphry D. Final Exit: The Practicalities of Self-Deliverance and Assisted Suicide for the Dying. Eugene, OR: The Hemlock Society (distributed by Carol Publishing, Secaucus, NJ), 1991.

18 Conwell Y, Caine ED. Rational suicide and the right to die: Reality and myth. N Engl J Med 1991;325:1100–1103.

QUESTIONS

1 Would the social consequences of legalizing physician-assisted suicide be less problematic than the social consequences of legalizing voluntary active euthanasia?

2 Should physician-assisted suicide be legalized? If so, should physicians be permitted to supervise or directly aid a patient in committing suicide, or should they be limited to providing information and means?

Opinion of the Court in *Washington v. Glucksberg*

Chief Justice William H. Rehnquist

At issue in this case is the constitutionality of Washington State's ban on assisted suicide—in particular, whether it violates the Due Process Clause of the Fourteenth Amendment. Although the Supreme Court unanimously upholds

United States Supreme Court. 521 U.S. 702 (1997).

Washington's assisted-suicide ban, the fact that this case has produced five separate concurring opinions indicates that the Court remains fragmented on the most appropriate way of constructing the underlying issues. Chief Justice Rehnquist, in this opinion joined by four other justices, rejects the contention (asserted by the Ninth Circuit Court of Appeals) that a competent, terminally ill adult can claim a constitutionally protected right to physician assistance in suicide. On his analysis, no such liberty interest is protected by the Due Process Clause of the Fourteenth Amendment; thus, no basis exists for a fundamental-right claim. It follows, he argues, that the constitutionality of Washington's assisted-suicide ban can be established merely by showing that the ban is rationally related to legitimate government interests. In order to display how this requirement is clearly met, the Chief Justice identifies and discusses the relevant state interests.

The question presented in this case is whether Washington's prohibition against "caus[ing]" or "aid[ing]" a suicide offends the Fourteenth Amendment to the United States Constitution. We hold that it does not.

It has always been a crime to assist a suicide in the State of Washington. In 1854, Washington's first Territorial Legislature outlawed "assisting another in the commission of self-murder." Today, Washington law provides: "A person is guilty of promoting a suicide attempt when he knowingly causes or aids another person to attempt suicide." Wash. Rev. Code 9A.36.060(1) (1994). "Promoting a suicide attempt" is a felony, punishable by up to five years' imprisonment and up to a $10,000 fine. At the same time, Washington's Natural Death Act, enacted in 1979, states that the "withholding or withdrawal of life-sustaining treatment" at a patient's direction "shall not, for any purpose, constitute a suicide."

Petitioners in this case are the State of Washington and its Attorney General. Respondents Harold Glucksberg, M.D., Abigail Halperin, M.D., Thomas A. Preston, M.D., and Peter Shalit, M.D., are physicians who practice in Washington. These doctors occasionally treat terminally ill, suffering patients, and declare that they would assist these patients in ending their lives if not for Washington's assisted-suicide ban. In January 1994, respondents, along with three gravely ill, pseudonymous plaintiffs who have since died and Compassion in Dying, a nonprofit organization that counsels people considering physician-assisted suicide, sued in the United States District Court, seeking a declaration that Wash. Rev. Code 9A.36.060(1) (1994) is, on its face, unconstitutional. *Compassion in Dying v. Washington* (WD Wash. 1994).

The plaintiffs asserted "the existence of a liberty interest protected by the Fourteenth Amendment which extends to a personal choice by a mentally competent, terminally ill adult to commit physician-assisted suicide." Relying primarily on *Planned Parenthood v. Casey* (1992) and *Cruzan v. Director, Missouri Dept. of Health* (1990), the District Court agreed and concluded that Washington's assisted-suicide ban is unconstitutional because it "places an undue burden on the exercise of [that] constitutionally protected liberty interest." The District Court also decided that the Washington statute violated the Equal Protection Clause's requirement that "'all persons similarly situated . . . be treated alike.'"

A panel of the Court of Appeals for the Ninth Circuit reversed, emphasizing that "[i]n the two hundred and five years of our existence no constitutional right to aid in killing oneself has ever been asserted and upheld by a court of final jurisdiction." *Compassion in Dying v. Washington* (1995). The Ninth Circuit reheard the case en banc, reversed the panel's decision, and affirmed the District Court. *Compassion in Dying v. Washington* (1996). Like the District Court, the en banc Court of Appeals emphasized our *Casey* and *Cruzan* decisions. The court also discussed what is described as "historical" and "current societal attitudes" toward suicide and assisted suicide, and concluded that "the Constitution encompasses a due process liberty interest in controlling the time and manner of one's death—that there is, in short, a constitutionally-recognized 'right to die.'" After "[w]eighing and then balancing" this interest against Washington's various interests, the court held that the State's assisted-suicide ban was unconstitutional "as applied to terminally ill competent adults who wish to hasten their deaths with medication prescribed by their physicians." The court did not reach the District Court's equal-protection holding. We granted certiorari and now reverse.

I

We begin, as we do in all due-process cases, by examining our Nation's history, legal traditions, and practices. In almost every State—indeed, in almost every western democracy—it is a crime to assist a suicide. The States' assisted-suicide bans are not innovations. Rather, they are longstanding expressions of the States' commitment to the protection and preservation of all human life. Indeed, opposition to and condemnation of suicide—and, therefore, of assisting suicide—are consistent and enduring themes of our philosophical, legal, and cultural heritages.

More specifically, for over 700 years, the Anglo-American common-law tradition has punished or otherwise disapproved of both suicide and assisting suicide. . . .

For the most part, the early American colonies adopted the common-law approach. . . . [For example,] Virginia . . . required ignominious burial for suicides, and their estates were forfeit to the crown.

Over time, however, the American colonies abolished these harsh common-law penalties. . . . [H]owever, . . . the movement away from the common law's harsh sanctions did not represent an acceptance of suicide; rather, . . . this change reflected the growing consensus that it was unfair to punish the suicide's family for his wrongdoing. . . . [C]ourts continued to condemn [suicide] as a grave public wrong.

That suicide remained a grievous, though non-felonious, wrong is confirmed by the fact that colonial and early state legislatures and courts did not retreat from prohibiting assisting suicide. . . . And the prohibitions against assisting suicide never contained exceptions for those who were near death. . . .

The earliest American statute explicitly to outlaw assisting suicide was enacted in New York in 1828. . . . By the time the Fourteenth Amendment was ratified, it was a crime in most States to assist a suicide. . . .

Though deeply rooted, the States' assisted-suicide bans have in recent years been reexamined and, generally, reaffirmed. Because of advances in medicine and technology, Americans today are increasingly likely to die in institutions, from chronic illnesses. Public concern and democratic action are therefore sharply focused on how best to protect dignity and independence at the end of life, with the result that there have been many significant changes in state laws and in the attitudes these laws reflect. Many States, for example, now permit "living wills," surrogate health-care decisionmaking, and the withdrawal or refusal of life-sustaining medical treatment. At the same time, however, voters and legislators continue for the most part to reaffirm their States' prohibitions on assisting suicide. . . .

. . . Against this backdrop of history, tradition, and practice, we now turn to respondents' constitutional claim.

II

The Due Process Clause guarantees more than fair process, and the "liberty" it protects includes more than the absence of physical restraint. The Clause also provides heightened protection against government interference with certain fundamental rights and liberty interests. In a long line of cases, we have held that, in addition to the specific freedoms protected by the Bill of Rights, the "liberty" specially protected by the Due Process Clause includes the rights to marry, to have children, to direct the education and upbringing of one's children, to marital privacy, to use contraception, to bodily integrity, and to abortion. We have also assumed, and strongly suggested, that the Due Process Clause protects the traditional right to refuse unwanted lifesaving medical treatment.

But we "ha[ve] always been reluctant to expand the concept of substantive due process because guideposts for responsible decisionmaking in this unchartered area are scarce and open-ended." By extending constitutional protection to an asserted right or liberty interest, we, to a great extent, place the matter outside the arena of public debate and legislative action. We must therefore "exercise the utmost care whenever we are asked to break new ground in this field," lest the liberty protected by the Due Process Clause be subtly transformed into the policy preferences of the members of this Court.

Our established method of substantive-due-process analysis has two primary features: First, we have regularly observed that the Due Process Clause specially protects those fundamental rights and liberties which are, objectively, "deeply rooted in this Nation's history and tradition" and "implicit in the concept of ordered liberty," such that "neither liberty nor justice would exist if they were sacrificed." Second, we have required in substantive-due-process cases a "careful description" of the asserted fundamental liberty interest. Our Nation's history, legal traditions, and practices thus provide the crucial "guideposts for responsible decisionmaking" that direct and restrain our exposition of the Due Process Clause. As we stated recently . . . , the Fourteenth Amendment "forbids the government to infringe . . . 'fundamental' liberty interests *at all,* no matter what process is provided, unless the infringement is narrowly tailored to serve a compelling state interest." . . .

Turning to the claim at issue here, the Court of Appeals stated that "[p]roperly analyzed, the first issue to be resolved is whether there is a liberty interest in determining the time and manner of one's death," or, in other words, "[i]s there a right to die?" Similarly, respondents assert a "liberty to choose how to die" and a right to "control of one's final days," and describe the asserted liberty as "the right to choose a humane, dignified death" and "the liberty to shape death." As noted above, we have a tradition of carefully formulating the interest at stake in substantive-due-process cases. For example, although *Cruzan* is often described as a "right to die" case, we were, in fact, more precise: we assumed that the Constitution granted competent persons a "constitutionally protected right to refuse lifesaving hydration and nutrition." The Washington statute at issue in this case prohibits "aid[ing] another person to attempt suicide," Wash. Rev. Code §9A.36.060(1) (1994), and, thus, the question before us is whether the "liberty" specially protected by the Due Process Clause includes a right to commit suicide which itself includes a right to assistance in doing so.

We now inquire whether this asserted right has any place in our Nation's traditions. Here, as discussed above, we are confronted with a consistent and almost universal tradition that has long rejected the asserted right, and continues explicitly to reject it today, even for terminally ill, mentally competent adults. To hold for respondents, we would have to reverse centuries of legal doctrine and practice, and strike down the considered policy choice of almost every State.

Respondents contend, however, that the liberty interest they assert *is* consistent with this Court's substantive-due-process line of cases, if not with this Nation's history and practice. Pointing to *Casey* and *Cruzan,* respondents read our jurisprudence in this area as reflecting a general tradition of "self-sovereignty" and as teaching that the "liberty" protected by the Due Process Clause includes "basic and intimate exercises of personal autonomy." According to respondents, our liberty jurisprudence, and the broad, individualistic principles it reflects, protects the "liberty of competent, terminally ill adults to make end-of-life decisions free of undue government interference." The question presented in this case, however, is whether the protections of the Due Process Clause include a right to commit suicide with another's assistance. With this "careful description" of respondents' claim in mind, we turn to *Casey* and *Cruzan.*

In *Cruzan,* we considered whether Nancy Beth Cruzan, who had been severely injured in an automobile accident and was in a persistive vegetative state, "ha[d] a right under the United States Constitution which would require the hospital to withdraw life-sustaining treatment" at her parents' request. We began with the observation that "[a]t common law, even the touching of one person by another without consent and without legal justification was a battery." We then discussed the related rule that "informed consent is generally required for medical treatment." After reviewing a long line of relevant state cases, we concluded that "the common-law doctrine of informed consent is viewed as generally encompassing the right of a competent individual to refuse medical treatment." Next, we reviewed our own cases on the subject, and stated that "[t]he principle that a competent person has a constitutionally protected liberty interest in refusing unwanted medical treatment may be inferred from our prior decisions." Therefore, "for purposes of [that] case, we assume[d] that the United States Constitution would grant a competent person a constitutionally protected right to refuse lifesaving hydration and nutrition." We concluded that, notwithstanding this right, the Constitution permitted Missouri to require clear and convincing evidence of an incompetent patient's wishes concerning the withdrawal of life-sustaining treatment.

Respondents contend that in *Cruzan* we "acknowledged that competent, dying persons have the right to direct the removal of life-sustaining medical treatment and thus hasten death," and that "the constitutional principle behind recognizing the patient's liberty to direct the withdrawal of artificial life support applies at least as strongly to the choice to hasten impending death by consuming lethal medication." Similarly, the Court of Appeals concluded that "*Cruzan,* by recognizing a liberty interest that includes the refusal of artificial provision of life-sustaining food and water, necessarily recognize[d] a liberty interest in hastening one's own death."

The right assumed in *Cruzan,* however, was not simply deduced from abstract concepts of personal autonomy. Given the common-law rule that forced medication was a battery, and the long legal tradition protecting the decision to refuse unwanted medical treatment, our assumption was entirely consistent with this Nation's history and constitutional traditions. The decisions to commit suicide with the assistance of another may be just as personal and profound as the decision to refuse unwanted medical treatment, but it has never enjoyed similar legal protection. Indeed, the two acts are widely and reasonably regarded as quite distinct. See *Quill v. Vacco* (1997). In *Cruzan* itself, we recognized that most States outlawed assisted suicide—and even more do today—and we certainly gave no intimation that the right to refuse unwanted medical treatment could be somehow transmuted into a right to assistance in committing suicide.

Respondents also rely on *Casey.* There, the Court's opinion concluded that "the essential holding of *Roe v. Wade* should be retained and once again reaffirmed." We held, first, that a woman has a right, before her fetus is viable, to an abortion "without undue interference from the State"; second, that States may restrict post-viability abortions, so long as exceptions are made to protect a woman's life and health; and third, that the State has legitimate interests throughout a pregnancy in protecting the health of the woman and the life of the unborn child. In reaching this conclusion, the opinion discussed in some detail this Court's substantive-due-process tradition of interpreting the Due Process Clause to protect certain fundamental rights and "personal decisions relating to marriage, procreation, contraception, family relationships, child rearing, and education," and noted that many of those rights and liberties "involv[e] the most intimate and personal choices a person may make in a lifetime."

The Court of Appeals, like the District Court, found *Casey* "'highly instructive'" and "'almost prescriptive'" for determining "'what liberty interest may inhere in a terminally ill person's choice to commit suicide'":

> Like the decision of whether or not to have an abortion, the decision how and when to die is one of "the most intimate and personal choices a person may make in a lifetime," a choice "central to personal dignity and autonomy."

. . . That many of the rights and liberties protected by the Due Process Clause sound in personal autonomy does not warrant the sweeping conclusion that any and all important, intimate, and personal decisions are so protected, and *Casey* did not suggest otherwise.

The history of the law's treatment of assisted suicide in this country has been and continues to be one of the rejection of nearly all efforts to permit it. That being the case, our decisions lead us to conclude that the asserted "right" to assistance in committing suicide is not a fundamental liberty interest protected by the Due Process Clause. The Constitution also requires, however, that Washington's assisted-suicide ban be rationally related to legitimate government interests. This requirement is unquestionably met here. As the court below recognized, Washington's assisted-suicide ban implicates a number of state interests.

First, Washington has an "unqualified interest in the preservation of human life." The State's prohibition on assisted suicide, like all homicide laws, both reflects and advances its commitment to this interest. This interest is symbolic and aspirational as well as practical:

> While suicide is no longer prohibited or penalized, the ban against assisted suicide and euthanasia shores up the notion of limits in human relationships. It reflects the gravity with which we view the decision to take one's own life or the life of another, and our reluctance to encourage or promote these decisions. New York State Task Force on Life and the Law, When Death Is Sought: Assisted Suicide and Euthanasia in the Medical Context 131–132 (May 1994) (hereinafter New York Task Force).

Respondents admit that "[t]he State has a real interest in preserving the lives of those who can still contribute to society and enjoy life." The Court of Appeals also recognized Washington's interest in protecting life, but held that the "weight" of this interest depends on the "medical condition and the wishes of the person whose life is at stake." Washington, however, has rejected this sliding-scale approach and, through its assisted-suicide ban, insists that all persons' lives, from beginning to end, regardless of physical or mental condition, are under the full protection of the law. As we have previously affirmed, the States "may properly decline to make judgments about the 'quality' of life that a particular individual may enjoy." This remains true, as *Cruzan* makes clear, even for those who are near death.

Relatedly, all admit that suicide is a serious public-health problem, especially among persons in otherwise vulnerable groups. The State has an interest in preventing suicide, and in studying, identifying, and treating its causes.

Those who attempt suicide—terminally ill or not—often suffer from depression or other mental disorders. See New York Task Force 13–22, 126–128 (more than 95% of those who commit suicide had a major psychiatric illness at the time of death; among the terminally ill, uncontrolled pain is a "risk factor" because it contributes to depression). Research indicates . . . that many people who request physician-assisted suicide withdraw that request if their depression and pain are treated. The New York Task Force, however, expressed its concern that, because depression is difficult to diagnose, physicians and medical professionals often fail to respond adequately to seriously ill patients' needs. Thus, legal physician-assisted suicide could make it more difficult for the State to protect depressed or mentally ill persons, or those who are suffering from untreated pain, from suicidal impulses.

The State also has an interest in protecting the integrity and ethics of the medical profession. In contrast to the Court of Appeals' conclusion that "the integrity of the medical profession would [not] be threatened in any way by [physician-assisted suicide]," the American Medical Association, like many other medical and physicians' groups, has concluded that "[p]hysician-assisted suicide is fundamentally incompatible with the physician's role as healer." American Medical Association, Code of Ethics §2.211 (1994). And physician-assisted suicide could, it is argued, undermine the trust that is essential to the doctor-patient relationship by blurring the time-honored line between healing and harming.

Next, the State has an interest in protecting vulnerable groups—including the poor, the elderly, and disabled persons—from abuse, neglect, and mistakes. The Court of Appeals dismissed the State's concern that disadvantaged persons might be pressured into physician-assisted suicide as "ludicrous on its face." We have recognized, however, the real risk of subtle coercion and undue influence in end-of-life situations. Similarly, the New York Task Force warned that "[l]egalizing physician-assisted suicide would pose profound risks to many individuals who are ill and vulnerable. . . . The risk of harm is greatest for the many individuals in our society whose autonomy and well-being are already compromised by poverty, lack of access to good medical care, advanced age, or membership in a stigmatized social group." New York Task Force 120. If physician-assisted suicide were permitted, many might resort to it to spare their families the substantial financial burden of end-of-life health-care costs.

The State's interest here goes beyond protecting the vulnerable from coercion; it extends to protecting disabled and terminally ill people from prejudice, negative and inaccurate stereotypes, and "societal indifference." The State's assisted-suicide ban reflects and reinforces its policy that the lives of terminally ill, disabled, and elderly people must be no less valued than the lives of the young and healthy, and that a seriously disabled person's suicidal impulses should be interpreted and treated the same way as anyone else's.

Finally, the State may fear that permitting assisted suicide will start it down the path to voluntary and perhaps even involuntary euthanasia. The Court of Appeals struck down Washington's assisted-suicide ban only "as applied to competent, terminally ill adults who wish to hasten their deaths by obtaining medication prescribed by their doctors." Washington insists, however, that the impact of the court's decision will not and cannot be so limited. If suicide is protected as a matter of constitutional right, it is argued, "every man and woman in the United States must enjoy it." The Court of Appeals' decision, and its expansive reasoning, provide ample support for the State's concerns. The court noted, for example, that the "decision of a duly appointed surrogate decision maker is for all legal purposes the decision of the patient himself," that "in some instances, the patient may be unable to self-administer the drugs and . . . administration by the physician . . . may be the only way the patient may be able to receive them," and that not only physicians, but also family members and loved ones, will inevitably participate in assisting suicide. Thus, it turns out that what is couched as a limited right to "physician-assisted suicide" is likely, in effect, a much broader license, which could prove extremely difficult to police and contain. Washington's ban on assisting suicide prevents such erosion. . . .

We need not weigh exactly the relative strengths of these various interests. They are unquestionably important and legitimate, and Washington's ban on assisted suicide is at least reasonably related to their promotion and protection. We therefore hold that Wash. Rev. Code §9A36.060(1) (1994) does not violate the Fourteenth Amendment, either on its face or "as applied to competent, terminally ill adults who wish to hasten their deaths by obtaining medication prescribed by their doctors."

Throughout the Nation, Americans are engaged in an earnest and profound debate about the morality, legality, and practicality of physician-assisted suicide. Our holding permits this debate to continue, as it should in a democratic society. The decision of the en banc Court of Appeals is reversed. . . .

QUESTIONS

1 How important is a terminally ill person's interest in controlling the time and manner of death?
2 Chief Justice Rehnquist points out that the Court's holding in this case permits the debate over physician-assisted suicide to continue. Would you endorse legalization of physician-assisted suicide in your state?

Concurring Opinion in *Washington v. Glucksberg* and *Vacco v. Quill*

Justice Sandra Day O'Connor

In this concurring opinion, Justice O'Connor emphasizes that, in both Washington and New York (the setting of *Vacco*), there are presently no legal barriers to terminally ill patients' obtaining adequate pain-relieving medication, "even to the point of causing unconsciousness and hastening death." If terminally ill patients did not, in fact, have access to such palliative care, she seems to suggest, there might be grounds for a different conclusion regarding physician-assisted suicide.

Death will be different for each of us. For many, the last days will be spent in physical pain and perhaps the despair that accompanies physical deterioration and a loss of control of basic bodily and mental functions. Some will seek medication to alleviate that pain and other symptoms.

The Court frames the issue in *Washington v. Glucksberg* as whether the Due Process Clause of the Constitution protects a "right to commit suicide which itself includes a right to assistance in doing so," and concludes that our Nation's

United States Supreme Court, 521 U.S. 702 (1997).

history, legal traditions, and practices do not support the existence of such a right. I join the Court's opinions because I agree that there is no generalized right to "commit suicide." But respondents urge us to address the narrower question whether a mentally competent person who is experiencing great suffering has a constitutionally cognizable interest in controlling the circumstances of his or her imminent death. I see no need to reach that question in the context of the facial challenges to the New York and Washington laws at issue here. ("The Washington statute at issue in this case prohibits 'aid[ing] another person to attempt suicide,' . . . and, thus, the question before us is whether the 'liberty' specially protected by the Due Process Clause includes a right to commit suicide which itself includes a right to assistance in doing so"). The parties and *amici* agree that in these States a patient who is suffering from a terminal illness and who is experiencing great pain has no legal barriers to obtaining medication, from qualified physicians, to alleviate that suffering, even to the point of causing unconsciousness and hastening death. In this light, even assuming that we would recognize such an interest, I agree that the State's interests in protecting those who are not truly competent or facing imminent death, or those whose decisions to hasten death would not truly be voluntary, are sufficiently weighty to justify a prohibition against physician-assisted suicide.

Every one of us at some point may be affected by our own or a family member's terminal illness. There is no reason to think the democratic process will not strike the proper balance between the interests of terminally ill, mentally competent individuals who would seek to end their suffering and the State's interests in protecting those who might seek to end life mistakenly or under pressure. As the Court recognizes, States are presently undertaking extensive and serious evaluation of physician-assisted suicide and other related issues. In such circumstances, "the . . . challenging task of crafting appropriate procedures for safeguarding . . . liberty interests is entrusted to the 'laboratory' of the States . . . in the first instance."

In sum, there is no need to address the question whether suffering patients have a constitutionally cognizable interest in obtaining relief from the suffering that they may experience in the last days of their lives. There is no dispute that dying patients in Washington and New York can obtain palliative care, even when doing so would hasten their deaths. The difficulty in defining terminal illness and the risk that a dying patient's request for assistance in ending his or her life might not be truly voluntary justifies the prohibitions on assisted suicide we uphold here.

QUESTIONS

1 If there are no *legal* barriers to terminally ill patients' obtaining adequate palliative care, does it follow that patients actually have access to such care?

2 To the extent that terminally ill patients actually have access to adequate palliative care, "even to the point of causing unconsciousness and hastening death," is there a compelling need to legalize physician-assisted suicide?

Voluntary Death: A Comparison of Terminal Dehydration and Physician-Assisted Suicide

Franklin G. Miller and Diane E. Meier

Miller and Meier argue that terminal dehydration should be more explicitly recognized as an alternative to physician-assisted suicide. Because competent patients who have terminal or incurable illnesses are already free to forgo nutrition and hydration, and thus bring about their deaths by terminal dehydration, the authors suggest that there may be no compelling need to legalize physician-assisted suicide. They point out various advantages that terminal dehydration has over physician-assisted suicide, arguing in particular that there is a stronger moral basis for voluntary death by terminal dehydration than by physician-assisted suicide. Miller and Meier briefly discuss concerns about the humaneness of terminal dehydration and also briefly discuss issues associated with the integration of terminal dehydration into clinical practice.

The deeply divisive question of whether to legalize physician-assisted suicide has become a pressing matter of public policy at a time of radical change in the U.S. health care system. Managed care has expanded rapidly and now serves as the form of health care coverage for more than half of Americans with health insurance. Although this organizational change seems to have reduced the growth of health care expenditures, approximately 40 million Americans (15% of the population) continue to lack health insurance. That a legal option of physician-assisted suicide could become a "quick fix" for dying patients is a serious risk in view of the built-in incentives of managed care plans to limit treatment, coupled with the documented deficiencies of physicians in providing adequate pain relief and diagnosing and treating depression in terminally ill patients.

Given the potential for abuse if physician-assisted suicide were to be legalized in a climate of overarching cost containment in health care, careful consideration of alternative ways for patients to retain some control over the timing and circumstances of death seems warranted. The debate over legalizing physician-assisted suicide has failed to give due attention to terminal dehydration as an alternative. With terminal dehydration, competent patients who have terminal or incurable illness seek voluntary death by forgoing artificial nutrition and hydration or by ceasing to eat and drink. Terminal dehydration, accompanied by standard measures of palliative care, offers patients a way to escape agonizing, incurable conditions that they consider to be worse than death, without requiring transformation of the law and medical ethics.

In this article, we analyze clinical, ethical, and policy issues relating to terminal dehydration as an alternative to physician-assisted suicide, building on the foundation

Reprinted with permission of the publisher from *Annals of Internal Medicine,* vol. 128, no. 7 (April 1, 1998), pp. 559–562. Many references omitted.

laid in 1993 by Bernat and colleagues (1) in their seminal article on patient refusal of hydration and nutrition. This topic warrants revisiting in light of the Oregon referendums to legalize physician-assisted suicide and recent federal court decisions on this issue. A balanced assessment of physician-assisted suicide and terminal dehydration is important because each method has substantial advantages and disadvantages.

MERITS OF TERMINAL DEHYDRATION

Evidence indicates that death by terminal dehydration is not painful and that attendant physical discomfort can be adequately alleviated. Pain and suffering caused by the underlying disease can be treated by standard palliative measures, including administration of sedation to the level of unconsciousness as a last resort.

A stronger moral basis exists for voluntary death by terminal dehydration than by physician-assisted suicide. The right to forgo food and water, whether by mouth or by artificial means, derives from the fundamental right of competent patients to refuse medical treatment and to be free of unwanted bodily intrusion. Physicians are morally obligated to honor a competent patient's refusal of food and water, but they are not morally obligated to comply with a competent patient's request for lethal medication. Although physician-assisted suicide may be justifiable as a last resort in extraordinary cases, a patient's right to assisted suicide does not carry the same moral force as a patient's right to forgo treatment. This difference can be seen by considering the significance of thwarting these two paths to voluntary death. Force-feeding a competent patient who clearly refuses food and water violates autonomy, liberty, and dignity. In contrast, refusal of a carefully considered request for physician-assisted suicide interferes with a patient's self-determination but does not amount to a personal assault. Moreover, the patient whose request for physician-assisted suicide is denied remains free to exercise the right to voluntary death by forgoing food and water.

Self-Determination

Terminal dehydration offers a method of voluntary death that is entirely under the control of competent patients; it is not necessary for the physician to intervene by prescribing or administering lethal medication. Death by terminal dehydration demands a resolute determination to resist food and water. Because it typically takes several days to a few weeks for death to occur by this means, the patient who seeks death by terminal dehydration retains an opportunity to change his or her mind. In contrast, the patient who ingests a lethal dose of medication quickly loses consciousness and rapidly progresses to death. This difference in time to death means that terminal dehydration, unlike physician-assisted suicide, cannot be accomplished impulsively.

Physician-assisted suicide, because it involves prescribing lethal medication, could subject patients to greater external influence in favor of death than that associated with terminal dehydration. Owing to the cultural authority of medicine, a prescription of lethal medication may carry social legitimization for some patients and signify that it is medically appropriate for the patient to hasten death. Terminal dehydration lacks this legitimization. The physician may accept the patient's decision to die by terminal dehydration, but no affirmative act by the physician is required.

Access

In 1996, the U.S. Court of Appeals for the Second Circuit held that prohibiting physician-assisted suicide violates "equal protection." It argued that it is unfair to permit competent, dying patients to die by forgoing life-sustaining treatment but prohibit physician-assisted suicide for equally competent, dying patients who are not able to hasten death by stopping a treatment (2). The option of terminal dehydration, which the court did not consider, undercuts this argument: It is available to all suffering patients who are able to make decisions, including patients who are not receiving life-sustaining treatment. Accordingly, terminal dehydration is more widely available than physician-assisted suicide, which is limited to patients who can ingest lethal medication. Even a patient with a condition as debilitating as the "locked-in syndrome" can seek death by terminal dehydration. The setting, however, may influence the availability of terminal dehydration because caregivers in some nursing homes and hospitals may be reluctant to comply with a patient's refusal of food and water.

Professional Integrity

Several noted physician-ethicists have argued that physician-assisted suicide is always wrong because it violates the healing vocation of medicine (3, 4). Although this absolute claim is open to challenge, the prescription or administration of lethal medication by physicians poses a serious threat to their professional integrity. A request for physician-assisted suicide by a competent, dying patient who is suffering intolerably places the physician in a moral conflict between the duty to relieve suffering and the duty not to kill or to help kill. With terminal dehydration, the physician is not responsible for providing the means of death and therefore is not subjected to such a conflict. Terminal dehydration remains morally challenging, however, in view of professional commitments to preserve life and to help terminally ill patients cope until death arrives naturally. Physicians retain the right to advocate in favor of the patient's continued life as long as they refrain from coercion.

Social Implications

No controversial change in the law or public policy is required to permit patients to die by terminal dehydration. Because the legitimacy of terminal dehydration derives from the patient's legal and moral right to refuse medical treatment, wider understanding and use of this option is apt to be less socially divisive than legalization of physician-assisted suicide. Terminal dehydration can be used openly by patients, which is a distinct advantage as long as physician-assisted suicide remains illegal.

The reluctance of many physicians to confront death and to undertake the demanding work of palliative care, coupled with incentives that operate within managed care, creates the potential for physician-assisted suicide to become a "quick fix." Physician-assisted suicide offers a swift exit, putting an end to the patient's suffering and the need for costly continued care. The determination and patience required to die by terminal dehydration, compared with the relative ease of ingesting lethal medication, make terminal dehydration much less likely to become routine for terminally ill patients.

IS TERMINAL DEHYDRATION HUMANE?

Many of the features that make terminal dehydration potentially superior to physician-assisted suicide derive from the relatively long interval between the patient's decision to die by forgoing nutrition and hydration and the occurrence of death. However, this factor also accounts for some of the major difficulties of this method. Terminal dehydration can be made painless but not swift. Although death by terminal dehydration normally takes several days to occur, some case reports indicate a period of 3 to 4 weeks from when the process is started to when the patient dies. The time required for death by terminal dehydration is likely to make this method seem less humane than physician-assisted suicide. Indeed, it may seem repugnant that a competent, informed patient who resolutely seeks voluntary death must stop eating and drinking and wait for an undetermined period for death to arrive. The vigil of family members awaiting their loved one's death may be burdensome and stressful. Moreover, minimal drinking in response to thirst or the urging of concerned relatives may further prolong the process of dying. Those who die by terminal dehydration typically lapse into unconsciousness before death, which may seem intolerable to some patients and their family members.

The difference between the lengths of time it takes to die of terminal dehydration and of physician-assisted suicide should be assessed in light of regulations likely to govern any legalized access to physician-assisted suicide. The Oregon Death with Dignity Act mandates a 2-week waiting period after a request for physician-assisted suicide. A waiting period of similar length is described in a model statute for legalizing physician-assisted suicide (5). Most patients who seek death by terminal dehydration would achieve their goal within 2 weeks.

Does terminal dehydration require more determination and fortitude than can be reasonably expected? Patients seeking death may be reluctant to accept terminal dehydration out of fear that their physicians and family members will not provide the support and care required to make this a tolerable option. Patients who choose this means of voluntary death remain vulnerable to persuasive pressure from family members or physicians to change their mind. They may succumb to such pressures either because life has again begun to seem worthwhile or because emotional and physical fatigue limits their ability to persist, forcing them to endure an unwanted existence.

Physician-assisted suicide also has deficiencies as a humane means of voluntary death. The patient may botch the suicide attempt and possibly be left in a condition worse than that resulting from the terminal illness. Family or friends have felt compelled in some cases to place a plastic bag over the head of a person attempting physician-assisted suicide to complete the deed. Those who assist in a loved one's death by giving them pills or applying a plastic bag may suffer debilitating guilt and a prolonged and complicated bereavement.

Some patients who seek death may feel that terminal dehydration is, at best, less desirable than physician-assisted suicide. They may choose terminal dehydration only because legal or ethical concerns prevent their physicians from complying with a request for lethal medication. However, anecdotal evidence suggests that terminal dehydration can provide a peaceful and dignified process of dying.

INTEGRATING TERMINAL DEHYDRATION INTO CLINICAL PRACTICE

Like patients who request physician-assisted suicide, patients who seek death by terminal dehydration may be depressed or may be motivated by concerns about being a burden to others. Clinicians involved in the care of patients who decide to forgo food and water must be sure that the patient is able to make decisions and that the patient's decision is informed and voluntary. Moreover, support from a physician may help counteract the patient's fear of being a burden. Because some data show an association between depression and a desire to hasten death, physicians are justified in encouraging a trial of antidepressant therapy, counseling, or both before supporting a patient's decision to die by terminal dehydration. To obviate undue influence from the physician, the initiative to explore the option of terminal dehydration should come from the patient.

Clinicians should continue to provide palliative care to patients who seek voluntary death by terminal dehydration, even if they view the patient's decision as problematic or unwarranted. Competent patients have the right to forgo food and water. Although physicians may legitimately deny a patient's request for assisted suicide, they have the responsibility to provide palliative care to patients who have resolutely chosen voluntary death. Just as a physician must continue to provide palliative care for a competent patient who refuses to have surgery and is dying of sepsis from a gangrenous extremity, palliation remains a physician's obligation for a patient who chooses to die by terminal dehydration. Patients who voluntarily choose this option after being informed about their alternatives should be assured that they will not be abandoned and that every effort will be made to promote comfort until death arrives. This commitment to provide palliative care also helps alleviate the distress of family members.

RESPONSE TO EXTRAORDINARY CASES

No adult of sound mind should be forced to endure an existence that he or she rationally considers to be intolerable. Accordingly, the physician has a moral obligation not to foreclose the option of voluntary death. We acknowledge that, in rare cases, physician-assisted suicide offers a superior alternative to terminal dehydration. Nonetheless, the existence of a small number of compelling cases does not, by itself, warrant a change in policy in favor of legalizing physician-assisted suicide. We do not view legalization of physician-assisted death as a matter of individual rights. The debate should focus on whether legalization of physician-assisted suicide will enable our society to provide better care for dying and incurably ill patients, without causing intolerable abuses. The already-available option of terminal dehydration deserves careful consideration as an alternative to physician-assisted suicide.

REFERENCES

1 Bernat JL, Gert B, Mogielnicki RP. Patient refusal of hydration and nutrition: an alternative to physician-assisted suicide or voluntary active euthanasia. Arch Intern Med. 1993;153:2723–8.
2 *Quill v. Vacco,* 80 F. 3d 716 (2d Cir. 1996).
3 Kass LR. Neither for love nor money: why doctors must not kill. Public Interest. 1989;94:25–46.
4 Pellegrino ED. Doctors must not kill. J Clin Ethics. 1992;3:95–102.
5 Baron CH, Bergstresser C, Brock DW, Cole GF, Dorfman NS, Johnson JA, et al. A model state act to authorize and regulate physician-assisted suicide. Harvard Journal of Legislation. 1996;33:1–34.

QUESTIONS

1 Does the availability of terminal dehydration provide the basis of a compelling argument against the legalization of physician-assisted suicide?
2 If you were terminally ill and enduring significant pain and/or indignity, would you welcome the possibility of physician-assisted suicide? Would terminal dehydration serve your purposes just as well?

SUGGESTED ADDITIONAL READINGS FOR CHAPTER 2

BATTIN, MARGARET P., ROSAMOND RHODES, and ANITA SILVERS, eds.: *Physician-Assisted Suicide: Expanding the Debate.* New York: Routledge, 1998. The essays in Part Two of this extensive collection debate the projected impact of physician-assisted suicide on vulnerable patients. Part Three considers physician-assisted suicide in reference to the practice of medicine. Part Four provides contrasting viewpoints on the issue of legalization, and Part Five presents religious perspectives.

GOMEZ, CARLOS F.: *Regulating Death: Euthanasia and the Case of The Netherlands.* New York: Free Press, 1991. Gomez describes and criticizes the practices of (active) euthanasia in the Netherlands. He argues that the Dutch system is plagued with inadequate controls

Hastings Center Report, vol. 22, March–April 1992. This issue provides a collection of articles on (active) euthanasia and physician-assisted suicide. In particular, Dan W. Brock offers an extensive defense of voluntary active euthanasia, which Daniel Callahan opposes in "When Self-Determination Runs Amok."

LEGEMAATE, JOHAN: "The Dutch Euthanasia Act and Related Issues." *Journal of Law and Medicine,* vol. 11, February 2004, pp. 312–323. Legemaate provides a discussion of the 2002 Dutch Termination of Life on Request and Assisted Suicide Act. He sets this legislation in historical context and considers international reactions to it. The full text of the act itself is included as an appendix to the article.

MILLER, FRANKLIN G., et al.: "Regulating Physician-Assisted Death." *New England Journal of Medicine,* vol. 331, July 14, 1994, pp. 119–123. A group of six authors, well known in bioethics, argues for the legalization of "physician-assisted death"—that is, both physician-assisted suicide and voluntary active euthanasia—in accordance with a detailed proposal for regulation of the practice.

THE NEW YORK STATE TASK FORCE ON LIFE AND THE LAW: *When Death Is Sought: Assisted Suicide and Euthanasia in the Medical Context.* Albany: Health Education Services, 1994. Providing an extensive analysis of clinical, legal, and ethical considerations, the task force unanimously recommends that the laws prohibiting assisted suicide and (active) euthanasia in New York not be changed.

PELLEGRINO, EDMUND D.: "Doctors Must Not Kill." *The Journal of Clinical Ethics,* vol. 3, Summer 1992, pp. 95–102. Pellegrino contends that (1) the moral arguments in favor of (active) euthanasia are flawed, (2) killing by physicians would seriously distort the healing relationship, and (3) the social consequences of allowing such killing would be very detrimental.

QUILL, TIMOTHY E., and MARGARET P. BATTIN, eds.: *Physician-Assisted Dying: The Case for Palliative Care and Patient Choice.* Baltimore: Johns Hopkins University Press, 2004. The collection of essays in this book has been assembled to present an overall case for the legalization of physician-assisted death.

QUILL, TIMOTHY E., BERNARD LO, and DAN W. BROCK: "Palliative Options of Last Resort: A Comparison of Voluntarily Stopping Eating and Drinking, Terminal Sedation, Physician-Assisted Suicide, and Voluntary Active Euthanasia." *JAMA,* vol. 278, December 17, 1997, pp. 2099–2104. The authors compare and contrast the four identified practices, presenting both a clinical and an ethical analysis. They also provide a brief discussion of appropriate safeguards for hastening death by any of the methods under discussion.

STEINBOCK, BONNIE, and ALASTAIR NORCROSS, eds.: *Killing and Letting Die,* 2d ed. New York: Fordham University Press, 1994. This anthology provides a wealth of material on the distinction between killing and letting die.

CHAPTER 3

The Death Penalty

Strong convictions are firmly entrenched on both sides of the death penalty controversy. From one side, we hear in forceful tones that "murderers deserve to die." We are also told that no lesser punishment than the death penalty will suffice to deter potential murderers. From the other side of the controversy, in tones of equal conviction, we are told that the death penalty is a cruel and barbarous practice, effectively serving no purpose that could not be equally well served by a more humane punishment. "How long," it is asked, "must we indulge this uncivilized and pointless lust for revenge?" In the face of such strongly held but opposed views, each of us is invited to confront an important ethical issue: the morality of the death penalty. Before approaching the death penalty in its ethical dimensions, however, it will be helpful to briefly discuss its constitutional dimensions. Many of the considerations raised in discussions of the constitutionality of the death penalty parallel those raised in discussions of its morality.

THE CONSTITUTIONALITY OF THE DEATH PENALTY

The Eighth Amendment to the Constitution of the United States explicitly prohibits the infliction of *cruel and unusual* punishment. If the death penalty is a cruel and unusual punishment, it is unconstitutional. But is it cruel and unusual? In a landmark case, *Furman v. Georgia* (1972), the United States Supreme Court ruled that the death penalty was unconstitutional *as then administered*. The Court did not rule, however, that the death penalty is unconstitutional *by its very nature*. Indeed, subsequent developments in the Court have led to the conclusion that the death penalty is constitutionally permissible—as long as it is administered in accordance with certain procedural requirements.

The decision reached in *Furman* was by a mere five-to-four majority. Moreover, there was a basic divergence of viewpoint among those who voted with the majority. Both Justice Marshall and Justice Brennan argued straightforwardly that the death penalty is a cruel and unusual punishment *by its very nature*. From this perspective, it would not matter how much the procedures of its administration might be modified. It would still remain a cruel and unusual punishment. Among the reasons advanced to support this contention, two are especially noteworthy: (1) The death penalty is excessive in the sense of being unnecessary; lesser penalties are capable of serving the desired legislative purpose. (2) The death penalty is abhorrent to currently existing moral values.

The other three justices (Douglas, White, and Stewart) who voted with the majority did not commit themselves to the position that the death penalty is unconstitutional *by its very nature*. Leaving this underlying issue unresolved, they simply advanced the more guarded contention that the death penalty was unconstitutional *as then administered*. In their view, the death penalty was unconstitutional primarily because it was being administered in an arbitrary and capricious manner. The essence of their argument can be reconstructed in the following way. The death penalty is typically imposed at the discretion of a jury (or sometimes a judge). The absence of explicit standards to govern the decision between life and death allows a wide range of unchecked prejudice to operate freely under the heading of *discretion*. For example, discretion seems to have rendered blacks more prone than whites to the death penalty. Such standardless discretion violates not only the Eighth Amendment but also the Fourteenth Amendment, which guarantees "due process of law."

As matters developed in the wake of *Furman,* it was the Court's objection to *standardless discretion* that provided an opening for the many individual states still eager to retain the death penalty as a viable component of their legal systems. These states were faced with the challenge of devising procedures for imposing the death penalty that would not be open to the charge of standardless discretion. Two such approaches gained prominence. (1) Some states (e.g., North Carolina) moved to dissolve the objection of standardless discretion by simply making the death penalty *mandatory* for certain crimes. (2) Other states (e.g., Georgia) took an equally obvious approach, attempting to establish standards that would provide guidance for the jury (or the judge) in deciding between life and death.

Subsequent developments have led to the conclusion that the second approach is constitutionally acceptable, whereas the first is not. In *Woodson v. North Carolina* (1976), the Court ruled (although by a mere five-to-four majority) that mandatory death sentences are unconstitutional. In *Gregg v. Georgia* (1976), however, the Court ruled (with only Justice Marshall and Justice Brennan dissenting) that the death penalty is not unconstitutional when imposed at the discretion of a jury for the *crime of murder,*[1] as long as appropriate safeguards are provided against any arbitrary or capricious imposition. Most important, there must be explicit standards established for the guidance of jury deliberations. The attitude of the Court in this

---

[1]In *Gregg,* the Supreme Court considered only the constitutionality of imposing the death penalty for the *crime of murder*. In *Coker v. Georgia* (1977), the Court subsequently considered the constitutionality of imposing the death penalty for the *crime of rape*. Holding death to be a "grossly disproportionate" punishment for the crime of rape, the Court declared such an employment of the death penalty unconstitutional. Although the Court has never retreated from its holding in *Gregg* that the death penalty is a constitutionally permissible form of punishment for the crime of murder, it has on occasion provided further clarification about procedural requirements for the imposition of the death penalty and has recently placed some notable restrictions on the scope of those who may be executed. In *Atkins v. Virginia* (2002), the Court ruled that the execution of a mentally retarded criminal is unconstitutional. In *Roper v. Simmons* (2005), the Court ruled that it is unconstitutional to execute killers who committed their crimes when they were younger than eighteen.

regard is made clear by Justices Stewart, Powell, and Stevens in their opinion in *Gregg,* which appears in this chapter. Also appearing in this chapter is the dissenting opinion of Justice Marshall.

THE ETHICAL ISSUE

In any discussion of the morality of the death penalty, it is important to remember that the death penalty is a kind of punishment. Indeed, it is normally thought to be the most serious kind of punishment; hence it is called *capital* punishment. Most philosophers agree that punishment in general (as contrasted with capital punishment in particular) is a morally justified social practice. For one thing, however uneasy we might feel about inflicting harm on another person, it is hard to visualize a complex society managing to survive without an established legal system of punishment. However, to say that most philosophers agree that punishment is a morally justified social practice is not to say that there are no dissenters from this view. Some argue that it is possible to structure society in ways that would not necessitate commitment to a legal system of punishment as we know it. One suggested possibility is that undesirable social behavior could be adequately kept in check by therapeutic treatment rather than by traditional kinds of punishment. Such a system would seem to have the advantage of being more humane, but surely it is implausible to believe that present therapeutic techniques are anywhere near adequate to the task. Perhaps future advances in the behavioral sciences will render such an alternative more viable. If so, it may one day be plausible to argue that the whole practice of (nontherapeutic) punishment must be rejected on moral grounds. Still, for now, there is widespread agreement on the moral defensibility of punishment as an overall social practice. What stands out as an open and hotly debated ethical issue is whether or not the death penalty, as a distinctive kind of punishment, should continue to play a role in our legal system of punishment.

Those in favor of retaining the death penalty are commonly called *retentionists.* Retentionists differ among themselves regarding the kinds of cases in which they find it appropriate to employ the death penalty. They also differ among themselves regarding the supporting arguments they find acceptable. But anyone who supports the retention of the death penalty—for employment in whatever kinds of cases and for whatever reasons—is by definition a retentionist. Those in favor of abolishing the death penalty are commonly called *abolitionists.* Abolitionists, by definition, refuse to support any employment of the death penalty. Like the retentionists, however, they differ among themselves concerning the supporting arguments they find acceptable.

There is one extreme, and not widely embraced, abolitionist line of thought. It is based on the belief that the sanctity of human life demands absolute nonviolence. On this view, killing of any kind, for whatever reason, is always and everywhere morally wrong. No one has the right to take a human life—not in self-defense, not in war, not in any circumstance. Thus, since the death penalty obviously involves a kind of killing, it is a morally unacceptable form of punishment and must be abolished. This general view, which is associated with the Quakers and other pacifists, has struck most moral philosophers as implausible. Can we really think that killing, when it is the only course that will save oneself from an unprovoked violent assault, is morally wrong? Can we really think that it would be morally wrong to kill a terrorist if that were the *only* possible way of stopping him or her from exploding a bomb in the midst of a kindergarten class? The defender of absolute nonviolence is sometimes inclined to argue at this point that violence will only breed violence. There may indeed be much truth in this claim. Still, most people do not believe that such a claim provides adequate support for the contention that *all* killing is morally wrong, and, if some killing is morally acceptable, perhaps the death penalty is as well. What arguments can be made on its behalf?

RETENTIONIST ARGUMENTS

Broadly speaking, arguments for the retention of the death penalty usually emphasize either (1) considerations of *justice* or (2) considerations of *social utility*. Those who emphasize considerations of justice typically develop their case along the following line: When the moral order is upset by the commission of an offense, it is only right that the disorder be rectified by punishment that is equal to or proportional to the offense. This view is reflected in remarks such as "The scales of justice demand retribution" and "The offender must pay for the crime." Along this line, the philosopher Immanuel Kant (1724–1804) is famous for his unequivocal defense of the *lex talionis*—the law (or principle) of retaliation, often expressed as "an eye for an eye." According to this principle, punishment is to be inflicted in a measure that will equalize the offense. And, when the offense is murder, *only* capital punishment is sufficient to equalize it.

In one of this chapter's readings, Igor Primoratz argues for retention of the death penalty on retributive grounds. Stephen Nathanson, an abolitionist, provides a contrasting point of view. Nathanson argues that no adequate retributive rationale can be provided for the death penalty.

Although the demand for retribution continues to play a prominent role in the overall case for the death penalty, many retentionists (and, obviously, abolitionists as well) have come to feel quite uneasy with the notion of imposing the death penalty "because the wrongdoer *deserves* it." Perhaps this uneasiness can be traced, at least in part, to our growing awareness of the way in which social conditions, such as ghetto living, seem to spawn criminal activity. If so, then it seems that we have arrived at a point of intersection with a venerable—and vexing—philosophical problem: the problem of "freedom and determinism." Pure retributive thinking seems to presuppose a radical sense of human freedom and its correlate: a radical sense of personal responsibility and accountability for one's actions. This is undoubtedly why retentionists who espouse a retributive rationale often insist that the death penalty does not constitute a denial of the wrongdoer's dignity and worth as a human being. On the contrary, they say, the death penalty reaffirms the dignity and worth of a convicted murderer—by holding the person strictly responsible for the crime that has been committed and giving the person what he or she deserves. Of course, if someone is uneasy with the radical sense of human freedom that seems to underlie pure retributive thinking, that person will surely be uneasy with the retributive rationale for retention of the death penalty. But we must also consider the utilitarian side of the retentionist coin.

Since considerations of social utility are commonly advanced in defense of the practice of punishment in general, it is not surprising to find that they are also commonly advanced in defense of retaining the death penalty. Utilitarianism, as a distinct school of moral philosophy, locates the primary justification of punishment in its social utility. Utilitarians recognize that punishment consists of the infliction of evil on another person, but they hold that such evil is far outweighed by the future benefits that will accrue to society. Imprisonment, for example, might lead to such socially desirable effects as (1) *rehabilitation* of the criminal, (2) *incapacitation,* whereby we achieve temporary or permanent protection from the imprisoned criminal, and (3) *deterrence* of other potential criminals. When utilitarian considerations are recruited in support of the retention of the *death* penalty, it is clear that rehabilitation of the criminal can play no part in the case. But retentionists do frequently promote considerations of incapacitation and deterrence.

Retentionists who appeal to considerations of incapacitation typically argue that the death penalty is the only effective way to protect society from a certain subset of convicted murderers—namely, those who are at once *violence-prone and irreformable.* (Notice that an important difficulty here would be specifying effective criteria for the identification of those already convicted murderers who are truly violence-prone and irreformable.) Life imprisonment, it is said, cannot assure society of the needed protection, because even if "life imprisonment" were really life imprisonment—that is, even if a sentence of life imprisonment excluded the possibility of parole—violence-prone and irreformable inmates would still pose an imminent threat to prison guards and fellow inmates. Furthermore, escape is always possible. Thus, the death penalty is the only truly effective way of achieving societal protection against the continuing threat posed by some convicted murderers.

According to many retentionists, however, the fundamental justification for retaining the death penalty lies in the fact that the death penalty is a *uniquely effective deterrent.* But is this central factual claim true? Is the death penalty really a more substantial deterrent than life imprisonment or even long-term imprisonment? At this point, a natural move is to look to the findings of the social sciences, but many scholars familiar with the social science literature on this issue would say that the available evidence is conflicting and ultimately inconclusive. If it is true that empirical studies have failed to resolve the central factual question, what else can be said about the deterrence rationale for the death penalty?

Many retentionists, willing to acknowledge that scientific findings are inconclusive, argue that we must simply rely on common sense. Since people typically fear death much more than they fear life imprisonment, it just stands to reason, they say, that the death penalty is superior to life imprisonment as a deterrent. Although the threat of life imprisonment or even long-term imprisonment may well be sufficient to deter many would-be murderers, the threat of execution would deter an even greater number. Thus, the death penalty ought to be retained in our system of criminal justice because common sense testifies to the fact that it is a more substantial deterrent than life imprisonment.

The commonsense argument for the death penalty as a uniquely effective deterrent might be countered with the following claim: it does not follow from the mere fact that one punishment is more severe than another that the former will be a more substantial deterrent than the latter. Indeed, it might be the case that anyone *capable of being deterred* from murder by the threat of the death penalty would be equally well deterred by the threat of life imprisonment. Jeffrey Reiman makes this counterargument, among others, as he takes issue in this chapter with the commonsense argument for the death penalty as a uniquely effective deterrent. Providing a contrasting view, Louis P. Pojman argues in this chapter that commonsense or anecdotal evidence is sufficient to establish the conclusion that the death penalty is a uniquely effective deterrent.

There is one other important argument made by retentionists dedicated to the deterrence rationale. This argument, often referred to as the *best bet argument,* has been most prominently advanced by Ernest van den Haag, a well-known retentionist who has also recurrently advanced the commonsense argument. The best bet argument takes uncertainty—our uncertainty whether or not the death penalty is a uniquely effective deterrent—as its point of departure. If we retain the death penalty, the argument goes, we run the risk of needlessly eradicating the lives of convicted murderers; perhaps the death penalty is *not* a uniquely effective deterrent. On the other hand, if we abolish the death penalty, we run the risk of innocent people becoming future murder victims; perhaps the death penalty is a uniquely effective deterrent. Faced with such uncertainty, the argument concludes, it is our moral obligation to retain the death penalty. Whichever way we go, there is a risk to be run, but it is better from a moral point of view to risk the lives of the guilty than to risk the lives of the innocent. "I believe we have no right to risk additional future victims of murder for the sake of sparing convicted murderers."[2]

Pojman makes clear in this chapter that he endorses the best bet argument, but a critic might respond as follows. In claiming that retention risks the lives of the guilty, whereas abolition risks the lives of the innocent, the best bet argument overlooks the possibility that retention of the death penalty has what is sometimes called "a counter-deterrent effect." The idea here is that state-sponsored killing in the form of execution has a brutalizing effect on society, that it actually weakens inhibitions on the part of the populace against killing. Thus, in the long run, there might well be more murders in a retentionist society than there would be in an abolitionist society. So it is not correct to say that retention of the death penalty risks only guilty lives; relative to the possibility that the death penalty has a counter-deterrent effect, retention also places innocent lives at risk. Reiman argues along very similar lines in this chapter, although he develops his argument in terms of "a deterrent effect from not executing" rather than "a counter-deterrent effect" of executing.

THE CASE FOR ABOLITION

What can be said of the abolitionist case against the death penalty? Most abolitionists do not care to argue the extreme position, already discussed, of absolute nonviolence, yet they typically do want to commit themselves seriously to the "sanctity of human life." They emphasize the inherent worth and dignity of each individual and insist that the taking of a human life, although perhaps sometimes

---

[2]Ernest van den Haag, "On Deterrence and the Death Penalty," *Ethics,* vol. 78, July 1968, p. 287.

morally permissible, is a very serious matter and not to be permitted in the absence of weighty overriding reasons. At face value, they argue, the death penalty is cruel and inhumane; since retentionists have failed to advance substantial reasons in its defense, it must be judged a morally unacceptable practice. Against retentionist arguments based on retribution as a demand of justice, abolitionists often argue that the "demand of justice" is nothing but a mask for a barbarous vengeance. At a more fundamental level, they simply argue that justice does not require the death penalty for the crime of murder. Against retentionist arguments based on considerations of social utility, abolitionists simply argue that other, more humane punishments will serve equally well. We do not need the death penalty to incapacitate convicted murderers because life imprisonment without the possibility of parole can provide us with a sufficient measure of societal protection. Also, since there is no reason to believe that the death penalty is a uniquely effective deterrent, retention cannot be justified on the basis of considerations of deterrence.

In addition to advancing arguments that directly counter retentionist claims, abolitionists often incorporate two further arguments into their overall case against the death penalty. The first of these arguments can be stated as follows: It is impossible to guarantee that mistakes will not be made in the administration of punishment, but this factor is especially important in the case of the death penalty, because only *capital* punishment is irrevocable. That is, only the death penalty eradicates the possibility of compensating an innocent person who has been wrongly punished. A second abolitionist argument focuses attention on patterns of discrimination in the administration of the death penalty. In our society, according to one version of the argument, blacks are more likely to receive the death penalty than whites, and the poor and uneducated are more likely to receive the death penalty than the affluent and educated. A retentionist counter to each of these abolitionist arguments is provided in this chapter by Primoratz.

According to a more recent construction of the racial bias problem, it is the *race of the victim,* rather than the *race of the killer,* that is the operative racial factor—and a very significant one—in the administration of the death penalty. "Other things being equal, the studies show, killers of white people are more likely to receive death sentences than killers of blacks."[3] Although the moral implications of this finding may be arguable, many contemporary abolitionists insist that racial disparities in the administration of the death penalty, at least in combination with other perceived procedural irregularities, provide a compelling moral objection to retention of the death penalty.

In this chapter's final reading, David Dolinko offers an analysis of three procedural arguments against the death penalty. In addition to considering the *mistake* argument and the *discrimination* argument, he also offers some commentary on the *arbitrariness* argument. In Dolinko's view, the mistake argument is the most powerful procedural argument against the death penalty. Indeed, an abolitionist interested in pressing the mistake argument might make reference to some notable factual findings reported in September 2004 by the Death Penalty Information Center. A total of 116 death-row inmates in the United States have been exonerated

[3]Erik Eckholm, "Studies Find Death Penalty Tied to Race of the Victims," *New York Times,* February 24, 1995, p. B1.

since 1973, and forty-nine of these exonerations have taken place in the 1997–2004 period, DNA evidence playing an important role in several of these more recent exonerations.[4] In January 2003, Illinois Governor George Ryan—citing seventeen cases in which Illinois death-row inmates had been exonerated and calling attention to multiple procedural problems plaguing that state's capital punishment system— commuted the death sentences of all Illinois death-row inmates.

Thomas A. Mappes

[4]"Innocence and the Crisis in the American Death Penalty," September 2004. This report is available on the DPIC website (www.deathpenaltyinfo.org).

Opinion in *Gregg v. Georgia*

Justices Potter Stewart, Lewis F. Powell, Jr., and John Paul Stevens

The state of Georgia reacted to the United States Supreme Court's decision in *Furman v. Georgia* (1972) by drafting a death penalty statute calculated to avoid the Court's objection to standardless discretion. Georgia's approach, in contrast to the approach of those states that made the death penalty mandatory for certain crimes, embodied an effort to specify standards that would guide a jury (or a judge) in deciding between the death penalty and life imprisonment. In this case, with only Justice Marshall and Justice Brennan dissenting, the Court upheld the constitutionality of imposing the death penalty for the crime of murder under the law of Georgia.

Justices Stewart, Powell, and Stevens initially consider the contention that the death penalty for the crime of murder is, under all circumstances, cruel and unusual punishment, thus unconstitutional. On their analysis, a punishment is cruel and unusual if it fails to accord with "evolving standards of decency." Moreover, even if a punishment does accord with contemporary values, it must still be judged cruel and unusual if it fails to accord with the "dignity of man," the "basic concept underlying the Eighth Amendment." They take this second stipulation to rule out "excessive" punishment, identified as (1) that which involves the unnecessary and wanton infliction of pain or (2) that which is grossly out of proportion to the severity of the crime. In light of these considerations, Justices Stewart, Powell, and Stevens argue that the imposition of the death penalty for the crime of murder does not invariably violate the Constitution. They contend that legislative developments since *Furman* have made clear that the death penalty is acceptable to contemporary society. Moreover, they contend, the death penalty is not invariably excessive: (1) It may properly be considered necessary to achieve two principal social purposes—retribution and deterrence. (2) When the death penalty is imposed for the crime of murder, it may properly be considered not disproportionate to the severity of the crime.

United States Supreme Court. 428 U.S. 153 (1976).

Turning their attention to the death sentence imposed under the law of Georgia in this case, Justices Stewart, Powell, and Stevens maintain that a carefully drafted statute, ensuring "that the sentencing authority is given adequate information and guidance," makes it possible to avoid imposing the death penalty in an arbitrary or capricious manner. The revised Georgia statutory system under which Gregg was sentenced to death, they conclude, does not violate the Constitution.

The issue in this case is whether the imposition of the sentence of death for the crime of murder under the law of Georgia violates the Eighth and Fourteenth Amendments.

I

The petitioner, Troy Gregg, was charged with committing armed robbery and murder. In accordance with Georgia procedure in capital cases, the trial was in two stages, a guilt stage and a sentencing stage. . . .

. . . The jury found the petitioner guilty of two counts of armed robbery and two counts of murder.

At the penalty stage, which took place before the same jury, . . . the trial judge instructed the jury that it could recommend either a death sentence or a life prison sentence on each count. . . . The jury returned verdicts of death on each count.

The Supreme Court of Georgia affirmed the convictions and the imposition of the death sentences for murder. . . . The death sentences imposed for armed robbery, however, were vacated on the grounds that the death penalty had rarely been imposed in Georgia for that offense. . . .

II

. . . The Georgia statute, as amended after our decision in *Furman v. Georgia* (1972), retains the death penalty for six categories of crime: murder, kidnaping for ransom or where the victim is harmed, armed robbery, rape, treason, and aircraft hijacking. . . .

III

We address initially the basic contention that the punishment of death for the crime of murder is, under all circumstances, "cruel and unusual" in violation of the Eighth and Fourteenth Amendments of the Constitution. In Part IV of this opinion, we will consider the sentence of death imposed under the Georgia statutes at issue in this case.

The Court on a number of occasions has both assumed and asserted the constitutionality of capital punishment. In several cases that assumption provided a necessary foundation for the decision, as the Court was asked to decide whether a particular method of carrying out a capital sentence would be allowed to stand under the Eighth Amendment. But until *Furman v. Georgia* (1972), the Court never confronted squarely the fundamental claim that the punishment of death always, regardless of the enormity of the offense or the procedure followed in imposing the sentence, is cruel and unusual punishment in violation of the Constitution. Although this issue was presented and addressed in *Furman,* it was not resolved by the Court. Four Justices would have held that capital punishment is not unconstitutional *per se;* two justices would have reached the opposite conclusion; and three Justices, while agreeing that the statutes then before the Court were invalid as applied, left open the question whether such punishment may ever be imposed. We now hold that the punishment of death does not invariably violate the Constitution.

A

The history of the prohibition of "cruel and unusual" punishment already has been reviewed at length. The phrase first appeared in the English Bill of Rights of 1689, which was drafted by Parliament at the accession of William and Mary. The English version appears to have been directed against punishments unauthorized by statute and beyond the jurisdiction of the sentencing court, as well as those disproportionate to the offense involved. The American draftsmen, who adopted the English phrasing in drafting the Eighth Amendment, were primarily concerned, however, with proscribing "tortures" and other "barbarous" methods of punishment.

In the earliest cases raising Eighth Amendment claims, the Court focused on particular methods of execution to determine whether they were too cruel to pass constitutional muster. The constitutionality of the sentence of death itself was not at issue, and the criterion used to evaluate the mode of execution was its similarity to "torture" and other "barbarous" methods. . . .

But the Court has not confined the prohibition embodied in the Eighth Amendment to "barbarous" methods that were generally outlawed in the 18th century. Instead, the Amendment has been interpreted in a flexible and dynamic manner. The Court early recognized that a "principle to be vital must be capable of wider application than the mischief which gave it birth." Thus the Clause forbidding "cruel and unusual" punishments "is not fastened to the obsolete but may acquire meaning as public opinion becomes enlightened by a humane justice." . . .

It is clear from the foregoing precedents that the Eighth Amendment has not been regarded as a static concept. As Mr. Chief Justice Warren said, in an oftquoted phrase, "[t]he Amendment must draw its meaning from the evolving standards of decency that mark the progress of a maturing society." Thus, an assessment of contemporary values concerning the infliction of a challenged sanction is relevant to the application of the Eighth Amendment. As we develop below more fully, this assessment does not call for a subjective judgment. It requires, rather, that we look to objective indicia that reflect the public attitude toward a given sanction.

But our cases also make clear that public perceptions of standards of decency with respect to criminal sanctions are not conclusive. A penalty also must accord with "the dignity of man," which is the "basic concept underlying the Eighth Amendment." This means, at least, that the punishment not be "excessive." When a form of punishment in the abstract (in this case, whether capital punishment may ever be imposed as a sanction for murder) rather than in the particular (the propriety of death as a penalty to be applied to a specific defendant for a specific crime) is under consideration, the inquiry into "excessiveness" has two aspects. First, the punishment must not involve the unnecessary and wanton infliction of pain. Second, the punishment must not be grossly out of proportion to the severity of the crime.

B

Of course, the requirements of the Eighth Amendment must be applied with an awareness of the limited role to be played by the courts. This does not mean that judges have no role to play, for the Eighth Amendment is a restraint upon the exercise of legislative power. . . .

But, while we have an obligation to insure that constitutional bounds are not overreached, we may not act as judges as we might as legislators. . . .

Therefore, in assessing a punishment selected by a democratically elected legislature against the constitutional measure, we presume its validity. We may not require the legislature to select the least severe penalty possible so long as the penalty selected is not cruelly inhumane or disproportionate to the crime involved. And a heavy burden rests on those who would attack the judgment of the representatives of the people.

This is true in part because the constitutional test is intertwined with an assessment of contemporary standards and the legislative judgment weighs heavily in ascertaining such standards. "[I]n a democratic society legislatures, not courts, are constituted to respond to the will and consequently the moral values of the people."

The deference we owe to the decisions of the state legislatures under our federal system is enhanced where the specification of punishments is concerned, for "these are peculiarly questions of legislative policy." Caution is necessary lest this Court become, "under the aegis of the Cruel and Unusual Punishment Clause, the ultimate arbiter of the standards of criminal responsibility . . . throughout the country." A decision that a given punishment is impermissible under the Eighth Amendment cannot be reversed short of a constitutional amendment. The ability of the people to express their preference through the normal democratic processes, as well as through ballot referenda, is shut off. Revisions cannot be made in the light of further experience.

C

In the discussion to this point we have sought to identify the principles and considerations that guide a court in addressing an Eighth Amendment claim. We now consider specifically whether the sentence of death for the crime of murder is a *per se* violation of the Eighth and Fourteenth Amendments to the Constitution. We note first that history and precedent strongly support a negative answer to this question.

The imposition of the death penalty for the crime of murder has a long history of acceptance both in the United States and in England. . . .

It is apparent from the text of the Constitution itself that the existence of capital punishment was accepted by the Framers. At the time the Eighth Amendment was ratified, capital punishment was a common sanction in every State. Indeed, the First Congress of the United States enacted legislation providing death as the penalty for specified crimes. . . .

For nearly two centuries, this Court, repeatedly and often expressly, has recognized that capital punishment is not invalid *per se*. . . .

Four years ago, the petitioners in *Furman* and its companion cases predicated their argument primarily upon the asserted proposition that standards of decency had evolved to the point where capital punishment no longer could be tolerated. The petitioners in those cases said, in effect, that the evolutionary process had come to an end, and that standards of decency required that the Eighth Amendment be construed finally as prohibiting capital punishment for any crime regardless of its depravity and impact on society. This view was accepted by two Justices. Three other Justices were unwilling to go so far; focusing on the procedures by which convicted defendants were selected for the death penalty rather than on the actual punishment inflicted, they joined in the conclusion that the statutes before the Court were constitutionally invalid.

The petitioners in the capital cases before the Court today renew the "standards of decency" argument, but developments during the four years since *Furman* have undercut substantially the assumptions upon which their argument rested. Despite the continuing debate, dating back to the 19th century, over the morality and utility of capital punishment, it is now evident that a large proportion of American society continues to regard it as an appropriate and necessary criminal sanction.

The most marked indication of society's endorsement of the death penalty for murder is the legislative response to *Furman*. The legislatures of at least 35 States have enacted new statutes that provide for the death penalty for at least some crimes that result in the death of another person. And the Congress of the United States, in 1974, enacted a statute providing the death penalty for aircraft piracy that results in death. These recently adopted statutes have attempted to address the concerns expressed by the Court in *Furman* primarily (i) by specifying the factors to be weighed and the procedures to be followed in deciding when to impose a capital sentence, or (ii) by making the death penalty mandatory for specified crimes. But all of the post-*Furman* statutes make clear that capital punishment itself has not been rejected by the elected representatives of the people. . . .

The jury also is a significant and reliable objective index of contemporary values because it is so directly involved. The Court has said that "one of the most important functions any jury can perform in making . . . a selection [between life imprisonment and death for a defendant convicted in a capital case] is to maintain a link between contemporary community values and the penal system." It may be true that evolving standards have influenced juries in recent decades to be more discriminating in imposing the sentence of death. But the relative infrequency of jury verdicts imposing the death sentence does not indicate rejection of capital punishment *per se*. Rather, the reluctance of juries in many cases to impose the sentence may well reflect the humane feeling that this most irrevocable of sanctions should be reserved for a small number of extreme cases. Indeed, the actions of juries in many States since *Furman* are fully compatible with the legislative judgments, reflected in the new statutes, as to the continued utility and necessity of capital punishment in appropriate cases. At the close of 1974 at least 254 persons had been sentenced to death since *Furman,* and by the end of March 1976, more than 460 persons were subject to death sentences.

As we have seen, however, the Eighth Amendment demands more than that a challenged punishment be acceptable to contemporary society. The Court also must ask whether it comports with the basic concept of human dignity at the core of the Amendment. Although we cannot "invalidate a category of penalties because we deem less severe penalties adequate to serve the ends of penology," the sanction imposed cannot be so totally without penological justification that it results in the gratuitous infliction of suffering.

The death penalty is said to serve two principal social purposes: retribution and deterrence of capital crimes by prospective offenders.[1]

In part, capital punishment is an expression of society's moral outrage at particularly offensive conduct. This function may be unappealing to many, but it is essential in an ordered society that asks its citizens to rely on legal processes rather than self-help to vindicate their wrongs.

> The instinct of retribution is part of the nature of man, and channeling that instinct in the administration of criminal justice serves an important purpose in promoting the stability of a society governed by law. When people begin to believe that organized society is unwilling or unable to impose upon criminal offenders the punishment they "deserve," then there are sown the seeds of anarchy—of self-help, vigilante justice, and lynch law. *Furman v. Georgia* (Stewart, J., concurring).

"Retribution is no longer the dominant objective of the criminal law," but neither is it a forbidden objective nor one inconsistent with our respect for the dignity of men. Indeed, the decision that capital punishment may be the appropriate sanction in extreme cases is an expression of the community's belief that certain crimes are themselves so grievous an affront to humanity that the only adequate response may be the penalty of death.

Statistical attempts to evaluate the worth of the death penalty as a deterrent to crimes by potential offenders have occasioned a great deal of debate. The results simply have been inconclusive. . . .

Although some of the studies suggest that the death penalty may not function as a significantly greater deterrent than lesser penalties, there is no convincing empirical evidence either supporting or refuting this view. We may nevertheless assume safely that there are murderers, such as those who act in passion, for whom the threat of death has little or no deterrent effect. But for many others, the death penalty undoubtedly is a significant deterrent. There are carefully contemplated murders, such as murder for hire, where the possible penalty of death may well enter into the cold calculus that precedes the decision to act. And there are some categories of murder, such as murder by a life prisoner, where other sanctions may not be adequate.

The value of capital punishment as a deterrent of crime is a complex factual issue the resolution of which properly rests with the legislatures, which can evaluate the results of statistical studies in terms of their own local conditions and with a flexibility of approach that is not available to the courts. Indeed, many of the post-*Furman* statutes reflect just such a responsible effort to define those crimes and those criminals for which capital punishment is most probably an effective deterrent.

In sum, we cannot say that the judgment of the Georgia Legislature that capital punishment may be necessary in some cases is clearly wrong. Considerations of federalism, as well as respect for the ability of a legislature to evaluate, in terms of its particular State, the moral consensus concerning the death penalty and its social utility as a sanction, require us to conclude, in the absence of more convincing evidence, that the infliction of death as a punishment for murder is not without justification and thus is not unconstitutionally severe.

Finally, we must consider whether the punishment of death is disproportionate in relation to the crime for which it is imposed. There is no question that death as a punishment is unique in its severity and irrevocability. When a defendant's life is at stake, the Court has been particularly sensitive to insure that every safeguard is observed. But we are concerned here only with the imposition of capital punishment for the crime of murder, and when a life has been taken deliberately by the offender,[2] we cannot say that the punishment is invariably disproportionate to the crime. It is an extreme sanction, suitable to the most extreme of crimes.

We hold that the death penalty is not a form of punishment that may never be imposed, regardless of the circumstances of the offense, regardless of the character of the offender, and regardless of the procedure followed in reaching the decision to impose it.

IV

We now consider whether Georgia may impose the death penalty on the petitioner in this case.

A

While *Furman* did not hold that the infliction of the death penalty *per se* violates the Constitution's ban on cruel and unusual punishments, it did recognize that the penalty of death is different in kind from any other punishment imposed under our system of criminal justice. Because of the uniqueness of the death penalty, *Furman* held that it could not be imposed under sentencing procedures that created a substantial risk that it would be inflicted in an arbitrary and capricious manner. . . .

Furman mandates that where discretion is afforded a sentencing body on a matter so grave as the determination of whether a human life should be taken or spared, that discretion must be suitably directed and limited so as to minimize the risk of wholly arbitrary and capricious action.

It is certainly not a novel proposition that discretion in the area of sentencing be exercised in an informed manner. We have long recognized that "[f]or the determination of sentences, justice generally requires . . . that there be taken into account the circumstances of the offense together with the character and propensities of the offender." . . .

Jury sentencing has been considered desirable in capital cases in order "to maintain a link between contemporary community values and the penal system—a link without which the determination of punishment could hardly reflect 'the evolving standards of decency that mark the progress of a maturing society.'" But it creates special problems. Much of the information that is relevant to the sentencing decision may have no relevance to the question of guilt, or may even be extremely prejudicial to a fair determination of that question. This problem, however, is scarcely insurmountable. Those who have studied the question suggest that a bifurcated procedure—one in which the question of sentence is not considered until the determination of guilt has been made—is the best answer. . . . When a human life is at stake and when the jury must have information prejudicial to the question of guilt but relevant to the question of penalty in order to impose a rational sentence, a bifurcated system is more likely to ensure elimination of the constitutional deficiencies identified in *Furman.*

But the provision of relevant information under fair procedural rules is not alone sufficient to guarantee that the information will be properly used in the imposition of punishment, especially if sentencing is performed by a jury. Since the members of a jury will have had little, if any, previous experience in sentencing, they are unlikely to be skilled in dealing with the information they are given. To the extent that this problem is inherent in jury sentencing, it may not be totally correctable. It seems clear, however, that the problem will be alleviated if the jury is given guidance regarding the factors about the crime and the defendant that the State, representing organized society, deems particularly relevant to the sentencing decision. . . .

While some have suggested that standards to guide a capital jury's sentencing deliberations are impossible to formulate, the fact is that such standards have been developed. When the drafters of the Model Penal Code faced this problem, they concluded "that it is within the realm of possibility to point to the main circumstances of aggravation and of mitigation that should be weighed *and weighed against each other* when they are presented in a concrete case.[3] While such standards are by necessity somewhat general, they do provide guidance to the sentencing authority and thereby reduce the likelihood that it will impose a sentence that fairly can be called capricious or arbitrary. Where the sentencing authority is required to specify the factors it relied upon in reaching its decision, the further safeguard of meaningful appellate review is available to ensure that death sentences are not imposed capriciously or in a freakish manner.

In summary, the concerns expressed in *Furman* that the penalty of death not be imposed in an arbitrary or capricious manner can be met by a carefully drafted statute that ensures that the sentencing authority is given adequate information and guidance. As a general proposition these concerns are best met by a system that provides for a bifurcated proceeding at which the sentencing authority is apprised of the information relevant to the imposition of sentence and provided with standards to guide its use of the information.

We do not intend to suggest that only the above-described procedures would be permissible under *Furman* or that any sentencing system constructed along these general lines would inevitably satisfy the concerns of *Furman,* for each distinct system must be examined on an individual basis. Rather, we have embarked upon this general exposition to make clear that it is possible to construct capital-sentencing systems capable of meeting *Furman*'s constitutional concerns.

B

We now turn to consideration of the constitutionality of Georgia's capital-sentencing procedures. In the wake of *Furman,* Georgia amended its capital punishment statute, but chose not to narrow the scope of its murder provisions. Thus, now as before *Furman,* in Georgia "[a] person commits murder when he unlawfully and with malice aforethought, either express or implied, causes the death of another human being." All persons convicted of murder "shall be punished by death or by imprisonment for life."

Georgia did act, however, to narrow the class of murderers subject to capital punishment by specifying 10 statutory aggravating circumstances, one of which must be found by the jury to exist beyond a reasonable doubt before a death sentence can ever be imposed. In addition, the jury is authorized to consider any other appropriate aggravating or mitigating circumstances. The jury is not required to find any mitigating circumstance in order to make a recommendation of mercy that is binding on the trial court, but it must find a *statutory* aggravating circumstance before recommending a sentence of death.

These procedures require the jury to consider the circumstances of the crime and the criminal before it recommends sentence. No longer can a Georgia jury do as Furman's jury did: reach a finding of the defendant's guilt and then, without guidance or direction, decide whether he should live or die. Instead, the jury's attention is directed to the specific circumstances of the crime: Was it committed in the course of another capital felony? Was it committed for money? Was it committed upon a peace officer or judicial officer? Was it committed in a particularly heinous way or in a manner that endangered the lives of many persons? In addition, the jury's attention is focused on the characteristics of the person who committed the crime: Does he have a record of prior convictions for capital offenses? Are there any special facts about this defendant that mitigate against imposing capital punishment (*e.g.,* his youth, the extent of his cooperation with the police, his emotional state at the time of the crime). As a result, while some jury discretion still exists, "the discretion to be exercised is controlled by clear and objective standards so as to produce non-discriminatory application."

As an important additional safeguard against arbitrariness and caprice, the Georgia statutory scheme provides for automatic appeal of all death sentences to the State's Supreme Court. That court is required by statute to review each sentence of death and determine whether it was imposed under the influence of passion or prejudice, whether the evidence supports the jury's finding of a statutory aggravating circumstance, and whether the sentence is disproportionate compared to those sentences imposed in similar cases.

In short, Georgia's new sentencing procedures require as a prerequisite to the imposition of the death penalty specific jury findings as to the circumstances of the crime or the character of the defendant. Moreover, to guard further against a situation comparable to that presented in *Furman,* the Supreme Court of Georgia compares each death sentence with the sentences imposed on similarly situated defendants to ensure that the sentence of death in a particular case is not disproportionate. On their face these procedures seem to satisfy the concerns of *Furman.* No longer should there be "no meaningful basis for distinguishing the few cases in which [the death penalty] is imposed from the many cases in which it is not." . . .

V

The basic concern of *Furman* centered on those defendants who were being condemned to death capriciously and arbitrarily. Under the procedures before the Court in that case, sentencing authorities were not directed to give attention to the nature or circumstances of the crime committed or to the character or record of the defendant. Left unguided, juries imposed the death sentence in a way that could only be called freakish. The new Georgia sentencing procedures, by contrast, focus the jury's attention on the particularized nature of the crime and the particularized characteristics of the individual defendant. While the jury is permitted to consider any aggravating or mitigating circumstances, it must find and identify at least one statutory aggravating factor before it may impose a penalty of death. In this way the jury's discretion is channeled. No longer can a jury wantonly and freakishly impose the death sentence; it is always circumscribed by the legislative guidelines. In addition, the review function of the Supreme Court of Georgia affords additional assurance that the concerns that prompted our decision in *Furman* are not present to any significant degree in the Georgia procedure applied here.

For the reasons expressed in this opinion, we hold that the statutory system under which Gregg was sentenced to death does not violate the Constitution. Accordingly, the judgment of the Georgia Supreme Court is affirmed.

NOTES

1 Another purpose that has been discussed is the incapacitation of dangerous criminals and the consequent prevention of crimes that they may otherwise commit in the future.

2 We do not address here the question whether the taking of the criminal's life is a proportionate sanction where no victim has been deprived of life—for example, when capital punishment is imposed for rape, kidnaping, or armed robbery that does not result in the death of any human being.

3 The Model Penal Code proposes the following standards:

"(3) Aggravating Circumstances.

"(a) The murder was committed by a convict under sentence of imprisonment.

"(b) The defendant was previously convicted of another murder or of a felony involving the use or threat of violence to the person.

"(c) At the time the murder was committed the defendant also committed another murder.

"(d) The defendant knowingly created a great risk of death to many persons.

"(e) The murder was committed while the defendant was engaged or was an accomplice in the commission of, or an attempt to commit, or flight after committing or attempting to commit robbery, rape or deviate sexual intercourse by force or threat of force, arson, burglary or kidnaping.

"(f) The murder was committed for the purpose of avoiding or preventing a lawful arrest or effecting an escape from lawful custody.

"(g) The murder was committed for pecuniary gain.

"(h) The murder was especially heinous, atrocious or cruel, manifesting exceptional depravity.

"(4) Mitigating Circumstances.

"(a) The defendant has no significant history of prior criminal activity.

"(b) The murder was committed while the defendant was under the influence of extreme mental or emotional disturbance.

"(c) The victim was a participant in the defendant's homicidal conduct or consented to the homicidal act.

"(d) The murder was committed under circumstances which the defendant believed to provide a moral justification or extenuation for his conduct.

"(e) The defendant was an accomplice in a murder committed by another person and his participation in the homicidal act was relatively minor.

"(f) The defendant acted under duress or under the domination of another person.

"(g) At the time of the murder, the capacity of the defendant to appreciate the criminality [wrongfulness] of his conduct or to conform his conduct to the requirements of law was impaired as a result of mental disease or defect or intoxication.

"(h) The youth of the defendant at the time of the crime." ALI Model Penal Code § 210.6 (Proposed Official Draft 1962).

QUESTIONS

1 With regard to the imposition of the death penalty for the crime of murder, Justices Stewart, Powell, and Stevens write, "We cannot say that the punishment is invariably disproportionate to the crime." The Georgia statute under which Gregg was sentenced, however, retained the death penalty not only for the crime of murder but also for "kidnaping for ransom or where the victim is harmed, armed robbery, rape, treason, and aircraft hijacking." In your view, is the death penalty a disproportionate punishment for such crimes?

2 In note 3, we find a set of proposed model standards for the guidance of a jury in deciding whether a murderer warrants the death penalty or a lesser penalty—typically, life imprisonment. Is the proposed set of aggravating circumstances (those whose presence should incline a jury toward the death penalty) defensible and complete? Is the proposed set of mitigating circumstances (those whose presence should incline a jury away from the death penalty) defensible and complete?

Dissenting Opinion in *Gregg v. Georgia*

Justice Thurgood Marshall

Justice Marshall reaffirms the conclusion he had reached in *Furman v. Georgia* (1972): The death penalty is unconstitutional for two individually sufficient reasons. (1) It is excessive. (2) The American people, if fully informed, would consider it morally unacceptable. He insists that his conclusion in *Furman* has not been undercut by subsequent developments. Despite the fact that legislative activity since *Furman* would seem to indicate that the American people do not consider the death penalty morally unacceptable, Justice Marshall continues to maintain that the citizenry, *if fully informed,* would consider it morally unacceptable. At any rate, he maintains, the death penalty is unconstitutional

United States Supreme Court. 428 U.S. 153 (1976).

because it is excessive—that is, unnecessary to accomplish a legitimate legislative purpose. Neither deterrence nor retribution, the principal purposes asserted by Justices Stewart, Powell, and Stevens, can sustain the death penalty as nonexcessive in Justice Marshall's view. Since the available evidence does not show the death penalty to be a more effective deterrent than life imprisonment, he contends, the death penalty is not necessary to promote the goal of deterrence. Moreover, the death penalty is unnecessary to "further any legitimate notion of retribution." According to Justice Marshall, the notion that a murderer "deserves" death constitutes a denial of the wrongdoer's dignity and worth and, thus, is fundamentally at odds with the Eighth Amendment.

In *Furman v. Georgia* (1972) (concurring opinion), I set forth at some length my views on the basic issue presented to the Court in [this case]. The death penalty, I concluded, is a cruel and unusual punishment prohibited by the Eighth and Fourteenth Amendments. That continues to be my view.

I have no intention of retracing the "long and tedious journey" that led to my conclusion in *Furman*. My sole purposes here are to consider the suggestion that my conclusion in *Furman* has been undercut by developments since then, and briefly to evaluate the basis for my Brethren's holding that the extinction of life is a permissible form of punishment under the Cruel and Unusual Punishments Clause.

In *Furman* I concluded that the death penalty is constitutionally invalid for two reasons. First, the death penalty is excessive. And second, the American people, fully informed as to the purposes of the death penalty and its liabilities, would in my view reject it as morally unacceptable.

Since the decision in *Furman,* the legislatures of 35 States have enacted new statutes authorizing the imposition of the death sentence for certain crimes, and Congress has enacted a law providing the death penalty for air piracy resulting in death. I would be less than candid if I did not acknowledge that these developments have a significant bearing on a realistic assessment of the moral acceptability of the death penalty to the American people. But if the constitutionality of the death penalty turns, as I have urged, on the opinion of an *informed* citizenry, then even the enactment of new death statutes cannot be viewed as conclusive. In *Furman,* I observed that the American people are largely unaware of the information critical to a judgment on the morality of the death penalty, and concluded that if they were better informed they would consider it shocking, unjust, and unacceptable. A recent study, conducted after the enactment of the post-*Furman* statutes, has confirmed that the American people know little about the death penalty, and that the opinions of an informed public would differ significantly from those of a public unaware of the consequences and effects of the death penalty.

Even assuming, however, that the post-*Furman* enactment of statutes authorizing the death penalty renders the prediction of the views of an informed citizenry an uncertain basis for a constitutional decision, the enactment of those statutes has no bearing whatsoever on the conclusion that the death penalty is unconstitutional because it is excessive. An excessive penalty is invalid under the Cruel and Unusual Punishments Clause "even though popular sentiment may favor" it. The inquiry here, then, is simply whether the death penalty is necessary to accomplish the legitimate legislative purposes in punishment, or whether a less severe penalty—life imprisonment—would do as well.

The two purposes that sustain the death penalty as nonexcessive in the Court's view are general deterrence and retribution. In *Furman,* I canvassed the relevant data on the deterrent effect of capital punishment. The state of knowledge at that point, after literally centuries of debate, was summarized as follows by a United Nations Committee:

> It is generally agreed between the retentionists and abolitionists, whatever their opinions about the validity of comparative studies of deterrence, that the data which now exist show no correlation between the existence of capital punishment and lower rates of capital crime.

The available evidence, I concluded in *Furman,* was convincing that "capital punishment is not necessary as a deterrent to crime in our society." . . .

. . . The evidence I reviewed in *Furman* remains convincing, in my view, that "capital punishment is not necessary as a deterrent to crime in our society." The justification for the death penalty must be found elsewhere.

The other principal purpose said to be served by the death penalty is retribution. The notion that retribution can serve as a moral justification for the sanction of death finds credence in the opinion of my Brothers STEWART, POWELL, and STEVENS. . . . It is this notion that I find to be the most disturbing aspect of today's unfortunate [decision].

The concept of retribution is a multifaceted one, and any discussion of its role in the criminal law must be undertaken with caution. On one level, it can be said that the notion of retribution or reprobation is the basis of our insistence that only those who have broken the law be punished, and in this sense the notion is quite obviously central to a just system of criminal sanctions. But our recognition that retribution plays a crucial role in determining who may be punished by no means requires approval of retribution as a general justification for punishment. It is the question whether retribution can provide a moral justification for punishment—in particular, capital punishment—that we must consider.

My Brothers STEWART, POWELL, and STEVENS offer the following explanation of the retributive justification for capital punishment:

> The instinct for retribution is part of the nature of man, and channeling that instinct in the administration of criminal justice serves an important purpose in promoting the stability of a society governed by law. When people begin to believe that organized society is unwilling or unable to impose upon criminal offenders the punishment they "deserve," then there are sown the seeds of anarchy—of self-help, vigilante justice, and lynch law.

This statement is wholly inadequate to justify the death penalty. As my Brother BRENNAN stated in *Furman,* "[t]here is no evidence whatever that utilization of imprisonment rather than death encourages private blood feuds and other disorders." It simply defies belief to suggest that the death penalty is necessary to prevent the American people from taking the law into their own hands.

In a related vein, it may be suggested that the expression of moral outrage through the imposition of the death penalty serves to reinforce basic moral values—that it marks some crimes as particularly offensive and therefore to be avoided. The argument is akin to a deterrence argument, but differs in that it contemplates the individual's shrinking from antisocial conduct, not because he fears punishment, but because he has been told in the strongest possible way that the conduct is wrong. This contention, like the previous one, provides no support for the death penalty. It is inconceivable that any individual concerned about conforming his conduct to what society says is "right" would fail to realize that murder is "wrong" if the penalty were simply life imprisonment.

The foregoing contentions—that society's expression of moral outrage through the imposition of the death penalty pre-empts the citizenry from taking the law into its own hands and reinforces moral values—are not retributive in the purest sense. They are essentially utilitarian in that they portray the death penalty as valuable because of its beneficial results. These justifications for the death penalty are inadequate because the penalty is, quite clearly I think, not necessary to the accomplishment of those results.

There remains for consideration, however, what might be termed the purely retributive justification for the death penalty—that the death penalty is appropriate, not because of its beneficial effect on society, but because the taking of the murderer's life is itself morally good. Some of the language of the opinion of my Brothers STEWART, POWELL, and STEVENS . . . appears positively to embrace this notion of retribution for its own sake as a justification for capital punishment. They state:

> [T]he decision that capital punishment may be the appropriate sanction in extreme cases is an expression of the community's belief that certain crimes are themselves so grievous an affront to humanity that the only adequate response may be the penalty of death.

They then quote with approval from Lord Justice Denning's remarks before the British Royal Commission on Capital Punishment:

> The truth is that some crimes are so outrageous that society insists on adequate punishment, because the wrong-doer deserves it, irrespective of whether it is a deterrent or not.

Of course, it may be that these statements are intended as no more than observations as to the popular demands that it is thought must be responded to in order to prevent anarchy. But the implication of the statements appears to me to be quite different— namely, that society's judgment that the murderer "deserves" death must be respected not simply because the preservation of order requires it, but because it is appropriate that society make the judgment and carry it out. It is this latter notion, in particular, that I consider to be fundamentally at odds with the Eighth Amendment. The mere fact that the community demands the murderer's life in return for the evil he has done cannot sustain the death penalty, for as JUSTICES STEWART, POWELL, and STEVENS remind us, "the Eighth Amendment demands more than that a challenged punishment be acceptable to contemporary society." To be sustained under the Eighth Amendment, the death penalty must "compor[t] with the basic concept of human dignity at the core of the Amendment;" the objective in imposing it must be "[consistent] with our respect for the dignity of [other] men." Under these standards, the taking of life "because the wrongdoer deserves it" surely must fail, for such a punishment has as its very basis the total denial of the wrongdoer's dignity and worth.

The death penalty, unnecessary to promote the goal of deterrence or to further any legitimate notion of retribution, is an excessive penalty forbidden by the Eighth and Fourteenth Amendments. I respectfully dissent from the Court's judgment upholding the [sentence] of death imposed upon the [petitioner in this case].

QUESTIONS

1 Is Justice Marshall correct in claiming that the American people, *if fully informed* about the death penalty, would consider it morally unacceptable?
2 Is the death penalty, as Justice Marshall claims, "unnecessary to promote the goal of deterrence or to further any legitimate notion of retribution"?

A Life for a Life

Igor Primoratz

Primoratz endorses a retributive rationale for the retention of the death penalty and defends this rationale against commonly made abolitionist arguments. He rejects the idea that the death penalty violates a murderer's right to life and insists that there is no contradiction involved in a system of criminal law that prohibits murder and yet allows the state to administer the death penalty. He also defends the retributive rationale against arguments claiming to show that the death penalty is in reality a disproportionate penalty for the crime of murder. Finally, Primoratz argues that neither the possibility of executing an innocent person nor the discriminatory application of the death penalty can provide a credible basis for abolition.

. . . According to the retributive theory, consequences of punishment, however important from the practical point of view, are irrelevant when it comes to its justi-fication; *the* moral consideration is its justice. Punishment is morally justified inso-far as it is meted out as retribution for the offense committed. When someone has committed an offense, he deserves to be punished: it is just, and consequently jus-tified, that he be punished. The offense is the sole ground of the state's right and duty to punish. It is also the measure of legitimate punishment: the two ought to be proportionate. So the issue of capital punishment within the retributive approach comes down to the question, Is this punishment ever proportionate retribution for the offense committed, and thus deserved, just, and justified?

The classic representatives of retributivism believed that it was, and that it was the only proportionate and hence appropriate punishment, if the offense was *murder*— that is, criminal homicide perpetrated voluntarily and intentionally or in wanton

From Igor Primoratz, *Justifying Legal Punishment* (1989), pp. 158–159, 161–166. Reprinted with the permission of Humanities Press International, Atlantic Highlands, NJ.

disregard of human life. In other cases, the demand for proportionality between offense and punishment can be satisfied by fines or prison terms;[1] the crime of murder, however, is an exception in this respect, and calls for the literal interpretation of the *lex talionis*. The uniqueness of this crime has to do with the uniqueness of the value which has been deliberately or recklessly destroyed. We come across this idea as early as the original formulation of the retributive view—the biblical teaching on punishment: "You shall accept no ransom for the life of a murderer who is guilty of death; but he shall be put to death."[2] The rationale of this command—one that clearly distinguishes the biblical conception of the criminal law from contemporaneous criminal law systems in the Middle East—is that man was not only created *by* God, like every other creature, but also, alone among all the creatures, *in the image of God:*

> That man was made in the image of God . . . is expressive of the peculiar and supreme worth of man. Of all creatures, Genesis 1 relates, he alone possesses this attribute, bringing him into closer relation to God than all the rest and conferring upon him the highest value. . . . This view of the uniqueness and supremacy of human life. . . places life beyond the reach of other values. The idea that life may be measured in terms of money or other property. . . is excluded. Compensation of any kind is ruled out. The guilt of the murderer is infinite because the murdered life is invaluable; the kinsmen of the slain man are not competent to say when he has been paid for. An absolute wrong has been committed, a sin against God which is not subject to human discussion. . . . Because human life is invaluable, to take it entails the death penalty.[3]

This view that the value of human life is not commensurable with other values, and that consequently there is only one truly equivalent punishment for murder, namely death, does not necessarily presuppose a theistic outlook. It can be claimed that, simply because we have to be alive if we are to experience and realize any other value at all, there is nothing equivalent to the murderous destruction of a human life except the destruction of the life of the murderer. Any other retribution, no matter how severe, would still be less than what is proportionate, deserved, and just. As long as the murderer is alive, no matter how bad the conditions of his life may be, there are always at least *some* values he can experience and realize. This provides a plausible interpretation of what the classical representatives of retributivism as a philosophical theory of punishment, such as Kant and Hegel, had to say on the subject.[4]

It seems to me that this is essentially correct. With respect to the larger question of the justification of punishment in general, it is the retributive theory that gives the right answer. Accordingly, capital punishment ought to be retained where it obtains, and reintroduced in those jurisdictions that have abolished it, although we have no reason to believe that, as a means of deterrence, it is any better than a very long prison term. It ought to be retained, or reintroduced, for one simple reason: that justice be done in cases of murder, that murderers be punished according to their deserts.

There are a number of arguments that have been advanced against this rationale of capital punishment. . . .

[One] abolitionist argument . . . simply says that capital punishment is illegitimate because it violates the right to life, which is a fundamental, absolute, sacred right belonging to each and every human being, and therefore ought to be respected even in a murderer.[5]

If any rights are fundamental, the right to life is certainly one of them; but to claim that it is absolute, inviolable under any circumstances and for any reason, is a different matter. If an abolitionist wants to argue his case by asserting an absolute right to life, she will also have to deny moral legitimacy to taking human life in war, revolution, and self-defense. This kind of pacifism is a consistent but farfetched and hence implausible position.

I do not believe that the right to life (nor, for that matter, any other right) is absolute. I have no general theory of rights to fall back upon here; instead, let me pose a question. Would we take seriously the claim to an absolute, sacred, inviolable right to life—coming from the mouth of a *confessed murderer*? I submit that we would not, for the obvious reason that it is being put forward by the person who confessedly denied another human being this very right. But if the murderer cannot plausibly claim such a right for himself, neither can *anyone else* do that in his behalf. This suggests that there is an element of reciprocity in our general rights, such as the right to life or property. I can convincingly claim these rights only so long as I acknowledge and respect the same rights of others. If I violate the rights of others, I thereby lose the same rights. If I am a murderer, I have no *right* to live.

Some opponents of capital punishment claim that a criminal law system which includes this punishment is contradictory, in that it prohibits murder and at the same time provides for its perpetration: "It is one and the same legal regulation which prohibits the individual from murdering, while allowing the state to murder. . . . This is obviously a terrible irony, an abnormal and immoral logic, against which everything in us revolts."[6]

This seems to be one of the more popular arguments against the death penalty, but it is not a good one. If it were valid, it would prove too much. Exactly the same might be claimed of other kinds of punishment: of prison terms, that they are "contradictory" to the legal protection of liberty; of fines, that they are "contradictory" to the legal protection of property. Fortunately enough, it is not valid, for it begs the question at issue. In order to be able to talk of the state as "murdering" the person it executes, and to claim that there is "an abnormal and immoral logic" at work here, which thrives on a "contradiction," one has to use the word "murder" in the very same sense—that is, in the usual sense, which implies the idea of the *wrongful* taking the life of another—both when speaking of what the murderer has done to the victim and of what the state is doing to him by way of punishment. But this is precisely the question at issue: whether capital punishment *is* "murder," whether it is wrongful or morally justified and right.

The next two arguments attack the retributive rationale of capital punishment by questioning the claim that it is only this punishment that satisfies the demand for proportion between offense and punishment in the case of murder. The first points out that any two human lives are different in many important respects, such as age, health, physical and mental capability, so that it does not make much sense to consider them equally valuable. What if the murdered person was very old, practically at the very end of her natural life, while the murderer is young, with most of his life still ahead of him, for instance? Or if the victim was gravely and incurably ill, and thus doomed to live her life in suffering and hopelessness, without being able to experience almost anything that makes a human life worth living, while the murderer is in every respect capable of experiencing and enjoying things life has to offer? Or the other way round? Would not the death penalty in such cases amount either to taking a more valuable life as a punishment for destroying a less valuable one, or *vice versa*? Would it not be either too much, or too little, and in both cases disproportionate, and thus unjust and wrong, from the standpoint of the retributive theory itself?[7]

Any plausibility this argument might appear to have is the result of a conflation of differences between, and value of, human lives. No doubt, any two human lives are *different* in innumerable ways, but this does not entail that they are not *equally valuable*. I have no worked-out general theory of equality to refer to here, but I do not think that one is necessary in order to do away with this argument. The modern humanistic and democratic tradition in ethical, social, and political thought is based on the idea that all human beings are equal. This finds its legal expression in the principle of equality of people under the law. If we are not willing to give up this principle, we have to stick to the assumption that, all differences notwithstanding, any two human lives, *qua* human lives, are equally valuable. If, on the other hand, we allow that, on the basis of such criteria as age, health, or mental or physical ability, it can be claimed that the life of one person is more or less valuable than the life of another, and we admit such claims in the sphere of law, including criminal law, we shall thereby give up the principle of equality of people under the law. In all consistency, we shall not be able to demand that property, physical and personal integrity, and all other rights and interests of individuals be given equal consideration in courts of law either—that is, we shall have to accept systematic discrimination between individuals on the basis of the same criteria across the whole field. I do not think anyone would seriously contemplate an overhaul of the whole legal system along these lines.

The second argument having to do with the issue of proportionality between murder and capital punishment draws our attention to the fact that the law normally provides for a certain period of time to elapse between the passing of a death sentence and its execution. It is a period of several weeks or months; in some cases it extends to years. This period is bound to be one of constant mental anguish for the condemned. And thus, all things considered, what is inflicted on him is disproportionately hard and hence unjust. It would be proportionate and just only in the case of "a criminal who had warned his victim of the date at which he would inflict a horrible death on him and who, from that moment onward, had confined him at his mercy for months."[8]

The first thing to note about this argument is that it does not support a full-fledged abolitionist stand; if it were valid, it would not show that capital punishment is *never* proportionate and just, but only that it is *very rarely* so. Consequently, the conclusion would not be that it ought to be abolished outright, but only that it ought to be restricted to those cases that would satisfy the condition cited above. Such cases do happen, although, to be sure, not very often; the murder of Aldo Moro, for instance, was of this kind. But this is not the main point. The main point is that the argument actually does not hit at capital punishment itself, although it is presented with that aim in view. It hits at something else: a particular way of carrying out this punishment, which is widely adopted in our time. Some hundred years ago and more, in the Wild West, they frequently hanged the man convicted to die almost immediately after pronouncing the sentence. I am not arguing here that we should follow this example today; I mention this piece of historical fact only in order to show that the interval between sentencing someone to death and carrying out the sentence is not a *part* of capital punishment itself. However unpalatable we might find those Wild West hangings, whatever objections we might want to voice against the speed with which they followed the sentencing, surely we shall not deny them the *description* of "executions." So the implication of the argument is not that we ought to do away with capital punishment altogether, nor that we ought to restrict it to those cases of murder where the murderer had warned the victim weeks or months in advance of what he was going to do to her, but that we ought to reexamine the procedure of carrying out this kind of punishment. We ought to weigh the reasons for having this interval between the sentencing and executing against the moral and human significance of the repercussions such an interval inevitably carries with it.

These reasons, in part, have to do with the possibility of miscarriages of justice and the need to rectify them. Thus we come to the argument against capital punishment which, historically, has been the most effective of all: many advances of the abolitionist movement have been connected with discoveries of cases of judicial errors. Judges and jurors are only human, and consequently some of their beliefs and decisions are bound to be mistaken. Some of their mistakes can be corrected upon discovery; but precisely those with most disastrous repercussions— those which result in innocent people being executed—can never be rectified. In all other cases of mistaken sentencing we can revoke the punishment, either completely or in part, or at least extend compensation. In addition, by exonerating the accused we give moral satisfaction. None of this is possible after an innocent person has been executed; capital punishment is essentially different from all other penalties by being completely irrevocable and irreparable.[9] Therefore, it ought to be abolished.

A part of my reply to this argument goes along the same lines as what I had to say on the previous one. It is not so far-reaching as abolitionists assume; for it would be quite implausible, even fanciful, to claim that there have *never* been cases of murder which left no room whatever for reasonable doubt as to the guilt and full responsibility of the accused. Such cases may not be more frequent than those others, but they do happen. Why not retain the death penalty at least for them?

Actually, this argument, just as the preceding one, does not speak out against capital punishment itself, but against the existing procedures for trying capital cases. Miscarriages of justice result in innocent people being sentenced to death and executed, even in the criminal law systems in which greatest care is taken to ensure that it never comes to that. But this does not stem from the intrinsic nature of the institution of capital punishment; it results from deficiencies, limitations, and imperfections of the criminal law procedures in which this punishment is meted out. Errors of justice do not demonstrate the need to do away with capital punishment; they simply make it incumbent on us to do everything possible to improve even further procedures of meting it out.

To be sure, this conclusion will not find favor with a diehard abolitionist. "I shall ask for the abolition of Capital Punishment until I have the infallibility of human judgement demonstrated to me," that is, as long as there is even the slightest possibility that innocent people may be executed because of judicial errors, Lafayette said in his day.[10] Many an opponent of this kind of punishment will say the same today. The demand to do away with capital punishment altogether, so as to eliminate even the smallest chance of that ever happening—the chance which, admittedly, would remain even after everything humanly possible has been done to perfect the procedure, although then it would be very slight indeed—is actually a demand to give a privileged position to murderers as against all other offenders, big and small. For if we acted on this demand, we would bring about a situation in which proportionate penalties would be meted out for all offenses, *except* for murder. Murderers would not be receiving the only punishment truly proportionate to their crimes, the punishment of death, but some other, lighter, and thus disproportionate penalty. All other offenders would be punished according to their deserts; only murderers would be receiving less than *they* deserve. In all other cases justice would be done in full; only in cases of the gravest of offenses, the crime of murder, justice would not be carried out in full measure. It is a great and tragic miscarriage of justice when an innocent person is mistakenly sentenced to death and executed, but systematically giving murderers advantage over all other offenders would also be a grave injustice. Is the fact that, as long as capital punishment is retained, there is a possibility that over a number of years, or even decades, an injustice of the first kind may be committed, unintentionally and unconsciously, reason enough to abolish it altogether, and thus end up with a system of punishments in which injustices of the second kind are perpetrated daily, consciously, and inevitably?[11]

There is still another abolitionist argument that actually does not hit out against capital punishment itself, but against something else. Figures are sometimes quoted which show that this punishment is much more often meted out to the uneducated and poor than to the educated, rich, and influential people; in the United States, much more often to blacks than to whites. These figures are adduced as a proof of the inherent injustice of this kind of punishment. On account of them, it is claimed that capital punishment is not a way of doing justice by meting out deserved punishment to murderers, but rather a means of social discrimination and perpetuation of social injustice.

I shall not question these findings, which are quite convincing, and anyway, there is no need to do that in order to defend the institution of capital punishment. For there seems to be a certain amount of discrimination and injustice not only in sentencing people to death and executing them, but also in meting out other penalties. The social structure of the death rows in American prisons, for instance, does not seem to be basically different from the general social structure of American penitentiaries. If this argument were valid, it would call not only for abolition of the penalty of death, but for doing away with other penalties as well. But it is not valid; as Burton Leiser has pointed out,

> . . . this is not an argument, either against the death penalty or against any other form of punishment. It is an argument against the unjust and inequitable distribution of penalties.

If the trials of wealthy men are less likely to result in convictions than those of poor men, then something must be done to reform the procedure in criminal courts. If those who have money and standing in the community are less likely to be charged with serious offenses than their less affluent fellow citizens, then there should be a major overhaul of the entire system of criminal justice. . . . But the maldistribution of penalties is no argument against any particular form of penalty.[12]

NOTES

1 Cf. I. Primoratz, *Justifying Legal Punishment* (Atlantic Highlands, N.J.: Humanities Press, 1989), pp. 85–94.

2 Numbers 35.31 (R.S.V.).

3 M. Greenberg, "Some Postulates of Biblical Criminal Law," in J. Goldin (ed.), *The Jewish Expression* (New York: Bantam, 1970), pp. 25–26. (Post-biblical Jewish law evolved toward the virtual abolition of the death penalty, but that is of no concern here.)

4 "There is no *parallel* between death and even the most miserable life, so that there is no equality of crime and retribution [in the case of murder] unless the perpetrator is judicially put to death" (I. Kant, "The Metaphysics of Morals," *Kant's Political Writings,* ed. H. Reiss, trans. H. B. Nisbet [Cambridge: Cambridge University Press, 1970], p. 156). "Since life is the full compass of a man's existence, the punishment [for murder] cannot simply consist in a 'value', for none is great enough, but can consist only in taking away a second life" (G. W. F. Hegel, *Philosophy of Right,* trans. T. M. Knox [Oxford: Oxford University Press, 1965], p. 247).

5 For an example of this view, see L. N. Tolstoy, *Smertnaya kazn i hristianstvo* (Berlin: I. P. Ladizhnikov, n.d.), pp. 40–41.

6 S. V. Vulović, *Problem smrtne kazne* (Belgrade: Geca Kon, 1925), pp. 23–24.

7 Cf. W. Blackstone, *Commentaries on the Laws of England,* 4th ed., ed. J. DeWitt Andrews (Chicago: Callaghan & Co., 1899), p. 1224.

8 A. Camus, "Reflections on the Guillotine," *Resistance, Rebellion and Death,* trans. J. O'Brien (London: Hamish Hamilton, 1961), p. 143.

9 For an interesting critical discussion of this point, see M. Davis, "Is the Death Penalty Irrevocable?" *Social Theory and Practice* 10 (1984).

10 Quoted in E. R. Calvert, *Capital Punishment in the Twentieth Century* (London: G. P. Putnam's Sons, 1927), p. 132.

11 For a criticism of this argument, see L. Sebba, "On Capital Punishment—a Comment," *Israel Law Review* 17 (1982), pp. 392–395.

12 B. M. Leiser, *Liberty, Justice and Morals: Contemporary Value Conflicts* (New York: Macmillan, 1973), p. 225.

QUESTIONS

1 Would you endorse a retributive rationale for the retention of the death penalty? If so, would you say that *all* murderers deserve to die or just *some*? If just some deserve to die, which ones?

2 If blacks are more likely to receive the death penalty than whites, if the poor and uneducated are more likely to receive the death penalty than the affluent and educated, does it follow that we should abolish the death penalty?

An Eye for an Eye?

Stephen Nathanson

Nathanson, an abolitionist, distinguishes between *equality* retributivism and *proportional* retributivism and argues that neither of these retributive approaches can provide a justification for the death penalty. In his view: (1) Equality retributivism—committed to the principle that punishment should be equal to the crime ("an eye for an eye")—fails because it does not provide a systematically satisfactory criterion for determining appropriate punishment. (2) Proportional retributivism—committed to the principle that punishment should be proportional to the crime—fails because it does not require that murderers be executed. Nathanson also argues that a societal decision to abolish the death penalty would convey two important symbolic messages. First, we would thereby express our respect for the dignity of all human beings, even those guilty of murder. Second, in restraining the expression of our anger against murderers, we would reinforce the conviction that only defensive violence is justifiable.

Suppose we . . . try to determine what people deserve from a strictly moral point of view. How shall we proceed?

The most usual suggestion is that we look at a person's actions because what someone deserves would appear to depend on what he or she does. A person's actions, it seems, provide not only a basis for a moral appraisal of the person but also a guide to how he should be treated. According to the *lex talionis* or principle of "an eye for an eye," we ought to treat people as they have treated others. What people deserve as recipients of rewards or punishments is determined by what they do as agents.

This is a powerful and attractive view, one that appears to be backed not only by moral common sense but also by tradition and philosophical thought. The most famous statement of philosophical support for this view comes from Immanuel Kant, who linked it directly with an argument for the death penalty. Discussing the problem of punishment, Kant writes,

> What kind and what degree of punishment does legal justice adopt as its principle and standard? None other than the principle of equality . . . the principle of not treating one side more favorably than the other. Accordingly, any undeserved evil that you inflict on someone else among the people is one that you do to yourself. If you vilify, you vilify yourself; if you steal from him, you steal from yourself; if you kill him, you kill yourself. Only the law of retribution (*jus talionis*) can determine exactly the kind and degree of punishment.[1]

Kant's view is attractive for a number of reasons. First, it accords with our belief that what a person deserves is related to what he does. Second, it appeals to a moral standard and does not seem to rely on any particular legal or political institutions.

Reprinted with permission of Rowman & Littlefield, Publishers, from Stephen Nathanson, *An Eye for an Eye?* (1987), pp. 72–77, 138–140, 145.

Third, it seems to provide a measure of appropriate punishment that can be used as a guide to creating laws and instituting punishments. It tells us that the punishment is to be identical with the crime. Whatever the criminal did to the victim is to be done in turn to the criminal.

In spite of the attractions of Kant's view, it is deeply flawed. When we see why, it will be clear that the whole "eye for an eye" perspective must be rejected.

PROBLEMS WITH THE EQUAL PUNISHMENT PRINCIPLE

. . . [Kant's view] does not provide an adequate criterion for determining appropriate levels of punishment.

. . . We can see this, first, by noting that for certain crimes, Kant's view recommends punishments that are not morally acceptable. Applied strictly, it would require that we rape rapists, torture torturers, and burn arsonists whose acts have led to deaths. In general, where a particular crime involves barbaric and inhuman treatment, Kant's principle tells us to act barbarically and inhumanly in return. So, in some cases, the principle generates unacceptable answers to the question of what constitutes appropriate punishment.

This is not its only defect. In many other cases, the principle tells us nothing at all about how to punish. While Kant thought it obvious how to apply his principle in the case of murder, his principle cannot serve as a general rule because it does not tell us how to punish many crimes. Using the Kantian version or the more common "eye for an eye" standard, what would we decide to do to embezzlers, spies, drunken drivers, airline hijackers, drug users, prostitutes, air polluters, or persons who practice medicine without a license? If one reflects on this question, it becomes clear that there is simply no answer to it. We could not in fact design a system of punishment simply on the basis of the "eye for an eye" principle.

In order to justify using the "eye for an eye" principle to answer our question about murder and the death penalty, we would first have to show that it worked for a whole range of cases, giving acceptable answers to questions about amounts of punishment. Then, having established it as a satisfactory general principle, we could apply it to the case of murder. It turns out, however, that when we try to apply the principle generally, we find that it either gives wrong answers or no answers at all. Indeed, I suspect that the principle of "an eye for an eye" is no longer even a principle. Instead, it is simply a metaphorical disguise for expressing belief in the death penalty. People who cite it do not take it seriously. They do not believe in a kidnapping for a kidnapping, a theft for a theft, and so on. Perhaps "an eye for an eye" once was a genuine principle, but now it is merely a slogan. Therefore, it gives us no guidance in deciding whether murderers deserve to die.

In reply to these objections, one might defend the principle by saying that it does not require that punishments be strictly identical with crimes. Rather, it requires only that a punishment produce an amount of suffering in the criminal which is equal to the amount suffered by the victim. Thus, we don't have to hijack airplanes belonging to airline hijackers, spy on spies, etc. We simply have to reproduce in them the harm done to others.

Unfortunately, this reply really does not solve the problem. It provides no answer to the first objection, since it would still require us to behave barbarically in our treatment of those who are guilty of barbaric crimes. Even if we do not reproduce their actions exactly, any action which caused equal suffering would itself be barbaric. Second, in trying to produce equal amounts of suffering, we run into many problems. Just how much suffering is produced by an airline hijacker or a spy? And how do we apply this principle to prostitutes or drug users, who may not produce any suffering at all? We have rough ideas about how serious various crimes are, but this may not correlate with any clear sense of just how much harm is done.

Furthermore, the same problem arises in determining how much suffering a particular punishment would produce for a particular criminal. People vary in their tolerance of pain and in the amount of unhappiness that a fine or a jail sentence would cause them. Recluses will be less disturbed by banishment than extroverts. Nature lovers will suffer more in prison than people who are indifferent to natural beauty. A literal application of the principle would require that we tailor punishments to individual sensitivities, yet this is at best impractical. To a large extent, the legal system must work with standardized and rather crude estimates of the negative impact that punishments have on people.

The move from calling for a punishment that is identical to the crime to favoring one that is equal in the harm done is no help to us or to the defense of the principle. "An eye for an eye" tells us neither what people deserve nor how we should treat them when they have done wrong.

PROPORTIONAL RETRIBUTIVISM

The view we have been considering can be called "equality retributivism," since it proposes that we repay criminals with punishments equal to their crimes. In the light of problems like those I have cited, some people have proposed a variation on this view, calling not for equal punishments but rather for punishments which are *proportional* to the crime. In defending such a view as a guide for setting criminal punishments, Andrew von Hirsch writes:

> If one asks how severely a wrongdoer deserves to be punished, a familiar principle comes to mind: Severity of punishment should be commensurate with the seriousness of the wrong. Only grave wrongs merit severe penalties; minor misdeeds deserve lenient punishments. Disproportionate penalties are undeserved—severe sanctions for minor wrongs or vice versa. This principle has variously been called a principle of "proportionality" or "just deserts"; we prefer to call it commensurate deserts.[2]

Like Kant, von Hirsch makes the punishment which a person deserves depend on that person's actions, but he departs from Kant in substituting proportionality for equality as the criterion for setting the amount of punishment.

In implementing a punishment system based on the proportionality view, one would first make a list of crimes, ranking them in order of seriousness. At one end would be quite trivial offenses like parking meter violations, while very serious crimes such as murder would occupy the other. In between, other crimes would be ranked according to their relative gravity. Then a corresponding scale of punishments would be constructed, and the two would be correlated. Punishments would be proportionate to crimes so long as we could say that the more serious the crime was, the higher on the punishment scale was the punishment administered.

This system does not have the defects of equality retributivism. It does not require that we treat those guilty of barbaric crimes barbarically. This is because we can set the upper limit of the punishment scale so as to exclude truly barbaric punishments. Second, unlike the equality principle, the proportionality view is genuinely general, providing a way of handling all crimes. Finally, it does justice to our ordinary belief that certain punishments are unjust because they are too severe or too lenient for the crime committed.

The proportionality principle does, I think, play a legitimate role in our thinking about punishments. Nonetheless, it is no help to death penalty advocates, because it does not require that murderers be executed. All that it requires is that if murder is the most serious crime, then murder should be punished by the most severe punishment on the scale. The principle does not tell us what this punishment should be, however, and it is quite compatible with the view that the most severe punishment should be a long prison term.

This failure of the theory to provide a basis for supporting the death penalty reveals an important gap in proportional retributivism. It shows that while the theory is general in scope, it does not yield any *specific* recommendations regarding punishment. It tells us, for example, that armed robbery should be punished more severely than embezzling and less severely than murder, but it does not tell us how much to punish any of these. This weakness is, in effect, conceded by von Hirsch, who admits that if we want to implement the "commensurate deserts" principle, we must supplement it with information about what level of punishment is needed to deter crimes.[3] In a later discussion of how to "anchor" the punishment system, he deals with this problem in more depth, but the factors he cites as relevant to making specific judgments (such as available prison space) have nothing to do with what people deserve. He also seems to suggest that a range of punishments may be appropriate for a particular crime. This runs counter to the death penalty supporter's sense that death alone is appropriate for some murderers.[4]

Neither of these retributive views, then, provides support for the death penalty. The equality principle fails because it is not in general true that the appropriate punishment for a crime is to do to the criminal what he has done to others. In some cases this is immoral, while in others it is impossible. The proportionality principle may be correct, but by itself it cannot determine specific punishments for specific crimes. Because of its flexibility and open-endedness, it is compatible with a great range of different punishments for murder.[5] . . .

THE SYMBOLISM OF ABOLISHING THE DEATH PENALTY

What is the symbolic message that we would convey by deciding to renounce the death penalty and to abolish its use?

I think that there are two primary messages. The first is the most frequently emphasized and is usually expressed in terms of the sanctity of human life, although I think we could better express it in terms of respect for human dignity.

One way we express our respect for the dignity of human beings is by abstaining from depriving them of their lives, even if they have done terrible deeds. In defense of human well-being, we may punish people for their crimes, but we ought not to deprive them of everything, which is what the death penalty does.

If we take the life of a criminal, we convey the idea that by his deeds he has made himself worthless and totally without human value. I do not believe that we are in a position to affirm that of anyone. We may hate such a person and feel the deepest anger against him, but when he no longer poses a threat to anyone, we ought not to take his life.

But, one might ask, hasn't the murderer forfeited whatever rights he might have had to our respect? Hasn't he, by his deeds, given up any rights that he had to decent treatment? Aren't we morally free to kill him if we wish?

These questions express important doubts about the obligation to accord any respect to those who have acted so deplorably, but I do not think that they prove that any such forfeiture has occurred. Certainly, when people murder or commit other crimes, they do forfeit some of the rights that are possessed by the law-abiding. They lose a certain right to be left alone. It becomes permissible to bring them to trial and, if they are convicted, to impose an appropriate—even a dreadful—punishment on them.

Nonetheless, they do not forfeit all their rights. It does not follow from the vileness of their actions that we can do anything whatsoever to them. This is part of the moral meaning of the constitutional ban on cruel and unusual punishments. No matter how terrible a person's deeds, we may not punish him in a cruel and unusual way. We may not torture him, for example. His right not to be tortured has not been forfeited. Why do these limits hold? Because this person remains a human being, and we think that there is something in him that we must continue to respect in spite of his terrible acts.

One way of seeing why those who murder still deserve some consideration and respect is by reflecting again on the idea of what it is to *deserve* something. In most contexts, we think that what people deserve depends on what they have done, intended, or tried to do. It depends on features that are qualities of individuals. The best person for the job deserves to be hired. The person who worked especially hard deserves our gratitude. We can call the concept that applies in these cases *personal* desert.

There is another kind of desert, however, that belongs to people by virtue of their humanity itself and does not depend on their individual efforts or achievements. I will call this impersonal kind of desert *human* desert. We appeal to this concept when we think that everyone deserves a certain level of treatment no matter what their individual qualities are. When the signers of the Declaration of Independence affirmed that people had inalienable rights to "life, liberty, and the pursuit of happiness," they were appealing to such an idea. These rights do not have to be earned by people. They are possessed "naturally," and everyone is bound to respect them.

According to the view that I am defending, people do not lose all of their rights when they commit terrible crimes. They still deserve some level of decent treatment simply because they remain living, functioning human beings. This level of moral desert need not be earned, and it cannot be forfeited. This view may sound controversial, but in fact everyone who believes that cruel and unusual punishment should be forbidden implicitly agrees with it. That is, they agree that even after someone has committed a terrible crime, we do not have the right to do anything whatsoever to him.

What I am suggesting is that by renouncing the use of death as a punishment, we express and reaffirm our belief in the inalienable, unforfeitable core of human dignity.

Why is this a worthwhile message to convey? It is worth conveying because this belief is both important and precarious. Throughout history, people have found innumerable reasons to degrade the humanity of one another. They have found qualities in others that they hated or feared, and even when they were not threatened by these people, they have sought to harm them, deprive them of their liberty, or take their lives from them. They have often felt that they had good reasons to do these things, and they have invoked divine commands, racial purity, and state security to support their deeds.

These actions and attitudes are not relics of the past. They remain an awful feature of the contemporary world. By renouncing the death penalty, we show our determination to accord at least minimal respect even to those whom we believe to be personally vile or morally vicious. This is, perhaps, why we speak of the *sanctity* of human life rather than its value or worth. That which is sacred remains, in some sense, untouchable, and its value is not dependent on its worth or usefulness to us. Kant expressed this ideal of respect in the famous second version of the Categorical Imperative: "So act as to treat humanity, whether in thine own person or in that of any other, in every case as an end withal, never as a means only." . . .

[THE SECOND SYMBOLIC MESSAGE]

. . . When the state has a murderer in its power and could execute him but does not, this conveys the idea that even though this person has done wrong and even though we may be angry, outraged, and indignant with him, we will nonetheless control ourselves in a way that he did not. We will not kill him, even though we could do so and even though we are angry and indignant. We will exercise restraint, sanctioning killing only when it serves a protective function.

Why should we do this? Partly out of a respect for human dignity. But also because we want the state to set an example of proper behavior. We do not want to encourage people to resort to violence to settle conflicts when there are other ways available. We want to avoid the cycle of violence that can come from retaliation and counter-retaliation. Violence is a contagion that arouses hatred and anger, and if unchecked, it simply leads to still more violence. The state can convey the message that the contagion must be stopped, and the most effective principle for stopping it is the idea that only defensive violence is justifiable. Since the death penalty is not an instance of defensive violence, it ought to be renounced.

We show our respect for life best by restraining ourselves and allowing murderers to live, rather than by following a policy of a life for a life. Respect for life and restraint of violence are aspects of the same ideal. The renunciation of the death penalty would symbolize our support of that ideal.

NOTES

1 Kant, *Metaphysical Elements of Justice,* translated by John Ladd (Indianapolis: Bobbs-Merrill, 1965), 101.
2 *Doing Justice* (New York: Hill & Wang, 1976), 66; reprinted in *Sentencing,* edited by H. Gross and A. von Hirsch (Oxford University Press, 1981), 243. For a more recent discussion and further defense by von Hirsch, see his *Past or Future Crimes* (New Brunswick, N.J.: Rutgers University Press, 1985).
3 Von Hirsch, *Doing Justice,* 93–94. My criticisms of proportional retributivism are not novel. For helpful discussions of the view, see Hugo Bedau, "Concessions to Retribution in Punishment," in *Justice and Punishment,* edited by J. Cederblom and W. Blizek (Cambridge, Mass.: Ballinger, 1977), and M. Golding, *Philosophy of Law* (Englewood Cliffs, N.J.: Prentice Hall, 1975), 98–99.
4 See von Hirsch, *Past or Future Crimes,* ch. 8.
5 For more positive assessments of these theories, see Jeffrey Reiman, "Justice, Civilization, and the Death Penalty," *Philosophy and Public Affairs* 14 (1985): 115–48; and Michael Davis, "How to Make the Punishment Fit the Crime," *Ethics* 93 (1983).

QUESTIONS

1 To what extent, if at all, should the principle of "an eye for an eye" be incorporated into our system of criminal justice?
2 Can a retributive rationale for retention of the death penalty be defended against the objections presented by Nathanson?
3 Does Nathanson's appeal to "the symbolism of abolishing the death penalty" provide a compelling argument for abolition? Could a retentionist develop a compelling argument based on the symbolism of *retaining* the death penalty?

Deterrence and the Death Penalty

Louis P. Pojman

Pojman acknowledges that there is no conclusive statistical evidence supporting the claim that the death penalty is a uniquely effective deterrent. Nevertheless, he espouses the deterrence rationale for retention of the death penalty, and he does so on the basis of (1) the so-called best bet argument and (2) commonsense or anecdotal evidence. The best bet argument, predicated on our uncertainty concerning the deterrent effect of the death penalty (i.e., whether or not it is a uniquely effective deterrent), leads to the conclusion that we must retain the death penalty because running the risk of needlessly eradicating the lives of convicted murderers is morally better than running the risk of innocent people becoming future murder victims. In discussing the commonsense case for the death penalty as a uniquely effective deterrent, Pojman argues in particular that, since the death penalty is the most feared (humane) punishment, it follows that the death penalty is a superior deterrent.

The utilitarian argument for capital punishment is that it deters would-be offenders from committing first-degree murder. Thorstein Sellin's study of comparing states with and without capital punishment concludes that the death penalty is not a better deterrent of homicides than imprisonment.[1] On the other hand, Isaac Ehrlich's study, the most thorough study to date, takes into account the problems of complex sociological data in terms of race, heredity, regional lines, standards of housing, education, opportunities, cultural patterns, intelligence, and so forth, and concludes that the death penalty does deter. His simultaneous equation regression model suggests that over the period 1933–1969 "an additional execution per year . . . may have resulted on the average in 7 or 8 fewer murders."[2] It should be noted that Ehrlich began his study as an abolitionist, but his data forced him to change his position. However, Ehrlich's study has been criticized, largely for technical reasons, so that his conclusion that we have significant statistical evidence that the death penalty deters better than prison sentences is not conclusive.[3] The problems seem to be that there are simply too many variables to control in comparing demographic patterns (culture, heredity, poverty, education, religion, and general environmental factors) and that the death penalty isn't carried out frequently enough to have the effect that it might have under circumstances of greater use. . . . A consensus is wanting, so that at present we must conclude that we lack strong statistical evidence that capital punishment deters. But this should not be construed as evidence against the deterrence thesis. There is no such evidence for nondeterrence either. The statistics available are simply inconclusive either way.

Precisely on the basis of this inconclusivity with regard to the evidence, some abolitionists . . . argue that deterrence cannot be the moral basis for capital punishment. . . . I think [they are] wrong about this. There is some nonstatistical evidence based on common sense that gives credence to the hypothesis that the threat of the death penalty deters and that it does so better than long prison sentences. I will discuss the commonsense case below, but first I want to present an argument for the deterrent effect of capital punishment that is agnostic as to whether the death penalty deters better than lesser punishments.

Ernest van den Haag has set forth what he calls the Best Bet Argument.[4] He argues that even though we don't know for certain whether the death penalty deters or prevents other murders, we should bet that it does. Indeed, due to our ignorance, any social policy we take is a gamble. Not to choose capital punishment for first-degree murder is as much a bet that capital punishment doesn't deter as choosing the policy is a bet that it does. There is a significant difference in the betting, however, in that to bet against capital punishment is to bet against the innocent and for the murderer, while to bet for it is to bet against the murderer and for the innocent. . . .

Suppose that we choose a policy of capital punishment for capital crimes. In this case we are betting that the death of some murderers will be more than compensated for by the lives of some innocents not being murdered (either by these murderers or others who would have murdered). If we're right, we have saved the lives of the innocent. If we're wrong, unfortunately, we've sacrificed the lives of some murderers. But say we choose not to have a social policy of capital punishment. If capital punishment doesn't work as a deterrent, we've come out ahead, but if it does work, then we've missed an opportunity to save innocent lives. If we value the saving of innocent lives more highly than the loss of the guilty, then to bet on a policy of capital punishment turns out to be rational. . . .

. . . As van den Haag writes, "Though we have no proof of the positive deterrence of the penalty, we also have no proof of zero or negative effectiveness. I believe we have no right to risk additional future victims of murder for the sake of sparing convicted murderers; on the contrary, our moral obligation is to risk the possible ineffectiveness of executions."[5] . . .

. . . [I]f you had to choose between saving an innocent person and saving one who had just committed cold-blooded murder, which would you choose? We generally judge that conscientiously moral people are more worthy than viciously immoral ones, that the innocent are more worthy of aid than those who are guilty of squandering aid. Van den Haag's argument only formalizes these comparisons and applies them to the practice of capital punishment. Some humans are worth more than others, and some have forfeited their right not to be killed, whereas most people have not. Our practices should take this into account. . . .

[It is not true] that we have no evidence at all about the deterrent effect of capital punishment. . . . We have evidence, though not statistical proof, based on commonsense experience, which makes the case for deterrence even stronger than the Best Bet Argument. I now turn to the Argument from Anecdotal Evidence, a commonsense argument.

THE ARGUMENT FROM ANECDOTAL EVIDENCE

Abolitionists like Stephen Nathanson argue that because the statistical evidence in favor of the deterrent effect of capital punishment is indecisive, we have no basis for concluding that it is a better deterrent than long prison sentences.[6] If I understand these opponents, their argument presents us with an exclusive disjunct: Either we must have conclusive statistical evidence (i.e., a proof) for the deterrent effect of the death penalty, or we have no grounds for supposing that the death penalty deters. Many people accept this argument. Just this morning a colleague said to me, "There is no statistical evidence that the death penalty deters," as if to dismiss the argument from deterrence altogether. This is premature judgment, for the argument commits the fallacy of supposing that only two opposites are possible. There is a middle position that holds that while we cannot prove conclusively that the death penalty deters, the weight of evidence supports its deterrence. Furthermore, I think there are too many variables to hold constant for us to prove via statistics the deterrence hypothesis, and even if the requisite statistics were available, we could question whether they were cases of mere correlation versus causation. On the other hand, commonsense or anecdotal evidence may provide insight into the psychology of human motivation, providing evidence that fear of the death penalty deters some types of would-be criminals from committing murder. Granted, people are sometimes deceived about their motivation. But usually they are not deceived, and, as a rule, we should presume they know their motives until we have evidence to the contrary. The general commonsense argument goes like this:

1 What people (including potential criminals) fear more will have a greater deterrent effect on them.

2 People (including potential criminals) fear death more than they do any other humane punishment.

3 The death penalty is a humane punishment.

4 Therefore, people (including criminals) will be deterred more by the death penalty than by any other humane punishment.

Since the purpose of this argument is to show that the death penalty very likely deters more than long-term prison sentences, I am assuming it is *humane,* that is, acceptable to the moral sensitivities of the majority in our society. Torture might deter even more, but it is not considered humane. . . .

Common sense informs us that most people would prefer to remain out of jail, that the threat of public humiliation is enough to deter some people, that a sentence of twenty years will deter most people more than a sentence of two years, that a life sentence will deter most would-be criminals more than a sentence of twenty years. I think that we have commonsense evidence that the death penalty is a better deterrent than prison sentences. For one thing, as Richard Herrnstein and James Q. Wilson have argued in *Crime and Human Nature,* a great deal of crime is committed on a cost-benefit schema, wherein the criminal engages in some form of risk assessment as to his or her chances of getting caught and punished in some manner. If he or she estimates the punishment mild, the crime becomes inversely attractive, and vice versa. The fact that those who are condemned to death do everything in their power to get their sentences postponed or reduced to long-term prison sentences, in a way lifers do not, shows that they fear death more than life in prison.

The point is this: Imprisonment constitutes one evil, the loss of freedom, but the death penalty imposes a more severe loss, that of life itself. If you lock me up, I may work for a parole or pardon, I may learn to live stoically with diminished freedom, and I can plan for the day when my freedom has been restored. But if I believe that my crime may lead to death, or loss of freedom followed by death, then I have more to fear than mere imprisonment. I am faced with a great evil plus an even greater evil. I fear death more than imprisonment because it alone takes from me all future possibility. . . .

Some of the commonsense evidence is anecdotal as the following quotation shows. British member of Parliament Arthur Lewis explains how he was converted from an abolitionist to a supporter of the death penalty:

> One reason that has stuck in my mind, and which has proved [deterrence] to me beyond question, is that there was once a professional burglar in [my] constituency who consistently boasted of the fact that he had spent about one-third of his life in prison. . . . He said to me "I am a professional burglar. Before we go out on a job we plan it down to every detail. Before we go into the boozer to have a drink we say 'Don't forget, no shooters'—shooters being guns." He adds "We did our job and didn't have shooters because at that time there was capital punishment. Our wives, girlfriends and our

mums said, 'Whatever you do, do not carry a shooter because if you are caught you might be topped [executed].' If you do away with capital punishment they will all be carrying shooters."[7]

It is difficult to know how widespread this reasoning is. My own experience corroborates this testimony. Growing up in the infamous Cicero, Illinois, home of Al Capone and the Mafia, I had friends who went into crime, mainly burglary and larceny. It was common knowledge that one stopped short of killing in the act of robbery. A prison sentence could be dealt with—especially with a good lawyer—but being convicted of murder, which at that time included a reasonable chance of being electrocuted, was an altogether different matter. No doubt exists in my mind that the threat of the electric chair saved the lives of some of those who were robbed in my town. No doubt some crimes are committed in the heat of passion or by the temporally (or permanently) insane, but some are committed through a process of risk assessment. Burglars, kidnappers, traitors and vindictive people will sometimes be restrained by the threat of death. We simply don't know how much capital punishment deters, but this sort of commonsense, anecdotal evidence must be taken into account in assessing the institution of capital punishment.

John Stuart Mill admitted that capital punishment does not inspire terror in hardened criminals, but it may well make an impression on prospective murderers. "As for what is called the failure of the death punishment, who is able to judge of that? We partly know who those are whom it has not deterred; but who is there who knows whom it has deterred, or how many human beings it has saved who would have lived to be murderers if that awful association had not been thrown round the idea of murder from their earliest infancy."[8] Mill's points are well taken: (1) Not everyone will be deterred by the death penalty, but some will; (2) The potential criminal need not consciously calculate a cost-benefit analysis regarding his crime to be deterred by the threat. The idea of the threat may have become a subconscious datum "from their earliest infancy." The repeated announcement and regular exercise of capital punishment may have deep causal influence. . . .

It seems likely that the death penalty does not deter as much as it could due to its inconsistent and rare use. . . . If potential murderers perceived the death penalty as a highly probable outcome of murder, would they not be more reluctant to kill? . . .

If the Best Bet Argument is sound, or if the death penalty does deter would-be murderers, as common sense suggests, then we should support some uses of the death penalty. It should be used for those who commit first-degree murder, for whom no mitigating factors are present, and especially for those who murder police officers, prison guards, and political leaders. Many states rightly favor it for those who murder while committing another crime, e.g., burglary or rape. It should also be used for treason and terrorist bombings.

NOTES

1 Thorstein Sellin, *The Death Penalty* (1959) reprinted in *The Death Penalty in America,* ed. Hugo Bedau (Anchor Books, 1967).

2 Isaac Ehrlich, "The Deterrent Effect of Capital Punishment: A Question of Life and Death," *American Economic Review* 65 (June 1975): 397–417.

3 See for example David Baldus and James Cole, "A Comparison of the Work of Thorstein Sellin and Isaac Ehrlich on the Deterrent Effect of Capital Punishment," *Yale Law Journal* 85 (1975).

4 Ernest van den Haag, "On Deterrence and the Death Penalty," *Ethics* 78 (July 1968).

5 Ibid.

6 Stephen Nathanson, *An Eye for an Eye?* (Lanham, Md.: Rowman & Littlefield, 1987). Chap. 2.

7 British *Parliamentary Debates,* fifth series, vol. 23, issue 1243, House of Commons, 11 May 1982. Quoted in Tom Sorell, *Moral Theory and Capital Punishment* (Oxford: Blackwell, 1987), 36.

8 *Parliamentary Debates,* third series, April 21, 1868. Reprinted in Peter Singer, ed., *Applied Ethics* (Oxford University Press, 1986), 97–104.

QUESTIONS

1 Is commonsense or anecdotal evidence sufficient to establish the conclusion that the death penalty is a uniquely effective deterrent?

2 Is the life of a convicted murderer worth as much as the life of a potential murder victim?

3 Would you endorse either of the following claims? (a) We should abolish the death penalty unless retentionists can prove that it is a uniquely effective deterrent. (b) We should retain the death penalty unless abolitionists can prove that it is not a uniquely effective deterrent.

Common Sense, the Deterrent Effect of the Death Penalty, and the Best Bet Argument

Jeffrey Reiman

Reiman directly counters the commonsense argument for the death penalty as a uniquely effective deterrent, and he also takes issue with the best bet argument. He initially considers the commonsense argument in a version put forth by Ernest van den Haag and presents three counterarguments. In developing his third counterargument, Reiman relies on the claim that abolition of the death penalty would have a civilizing impact on society, and thus he speaks of "a deterrent effect from *not executing*." Subsequently, in formulating a reply to the views of Pojman in the previous selection, Reiman deepens his critique of the commonsense argument by focusing attention on what he calls "the continuously rising disinclination premise." (This part of Reiman's overall critique is best understood in conjunction with the first of his three initial counterarguments.) Reiman concludes by advancing two counterarguments against the best bet argument.

Reprinted with permission of Rowman & Littlefield Publishers from Louis P. Pojman and Jeffrey Reiman, *The Death Penalty: For and Against* (1998), pp. 102–107, 156–161.

Conceding that it has not been proven that the death penalty deters more murders than life imprisonment, Ernest van den Haag has argued that neither has it been proven that the death penalty does not deter more murders.[1] Thus, his argument goes, we must follow common sense, which teaches that the higher the cost of something, the fewer the people who will choose it. Therefore, at least some potential murderers who would not be deterred by life imprisonment will be deterred by the death penalty. Van den Haag continues:

> [O]ur experience shows that the greater the threatened penalty, the more it deters. . . .
>
> Life in prison is still life, however unpleasant. In contrast, the death penalty does not just threaten to make life unpleasant—it threatens to take life altogether. This difference is perceived by those affected. We find that when they have the choice between life in prison and execution, 99% of all prisoners under sentence of death prefer life in prison. . . .
>
> From this unquestioned fact a reasonable conclusion can be drawn in favor of the superior deterrent effect of the death penalty. Those who have the choice in practice . . . fear death more than they fear life in prison. . . . If they do, it follows that the threat of the death penalty, all other things equal, is likely to deter more than the threat of life in prison. One is most deterred by what one fears most. From which it follows that whatever statistics fail, or do not fail, to show, the death penalty is likely to be more deterrent than any other.[2]

Those of us who recognize how commonsensical it was, and still is, to believe that the sun moves around the earth will be less willing than van den Haag to follow common sense here, especially when it comes to doing something awful to our fellows. Moreover, there are good reasons for doubting common sense on this matter. Here are three.

1. From the fact that one penalty is more feared than another, it does not follow that the more feared penalty will deter more than the less feared, unless we know that the less feared penalty is not fearful enough to deter everyone who can be deterred—and this is just what we don't know with regard to the death penalty. This point is crucial because it shows that *the commonsense argument includes a premise that cannot be based on common sense,* namely, that the deterrence impact of a penalty rises without limit in proportion to the fearfulness of the penalty. All that common sense could possibly indicate is that deterrence impact increases with fearfulness of penalty *within a certain normally experienced range.* Since few of us ever face a choice between risking death and risking lifetime confinement, common sense has no resources for determining whether this difference in fearfulness is still within the range that increases deterrence. To figure that out, we will have to turn to social science—as a matter of common sense! And when we do, we find that most of the research we have on the comparative deterrent impact of execution versus life imprisonment suggests that there is no difference in deterrent impact between the death penalty and life imprisonment.

Since it seems to me that whoever would be deterred by a given likelihood of death would be deterred by an *equal* likelihood of life behind bars, I suspect that the commonsense argument only seems plausible because we evaluate it while unconsciously assuming that potential criminals will face larger likelihoods of death sentences than of life sentences. If the likelihoods were equal, it seems to me that where life imprisonment were improbable enough to make it too distant a possibility to worry much about, a similar low probability of death would have the same effect. After all, we are undeterred by small likelihoods of death every time we walk the streets. And if life imprisonment were sufficiently probable to pose a real deterrent threat, it would pose as much of a deterrent threat as death. And then it seems that any lengthy prison sentence—say, twenty years—dependably imposed and not softened by parole, would do the same.

2. In light of the fact that the number of privately owned guns in America is substantially larger than the number of households in America, as well as the fact that about twelve hundred suspected felons are killed or wounded by the police in the line of duty every year, it must be granted that anyone contemplating committing a crime already faces a substantial risk of ending up dead as a result. It's hard to see why anyone *who is not already deterred by this* would be deterred by the addition of the more distant risk of death after apprehension, conviction, and appeal.

3. Van den Haag has maintained that deterrence works not only by means of cost-benefit calculations made by potential criminals, but also by the lesson about the wrongfulness of murder that is slowly learned in a society that subjects murderers to the ultimate punishment.[3] If, however, I am correct in claiming that the refusal to execute even those who deserve it has a civilizing effect, then the refusal to execute also teaches a lesson about the wrongfulness of murder. My claim here is admittedly speculative, but no more so than van den Haag's to the contrary. And my view has the added virtue of accounting for the failure of research to show an increased deterrent effect from executions, *without having to deny the plausibility of van den Haag's commonsense argument that at least some additional potential murderers will be deterred by the prospect of the death penalty.* If there is a deterrent effect from *not executing,* then it is understandable that while executions will deter some murderers, this effect will be balanced out by the weakening of the deterrent effect of not executing, such that no net reduction in murders will result.[4] This, by the way, also disposes of van den Haag's argument that, in the absence of knowledge one way or the other on the deterrent effect of executions, we should execute murderers rather than risk the lives of innocent people whose murders might have been deterred if we had executed. If there is a deterrent effect of not executing, it follows that we risk innocent lives either way. And if this is so, it seems that the only reasonable course of action is to refrain from imposing what we know is a horrible fate.

I conclude then that we have no good reason to think that we need the death penalty to protect innocent people from murder. Life in prison (or, at least, a lengthy prison term without parole) dependably meted out, will do as well. . . .

REPLY TO LOUIS P. POJMAN

. . . Pojman, contending that the research has not proven that the death penalty does not deter more than life imprisonment, seeks to bolster his case by putting forth the so-called best bet argument, which he takes to be agnostic on the issue of whether the death penalty is a superior deterrent to imprisonment, and he follows this argument with the commonsense argument, which purports to prove that, whatever the research shows, the death penalty is a greater deterrent after all. Since I think that the best bet argument is not really agnostic, but in fact gets some of its force from the commonsense argument, I take up the commonsense argument first.

We have already seen the commonsense argument formulated by Ernest van den Haag. . . . Pojman follows suit. The argument starts from the premise that "what people (including potential criminals) fear more will have a greater deterrent effect on them," and it goes on to say that, since people fear death more than life in prison, they "will be deterred more by the death penalty" than by other available punishments, such as life in prison. I [contend] . . . that the first premise here is a nonstarter. As David Conway pointed out, the fact that one penalty is feared more than another does not imply that the more feared penalty deters more than the less feared, since the less feared penalty may already deter me as much as I can be deterred. Says Conway,

> given the choice, I would strongly prefer one thousand years in hell to eternity there. Nonetheless, if one thousand years in hell were the penalty for some action, it would be quite sufficient to deter me from performing that action. The additional years would do nothing to discourage me further. Similarly, the prospect of the death penalty, while worse, may not have any greater deterrent effect than does that of life imprisonment.[5]

Since this argument was made more than twenty years ago and still has not deterred van den Haag . . . and now Pojman from using the commonsense argument, I am convinced that more must be said to show just how devastating the implications of this point are for any version of the commonsense argument. Conway's argument shows that the commonsense argument contains a questionable premise, namely, the idea that *people's disinclination to act in some way rises continuously and without limit as the fearsomeness of the penalty for that act rises.* Without this premise, the commonsense argument fails. If people's disinclination doesn't keep rising but instead tops out at some point, it is no longer possible to infer from the greater fearfulness of the death penalty its greater deterrent impact since people's disinclination may have topped out at life imprisonment. What is really devastating about Conway's point is that the continuously rising disinclination premise is part of a technical theory, and no part of common sense. Those who put forth the commonsense argument are really putting forth a theory that isn't commonsensical at all, and they're calling it common sense!

What theory is this that underlies the idea that disinclination continuously correlates with fearfulness? It is some version of psychological hedonism of the sort that one finds in textbooks of neoclassical economic theory, in which people are thought to seek continuously to maximize their net satisfaction. What we have here, then, is not the behavior of commonsense folks. It's the behavior of idealized rational consumers! The giveaway is Pojman's claim that criminals do cost-benefit analyses before deciding to break the law. Beware of equivocation here. I don't doubt that would-be criminals consider costs and benefits of potential crimes in a rough manner. I will shortly suggest a "model" of how they do so. What is highly implausible, however, is that criminals do cost-benefit analyses in the technical sense of that term, such that every increment of cost and every increment of benefit are taken into account. This is what we have to think at least a significant number of criminals are doing in order to ignore the social science findings and insist, as Pojman (and van den Haag . . .) do, that an increase in penalty from life in prison to execution will figure in the motivation of potential murderers enough to deter additional murders. And that is simply implausible. . . .

. . . Rather than finely calibrating their reactions to increasingly negative outcomes, commonsense people seem to batch negative outcomes into qualitative groupings, such as "worth a great effort to avoid," "worth a substantial effort to avoid," and "worth only a minor effort to avoid." So being killed painfully or painlessly, being locked in prison for your whole life or for much of your life, being paralyzed, being blinded, and losing both arms or both legs are all, irrespective of their relative differences in awfulness, worth a great effort to avoid. Breaking a bone, losing a finger, getting a serious (but not permanently damaging) beating, and being injured seriously (but not gravely and permanently) in a car accident are worth a substantial effort to avoid. And getting a splinter, stubbing a toe, and falling in the street, as well as worse but very unlikely things, such as getting hit by lightning, killed in a train derailment, or contracting a rare and terrible disease, are worth only a minor effort to avoid.

I do not insist on the details of this description. I say only that it is something like what commonsensically rational people do in the face of statistically possible negative outcomes, and there's nothing irrational about it, unless one is already assuming a theory of rationality, such as that used in economics. Then, when you think of potential criminals, it's only commonsensical to suppose that they do the same, treating any serious criminal penalty as "worth a great effort to avoid." I contend that the so-called cost-benefit analyses that Pojman thinks some criminals engage in amount to no finer calculation than this. And this is not only closer to the actual way in which commonsense folks treat risks, it also fits perfectly with the majority of social science studies on the death penalty, which show that the difference between life in prison and death does not alter people's inclination or disinclination to commit murder—just as if would-be murderers had batched these two penalties under one rubric and acted accordingly. I conclude that the commonsense argument for the death penalty is an impostor. It is a theory of rational behavior and not even a very plausible one. The commonsense argument fails for lack of common sense. . . .

I turn now to the best bet argument. The best bet argument holds that, because execution *might* deter murderers, it is better to execute murderers than not to. Executing murderers may deter someone from killing an innocent person, and if not, all we have lost is one dead murderer. Not executing may have no impact on future criminals, but if there are any who would have been deterred by execution, then we have failed to stop the killing of an innocent person. Since it seems worse to fail to stop the killing of the innocent than to kill a murderer without a deterrent gain, our best bet is to execute murderers.

I put off dealing with the best bet argument until now because that argument looks very weak without the commonsense argument accompanying it. For unless there is some reason to expect the death penalty to be a superior deterrent to life in prison, the best bet argument calls for the merest toying with human beings, which seems offensive even when the human beings are murderers. It is one thing to kill murderers when there is reason to think it will protect innocents, but to kill them because of the bare possibility that this might happen seems like exactly the kind of disrespectful treatment of the murderer that Kant condemned. So, without either a showing from social science or from common sense that the death penalty is likely to save lives, I think the best bet argument fails.

Some people may resist this conclusion, holding that, since murderers are of less worth than innocent people . . . , the bare possibility that executing a murderer might save an innocent is enough to justify the death penalty as our best bet. There is, I think, a further argument against this approach that I think refutes it finally. Recall that [earlier] I argued that, by refraining from executing murderers, the state will contribute to the general repugnance of murder, and I speculated that *this will lead to fewer murders over time*. Moreover, there is a line of social science research defending the so-called brutalization hypothesis, which purports to show that murders increase in the period following executions and that these are real increases (not just changes in timing). If either or both of these claims are plausible, then the outcomes facing us in the best bet argument are dramatically changed. Now, in addition to no evidence that the death penalty deters more murders, there is the additional possibility that the death penalty increases the number of murders. Then, there is no reason to bet on executions over life imprisonment in the name of future innocent victims. Executions may protect them or jeopardize them. With that, the best bet argument evaporates.

NOTES

1 Ernest van den Haag and John P. Conrad, *The Death Penalty: A Debate* (New York: Plenum, 1983), 65.
2 Ibid., 68–69.
3 Ibid., 63.
4 A related claim has been made by those who defend the so-called brutalization hypothesis by presenting evidence to show that murders increase following an execution. See, for example, William J. Bowers and Glenn L. Pierce, "Deterrence or Brutalization: What Is the Effect of Executions?" *Crime and Delinquency* 26, no. 4 (October 1980): 453–84. Bowers and Pierce conclude that each execution gives rise to two additional homicides in the month following and that these are real additions, not just a change in timing of the homicides (481). My claim, it should be noted, is not identical to this, since, as I indicate in the text, what I call "the deterrent effect of not executing" is not something whose impact is to be seen immediately following executions, but an effect that occurs over the long haul; further, my claim is compatible with finding no net increase in murders due to executions. Nonetheless, should the brutalization hypothesis be borne out by further studies, it would certainly lend support to the notion that there is a deterrent effect of not executing.
5 David A. Conway, "Capital Punishment and Deterrence: Some Considerations in Dialogue Form," *Philosophy and Public Affairs* 3, no. 4 (Summer 1974), 433.

QUESTIONS

1 Can the commonsense argument for the death penalty as a uniquely effective deterrent be defended against the counterarguments advanced by Reiman?

2 Is it plausible to believe that abolition of the death penalty would produce "a deterrent effect from not executing"?

3 If we are unsure whether or not the death penalty is a uniquely effective deterrent, does our uncertainty favor retention, abolition, or neither?

Procedural Arguments Against the Death Penalty

David Dolinko

Dolinko identifies three procedural arguments employed by abolitionists against the death penalty: (1) the arbitrariness argument, (2) the discrimination argument, and (3) the mistake argument. In his critical examination of these three arguments, he sometimes incorporates a discussion of both retentionist counterarguments and abolitionist responses to these counterarguments. Dolinko's analysis ultimately suggests that the mistake argument is the most powerful procedural argument against the death penalty.

. . . Abolitionists . . . rely . . . on a number of *procedural* arguments—claims that one or another serious flaw infects the methods used to select those killers who will actually be executed. (The following discussion of procedural arguments is a condensed version of that in Dolinko, 1986.)

Procedural arguments can be dismissed by insisting that capital punishment systems need not exhibit the particular features of the American system. But speculation about hypothetical utopian systems does little to blunt the critique of what is, after all, almost the only functioning death penalty in a modern industrialized democracy. (Japan, where capital punishment is shrouded in remarkable secrecy, is believed to have executed about 35 people during the 1990s.)

One procedural argument is that capital punishment is inflicted "arbitrarily"—without any rational, principled distinction between the murderers who are executed and the far larger number who receive prison sentences. (In the United States in recent years, only some 6.25–12.5 percent of persons convicted of potentially capital murder have actually received death sentences; see figures in Bedau, 1997: 31–2.) The most explicit, detailed version of this argument contends that most of the crucial steps in a homicide prosecution that results in execution are taken "under no standards at all or under pseudo-standards without discoverable meaning" (Black, 1981: 29). No articulated standard, for example, controls a prosecutor's discretionary decision to bring capital charges in the first place or to reject a plea to a lesser offense. And the concept of "premeditation," frequently a prerequisite

Reprinted with permission of the publisher from *A Companion to Applied Ethics* (2003), edited by R. G. Frey and Christopher Heath Wellman, pp. 83–87. © 2003 by Blackwell Publishing Ltd.

for a capital murder conviction, is an example of a "pseudo-standard" in those (many) states where juries are told that "premeditation" can occur in a single instant and need occur no more than a moment before the killing.

Another procedural argument, which many people find more troubling, is that capital punishment is inflicted in a racially discriminatory manner. This claim is supported by many empirical studies which show that killers of whites are more likely to be sentenced to death than killers of blacks. A 1990 review of then-existing research by the US government's General Accounting Office reported that "In 82 percent of the studies, race of victim was found to influence the likelihood of being charged with capital murder or receiving the death penalty," a finding "remarkably consistent across data sets, states, data collection methods, and analytic techniques" (Bedau, 1997: 271). Controlling for a variety of legitimate, relevant non-racial variables reduced but did not eliminate the evidence of race-of-victim bias.

The most prominent retentionist academic, Ernest Van Den Haag, has dismissed both of these arguments by insisting that the justice of executing any individual killer depends wholly on whether execution is what that individual deserves, and is unaffected by whether others who deserve death are more leniently treated either "arbitrarily" or for racially biased reasons (Van Den Haag, 1982). That response is question-begging with regard to the arbitrariness argument, whose crucial claim is the lack of any rational method for determining which killers "deserve" death. Moreover, it assumes an idiosyncratic, narrow view of justice as having no *comparative* dimension. Yet justice has been equated with "treating like cases alike" as persistently as with "giving each his due"—indeed, both characterizations stem from the same passage in Aristotle. Besides, if we do take a wholly non-comparative view of justice, we are given no convincing reason to believe justice, so conceived, must always be preferred to equality—Van Den Haag's premise for inferring that undeserved leniency to some murderers cannot impugn the propriety of executing those who receive their "just deserts."

Whatever the weaknesses of Van Den Haag's position, however, the arbitrariness and discrimination arguments do invite serious objections. The empirical basis for the arbitrariness argument is questionable. Proponents tend to focus wholly on whether capital decision-makers are bound by *explicit* rules that effectively constrain their discretion. Yet decisions not subject to explicit rules may none the less be made in a consistent, rationally explicable manner—and standards vague and indeterminate in theory may in practice receive a narrow and principled interpretation. Indeed, some empirical studies of capital sentencing suggest that a small number of factors will predict the sentences in capital cases rather accurately, so that these sentences are much less "arbitrary" than abolitionists assume.

The empirical evidence of race-of-victim discrimination, while not wholly conclusive, is powerful, and certainly far stronger than the evidence of "arbitrariness." Yet this evidence is open to conflicting interpretations. For example, polls reveal more hostility to capital punishment among blacks than whites, which might translate into less community support for pressing capital charges in cases with black victims. Then, too, the great majority of murders are intra-racial—meaning black victims tend to die at the hands of black killers—so prosecutors trying to avoid an appearance of bias against black defendants might end up appearing to discount the lives of black victims.

Regardless of the plausibility of explaining away the race-of-victim effect in these or similar ways, the discrimination argument shares one big defect with the arbitrariness argument. Neither depends on any special feature of death as a punishment—each, if valid, indicts the criminal justice system regardless of what penalty is reserved for the very worst crimes. Suppose, for example, that the criminal justice system is as riddled with standardless discretion as proponents of the arbitrariness argument allege. Then *whatever* penalty is employed against those convicted of "the worst crimes" would be imposed in a manner too shockingly capricious and irrational to be morally legitimate. One killer might receive life without parole, another life *with* parole, a third a five-year sentence, while a fourth goes free altogether—all as the upshot of decisions made "under no standards at all or under pseudo-standards without discoverable meaning." Now assume that killers of whites are more likely to receive death sentences than killers of blacks because prejudiced prosecutors, judges, and juries value white lives more highly than black lives. Abolishing capital punishment would not affect those prejudices, so killers of whites would then receive the most severe *non*-capital punishment disproportionately often compared to killers of blacks. What both arguments suggest, then, is not that capital punishment should be abolished but that the mechanism for picking out "the worst criminals" and inflicting on them whatever is our most severe penalty needs thoroughgoing reform if it is to be morally acceptable.

Of course, death is not merely the most severe punishment in the contemporary repertoire, it is qualitatively different from even the lengthiest prison sentence in taking *everything* from the criminal and in doing so *irrevocably*. But the arbitrariness and discrimination arguments do not trade on those features of capital punishment. In particular, their force does not stem from a fear that we might discover we have executed someone either "arbitrarily" or for discriminatory reasons and be unable to revoke the punishment and make amends. They are *systemic* arguments—that no principled criteria distinguish *the class* of murderers who get executed; that killers of whites *as a class* are more harshly treated—not claims that in particular, identifiable cases we may discover arbitrariness or discrimination.

A third procedural argument, however, appeals squarely to the unique irrevocability of capital punishment. This is the claim that the unavoidable imperfections of all human fact-finding and decision procedures make mistakes in capital sentencing inevitable. Every now and then—perhaps extremely rarely, but *sometimes*—innocent people will be convicted of capital crimes, sentenced to death, and in at least some instances will actually end up being executed. (Talk of "innocent people" here is an oversimplification because there are other capital sentencing "mistakes," like finding a killing premeditated when it was actually impulsive, convicting of murder a defendant who actually killed in legitimate self-defense, or erroneously rejecting a valid insanity defense.) This argument does derive its force from the chilling prospect of learning that a person has been erroneously executed and being unable to call off the punishment or compensate the hideously mistreated innocent. It has been an increasingly influential argument with Americans in recent years in the wake of several widely reported instances of death row prisoners winning release after new evidence established their innocence. Most notably, the governor of Illinois ordered a moratorium on executions in that state in January 2000 after the exoneration of the thirteenth death-row prisoner found to have been wrongly convicted there since 1977.

Retentionists have two responses to the mistake argument. The first is that abolitionists grossly exaggerate the likelihood of executing innocent persons. Actually, retentionists assert, the multiple layers of review and due process protections built into the American capital-punishment system make it extraordinarily unlikely that a genuinely innocent person will ever be executed. When abolitionists note that more than ninety prisoners have been released from American death rows since 1973 when evidence of their wrongful convictions emerged, retentionists counter that this merely reinforces their claim that the system works to ferret out erroneous capital convictions before mistaken executions ever occur.

Second, retentionists argue that the risk of mistake is only one moral consideration relevant to whether execution is morally permissible, and can be outweighed or overridden by competing moral considerations (just as we regard the use of automobiles as morally legitimate despite knowing their use will cause the deaths of faultless individuals). In particular, it could be permissible to run the risk of someday executing an innocent person so long as capital punishment provides sufficiently large countervailing benefits either by way of increased deterrence— yielding a net *saving* of innocent lives—or by "doing justice," giving the worst killers their retributivist just deserts.

Abolitionists challenge both of these responses to the mistake argument. They insist that execution of the innocent is not so remote a possibility, claiming that at least twenty-four such miscarriages occurred in the 1900s (Radelet et al., 1992). The protections and reviews supposedly built into the system, they argue, are frequently more apparent than real, given the often abysmally poor legal representation of indigent capital defendants at trial and the formidable legal barriers to meaningful post-conviction review, especially review of the substantive correctness of the outcome as opposed to whether procedural errors were committed. Tellingly, actual instances of overturned capital convictions often arise from the almost fortuitous intervention of media figures, college students, and other actors wholly outside the formal criminal justice system.

As for the benefits of capital punishment outweighing the risk of mistake, recall first that there is little evidence of death's superior deterrent efficacy. And "doing justice" can provide a retributive "benefit" sufficient to justify risking execution of the innocent only if we agree both that some murderers deserve death as their punishment, and that it would therefore be *unjust* to give them a lesser penalty. . . .

REFERENCES

Bedau, H. A. (ed.) (1997) *The Death Penalty in America: Current Controversies.* New York and Oxford: Oxford University Press.

Black, C. (1981) *Capital Punishment: The Inevitability of Caprice and Mistake,* 2nd edn. New York: W. W. Norton.

Dolinko, D. (1986) How to criticize the death penalty. *Journal of Criminal Law and Criminology,* 77: 546–601.

Radelet, M. L., Bedau, H. A., and Putnam, C. E. (1992) *In Spite of Innocence: Erroneous Convictions in Capital Cases.* Boston: Northeastern University Press.

Van Den Haag, E. (1982) In defense of the death penalty: a practical and moral analysis. In H. A. Bedau (ed.), *The Death Penalty in America,* 3rd edn. Oxford: Oxford University Press.

QUESTIONS

1 If it is true that the race of the victim is a significant factor in the imposition of the death penalty, does it follow that the death penalty should be abolished?

2 Is the mistake argument in itself sufficient to make the case for abolition?

3 Are procedural arguments against the death penalty collectively sufficient to make the case for abolition?

SUGGESTED ADDITIONAL READINGS FOR CHAPTER 3

BAIRD, ROBERT M., and STUART E. ROSENBAUM, eds.: *Punishment and the Death Penalty: The Current Debate.* Amherst, N.Y.: Prometheus, 1995. Part One of this anthology provides a set of articles on the justification of punishment. Part Two provides a wide range of articles on the death penalty.

BEDAU, HUGO ADAM: "Capital Punishment." In Hugh LaFollette, ed., *The Oxford Handbook of Practical Ethics.* Oxford: Oxford University Press, 2003, pp. 705–733. Bedau, a prominent abolitionist, offers commentary on numerous retentionist and abolitionist arguments, concluding his discussion with a consideration of "the best argument for abolition."

BERNS, WALTER: *For Capital Punishment.* New York: Basic, 1979. In this book, which provides a wide-ranging discussion of issues relevant to the death penalty controversy, Berns insists that capital punishment can be defended effectively on retributive grounds.

BLACK, CHARLES L., JR.: *Capital Punishment: The Inevitability of Caprice and Mistake,* 2d ed. New York: Norton, 1981. Black argues for abolition on the grounds that it is virtually impossible to eliminate arbitrariness and mistake from the numerous decisions that lead to the imposition of the death penalty.

DAVIS, MICHAEL: "Death, Deterrence, and the Method of Common Sense." *Social Theory and Practice,* vol. 7, Summer 1981, pp. 146–177. Davis argues that common sense is sufficient to establish the claim that death is the most effective deterrent. For other reasons, however, he is unwilling to endorse retention of the death penalty.

NATHANSON, STEPHEN: *An Eye for an Eye? The Immorality of Punishing by Death,* 2d ed. Lanham, Md.: Rowman & Littlefield, 2001. Nathanson touches on all aspects of the death penalty controversy and constructs an overall case for abolition.

POJMAN, LOUIS P., and JEFFREY REIMAN: *The Death Penalty: For and Against.* Lanham, Md.: Rowman & Littlefield, 1998. Each author first contributes a long essay, Pojman arguing for retention of the death penalty and Reiman arguing for abolition. Then each author provides a shorter essay in reply to the views of the other.

REIMAN, JEFFREY H.: "Justice, Civilization, and the Death Penalty: Answering van den Haag." *Philosophy and Public Affairs,* vol. 14, Spring 1985, pp. 115–148. Reiman argues that "abolition of the death penalty is part of the civilizing mission of modern states." In his view, although it is just to execute murderers, it is not unjust to forgo execution and punish murderers with long-term imprisonment. Counterarguments by Ernest van den Haag can be found in the same issue—"Refuting Reiman and Nathanson" (pp. 165–176).

RYAN, GEORGE: "'I Must Act'." In Hugo Adam Bedau and Paul G. Cassell, eds., *Debating the Death Penalty*. New York: Oxford University Press, 2004, pp. 218–234. This is the text of the January 11, 2003, speech in which the Illinois governor, arguing that "the Illinois capital punishment system is broken," announces that he is commuting the death sentences of all Illinois death-row inmates.

SORELL, TOM: "Aggravated Murder and Capital Punishment." *Journal of Applied Philosophy*, vol. 10, 1993, pp. 201–213. Sorell appeals to both John Stuart Mill and Immanuel Kant in constructing a "hybrid argument," which "provides at least the basis for a sound defense of execution for the most serious murders."

VAN DEN HAAG, ERNEST, and JOHN P. CONRAD: *The Death Penalty: A Debate*. New York: Plenum, 1983. Van den Haag (a retentionist) and Conrad (an abolitionist) touch on all aspects of the death penalty controversy as they develop their respective cases and critically respond to each other's arguments.

CHAPTER 4

Sex and Marriage

This chapter begins with a discussion of sexual morality. The focus then shifts to the closely related topic of same-sex marriage, where the central issue is whether marriage—traditionally understood as restricted to opposite-sex couples—should be reconceptualized and made available to same-sex couples as well as opposite-sex couples.

Individuals are sometimes described as having "loose morals" when their *sexual* behavior is out of line with what is considered morally appropriate. But assessments of morally appropriate sexual behavior vary enormously. Conventionalists consider sex morally appropriate only within the bounds of (opposite-sex) marriage. Some conventionalists even insist that there are substantial moral restrictions on sex *within marriage;* they are committed to the principle that sexual activity may not take place in a way that cuts off the possibility of procreation. More liberal thinkers espouse various degrees of permissiveness. Some would allow a full and open promiscuity; some would not. Some would allow homosexual sex; some would not.

CONVENTIONAL SEXUAL MORALITY

According to conventional sexual morality, sex is morally legitimate only within the bounds of marriage; nonmarital sex is immoral.[1] The category of *nonmarital sex* is applicable to any sexual relation other than that between marriage partners. Thus, it includes sexual relations between single people as well as adulterous sexual relations. Both religious and nonreligious arguments are advanced in support of conventional sexual morality, but our concern here is with the nonreligious arguments that are advanced in its defense.

One common defense of the traditional convention that sex is permissible only within the bounds of marriage is based on considerations of *social utility.* It takes

---

[1]Conventional sexual morality as discussed here is to be understood as presupposing the traditional conception that marriage necessarily involves one man and one woman—that is, an opposite-sex couple. In theory, of course, one could maintain that nonmarital sex is immoral but refuse to rule out the possibility of same-sex marriage. The resulting view, while perhaps *conventional* in one sense, would be very unconventional in another.

the following form: A stable family life is absolutely essential for the proper raising of children and the consequent welfare of society as a whole. But the limitation
of sex to marriage is a necessary condition of forming and maintaining stable family units. The availability of sex within marriage will reinforce the loving relationship between husband and wife, the *exclusive* availability of sex within marriage
will lead most people to get married and to stay married, and the unavailability of
extramarital sex will keep the marriage strong. Therefore, the convention that sex
is permissible only within the bounds of marriage is solidly based on considerations
of social utility.

This argument is criticized in various ways. Sometimes it is argued that stable
family units are not really so essential. More commonly, it is argued that the availability of nonmarital sex does not really undercut family life. Whereas adultery
might very well undermine a marital relationship, it is argued, premarital sex can
prepare one for marriage. At any rate, it is pointed out, people continue to marry
even after they have had somewhat free access to sexual relations.

Another prominent defense of conventional sexual morality is intimately bound up
with *natural law theory,* an approach to ethics that is historically associated with the
medieval philosopher and theologian Thomas Aquinas (1225–1274). The fundamental principle of natural law theory may be expressed in rather rough form as follows:
Actions are morally appropriate insofar as they accord with our nature and end as
human beings and morally inappropriate insofar as they fail to accord with our nature
and end as human beings. With regard to sexual morality, Aquinas argues as follows:

> . . . [T]he emission of semen ought to be so ordered that it will result in both the pro-
> duction of the proper offspring and in the upbringing of this offspring.
>
> It is evident from this that every emission of semen, in such a way that generation can-
> not follow, is contrary to the good for man. And if this be done deliberately, it must be a
> sin. Now, I am speaking of a way from which, *in itself,* generation could not result; such
> would be any emission of semen apart from the natural union of male and female. For
> which reason, sins of this type are called *contrary to nature.* . . .
>
> Likewise, it must also be contrary to the good for man if the semen be emitted under con-
> ditions such as generation could result but the proper upbringing would be prevented. . . . .
>
> Now, it is abundantly evident that the female in the human species is not at all able to
> take care of the upbringing of offspring by herself, since the needs of human life demand
> many things which cannot be provided by one person alone. Therefore, it is appropriate
> to human nature that a man remain together with a woman after the generative act, and
> not leave her immediately to have such relations with another woman, as is the practice
> with fornicators. . . .
>
> Now we call this society *matrimony.* Therefore, matrimony is natural for man, and
> promiscuous performance of the sexual act, outside matrimony, is contrary to man's
> good. For this reason, it must be a sin.[2]

According to Aquinas, procreation is the natural purpose or end of sexual activity. Accordingly, sexual activity is morally legitimate only when it accords with this
fundamental aspect of human nature. Since sex is for the purpose of procreation,
and since the proper upbringing of children can occur only within the framework

---

[2]Thomas Aquinas, *On the Truth of the Catholic Faith,* Book Three, "Providence," Part II, trans.
Vernon J. Bourke (New York: Doubleday, 1956).

of marriage, nonmarital sex violates the natural law; it is thereby immoral. In this way, then, Aquinas constructs a defense of conventional sexual morality.

Notice, however, that Aquinas is also committed to substantial restrictions on marital sex itself. Since procreation is the natural purpose or end of sexual activity, he contends, any sexual act that cuts off the possibility of procreation is "contrary to nature." It follows that such practices as oral intercourse, anal intercourse, mutual masturbation, and the use of artificial birth control are illicit, even within marriage. Of course, Aquinas also condemns masturbation and homosexual intercourse as "contrary to nature."

One common criticism of Aquinas's point of view on sexual morality centers on his insistence that sexual activity must not frustrate its natural purpose—procreation. Granted, it is said, procreation is in a biological sense the *natural* purpose of sex. Still, the argument goes, it is not clear that sexual activity cannot legitimately serve other important human purposes. Why cannot sex legitimately function as a means for the expression of love? Why, for that matter, cannot sex legitimately function simply as a source of intense (recreational) pleasure?

In contemporary times, Aquinas's point of view on sexual morality is essentially incorporated in the formal teaching of the Roman Catholic church. In the 1968 papal encyclical *Humanae Vitae,* artificial birth control is once again identified as immoral, a violation of the natural law: "Each and every marriage act must remain open to the transmission of life."[3] In a subsequent Vatican document, entitled "Declaration on Some Questions of Sexual Ethics," the natural law framework of Aquinas is equally apparent.[4] "The deliberate use of the sexual faculties outside of normal conjugal relations essentially contradicts its finality." "Homosexual acts are disordered by their very nature." "Masturbation is an intrinsically and seriously disordered act."[5]

In one of this chapter's readings, Vincent C. Punzo provides a somewhat distinctive defense of conventional sexual morality. At the core of his argument is the idea of existential integrity. In Punzo's view, existential integrity is compromised whenever sexual intercourse is detached from the framework of commitment that is constitutive of marriage.[6]

THE LIBERAL VIEW

In vivid contrast to conventional sexual morality is an approach that will be referred to here as the *liberal* view of sexual morality. Liberals reject as unfounded the conventionalist claim that nonmarital sex is immoral. They also reject the related claim (made by some conventionalists) that sex is immoral if it cuts off the possibility of procreation. Nor are liberals willing to accept the claim (defended

[3]Pope Paul VI, *Humanae Vitae* (1968), section 11. This encyclical is widely reprinted. See, for example, Robert Baker and Frederick Elliston, eds., *Philosophy and Sex,* new rev. ed. (Buffalo, NY.: Prometheus, 1975), pp. 167–184.

[4]This document was issued by the Sacred Congregation for the Doctrine of the Faith and approved by Pope Paul VI. *The Pope Speaks,* vol. 21, no. 1 (1976), pp. 60–73.

[5]Ibid., pp. 67, 66, 67.

[6]Although Punzo's thinking clearly reflects the traditional presumption that marriage necessarily involves an opposite-sex couple, there is no apparent reason why a Punzo-like approach to the issue of sexual morality could not be combined with an endorsement of same-sex marriage.

by some nonconventionalists) that *sex without love* is immoral. Yet liberals insist that there are important moral restrictions on sexual activity. In the liberal view, sexual activity (like any other type of human activity) is morally objectionable to the extent that it is incompatible with a justified moral rule or principle. Accordingly, it is argued, the way to construct a defensible account of sexual morality is simply to work out the implications of relevant moral rules or principles in the area of sexual behavior.

In this vein, since it is widely acknowledged that the infliction of personal harm is morally objectionable, *some* sexual activity may be identified as immoral simply because it involves one person inflicting harm on another. For example, the seduction of a minor who does not even know "what it's all about" is morally objectionable on the grounds that the minor will almost inevitably be psychologically harmed. Rape, of course, is a moral outrage, in no small part because it typically involves the infliction of both physical and psychological harm. Its immorality, however, can also be established by reference to another widely acknowledged (when properly understood) moral principle—roughly, the principle that it is wrong for one person to "use" another person.

Since the domain of sexual interaction seems to offer ample opportunity for "using" another person, the concept of using is worthy of special attention in this context. In one of this chapter's selections, Thomas A. Mappes attempts to clarify what he calls the morally significant sense of "using another person." His ultimate aim is to determine the conditions under which someone would be guilty of *sexually* using another person, and the essence of his view is that the sexual using of another person takes place whenever there is a violation of the requirement of *voluntary informed consent* (to sexual interaction). Mappes especially emphasizes both *deception* and *coercion* as mechanisms for the sexual using of another person.

Is nonmarital sex immoral? Is sex that cuts off the possibility of procreation immoral? Is sex without love immoral? According to the liberal, *no* sexual activity is immoral unless a well-established moral rule or principle is transgressed. Does one's sexual activity involve the infliction of harm on another? Does it involve the using of another? Does it involve promise breaking, another commonly recognized ground of moral condemnation? If the answer to such questions is no, the liberal maintains, then the sexual activity in question is perfectly acceptable from a moral point of view.

According to the liberal, then, we must conclude that nonmarital sex is, in many cases, morally acceptable. Sexual partners may share some degree of mutual affection or love, or they may merely share a mutual desire to attain sexual satisfaction. The sexual interaction may be heterosexual or homosexual. Or there may be no *interaction* at all; the sexual activity may be masturbation. But what about the morality of adultery, an especially noteworthy type of nonmarital sex? As the marriage bond is usually understood, the liberal might respond, there is present in cases of adultery a distinctive ground of moral condemnation. To the extent that marriage involves a pledge of sexual exclusivity, as is typically the case, then adulterous behavior seems to involve a serious breaking of trust. However, the liberal would insist, if marriage partners have entered into a so-called open marriage, with no pledge of sexual exclusivity, then this special ground of moral condemnation evaporates.

If the liberal approach to sexual morality is correct, it is nevertheless important to recognize that a particular sexual involvement could be morally acceptable and yet unwise or imprudent—that is, not in a person's best long-term interests. For example, an individual might very well decide to steer clear of casual sex, not because it is immoral but because of a conviction (perhaps based on experience) that it is not compatible with personal happiness.

THE SEX WITH LOVE APPROACH

There is one additional point of view on sexual morality that is sufficiently common to warrant explicit recognition. One may, after all, find conventional sexual morality unwarranted and yet be inclined to stop short of granting moral approval to the promiscuity that is found morally acceptable on the liberal view. This intermediate point of view can be identified as the *sex with love* approach. Defenders of this approach typically insist that sex without love reduces a humanly significant activity to a merely mechanical performance, which in turn leads to the disintegration (fragmentation) of the human personality. They differ among themselves, however, as to whether the love necessary to warrant a sexual relationship must be an *exclusive* love or whether it may be a *nonexclusive* love. Those who argue that it must be exclusive nevertheless grant that *successive* sexual liaisons are not objectionable. Those who argue that the love may be nonexclusive necessarily presume that a person is capable of simultaneously loving several persons. On their view, even *simultaneous* love affairs are not objectionable. Whether exclusive or nonexclusive love is taken to be the relevant standard, proponents of the sex with love approach usually argue that their view allows for sexual freedom in a way that avoids the alleged dehumanizing effects of mere promiscuity. Where sex and love remain united, it is argued, there is no danger of dehumanization and psychological disintegration. The liberal might respond: If psychological disintegration is a justifiable fear, which can be doubted, such a consideration shows not that sex without love is immoral but only that it is imprudent.

HOMOSEXUALITY AND MORALITY

Is homosexual sex immoral? While the advocate of conventional sexual morality vigorously condemns it, the liberal typically maintains that homosexual sex is no more immoral in itself than heterosexual sex. There are, however, many people who reject conventional sexual morality but nevertheless remain morally opposed to homosexual sex. Are such people correct in thinking that homosexual sex is morally problematic in a way that heterosexual sex is not? A homosexual, in the most generic sense, is a person (male or female) whose dominant sexual preference is for a person of the same sex. In common parlance, however, the term *homosexual* is often taken to designate a male, whereas the term *lesbian* is used to designate a female. It is apparently true that male homosexual sex occasions a higher degree of societal indignation than female homosexual sex, but it is implausible to believe that there is any morally relevant difference between the two.

There is no lack of invective against the practice of homosexuality. For example, the following claims are often asserted: (1) Homosexual sex is repulsive and highly offensive. (2) Homosexuality as a way of life is totally given over to promiscuity and is not conducive to enduring human relationships. (3) Homosexuals make the streets unsafe for our children. (4) Homosexual sex is a perversion, a sin against nature. (5) The practice of homosexuality threatens to undermine our social fabric.

It is important to assess the extent to which such claims support the view that homosexual sex is morally objectionable. With regard to (1), it may, in fact, be true that many people find homosexual acts repulsive and offensive, but it is also true that many people find eating liver repulsive and offensive, and no one thinks that this fact in itself establishes the conclusion that eating liver is morally objectionable. With regard to (2), it may be true that many homosexuals are promiscuous, but it can be argued that society's attitude toward homosexuality is responsible for making homosexual relationships extremely difficult to sustain. With regard to (3), it may be true that *some* homosexuals prey upon children (as do some heterosexuals), and surely this is morally reprehensible, but still we find ourselves left with the more typical case in which homosexual sex takes place between consenting adults. John Corvino, in one of the readings in this chapter, incorporates many of these points into an overall defense of the practice of homosexuality.

Although the "unnaturalness argument" (4) is sometimes employed against such "perversions" as masturbation and (heterosexual) oral-genital sex practices, it is especially prominent as an argument against homosexual sex. Corvino critically analyzes the claim that homosexual sex is immoral because it is unnatural. He concludes that homosexual sex is not *unnatural* in any morally relevant sense. Corvino also takes issue with argument (5). He denies that the practice of homosexuality constitutes a threat to society. It is not always clear what proponents of (5) have in mind in asserting that the practice of homosexuality represents a threat to our social fabric. In what way is the alleged societal harm supposed to arise? Proponents of (5) often claim that societal acceptance of homosexuals and homosexual sex would—in some way—have a detrimental impact on the institutions of marriage and family. In response, it can be argued that societal acceptance of homosexuals and homosexual sex would, on balance, have beneficial rather than detrimental social consequences.

SEXUAL MORALITY AND FEMINIST CRITIQUE

Feminists typically renounce conventional sexual morality. A central feminist goal is to eradicate structures of oppression,[7] and feminists ordinarily consider conventional sexual morality an oppressive value system. For one thing, according to many feminists, this traditional standard embodies a norm of "compulsory heterosexuality" and thus is oppressive to lesbians and gay males. Further, many feminists would say, conventional sexual morality is systematically linked with an inegalitarian conception of marriage and traditional sex roles and thus is deeply implicated

---

[7]See the article by Iris M. Young in Chapter 8 for an extensive discussion of the concept of oppression.

in the patriarchal oppression of women. A related point is embodied in the feminist complaint against the double standard often associated with conventional sexual morality. The concern here is that conventional sexual morality has been put forth as a standard for both men and women, but only women have really been expected to follow it.

What attitude might feminists take toward the liberal view of sexual morality? Two prominent feminist philosophers write:

> According to liberals . . . , consenting adults should be free to express and explore their sexuality in whatever way they choose within the context of a mature and private relationship. Some feminists share the liberal view, but others argue that liberals are blind to the unequal economic and social realities that form the context in which this so-called free sexual expression occurs. In addition, feminists disagree strongly over whether certain sexual practices are so inherently degrading to women that they should not be tolerated under any conditions.[8]

The moral legitimacy of sadomasochistic sexual practices is an example of an issue that occasions strong disagreement among feminists. Some feminists argue that sadomasochistic sexual practices are morally objectionable even if they are genuinely consensual. The implications of eroticizing dominance/subordination relationships are a principal concern in this regard.

Even feminists who are somewhat sympathetic to the emphasis placed by the liberal tradition on the moral legitimacy of consensual sexual interactions often insist that this emphasis must be corrected or qualified in certain ways. For example, many feminists would challenge the idea that sexual relationships can be genuinely consensual if there are significant social inequalities between the two sexual partners. In particular, it is said, the relative lack of power that typically characterizes women relative to men in a patriarchal society creates a significant obstacle to women giving genuine consent to heterosexual interactions.

SAME-SEX MARRIAGE

As traditionally understood and defined, marriage is restricted to two people—one woman and one man, an opposite-sex couple. Should this traditional understanding and definition be reconfigured and opened up in order to make room for same-sex marriage, or is a society justified in denying same-sex couples access to marriage?

One productive way of approaching this question is by reference to the purpose or purposes that underlie the institution of marriage. Marriage is widely believed to be a social institution of great, even fundamental importance. But very different accounts may be offered about the underlying sense of marriage as a social institution. One well-known approach, deeply rooted in both religion and secular tradition, sees procreation and the raising of children as the dominant, if not sole, purpose of marriage. A contrasting approach is unwilling to connect the social sense of marriage so exclusively with procreation and the raising of children. On this view, although procreation and the raising of children may be one important

---

[8]Alison M. Jaggar and Paula S. Rothenberg, *Feminist Frameworks,* 3d ed. (New York: McGraw-Hill, 1993), p. 286.

purpose effectively served by marriage, the underlying sense of marriage as a social institution cannot be articulated fully without reference to other notable purposes effectively served by marriage.

In this chapter, both Maggie Gallagher and Jonathan Rauch directly confront the question: What is marriage for? Both are concerned with capturing the social sense underlying the institution of marriage, but they offer very different answers. Gallagher locates the underlying social sense of marriage in the fact that this institution functions to provide children with "loving, committed mothers and fathers." Accordingly, she claims, societal endorsement of same-sex marriage is incompatible with "the central meaning of marriage." Rauch is willing to acknowledge that raising children is one of the important social purposes served by the institution of marriage, but he argues that two other purposes effectively served by marriage— domesticating males and providing reliable caregivers—play a significant role in an overall account of the "social meaning" of marriage. Because these latter two purposes can also be served by same-sex marriage, he argues, society has a compelling interest in the acceptance of same-sex marriage. One might also point out that the public recognition and support provided by marriage for the loving, committed relationship of two people is of great benefit to the couple themselves, although Rauch himself apparently thinks that this consideration has no direct relevance in an overall account of the social meaning of marriage.

Some opposition to same-sex marriage is based solely on a moral condemnation of homosexual sex, but, that argument aside, the most prominent argument against same-sex marriage asserts that societal acceptance of same-sex marriage would have detrimental social consequences. In various versions of this argument—all closely related—it is said that acceptance of same-sex marriage would have a negative impact on opposite-sex marriage or undermine the very institution of marriage, that it would be destructive of family structure and family values, and that it would be harmful to children. The most prominent argument in support of same-sex marriage is based on considerations of equality: To deny same-sex couples the benefits of marriage that are available to opposite-sex couples is a denial of equality— in essence, a form of discrimination against homosexuals. Proponents of same-sex marriage also frequently press the analogy between a ban on same-sex marriage and a ban on interracial marriage. Further, proponents of same-sex marriage often ask: If procreation is supposed to be so centrally connected with marriage, why are heterosexual couples allowed to marry even if they are incapable of having children or unwilling to do so? Opponents of same-sex marriage often offer counters to these various arguments, as Gallagher does in this chapter. One other especially prominent argument put forth by opponents of same-sex marriage raises the following challenge: If we once redefine marriage to allow for same-sex marriage, on what basis could we resist another redefinition of marriage to allow for polygamy or other forms of "plural" marriage?

In 1993, a ruling of the Hawaii Supreme Court seemed to indicate that Hawaii's ban on same-sex marriage would ultimately be found in violation of the equal protection provision of the Hawaii Constitution, but before that state's highest court formally reached such a conclusion, Hawaii voters adopted, in 1998, a constitutional amendment banning same-sex marriage. Meanwhile, responsive to the prospect of legalized same-sex marriage in Hawaii, the United States Congress enacted the 1996 Defense of Marriage Act. This act specifies that no state is required to recognize the same-sex marriages of another state and also declares that, for purposes of federal law, "the word 'marriage' means only a legal union between one man and one woman as husband and wife." In a subsequent development, Vermont became the first American state to make "civil unions" available to same-sex couples. This result was achieved through legislative action that emerged in response to a 1999 Vermont Supreme Court ruling. The basic idea of civil unions is that same-sex couples can be granted access to the many legal benefits of marriage without being granted access to "marriage" itself. Only in 2004 did an American state formally legalize same-sex marriage; that state was Massachusetts.

At issue in the case of *Goodridge v. Department of Public Health* (2003) was whether the Massachusetts ban on same-sex marriage was consistent with the Massachusetts Constitution. In a four-to-three decision, the Massachusetts Supreme Judicial Court ruled that the ban was unconstitutional because it violated both the *equal protection* and *due process* provisions of the Massachusetts Constitution. As a result of this ruling, same-sex marriage became legally available in Massachusetts in March 2004. A substantial excerpt from the majority opinion of Chief Justice Margaret H. Marshall is reprinted in this chapter, as is the dissenting opinion of Justice Martha B. Sosman.

At present, same-sex marriage has been legalized in the Netherlands, Belgium, Spain, and Canada. In the United States, Connecticut has followed the lead of Vermont in recognizing civil unions for same-sex couples, but no other state has joined Massachusetts in recognizing same-sex marriages. Further, at least seventeen states to date have amended their constitutions to incorporate bans on same-sex marriage, and debate is expected to continue about the proposed Federal Marriage Amendment, calculated to ban same-sex marriage throughout the country.

Thomas A. Mappes

Morality and Human Sexuality

Vincent C. Punzo

Punzo begins by arguing that there is a morally significant difference between sexual intercourse and other types of human activity. Then, emphasizing the historical aspect of the human self, he constructs an argument against premarital sexual intercourse. Marriage, in his view, is constituted by the mutual and total commitment of a man and a woman. Apart from this framework of commitment, he argues, sexual unions are "morally deficient because they lack existential integrity." Although Punzo is essentially a proponent of conventional sexual morality, he understands marriage in such a way that he does not condemn "preceremonial" intercourse. He insists that the commitment constitutive of marriage can exist prior to and apart from any legal or ceremonial formalities.

If one sees man's moral task as being simply that of not harming anyone, that is if one sees this task in purely negative terms, he will certainly not accept the argument to be presented in the following section. However, if one accepts the notion of the morality of aspiration, if one accepts the view that man's moral task involves the positive attempt to live up to what is best in man, to give reality to what he sees to be the perfection of himself as a human subject, the argument may be acceptable.

SEXUALITY AND THE HUMAN SUBJECT

[Prior discussion] has left us with the question as to whether sexual intercourse is a type of activity that is similar to choosing a dinner from a menu. This question is of utmost significance in that one's view of the morality of premarital intercourse seems to depend on the significance that one gives to the sexual encounter in human life. Those such as [John] Wilson and [Eustace] Chesser who see nothing immoral about the premarital character of sexual intercourse seem to see sexual intercourse as being no different from myriad of other purely aesthetic matters. This point is seen in Chesser's questioning of the reason for demanding permanence in the relationship of sexual partners when we do not see such permanence as being important to other human relationships.[1] It is also seen in his asking why we raise a moral issue about premarital coition when two people may engage in it, with the resulting social and psychological consequences being no different than if they had gone to a movie.[2]

Wilson most explicitly makes a case for the view that sexual intercourse does not differ significantly from other human activities. He holds that people think that there is a logical difference between the question "Will you engage in sexual intercourse with me?" and the question, "Will you play tennis with me?" only because they are influenced by the acquisitive character of contemporary society.[3] Granted that the two questions may be identical from the purely formal perspective of logic, the ethician must move beyond this perspective to a consideration of their content. Men and women find themselves involved in many different relationships: for example, as buyer-seller, employer-employee, teacher-student, lawyer-client, and partners or competitors in certain games such as tennis or bridge. Is there any morally significant difference between these relationships and sexual intercourse? We cannot examine all the possible relationships into which a man and woman can enter, but we will consider the employer-employee relationship in order to get some perspective on the distinctive character of the sexual relationship.

A man pays a woman to act as his secretary. What rights does he have over her in such a situation? The woman agrees to work a certain number of hours during the day taking dictation, typing letters, filing reports, arranging appointments and flight schedules, and greeting clients and competitors. In short, we can say that the man has rights to certain of the woman's services or skills. The use of the word "services" may lead some to conclude that this relationship is not significantly different from the relationship between a prostitute and her client in that the prostitute also offers her "services."

It is true that we sometimes speak euphemistically of a prostitute offering her services to a man for a sum of money, but if we are serious about our quest for the difference between the sexual encounter and other types of human relationships, it is necessary to drop euphemisms and face the issue directly. The man and woman who engage in sexual intercourse are giving their bodies, the most intimate physical expression of themselves, over to the other. Unlike the man who plays tennis with a woman, the man who has sexual relations with her has literally entered her. A man and woman engaging in sexual intercourse have united themselves as intimately and as totally as is physically possible for two human beings. Their union is not simply a union of organs, but is as intimate and as total a physical union of two selves as is possible of achievement. Granted the character of this union, it seems strange to imply that there is no need for a man and a woman to give any more thought to the question of whether they should engage in sexual intercourse than to the question of whether they should play tennis.

In opposition to Wilson, I think that it is the acquisitive character of our society that has blinded us to the distinction between the two activities. Wilson's and Chesser's positions seem to imply that exactly the same moral considerations ought to apply to a situation in which a housewife is bartering with a butcher for a few pounds of pork chops and the situation in which two human beings are deciding whether sexual intercourse ought to be an ingredient of their relationship. So long as the butcher does not put his thumb on the scale in the weighing process, so long as he is truthful in stating that the meat is actually pork, so long as the woman pays the proper amount with the proper currency, the trade is perfectly moral. Reflecting on sexual intercourse from the same sort of economic perspective, one can say that so long as the sexual partners are truthful in reporting their freedom from contagious venereal diseases and so long as they are truthful in reporting that they are interested in the activity for the mere pleasure of it or to try out their sexual techniques, there is nothing immoral about such activity. That in the one case pork chops are being exchanged for money whereas in the other the decision concerns the most complete and intimate merging of one's self with another makes no difference to the moral evaluation of the respective cases.

It is not surprising that such a reductionistic outlook should pervade our thinking on sexual matters, since in our society sexuality is used to sell everything from shave cream to underarm deodorants, to soap, to mouthwash, to cigarettes, and to automobiles. Sexuality has come to play so large a role in our commercial lives that it is not surprising that our sexuality should itself come to be treated as a commodity governed by the same moral rules that govern any other economic transaction.

Once sexuality is taken out of this commercial framework, once the character of the sexual encounter is faced directly and squarely, we will come to see that Doctor Mary Calderone has brought out the type of questions that ought to be asked by those contemplating the introduction of sexual intercourse into their relationships: "How many times, and how casually, are you willing to invest a portion of your total self, and to be the custodian of a like investment from the other person, without the sureness of knowing that these investments are being made for keeps?"[4] These questions come out of the recognition that the sexual encounter is a definitive experience, one in which the physical intimacy and merging involves also a merging of the non-physical dimensions of the partners. With these questions, man moves beyond the negative concern with avoiding his or another's physical and psychological harm to the question of what he is making of himself and what he is contributing to the existential formation of his partner as a human subject.

If we are to make a start toward responding to Calderone's questions we must cease talking about human selfhood in abstraction. The human self is an historical as well as a physical being. He is a being who is capable of making at least a portion of his past an object of his consciousness and thus is able to make this past play a conscious role in his present and in his looking toward the future. He is also a being who looks to the future, who faces tomorrow with plans, ideals, hopes, and fears. The very being of a human self involves his past and his movement toward the future. Moreover, the human self is not completely shut off in his own past and future. Men and women are capable of consciously and purposively uniting themselves in a common career and venture. They can commit themselves to sharing the future with another, sharing it in all its aspects—in its fortunes and misfortunes, in its times of happiness and times of tragedy. Within the lives of those who have so committed themselves to each other, sexual intercourse is a way of asserting and confirming the fullness and totality of their mutual commitment.

Unlike those who have made such a commitment and who come together in the sexual act in the fullness of their selfhood, those who engage in premarital sexual unions and who have made no such commitment act as though they can amputate their bodily existence and the most intimate physical expression of their selfhood from their existence as historical beings. Granting that there may be honesty on the verbal level in that two people engaging in premarital intercourse openly state that they are interested only in the pleasure of the activity, the fact remains that such unions are morally deficient because they lack existential integrity in that there is a total merging and union on a physical level, on the one hand, and a conscious decision not to unite any other dimension of themselves, on the other hand. Their sexual union thus involves a "depersonalization" of their bodily existence, an attempt to cut off the most intimate physical expression of their respective selves from their very selfhood. The mutual agreement of premarital sex partners is an agreement to merge with the other not as a self, but as a body which one takes unto oneself, which one possesses in a most intimate and total fashion for one's own pleasure or designs, allowing the other to treat oneself in the same way. It may be true that no physical or psychological harm may result from such unions, but such partners have failed to existentially incorporate human sexuality, which is at the very least the most intimate physical expression of the human self, into the character of this selfhood.

In so far as premarital sexual unions separate the intimate and total physical union that is sexual intercourse from any commitment to the self in his historicity, human sexuality, and consequently the human body, have been fashioned into external things or objects to be handed over totally to someone else, whenever one feels that he can get possession of another's body, which he can use for his own purposes.[5] The human body has thus been treated no differently from the pork chops spoken of previously or from any other object or commodity, which human beings exchange and haggle over in their day-to-day transactions. One hesitates to use the word that might be used to capture the moral value that has been sacrificed in premarital unions because in our day the word has taken on a completely negative meaning at best, and, at worst, it has become a word used by "sophisticates" to mock or deride certain attitudes toward human sexuality. However, because the word "chastity" has been thus abused is no reason to leave it in the hands of those who have misrepresented the human value to which it gives expression.

The chaste person has often been described as one intent on denying his sexuality. The value of chastity as conceived in this section is in direct opposition to this description. It is the unchaste person who is separating himself from his sexuality, who is willing to exchange human bodies as one would exchange money for tickets to a baseball game—honestly and with no commitment of self to self. Against this alienation of one's sexuality from one's self, an alienation that makes one's sexuality an object, which is to be given to another in exchange for his objectified sexuality, chastity affirms the integrity of the self in his bodily and historical existence. The sexuality of man is seen as an integral part of his subjectivity. Hence, the chaste man rejects depersonalized sexual relations as a reduction of man in his most intimate physical being to the status of an object or pure instrument for another. He asserts that man is a subject and end in himself, not in some trans-temporal, nonphysical world, but in the historical-physical world in which he carries on his moral task and where he finds his fellow man. He will not freely make of himself in his bodily existence a thing to be handed over to another's possession, nor will he ask that another treat his own body in this way. The total physical intimacy of sexual intercourse will be an expression of total union with the other self on all levels of their beings. Seen from this perspective, chastity is one aspect of man's attempt to attain existential integrity, to accept his body as a dimension of his total personality.

In concluding this section, it should be noted that I have tried to make a case against the morality of premarital sexual intercourse even in those cases in which the partners are completely honest with each other. There is reason to question whether the complete honesty, to which those who see nothing immoral in such unions refer, is as a matter of fact actually found very often among premarital sex partners. We may well have been dealing with textbook cases which present these unions in their best light. One may be pardoned for wondering whether sexual intercourse often occurs under the following conditions: "Hello, my name is Josiah. I am interested in having a sexual experience with you. I can assure you that I am good at it and that I have no communicable disease. If it sounds good to you and if you have taken the proper contraceptive precautions, we might have a go at it. Of course, I want to make it clear to you that I am interested only in the sexual experience and that I have no intention of making any long-range commitment to you."

If those, who defend the morality of premarital sexual unions so long as they are honestly entered into, think that I have misrepresented what they mean by honesty, then they must specify what they mean by an honest premarital union. . . .

MARRIAGE AS A TOTAL HUMAN COMMITMENT

The preceding argument against the morality of premarital sexual unions was not based on the view that the moral character of marriage rests on a legal certificate or on a legal or religious ceremony. The argument was not directed against "preceremonial" intercourse, but against premarital intercourse. Morally speaking, a man and woman are married when they make the mutual and total commitment to share the problems and prospects of their historical existence in the world. . . .

. . . A total commitment to another means a commitment to him in his historical existence. Such a commitment is not simply a matter of words or of feelings, however strong. It involves a full existential sharing on the part of two beings of the burdens, opportunities, and challenges of their historical existence.

Granted the importance that the character of their commitment to each other plays in determining the moral quality of a couple's sexual encounter, it is clear that there may be nothing immoral in the behavior of couples who engage in sexual intercourse before participating in the marriage ceremony. For example, it is foolish to say that two people who are totally committed to each other and who have made all the arrangements to live this commitment are immoral if they engage in sexual intercourse the night before the marriage ceremony. Admittedly this position can be abused by those who have made a purely verbal commitment, a commitment, which will be carried out in some vague and ill-defined future. At some time or other, they will unite their two lives totally by setting up house together and by actually undertaking the task of meeting the economic, social, legal, medical responsibilities that are involved in living this commitment. Apart from the reference to a vague and amorphous future time when they will share the full responsibility for each other, their commitment presently realizes itself in going to dances, sharing a box of popcorn at Saturday night movies, and sharing their bodies whenever they can do so without taking too great a risk of having the girl become pregnant.

Having acknowledged that the position advanced in this section can be abused by those who would use the word "commitment" to rationalize what is an interest only in the body of the other person, it must be pointed out that neither the ethician nor any other human being can tell two people whether they actually have made the commitment that is marriage or are mistaking a "warm glow" for such a commitment. There comes a time when this issue falls out of the area of moral philosophy and into the area of practical wisdom. . . .

The characterization of marriage as a total commitment between two human beings may lead some to conclude that the marriage ceremony is a wholly superfluous affair. It must be admitted that people may be morally married without having engaged in a marriage ceremony. However, to conclude from this point that the ceremony is totally meaningless is to lose sight of the social character of human beings. The couple contemplating marriage do not exist in a vacuum, although there may be times when they think they do. Their existences reach out beyond their union to include other human beings. By making their commitment a matter of public record, by solemnly expressing it before the law and in the presence of their respective families and friends and, if they are religious people, in the presence of God and one of his ministers, they sink the roots of their commitment more deeply and extensively in the world in which they live, thus taking steps to provide for the future growth of their commitment to each other. The public expression of this commitment makes it more fully and more explicitly a part of a couple's lives and of the world in which they live. . . .

NOTES

1 Eustace Chesser, *Unmarried Love* (New York: Pocket Books, 1965), p. 29.
2 *Ibid.,* pp. 35–36, see also p. 66.
3 John Wilson, *Logic and Sexual Morality* (Baltimore, Md.: Penguin Books, 1965). See footnote 1, p. 67.
4 Mary Steichen Calderone, "The Case for Chastity," *Sex in America,* ed. by Henry Anatole Grunwald (New York: Bantam Books, 1964), p. 147.
5 The psychoanalyst Rollo May makes an excellent point in calling attention to the tendency in contemporary society to exploit the human body as if it were only a machine. Rollo May, "The New Puritanism," *Sex in America,* pp. 161–164.

QUESTIONS

1 Could the idea of existential integrity be developed in such a way as to provide a justification for the sex with love approach instead of conventional sexual morality?
2 Punzo says that no one is capable of telling "two people whether they actually have made the commitment that is marriage or are mistaking a 'warm glow' for such a commitment." What factors should a couple consider in attempting to resolve this question?

Sexual Morality and the Concept of Using Another Person

Thomas A. Mappes

Advocating a liberal approach to sexual morality, Mappes attempts to determine the conditions under which someone would be guilty of *sexually* using another person. On his view, the morally significant sense of "using another person" is best understood in reference to the notion of voluntary informed consent. Accordingly, his central thesis is that one person (A) is guilty of sexually using another person (B) "if and only if A intentionally acts in a way that violates the requirement that B's sexual interaction with A be based on B's voluntary informed consent."

Mappes emphasizes the importance of deception and coercion as mechanisms for the sexual using of another person, but he also insists that such using can result from "taking advantage of someone's desperate situation."

The central tenet of *conventional* sexual morality is that nonmarital sex is immoral. A somewhat less restrictive sexual ethic holds that *sex without love* is immoral. If neither of these positions is philosophically defensible, and I would contend that neither is, it does not follow that there are no substantive moral restrictions on human sexual interaction. *Any* human interaction, including sexual interaction, may be judged morally objectionable to the extent that it transgresses a justified moral rule or principle. The way to construct a detailed account of sexual morality, it would seem, is simply to work out the implications of relevant moral rules or principles in the area of human sexual interaction.

As one important step in the direction of such an account, I will attempt to work out the implications of an especially relevant moral principle, the principle that it is wrong for one person to use another person. However ambiguous the expression "using another person" may seem to be, there is a determinate and clearly specifiable sense according to which using another person is morally objectionable. Once this morally significant sense of "using another person" is identified and explicated, the concept of using another person can play an important role in the articulation of a defensible account of sexual morality.

I   THE MORALLY SIGNIFICANT SENSE OF "USING ANOTHER PERSON"

Historically, the concept of using another person is associated with the ethical system of Immanuel Kant. According to a fundamental Kantian principle, it is morally wrong for A to use B *merely as a means* (to achieve A's ends). Kant's principle does not rule out A using B as a means, only A using B *merely* as a means, that is, in a way incompatible with respect for B as a person. In the ordinary course of life, it is surely unavoidable (and morally unproblematic) that each of us in numerous ways uses others as a means to achieve our various ends. A college teacher uses students as a means to achieve his or her livelihood. A college student uses instructors as a means of gaining knowledge and skills. Such human interactions, presumably based on the voluntary participation of the respective parties, are quite compatible with the idea of respect for persons. But respect for persons entails that each of us recognize the rightful authority of other persons (as rational beings) to conduct their individual lives as they see fit. We may legitimately recruit others to participate in the satisfaction of our personal ends, but they are used merely as a means whenever we undermine the voluntary or informed character of their consent to interact with us in some desired way. A coerces B at knife point to hand over $200. A uses B merely as a means. If A had requested of B a gift of $200, leaving B free to determine whether or not to make the gift, A would have proceeded in a manner compatible with respect for B as a person. C deceptively rolls back the odometer of a car and thereby manipulates D's decision to buy the car. C uses D merely as a means.

On the basis of these considerations, I would suggest that the morally significant sense of "using another person" is best understood by reference to the notion of *voluntary informed consent*. More specifically, A immorally uses B if and only if A intentionally acts in a way that violates the requirement that B's involvement with A's ends be based on B's voluntary informed consent. If this account is correct, using another person (in the morally significant sense) can arise in at least two important ways: via *coercion,* which is antithetical to voluntary consent, and via *deception,* which undermines the informed character of voluntary consent.

The notion of voluntary informed consent is very prominent in the literature of biomedical ethics and is systematically related to the much emphasized notion of (patient) autonomy. We find in the famous words of Supreme Court Justice Cardozo a ringing affirmation of patient autonomy. "Every human being of adult years and sound mind has a right to determine what shall be done with his own body." Because respect for individual autonomy is an essential part of respect for persons, if medical professionals (and biomedical researchers) are to interact with their patients (and research subjects) in an acceptable way, they must respect individual autonomy. That is, they must respect the self-determination of the patient/subject, the individual's right to determine what shall be done with his or her body. This means that they must not act in a way that violates the requirement of voluntary informed consent. Medical procedures must not be performed without the consent of competent patients; research on human subjects must not be carried out without the consent of the subjects involved. Moreover, consent must be voluntary; coercion undermines individual autonomy. Consent must also be informed; lying or withholding relevant information undercuts rational decision making and thereby undermines individual autonomy.

To further illuminate the concept of using that has been proposed, I will consider in greater detail the matter of research involving human subjects. In the sphere of researcher-subject interaction, just as in the sphere of human sexual interaction, there is ample opportunity for immorally using another person. If a researcher is engaged in a study that involves human subjects, we may presume that the "end" of the researcher is the successful completion of the study. (The researcher may desire this particular end for any number of reasons: the speculative understanding it will provide, the technology it will make possible, the eventual benefit of humankind, increased status in the scientific community, a raise in pay, etc.) The work, let us presume, strictly requires the use (employment) of human research subjects. The researcher, however, immorally uses other people only if he or she intentionally acts in a way that violates the requirement that the participation of research subjects be based on their voluntary informed consent.

Let us assume that in a particular case participation as a research subject involves some rather significant risks. Accordingly, the researcher finds that potential subjects are reluctant to volunteer. At this point, if an unscrupulous researcher is willing to resort to the immoral using of other people (to achieve his or her own ends), two manifest options are available—deception and coercion. By way of deception, the researcher might choose to lie about the risks involved. For example, potential subjects could be explicitly told that there are no significant risks associated with research participation. On the other hand, the researcher could simply withhold a full disclosure of risks. Whether pumped full of false information or simply deprived of relevant information, the potential subject is intentionally deceived in such a way as to be led to a decision that furthers the researcher's ends. In manipulating the decision making process of the potential subject in this way, the researcher is guilty of immorally using another person.

To explain how an unscrupulous researcher might immorally use another person via coercion, it is helpful to distinguish two basic forms of coercion.[1] "Occurrent" coercion involves the use of physical force. "Dispositional" coercion involves the threat of harm. If I am forcibly thrown out of my office by an intruder, I am the victim of occurrent coercion. If, on the other hand, I leave my office because an intruder has threatened to shoot me if I do not leave, I am the victim of dispositional coercion. The victim of occurrent coercion literally has no choice in what happens. The victim of dispositional coercion, in contrast, does intentionally choose a certain course of action. However, one's choice, in the face of the threat of harm, is less than fully voluntary.

It is perhaps unlikely that even an unscrupulous researcher would resort to any very explicit measure of coercion. Deception, it seems, is less risky. Still, it is well known that Nazi medical experimenters ruthlessly employed coercion. By way of occurrent coercion, the Nazis literally forced great numbers of concentration camp victims to participate in experiments that entailed their own death or dismemberment. And if some concentration camp victims "volunteered" to participate in Nazi research to avoid even more unspeakable horrors, clearly we must consider them victims of dispositional coercion. The Nazi researchers, employing coercion, immorally used other human beings with a vengeance.

II DECEPTION AND SEXUAL MORALITY

To this point, I have been concerned to identify and explicate the morally significant sense of "using another person." On the view proposed, A immorally uses B if and only if A intentionally acts in a way that violates the requirement that B's involvement with A's ends be based on B's voluntary informed consent. I will now apply this account to the area of human sexual interaction and explore its implications. For economy of expression in what follows, "using" (and its cognates) is to be understood as referring only to the morally significant sense.

If we presume a state of affairs in which A desires some form of sexual interaction with B, we can say that this desired form of sexual interaction with B is A's end. Thus A sexually *uses* B if and only if A intentionally acts in a way that violates the requirement that B's sexual interaction with A be based on B's voluntary informed consent. It seems clear then that A may sexually use B in at least two distinctive ways, (1) via coercion and (2) via deception. However, before proceeding to discuss deception and then the more problematic case of coercion, one important point must be made. In emphasizing the centrality of coercion and deception as mechanisms for the sexual using of another person, I have in mind sexual interaction with a fully competent adult partner. We should also want to say, I think, that sexual interaction with a child inescapably involves the sexual using of another person. Even if a child "consents" to sexual interaction, he or she is, strictly speaking, incapable of *informed* consent. It's a matter of being *incompetent* to give consent.

Similarly, to the extent that a mentally retarded person is rightly considered incompetent, sexual interaction with such a person amounts to the sexual using of that person, unless someone empowered to give "proxy consent" has done so. (In certain circumstances, sexual involvement might be in the best interests of a mentally retarded person.) We can also visualize the case of an otherwise fully competent adult temporarily disordered by drugs or alcohol. To the extent that such a person is rightly regarded as temporarily incompetent, winning his or her "consent" to sexual interaction could culminate in the sexual using of that person.

There are a host of clear cases in which one person sexually uses another precisely because the former employs deception in a way that undermines the informed character of the latter's consent to sexual interaction. Consider this example. One person, A, has decided, as a matter of personal prudence based on past experience, not to become sexually involved outside the confines of a loving relationship. Another person, B, strongly desires a sexual relationship with A but does not love A. B, aware of A's unwillingness to engage in sex without love, professes love for A, thereby hoping to win A's consent to a sexual relationship. B's ploy is successful; A consents. When the smoke clears and A becomes aware of B's deception, it would be both appropriate and natural for A to complain, "I've been used."

In the same vein, here are some other examples. (1) Mr. A is aware that Ms. B will consent to sexual involvement only on the understanding that in time the two will be married. Mr. A has no intention of marrying Ms. B but says that he will. (2) Ms. C has herpes and is well aware that Mr. D will never consent to sex if he knows of her condition. When asked by Mr. D, Ms. C denies that she has herpes. (3) Mr. E knows that Ms. F will not consent to sexual intercourse in the absence of responsible birth control measures. Mr. E tells Ms. F that he has had a vasectomy, which is not the case. (4) Ms. G knows that Mr. H would not consent to sexual involvement with a married woman. Ms. G is married but tells Mr. H that she is single. (5) Ms. I is well aware that Ms. J is interested in a stable lesbian relationship and will not consent to become sexually involved with someone who is bisexual. Ms. I tells Ms. J that she is exclusively homosexual, whereas the truth is that she is bisexual.

If one person's consent to sex is predicated on false beliefs that have been intentionally and deceptively inculcated by one's sexual partner in an effort to win the former's consent, the resulting sexual interaction involves one person sexually using another. In each of the above cases, one person explicitly *lies* to another. False information is intentionally conveyed to win consent to sexual interaction, and the end result is the sexual using of another person.

As noted earlier, however, lying is not the only form of deception. Under certain circumstances, the simple withholding of information can be considered a form of deception. Accordingly, it is possible to sexually use another person not only by (deceptively) lying about relevant facts but also by (deceptively) not disclosing relevant facts. If A has good reason to believe that B would refuse to consent to sexual interaction should B become aware of certain factual information, and if A withholds disclosure of this information in order to enhance the possibility of gaining B's consent, then, if B does consent, A sexually uses B via deception. One example will suffice. Suppose that Mr. A meets Ms. B in a singles bar. Mr. A realizes immediately that Ms. B is the sister of Ms. C, a woman that Mr. A has been sexually involved with for a long time. Mr. A, knowing that it is very unlikely that Ms. B will consent to sexual interaction if she becomes aware of Mr. A's involvement with her sister, decides not to disclose this information. If Ms. B eventually consents to sexual interaction, since her consent is the product of Mr. A's deception, it is rightly thought that she has been sexually used by him.

III   COERCION AND SEXUAL MORALITY

We have considered the case of deception. The present task is to consider the more difficult case of coercion. Whereas deception functions to undermine the *informed* character of voluntary consent (to sexual interaction), coercion either obliterates consent entirely (the case of occurrent coercion) or undermines the voluntariness of consent (the case of dispositional coercion).

Forcible rape is the most conspicuous, and most brutal, way of sexually using another person via coercion.[2] Forcible rape may involve either occurrent coercion or dispositional coercion. A man who rapes a woman by the employment of sheer physical force, by simply overpowering her, employs occurrent coercion. There is literally no sexual *interaction* in such a case; only the rapist performs an action. In no sense does the woman consent to or participate in sexual activity. She has no choice in what takes place, or rather, physical force results in her choice being simply beside the point. The employment of occurrent coercion for the purpose of rape "objectifies" the victim in the strongest sense of that term. She is treated like a physical object. One does not interact with physical objects; one acts upon them. In a perfectly ordinary (not the morally significant) sense of the term, we "use" physical objects. But when the victim of rape is treated as if she were a physical object, there we have one of the most vivid examples of the immoral using of another person.

Frequently, forcible rape involves not occurrent coercion (or not *only* occurrent coercion) but dispositional coercion.[3] In dispositional coercion, the relevant factor is not physical force but the threat of harm. The rapist threatens his victim with immediate and serious bodily harm. For example, a man threatens to kill or beat a woman if she resists his sexual demands. She "consents," that is, she submits to his demands. He may demand only passive participation (simply not struggling against him) or he may demand some measure of active participation. Rape that employs dispositional coercion is surely just as wrong as rape that employs occurrent coercion, but there is a notable difference in the mechanism by which the rapist uses his victim in the two cases. With occurrent coercion, the victim's consent is entirely bypassed. With dispositional coercion, the victim's consent is not bypassed. It is coerced. Dispositional coercion undermines the *voluntariness* of consent. The rapist, by employing the threat of immediate and serious bodily harm, may succeed in bending the victim's will. He may gain the victim's "consent." But he uses another person precisely because consent is coerced.

The relevance of occurrent coercion is limited to the case of forcible rape. Dispositional coercion, a notion that also plays an indispensable role in an overall account of forcible rape, now becomes our central concern. Although the threat of immediate and serious bodily harm stands out as the most brutal way of coercing consent to sexual interaction, we must not neglect the employment of other kinds of threats to this same end. There are numerous ways in which one person can effectively harm, and thus effectively threaten, another. Accordingly, for example, consent to sexual interaction might be coerced by threatening to damage someone's reputation. If a person consents to sexual interaction to avoid a threatened harm, then that person has been sexually used (via dispositional coercion). In the face of a threat, of course, it remains possible that a person will refuse to comply with another's sexual demands. It is probably best to describe this sort of situation as a case not of coercion, which entails the *successful* use of threats to gain compliance, but of *attempted* coercion. Of course, the moral fault of an individual emerges with the *attempt* to coerce. A person who attempts murder is morally blameworthy even if the attempt fails. The same is true for someone who fails in an effort to coerce consent to sexual interaction.

Consider now each of the following cases:

Case 1   Mr. Supervisor makes a series of increasingly less subtle sexual overtures to Ms. Employee. These advances are consistently and firmly rejected by Ms. Employee. Eventually, Mr. Supervisor makes it clear that the granting of "sexual favors" is a condition of her continued employment.

Case 2   Ms. Debtor borrowed a substantial sum of money from Mr. Creditor, on the understanding that she would pay it back within one year. In the meantime, Ms. Debtor has become sexually attracted to Mr. Creditor, but he does not share her interest. At the end of the one-year period, Mr. Creditor asks Ms. Debtor to return the money. She says she will be happy to return the money so long as he consents to sexual interaction with her.

Case 3   Mr. Theatergoer has two tickets to the most talked-about play of the season. He is introduced to a woman whom he finds sexually attractive and who shares his interest in the theater. In the course of their conversation, she expresses disappointment that the play everyone is talking about is sold out; she would love to see it. At this point, Mr. Theatergoer suggests that she be his guest at the theater. "Oh, by the way," he says, "I always expect sex from my dates."

Case 4   Ms. Jetsetter is planning a trip to Europe. She has been trying for some time to develop a sexual relationship with a man who has shown little interest in her. She knows, however, that he has always wanted to go to Europe and that it is only lack of money that has deterred him. Ms. Jetsetter proposes that he come along as her traveling companion, all expenses paid, on the express understanding that sex is part of the arrangement.

Cases 1 and 2 involve attempts to sexually use another person whereas cases 3 and 4 do not. To see why this is so, it is essential to introduce a distinction between two kinds of proposals, viz., the distinction between *threats* and *offers*.[4] The logical form of a threat differs from the logical form of an offer in the following way. Threat: "If you *do not* do what I am proposing you do, I will bring about an *undesirable consequence* for you." Offer: "If you *do* what I am proposing you do, I will bring about a *desirable consequence* for you." The person who makes a threat attempts to gain compliance by attaching an undesirable consequence to the alternative of noncompliance. This person attempts to *coerce* consent. The person who makes an offer attempts to gain compliance by attaching a desirable consequence to the alternative of compliance. This person attempts not to coerce but to *induce* consent.

Since threats are morally problematic in a way that offers are not, it is not uncommon for threats to be advanced in the language of offers. Threats are represented as if they were offers. An armed assailant might say, "I'm going to make you an *offer*. If you give me your money, I will allow you to go on living." Though this proposal on the surface has the logical form of an offer, it is in reality a threat. The underlying sense of the proposal is this: "If you do not give me your money, I will kill you." If, in a given case, it is initially unclear whether a certain proposal is to count as a threat or an offer, ask the following question. Does the proposal in question have the effect of making a person *worse off upon noncompliance*? The recipient of an offer, upon noncompliance, *is not worse off* than he or she was before the offer. In contrast, the recipient of a threat, upon noncompliance, *is worse off* than he or she was before the threat. Since the "offer" of our armed assailant has the effect, upon noncompliance, of rendering its recipient worse off (relative to the preproposal situation of the recipient), the recipient is faced with a threat, not an offer.

The most obvious way for a coercer to attach an undesirable consequence to the path of noncompliance is by threatening to render the victim of coercion materially worse off than he or she has heretofore been. Thus a person is threatened with loss of life, bodily injury, damage to property, damage to reputation, etc. It is important to realize, however, that a person can also be effectively coerced by being threatened with the withholding of something (in some cases, what we would call a "benefit") to which the person is entitled. Suppose that A is mired in quicksand and is slowly but surely approaching death. When B happens along, A cries out to B for assistance. All B need do is throw A a rope. B is quite willing to accommodate A, "provided you pay me $100,000 over the next ten years." Is B making A an offer? Hardly! B, we must presume, stands under a moral obligation to come to the aid of a person in serious distress, at least when such assistance entails no significant risk, sacrifice of time, etc. A is entitled to B's assistance. Thus, in reality, B attaches an undesirable consequence to A's noncompliance with the proposal that A pay B $100,000. A is undoubtedly better off that B has happened along, but A is not rendered better off *by B's proposal*. Before B's proposal, A legitimately expected assistance from B, "no strings attached." In attaching a very unwelcome string, B's proposal effectively renders A worse off. What B proposes, then, is not an offer of assistance. Rather, B threatens A with the withholding of something (assistance) that A is entitled to have from B.

Since threats have the effect of rendering a person worse off upon noncompliance, it is ordinarily the case that a person does not welcome (indeed, despises) them. Offers, on the other hand, are ordinarily welcome to a person. Since an offer provides no penalty for noncompliance with a proposal but only an inducement for compliance, there is *in principle* only potential advantage in being confronted with an offer. In real life, of course, there are numerous reasons why a person may be less than enthusiastic about being presented with an offer. Enduring the presentation of trivial offers does not warrant the necessary time and energy expenditures. Offers can be both annoying and offensive; certainly this is true of some sexual offers. A person might also be unsettled by an offer that confronts him or her with a difficult decision. All this, however, is compatible with the fact that an offer is fundamentally welcome to a rational person in the sense that the *content* of an offer necessarily widens the field of opportunity and thus provides, in principle, only potential advantage.

With the distinction between threats and offers clearly in view, it now becomes clear why cases 1 and 2 do indeed involve attempts to sexually use another person whereas cases 3 and 4 do not. Cases 1 and 2 embody threats, whereas cases 3 and 4 embody offers. In case 1, Mr. Supervisor proposes sexual interaction with Ms. Employee and, in an effort to gain compliance, threatens her with the loss of her job. Mr. Supervisor thereby attaches an undesirable consequence to one of Ms. Employee's alternatives, the path of noncompliance. Typical of the threat situation, Mr. Supervisor's proposal has the effect of rendering Ms. Employee worse off upon noncompliance. Mr. Supervisor is attempting via (dispositional) coercion to sexually use Ms. Employee. The situation in case 2 is similar. Ms. Debtor, as *she* might be inclined to say, "offers" to pay Mr. Creditor the money she owes him *if* he consents to sexual interaction with her. In reality, Ms. Debtor is threatening Mr. Creditor, attempting to coerce his consent to sexual interaction, attempting to sexually use him. Though Mr. Creditor is not now in possession of the money Ms. Debtor owes him, he is *entitled* to receive it from her at this time. She threatens to deprive him of something to which he is entitled. Clearly, her proposal has the effect of rendering him worse off upon noncompliance. Before her proposal, he had the legitimate expectation, "no strings attached," of receiving the money in question.

Cases 3 and 4 embody offers; neither involves an attempt to sexually use another person. Mr. Theatergoer simply provides an inducement for the woman he has just met to accept his proposal of sexual interaction. He offers her the opportunity to see the play that everyone is talking about. In attaching a desirable consequence to the alternative of compliance, Mr. Theatergoer in no way threatens or attempts to coerce his potential companion. Typical of the offer situation, his proposal does not have the effect of rendering her worse off upon noncompliance. She now has a new opportunity; if she chooses to forgo this opportunity, she is no worse off. The situation in case 4 is similar. Ms. Jetsetter provides an inducement for a man that she is interested in to accept her proposal of sexual involvement. She offers him the opportunity to see Europe, without expense, as her traveling companion. Before Ms. Jetsetter's proposal, he had no prospect of a European trip. If he chooses to reject her proposal, he is no worse off than he has heretofore been. Ms. Jetsetter's proposal embodies an offer, not a threat. She cannot be accused of attempting to sexually use her potential traveling companion.

Consider now two further cases, 5 and 6, each of which develops in the following way. Professor Highstatus, a man of high academic accomplishment, is sexually attracted to a student in one of his classes. He is very anxious to secure her consent to sexual interaction. Ms. Student, confused and unsettled by his sexual advances, has begun to practice "avoidance behavior." To the extent that it is possible, she goes out of her way to avoid him.

Case 5   Professor Highstatus tells Ms. Student that, though her work is such as to entitle her to a grade of B in the class, she will be assigned a D unless she consents to sexual interaction.

Case 6 Professor Highstatus tells Ms. Student that, though her work is such as to entitle her to a grade of B, she will be assigned an A if she consents to sexual interaction.

It is clear that case 5 involves an attempt to sexually use another person. Case 6, however, at least at face value, does not. In case 5, Professor Highstatus *threatens* to deprive Ms. Student of the grade she deserves. In case 6, he *offers* to assign her a grade that is higher than she deserves. In case 5, Ms. Student would be worse off upon noncompliance with Professor Highstatus's proposal. In case 6, she would not be worse off upon noncompliance with his proposal. In saying that case 6 does not involve an attempt to sexually use another person, it is not being asserted that Professor Highstatus is acting in a morally legitimate fashion. In offering a student a higher grade than she deserves, he is guilty of abusing his institutional authority. He is under an obligation to assign the grades that students earn, as defined by the relevant course standards. In case 6, Professor Highstatus is undoubtedly acting in a morally reprehensible way, but in contrast to case 5, where it is fair to say that he both abuses his institutional authority *and* attempts to sexually use another person, we can plausibly say that in case 6 his moral failure is limited to abuse of his institutional authority.

There remains, however, a suspicion that case 6 might after all embody an attempt to sexually use another person. There is no question that the literal content of what Professor Highstatus conveys to Ms. Student has the logical form of an offer and not a threat. Still, is it not the case that Ms. Student may very well feel threatened? Professor Highstatus, in an effort to secure consent to sexual interaction, has announced that he will assign Ms. Student a higher grade than she deserves. Can she really turn him down without substantial risk? Is he not likely to retaliate? If she spurns him, will he not lower her grade or otherwise make it harder for her to succeed in her academic program? He does, after all, have power over her. Will he use it to her detriment? Surely he is not above abusing his institutional authority to achieve his ends; this much is abundantly clear from his willingness to assign a grade higher than a student deserves.

Is Professor Highstatus naive to the threat that Ms. Student may find implicit in the situation? Perhaps. In such a case, if Ms. Student reluctantly consents to sexual interaction, we may be inclined to say that he has *unwittingly* used her. More likely, Professor Highstatus is well aware of the way in which Ms. Student will perceive his proposal. He knows that threats need not be verbally expressed. Indeed, it may even be the case that he consciously exploits his underground reputation. "Everyone knows what happens to the women who reject Professor Highstatus's little offers." To the extent, then, that Professor Highstatus intends to convey a threat in case 6, he is attempting via coercion to sexually use another person.

Many researchers "have pointed out the fact that the possibility of sanctions for noncooperation is implicit in all sexual advances across authority lines, as between teacher and student."[5] I do not think that this consideration should lead us to the conclusion that a person with an academic appointment is obliged in all circumstances to refrain from attempting to initiate sexual involvement with one of his or her students. Still, since even "good faith" sexual advances may be ambiguous in the eyes of a student, it is an interesting question what precautions an instructor must take to avoid unwittingly coercing a student to consent to sexual interaction.

Much of what has been said about the professor/student relationship in an academic setting can be applied as well to the supervisor/subordinate relationship in an employment setting. A manager who functions within an organizational structure is required to evaluate fairly his or her subordinates according to relevant corporate or institutional standards. An unscrupulous manager, willing to abuse his or her institutional authority in an effort to win the consent of a subordinate to sexual interaction, can advance threats and/or offers related to the managerial task of employee evaluation. An employee whose job performance is entirely satisfactory can be threatened with an unsatisfactory performance rating, perhaps leading to termination. An employee whose job performance is excellent can be threatened with an unfair evaluation, designed to bar the employee from recognition, merit pay, consideration for promotion, etc. Such threats, when made in an effort to coerce employee consent to sexual interaction, clearly embody the attempt to sexually use another person. On the other hand, the manager who (abusing his or her institutional authority) offers to provide an employee with an inflated evaluation as an inducement for consent to sexual interaction does not, at face value, attempt to sexually use another person. Of course, all of the qualifications introduced in the discussion of case 6 above are applicable here as well.

IV THE IDEA OF A COERCIVE OFFER

In section III, I have sketched an overall account of sexually using another person *via coercion*. In this section, I will consider the need for modifications or extensions of the suggested account. As before, certain case studies will serve as points of departure.

Case 7 Ms. Starlet, a glamorous, wealthy, and highly successful model, wants nothing more than to become a movie superstar. Mr. Moviemogul, a famous producer, is very taken with Ms. Starlet's beauty. He invites her to come to his office for a screen test. After the screen test, Mr. Moviemogul tells Ms. Starlet that he is prepared to make her a star, on the condition that she agree to sexual involvement with him. Ms. Starlet finds Mr. Moviemogul personally repugnant; she is not at all sexually attracted to him. With great reluctance, she agrees to his proposal.

Has Mr. Moviemogul sexually used Ms. Starlet? No. He has made her an offer that she has accepted, however reluctantly. The situation would be quite different if it were plausible to believe that she was, before acceptance of his proposal, *entitled* to his efforts to make her a star. Then we could read case 7 as amounting to his threatening to deprive her of something to which she was entitled. But what conceivable grounds could be found for the claim that Mr. Moviemogul, before Ms. Starlet's acceptance of his proposal, is under an obligation to make her a star? He does not threaten her; he makes her an offer. Even if there are other good grounds for morally condemning his action, it is a mistake to think that he is guilty of coercing consent.

But some would assert that Mr. Moviemogul's offer, on the grounds that it confronts Ms. Starlet with an overwhelming inducement, is simply an example of a *coercive offer*. The more general claim at issue is that offers are coercive precisely inasmuch as they are extremely enticing or seductive. Though there is an important reality associated with the notion of a coercive offer, a reality that must shortly be confronted, we ought not embrace the view that an offer is coercive merely because it is extremely enticing or seductive. Virginia Held is a leading proponent of the view under attack here. She writes:

> A person unable to spurn an offer may act as unwillingly as a person unable to resist a threat. Consider the distinction between rape and seduction. In one case constraint and threat are operative, in the other inducement and offer. If the degree of inducement is set high enough in the case of seduction, there may seem to be little difference in the extent of coercion involved. In both cases, persons may act against their own wills.[6]

Certainly a rape victim who acquiesces at knife point is forced to act *against her will*. Does Ms. Starlet, however, act against her will? We have said that she consents "with great reluctance" to sexual involvement, but she does not act against her will. She *wants* very much to be a movie star. I might want very much to be thin. She regrets having to become sexually involved with Mr. Moviemogul as a means of achieving what she wants. I might regret very much having to go on a diet to lose weight. If we say that Ms. Starlet acts against her will in case 7, then we must say that I am acting against my will in embracing "with great reluctance" the diet I despise.

A more important line of argument against Held's view can be advanced on the basis of the widely accepted notion that there is a moral presumption against coercion. Held herself embraces this notion and very effectively clarifies it:

> . . . [A]lthough coercion is not *always* wrong (quite obviously: one coerces the small child not to run across the highway, or the murderer to drop his weapon), there is a presumption against it. . . . This has the standing of a fundamental moral principle. . . .
>
> What can be concluded at the moral level is that we have a *prima facie* obligation not to employ coercion.[7] [all italics hers]

But it would seem that acceptance of the moral presumption against coercion is not compatible with the view that offers become coercive precisely inasmuch as they become extremely enticing or seductive. Suppose you are my neighbor and regularly spend your Saturday afternoon on the golf course. Suppose also that you are a skilled gardener. I am anxious to convince you to do some gardening work for me and it must be done this Saturday. I offer you $100, $200, $300, . . . in an effort to make it worth your while to sacrifice your recreation and undertake my gardening. At some point, my proposal becomes very enticing. Yet, at the same time in no sense is my proposal becoming morally problematic. If my proposal were becoming coercive, surely our moral sense would be aroused.

Though it is surely not true that the extremely enticing character of an offer is sufficient to make it coercive, we need not reach the conclusion that no sense can be made out of the notion of a coercive offer. Indeed, there is an important social reality that the notion of a coercive offer appears to capture, and insight into this reality can be gained by simply taking note of the sort of case that most draws us to the language of "coercive offer." Is it not a case in which the recipient of an offer is in circumstances of genuine need, and acceptance of the offer seems to present the only realistic possibility for alleviating the need? Assuming that this sort of case is the heart of the matter, it seems that we cannot avoid introducing some sort of distinction between *genuine needs* and *mere wants*. Though the philosophical difficulties involved in drawing this distinction are not insignificant, I nevertheless claim that we will not achieve any clarity about the notion of a coercive offer, at least in this context, except in reference to it. Whatever puzzlement we may feel with regard to the host of borderline cases that can be advanced, it is nevertheless true, for example, that I *genuinely need* food and that I *merely want* a backyard tennis court. In the same spirit, I think it can be acknowledged by all that Ms. Starlet, though she *wants* very much to be a star, does not in any relevant sense *need* to be a star. Accordingly, there is little plausibility in thinking that Mr. Moviemogul makes her a coercive offer. The following case, in contrast, can more plausibly be thought to embody a coercive offer.

Case 8   Mr. Troubled is a young widower who is raising his three children. He lives in a small town and believes that it is important for him to stay there so that his children continue to have the emotional support of other family members. But economic times are tough. Mr. Troubled has been laid off from his job and has not been able to find another. His unemployment benefits have ceased and his relatives are in no position to help him financially. If he is unable to come up with the money for his mortgage payments, he will lose his rather modest house. Ms. Opportunistic lives in the same town. Since shortly after the death of Mr. Troubled's wife, she has consistently made sexual overtures in his direction. Mr. Troubled, for his part, does not care for Ms. Opportunistic and has made it clear to her that he is not interested in sexual involvement with her. She, however, is well aware of his present difficulties. To win his consent to a sexual affair, Ms. Opportunistic offers to make mortgage payments for Mr. Troubled on a continuing basis.

Is Ms. Opportunistic attempting to sexually use Mr. Troubled? The correct answer is yes, even though we must first accept the conclusion that her proposal embodies an offer and not a threat. If Ms. Opportunistic were threatening Mr. Troubled, her proposal would have the effect of rendering him worse off upon noncompliance. But this is not the case. If he rejects her proposal, his situation will not worsen; he will simply remain, as before, in circumstances of extreme need. It might be objected at this point that Ms. Opportunistic does in fact threaten Mr. Troubled. She threatens to deprive him of something to which he is entitled, namely, the alleviation of a genuine need. But this approach is defensible only if, before acceptance of her proposal, he is entitled to have his needs alleviated *by her*. And whatever Mr. Troubled and his children are entitled to from their society as a whole—they are perhaps slipping through the "social safety net"—it cannot be plausibly maintained that Mr. Troubled is entitled to have his mortgage payments made *by Ms. Opportunistic*.

Yet, though she does not threaten him, she is attempting to sexually use him. How can this conclusion be reconciled with our overall account of sexually using another person? First of all, I want to suggest that nothing hangs on whether or not we decide to call Ms. Opportunistic's offer "coercive." More important than the label "coercive offer" is an appreciation of the social reality that inclines us to consider the label appropriate. The label most forcefully asserts itself when we reflect on what Mr. Troubled is likely to say after accepting the offer. "I really had no choice." "I didn't want to accept her offer but what could I do? I have my children to think about." Both Mr. Troubled and Ms. Starlet (in our previous case) *reluctantly* consented to sexual interaction, but I think it can be agreed that Ms. Starlet had a choice in a way that Mr. Troubled did not. Mr. Troubled's choice was *severely constrained by his needs,* whereas Ms. Starlet's was not. As for Ms. Opportunistic, it seems that we might describe her approach as in some sense exploiting or taking advantage of Mr. Troubled's desperate situation. It is not so much, as we would say in the case of threats, that she coerces him or his consent, but rather that she achieves her aim of winning consent by taking advantage of the fact that he is already "under coercion," that is, his choice is severely constrained by his need. If we choose to describe what has taken place as a "coercive offer," we should remember that Mr. Troubled is "coerced" (constrained) by his own need or perhaps by preexisting factors in his situation rather than by Ms. Opportunistic or her offer.

Since it is not quite right to say that Ms. Opportunistic is attempting to coerce Mr. Troubled, even if we are prepared to embrace the label "coercive offer," we cannot simply say, as we would say in the case of threats, that she is attempting to sexually use him *via coercion.* The proper account of the way in which Ms. Opportunistic attempts to sexually use Mr. Troubled is somewhat different. Let us say simply that she attempts to sexually use him *by taking advantage of his desperate situation.* The sense behind this distinctive way of sexually using someone is that a person's choice situation can sometimes be subject to such severe prior constraints that the possibility of *voluntary* consent to sexual interaction is precluded. A advances an offer calculated to gain B's reluctant consent to sexual interaction by confronting B, who has no apparent way of alleviating a genuine need, with an opportunity to do so, but makes this opportunity contingent upon consent to sexual interaction. In such a case, should we not say simply that B's need, when coupled with a lack of viable alternatives, results in B being incapable of *voluntarily* accepting A's offer? Thus A, in making an offer which B "cannot refuse," although not coercing B, nevertheless does intentionally act in a way that violates the requirement that B's sexual interaction with A be based upon B's voluntary informed consent. Thus A sexually uses B.

The central claim of this paper is that A sexually uses B if and only if A intentionally acts in a way that violates the requirement that B's sexual interaction with A be based on B's voluntary informed consent. Clearly, deception and coercion are important mechanisms whereby sexual using takes place. But consideration of case 8 has led us to the identification of yet another mechanism. In summary, then, limiting attention to cases of sexual interaction with a fully competent adult partner, A can sexually use B not only (1) by deceiving B or (2) by coercing B but also (3) by taking advantage of B's desperate situation.

NOTES

1 I follow here an account of coercion developed by Michael D. Bayles in "A Concept of Coercion," in J. Roland Pennock and John W. Chapman, eds., *Coercion: Nomos XIV* (Chicago: Aldine-Atherton, 1972), pp. 16–29.

2 Statutory rape, sexual relations with a person under the legal age of consent, can also be construed as the sexual using of another person. In contrast to forcible rape, however, statutory rape need not involve coercion. The victim of statutory rape may freely "consent" to sexual interaction but, at least in the eyes of the law, is deemed incompetent to consent.

3 A man wrestles a woman to the ground. She is the victim of occurrent coercion. He threatens to beat her unless she submits to his sexual demands. Now she becomes the victim of dispositional coercion.

4 My account of this distinction largely derives from Robert Nozick, "Coercion," in Sidney Morgenbesser, Patrick Suppes, and Morton White, eds., *Philosophy, Science, and Method* (New York: St. Martin's Press, 1969), pp. 440–472, and from Michael D. Bayles, "Coercive Offers and Public Benefits," *The Personalist* 55, no. 2 (Spring 1974), 139–144.

5 The National Advisory Council on Women's Educational Programs, *Sexual Harassment: A Report on the Sexual Harassment of Students* (August 1980), p. 12.

6 Virginia Held, "Coercion and Coercive Offers," in *Coercion: Nomos XIV,* p. 58.

7 *Ibid.,* pp. 61, 62.

QUESTIONS

1 Is there a morally relevant sense of *sexually* using another person that is not captured by reference to the notion of voluntary informed consent?

2 What is promiscuity? Is promiscuity immoral?

3 Is prostitution immoral?

Why Shouldn't Tommy and Jim Have Sex?
A Defense of Homosexuality

John Corvino

Corvino rejects the view that homosexual sex is immoral. He responds directly to two recurrent arguments against homosexual sex: (1) that it is unnatural and (2) that it is harmful. In discussing the unnaturalness argument, Corvino distinguishes various senses of "unnatural." His overall conclusion in this regard is that homosexual sex is not *unnatural* in any morally relevant sense. Corvino also defends the practice of homosexuality against the charge that it is harmful. He takes issue both with the claim that the practice of homosexuality is harmful to those who engage in it and with the claim that others (children in particular and society in general) are threatened by it.

Tommy and Jim are a homosexual couple I know. Tommy is an accountant; Jim is a botany professor. They are in their forties and have been together fourteen years, the last five of which they've lived in a Victorian house that they've lovingly restored. Although their relationship has had its challenges, each has made sacrifices for the sake of the other's happiness and the relationship's long-term success.

I assume that Tommy and Jim have sex with each other (although I've never bothered to ask). Furthermore, I contend that they probably *should* have sex with each other. For one thing, sex is pleasurable. But it is also much more than that: a sexual relationship can unite two people in a way that virtually nothing else can. It can be an avenue of growth, of communication, and of lasting interpersonal fulfillment. These are reasons why most heterosexual couples have sex even if they don't want children, don't want children yet, or don't want additional children. And if these reasons are good enough for most heterosexual couples, then they should be good enough for Tommy and Jim.

Of course, having a reason to do something does not preclude there being an even better reason for not doing it. Tommy might have a good reason for drinking orange juice (it's tasty and nutritious) but an even better reason for not doing so (he's allergic). The point is that one would need a pretty good reason for denying a sexual relationship to Tommy and Jim, given the intense benefits widely associated with such relationships. The question I shall consider in this paper is thus quite simple: Why shouldn't Tommy and Jim have sex?[1]

HOMOSEXUAL SEX IS "UNNATURAL"

Many contend that homosexual sex is "unnatural." But what does that mean? Many things that people value—clothing, houses, medicine, and government, for example—are unnatural in some sense. On the other hand, many things that people detest—disease, suffering, and death, for example—are "natural" in the sense that they occur "in nature." If the unnaturalness charge is to be more than empty rhetorical flourish, those who levy it must specify what they mean. Borrowing from Burton Leiser, I will examine several possible meanings of "unnatural."[2]

What Is Unusual or Abnormal Is Unnatural

One meaning of "unnatural" refers to that which deviates from the norm, that is, from what most people do. Obviously, most people engage in heterosexual relationships. But does it follow that it is wrong to engage in homosexual relationships? Relatively few people read Sanskrit, pilot ships, play the mandolin, breed goats, or write with both hands, yet none of these activities is immoral simply because it is unusual. As the Ramsey Colloquium, a group of Jewish and Christian scholars who oppose homosexuality, writes, "The statistical frequency of an act does not determine its moral status."[3] So while homosexuality might be unnatural in the sense of being unusual, that fact is morally irrelevant.

What Is Not Practiced by Other Animals Is Unnatural

Some people argue, "Even animals know better than to behave homosexually; homosexuality must be wrong." This argument is doubly flawed. First, it rests on a false premise. Numerous studies—including Anne Perkins's study of "gay" sheep and George and Molly Hunt's study of "lesbian" seagulls—have shown that some animals do form homosexual pair-bonds.[4] Second, even if animals did not behave homosexually, that fact would not prove that homosexuality is immoral. After all, animals don't cook their food, brush their teeth, participate in religious worship, or attend college; human beings do all of these without moral censure. Indeed, the idea that animals could provide us with our standards—especially our sexual standards—is simply amusing.

What Does Not Proceed from Innate Desires Is Unnatural

Recent studies suggesting a biological basis for homosexuality have resulted in two popular positions. One side proposes that homosexual people are "born that way" and that it is therefore natural (and thus good) for them to form homosexual relationships. The other side maintains that homosexuality is a lifestyle choice, which is therefore unnatural (and thus wrong). Both sides assume a connection between the origin of homosexual orientation, on the one hand, and the moral value of homosexual activity, on the other. And insofar as they share that assumption, both sides are wrong.

Consider first the pro-homosexual side: "They are born that way; therefore it's natural and good." This inference assumes that all innate desires are good ones (i.e., that they should be acted upon). But that assumption is clearly false. Research suggests that some people are born with a predisposition toward violence, but such people have no more right to strangle their neighbors than anyone else. So while people like Tommy and Jim may be born with homosexual tendencies, it doesn't follow that they ought to act on them. Nor does it follow that they ought *not* to act on them, even if the tendencies are not innate. I probably do not have any innate tendency to write with my left hand (since I, like everyone else in my family, have always been right-handed), but it doesn't follow that it would be immoral for me to do so. So simply asserting that homosexuality is a lifestyle choice will not show that it is an immoral lifestyle choice.

Do people "choose" to be homosexual? People certainly don't seem to choose their sexual *feelings,* at least not in any direct or obvious way. (Do you? Think about it.) Rather, they find certain people attractive and certain activities arousing, whether they "decide" to or not. Indeed, most people at some point in their lives wish that they could control their feelings more—for example, in situations of unrequited love—and find it frustrating that they cannot. What they *can* control to a considerable degree is how and when they act upon those feelings. In that sense, both homosexuality and heterosexuality involve lifestyle choices. But in either case, determining the origin of the feelings will not determine whether it is moral to act on them.

What Violates an Organ's Principal Purpose Is Unnatural

Perhaps when people claim that homosexual sex is unnatural they mean that it cannot result in procreation. The idea behind the argument is that human organs have various natural purposes: eyes are for seeing, ears are for hearing, genitals are for procreating. According to this argument, it is immoral to use an organ in a way that violates its particular purpose.

Many of our organs, however, have multiple purposes. Tommy can use his mouth for talking, eating, breathing, licking stamps, chewing gum, kissing women, or kissing Jim; and it seems rather arbitrary to claim that all but the last use are "natural." (And if we say that some of the other uses are "unnatural, but not immoral," we have failed to specify a morally relevant sense of the term "natural.")

Just because people can and do use their sexual organs to procreate, it does not follow that they should not use them for other purposes. Sexual organs seem very well suited for expressing love, for giving and receiving pleasure, and for celebrating, replenishing, and enhancing a relationship—even when procreation is not a factor. Unless opponents of homosexuality are prepared to condemn heterosexual couples who use contraception or individuals who masturbate, they must abandon this version of the unnaturalness argument. Indeed, even the Roman Catholic Church, which forbids contraception and masturbation, approves of sex for sterile couples and of sex during pregnancy, neither of which can lead to procreation. The Church concedes here that intimacy and pleasure are morally legitimate purposes for sex, even in cases where procreation is impossible. But since homosexual sex can achieve these purposes as well, it is inconsistent for the Church to condemn it on the grounds that it is not procreative. . . .

What Is Disgusting or Offensive Is Unnatural

It often seems that when people call homosexuality "unnatural" they really just mean that it's disgusting. But plenty of morally neutral activities—handling snakes, eating snails, performing autopsies, cleaning toilets, and so on—disgust people. Indeed, for centuries, most people found interracial relationships disgusting, yet that feeling—which has by no means disappeared—hardly proves that such relationships are wrong. In sum, the charge that homosexuality is unnatural, at least in its most common forms, is longer on rhetorical flourish than on philosophical cogency. At best it expresses an aesthetic judgment, not a moral judgment.

HOMOSEXUAL SEX IS HARMFUL

One might instead argue that homosexuality is harmful. The Ramsey Colloquium, for instance, argues that homosexuality leads to the breakdown of the family and, ultimately, of human society, and it points to the "alarming rates of sexual promiscuity, depression, and suicide and the ominous presence of AIDS within the homosexual subculture."[5] Thomas Schmidt marshals copious statistics to show that homosexual activity undermines physical and psychological health.[6] Such charges, if correct, would seem to provide strong evidence against homosexuality. But are the charges correct? And do they prove what they purport to prove?

One obvious (and obviously problematic) way to answer the first question is to ask people like Tommy and Jim. It would appear that no one is in a better position to judge the homosexual lifestyle than those who know it firsthand. Yet it is unlikely that critics would trust their testimony. Indeed, the more homosexual people try to explain their lives, the more critics accuse them of deceitfully promoting an agenda. (It's like trying to prove that you're not crazy. The more you object, the more people think, "That's exactly what a crazy person would say.")

One might instead turn to statistics. An obvious problem with this tack is that both sides of the debate bring forth extensive statistics and "expert" testimony, leaving the average observer confused. There is a more subtle problem as well. Because of widespread antigay sentiment, many homosexual people won't acknowledge their romantic feelings to themselves, much less to researchers. I have known a number of gay men who did not "come out" until their forties and fifties, and no amount of professional competence on the part of interviewers would have been likely to open their closets sooner. Such problems compound the usual difficulties of finding representative population samples for statistical study.

Yet even if the statistical claims of gay rights opponents were true, they would not prove what they purport to prove, for several reasons. First, as any good statistician realizes, correlation does not equal cause. Even if homosexual people were more likely to commit suicide, be promiscuous, or contract AIDS than the general population, it would not follow that their homosexuality causes them to do these things. An alternative—and very plausible—explanation is that these phenomena, like the disproportionately high crime rates among African Americans, are at least partly a function of society's treatment of the group in question. Suppose you were told from a very early age that the romantic feelings that you experienced were sick, unnatural, and disgusting. Suppose further that expressing these feelings put you at risk of social ostracism or, worse yet, physical violence. Is it not plausible that you would, for instance, be more inclined to depression than you would be without such obstacles? And that such depression could, in its extreme forms, lead to suicide or other self-destructive behaviors? (It is indeed remarkable that couples like Tommy and Jim continue to flourish in the face of such obstacles.)

A similar explanation can be given for the alleged promiscuity of homosexuals. The denial of legal marriage, the pressure to remain in the closet, and the overt hostility toward homosexual relationships are all more conducive to transient, clandestine encounters than they are to long-term unions. As a result, that which is challenging enough for heterosexual couples—settling down and building a life together—becomes far more challenging for homosexual couples.

Indeed, there is an interesting tension in the critics' position here. Opponents of homosexuality commonly claim that "marriage and the family . . . are fragile institutions in need of careful and continuing support."[7] And they point to the increasing prevalence of divorce and premarital sex among heterosexuals as evidence that such support is declining. Yet they refuse to concede that the complete absence of similar support for homosexual relationships might explain many of the alleged problems of homosexuals. The critics can't have it both ways: if heterosexual marriages are in trouble despite the various social, economic, and legal incentives for keeping them together, society should be little surprised that homosexual relationships—which not only lack such supports, but face overt hostility—are difficult to maintain.

One might object that if social ostracism were the main cause of homosexual people's problems, then homosexual people in more "tolerant" cities like New York and San Francisco should exhibit fewer such problems than their small-town counterparts; yet statistics do not seem to bear this out. This objection underestimates the extent of antigay sentiment in our society. By the time many gay and lesbian people move to urban centers, they have already been exposed to (and may have internalized) considerable hostility toward homosexuality. Moreover, the visibility of homosexuality in urban centers makes gay and lesbian people there more vulnerable to attack (and thus more likely to exhibit certain difficulties). Finally, note that urbanites *in general* (not just homosexual urbanites) tend to exhibit higher rates of promiscuity, depression, and sexually transmitted disease than the rest of the population.

But what about AIDS? Opponents of homosexuality sometimes claim that even if homosexual sex is not, strictly speaking, immoral, it is still a bad idea, since it puts people at risk for AIDS and other sexually transmitted diseases. But that claim is misleading: it is infinitely more risky for Tommy to have sex with a woman who is HIV-positive than with Jim, who is HIV-negative. Obviously, it's not homosexuality that's harmful, it's the virus; and the virus may be carried by both heterosexual and homosexual people.

Now it may be true (in the United States, at least) that homosexual males are statistically more likely to carry the virus than heterosexual females and thus that homosexual sex is *statistically* more risky than heterosexual sex (in cases where the partner's HIV status is unknown). But opponents of homosexuality need something stronger than this statistical claim. For if it is wrong for men to have sex with men because their doing so puts them at a higher AIDS risk than heterosexual sex, then it is also wrong for women to have sex with men because their doing so puts them at a higher AIDS risk than homosexual sex (lesbians as a group have the lowest incidence of AIDS). Purely from the standpoint of AIDS risk, women ought to prefer lesbian sex.

If this response seems silly, it is because there is obviously more to choosing a romantic or sexual partner than determining AIDS risk. And a major part of the decision, one that opponents of homosexuality consistently overlook, is considering whether one can have a mutually fulfilling relationship with the partner. For many people like Tommy and Jim, such fulfillment—which most heterosexuals recognize to be an important component of human flourishing—is only possible with members of the same sex.

Of course, the foregoing argument hinges on the claim that homosexual sex can only cause harm indirectly. Some would object that there are certain activities—anal sex, for instance—that for anatomical reasons are intrinsically harmful. But an argument against anal intercourse is by no means tantamount to an argument against homosexuality: neither all nor only homosexuals engage in anal sex. There are plenty of other things for both gay men and lesbians to do in bed. Indeed, for women, it appears that the most common forms of homosexual activity may be *less* risky than penile-vaginal intercourse, since the latter has been linked to cervical cancer.[8]

In sum, there is nothing *inherently* risky about sex between persons of the same gender. It is only risky under certain conditions: for instance, if they exchange diseased bodily fluids or if they engage in certain "rough" forms of sex that could cause tearing of delicate tissue. Heterosexual sex is equally risky under such conditions. Thus, even if statistical claims like those of Schmidt and the Ramsey Colloquium were true, they would not prove that homosexuality is immoral. At best, they would prove that homosexual people—like everyone else—ought to take great care when deciding to become sexually active.

Of course, there's more to a flourishing life than avoiding harm. One might argue that even if Tommy and Jim are not harming each other by their relationship, they are still failing to achieve the higher level of fulfillment possible in a heterosexual relationship, which is rooted in the complementarity of male and female. But this argument just ignores the facts: Tommy and Jim are homosexual *precisely because* they find relationships with men (and, in particular, with each other) more fulfilling than relationships with women. Even evangelicals (who have long advocated "faith healing" for homosexuals) are beginning to acknowledge that the choice for most homosexual people is not between homosexual relationships and heterosexual relationships, but rather between homosexual relationships and celibacy. What the critics need to show, therefore, is that no matter how loving, committed, mutual, generous, and fulfilling the relationship may be, Tommy and Jim would flourish more if they were celibate. Given the evidence of their lives (and of others like them), this is a formidable task indeed.

Thus far I have focused on the allegation that homosexuality harms those who engage in it. But what about the allegation that homosexuality harms other, non-consenting parties? Here I will briefly consider two claims: that homosexuality threatens children and that it threatens society.

Those who argue that homosexuality threatens children may mean one of two things. First, they may mean that homosexual people are child molesters. Statistically, the vast majority of reported cases of child sexual abuse involve young girls and their fathers, stepfathers, or other familiar (and presumably heterosexual) adult males. But opponents of homosexuality argue that when one adjusts for relative percentage in the population, homosexual males appear more likely than heterosexual males to be child molesters. As I argued above, the problems with obtaining reliable statistics on homosexuality render such calculations difficult. Fortunately, they are also unnecessary.

Child abuse is a terrible thing. But when a heterosexual male molests a child (or rapes a woman or commits assault), the act does not reflect upon all heterosexuals. Similarly, when a homosexual male molests a child, there is no reason why that act should reflect upon all homosexuals. Sex with adults of the same sex is one thing; sex with *children* of the same sex is quite another. Conflating the two not only slanders innocent people, it also misdirects resources intended to protect children. Furthermore, many men convicted of molesting young boys are sexually attracted to adult women and report no attraction to adult men. To call such men "homosexual," or even "bisexual," is probably to stretch such terms too far.

Alternatively, those who charge that homosexuality threatens children might mean that the increasing visibility of homosexual relationships makes children more likely to become homosexual. The argument for this view is patently circular. One cannot prove that doing X is bad by arguing that it causes other people to do X, which is bad. One must first establish independently that X is bad. That said, there is not a shred of evidence to demonstrate that exposure to homosexuality leads children to become homosexual.

But doesn't homosexuality threaten society? A Roman Catholic priest once put the argument to me as follows: "Of course homosexuality is bad for society. If everyone were homosexual, there would be no society." Perhaps it is true that if everyone were homosexual, there would be no society. But if everyone were a celibate priest, society would collapse just as surely, and my friend the priest didn't seem to think that he was doing anything wrong simply by failing to procreate. . . .

From the fact that the continuation of society requires procreation, it does not follow that *everyone* must procreate. Moreover, even if such an obligation existed, it would not preclude homosexuality. At best, it would preclude *exclusive* homosexuality: homosexual people who occasionally have heterosexual sex can procreate just fine. And given artificial insemination, even those who are exclusively homosexual can procreate. In short, the priest's claim—if everyone were homosexual, there would be no society—is false; and even if it were true, it would not establish that homosexuality is immoral. . . .

I have argued that Tommy and Jim's sexual relationship harms neither them nor society. On the contrary, it benefits both. It benefits them because it makes them happier—not merely in a short-term, hedonistic sense, but in a long-term, "big picture" sort of way. And, in turn, it benefits society, since it makes Tommy and Jim more stable, more productive, and more generous than they would otherwise be. In short, their relationship—including its sexual component—provides the same kinds of benefits that infertile heterosexual relationships provide (and perhaps other benefits as well). Nor should we fear that accepting their relationship and others like it will cause people to flee in droves from the institution of heterosexual marriage. After all, . . . the usual response to a gay person is not "How come *he* gets to be gay and I don't?" . . .

NOTES

1 Although my central example in the paper is a gay male couple, much of what I say will apply mutatis mutandis to lesbians as well, since many of the same arguments are used against them. This is not to say gay male sexuality and lesbian sexuality are largely similar or that discussions of the former will cover all that needs to be said about the latter. Furthermore, the fact that I focus on a long-term, committed relationship should not be taken to imply any judgment about homosexual activity outside of such unions. If the argument of this paper is successful, then the evaluation of homosexual activity outside of committed unions should be largely (if not entirely) similar to the evaluation of *hetero*sexual activity outside of committed unions.

2 Burton M. Leiser, *Liberty, Justice, and Morals: Contemporary Value Conflicts* (New York: Macmillan, 1986), 51–57.

3 The Ramsey Colloquium, "The Homosexual Movement," *First Things* (March 1994), 15–20.

4 For an overview of some of these studies, see Simon LeVay, *Queer Science* (Boston: MIT Press, 1996), chap. 10.

5 The Ramsey Colloquium, "Homosexual Movement," 19.

6 Thomas Schmidt, "The Price of Love" in *Straight and Narrow? Compassion and Clarity in the Homosexuality Debate* (Downers Grove, IL: InterVarsity Press, 1995), chap. 6.

7 The Ramsey Colloquium, "Homosexual Movement," 19.

8 See S. R. Johnson, E. M. Smith, and S. M. Guenther, "Comparison of Gynecological Health Care Problems Between Lesbian and Bisexual Women," *Journal of Reproductive Medicine* 32 (1987), 805–811.

QUESTIONS

1 Is homosexual sex unnatural? If so, does it follow that homosexual sex is immoral?

2 Is the practice of homosexuality harmful to those who engage in it?

3 Does the practice of homosexuality represent a threat to society? If so, in what way and to what extent?

Majority Opinion in *Goodridge v. Department of Public Health*

Chief Justice Margaret H. Marshall

Chief Justice Marshall argues that the Massachusetts ban on same-sex marriage is incompatible with the Massachusetts Constitution on both *equal protection* and *due process* grounds. She employs a "rational basis" standard of review in her analysis, holding that there is no need to consider whether the case might also require analysis on the basis of the more demanding "strict judicial scrutiny" standard—because the Massachusetts ban on same-sex marriage cannot even survive rational basis analysis. Chief Justice Marshall considers three legislative rationales put forward by the Massachusetts Department of Public Health to justify denying same-sex couples access to civil marriage. On her view, none of these rationales successfully provides a rational basis for the Massachusetts ban on same-sex marriage. Frequently emphasizing the fundamental social importance of the institution of marriage, Chief Justice Marshall also asserts that civil marriage is essentially characterized by the exclusive and permanent commitment of marriage partners to each other.

Marriage is a vital social institution. The exclusive commitment of two individuals to each other nurtures love and mutual support; it brings stability to our society. For those who choose to marry, and for their children, marriage provides an abundance of legal, financial, and social benefits. In return it imposes weighty legal, financial, and social obligations. The question before us is whether, consistent with the Massachusetts

Supreme Judicial Court of Massachusetts. 440 Mass. 309 (2003).

Constitution, the commonwealth may deny the protections, benefits, and obligations conferred by civil marriage to two individuals of the same sex who wish to marry. We conclude that it may not. The Massachusetts Constitution affirms the dignity and equality of all individuals. It forbids the creation of second-class citizens. In reaching our conclusion we have given full deference to the arguments made by the commonwealth. But it has failed to identify any constitutionally adequate reason for denying civil marriage to same-sex couples. . . .

I

The plaintiffs are fourteen individuals from five Massachusetts counties. As of April 11, 2001, the date they filed their complaint, the plaintiffs Gloria Bailey, sixty years old, and Linda Davies, fifty-five years old, had been in a committed relationship for thirty years; the plaintiffs Maureen Brodoff, forty-nine years old, and Ellen Wade, fifty-two years old, had been in a committed relationship for twenty years and lived with their twelve-year-old daughter; the plaintiffs Hillary Goodridge, forty-four years old, and Julie Goodridge, forty-three years old, had been in a committed relationship for thirteen years and lived with their five-year-old daughter; the plaintiffs Gary Chalmers, thirty-five years old, and Richard Linnell, thirty-seven years old, had been in a committed relationship for thirteen years and lived with their eight-year-old daughter and Richard's mother; the plaintiffs Heidi Norton, thirty-six years old, and Gina Smith, thirty-six years old, had been in a committed relationship for eleven years and lived with their two sons, ages five years and one year; the plaintiffs Michael Horgan, forty-one years old, and David Balmelli, forty-one years old, had been in a committed relationship for seven years; and the plaintiffs David Wilson, fifty-seven years old, and Robert Compton, fifty-one years old, had been in a committed relationship for four years and had cared for David's mother in their home after a serious illness until she died.

The plaintiffs . . . have employed such legal means as are available to them—for example, joint adoption, powers of attorney, and joint ownership of real property— to secure aspects of their relationships. Each plaintiff attests a desire to marry his or her partner in order to affirm publicly their commitment to each other and to secure the legal protections and benefits afforded to married couples and their children. . . .

In March and April 2001, each of the plaintiff couples attempted to obtain a marriage license from a city or town clerk's office. . . . In each case, the clerk either refused to accept the notice of intention to marry or denied a marriage license to the couple on the ground that Massachusetts does not recognize same-sex marriage. . . .

On April 11, 2001, the plaintiffs filed suit in the Superior Court against the [Department of Public Health]. . . .

A Superior Court judge ruled for the department. In a memorandum of decision and order dated May 7, 2002, he dismissed the plaintiffs' claim that the marriage statutes should be construed to permit marriage between persons of the same sex. . . . Turning to the constitutional claims, he held that the marriage exclusion does not offend the liberty, freedom, equality, or due process provisions of the Massachusetts

Constitution, and that the Massachusetts Declaration of Rights does not guarantee "the fundamental right to marry a person of the same sex." He concluded that prohibiting same-sex marriage rationally furthers the legislature's legitimate interest in safeguarding the "primary purpose" of marriage, "procreation." The legislature may rationally limit marriage to opposite-sex couples, he concluded, because those couples are "theoretically . . . capable of procreation," they do not rely on "inherently more cumbersome" noncoital means of reproduction, and they are more likely than same-sex couples to have children, or more children.

After the complaint was dismissed and summary judgment entered for the defendants, the plaintiffs appealed. Both parties requested direct appellate review, which we granted. . . .

[II]

A

The . . . question is whether, as the department claims, government action that bars same-sex couples from civil marriage constitutes a legitimate exercise of the state's authority to regulate conduct, or whether, as the plaintiffs claim, this categorical marriage exclusion violates the Massachusetts Constitution. We have recognized the long-standing statutory understanding, derived from the common law, that "marriage" means the lawful union of a woman and a man. But that history cannot and does not foreclose the constitutional question.

The plaintiffs' claim that the marriage restriction violates the Massachusetts Constitution can be analyzed in two ways. Does it offend the constitution's guarantees of equality before the law? Or do the liberty and due process provisions of the Massachusetts Constitution secure the plaintiffs' right to marry their chosen partner? In matters implicating marriage, family life, and the upbringing of children, the two constitutional concepts frequently overlap, as they do here. . . .

We begin by considering the nature of civil marriage itself. Simply put, the government creates civil marriage. In Massachusetts, civil marriage is, and since precolonial days has been, precisely what its name implies: a wholly secular institution. No religious ceremony has ever been required to validate a Massachusetts marriage. . . .

Without question, civil marriage enhances the "welfare of the community." It is a "social institution of the highest importance." Civil marriage anchors an ordered society by encouraging stable relationships over transient ones. It is central to the way the commonwealth identifies individuals, provides for the orderly distribution of property, ensures that children and adults are cared for and supported whenever possible from private rather than public funds, and tracks important epidemiological and demographic data.

Marriage also bestows enormous private and social advantages on those who choose to marry. Civil marriage is at once a deeply personal commitment to another human being and a highly public celebration of the ideals of mutuality, companionship, intimacy, fidelity, and family. "It is an association that promotes a way of life, not causes; a harmony in living, not political faiths; a bilateral loyalty, not commercial or social projects." Because it fulfills yearnings for security, safe haven, and

connection that express our common humanity, civil marriage is an esteemed institution, and the decision whether and whom to marry is among life's momentous
acts of self-definition.

Tangible as well as intangible benefits flow from marriage. The marriage license
grants valuable property rights to those who meet the entry requirements, and who
agree to what might otherwise be a burdensome degree of government regulation
of their activities. . . .

The benefits accessible only by way of a marriage license are enormous, touching nearly every aspect of life and death. The department states that "hundreds of
statutes" are related to marriage and to marital benefits. . . .

Without the right to marry—or more properly, the right to choose to marry—one
is excluded from the full range of human experience and denied full protection of
the laws for one's "avowed commitment to an intimate and lasting human relationship." Because civil marriage is central to the lives of individuals and the welfare
of the community, our laws assiduously protect the individual's right to marry
against undue government incursion. Laws may not "interfere directly and substantially with the right to marry."

Unquestionably, the regulatory power of the commonwealth over civil marriage
is broad, as is the commonwealth's discretion to award public benefits. Individuals
who have the choice to marry each other and nevertheless choose not to may properly be denied the legal benefits of marriage. But that same logic cannot hold for a
qualified individual who would marry if she or he only could.

B

For decades, indeed centuries, in much of this country (including Massachusetts)
no lawful marriage was possible between white and black Americans. That long
history availed not when the Supreme Court of California held in 1948 that a legislative prohibition against interracial marriage violated the due process and equality guarantees of the Fourteenth Amendment, *Perez v. Sharp* (1948), or when,
nineteen years later, the United States Supreme Court also held that a statutory bar
to interracial marriage violated the Fourteenth Amendment, *Loving v. Virginia*
(1967). As both *Perez* and *Loving* make clear, the right to marry means little if it
does not include the right to marry the person of one's choice, subject to appropriate government restrictions in the interests of public health, safety, and welfare. In
this case, as in *Perez* and *Loving,* a statute deprives individuals of access to an institution of fundamental legal, personal, and social significance—the institution of
marriage—because of a single trait: skin color in *Perez* and *Loving,* sexual orientation here. As it did in *Perez* and *Loving,* history must yield to a more fully developed understanding of the invidious quality of the discrimination.

The Massachusetts Constitution protects matters of personal liberty against government incursion as zealously, and often more so, than does the federal Constitution,
even where both constitutions employ essentially the same language. . . .

The individual liberty and equality safeguards of the Massachusetts Constitution
protect both "freedom from" unwarranted government intrusion into protected
spheres of life and "freedom to" partake in benefits created by the state for the

common good. Both freedoms are involved here. Whether and whom to marry, how to express sexual intimacy, and whether and how to establish a family—these are among the most basic of every individual's liberty and due process rights. And central to personal freedom and security is the assurance that the laws will apply equally to persons in similar situations. "Absolute equality before the law is a fundamental principle of our own Constitution." The liberty interest in choosing whether and whom to marry would be hollow if the commonwealth could, without sufficient justification, foreclose an individual from freely choosing the person with whom to share an exclusive commitment in the unique institution of civil marriage.

The Massachusetts Constitution requires, at a minimum, that the exercise of the state's regulatory authority not be "arbitrary or capricious." Under both the equality and liberty guarantees, regulatory authority must, at very least, serve "a legitimate purpose in a rational way"; a statute must "bear a reasonable relation to a permissible legislative objective." Any law failing to satisfy the basic standards of rationality is void.

The plaintiffs challenge the marriage statute on both equal protection and due process grounds. With respect to each such claim, we must first determine the appropriate standard of review. Where a statute implicates a fundamental right or uses a suspect classification, we employ "strict judicial scrutiny." For all other statutes, we employ the "'rational basis' test." For due process claims, rational basis analysis requires that statutes "bear[ ] a real and substantial relation to the public health, safety, morals, or some other phase of the general welfare." For equal protection challenges, the rational basis test requires that "an impartial lawmaker could logically believe that the classification would serve a legitimate public purpose that transcends the harm to the members of the disadvantaged class."

The department argues that no fundamental right or "suspect" class is at issue here, and rational basis is the appropriate standard of review. For the reasons we explain below, we conclude that the marriage ban does not meet the rational basis test for either due process or equal protection. Because the statute does not survive rational basis review, we do not consider the plaintiffs' arguments that this case merits strict judicial scrutiny.

The department posits three legislative rationales for prohibiting same-sex couples from marrying: (1) providing a "favorable setting for procreation"; (2) ensuring the optimal setting for child rearing, which the department defines as "a two-parent family with one parent of each sex"; and (3) preserving scarce state and private financial resources. We consider each in turn.

The judge in the Superior Court endorsed the first rationale, holding that "the state's interest in regulating marriage is based on the traditional concept that marriage's primary purpose is procreation." This is incorrect. Our laws of civil marriage do not privilege procreative heterosexual intercourse between married people above every other form of adult intimacy and every other means of creating a family. . . . Fertility is not a condition of marriage, nor is it grounds for divorce. People who have never consummated their marriage, and never plan to, may be and stay married. People who cannot stir from their deathbed may marry. While it is certainly true that many, perhaps most, married couples have children together (assisted or unassisted), it is the exclusive and permanent commitment of the marriage partners to one another, not the begetting of children, that is the sine qua non of civil marriage.

Moreover, the commonwealth affirmatively facilitates bringing children into a family regardless of whether the intended parent is married or unmarried, whether the child is adopted or born into a family, whether assistive technology was used to conceive the child, and whether the parent or her partner is heterosexual, homosexual, or bisexual. If procreation were a necessary component of civil marriage, our statutes would draw a tighter circle around the permissible bounds of nonmarital childbearing and the creation of families by noncoital means. . . .

The "marriage is procreation" argument singles out the one unbridgeable difference between same-sex and opposite-sex couples, and transforms that difference into the essence of legal marriage. Like "Amendment 2" to the Constitution of Colorado, which effectively denied homosexual persons equality under the law and full access to the political process, the marriage restriction impermissibly "identifies persons by a single trait and then denies them protection across the board." In so doing, the state's action confers an official stamp of approval on the destructive stereotype that same-sex relationships are inherently unstable and inferior to opposite-sex relationships and are not worthy of respect.

The department's first stated rationale, equating marriage with unassisted heterosexual procreation, shades imperceptibly into its second: that confining marriage to opposite-sex couples ensures that children are raised in the "optimal" setting. Protecting the welfare of children is a paramount state policy. Restricting marriage to opposite-sex couples, however, cannot plausibly further this policy. . . .

The department has offered no evidence that forbidding marriage to people of the same sex will increase the number of couples choosing to enter into opposite-sex marriages in order to have and raise children. There is thus no rational relationship between the marriage statute and the commonwealth's proffered goal of protecting the "optimal" child rearing unit. Moreover, the department readily concedes that people in same-sex couples may be "excellent" parents. . . . Given the wide range of public benefits reserved only for married couples, we do not credit the department's contention that the absence of access to civil marriage amounts to little more than an inconvenience to same-sex couples and their children. Excluding same-sex couples from civil marriage will not make children of opposite-sex marriages more secure, but it does prevent children of same-sex couples from enjoying the immeasurable advantages that flow from the assurance of "a stable family structure in which children will be reared, educated, and socialized." . . .

The third rationale advanced by the department is that limiting marriage to opposite-sex couples furthers the legislature's interest in conserving scarce state and private financial resources. The marriage restriction is rational, it argues, because the General Court logically could assume that same-sex couples are more financially independent than married couples and thus less needy of public marital benefits, such as tax advantages, or private marital benefits, such as employer-financed health plans that include spouses in their coverage.

An absolute statutory ban on same-sex marriage bears no rational relationship to the goal of economy. First, the department's conclusory generalization—that same-sex couples are less financially dependent on each other than opposite-sex couples—ignores that many same-sex couples, such as many of the plaintiffs in this case, have children and other dependents (here, aged parents) in their care. The department does not contend, nor could it, that these dependents are less needy or deserving than the dependents of married couples. Second, Massachusetts marriage laws do not condition receipt of public and private financial benefits to married individuals on a demonstration of financial dependence on each other; the benefits are available to married couples regardless of whether they mingle their finances or actually depend on each other for support.

The department suggests additional rationales for prohibiting same-sex couples from marrying, which are developed by some amici. It argues that broadening civil marriage to include same-sex couples will trivialize or destroy the institution of marriage as it has historically been fashioned. Certainly our decision today marks a significant change in the definition of marriage as it has been inherited from the common law, and understood by many societies for centuries. But it does not disturb the fundamental value of marriage in our society.

Here, the plaintiffs seek only to be married, not to undermine the institution of civil marriage. They do not want marriage abolished. They do not attack the binary nature of marriage, the consanguinity provisions, or any of the other gatekeeping provisions of the marriage licensing law. Recognizing the right of an individual to marry a person of the same sex will not diminish the validity or dignity of opposite-sex marriage, any more than recognizing the right of an individual to marry a person of a different race devalues the marriage of a person who marries someone of her own race. If anything, extending civil marriage to same-sex couples reinforces the importance of marriage to individuals and communities. That same-sex couples are willing to embrace marriage's solemn obligations of exclusivity, mutual support, and commitment to one another is a testament to the enduring place of marriage in our laws and in the human spirit. . . .

The marriage ban works a deep and scarring hardship on a very real segment of the community for no rational reason. The absence of any reasonable relationship between, on the one hand, an absolute disqualification of same-sex couples who wish to enter into civil marriage and, on the other, protection of public health, safety, or general welfare, suggests that the marriage restriction is rooted in persistent prejudices against persons who are (or who are believed to be) homosexual. "The Constitution cannot control such prejudices but neither can it tolerate them. Private biases may be outside the reach of the law, but the law cannot, directly or indirectly, give them effect." Limiting the protections, benefits, and obligations of civil marriage to opposite-sex couples violates the basic premises of individual liberty and equality under law protected by the Massachusetts Constitution. . . .

QUESTIONS

1 Can any of the legislative rationales explicity rejected by Chief Justice Marshall provide a rational basis for the Massachusetts ban on same-sex marriage?

2 Do you agree with Chief Justice Marshall that the legal acceptance of same-sex marriage "will not diminish the validity or dignity of opposite-sex marriage"?

3 Chief Justice Marshall leaves aside the question of whether there is "a fundamental right" under the Massachusetts Constitution to marry a person of the same sex. Is it plausible to think that there might be such a right under the United States Constitution?

Dissenting Opinion in *Goodridge v. Department of Public Health*

Justice Martha B. Sosman

Justice Sosman takes the majority opinion to task for a misapplication of the rational basis test in this case. She insists that the rational basis standard does not require that a legislative rationale be persuasive, only that it satisfy "a minimal threshold of rationality." Justice Sosman focuses attention on the unsettled nature of presently available evidence in support of the claim that families headed by same-sex partners are as successful in raising children as families headed by opposite-sex partners. Mindful of legitimate worries about undesirable social consequences, she concludes that the legislature does have a rational basis for resisting a redefinition of marriage that provides access to same-sex couples.

In applying the rational basis test to any challenged statutory scheme, the issue is not whether the legislature's rationale behind that scheme is persuasive to us, but only whether it satisfies a minimal threshold of rationality. Today, rather than apply that test, the court announces that, because it is persuaded that there are no differences between same-sex and opposite-sex couples, the legislature has no rational basis for treating them differently with respect to the granting of marriage licenses. Reduced to its essence, the court's opinion concludes that, because same-sex couples are now raising children, and withholding the benefits of civil marriage from their union makes it harder for them to raise those children, the state must therefore provide the benefits of civil marriage to same-sex couples just as it does to opposite-sex couples. Of course, many people are raising children outside the confines of traditional marriage, and, by definition, those children are being deprived of the various benefits that would flow if they were being raised in a household with married parents. That does not mean that the legislature must accord the full benefits of marital status on every household raising children. Rather, the legislature need only have some rational basis for concluding that, at present, those alternate family structures have not yet been conclusively shown to be the equivalent of the marital family structure that has established itself as a successful one over a period of centuries. People are of course at liberty to raise their children in various family structures, as long as they are not literally harming their children by doing so. That does not mean that the state is required to provide identical forms of encouragement, endorsement, and support to all of the infinite variety of household structures that a free society permits.

Based on our own philosophy of child rearing, and on our observations of the children being raised by same-sex couples to whom we are personally close, we may be of the view that what matters to children is not the gender, or sexual orientation, or even the number of the adults who raise them, but rather whether those adults provide the children with a nurturing, stable, safe, consistent, and

Supreme Judicial Court of Massachusetts. 440 Mass. 309 (2003).

supportive environment in which to mature. Same-sex couples can provide their children with the requisite nurturing, stable, safe, consistent, and supportive environment in which to mature, just as opposite-sex couples do. It is therefore understandable that the court might view the traditional definition of marriage as an unnecessary anachronism, rooted in historical prejudices that modern society has in large measure rejected and biological limitations that modern science has overcome.

It is not, however, our assessment that matters. Conspicuously absent from the court's opinion today is any acknowledgment that the attempts at scientific study of the ramifications of raising children in same-sex couple households are themselves in their infancy and have so far produced inconclusive and conflicting results. Notwithstanding our belief that gender and sexual orientation of parents should not matter to the success of the child-rearing venture, studies to date reveal that there are still some observable differences between children raised by opposite-sex couples and children raised by same-sex couples. Interpretation of the data gathered by those studies then becomes clouded by the personal and political beliefs of the investigators, both as to whether the differences identified are positive or negative, and as to the untested explanations of what might account for those differences. (This is hardly the first time in history that the ostensible steel of the scientific method has melted and buckled under the intense heat of political and religious passions.) Even in the absence of bias or political agenda behind the various studies of children raised by same-sex couples, the most neutral and strict application of scientific principles to this field would be constrained by the limited period of observation that has been available. Gay and lesbian couples living together openly, and official recognition of them as their children's sole parents, comprise a very recent phenomenon, and the recency of that phenomenon has not yet permitted any study of how those children fare as adults and at best minimal study of how they fare during their adolescent years. The legislature can rationally view the state of the scientific evidence as unsettled on the critical question it now faces: Are families headed by same-sex parents equally successful in rearing children from infancy to adulthood as families headed by parents of opposite sexes? Our belief that children raised by same-sex couples should fare the same as children raised in traditional families is just that: a passionately held but utterly untested belief. The legislature is not required to share that belief but may, as the creator of the institution of civil marriage, wish to see the proof before making a fundamental alteration to that institution.

Although ostensibly applying the rational basis test to the civil marriage statutes, it is abundantly apparent that the court is in fact applying some undefined stricter standard to assess the constitutionality of the marriage statutes' exclusion of same-sex couples. While avoiding any express conclusion as to any of the proffered routes by which that exclusion would be subjected to a test of strict scrutiny—infringement of a fundamental right, discrimination based on gender, or discrimination against gays and lesbians as a suspect classification—the opinion repeatedly alludes to those concepts in a prolonged and eloquent prelude before articulating its view that the exclusion lacks even a rational basis. . . .

In short, while claiming to apply a mere rational basis test, the court's opinion works up an enormous head of steam by repeated invocations of avenues by which to subject the statute to strict scrutiny, apparently hoping that that head of steam will generate momentum sufficient to propel the opinion across the yawning chasm of the very deferential rational basis test.

Shorn of these emotion-laden invocations, the opinion ultimately opines that the legislature is acting irrationally when it grants benefits to a proven successful family structure while denying the same benefits to a recent, perhaps promising, but essentially untested alternate family structure. Placed in a more neutral context, the court would never find any irrationality in such an approach. For example, if the issue were government subsidies and tax benefits promoting use of an established technology for energy efficient heating, the court would find no equal protection or due process violation in the legislature's decision not to grant the same benefits to an inventor or manufacturer of some new, alternative technology who did not yet have sufficient data to prove that that new technology was just as good as the established technology. That the early results from preliminary testing of the new technology might look very promising, or that the theoretical underpinnings of the new technology might appear flawless, would not make it irrational for the legislature to grant subsidies and tax breaks to the established technology and deny them to the still unproved newcomer in the field. While programs that affect families and children register higher on our emotional scale than programs affecting energy efficiency, our standards for what is or is not "rational" should not be bent by those emotional tugs. Where, as here, there is no ground for applying strict scrutiny, the emotionally compelling nature of the subject matter should not affect the manner in which we apply the rational basis test.

Or, to the extent that the court is going to invoke such emotion-laden and value-laden rhetoric as a means of heightening the degree of scrutiny to be applied, the same form of rhetoric can be employed to justify the legislature's proceeding with extreme caution in this area. In considering whether the legislature has a rational reason for postponing a dramatic change to the definition of marriage, it is surely pertinent to the inquiry to recognize that this proffered change affects not just a load-bearing wall of our social structure but the very cornerstone of that structure. Before making a fundamental alteration to that cornerstone, it is eminently rational for the legislature to require a high degree of certainty as to the precise consequences of that alteration, to make sure that it can be done safely, without either temporary or lasting damage to the structural integrity of the entire edifice. The court today blithely assumes that there are no such dangers and that it is safe to proceed, an assumption that is not supported by anything more than the court's blind faith that it is so.

More importantly, it is not our confidence in the lack of adverse consequences that is at issue, or even whether that confidence is justifiable. The issue is whether it is rational to reserve judgment on whether this change can be made at this time without damaging the institution of marriage or adversely affecting the critical role it has played in our society. Absent consensus on the issue (which obviously does not exist), or unanimity amongst scientists studying the issue (which also does not exist), or a more prolonged period of observation of this new family structure (which has not yet been possible), it is rational for the legislature to postpone any redefinition of marriage that would include same-sex couples until such time as it is certain that that redefinition will not have unintended and undesirable social consequences. Through the political process, the people may decide when the benefits of extending civil marriage to same-sex couples have been shown to outweigh whatever risks—be they palpable or ephemeral—are involved. However minimal the risks of that redefinition of marriage may seem to us from our vantage point, it is not up to us to decide what risks society must run, and it is inappropriate for us to abrogate that power to ourselves merely because we are confident that "it is the right thing to do."

As a matter of social history, today's opinion may represent a great turning point that many will hail as a tremendous step toward a more just society. As a matter of constitutional jurisprudence, however, the case stands as an aberration. To reach the result it does, the court has tortured the rational basis test beyond recognition. I fully appreciate the strength of the temptation to find this particular law unconstitutional—there is much to be said for the argument that excluding gay and lesbian couples from the benefits of civil marriage is cruelly unfair and hopelessly outdated; the inability to marry has a profound impact on the personal lives of committed gay and lesbian couples (and their children) to whom we are personally close (our friends, neighbors, family members, classmates, and coworkers); and our resolution of this issue takes place under the intense glare of national and international publicity. Speaking metaphorically, these factors have combined to turn the case before us into a "perfect storm" of a constitutional question. In my view, however, such factors make it all the more imperative that we adhere precisely and scrupulously to the established guideposts of our constitutional jurisprudence, a jurisprudence that makes the rational basis test an extremely deferential one that focuses on the rationality, not the persuasiveness, of the potential justifications for the classifications in the legislative scheme. I trust that, once this particular "storm" clears, we will return to the rational basis test as it has always been understood and applied. Applying that deferential test in the manner it is customarily applied, the exclusion of gay and lesbian couples from the institution of civil marriage passes constitutional muster. I respectfully dissent.

QUESTIONS

1 Is there any reason to believe that same-sex couples raising children cannot provide their children with a "nurturing, stable, safe, consistent, and supportive environment in which to mature"? Is there any reason to believe they cannot do so as well as opposite-sex couples?

2 In your view, are there any notable risks associated with changing the traditional definition of marriage in order to allow for same-sex marriage? Is it reasonable for a legislator to believe that it is too risky—at least at this time—to redefine marriage in this way?

What Marriage Is For: Children Need Mothers and Fathers

Maggie Gallagher

Gallagher expresses strong opposition to same-sex marriage. She argues against the view that marriage involves nothing more than public recognition of a couple's love and commitment. Asserting a contrasting view, she contends that the underlying sense of marriage as a fundamental social institution is that it bridges "the male-female divide so that children have loving, committed mothers and fathers." Accordingly, she argues, a societal endorsement of same-sex marriage would amount to no less than the abandonment of the central meaning of marriage. Gallagher also (1) argues that her view is compatible with the fact that the ability and willingness to have children is not a requirement for opposite-sex marriage, (2) contends that allowing only opposite-sex marriage does not amount to discrimination against gays and lesbians, and (3) denies that the refusal to accept same-sex marriage is analogous to laws against interracial marriage.

Gay marriage is no longer a theoretical issue. Canada has it. Massachusetts is expected to get it any day. The *Goodridge* decision there could set off a legal, political, and cultural battle in the courts of 50 states and in the U.S. Congress. Every politician, every judge, every citizen has to decide: Does same-sex marriage matter? If so, how and why?

The timing could not be worse. Marriage is in crisis, as everyone knows: High rates of divorce and illegitimacy have eroded marriage norms and created millions of fatherless children, whole neighborhoods where lifelong marriage is no longer customary, driving up poverty, crime, teen pregnancy, welfare dependency, drug abuse, and mental and physical health problems. And yet, amid the broader negative trends, recent signs point to a modest but significant recovery.

Divorce rates appear to have declined a little from historic highs; illegitimacy rates, after doubling every decade from 1960 to 1990, appear to have leveled off, albeit at a high level (33 percent of American births are to unmarried women); teen pregnancy and sexual activity are down; the proportion of homemaking mothers is up; marital fertility appears to be on the rise. Research suggests that married adults are more committed to marital permanence than they were twenty years ago. A new generation of children of divorce appears on the brink of making a commitment to lifelong marriage. In 1977, 55 percent of American teenagers thought a divorce should be harder to get; in 2001, 75 percent did.

A new marriage movement—a distinctively American phenomenon—has been born. The scholarly consensus on the importance of marriage has broadened and deepened; it is now the conventional wisdom among child welfare organizations. As a Child Trends research brief summed up: "Research clearly demonstrates that

Reprinted with permission of the author from *The Weekly Standard,* August 4/August 11, 2003, pp. 22–25.

family structure matters for children, and the family structure that helps children the most is a family headed by two biological parents in a low-conflict marriage. Children in single-parent families, children born to unmarried mothers, and children in stepfamilies or cohabiting relationships face higher risks of poor outcomes. . . . There is thus value for children in promoting strong, stable marriages between biological parents."

What will court-imposed gay marriage do to this incipient recovery of marriage? For, even as support for marriage in general has been rising, the gay marriage debate has proceeded on a separate track. Now the time has come to decide: Will unisex marriage help or hurt marriage as a social institution?

Why should it do either, some may ask? How can Bill and Bob's marriage hurt Mary and Joe? In an exchange with me in the just-released book *Marriage and Same Sex Unions: A Debate,* Evan Wolfson, chief legal strategist for same-sex marriage in the Hawaii case, *Baer v. Lewin,* argues there is "enough marriage to share." What counts, he says, "is not family structure, but the quality of dedication, commitment, self-sacrifice, and love in the household."

Family structure does not count. Then what is marriage for? Why have laws about it? Why care whether people get married or stay married? Do children need mothers and fathers, or will any sort of family do? When the sexual desires of adults clash with the interests of children, which carries more weight, socially and legally?

These are the questions that same-sex marriage raises. Our answers will affect not only gay and lesbian families, but marriage as a whole.

In ordering gay marriage on June 10, 2003, the highest court in Ontario, Canada, explicitly endorsed a brand new vision of marriage along the lines Wolfson suggests: "Marriage is, without dispute, one of the most significant forms of personal relationships. . . . Through the institution of marriage, individuals can publicly express their love and commitment to each other. Through this institution, society publicly recognizes expressions of love and commitment between individuals, granting them respect and legitimacy as a couple."

The Ontario court views marriage as a kind of Good Housekeeping Seal of Approval that government stamps on certain registered intimacies because, well, for no particular reason the court can articulate except that society likes to recognize expressions of love and commitment. In this view, endorsement of gay marriage is a no-brainer, for nothing really important rides on whether anyone gets married or stays married. Marriage is merely individual expressive conduct, and there is no obvious reason why some individuals' expression of gay love should hurt other individuals' expressions of non-gay love.

There is, however, a different view—indeed, a view that is radically opposed to this: Marriage is the fundamental, cross-cultural institution for bridging the male-female divide so that children have loving, committed mothers and fathers. Marriage is inherently normative: It is about holding out a certain kind of relationship as a social ideal, especially when there are children involved. Marriage is not simply an artifact of law; neither is it a mere delivery mechanism for a set of legal benefits that might as well be shared more broadly. The laws of marriage do not create marriage, but in societies ruled by law they help trace the boundaries and sustain the public meanings of marriage.

In other words, while individuals freely choose to enter marriage, society upholds the marriage option, formalizes its definition, and surrounds it with norms and reinforcements, so we can raise boys and girls who aspire to become the kind of men and women who can make successful marriages. Without this shared, public aspect, perpetuated generation after generation, marriage becomes what its critics say it is: a mere contract, a vessel with no particular content, one of a menu of sexual lifestyles, of no fundamental importance to anyone outside a given relationship.

The marriage idea is that children need mothers and fathers, that societies need babies, and that adults have an obligation to shape their sexual behavior so as to give their children stable families in which to grow up.

Which view of marriage is true? We have seen what has happened in our communities where marriage norms have failed. What has happened is not a flowering of libertarian freedom, but a breakdown of social and civic order that can reach frightening proportions. When law and culture retreat from sustaining the marriage idea, individuals cannot create marriage on their own.

In a complex society governed by positive law, social institutions require both social and legal support. To use an analogy, the government does not create private property. But to make a market system a reality requires the assistance of law as well as culture. People have to be raised to respect the property of others, and to value the traits of entrepreneurship, and to be law-abiding generally. The law cannot allow individuals to define for themselves what private property (or law-abiding conduct) means. The boundaries of certain institutions (such as the corporation) also need to be defined legally, and the definitions become socially shared knowledge. We need a shared system of meaning, publicly enforced, if market-based economies are to do their magic and individuals are to maximize their opportunities.

Successful social institutions generally function without people's having to think very much about how they work. But when a social institution is contested—as marriage is today—it becomes critically important to think and speak clearly about its public meanings.

Again, what is marriage for? Marriage is a virtually universal human institution. In all the wildly rich and various cultures flung throughout the ecosphere, in society after society, whether tribal or complex, and however bizarre, human beings have created systems of publicly approved sexual union between men and women that entail well-defined responsibilities of mothers and fathers. Not all these marriage systems look like our own, which is rooted in a fusion of Greek, Roman, Jewish, and Christian culture. Yet everywhere, in isolated mountain valleys, parched deserts, jungle thickets, and broad plains, people have come up with some version of this thing called marriage. Why?

Because sex between men and women makes babies, that's why. Even today, in our technologically advanced contraceptive culture, half of all pregnancies are unintended: Sex between men and women *still* makes babies. Most men and women are powerfully drawn to perform a sexual act that can and does generate life. Marriage is our attempt to reconcile and harmonize the erotic, social, sexual, and financial needs of men and women with the needs of their partner and their children.

How to reconcile the needs of children with the sexual desires of adults? Every society has to face that question, and some resolve it in ways that inflict horrendous cruelty on children born outside marriage. Some cultures decide these children don't matter: Men can have all the sex they want, and any children they create outside of marriage will be throwaway kids; marriage is for citizens—slaves and peasants need not apply. You can see a version of this elitist vision of marriage emerging in America under cover of acceptance of family diversity. Marriage will continue to exist as the social advantage of elite communities. The poor and the working class? Who cares whether their kids have dads? We can always import people from abroad to fill our need for disciplined, educated workers.

Our better tradition, and the only one consistent with democratic principles, is to hold up a single ideal for all parents, which is ultimately based on our deep cultural commitment to the equal dignity and social worth of all children. All kids need and deserve a married mom and dad. All parents are supposed to at least try to behave in ways that will give their own children this important protection. Privately, religiously, emotionally, individually, marriage may have many meanings. But this is the core of its public, shared meaning: Marriage is the place where having children is not only tolerated but welcomed and encouraged, because it gives children mothers and fathers.

Of course, many couples fail to live up to this ideal. Many of the things men and women have to do to sustain their own marriages, and a culture of marriage, are *hard.* Few people will do them consistently if the larger culture does not affirm the critical importance of marriage as a social institution. Why stick out a frustrating relationship, turn down a tempting new love, abstain from sex outside marriage, or even take pains not to conceive children out of wedlock if family structure does not matter? If marriage is not a shared norm, and if successful marriage is not socially valued, do not expect it to survive as the generally accepted context for raising children. If marriage is just a way of publicly celebrating private love, then there is no need to encourage couples to stick it out for the sake of the children. If family structure does not matter, why have marriage laws at all? Do adults, or do they not, have a basic obligation to control their desires so that children can have mothers and fathers?

The problem with endorsing gay marriage is not that it would allow a handful of people to choose alternative family forms, but that it would require society at large to gut marriage of its central presumptions about family in order to accommodate a few adults' desires.

The debate over same-sex marriage, then, is not some sideline discussion. It *is* the marriage debate. Either we win—or we lose the central meaning of marriage. The great threat unisex marriage poses to marriage as a social institution is not some distant or nearby slippery slope, it is an abyss at our feet. If we cannot explain why unisex marriage is, in itself, a disaster, we have already lost the marriage ideal.

Same-sex marriage would enshrine in law a public judgment that the desire of adults for families of choice outweighs the need of children for mothers and fathers. It would give sanction and approval to the creation of a motherless or fatherless family as a deliberately chosen "good." It would mean the law was neutral as to whether children had mothers and fathers. Motherless and fatherless families would be deemed just fine.

Same-sex marriage advocates are starlingly clear on this point. Marriage law, they repeatedly claim, has nothing to do with babies or procreation or getting mothers and fathers for children. In forcing the state legislature to create civil unions for gay couples, the high court of Vermont explicitly ruled that marriage in the state of Vermont has nothing to do with procreation. Evan Wolfson made the same point in *Marriage and Same Sex Unions:* "[I]sn't having the law pretend that there is only one family model that works (let alone exists) a lie?" He goes on to say that in law, "marriage is not just about procreation—indeed is not necessarily about procreation at all."

Wolfson is right that in the course of the sexual revolution the Supreme Court struck down many legal features designed to reinforce the connection of marriage to babies. The animus of elites (including legal elites) against the marriage idea is not brand new. It stretches back at least thirty years. That is part of the problem we face, part of the reason 40 percent of our children are growing up without their fathers.

It is also true, as gay-marriage advocates note, that we impose no fertility tests for marriage: Infertile and older couples marry, and not every fertile couple chooses procreation. But every marriage between a man and a woman is capable of giving any child they create or adopt a mother and a father. Every marriage between a man and a woman discourages either from creating fatherless children outside the marriage vow. In this sense, neither older married couples nor childless husbands and wives publicly challenge or dilute the core meaning of marriage. Even when a man marries an older woman and they do not adopt, his marriage helps protect children. How? His marriage means, if he keeps his vows, that he will not produce out-of-wedlock children.

Does marriage discriminate against gays and lesbians? Formally speaking, no. There are no sexual-orientation tests for marriage; many gays and lesbians do choose to marry members of the opposite sex, and some of these unions succeed. Our laws do not require a person to marry the individual to whom he or she is most erotically attracted, so long as he or she is willing to promise sexual fidelity, mutual caretaking, and shared parenting of any children of the marriage.

But marriage is unsuited to the wants and desires of many gays and lesbians, precisely because it is designed to bridge the male-female divide and sustain the idea that children need mothers and fathers. To make a marriage, what you need is a husband and a wife. Redefining marriage so that it suits gays and lesbians would require fundamentally changing our legal, public, and social conception of what marriage is in ways that threaten its core public purposes.

Some who criticize the refusal to embrace gay marriage liken it to the outlawing of interracial marriage, but the analogy is woefully false. The Supreme Court overturned anti-miscegenation laws because they frustrated the core purpose of marriage in order to sustain a racist legal order. Marriage laws, by contrast, were not invented to express animus toward homosexuals or anyone else. Their purpose is not negative, but positive: They uphold an institution that developed, over thousands of years, in thousands of cultures, to help direct the erotic desires of men and women into a relatively narrow but indispensably fruitful channel. We need men and women to marry and make babies for our society to survive. We have no similar public stake in any other family form—in the union of same-sex couples or the singleness of single moms.

Meanwhile, *cui bono*? To meet the desires of whom would we put our most basic social institution at risk? No good research on the marriage intentions of homosexual people exists. For what it's worth, the Census Bureau reports that 0.5 percent of households now consist of same-sex partners. To get a proxy for how many gay couples would avail themselves of the health insurance benefits marriage can provide, I asked the top 10 companies listed on the Human Rights Campaign's website as providing same-sex insurance benefits how many of their employees use this option. Only one company, General Motors, released its data. Out of 1.3 million employees, 166 claimed benefits for a same-sex partner, *one one-hundredth of one percent.*

People who argue for creating gay marriage do so in the name of high ideals: justice, compassion, fairness. Their sincerity is not in question. Nevertheless, to take the already troubled institution most responsible for the protection of children and throw out its most basic presumption in order to further adult interests in sexual freedom would not be high-minded. It would be morally callous and socially irresponsible.

If we cannot stand and defend this ground, then face it: The marriage debate is over. Dan Quayle was wrong. We lost.

QUESTIONS

1 Do you agree with Gallagher's construction of "the central meaning of marriage"? In any case, is societal endorsement of same-sex marriage incompatible with the central meaning of marriage?
2 Gallagher denies that the refusal to accept same-sex marriage is analogous to laws against interracial marriage. Do you agree?

For Better or Worse? The Case for Gay (and Straight) Marriage
Jonathan Rauch

Rauch situates his defense of gay (same-sex) marriage within the framework of an overall analysis of the *social meaning* of marriage, so one of his central tasks is to identify the underlying purpose or purposes of marriage as a social institution. He briefly considers and rejects a "Hayekian" argument against gay marriage and then confronts the "standard" or "child-centered" view of the purpose of marriage.

Reprinted with permission of the author from *The New Republic,* May 6, 1996, pp. 18–23. © 1996 by Jonathan Rauch.

Rauch makes a series of arguments against the child-centered view, focusing especially on a construction of that view that emphasizes the anatomical possibility of a married couple producing children. He acknowledges that raising children is one of the important social purposes served by the institution of marriage but argues that there are two additional purposes underlying that institution: domesticating males and providing reliable caregivers. Because these latter two purposes are also part of the social sense underlying the privileged status of marriage in our society, and because these two purposes can also be served by gay marriage, Rauch argues that society has a compelling interest in the acceptance of gay marriage. He concludes by claiming that there is a sense in which gay marriage should be *expected* for homosexuals, not merely permitted.

Whatever else marriage may or may not be, it is certainly falling apart. Half of today's marriages end in divorce, and, far more costly, many never begin—leaving mothers poor, children fatherless and neighborhoods chaotic. With timing worthy of Neville Chamberlain, homosexuals have chosen this moment to press for the right to marry. What's more, Hawaii's courts are moving toward letting them do so. I'll believe in gay marriage in America when I see it, but if Hawaii legalizes it, even temporarily, the uproar over this final insult to a besieged institution will be deafening.

Whether gay marriage makes sense—and whether straight marriage makes sense—depends on what marriage is actually for. Current secular thinking on this question is shockingly sketchy. Gay activists say: marriage is for love, and we love each other, therefore we should be able to marry. Traditionalists say: marriage is for children, and homosexuals do not (or should not) have children, therefore you should not be able to marry. That, unfortunately, pretty well covers the spectrum. I say "unfortunately" because both views are wrong. They misunderstand and impoverish the social meaning of marriage.

So what is marriage for? Modern marriage is, of course, based upon traditions that religion helped to codify and enforce. But religious doctrine has no special standing in the world of secular law and policy (the "Christian nation" crowd notwithstanding). If we want to know what and whom marriage is for in modern America, we need a sensible secular doctrine.

At one point, marriage in secular society was largely a matter of business: cementing family ties, providing social status for men and economic support for women, conferring dowries, and so on. Marriages were typically arranged, and "love" in the modern sense was no prerequisite. In Japan, remnants of this system remain, and it works surprisingly well. Couples stay together because they view their marriage as a partnership: an investment in social stability for themselves and their children. Because Japanese couples don't expect as much emotional fulfillment as we do, they are less inclined to break up. They also take a somewhat more relaxed attitude toward adultery. What's a little extracurricular love provided that each partner is fulfilling his or her many other marital duties?

In the West, of course, love is a defining element. The notion of lifelong love is charming, if ambitious, and certainly love is a desirable element of marriage. In society's eyes, however, it cannot be the defining element. You may or may not love your husband, but the two of you are just as married either way. You may love your mistress, but that certainly doesn't make her your spouse. Love helps make sense of marriage emotionally, but it is not terribly important in making sense of marriage from the point of view of social policy.

If love does not define the purpose of secular marriage, what does? Neither the law nor secular thinking provides a clear answer. Today marriage is almost entirely a voluntary arrangement whose contents are up to the people making the deal. There are few if any behaviors that automatically end a marriage. If a man beats his wife, which is about the worst thing he can do to her, he may be convicted of assault, but his marriage is not automatically dissolved. Couples can be adulterous ("open") yet remain married. They can be celibate, too; consummation is not required. All in all, it is an impressive and also rather astonishing victory for modern individualism that so important an institution should be so bereft of formal social instruction as to what should go on inside of it.

Secular society tells us only a few things about marriage. First, marriage depends on the consent of the parties. Second, the parties are not children. Third, the number of parties is two. Fourth, one is a man and the other a woman. Within those rules a marriage is whatever anyone says it is.

Perhaps it is enough simply to say that marriage is as it is and should not be tampered with. This sounds like a crudely reactionary position. In fact, however, of all the arguments against reforming marriage, it is probably the most powerful.

Call it a Hayekian argument, after the great libertarian economist F. A. Hayek, who developed this line of thinking in his book *The Fatal Conceit.* In a market system, the prices generated by impersonal forces may not make sense from any one person's point of view, but they encode far more information than even the cleverest person could ever gather. In a similar fashion, human societies evolve rich and complicated webs of nonlegal rules in the form of customs, traditions and institutions. Like prices, they may seem irrational or arbitrary.

But the very fact that they are the customs that have evolved implies that they embody a practical logic that may not be apparent to even a sophisticated analyst. And the web of custom cannot be torn apart and reordered at will because once its internal logic is violated it falls apart. Intellectuals, such as Marxists or feminists, who seek to deconstruct and rationally rebuild social traditions, will produce not better order but chaos.

So the Hayekian view argues strongly against gay marriage. It says that the current rules may not be best and may even be unfair. But they are all we have, and, once you say that marriage need not be male-female, soon marriage will stop being anything at all. You can't mess with the formula without causing unforeseen consequences, possibly including the implosion of the institution of marriage itself.

However, there are problems with the Hayekian position. It is untenable in its extreme form and unhelpful in its milder version. In its extreme form, it implies that no social reforms should ever be undertaken. Indeed, no laws should be passed, because they interfere with the natural evolution of social mores. How could Hayekians abolish slavery? They would probably note that slavery violates fundamental moral principles. But in so doing they would establish a moral platform from which to judge social rules, and thus acknowledge that abstracting social debate from moral concerns is not possible.

If the ban on gay marriage were only mildly unfair, and if the costs of changing it were certain to be enormous, then the ban could stand on Hayekian grounds. But, if there is any social policy today that has a fair claim to be scaldingly inhumane, it is the ban on gay marriage. As conservatives tirelessly and rightly point out, marriage is society's most fundamental institution. To bar any class of people from marrying as they choose is an extraordinary deprivation. When not so long ago it was illegal in parts of America for blacks to marry whites, no one could claim that this was a trivial disenfranchisement. Granted, gay marriage raises issues that interracial marriage does not; but no one can argue that the deprivation is a minor one.

To outweigh such a serious claim it is not enough to say that gay marriage might lead to bad things. Bad things happened as a result of legalizing contraception, but that did not make it the wrong thing to do. Besides, it seems doubtful that extending marriage to, say, another 3 or 5 percent of the population would have anything like the effects that no-fault divorce has had, to say nothing of contraception. By now, the "traditional" understanding of marriage has been sullied in all kinds of ways. It is hard to think of a bigger affront to tradition, for instance, than allowing married women to own property independently of their husbands or allowing them to charge their husbands with rape. Surely it is unfair to say that marriage may be reformed for the sake of anyone and everyone except homosexuals, who must respect the dictates of tradition.

Faced with these problems, the milder version of the Hayekian argument says not that social traditions shouldn't be tampered with at all, but that they shouldn't be tampered with lightly. Fine. In this case, no one is talking about casual messing around; both sides have marshaled their arguments with deadly seriousness. Hayekians surely have to recognize that appeals to blind tradition and to the risks inherent in social change do not, a priori, settle anything in this instance. They merely warn against frivolous change.

So we turn to what has become the standard view of marriage's purpose. Its proponents would probably like to call it a child-centered view, but it is actually an anti-gay view, as will become clear. Whatever you call it, it is the view of marriage that is heard most often, and in the context of the debate over gay marriage it is heard almost exclusively. In its most straightforward form it goes as follows (I quote from James Q. Wilson's fine book *The Moral Sense*):

> A family is not an association of independent people; it is a human commitment designed to make possible the rearing of moral and healthy children. Governments care—or ought to care—about families for this reason, and scarcely for any other.

Wilson speaks about "family" rather than "marriage" as such, but one may, I think, read him as speaking of marriage without doing any injustice to his meaning. The resulting proposition—government ought to care about marriage almost entirely because of children—seems reasonable. But there are problems. The first, obviously, is that gay couples may have children, whether through adoption, prior marriage or (for lesbians) artificial insemination. Leaving aside the thorny issue of gay adoption, the point is that if the mere presence of children is the test, then homosexual relationships can certainly pass it.

You might note, correctly, that heterosexual marriages are more likely to produce children than homosexual ones. When granting marriage licenses to heterosexuals, however, we do not ask how likely the couple is to have children. We assume that they are entitled to get married whether or not they end up with children. Understanding this, conservatives often make an interesting move. In seeking to justify the state's interest in marriage, they shift from the actual presence of children to the anatomical possibility of making them. Hadley Arkes, a political science professor and prominent opponent of homosexual marriage, makes the case this way:

> The traditional understanding of marriage is grounded in the 'natural teleology of the body'—in the inescapable fact that only a man and a woman, and only two people, not three, can generate a child. Once marriage is detached from that natural teleology of the body, what ground of principle would thereafter confine marriage to two people rather than some larger grouping? That is, on what ground of principle would the law reject the claim of a gay couple that their love is not confined to a coupling of two, but that they are woven into a larger ensemble with yet another person or two?

What he seems to be saying is that, where the possibility of natural children is nil, the meaning of marriage is nil. If marriage is allowed between members of the same sex, then the concept of marriage has been emptied of content except to ask whether the parties love each other. Then anything goes, including polygamy. This reasoning presumably is what those opposed to gay marriage have in mind when they claim that, once gay marriage is legal, marriage to pets will follow close behind.

But Arkes and his sympathizers make two mistakes. To see them, break down the claim into two components: (1) Two-person marriage derives its special status from the anatomical possibility that the partners can create natural children; and (2) Apart from (1), two-person marriage has no purpose sufficiently strong to justify its special status. That is, absent justification (1), anything goes.

The first proposition is wholly at odds with the way society actually views marriage. Leave aside the insistence that natural, as opposed to adopted, children define the importance of marriage. The deeper problem, apparent right away, is the issue of sterile heterosexual couples. Here the "anatomical possibility" crowd has a problem, for a homosexual union is, anatomically speaking, nothing but one variety of sterile union and no different even in principle: a woman without a uterus has no more potential for giving birth than a man without a vagina.

It may sound like carping to stress the case of barren heterosexual marriage: the vast majority of newlywed heterosexual couples, after all, can have children and probably will. But the point here is fundamental. There are far more sterile heterosexual unions in America than homosexual ones. The "anatomical possibility" crowd cannot have it both ways. If the possibility of children is what gives meaning to marriage, then a post-menopausal woman who applies for a marriage license should be turned away at the courthouse door. What's more, she should be hooted at and condemned for stretching the meaning of marriage beyond its natural basis and so reducing the institution to frivolity. People at the

Family Research Council or Concerned Women for America should point at her and say, "If she can marry, why not polygamy?"

Obviously, the "anatomical" conservatives do not say this, because they are sane. They instead flail around, saying that sterile men and women were at least born with the right-shaped parts for making children, and so on. Their position is really a nonposition. It says that the "natural children" rationale defines marriage when homosexuals are involved but not when heterosexuals are involved. When the parties to union are sterile heterosexuals, the justification for marriage must be something else. But what?

Now arises the oddest part of the "anatomical" argument. Look at proposition (2) above. It says that, absent the anatomical justification for marriage, anything goes. In other words, it dismisses the idea that there might be other good reasons for society to sanctify marriage above other kinds of relationships. Why would anybody make this move? I'll hazard a guess: to exclude homosexuals. Any rationale that justifies sterile heterosexual marriages can also apply to homosexual ones. For instance, marriage makes women more financially secure. Very nice, say the conservatives. But that rationale could be applied to lesbians, so it's definitely out.

The end result of this stratagem is perverse to the point of being funny. The attempt to ground marriage in children (or the anatomical possibility thereof) falls flat. But, having lost that reason for marriage, the anti-gay people can offer no other. In their fixation on excluding homosexuals, they leave themselves no consistent justification for the privileged status of *heterosexual* marriage. They thus tear away any coherent foundation that secular marriage might have, which is precisely the opposite of what they claim they want to do. If they have to undercut marriage to save it from homosexuals, so be it!

For the record, I would be the last to deny that children are one central reason for the privileged status of marriage. When men and women get together, children are a likely outcome; and, as we are learning in ever more unpleasant ways, when children grow up without two parents, trouble ensues. Children are not a trivial reason for marriage; they just cannot be the only reason.

What are the others? It seems to me that the two strongest candidates are these: domesticating men and providing reliable caregivers. Both purposes are critical to the functioning of a humane and stable society, and both are much better served by marriage—that is, by one-to-one lifelong commitment—than by any other institution.

Civilizing young males is one of any society's biggest problems. Wherever unattached males gather in packs, you see no end of trouble: wildings in Central Park, gangs in Los Angeles, soccer hooligans in Britain, skinheads in Germany, fraternity hazings in universities, grope-lines in the military and, in a different but ultimately no less tragic way, the bathhouses and wanton sex of gay San Francisco or New York in the 1970s.

For taming men, marriage is unmatched. "Of all the institutions through which men may pass—schools, factories, the military—marriage has the largest effect," Wilson writes in *The Moral Sense*. (A token of the casualness of current thinking about marriage is that the man who wrote those words could, later in the very same book, say that government should care about fostering families for "scarcely any other" reason than children.) If marriage—that is, the binding of men into couples—did nothing else, its power to settle men, to keep them at home and out of trouble, would be ample justification for its special status.

Of course, women and older men don't generally travel in marauding or orgiastic packs. But in their case the second rationale comes into play. A second enormous problem for society is what to do when someone is beset by some sort of burdensome contingency. It could be cancer, a broken back, unemployment or depression; it could be exhaustion from work or stress under pressure. If marriage has any meaning at all, it is that, when you collapse from a stroke, there will be at least one other person whose "job" is to drop everything and come to your aid; or that when you come home after being fired by the postal service there will be someone to persuade you not to kill the supervisor.

Obviously, both rationales—the need to settle males and the need to have people looked after—apply to sterile people as well as fertile ones, and apply to childless couples as well as to ones with children. The first explains why everybody feels relieved when the town delinquent gets married, and the second explains why everybody feels happy when an aging widow takes a second husband. From a social point of view, it seems to me, both rationales are far more compelling as justifications of marriage's special status than, say, love. And both of them apply to homosexuals as well as to heterosexuals.

Take the matter of settling men. It is probably true that women and children, more than just the fact of marriage, help civilize men. But that hardly means that the settling effect of marriage on homosexual men is negligible. To the contrary, being tied to a committed relationship plainly helps stabilize gay men. Even without marriage, coupled gay men have steady sex partners and relationships that they value and therefore tend to be less wanton. Add marriage, and you bring a further array of stabilizing influences. One of the main benefits of publicly recognized marriage is that it binds couples together not only in their own eyes but also in the eyes of society at large. Around the partners is woven a web of expectations that they will spend nights together, go to parties together, take out mortgages together, buy furniture at Ikea together, and so on—all of which helps tie them together and keep them off the streets and at home. Surely that is a very good thing, especially as compared to the closet-gay culture of furtive sex with innumerable partners in parks and bathhouses.

The other benefit of marriage—caretaking—clearly applies to homosexuals. One of the first things many people worry about when coming to terms with their homosexuality is: Who will take care of me when I'm ailing or old? Society needs to care about this, too, as the AIDS crisis has made horribly clear. If that crisis has shown anything, it is that homosexuals can and will take care of each other, sometimes with breathtaking devotion—and that no institution can begin to match the care of a devoted partner. Legally speaking, marriage creates kin. Surely society's interest in kin-creation is strongest of all for people who are unlikely to be supported by children in old age and who may well be rejected by their own parents in youth.

Gay marriage, then, is far from being a mere exercise in political point-making or rights-mongering. On the contrary, it serves two of the three social purposes that make marriage so indispensable and irreplaceable for heterosexuals. Two out of three may not be the whole ball of wax, but it is more than enough to give society a compelling interest in marrying off homosexuals.

There is no substitute. Marriage is the *only* institution that adequately serves these purposes. The power of marriage is not just legal but social. It seals its promise with the smiles and tears of family, friends and neighbors. It shrewdly exploits ceremony (big, public weddings) and money (expensive gifts, dowries) to deter casual commitment and to make bailing out embarrassing. Stag parties and bridal showers signal that what is beginning is not just a legal arrangement but a whole new stage of life. "Domestic partner" laws do none of these things.

I'll go further: far from being a substitute for the real thing, marriage-lite may undermine it. Marriage is a deal between a couple and society, not just between two people: society recognizes the sanctity and autonomy of the pair-bond, and in exchange each spouse commits to being the other's nurse, social worker and policeman of first resort. Each marriage is its own little society within society. Any step that weakens the deal by granting the legal benefits of marriage without also requiring the public commitment is begging for trouble.

So gay marriage makes sense for several of the same reasons that straight marriage makes sense. That would seem a natural place to stop. But the logic of the argument compels one to go a twist further. If it is good for society to have people attached, then it is not enough just to make marriage available. Marriage should also be *expected*. This, too, is just as true for homosexuals as for heterosexuals. So, if homosexuals are justified in expecting access to marriage, society is equally justified in expecting them to use it. I'm not saying that out-of-wedlock sex should be scandalous or that people should be coerced into marrying. The mechanisms of expectation are more subtle. When grandma cluck-clucks over a still-unmarried young man, or when mom says she wishes her little girl would settle down, she is expressing a strong and well-justified preference: one that is quietly echoed in a thousand ways throughout society and that produces subtle but important pressure to form and sustain unions. This is a good and necessary thing, and it will be as necessary for homosexuals as heterosexuals. If gay marriage is recognized, single gay people over a certain age should not be surprised when they are disapproved of or pitied. That is a vital part of what makes marriage work. It's stigma as social policy.

If marriage is to work it cannot be merely a "lifestyle option." It must be privileged. That is, it must be understood to be better, on average, than other ways of living. Not mandatory, not good where everything else is bad, but better: a general norm, rather than a personal taste. The biggest worry about gay marriage, I think, is that homosexuals might get it but then mostly not use it. Gay neglect of marriage wouldn't greatly erode the bonding power of heterosexual marriage (remember, homosexuals are only a tiny fraction of the population)—but it would certainly not help. And heterosexual society would rightly feel betrayed if, after legalization, homosexuals treated marriage as a minority taste rather than as a core institution of life. It is not enough, I think, for gay people to say we want the right to marry. If we do not use it, shame on us.

QUESTIONS

1 Is Rauch's suggested account of the social meaning of marriage defensible and complete?

2 Does society, as Rauch claims, have a compelling interest in the acceptance of same-sex marriage?

3 Marriage is traditionally understood as restricted to two partners, one man and one woman. If marriage is once redefined to make way for same-sex marriage, how would you react to a proposal to redefine marriage again, this time to make way for polygamy and other forms of "plural" marriage?

SUGGESTED ADDITIONAL READINGS FOR CHAPTER 4

BAIRD, ROBERT M., and STUART E. ROSENBAUM, eds.: *Same-Sex Marriage: The Moral and Legal Debate,* 2d ed. Amherst, N.Y.: Prometheus, 2004. This anthology groups articles under three headings: "The Massachusetts Decision and Reactions," "The Emotional Dimensions of the Debate," and "The Philosophical Arguments."

BAKER, ROBERT B., KATHLEEN J. WININGER, and FREDERICK A. ELLISTON, eds.: *Philosophy and Sex,* 3d ed. Amherst, N.Y.: Prometheus, 1998. Part I of this three-part anthology contains a number of articles relevant to the topic of sexual morality.

BELLIOTTI RAYMOND A.: *Good Sex: Perspectives on Sexual Ethics.* Lawrence: University Press of Kansas, 1993. Belliotti discusses mainstream philosophical views of sexual morality, considers Marxist and feminist perspectives, and then constructs his own theory, which he calls "sexual morality in five tiers."

CORVINO, JOHN, ed.: *Same Sex: Debating the Ethics, Science, and Culture of Homosexuality.* Lanham, Md.: Rowman & Littlefield, 1997. Part I of this book provides a collection of articles on the issue of the morality of homosexual sex. Religious as well as philosophical perspectives are included. Part II deals with the etiology of same-sex desire, and Part IV deals with public-policy issues.

JORDAN, JEFF: "Contra Same-Sex Marriage." In Robert M. Baird and Stuart E. Rosenbaum, eds., *Same-Sex Marriage: The Moral and Legal Debate,* 2d ed. Amherst, N.Y.: Prometheus, 2004, pp. 163–180. Jordan discusses three models of marriage, then argues against state recognition of same-sex marriage on the grounds that such recognition would violate two fundamental principles of liberalism.

KLEPPER, HOWARD: "Sexual Exploitation and the Value of Persons." *Journal of Value Inquiry,* vol. 27, December 1993, pp. 479–486. Klepper argues that the concept of sexually using another person cannot be reduced entirely to violations of the requirement of voluntary informed consent.

KRISTJÁNSSON, KRISTJÁN: "Casual Sex Revisited." *Journal of Social Philosophy,* vol. 29, Fall 1998, pp. 97–108. Kristjánsson essentially embraces the sex with love approach and develops an argument against promiscuity.

LEMONCHECK, LINDA: *Loose Women, Lecherous Men: A Feminist Philosophy of Sex.* New York: Oxford University Press, 1997. LeMoncheck's overall goal is to construct a feminist philosophy of sex. In Chapter 2, she engages the issue of promiscuity. In Chapter 3, she discusses sexual preference.

SULLIVAN, ANDREW, ed.: *Same-Sex Marriage: Pro and Con,* updated ed. New York: Vintage, 2004. This anthology provides an extensive collection of materials on the same-sex marriage debate. Historical, religious, and legal perspectives are included, and there are chapters dealing respectively with "the debate on the left," "the debate on the right," "same-sex marriage and parenthood," and "the polygamy and adultery debate."

WASSERSTROM, RICHARD: "Is Adultery Immoral?" In Richard Wasserstrom, ed., *Today's Moral Problems,* 3d ed. New York: Macmillan, 1985. This helpful article investigates the various arguments that can plausibly be made in support of the claim that adultery is immoral. Wasserstrom's analysis is especially valuable in focusing attention on the presuppositions of such arguments.

WEDGWOOD, RALPH: "The Fundamental Argument for Same-Sex Marriage." *Journal of Political Philosophy,* vol. 7, September 1999, pp. 225–242. Wedgwood presents an account of the institution of marriage, specifies "marriage's essential rationale," and argues that the state's refusal to recognize same-sex marriage involves an indefensible denial of equality.

CHAPTER 5

Pornography, Hate Speech, and Censorship

Efforts to place legal restrictions on the flow of pornographic material typically give rise to complaints of unwarranted censorship and unjustified intrusion into individual liberty. Proposals to regulate hate speech, whether on college campuses or in society more generally, typically give rise to similar complaints. This chapter deals first with the issue of restricting access to pornography and then with the issue of regulating hate speech.

Is a government—at the national, state, or local level—justified in limiting the access of *consenting adults* to pornographic materials? Censorship laws, in their most common form, seek to limit access to pornographic materials by prohibiting their distribution, sale, or exhibition. However, censorship laws might also take the form of prohibiting the production of pornography or even its possession.

COMMISSION REPORTS ON PORNOGRAPHY

In 1967, the Congress of the United States, labeling the traffic in obscene and pornographic materials "a matter of national concern," established the Commission on Obscenity and Pornography. This advisory commission, whose members were appointed by President Lyndon Johnson in January 1968, was charged with initiating a thorough study of obscenity and pornography and, on the basis of such a study, submitting recommendations for the regulation of obscene and pornographic materials. In September 1970, the commission transmitted its final report to the president and the Congress. Its fundamental recommendation was that all legislation prohibiting the sale, exhibition, or distribution of sexual materials to *consenting adults* be repealed. However, the commission recommended the continuation of legislation intended to protect nonconsenting adults from being confronted with sexually explicit material through public displays and unsolicited mailings. It also recommended the continuation of legislation prohibiting the commercial distribution of certain sexual material to juveniles. The commission based its fundamental rec-ommendation largely, though not exclusively, on its central factual finding: There is no evidence to support the contention that exposure to explicit sexual materials plays a significant role in the causation of either social harms (via antisocial behavior) or individual harms (such as severe emotional disturbance).

The report of the Commission on Obscenity and Pornography was unwelcome in many quarters. To begin with, only twelve of the commission's eighteen mem-bers voted in support of its fundamental recommendation. In fact, the report itself features a substantial minority report that questions the factual findings as well as the recommendations of the commission. President Richard Nixon contended that the report was completely unsatisfactory. Many members of Congress were also displeased, and there was a substantial public outcry that the commission's conclu-sions were "morally bankrupt." As a result, there was no significant movement to implement its fundamental recommendation.

In spring 1985, responsive to a request by President Ronald Reagan, Attorney General Edwin Meese III named an eleven-member commission to *reexamine* the problem of pornography in American society. The Attorney General's Commission on Pornography submitted its final report in July 1986. With regard to the issue of the harmfulness of pornography, some of the factual findings of this second com-mission (which will be called "the 1986 commission") stand in stark contrast to the central factual finding of the earlier commission (which will be called "the 1970 commission"). The 1986 commission, using the word *pornography* to refer to material that is "predominantly sexually explicit and intended primarily for the pur-pose of sexual arousal," thought it important to distinguish among (1) violent pornography, (2) nonviolent but degrading pornography, and (3) nonviolent and nondegrading pornography. The commission concluded that both category (1) and category (2) materials, but *not* category (3) materials, bear a causal relationship to undesirable attitudinal changes and acts of sexual violence. The thinking of the commission on these matters is exhibited in an excerpt from the *Final Report* that is reprinted in this chapter.

The 1970 commission, convinced of the essential harmlessness of pornography, embraced an explicit anticensorship stance. In contrast, the 1986 commission was fundamentally procensorship and endorsed (and, in fact, called for vigorous enforcement of) already existing laws that criminalize the sale, distribution, or exhibition of *legally obscene* pornographic materials. The relevant standard of legal obscenity—a category that does not enjoy First Amendment protection—was first enunciated by the United States Supreme Court in *Miller v. California* (1973). In accordance with "the Miller standard," material is legally obscene if three condi-tions are satisfied:

(a) . . . "the average person, applying contemporary community standards," would find that the work, taken as a whole, appeals to the prurient interest; (b) . . . the work depicts or describes, in a patently offensive way, sexual conduct specifically defined by the appli-cable state law; and (c) . . . the work, taken as a whole, lacks serious literary, artistic, political, or scientific value.[1]

[1]United States Supreme Court, 413 U.S. 15, 24.

The 1986 commission also called special attention to the problem of child pornography. Since the production of child pornography typically entails the sexual abuse of children, the commission pointed out that there is a distinctive and compelling rationale for laws that prohibit the production, as well as the sale, exhibition, or distribution, of child pornography.[2]

The 1986 commission reported that pornography in American society had undergone significant changes in the sixteen years that had passed between the two commission reports. Its finding was that pornography had become increasingly violent, increasingly degrading, and increasingly pervasive. Whether pornography has become even more violent and degrading since 1986 is perhaps difficult to say, but computer-generated images and Internet transmission seem to leave little doubt that pornography has become even more pervasive in American society.

LIBERTY-LIMITING PRINCIPLES

Laws limiting the access of consenting adults to pornographic materials, like all prohibitive laws, inevitably involve the limitation of individual liberty. Accordingly, one way of providing a framework for our discussion is to take notice of the kinds of grounds that may be advanced to justify the limitation of individual liberty. Four suggested liberty-limiting principles are especially noteworthy:[3]

1 The harm principle—Individual liberty is justifiably limited to prevent *harm to others.*

2 The principle of legal paternalism—Individual liberty is justifiably limited to prevent *harm to self.*

3 The principle of legal moralism—Individual liberty is justifiably limited to prevent *immoral behavior.*

4 The offense principle—Individual liberty is justifiably limited to prevent *offense to others.*

The *harm principle* is the most widely accepted liberty-limiting principle. Few will dispute that the law is within its proper bounds when it restricts actions whereby one person causes harm to others. (The category of *harm to others* is understood as encompassing not only personal injury but also damage to the general welfare of society.) What remains a lively source of debate is whether any, or all, of the other suggested principles are legitimate liberty-limiting principles. According to John Stuart Mill (1806–1873), only the harm principle is a legitimate liberty-limiting principle. Some brief excerpts from his famus essay *On Liberty* appear in this chapter. Although Mill need not be read as unsympathetic to the offense principle, he clearly and vigorously rejects both the principle of legal paternalism and the principle of legal moralism.

---

[2]This analysis is not intended to apply to *virtual* child pornography, which involves no actual child in its production. In *Ashcroft v. Free Speech Coalition,* 535 U.S. 234 (2002), the Supreme Court struck down a federal ban on "virtual child pornography."

[3]Joel Feinberg's discussion of such principles served as a guide for the formulations adopted here. *Social Philosophy* (Englewood Cliffs, N.J.: Prentice-Hall, 1973), chap. 2.

According to the *principle of legal paternalism,* the law may justifiably be invoked to prevent self-harm and, thus, "to protect individuals from themselves." Supporters of this principle think that the law rightfully serves much as a benevolent parent who limits his or her child's liberty in order to save the child from harm. Others, of course, often in the spirit of Mill, hotly contest the legitimacy of the principle of legal paternalism. It is said, for example, that government does not have the right to meddle in the private lives of its citizens. Although there is little doubt that there are presently numerous paternalistic features in our legal system, their justifiability remains a disputed issue. The widespread law that requires motorcyclists to wear protective head gear is one apparent example of a paternalistic law.

According to the *principle of legal moralism,* the law may justifiably be invoked to prevent immoral behavior or, as it is often expressed, to "enforce morals." Such things as kidnapping, murder, and fraud are undoubtedly immoral, but there would seem to be no need to appeal to the principle of legal moralism to justify laws against them. An appeal to the harm principle already provides a widely accepted independent justification. As a result, the principle of legal moralism usually comes to the fore only when so-called victimless crimes are under discussion. Is it justifiable to legislate against gambling, marijuana smoking, and certain forms of sexual behavior simply on the grounds that such activities are thought to be morally unacceptable? There are many such laws, and, to the extent that they are perceived as merely enforcing conventional morality, some critics call for their repeal on the grounds that the principle of legal moralism is an unacceptable liberty-limiting principle. To accept the principle of legal moralism, in Mill's words, is tantamount to permitting a "tyranny of the majority."

According to the *offense principle,* the law may justifiably be invoked to prevent offensive behavior in public. "Offensive" behavior is understood as behavior that causes shame, embarrassment, disgust, or other forms of psychic discomfort in onlookers. The offense principle, unlike the other principles under discussion here, is not ordinarily advanced to justify laws that would limit the access of *consenting* adults to pornographic materials. However, this principle is sometimes advanced to justify laws that protect *nonconsenting* adults from offensive displays of pornography.

IS THE CENSORSHIP OF PORNOGRAPHY JUSTIFIED?

Arguments in support of laws that would limit the access of consenting adults to pornographic materials can conveniently be organized by reference to the liberty-limiting principles on which they are based.

The most important procensorship argument is based on the *harm principle.* It is asserted that exposure to pornography is a significant causal factor in sex-related crimes, such as rape. Defenders of this thesis sometimes argue for their claim by citing examples of persons exposed to pornographic material who subsequently commit sex-related crimes. Such examples, however, fail to establish that the crime, which *follows* exposure to pornography, is a *causal result* of exposure to pornography.

Indeed, the 1970 commission reported that there is no evidence to support such a causal connection. On the other hand, the 1986 commission surveyed the available evidence and reported the existence of a causal connection between exposure to certain kinds of pornography (namely, *violent* pornography and *degrading* pornography) and acts of sexual violence. All of these matters continue to be hotly debated. However, since the harm principle is a widely accepted liberty-limiting principle, a formidable argument for censorship emerges to the extent that a causal connection between the use of pornography (or certain kinds of pornography) and antisocial behavior can be established.

A second procensorship argument is based on the *principle of legal paternalism*. It is said that those exposed to pornography will be harmed by such exposure. They will, it is thought, develop or reinforce emotional problems; they will render themselves incapable of love and other human relationships necessary for a happy and satisfying life. In a more abstract and possibly rhetorical version of this argument, it is alleged that frequent exposure to pornography "depersonalizes" or "dehumanizes," and presumably such effects are at least in a broad sense harmful to the individual. The argument based on the principle of legal paternalism is answered in two ways: (1) The alleged self-harm does not occur. (2) Regardless of the truth or falsity of the claim of self-harm, the principle of legal paternalism is not an acceptable liberty-limiting principle.

A third procensorship argument is based on the *principle of legal moralism*. It is claimed that there is a widespread consensus to the effect that pornography is morally repugnant.[4] Inasmuch as the principle of legal moralism seems to allow a community to enforce its moral convictions, it follows that the access of consenting adults to pornographic materials may rightfully be restricted. The argument based on the principle of legal moralism is answered in two ways: (1) The alleged consensus of moral opinion is nonexistent. (2) Regardless of the truth or falsity of the claim of an existing moral consensus, the principle of legal moralism is not an acceptable liberty-limiting principle.

The overall case against laws limiting the access of consenting adults to pornographic materials typically takes the following form: The principle of legal paternalism is an unacceptable liberty-limiting principle; the government should not meddle in the private affairs of its citizens, since such meddling is likely to produce more harm than it prevents. The principle of legal moralism is also an unacceptable liberty-limiting principle; to enforce the moral views of the majority is, in effect, to allow a "tyranny of the majority." A government can rightfully restrict the activity of consenting adults only on the grounds that such activity is *harmful to others*. At the present time, however, it has not been established that the access of consenting adults to pornographic materials presents a "clear and present danger." Thus, censorship, especially in view of the administrative nightmares it is likely to generate and the very real possibility that the power of the censor will be abused, is clearly unwarranted.

---

[4]The morality of pornography is an important ethical issue in its own right. To some extent, of course, one's moral assessment of pornography is a function of one's views on sexual morality in general.

FEMINISM AND PORNOGRAPHY

In recent years, an important critique of pornography has arisen from a feminist point of view. In contrast to more traditional critics of pornography, feminists do not ordinarily object to the sexual explicitness that is found in pornography. Rather, their concern is rooted in the fact that pornography typically portrays women in a degrading and dehumanizing way. Related to this central concern is a distinction that feminists ordinarily draw between *pornography* (which is morally and socially problematic) and *erotica* (which is not).

In one of this chapter's selections, Helen E. Longino defines pornography as "material that explicitly represents or describes degrading and abusive sexual behavior so as to endorse and/or recommend the behavior as described." Because pornography is *injurious* to women in a number of related ways, she maintains, its production and distribution are justifiably subject to control. In essence, then, Longino presents a procensorship argument based on the harm principle. However, not all feminists advocate the censorship of pornography. In another of this chapter's selections, Mark R. Wicclair vigorously defends an anticensorship stance within the framework of feminism. He emphasizes the values associated with the principle of freedom of expression and calls attention to the detrimental side effects of censorship. He also maintains, against the procensorship feminist, that the connection between pornography and harm to women is too speculative to warrant incurring the social costs of censorship.

REGULATING HATE SPEECH

In *On Liberty,* John Stuart Mill constructs a famous case for the free expression of opinion.[5] With regard to factual, scientific, philosophical, religious, moral, and political matters, he argues for complete freedom of expression. His underlying claim is that societal attempts to suppress unpopular and unorthodox opinions are more productive of harm than are the unregulated opinions themselves. On the other hand, Mill is not committed to the view that no restrictions whatsoever on expressions of opinion are justified. Sometimes expressions of opinion are overtly harmful to others (e.g., when speech is used to incite an angry mob to violence), and in such cases the harm principle would allow restrictions.

Hate speech, perhaps especially the use of slurs and epithets, confronts contemporary society with a profound dilemma. Should people be free to make racist, sexist, and homophobic statements? Should people be free to confront others directly with the hateful venom of slurs and epithets? On the one hand, freedom of expression is a deeply held value, enshrined in the First Amendment of the United States Constitution. On the other hand, not only do all morally sensitive people find hate speech offensive but, more important, the victims of hate speech are left to deal with its psychological fallout. Are the psychological harms produced by hate speech significant enough to override the presumption we ordinarily give to the principle of free expression? Are they sufficient to justify legal restrictions?

[5]The account of Mill's thinking provided in this paragraph follows Feinberg's analysis in "Limits to the Free Expression of Opinion," in Joel Feinberg and Hyman Gross, eds., *Philosophy of Law,* 5th ed. (Belmont, Calif.: Wadsworth, 1995), pp. 262–264.

In one of this chapter's selections, Andrew Altman provides an extensive analysis of the issue of hate-speech regulation on college campuses. He acknowledges that hate speech can cause serious psychological harms but does not believe that such harms can serve to justify hate-speech regulation, at least within the theoretical framework he identifies as *liberalism*. Altman focuses attention on one distinctive type of hate speech, characterized by the fact that a person is treated as a moral subordinate—that is, as having inferior moral status. It is this narrowly drawn class of hate speech—involving what he calls "the speech-act wrong of subordination"—that he believes can justifiably be targeted for regulation. Altman is unsympathetic to sweeping hate-speech regulation, but he does essentially endorse the sort of narrowly drawn hate-speech rules that were in effect at Stanford University in the early 1990s.

The Stanford code prohibited "speech or other expression" if three conditions were satisfied—that is, if it:

(a) is intended to insult or stigmatize an individual or a small number of individuals on the basis of their sex, race, color, handicap, religion, sexual orientation, or national and ethnic origin; and (b) is addressed directly to the individual or individuals whom it insults or stigmatizes; and (c) makes use of insulting or "fighting" words or non-verbal symbols.

Further clarification was provided for provision (c) as follows:

In [this] context . . . , insulting or "fighting" words or non-verbal symbols are those "which by their very utterance inflict injury or tend to incite to an immediate breach of the peace," and which are commonly understood to convey direct and visceral hatred or contempt for human beings on the basis of their sex, race, color, handicap, religion, sexual orientation, or national and ethnic origin.[6]

The prospects for crafting campus hate-speech codes in a way that can withstand constitutional scrutiny on First Amendment grounds are not very promising. Certainly, to date, courts have been thoroughly unsympathetic to campus hate-speech codes. For example, both a University of Michigan code and a University of Wisconsin System code have been struck down in federal courts, and in 1995 even the narrowly drawn Stanford code was declared unconstitutional in a California Superior Court decision. An excerpt from the court opinion in this latter case—*Corry v. Stanford University*—is included in this chapter. In this opinion, Judge Peter Stone argues that the Stanford hate-speech regulations are unconstitutionally overbroad and also embody an impermissible content-based regulation.[7]

Whether hate-speech regulation is discussed specifically in reference to college campuses or more broadly in reference to society as a whole, ethical evaluation is frequently intertwined with First Amendment analysis. *Village of Skokie v. National Socialist Party of America,* an important freedom-of-expression case decided by the

[6]The entire text of the Stanford regulations appears in the appendix to an article by Thomas Grey, "Civil Rights Versus Civil Liberties: The Case of Discriminatory Verbal Harassment," *Social Philosophy and Policy*, vol. 8, Spring 1991, pp. 81–107.

[7]Another dimension of *Corry* is not tracked in the court opinion as it appears in this chapter but played a significant role in the overall outcome of the case. As a *private* university, Stanford argued that its hate-speech code was not required to conform to First Amendment standards, because the First Amendment protects speech against restrictions put in place by *state* actors, not by private actors. Judge Stone ruled, however, in accordance with certain provisions of California law, themselves constitutionally sound, that the Stanford hate-speech code was required to conform to First Amendment standards.

Illinois Supreme Court in 1978, is included in this chapter. In *Skokie,* the court ruled that the American Nazi Party could not be prevented from displaying the swastika (which can be understood as hate speech against Jews) during the course of a planned demonstration in a predominantly Jewish community. In one other selection in this chapter, Charles R. Lawrence III analyzes the impact of face-to-face racial insults on those who are subjected to them. He argues that such insults are undeserving of First Amendment protection.

Thomas A. Mappes

On Liberty
John Stuart Mill

In these excerpts from his classic work *On Liberty* (1859), Mill first contends that society is warranted in restricting individual liberty only if an action is harmful to others, never because an action in one way or another is harmful to the person who performs the action. He clearly rejects both the principle of legal paternalism and the principle of legal moralism. Mill argues on utilitarian grounds for an exclusive adherence to the harm principle, holding that society will be better off by tolerating all expressions of individual liberty that involve no harm to others, rather than by "compelling each to live as seems good to the rest." Mill also constructs, again on a utilitarian foundation, an overall argument for the free expression of opinion.

. . . The object of this Essay is to assert one very simple principle, as entitled to govern absolutely the dealings of society with the individual in the way of compulsion and control, whether the means used be physical force in the form of legal penalties, or the moral coercion of public opinion. That principle is, that the sole end for which mankind are warranted, individually or collectively, in interfering with the liberty of action of any of their number, is self-protection. That the only purpose for which power can be rightfully exercised over any member of a civilized community, against his will, is to prevent harm to others. His own good, either physical or moral, is not a sufficient warrant. He cannot rightfully be compelled to do or forbear because it will be better for him to do so, because it will make him happier, because, in the opinions of others, to do so would be wise, or even right. These are good reasons for remonstrating with him, or reasoning with him, or persuading him, or entreating him, but not for compelling him, or visiting him with any evil in case he do otherwise. To justify that, the conduct from which it is desired to deter

Reprinted from the original edition of *On Liberty* (London, 1859).

him, must be calculated to produce evil to some one else. The only part of the conduct of any one, for which he is amenable to society, is that which concerns others. In the part which merely concerns himself, his independence is, of right, absolute. Over himself, over his own body and mind, the individual is sovereign.

It is, perhaps, hardly necessary to say that this doctrine is meant to apply only to human beings in the maturity of their faculties. We are not speaking of children, or of young persons below the age which the law may fix as that of manhood and womanhood. Those who are still in a state to require being taken care of by others, must be protected against their own actions as well as against external injury. . . .

. . . There is a sphere of action in which society, as distinguished from the individual, has, if any, only an indirect interest; comprehending all that portion of a person's life and conduct which affects only himself, or if it also affects others, only with their free, voluntary, and undeceived consent and participation. When I say only himself, I mean directly, and in the first instance: for whatever affects himself, may affect others *through* himself; and the objection which may be grounded on this contingency, will receive consideration in the sequel. This, then, is the appropriate region of human liberty. It comprises, first, the inward domain of consciousness; demanding liberty of conscience, in the most comprehensive sense; liberty of thought and feeling; absolute freedom of opinion and sentiment on all subjects, practical or speculative, scientific, moral, or theological. The liberty of expressing and publishing opinions may seem to fall under a different principle, since it belongs to that part of the conduct of an individual which concerns other people; but, being almost of as much importance as the liberty of thought itself, and resting in great part on the same reasons, is practically inseparable from it. Secondly, the principle requires liberty of tastes and pursuits; of framing the plan of our life to suit our own character; of doing as we like, subject to such consequences as may follow; without impediment from our fellow-creatures, so long as what we do does not harm them, even though they should think our conduct foolish, perverse, or wrong. Thirdly, from this liberty of each individual, follows the liberty, within the same limits, of combination among individuals; freedom to unite, for any purpose not involving harm to others: the persons combining being supposed to be of full age, and not forced or deceived.

No society in which these liberties are not, on the whole, respected, is free, whatever may be its form of government; and none is completely free in which they do not exist absolute and unqualified. The only freedom which deserves the name, is that of pursuing our own good in our own way, so long as we do not attempt to deprive others of theirs, or impede their efforts to obtain it. Each is the proper guardian of his own health, whether bodily, or mental and spiritual. Mankind are greater gainers by suffering each other to live as seems good to themselves, than by compelling each to live as seems good to the rest. . . .

OF THE LIBERTY OF THOUGHT AND DISCUSSION

. . . If all mankind minus one, were of one opinion, and only one person were of the contrary opinion, mankind would be no more justified in silencing that one person, than he, if he had the power, would be justified in silencing mankind. Were an opinion a personal possession of no value except to the owner; if to be obstructed in the enjoyment of it were simply a private injury, it would make some difference whether the injury was inflicted only on a few persons or on many. But the peculiar evil of silencing the expression of an opinion is, that it is robbing the human race; posterity as well as the existing generation; those who dissent from the opinion, still more than those who hold it. If the opinion is right, they are deprived of the opportunity of exchanging error for truth: if wrong, they lose, what is almost as great a benefit, the clearer perception and livelier impression of truth, produced by its collision with error.

It is necessary to consider separately these two hypotheses, each of which has a distinct branch of the argument corresponding to it. We can never be sure that the opinion we are endeavouring to stifle is a false opinion; and if we were sure, stifling it would be an evil still.

First: the opinion which it is attempted to suppress by authority may possibly be true. Those who desire to suppress it, of course deny its truth; but they are not infallible. They have no authority to decide the question for all mankind, and exclude every other person from the means of judging. To refuse a hearing to an opinion, because they are sure that it is false, is to assume that *their* certainty is the same thing as *absolute* certainty. All silencing of discussion is an assumption of infallibility. . . .

Let us now pass to the second division of the argument, and dismissing the supposition that any of the received opinions may be false, let us assume them to be true, and examine into the worth of the manner in which they are likely to be held, when their truth is not freely and openly canvassed. However unwillingly a person who has a strong opinion may admit the possibility that his opinion may be false, he ought to be moved by the consideration that however true it may be, if it is not fully, frequently, and fearlessly discussed, it will be held as a dead dogma, not a living truth. . . .

. . . If the cultivation of the understanding consists in one thing more than in another, it is surely in learning the grounds of one's own opinions. . . . He who knows only his own side of the case, knows little of that. His reasons may be good, and no one may have been able to refute them. But if he is equally unable to refute the reasons on the opposite side; if he does not so much as know what they are, he has no ground for preferring either opinion. . . . Nor is it enough that he should hear the arguments of adversaries from his own teachers, presented as they state them, and accompanied by what they offer as refutations. That is not the way to do justice to the arguments, or bring them into real contact with his own mind. He must be able to hear them from persons who actually believe them; who defend them in earnest, and do their very utmost for them. He must know them in their most plausible and persuasive form. . . .

. . . The fact . . . is, that not only the grounds of the opinion are forgotten in the absence of discussion, but too often the meaning of the opinion itself. The words which convey it, cease to suggest ideas, or suggest only a small portion of those they were originally employed to communicate. Instead of a vivid conception and a living belief, there remain only a few phrases retained by rote; or, if any part, the shell and husk only of the meaning is retained, the finer essence being lost. The great chapter in human history which this fact occupies and fills, cannot be too earnestly studied and meditated on. . . .

. . . We have hitherto considered only two possibilities: that the received opinion may be false, and some other opinion, consequently, true; or that, the received opinion being true, a conflict with the opposite error is essential to a clear apprehension and deep feeling of its truth. But there is a commoner case than either of these; when the conflicting doctrines, instead of being one true and the other false, share the truth between them; and the nonconforming opinion is needed to supply the remainder of the truth, of which the received doctrine embodies only a part. . . .

We have now recognised the necessity to the mental well-being of mankind (on which all their other well-being depends) of freedom of opinion, and freedom of the expression of opinion, on four distinct grounds; which we will now briefly recapitulate.

First, if any opinion is compelled to silence, that opinion may, for aught we can certainly know, be true. To deny this is to assume our own infallibility.

Secondly, though the silenced opinion be an error, it may, and very commonly does, contain a portion of truth; and since the general or prevailing opinion on any subject is rarely or never the whole truth, it is only by the collision of adverse opinions that the remainder of the truth has any chance of being supplied.

Thirdly, even if the received opinion be not only true, but the whole truth; unless it is suffered to be, and actually is, vigorously and earnestly contested, it will, by most of those who receive it, be held in the manner of a prejudice, with little comprehension or feeling of its rational grounds. And not only this, but, fourthly, the meaning of the doctrine itself will be in danger of being lost, or enfeebled, and deprived of its vital effect on the character and conduct: the dogma becoming a mere formal profession, inefficacious for good, but cumbering the ground, and preventing the growth of any real and heartfelt conviction, from reason or personal experience. . : .

QUESTIONS

1 Is it true, as Mill claims, that "mankind are greater gainers by suffering each other to live as seems good to themselves, than by compelling each to live as seems good to the rest"?
2 Would you endorse an argument for the censorship of pornography based on the principle of legal paternalism? Would you endorse a procensorship argument based on the principle of legal moralism?
3 Does Mill provide a compelling case for the free expression of opinion?

The Question of Harm

The Attorney General's Commission on Pornography

In considering the question of whether pornography is harmful, the Attorney General's Commission on Pornography (the 1986 commission) distinguishes among (1) violent pornography, (2) nonviolent but degrading pornography, and (3) nonviolent and nondegrading pornography. On its interpretation of the evidence, material in category (1) bears a causal relationship to undesirable

Reprinted from *Final Report* (Washington, D.C.: United States Department of Justice, July 1986).

attitudinal changes and to acts of sexual violence. The commission also asserts
that the same effects are causally connected with category (2) material. On the
other hand, the commission concludes that category (3) material does not bear a
causal relationship to acts of sexual violence. In a brief reference to the category
of child pornography, the commission emphasizes the way in which the
production of child pornography entails child abuse.

MATTERS OF METHOD

. . . The analysis of the hypothesis that pornography causes harm must start with the
identification of hypothesized harms, proceed to the determination of whether those
hypothesized harms are indeed harmful, and then conclude with the examination of
whether a causal link exists between the material and the harm. When the consequences of exposure to sexually explicit material are not harmful, or when there is
no causal relationship between exposure to sexually explicit material and some
harmful consequence, then we cannot say that the sexually explicit material is
harmful. But if sexually explicit material of some variety is causally related to, or
increases the incidence of, some behavior that *is* harmful, then it is safe to conclude
that the material is harmful. . . .

The Problem of Multiple Causation

The world is complex, and most consequences are "caused" by numerous factors.
Are highway deaths caused by failure to wear seat belts, failure of the automobile
companies to install airbags, failure of the government to require automobile companies to install airbags, alcohol, judicial leniency towards drunk drivers, speeding,
and so on and on? Is heart disease caused by cigarette smoking, obesity, stress, or
excess animal fat in our diets? As with most other questions of this type, the answers
can only be "all of the above," and so too with the problem of pornography. We have
concluded, for example, that some forms of sexually explicit material bear a causal
relationship both to sexual violence and to sex discrimination, but we are hardly so
naive as to suppose that were these forms of pornography to disappear the problems
of sex discrimination and sexual violence would come to an end.

If this is so, then what does it mean to identify a causal relationship? It means
that the evidence supports the conclusion that if there were none of the material
being tested, then the incidence of the consequences would be less. We live in a
world of multiple causation, and to identify a factor as a *cause* in such a world
means only that if this factor were eliminated while everything else stayed the same
then the problem would at least be lessened. In most cases it is impossible to say
any more than this, although to say this is to say quite a great deal. But when we
identify something as a cause, we do not deny that there are other causes, and we
do not deny that some of these other causes might bear an even *greater* causal connection than does some form of pornography. That is, it may be, for example, and
there is some evidence that points in this direction, that certain magazines focusing
on guns, martial arts, and related topics bear a closer causal relationship to sexual
violence than do some magazines that are, in a term we will explain shortly,

"degrading." If this is true, then the amount of sexual violence would be reduced more by eliminating the weaponry magazines and keeping the degrading magazines than it would be reduced by eliminating the degrading magazines and keeping the weaponry magazines. . . .

OUR CONCLUSIONS ABOUT HARM

We present in the following sections our conclusions regarding the harms we have investigated with respect to the various subdividing categories we have found most useful. . . .

Sexually Violent Material

The category of material on which most of the evidence has focused is the category of material featuring actual or unmistakably simulated or unmistakably threatened violence presented in sexually explicit fashion with a predominant focus on the sexually explicit violence. Increasingly, the most prevalent forms of pornography, as well as an increasingly prevalent body of less sexually explicit material, fit this description. Some of this material involves sado-masochistic themes, with the standard accoutrements of the genre, including whips, chains, devices of torture, and so on. But another theme of some of this material is not sado-masochistic, but involves instead the recurrent theme of a man making some sort of sexual advance to a woman, being rebuffed, and then raping the woman or in some other way violently forcing himself on the woman. In almost all of this material, whether in magazine or motion picture form, the woman eventually becomes aroused and ecstatic about the initially forced sexual activity, and usually is portrayed as begging for more. There is also a large body of material, more "mainstream" in its availability, that portrays sexual activity or sexually suggestive nudity coupled with extreme violence, such as disfigurement or murder. The so-called "slasher" films fit this description, as does some material, both in films and in magazines, that is less or more sexually explicit than the prototypical "slasher" film.

It is with respect to material of this variety that the scientific findings and ultimate conclusions of the 1970 Commission are least reliable for today, precisely because material of this variety was largely absent from that Commission's inquiries. It is not, however, absent from the contemporary world, and it is hardly surprising that conclusions about this material differ from conclusions about material not including violent themes.

When clinical and experimental research has focused particularly on sexually violent material, the conclusions have been virtually unanimous. In both clinical and experimental settings, exposure to sexually violent materials has indicated an increase in the likelihood of aggression. More specifically, the research, which is described in much detail later in this Report, shows a causal relationship between exposure to material of this type and aggressive behavior towards women.

Finding a link between aggressive behavior towards women and sexual violence, whether lawful or unlawful, requires assumptions not found exclusively in the experimental evidence. We see no reason, however, not to make these assumptions.

The assumption that increased aggressive behavior towards women is causally related, for an aggregate population, to increased sexual violence is significantly supported by the clinical evidence, as well as by much of the less scientific evidence. They are also to all of us assumptions that are plainly justified by our own common sense. This is not to say that all people with heightened levels of aggression will commit acts of sexual violence. But it is to say that over a sufficiently large number of cases we are confident in asserting that an increase in aggressive behavior directed at women will cause an increase in the level of sexual violence directed at women.

Thus we reach our conclusions by combining the results of the research with highly justifiable assumptions about the generalizability of more limited research results. Since the clinical and experimental evidence supports the conclusion that there is a causal relationship between exposure to sexually violent materials and an increase in aggressive behavior directed towards women, and since we believe that an increase in aggressive behavior towards women will in a population increase the incidence of sexual violence in that population, we have reached the conclusion, unanimously and confidently, that the available evidence strongly supports the hypothesis that substantial exposure to sexually violent materials as described here bears a causal relationship to antisocial acts of sexual violence and, for some subgroups, possibly to unlawful acts of sexual violence.

Although we rely for this conclusion on significant scientific empirical evidence, we feel it worthwhile to note the underlying logic of the conclusion. The evidence says simply that the images that people are exposed to bears a causal relationship to their behavior. This is hardly surprising. What would be surprising would be to find otherwise, and we have not so found. We have not, of course, found that the images people are exposed to are a greater cause of sexual violence than all or even many other possible causes the investigation of which has been beyond our mandate. Nevertheless, it would be strange indeed if graphic representations of a form of behavior, especially in a form that almost exclusively portrays such behavior as desirable, did not have at least some effect on patterns of behavior.

Sexual violence is not the only negative effect reported in the research to result from substantial exposure to sexually violent materials. The evidence is also strongly supportive of significant attitudinal changes on the part of those with substantial exposure to violent pornography. These attitudinal changes are numerous. Victims of rape and other forms of sexual violence are likely to be perceived by people so exposed as more responsible for the assault, as having suffered less injury, and as having been less degraded as a result of the experience. Similarly, people with a substantial exposure to violent pornography are likely to see the rapist or other sexual offender as less responsible for the act and as deserving of less stringent punishment.

These attitudinal changes have been shown experimentally to include a larger range of attitudes than those just discussed. The evidence also strongly supports the conclusion that substantial exposure to violent sexually explicit material leads to a greater acceptance of the "rape myth" in its broader sense—that women enjoy being coerced into sexual activity, that they enjoy being physically hurt in sexual context, and that as a result a man who forces himself on a woman sexually is in fact merely acceding to the "real" wishes of the woman, regardless of the extent to which she seems to be resisting. The myth is that a woman who says "no" really means "yes," and that men are justified in acting on the assumption that the "no" answer is indeed the "yes" answer. We have little trouble concluding that this attitude is both pervasive and profoundly harmful, and that any stimulus reinforcing or increasing the incidence of this attitude is for that reason alone properly designated as harmful.

. . . All of the harms discussed here, including acceptance of the legitimacy of sexual violence against women but not limited to it, are more pronounced when the sexually violent materials depict the woman as experiencing arousal, orgasm, or other form of enjoyment as the ultimate result of the sexual assault. This theme, unfortunately very common in the materials we have examined, is likely to be the major, albeit not the only, component of what it is in the materials in this category that causes the consequences that have been identified. . . .

Nonviolent Materials Depicting Degradation, Domination, Subordination, or Humiliation

. . . It appears that effects similar to, although not as extensive as that involved with violent material, can be identified with respect to . . . degrading material, but that these effects are likely absent when neither degradation nor violence is present.

An enormous amount of the most sexually explicit material available, as well as much of the material that is somewhat less sexually explicit, is material that we would characterize as "degrading," the term we use to encompass the undeniably linked characteristics of degradation, domination, subordination, and humiliation. The degradation we refer to is degradation of people, most often women, and here we are referring to material that, although not violent, depicts people, usually women, as existing solely for the sexual satisfaction of others, usually men, or that depicts people, usually women, in decidedly subordinate roles in their sexual relations with others, or that depicts people engaged in sexual practices that would to most people be considered humiliating. Indeed, forms of degradation represent the largely predominant proportion of commercially available pornography.

With respect to material of this variety, our conclusions are substantially similar to those with respect to violent material, although we make them with somewhat less assumption than was the case with respect to violent material. The evidence, scientific and otherwise, is more tentative, but supports the conclusion that the material we describe as degrading bears some causal relationship to the attitudinal changes we have previously identified. That is, substantial exposure to material of this variety is likely to increase the extent to which those exposed will view rape or other forms of sexual violence as less serious than they otherwise would have, will view the victims of rape and other forms of sexual violence as significantly more responsible, and will view the offenders as significantly less responsible. We also conclude that the evidence supports the conclusion that substantial exposure to material of this type will increase acceptance of the proposition that women like to be forced into sexual practices, and, once again, that the woman who says "no" really means "yes."

. . . We believe we are justified in drawing the following conclusions: Over a large enough sample of population that believes that many women like to be raped, that believes that sexual violence or sexual coercion is often desired or appropriate, and that believes that sex offenders are less responsible for their acts, [this population] will commit more acts of sexual violence or sexual coercion than would a population holding these beliefs to a lesser extent.

. . . Thus, we conclude that substantial exposure to materials of this type bears some causal relationship to the level of sexual violence, sexual coercion, or unwanted sexual aggression in the population so exposed.

We need mention as well that our focus on these more violent or more coercive forms of actual subordination of women should not diminish what we take to be a necessarily incorporated conclusion: Substantial exposure to materials of this type bears some causal relationship to the incidence of various nonviolent forms of discrimination against or subordination of women in our society. To the extent that these materials create or reinforce the view that women's function is disproportionately to satisfy the sexual needs of men, then the materials will have pervasive effects on the treatment of women in society far beyond the incidence of identifiable acts of rape or other sexual violence. We obviously cannot here explore fully all the forms in which women are discriminated against in contemporary society. Nor can we explore all of the causes of that discrimination against women. But we feel confident in concluding that the view of women as available for sexual domination is one cause of that discrimination, and we feel confident as well in concluding that degrading material bears a causal relationship to the view that women ought to subordinate their own desires and beings to the sexual satisfaction of men. . . .

Non-Violent and Non-Degrading Materials

Our most controversial category has been the category of sexually explicit materials that are not violent and are not degrading as we have used that term. They are materials in which the participants appear to be fully willing participants occupying substantially equal roles in a setting devoid of actual or apparent violence or pain. This category is in fact quite small in terms of currently available materials. There is some, to be sure, and the amount may increase as the division between the degrading and the non-degrading becomes more accepted, but we are convinced that only a small amount of currently available highly sexually explicit material is neither violent nor degrading. We thus talk about a small category, but one that should not be ignored.

We have disagreed substantially about the effects of such materials, and that should come as no surprise. We are dealing in this category with "pure" sex, as to which there are widely divergent views in this society. That we have disagreed among ourselves does little more than reflect the extent to which we are representative of the population as a whole. In light of that disagreement, it is perhaps more appropriate to explain the various views rather than indicate a unanimity that does not exist, within this Commission or within society, or attempt the preposterous task of saying that some fundamental view about the role of sexuality and portrayals of sexuality was accepted or defeated by such-and-such vote. We do not wish to give easy answers to hard questions, and thus feel better with describing the diversity of opinion rather than suppressing part of it.

In examining the material in this category, we have not had the benefit of extensive evidence. Research has only recently begun to distinguish the non-violent but degrading from material that is neither violent nor degrading, and we have all relied on a combination of interpretation of existing studies that may not have drawn the same divisions, studies that did draw these distinctions, clinical evidence, interpretation of victim testimony, and our own perceptions of the effect of images on human behavior. Although the social science evidence is far from conclusive, we are, on the current state of the evidence, persuaded that material of this type does not bear a causal relationship to rape and other acts of sexual violence. . . .

That there does not appear from the social science evidence to be a causal link with sexual violence, however, does not answer the question of whether such materials might not themselves simply for some other reason constitute a harm in themselves, or bear a causal link to consequences other than sexual violence but still taken to be harmful. And it is here that we and society at large have the greatest differences in opinion.

One issue relates to materials that, although undoubtedly consensual and equal, depict sexual practices frequently condemned in this and other societies. In addition, level of societal condemnation varies for different activities; some activities are condemned by some people, but not by others. We have discovered that to some significant extent the assessment of the harmfulness of materials depicting such activities correlates directly with the assessment of the harmfulness of the activities themselves. Intuitively and not experimentally, we can hypothesize that materials portraying such an activity will either help to legitimize or will bear some causal relationship to that activity itself. With respect to these materials, therefore, it appears that a conclusion about the harmfulness of these materials turns on a conclusion about the harmfulness of the activity itself. As to this, we are unable to agree with respect to many of these activities. Our differences reflect differences now extant in society at large, and actively debated, and we can hardly resolve them here.

A larger issue is the very question of promiscuity. Even to the extent that the behavior depicted is not inherently condemned by some or any of us, the manner of presentation almost necessarily suggests that the activities are taking place outside of the context of marriage, love, commitment, or even affection. Again, it is far from implausible to hypothesize that materials depicting sexual activity without marriage, love, commitment, or affection bear some causal relationship to sexual activity without marriage, love, commitment, or affection. There are undoubtedly many causes for what used to be called the "sexual revolution," but it is absurd to suppose that depictions or descriptions of uncommitted sexuality were not among them. Thus, once again our disagreements reflect disagreements in society at large, although not to as great an extent. Although there are many members of this society who can and have made affirmative cases for uncommitted sexuality, none of us believes it to be a good thing. A number of us, however, believe that the level of commitment in sexuality is a matter of choice among those who voluntarily engage in the activity. Others of us believe that uncommitted sexual activity is wrong for the individuals involved and harmful to society to the extent of its prevalence. Our view of the ultimate harmfulness of much of this material, therefore, is reflective of our individual views about the extent to whether sexual commitment is purely a matter of individual choice. . . .

THE SPECIAL HORROR OF CHILD PORNOGRAPHY

What is commonly referred to as "child pornography" is not so much a form of pornography as it is a form of sexual exploitation of children. The distinguishing characteristic of child pornography, as generally understood, is that actual children are photographed while engaged in some form of sexual activity, either with adults or with other children. To understand the very idea of child pornography requires understanding the way in which real children, whether actually identified or not, are photographed, and understanding the way in which the use of real children in photographs creates a special harm largely independent of the kinds of concerns often expressed with respect to sexually explicit materials involving only adults.

Thus, the necessary focus of an inquiry into child pornography must be on the process by which children, from as young as one week up to the age of majority, are induced to engage in sexual activity of one sort or another, and the process by which children are photographed while engaging in that activity. The inevitably permanent record of that sexual activity created by a photograph is rather plainly a harm to the children photographed. But even if the photograph were never again seen, the very activity involved in creating the photograph is itself an act of sexual exploitation of children, and thus the issues related to the sexual abuse of children and those related to child pornography are inextricably linked. Child pornography necessarily includes the sexual abuse of a real child, and there can be no understanding of the special problem of child pornography until there is understanding of the special way in which child pornography *is* child abuse. . . .

QUESTIONS

1 Is it possible to provide a workable definition of "degrading pornography," or is this concept hopelessly subjective?
2 Which of the following, if any, would you endorse: (1) the censorship of violent pornography; (2) the censorship of nonviolent but degrading pornography; (3) the censorship of nonviolent and nondegrading pornography?
3 In *Ohio v. Osborne* (1990), the United States Supreme Court ruled that it is constitutional for states to prohibit by law even the private *possession* of child pornography. In view of the special evil of child pornography, would you endorse such a law?

Pornography, Oppression, and Freedom:
A Closer Look

Helen E. Longino

Longino constructs a case against pornography from a feminist point of view. She begins by defining pornography in such a way as to distinguish it from both erotica and moral realism; pornography is "material that explicitly represents or describes degrading and abusive sexual behavior so as to endorse and/or recommend the behavior as described." In Longino's view, pornography is immoral not because it is sexually explicit but because it typically portrays women in a degrading and dehumanizing way. She explicitly identifies a number of related ways in which pornography is injurious to women. Because of pornography's injurious character, she concludes, its production and distribution are justifiably subject to control.

I INTRODUCTION

The much-touted sexual revolution of the 1960's and 1970's not only freed various modes of sexual behavior from the constraints of social disapproval, but also made possible a flood of pornographic material. According to figures provided by WAVPM (Women Against Violence in Pornography and Media), the number of pornographic magazines available at newsstands has grown from zero in 1953 to forty in 1977, while sales of pornographic films in Los Angeles alone have grown from $15 million in 1969 to $85 million in 1976.[1]

Traditionally, pornography was condemned as immoral because it presented sexually explicit material in a manner designed to appeal to "prurient interests" or a "morbid" interest in nudity and sexuality, material which furthermore lacked any redeeming social value and which exceeded "customary limits of candor." While these phrases, taken from a definition of "obscenity" proposed in the 1954 American Law Institute's *Model Penal Code,*[2] require some criteria of application to eliminate vagueness, it seems that what is objectionable is the explicit description or representation of bodily parts or sexual behavior for the purpose of inducing sexual stimulation or pleasure on the part of the reader or viewer. This kind of objection is part of a sexual ethic that subordinates sex to procreation and condemns all sexual interactions outside of legitimated marriage. It is this code which was the primary target of the sexual revolutionaries in the 1960's, and which has given way in many areas to more open standards of sexual behavior.

One of the beneficial results of the sexual revolution has been a growing acceptance of the distinction between questions of sexual mores and questions of morality. This distinction underlies the old slogan, "Make love, not war," and takes harm to others as the defining characteristic of immorality. What is immoral is behavior which causes injury to or violation of another person or people. Such injury may be physical or it may be psychological. To cause pain to another, to lie to another, to hinder another in the exercise of her or his rights, to exploit another, to degrade another, to misrepresent and slander another are instances of immoral behavior. Masturbation or engaging voluntarily in sexual intercourse with another consenting adult of the same or the other sex, as long as neither injury nor violation of either individual or another is involved, [is] not immoral. Some sexual behavior is morally objectionable, but not because of its sexual character. Thus, adultery is immoral not because it involves sexual intercourse with someone to whom one is not legally married, but because it involves breaking a promise (of sexual and emotional fidelity to one's spouse). Sadistic, abusive, or forced sex is immoral because it injures and violates another.

The detachment of sexual chastity from moral virtue implies that we cannot condemn forms of sexual behavior merely because they strike us as distasteful or subversive of the Protestant work ethic, or because they depart from standards of behavior we have individually adopted. It has thus seemed to imply that no matter how offensive we might find pornography, we must tolerate it in the name of freedom from illegitimate repression. I wish to argue that this is not so, that pornography is immoral because it is harmful to people.

II   WHAT IS PORNOGRAPHY?

I define pornography as *verbal or pictorial explicit representations of sexual behavior that,* in the words of the Commission on Obscenity and Pornography, *have as a distinguishing characteristic "the degrading and demeaning portrayal of the role and status of the human female . . . as a mere sexual object to be exploited and manipulated sexually."*[3] In pornographic books, magazines, and films, women are represented as passive and as slavishly dependent upon men. The role of female characters is limited to the provision of sexual services to men. To the extent that women's sexual pleasure is represented at all, it is subordinated to that of men and is never an end in itself as is the sexual pleasure of men. What pleases women is the use of their bodies to satisfy male desires. While the sexual objectification of women is common to all pornography, women are the recipients of even worse treatment in violent pornography, in which women characters are killed, tortured, gang-raped, mutilated, bound, and otherwise abused, as a means of providing sexual stimulation or pleasure to the male characters. It is this development which has attracted the attention of feminists and been the stimulus to an analysis of pornography in general.[4]

Not all sexually explicit material is pornography, nor is all material which contains representations of sexual abuse and degradation pornography.

A representation of a sexual encounter between adult persons which is characterized by mutual respect is, once we have disentangled sexuality and morality, not morally objectionable. Such a representation would be one in which the desires and experiences of each participant were regarded by the other participants as having a validity and a subjective importance equal to those of the individual's own desire and experiences. In such an encounter, each participant acknowledges the other participant's basic human dignity and personhood. Similarly, a representation of a nude human body (in whole or in part) in such a manner that the person shown maintains self-respect—e.g., is not portrayed in a degrading position—would not be morally objectionable. The educational films of the National Sex Forum, as well as a certain amount of erotic literature and art, fall into this category. While some erotic materials are beyond the standards of modesty held by some individuals, they are not for this reason immoral.

A representation of a sexual encounter which is not characterized by mutual respect, in which at least one of the parties is treated in a manner beneath her or his dignity as a human being, is no longer simple erotica. That a representation is of degrading behavior does not in itself, however, make it pornographic. Whether or not it is pornographic is a function of contextual features. Books and films may

contain descriptions or representations of a rape in order to explore the consequences of such an assault upon its victim. What is being shown is abusive or
degrading behavior which attempts to deny the humanity and dignity of the person
assaulted, yet the context surrounding the representation, through its exploration of
the consequences of the act, acknowledges and reaffirms her dignity. Such books
and films, far from being pornographic, are (or can be) highly moral, and fall into
the category of moral realism.

What makes a work a work of pornography, then, is not simply its representation
of degrading and abusive sexual encounters, but its implicit, if not explicit, approval
and recommendation of sexual behavior that is immoral, i.e., that physically or psychologically violates the personhood of one of the participants. Pornography, then, is
verbal or pictorial material which represents or describes sexual behavior that is
degrading or abusive to one or more of the participants *in such a way as to endorse
the degradation*. The participants so treated in virtually all heterosexual pornography
are women or children, so heterosexual pornography is, as a matter of fact, material
which endorses sexual behavior that is degrading and/or abusive to women and children. As I use the term "sexual behavior," this includes sexual encounters between
persons, behavior which produces sexual stimulation or pleasure for one of the participants, and behavior which is preparatory to or invites sexual activity. Behavior that
is degrading or abusive includes physical harm or abuse, and physical or psychological coercion. In addition, behavior which ignores or devalues the real interests,
desires, and experiences of one or more participants in any way is degrading. Finally,
that a person has chosen or consented to be harmed, abused, or subjected to coercion
does not alter the degrading character of such behavior.

Pornography communicates its endorsement of the behavior it represents by various features of the pornographic context: the degradation of the female characters
is represented as providing pleasure to the participant males and, even worse, to the
participant females, and there is no suggestion that this sort of treatment of others
is inappropriate to their status as human beings. These two features are together sufficient to constitute endorsement of the represented behavior. The contextual features which make material pornographic are intrinsic to the material. In addition to
these, extrinsic features, such as the purpose for which the material is presented—
i.e., the sexual arousal/pleasure/satisfaction of its (mostly) male consumers—or
an accompanying text, may reinforce or make explicit the endorsement. Representations which in and of themselves do not show or endorse degrading behavior may
be put into a pornographic context by juxtaposition with others that are degrading,
or by a text which invites or recommends degrading behavior toward the subject
represented. In such a case the whole complex—the series of representations or
representations with text—is pornographic.

The distinction I have sketched is one that applies most clearly to sequential
material—a verbal or pictorial (filmed) story—which represents an action and provides a temporal context for it. In showing the before and after, a narrator or film-
maker has plenty of opportunity to acknowledge the dignity of the person violated
or clearly to refuse to do so. It is somewhat more difficult to apply the distinction to
single still representations. The contextual features cited above, however, are clearly
present in still photographs or pictures that glamorize degradation and sexual violence.

Phonograph album covers and advertisements offer some prime examples of such glamorization. Their representations of women in chains (the Ohio Players), or bound by ropes and black and blue (the Rolling Stones) are considered high-quality commercial "art" and glossily prettify the violence they represent. Since the standard function of prettification and glamorization is the communication of desirability, these albums and ads are communicating the desirability of violence against women. Representations of women bound or chained, particularly those of women bound in such a way as to make their breasts, or genital or anal areas vulnerable to any passerby, endorse the scene they represent by the absence of any indication that this treatment of women is in any way inappropriate.

To summarize: Pornography is not just the explicit representation or description of sexual behavior, nor even the explicit representation or description of sexual behavior which is degrading and/or abusive to women. Rather, it is material that explicitly represents or describes degrading and abusive sexual behavior so as to endorse and/or recommend the behavior as described. The contextual features, moreover, which communicate such endorsement are intrinsic to the material; that is, they are features whose removal or alteration would change the representation or description.

This account of pornography is underlined by the etymology and original meaning of the word "pornography." *The Oxford English Dictionary* defines pornography as "Description of the life, manners, etc. of prostitutes and their patrons [from πόρνη (porne) meaning "harlot" and γράφειν (graphein) meaning "to write"]; hence the expression or suggestion of obscene or unchaste subjects in literature or art."[5]

Let us consider the first part of the definition for a moment. In the transactions between prostitutes and their clients, prostitutes are paid, directly or indirectly, for the use of their bodies by the client for sexual pleasure.[6] Traditionally males have obtained from female prostitutes what they could not or did not wish to get from their wives or women friends, who, because of the character of their relation to the male, must be accorded some measure of human respect. While there are limits to what treatment is seen as appropriate toward women as wives or women friends, the prostitute as prostitute exists to provide sexual pleasure to males. The female characters of contemporary pornography also exist to provide pleasure to males, but in the pornographic context no pretense is made to regard them as parties to a contractual arrangement. Rather, the anonymity of these characters makes each one Everywoman, thus suggesting not only that all women are appropriate subjects for the enactment of the most bizarre and demeaning male sexual fantasies, but also that this is their primary purpose. The recent escalation of violence in pornography—the presentation of scenes of bondage, rape, and torture of women for the sexual stimulation of the male characters or male viewers—while shocking in itself, is from this point of view merely a more vicious extension of a genre whose success depends on treating women in a manner beneath their dignity as human beings.

III PORNOGRAPHY: LIES AND VIOLENCE AGAINST WOMEN

What is wrong with pornography, then, is its degrading and dehumanizing portrayal of women (and *not* its sexual content). Pornography, by its very nature, requires that women be subordinate to men and mere instruments for the fulfillment of male fantasies. To accomplish this, pornography must lie. Pornography lies when it says that our sexual life is or ought to be subordinate to the service of men, that our pleasure consists in pleasing men and not ourselves, that we are depraved, that we are fit subjects for rape, bondage, torture, and murder. Pornography lies explicitly about women's sexuality, and through such lies fosters more lies about our humanity, our dignity, and our personhood.

Moreover, since nothing is alleged to justify the treatment of the female characters of pornography save their womanhood, pornography depicts all women as fit objects of violence by virtue of their sex alone. Because it is simply being female that, in the pornographic vision, justifies being violated, the lies of pornography are lies about all women. Each work of pornography is on its own libelous and defamatory, yet gains power through being reinforced by every other pornographic work. The sheer number of pornographic productions expands the moral issue to include not only assessing the morality or immorality of individual works, but also the meaning and force of the mass production of pornography.

The pornographic view of women is thoroughly entrenched in a booming portion of the publishing, film, and recording industries, reaching and affecting not only all who look to such sources for sexual stimulation, but also those of us who are forced into an awareness of it as we peruse magazines at newsstands and record albums in record stores, as we check the entertainment sections of city newspapers, or even as we approach a counter to pay for groceries. It is not necessary to spend a great deal of time reading or viewing pornographic material to absorb its male-centered definition of women. No longer confined within plain brown wrappers, it jumps out from billboards that proclaim "Live X-rated Girls!" or "Angels in Pain" or "Hot and Wild," and from magazine covers displaying a woman's genital area being spread open to the viewer by her own fingers.[7] Thus, even men who do not frequent pornographic shops and movie houses are supported in the sexist objectification of women by their environment. Women, too, are crippled by internalizing as self-images those that are presented to us by pornographers. Isolated from one another and with no source of support for an alternative view of female sexuality, we may not always find the strength to resist a message that dominates the common cultural media.

The entrenchment of pornography in our culture also gives it a significance quite beyond its explicit sexual messages. To suggest, as pornography does, that the primary purpose of women is to provide sexual pleasure to men is to deny that women are independently human or have a status equal to that of men. It is, moreover, to deny our equality at one of the most intimate levels of human experience. This denial is especially powerful in a hierarchical, class society such as ours, in which individuals feel good about themselves by feeling superior to others. Men in our society have a vested interest in maintaining their belief in the inferiority of the female sex, so that no matter how oppressed and exploited by the society in which they live and work, they can feel that they are at least superior to someone or some category of individuals—a woman or women. Pornography, by presenting women as wanton, depraved, and made for the sexual use of men, caters directly to that interest.[8] The very intimate nature of sexuality which makes pornography so corrosive also protects it from explicit public discussion. The consequent lack of any explicit social disavowal of the pornographic image of women enables this image to continue fostering sexist attitudes even as the society publicly proclaims its (as yet timid) commitment to sexual equality.

In addition to finding a connection between the pornographic view of women and the denial to us of our full human rights, women are beginning to connect the consumption of pornography with committing rape and other acts of sexual violence against women. Contrary to the findings of the Commission on Obscenity and Pornography a growing body of research is documenting (1) a correlation between exposure to representations of violence and the committing of violent acts generally, and (2) a correlation between exposure to pornographic materials and the committing of sexually abusive or violent acts against women.[9] While more study is needed to establish precisely what the causal relations are, clearly so-called hardcore pornography is not innocent.

From "snuff" films and miserable magazines in pornographic stores to *Hustler,* to phonograph album covers and advertisements, to *Vogue,* pornography has come to occupy its own niche in the communications and entertainment media and to acquire a quasi-institutional character (signaled by the use of diminutives such as "porn" or "porno" to refer to pornographic material, as though such familiar naming could take the hurt out). Its acceptance by the mass media, whatever the motivation, means a cultural endorsement of its message. As much as the materials themselves, the social tolerance of these degrading and distorted images of women in such quantities is harmful to us, since it indicates a general willingness to see women in ways incompatible with our fundamental human dignity and thus to justify treating us in those ways.[10] The tolerance of pornographic representations of the rape, bondage, and torture of women helps to create and maintain a climate more tolerant of the actual physical abuse of women.[11] The tendency on the part of the legal system to view the victim of a rape as responsible for the crime against her is but one manifestation of this.

In sum, pornography is injurious to women in at least three distinct ways:

1 Pornography, especially violent pornography, is implicated in the committing of crimes of violence against women.

2 Pornography is the vehicle for the dissemination of a deep and vicious lie about women. It is defamatory and libelous.

3 The diffusion of such a distorted view of women's nature in our society as it exists today supports sexist (i.e., male-centered) attitudes, and thus reinforces the oppression and exploitation of women.

Society's tolerance of pornography, especially pornography on the contemporary massive scale, reinforces each of these modes of injury: By not disavowing the lie, it supports the male-centered myth that women are inferior and subordinate creatures. Thus, it contributes to the maintenance of a climate tolerant of both psychological and physical violence against women. . . .

CONCLUSION

I have defined pornography in such a way as to distinguish it from erotica and from moral realism, and have argued that it is defamatory and libelous toward women, that it condones crimes against women, and that it invites tolerance of the social, economic, and cultural oppression of women. The production and distribution of pornographic material is thus a social and moral wrong. Contrasting both the current volume of pornographic production and its growing infiltration of the communications media with the status of women in this culture makes clear the necessity for its control. . . .

Appeals for action against pornography are sometimes brushed aside with the claim that such action is a diversion from the primary task of feminists—the elimination of sexism and of sexual inequality. This approach focuses on the enjoyment rather than the manufacture of pornography, and sees it as merely a product of sexism which will disappear when the latter has been overcome and the sexes are socially and economically equal. Pornography cannot be separated from sexism in this way: Sexism is not just a set of attitudes regarding the inferiority of women but the behaviors and social and economic rules that manifest such attitudes. Both the manufacture and distribution of pornography and the enjoyment of it are instances of sexist behavior. The enjoyment of pornography on the part of individuals will presumably decline as such individuals begin to accord women their status as fully human. A cultural climate which tolerates the degrading representation of women is not a climate which facilitates the development of respect for women. Furthermore, the demand for pornography is stimulated not just by the sexism of individuals but by the pornography industry itself. Thus, both as a social phenomenon and in its effect on individuals, pornography, far from being a mere product, nourishes sexism. The campaign against it is an essential component of women's struggle for legal, economic, and social equality, one which requires the support of all feminists.[12]

NOTES

1 *Women Against Violence in Pornography and Media Newspage,* Vol. II, No. 5, June 1978; and Judith Reisman in *Women Against Violence in Pornography and Media Proposal.*

2 American Law Institute *Model Penal Code,* sec. 251.4.

3 *Report of the Commission on Obscenity and Pornography* (New York: Bantam Books, 1970), p. 239. The Commission, of course, concluded that the demeaning content of pornography did not adversely affect male attitudes toward women.

4 Among recent feminist discussions are Diana Russell, "Pornography: A Feminist Perspective" and Susan Griffin, "On Pornography," *Chrysalis,* Vol. I, No. 4, 1978; and Ann Garry, "Pornography and Respect for Women," *Social Theory and Practice,* Vol. 4, Spring 1978, pp. 395–421.

5 *The Oxford English Dictionary,* Compact Edition (London: Oxford University Press, 1971), p. 2242.

6 In talking of prostitution here, I refer to the concept of, rather than the reality of, prostitution. The same is true of my remarks about relationships between women and their husbands or men friends.

7 This was a full-color magazine cover seen in a rack at the check-out counter of a corner delicatessen.

8 Pornography thus becomes another tool of capitalism. One feature of some contemporary pornography—the use of black and Asian women in both still photographs and films—exploits the racism as well as the sexism of its white consumers. For a discussion of the interplay between racism and sexism under capitalism as it relates to violent crimes against women, see Angela Y. Davis, "Rape, Racism, and the Capitalist Setting," *The Black Scholar*, Vol. 9, No. 7, April 1978.

9 Urie Bronfenbrenner, *Two Worlds of Childhood* (New York: Russell Sage Foundation, 1970); H.J. Eysenck and D.K.B. Nias, *Sex, Violence and the Media* (New York: St. Martin's Press, 1978); and Michael Goldstein, Harold Kant, and John Hartman, *Pornography and Sexual Deviance* (Berkeley: University of California Press, 1973); and the papers by Diana Russell, Pauline Bart, and Irene Diamond included in [Laura Lederer, ed., *Take Back the Night* (New York: William Morrow, 1980)].

10 This tolerance has a linguistic parallel in the growing acceptance and use of nonhuman nouns such as "chick," "bird," "filly," "fox," "doll," "babe," "skirt," etc., to refer to women, and of verbs of harm such as "fuck," "screw," "bang," to refer to sexual intercourse. See Robert Baker and Frederick Elliston, "'Pricks' and 'Chicks': A Plea for Persons." *Philosophy and Sex* (Buffalo, N.Y.: Prometheus Books, 1975).

11 This is supported by the fact that in Denmark the number of rapes committed has increased while the number of rapes reported to the authorities has decreased over the past twelve years. See *WAVPM Newspage,* Vol. II, No. 5, June, 1978, quoting M. Harry, "Denmark Today—The Causes and Effects of Sexual Liberty" (paper presented to The Responsible Society, London, England, 1976). See also Eysenck and Nias, *Sex, Violence and the Media* (New York: St. Martin's Press, 1978), pp. 120–124.

12 Many women helped me to develop and crystallize the ideas presented in this paper. I would especially like to thank Michele Farrell, Laura Lederer, Pamela Miller, and Dianne Romain for their comments in conversation and on the first written draft. Portions of this material were presented orally to members of the Society for Women in Philosophy and to participants in the workshops on "What Is Pornography?" at the Conference on Feminist Perspectives on Pornography, San Francisco, November 17, 18, and 19, 1978. Their discussion was invaluable in helping me to see problems and to clarify the ideas presented here.

QUESTIONS

1 Do you accept Longino's suggested definition of pornography? Is there a better definition?

2 Emphasizing the injurious impact of pornography on women, Longino concludes that "its control is necessary." What specific controls on the production and distribution of pornography would you endorse?

Feminism, Pornography, and Censorship
Mark R. Wicclair

Wicclair operates with the definition of pornography suggested by Longino. He argues, however, that censorship of pornography is not a legitimate means of achieving the aims of feminism, nor even the most effective means. In his view, there is a strong presumption against censorship; this presumption is based on the principle of freedom of expression, as well as the likely negative side effects of censorship. In rejecting the argument that censorship of pornography is a legitimate means of preventing harm to women, he claims that the connection between pornography and harm to women is too speculative to warrant incurring the costs of censorship. In addition to emphasizing the costs of censorship, Wicclair warns against overestimating its expected benefits. He concludes by presenting the procensorship feminist with a series of difficulties.

It is sometimes claimed that pornography is objectionable because it violates conventional standards of sexual morality. Although feminists tend to agree that pornography is objectionable, they reject this particular argument against it.[1] This argument is unacceptable to feminists because it is associated with an oppressive Puritanical sexual ethic that inhibits the sexual fulfillment of all people, but especially women. In order to understand why feminists find pornography objectionable, one has to keep in mind that they do not equate the terms "pornographic" and "sexually explicit." Rather, sexually explicit material is said to be "pornographic" only if it depicts and condones the exploitation, dehumanization, subordination, abuse, or denigration of women. By definition, then, all pornography is sexist and misogynistic. Some pornographic material has the additional feature of depicting and condoning acts of *violence* against women (e.g., rape, brutality, torture, sadism). Thus there is a world of difference between harmless "erotica" and pornography. Whereas erotica depicts sexual activity in a manner which is designed to produce sexual arousal and is therefore likely to be objectionable only to those who subscribe to a Puritanical sexual ethic, pornography is "material that explicitly represents or describes degrading and abusive sexual behavior so as to endorse and/or recommend the behavior as described."[2]

Despite the general agreement among feminists that pornography, understood in the way just described, is objectionable, they are sharply divided over the question of its *censorship*. Whereas some feminists find pornography to be so objectionable that they call for its censorship, others oppose this proposal.[3] I will argue that anyone who supports the aims of feminism and who seeks the liberation of all people should reject the censorship of pornography.[4]

When discussing censorship, it is important to keep in mind that there are very strong reasons to be wary of its use. In our society, the importance of the principle of freedom of expression—an anticensorship principle—is widely recognized. The ability to speak one's mind and to express ideas and feelings without the threat of legal penalties or government control is rightly perceived as an essential feature of a truly free society. Moreover, an environment that tolerates the expression of differing views about politics, art, lifestyles, etc., encourages progress and aids in the search for truth and justice. In addition to the many important values associated with the principle of freedom of expression, it is also necessary to consider likely negative side effects of censorship. There is a serious risk that once any censorship is allowed, the power to censor will, over time, expand in unintended and undesirable directions (the "slippery slope"). This is not mere speculation, for such an expansion of the power to censor is to be expected in view of the fact that it is extremely difficult, if not impossible, to formulate unequivocal and unambiguous criteria of censorship. Then, too, the power to censor can all too easily be abused or misused. Even though it may arise in a genuine effort to promote the general welfare and to protect certain rights, officials and groups might use the power to censor as a means to advance their own interests and values and to suppress the rights, interests, and values of others. Thus, given the value of freedom of expression and the many dangers associated with censorship, there is a strong *prima facie* case against censorship. In other words, advocates of censorship have the burden of showing that there are sufficiently strong overriding reasons which would justify it in a specific area.

Like racist and antisemitic material, sexist and misogynistic films, books, and magazines surely deserve condemnation. But censorship is another matter. In view of the strength of the case against censorship in general, it is unwise to advocate it merely to prevent depicting morally objectionable practices in a favorable light. Fortunately, proponents of the censorship of pornography tend to recognize this, for they usually base their call for censorship on a claim about the *effects* of pornography. Pornography, it is held, is *injurious* or *harmful* to women because it fosters the objectionable practices that it depicts. Pornography generally is said to promote the exploitation, humiliation, denigration, subordination, etc., of women; and pornography that depicts acts of violence against women is said to cause murder, rape, assault, and other acts of violence. On the basis of the "harm principle"—a widely accepted principle that allows us to restrict someone's freedom in order to prevent harm to others—it would appear to be justified to override the principle of freedom of expression and to restrict the freedom of would-be producers, distributors, sellers, exhibitors, and consumers of pornography. In short it seems that censorship of pornography is a legitimate means of preventing harm to women.

However, there are a number of problems associated with this attempt to justify censorship. To begin with, it is essential to recognize the important difference between words and images, on the one hand, and actions, on the other hand. A would-be rapist poses a *direct* threat to his intended victim, and by stopping him, we prevent an act of violence. But if there is a connection between the depiction of a rape—even one which appears to condone it—and someone's committing an act of violence against a woman, the connection is relatively *indirect;* and stopping the production, distribution, sale, and exhibition of depictions of rape does not directly restrict the freedom of would-be rapists to commit acts of violence against women. In recognition of the important difference between restricting words and images and preventing harmful behavior, exceptions to the principle of freedom of expression are generally thought to be justified only if words or images present a "clear and present danger" of harm or injury. Thus, to cite a standard example, it is justified to stop someone from falsely shouting "Fire!" in a crowded theater, for this exclamation is likely to cause a panic that would result in serious injury and even death.

It is doubtful that pornography satisfies the "clear and present danger" condition. For there does not seem to be conclusive evidence that establishes its *causal* significance. Most studies are limited to violent pornography. And even though some of these studies do suggest a *temporary* impact on *attitudes* (e.g., those who view violent pornography may be more likely to express the view that women seek and "enjoy" violence), this does not show that viewing violent pornography causes violent *behavior*. Moreover, there is some evidence suggesting that the effect on attitudes is only temporary and that it can be effectively counteracted by additional information.[5]

But even if there is no conclusive evidence that pornography causes harm, is it not reasonable to "play it safe," and does this not require censorship? Unfortunately, the situation is not as simple as this question appears to suggest. For one thing, it is sometimes claimed that exposure to pornography has a "cathartic" effect and that it therefore produces a net *reduction* in harm to women. This claim is based upon two assumptions, neither of which has been proven to be false: (1) Men who are not already violence-prone are more likely to be "turned off" than to be "turned on" by depictions of rape, brutality, dismemberment, etc. (2) For men in the latter category, exposure to pornography can function as a substitute for actually causing harm. It is also necessary to recall that there are significant values associated with the principle of freedom of expression, and that a failure to observe it involves a number of serious dangers. Since censorship has costs which are substantial and not merely speculative, the more speculative the connection between pornography and harm to women, the less basis there is for incurring the costs associated with censorship.

Just as it is easy to overlook the negative side of censorship, it is also common to overplay its positive effects. Surely it would be foolish to think that outlawing antisemitism in sexually explicit material would have halted the slaughter of Jews in Hitler Germany or that prohibiting racism in sexually explicit material would reduce the suffering of Blacks in South Africa. Similarly, in view of the violent nature of American society generally and the degree to which sexism persists to this day, it is unlikely that censorship of pornography by itself would produce any significant improvement in the condition of women in the United States. Fortunately, there are other, more effective and direct means of eliminating sexism than by censoring pornography. Passage and strict enforcement of the Equal Rights Amendment, electing feminists to local, state, and national political office, achieving genuine economic justice for women, and securing their reproductive freedom will do considerably more to foster the genuine liberation of women in the United States than will the censorship of pornography. With respect to rape and other acts of violence, it has often been noted that American society is extremely violent, and, sadly, there are no magic solutions to the problems of rape and violence. But the magnitude of the problem suggests that censoring pornography only addresses a symptom and not the underlying disease. Although there is still much dispute about the causes of violence generally and rape in particular, it is unlikely that there will be a serious reduction in acts of violence against women until there are rather drastic changes in the socioeconomic environment and in the criminal justice system.

Those who remain concerned about the possible contribution of pornography to violence and sexism should keep in mind that it can be "neutralized" in ways that avoid the dangers of censorship. One important alternative to government censorship is to help people understand why pornography is objectionable and why it and its message should be rejected. This can be accomplished by means of educational campaigns, discussions of pornography on radio and television and at public forums, letter writing, and educational picketing. In addition, attempts might be made to prevent or restrict the production, distribution, display, sale, and consumption of pornographic material by means of organized pickets, boycotts, and the like. Such direct measures by private citizens raise some troubling questions, but the dangers and risks which they pose are considerably less than those associated with government censorship.

There are several other reasons for questioning the view that the sexist and misogynistic nature of pornography justifies its censorship. Some of the more important of these include the following:

1 Although pornography depicts some practices that are both morally objectionable and illegal (e.g., rape, assault, torture), many of the practices depicted are morally repugnant *but do not break any law*. Thus, for example, our legal system does not explicitly prohibit men from treating women in a degrading or humiliating manner; and with some exceptions, it is not a crime to treat women exclusively as sex objects or to use them exclusively as means and not ends. But is it not odd to recommend making illegal the production, distribution, sale, and exhibition of materials that depict practices that are not themselves illegal?

2 It is essential that laws be clearly formulated and that vagueness be avoided. Vague laws can have a "chilling effect" on unobjectionable activities, and they tend to undermine the fair and effective enforcement of the law by giving police, prosecutors, and judges too much discretionary power. But those who call for the censorship of pornography on the grounds that it is sexist and misogynistic fail to recognize the difficulty of formulating laws which would have an acceptable degree of clarity and specificity. Proponents of censorship use terms like "degrading," "humiliating," "debasing," "exploitative," and "subordination of women." But these terms are far from unambiguous. In fact, they are highly subjective in the sense that different people have different criteria for deciding when something is degrading, humiliating, etc. For example, someone might think that the depiction of an unmarried female or a lesbian couple having and enjoying sex is "demeaning" or "debasing." Thus, in order to prevent censorship from being applied in unintended and undesirable ways, it is necessary to offer clear and unambiguous operational criteria for terms like "demeaning," "humiliating," etc. But the feasibility of articulating generally acceptable criteria of this sort remains highly doubtful.

3 Sexually explicit material that depicts violence against women or that depicts sexist practices is said to be subject to censorship only if it *condones* the objectionable practices. Thus, for example, news films, documentaries, and works which take a critical stance toward those practices are not to be censored. But it is exceedingly difficult in many cases to determine the "point of view" of films, books, photographs, etc.[6] If scholars who have advanced degrees in film, literature, and art can come to no general consensus about the "meaning" or "message" of certain works, is it plausible to think that prosecutors, judges, and juries are likely to fare any better?

4 Why call for the censorship of sexist and misogynistic books, magazines, films, and photographs only if they include an explicit depiction of *sexual activity*? There is no conclusive evidence showing that material that includes a depiction of sexual activity has a greater causal impact on attitudes and behavior.[7] Moreover, it will not do to claim that such material is not worthy of protection under the principle of freedom of expression. Surely, many works which include explicit depictions of sex are not totally devoid of significant and challenging ideas. Consequently, advocates of censorship are faced with a dilemma: Either they can call for the censorship of *all* material that contains objectionable images of women; or they can call for censorship only in the case of sexually explicit materials of that nature. If the first alternative is chosen, then given the pervasiveness of objectionable portrayals of women in art, literature, and the mass media, very little would be immune from censorship. But in view of the strong *prima facie* case against censorship, this seems unacceptable. On the other hand, if the second alternative is chosen, this invites the suspicion that the restriction to sexual material is based upon the very same Puritanical sexual ethic which feminists rightly tend to reject. I am not suggesting that feminists who call for censorship wish to champion sexual oppression. But it is noteworthy that many conservatives who generally do not support the aims of feminism align themselves with feminists who advocate censoring pornography.

5 Why call for censorship of materials only if they depict violence or other objectionable practices in relation to *women*? Wouldn't consistency require censoring *all* violence and material that portrays *anyone* in a derogatory light? But this is clearly unacceptable. For so much of our culture is permeated with images of violence and morally distasteful treatment of people that it is hard to think of many films, television programs, books, or magazines which would be totally immune from censorship. Censorship would be the rule rather than an exception, and such pervasive censorship is incompatible with a truly free society. It also won't do to limit censorship to members of historically oppressed groups (e.g., women, Blacks, Jews). First, it is very unlikely that such "preferential censorship" would be accepted by the majority for too long. Sooner or later others would object and/or press for protection too. Second, in view of the significant costs of censorship, even if it were limited to the protection of historically oppressed groups, it would not be justified unless there were a demonstrable "clear and present danger;" and this remains doubtful. But what about the view that only pornography should be subject to censorship because *women need special protection*? This position is also unacceptable. For since men are victimized by acts of racism, antisemitism, and violence, and since there is no evidence to prove that depictions of objectionable practices have a greater effect on behavior in pornographic material than they do in nonpornographic material, this position seems to be based on the sexist assumption that women need greater protection than men because they are "naturally" more fragile and vulnerable.

I have tried to show that censorship of pornography is neither the most effective nor a legitimate means to achieve the aims of feminism. Much pornographic material is morally repugnant, but there are less costly ways to express one's moral outrage and to attempt to "neutralize" pornography than by censorship. Moreover, pornography is only a relatively minor manifestation of the sexist practices and institutions that still pervade our society. Hence, the genuine liberation of women—and men—is best served by directly attacking those oppressive practices and institutions. It may be easier to identify and attack pornography—and to win some battles—but the payoff would be slight, and the negative side effects would be substantial.

NOTES

1 Just as the civil rights movement in the United States in the 1950's and 1960's included many people who were not Black, so one does not have to be a woman to be a feminist. As I am using the term, a feminist is any person who supports the fundamental goal of feminism: the liberation of women.

2 Helen E. Longino, "Pornography, Oppression, and Freedom: A Closer Look," in Laura Lederer, ed., *Take Back the Night* (New York: William Morrow and Company, Inc., 1980), p. 44. Longino also stipulates that the sexual activities depicted in pornography are degrading or abusive *to women.*

3 In response to the generally pro-censorship Women Against Violence in Pornography and Media, other feminists have organized the Feminist Anti-Censorship Taskforce.

4 Until recently, advocates of censorship have pressed for laws which prohibit or restrict the production, distribution, sale, and exhibition of pornographic material. However, pro-censorship feminists have hit upon a new strategy: Ordinances which stipulate that pornography is *sex discrimination,* enabling women to file sex discrimination lawsuits against producers, distributors, sellers, and exhibitors of pornography. Most of the criticisms of censorship which I discuss in this paper apply to both strategies.

5 For a discussion of research on the effects of pornography, see Edward Donnerstein and Neil Malamuth, eds., *Pornography and Sexual Aggression* (New York: Academic Press, 1984).

6 An informative illustration of how a film can resist unambiguous classification as either progressive or retrograde from a feminist perspective is provided in Lucy Fischer and Marcia Landy, *"The Eyes of Laura Mars:* A Binocular Critique," *Screen,* Vol. 23, Nos. 3–4 (September–October 1982).

7 In fact some researchers claim that the impact of depictions of violence is *greater* in material which is *not* pornographic. See, for example, the contribution of Edward Donnerstein and Daniel Linz to a section on pornography, "Pornography: Love or Death?" in *Film Comment,* Vol. 20, No. 6 (December 1984), pp. 34–35.

QUESTIONS

1 Does the easy availability of pornography pose a "clear and present danger" to women?

2 Considering the aims of feminism, are feminists well advised to endorse the censorship of pornography?

Opinion in *Village of Skokie v. National Socialist Party of America*

Illinois Supreme Court

This case originated when the village of Skokie, a Chicago suburb with a predominantly Jewish population, attempted to block certain activities planned by the National Socialist Party of America in conjunction with a demonstration in Skokie. The circuit court of Cook County issued an injunction against

Illinois Supreme Court. 373 N.E.2d 21 (1978).

(1) marching, walking, or parading while wearing the party uniform, (2) displaying the swastika, and (3) distributing pamphlets or displaying materials (e.g., slogans) that promote religious, ethnic, or racial hatred. An appellate court modified the original injunction so that party members were ordered only to refrain from displaying the swastika; the appellate court held the original injuction unconstitutional with regard to (1) and (3) above, but not with regard to (2). The Illinois Supreme Court affirmed the judgment of the appellate court with regard to (1) and (3) but reversed the judgment of the appellate court with regard to (2).

Referring to relevant decisions in the United States Supreme Court, the Illinois Supreme Court holds that display of the swastika is symbolic political speech and thus entitled to First Amendment protection. The court argues that display of the swastika does not fall within the definition of "fighting words." The court also argues that anticipation of a hostile audience cannot justify the prior restraint embodied in a court order against display of the swastika.

Plaintiff, the village of Skokie, filed a complaint in the circuit court of Cook County seeking to enjoin defendants, the National Socialist Party of America (the American Nazi Party) and 10 individuals as "officers and members" of the party, from engaging in certain activities while conducting a demonstration within the village. The circuit court issued an order enjoining certain conduct during the planned demonstration. The appellate court modified the injunction order, and, as modified, defendants are enjoined from "[i]ntentionally displaying the swastika on or off their persons, in the course of a demonstration, march, or parade." We allowed defendants' petition for leave to appeal.

The pleadings and the facts adduced at the hearing are fully set forth in the appellate court opinion, and only those matters necessary to the discussion of the issues will be repeated here. The facts are not disputed.

It is alleged in plaintiff's complaint that the "uniform of the National Socialist Party of America consists of the storm trooper uniform of the German Nazi Party embellished with the Nazi swastika"; that the plaintiff village has a population of about 70,000 persons of which approximately 40,500 persons are of "Jewish religion or Jewish ancestry" and of this latter number 5,000 to 7,000 are survivors of German concentration camps; that the defendant organization is "dedicated to the incitation of racial and religious hatred directed principally against individuals of Jewish faith or ancestry and non-Caucasians"; and that its members "have patterned their conduct, their uniform, their slogan and their tactics along the pattern of the German Nazi Party. . . ."

Defendants moved to dismiss the complaint. In an affidavit attached to defendants' motion to dismiss, defendant Frank Collin, who testified that he was "party leader," stated that on or about March 20, 1977, he sent officials of the plaintiff village a letter stating that the party members and supporters would hold a peaceable, public assembly in the village on May 1, 1977, to protest the Skokie Park District's requirement that the party procure $350,000 of insurance prior to the party's use of the Skokie public parks for public assemblies. The demonstration was to begin at 3 P.M., last 20 to 30 minutes, and consist of 30 to 50 demonstrators marching in single file, back and forth, in front of the village hall. The marchers were to wear uniforms which include a swastika emblem or armband. They were to carry a party banner containing a swastika emblem and signs containing such statements as "White Free Speech," "Free Speech for the White Man," and "Free Speech for White America." The demonstrators would not distribute handbills, make any derogatory statements directed to any ethnic or religious group, or obstruct traffic. They would cooperate with any reasonable police instructions or requests.

At the hearing on plaintiff's motion for an "emergency injunction" a resident of Skokie testified that he was a survivor of the Nazi holocaust. He further testified that the Jewish community in and around Skokie feels the purpose of the march in the "heart of the Jewish population" is to remind the two million survivors "that we are not through with you" and to show "that the Nazi threat is not over, it can happen again." Another resident of Skokie testified that as the result of defendants' announced intention to march in Skokie, 15 to 18 Jewish organizations, within the village and surrounding area, were called and a counter-demonstration of an estimated 12,000 to 15,000 people was scheduled for the same day. There was opinion evidence that defendants' planned demonstration in Skokie would result in violence.

The circuit court entered an order enjoining defendants from "marching, walking or parading in the uniform of the National Socialist Party of America; marching, walking or parading or otherwise displaying the swastika on or off their person; distributing pamphlets or displaying any materials which incite or promote hatred against persons of Jewish faith or ancestry or hatred against persons of any faith or ancestry, race or religion" within the village of Skokie. The appellate court, as earlier noted, modified the order so that defendants were enjoined only from intentional display of the swastika during the Skokie demonstration.

The appellate court opinion adequately discussed and properly decided those issues arising from the portions of the injunction order which enjoined defendants from marching, walking, or parading, from distributing pamphlets or displaying materials, and from wearing the uniform of the National Socialist Party of America. The only issue remaining before this court is whether the circuit court order enjoining defendants from displaying the swastika violates the first amendment rights of those defendants.

In defining the constitutional rights of the parties who come before this court, we are, of course, bound by the pronouncements of the United States Supreme Court in its interpretation of the United States Constitution. The decisions of that court, particularly *Cohen v. California* (1971), in our opinion compel us to permit the demonstration as proposed, including display of the swastika.

"It is firmly settled that under our Constitution the public expression of ideas may not be prohibited merely because the ideas are themselves offensive to some of their hearers," and it is entirely clear that the wearing of distinctive clothing can be symbolic expression of a thought or philosophy. The symbolic expression of thought falls within the free speech clause of the first amendment, and the plaintiff village has the heavy burden of justifying the imposition of a prior restraint upon defendants' right to freedom of speech.

The village of Skokie seeks to meet this burden by application of the "fighting words" doctrine first enunciated in *Chaplinsky v. New Hampshire* (1942). That doctrine was designed to permit punishment of extremely hostile personal communication likely to cause immediate physical response, "no words being 'forbidden except such as have a direct tendency to cause acts of violence by the persons to whom, individually, the remark is addressed.'" In *Cohen* the Supreme Court restated the description of fighting words as "those personally abusive epithets which, when addressed to the ordinary citizen, are, as a matter of common knowledge, inherently likely to provoke violent reaction." Plaintiff urges, and the appellate court has held, that the exhibition of the Nazi symbol, the swastika, addresses to ordinary citizens a message which is tantamount to fighting words. Plaintiff further asks this court to extend *Chaplinsky*, which upheld a statute punishing the use of such words, and hold that the fighting-words doctrine permits a prior restraint on defendants' symbolic speech. In our judgment we are precluded from doing so.

In *Cohen*, defendant's conviction stemmed from wearing a jacket bearing the words "Fuck the Draft" in a Los Angeles County courthouse corridor. The Supreme Court for reasons we believe applicable here refused to find that the jacket inscription constituted fighting words. That court stated:

> The constitutional right of free expression is powerful medicine in a society as diverse and populous as ours. It is designed and intended to remove governmental restraints from the arena of public discussion, putting the decision as to what views shall be voiced largely into the hands of each of us, in the hope that use of such freedom will ultimately produce a more capable citizenry and more perfect polity and in the belief that no other approach would comport with the premise of individual dignity and choice upon which our political system rests.
>
> To many, the immediate consequence of this freedom may often appear to be only verbal tumult, discord, and even offensive utterance. These are, however, within established limits, in truth necessary side effects of the broader enduring values which the process of open debate permits us to achieve. That the air may at times seem filled with verbal cacophony is, in this sense not a sign of weakness but of strength. We cannot lose sight of the fact that, in what otherwise might seem a trifling and annoying instance of individual distasteful abuse of a privilege, these fundamental societal values are truly implicated. . . . "so long as the means are peaceful, the communication need not meet standards of acceptability."
>
> Against this perception of the constitutional policies involved, we discern certain more particularized considerations that peculiarly call for reversal of this conviction. First, the principle contended for by the State seems inherently boundless. How is one to distinguish this from any other offensive word [emblem]? Surely the State has no right to cleanse public debate to the point where it is grammatically palatable to the most squeamish among us. Yet no readily ascertainable general principle exists for stopping short of that result were we to affirm the judgment below. For, while the particular four-letter word [emblem] being litigated here is perhaps more distasteful than most others of its genre, it is nevertheless often true that one man's vulgarity is another's lyric. Indeed, we think it is largely because governmental officials cannot make principled distinctions in this area that the Constitution leaves matters of taste and style so largely to the individual. . . .
>
> Finally, and in the same vein, we cannot indulge the facile assumption that one can forbid particular words without also running a substantial risk of suppressing ideas in the process. Indeed, governments might soon seize upon the censorship of particular words

[emblems] as a convenient guise for banning the expression of unpopular views. We have been able, as noted above, to discern little social benefit that might result from running the risk of opening the door to such grave results.

The display of the swastika, as offensive to the principles of a free nation as the memories it recalls may be, is symbolic political speech intended to convey to the public the beliefs of those who display it. It does not, in our opinion, fall within the definition of "fighting words," and that doctrine cannot be used here to overcome the heavy presumption against the constitutional validity of a prior restraint.

Nor can we find that the swastika, while not representing fighting words, is nevertheless so offensive and peace threatening to the public that its display can be enjoined. We do not doubt that the sight of this symbol is abhorrent to the Jewish citizens of Skokie, and that the survivors of the Nazi persecutions, tormented by their recollections, may have strong feelings regarding its display. Yet it is entirely clear that this factor does not justify enjoining defendants' speech. The *Cohen* court spoke to this subject:

> Finally, in arguments before this Court much has been made of the claim that Cohen's distasteful mode of expression was thrust upon unwilling or unsuspecting viewers, and that the State might therefore legitimately act as it did in order to protect the sensitive from otherwise unavoidable exposure to appellant's crude form of protest. Of course, the mere presumed presence of unwitting listeners or viewers does not serve automatically to justify curtailing all speech capable of giving offense. While this Court has recognized that government may properly act in many situations to prohibit intrusion into the privacy of the home of unwelcome views and ideas which cannot be totally banned from the public dialogue, we have at the same time consistently stressed that "we are often 'captives' outside the sanctuary of the home and subject to objectionable speech." The ability of government, consonant with the Constitution, to shut off discourse solely to protect others from hearing it is, in other words, dependent upon a showing that substantial privacy interests are being invaded in an essentially intolerable manner. Any broader view of this authority would effectively empower a majority to silence dissidents simply as a matter of personal predilections.

Similarly, the Court of Appeals for the Seventh Circuit, in reversing the denial of defendant Collin's application for a permit to speak in Chicago's Marquette Park, noted that courts have consistently refused to ban speech because of the possibility of unlawful conduct by those opposed to the speaker's philosophy. . . .

Rockwell v. Morris (1961) also involved an American Nazi leader, George Lincoln Rockwell, who challenged a bar to his use of a New York City park to hold a public demonstration where anti-Semitic speeches would be made. Although approximately 2½ million Jewish New Yorkers were hostile to Rockwell's message, the court ordered that a permit to speak be granted, stating:

> A community need not wait to be subverted by street riots and storm troopers; but, also, it cannot, by its policemen or commissioners, suppress a speaker, in prior restraint, on the basis of news reports, hysteria, or inference that what he did yesterday, he will do today. Thus, too, if the speaker incites others to immediate unlawful action he may be punished—in a proper case, stopped when disorder actually impends; but this is not to be confused with unlawful action from others who seek unlawfully to suppress or punish the speaker.

So, the unpopularity of views, their shocking quality, their obnoxiousness, and even their alarming impact is not enough. Otherwise, the preacher of any strange doctrine could be stopped; the anti-racist himself could be suppressed, if he undertakes to speak in "restricted" areas; and one who asks that public schools be open indiscriminately to all ethnic groups could be lawfully suppressed, if only he choose to speak where persuasion is needed most.

In summary, as we read the controlling Supreme Court opinions, use of the swastika is a symbolic form of free speech entitled to first amendment protections. Its display on uniforms or banners by those engaged in peaceful demonstrations cannot be totally precluded solely because that display may provoke a violent reaction by those who view it. Particularly is this true where, as here, there has been advance notice by the demonstrators of their plans so that they have become, as the complaint alleges, "common knowledge" and those to whom sight of the swastika banner or uniforms would be offense are forewarned and need not view them. A speaker who gives prior notice of his message has not compelled a confrontation with those who voluntarily listen.

As to those who happen to be in a position to be involuntarily confronted with the swastika, the following observations from *Erznoznik v. City of Jacksonville* (1975) are appropriate:

> The plain, if at all times disquieting, truth is that in our pluralistic society, constantly proliferating new and ingenious forms of expression, "we are inescapably captive audiences for many purposes." Much that we encounter offends our esthetic, if not our political and moral, sensibilities. Nevertheless, the Constitution does not permit government to decide which types of otherwise protected speech are sufficiently offensive to require protection for the unwilling listener or viewer. Rather, absent the narrow circumstances described above [home intrusion or captive audience], the burden normally falls upon the viewer to "avoid further bombardment of [his] sensibilities simply by averting [his] eyes."

Thus by placing the burden upon the viewer to avoid further bombardment, the Supreme Court has permitted speakers to justify the initial intrusion into the citizen's sensibilities.

We accordingly, albeit reluctantly, conclude that the display of the swastika cannot be enjoined under the fighting-words exception to free speech, nor can anticipation of a hostile audience justify the prior restraint. Furthermore, *Cohen* and *Erznoznik* direct the citizens of Skokie that it is their burden to avoid the offensive symbol if they can do so without unreasonable inconvenience. Accordingly, we are constrained to reverse that part of the appellate court judgment enjoining the display of the swastika. That judgment is in all other respects affirmed.

QUESTIONS

1 What meaning does display of the swastika have for the Jewish community? Does display of the swastika constitute "fighting words"?

2 In your view, did the circuit court, the appellate court, or the Illinois Supreme Court provide the most defensible resolution of this case?

Racist Speech as the Functional Equivalent of Fighting Words

Charles R. Lawrence III

Lawrence argues that face-to-face racial insults are unworthy of First Amendment protection. He gives two reasons: (1) Racial insults produce an immediate injury. (2) Racial insults typically have a preemptive effect on further speech and thus do not cohere with the underlying purpose of the First Amendment, which is presumably to foster the greatest amount of speech. Lawrence presents an analysis of the "speechlessness" often experienced by those subjected to racial insults. In his view, racial insults are less likely than other "fighting words" to produce violent responses, in part because of the relative powerlessness of those typically subjected to them. However, Lawrence argues that, since racial insults inhibit speech as much or more than other "fighting words," they are best understood as the "functional equivalent" of fighting words.

. . . When racist speech takes the form of face-to-face insults, catcalls, or other assaultive speech aimed at an individual or small group of persons, then it falls within the "fighting words" exception to first amendment protection. The Supreme Court has held [in *Chaplinsky v. New Hampshire* (1942)] that words that "by their very utterance inflict injury or tend to incite an immediate breach of the peace" are not constitutionally protected.

Face-to-face racial insults, like fighting words, are undeserving of first amendment protection for two reasons. The first reason is the immediacy of the injurious impact of racial insults. The experience of being called "nigger," "spic," "Jap," or "kike" is like receiving a slap in the face. The injury is instantaneous. There is neither an opportunity for intermediary reflection on the idea conveyed nor an opportunity for responsive speech. The harm to be avoided is both clear and present. The second reason that racial insults should not fall under protected speech relates to the purpose underlying the first amendment. If the purpose of the first amendment is to foster the greatest amount of speech, then racial insults disserve that purpose. Assaultive racist speech functions as a preemptive strike. The racial invective is experienced as a blow, not a proffered idea, and once the blow is struck, it is unlikely that dialogue will follow. Racial insults are undeserving of first amendment protection because the perpetrator's intention is not to discover truth or initiate dialogue but to injure the victim.

The fighting words doctrine anticipates that the verbal "slap in the face" of insulting words will provoke a violent response with a resulting breach of the peace. When racial insults are hurled at minorities, the response may be silence or flight rather than a fight, but the preemptive effect on further speech is just as complete as with fighting words. Women and minorities often report that they find themselves speechless in the face of discriminatory verbal attacks. This inability to respond is not the result of oversensitivity among these groups, as some individuals who oppose protective regulation have argued. Rather, it is the product of several factors, all of which reveal the non-speech character of the initial preemptive verbal assault. The first factor is that the visceral emotional response to personal attack precludes speech. Attack produces an instinctive, defensive psychological reaction. Fear, rage, shock, and flight all interfere with any reasoned response. Words like "nigger," "kike," and "faggot" produce physical symptoms that temporarily disable the victim, and the perpetrators often use these words with the intention of producing this effect. Many victims do not find words of response until well after the assault when the cowardly assaulter has departed.

A second factor that distinguishes racial insults from protected speech is the preemptive nature of such insults—the words by which to respond to such verbal attacks may never be forthcoming because speech is usually an inadequate response. When one is personally attacked with words that denote one's subhuman status and untouchability, there is little (if anything) that can be said to redress either the emotional or reputational injury. This is particularly true when the message and meaning of the epithet resonates with beliefs widely held in society. This preservation of widespread beliefs is what makes the face-to-face racial attack more likely to preempt speech than are other fighting words. The racist name-caller is accompanied by a cultural chorus of equally demeaning speech and symbols.

The subordinated victim of fighting words also is silenced by her relatively powerless position in society. Because of the significance of power and position, the categorization of racial epithets as "fighting words" provides an inadequate paradigm; instead one must speak of their "functional equivalent." The fighting words doctrine presupposes an encounter between two persons of relatively equal power who have been acculturated to respond to face-to-face insults with violence. The fighting words doctrine is a paradigm based on a white male point of view. In most situations, minorities correctly perceive that a violent response to fighting words will result in a risk to their own life and limb. Since minorities are likely to lose the fight, they are forced to remain silent and submissive. This response is most obvious when women submit to sexually assaultive speech or when the racist name-caller is in a more powerful position—the boss on the job or the mob. Certainly, we do not expect the black women crossing the Wisconsin campus to turn on their tormentors and pummel them. Less obvious, but just as significant, is the effect of pervasive racial and sexual violence and coercion on individual members of subordinated groups who must learn the survival techniques of suppressing and disguising rage and anger at an early age.

One of my students, a white, gay male, related an experience that is quite instructive in understanding the inadequacy and potential of the "fighting words" doctrine. In response to my request that students describe how they experienced the injury of racist speech, Michael told a story of being called "faggot" by a man on a subway. His description included all of the speech inhibiting elements I have noted previously. He found himself in a state of semi-shock, nauseous, dizzy, unable to muster the witty, sarcastic, articulate rejoinder he was accustomed to making. He suddenly was aware of the recent spate of gay-bashing in San Francisco, and how many of these had escalated from verbal encounters. Even hours later when the shock resided and his facility with words returned, he realized that any response was inadequate to counter the hundreds of years of societal defamation that one word—"faggot"—carried with it. Like the word "nigger" and unlike the word "liar," it is not sufficient to deny the truth of the word's application, to say, "I am not a faggot." One must deny the truth of the word's meaning, a meaning shouted from the rooftops by the rest of the world a million times a day. Although there are many of us who constantly and in myriad ways seek to counter the lie spoken in the meaning of hateful words like "nigger" and "faggot," it is a nearly impossible burden to bear when one encounters hateful speech face-to-face.

But there was another part of my discussion with Michael that is equally instructive. I asked if he could remember a situation when he had been verbally attacked with reference to his membership in a superordinate group. Had he ever been called a "honkie," a "chauvinist pig," or "mick"? (Michael is from a working class Irish family in Boston.) He said that he had been called some version of all three and that although he found the last one more offensive than the first two, he had not experienced—even in that subordinated role—the same disorienting powerlessness he had experienced when attacked for his membership in the gay community. The question of power, of the context of the power relationships within which speech takes place, must be considered as we decide how best to foster the freest and fullest dialogue within our communities. . . .

QUESTIONS

1 Does Lawrence provide a compelling analysis of the "speechlessness" often experienced by those who are subjected to racial insults?
2 Lawrence claims that "the fighting words doctrine is a paradigm based on a white male point of view." Do you agree?

Liberalism and Campus Hate Speech: A Philosophical Examination

Andrew Altman

Altman engages the issue of campus hate-speech regulation. He argues, within the liberal tradition, in favor of a very narrow form of hate-speech regulation, but he does not base his argument on the psychological harms produced by hate speech. Rather, in conjunction with an analysis of the typical function of slurs and epithets, he develops the concept of "the speech-act wrong of subordination," and he

Reprinted with permission of the author and the publisher from *Ethics,* vol. 103 (January 1993), pp. 302–317. Copyright © 1993 by the University of Chicago.

endorses hate-speech regulation that targets this particular speech-act wrong. Although Altman concedes that any hate-speech regulation violates the important liberal principle of viewpoint-neutrality, he argues that hate-speech regulation targeting the speech-act wrong of subordination can accommodate the deeper liberal concerns underlying that principle.

INTRODUCTION

In recent years a vigorous public debate has developed over freedom of speech within the academic community. The immediate stimulus for the debate has been the enactment by a number of colleges and universities of rules against hate speech. While some have defended these rules as essential for protecting the equal dignity of all members of the academic community, others have condemned them as intolerable efforts to impose ideological conformity on the academy.

Liberals can be found on both sides of this debate. Many see campus hate-speech regulation as a form of illegitimate control by the community over individual liberty of expression. They argue that hate-speech rules violate the important liberal principle that any regulation of speech be viewpoint-neutral. But other liberals see hate-speech regulation as a justifiable part of the effort to help rid society of discrimination and subordination based on such characteristics as race, religion, ethnicity, gender, and sexual preference.

In this article, I develop a liberal argument in favor of certain narrowly drawn rules prohibiting hate speech. The argument steers a middle course between those who reject all forms of campus hate-speech regulation and those who favor relatively sweeping forms of regulation. Like those who reject all regulation, I argue that rules against hate speech are not viewpoint-neutral. Like those who favor sweeping regulation, I accept the claim that hate speech can cause serious psychological harm to those at whom it is directed. However, I do not believe that such harm can justify regulation, sweeping or otherwise. Instead, I argue that some forms of hate speech inflict on their victims a certain kind of wrong, and it is on the basis of this wrong that regulation can be justified. The kind of wrong in question is one that is inflicted in virtue of the performance of a certain kind of speech-act characteristic of some forms of hate speech, and I argue that rules targeting this speech-act wrong will be relatively narrow in scope.[1]

HATE SPEECH, HARASSMENT, AND NEUTRALITY

Hate-speech regulations typically provide for disciplinary action against students for making racist, sexist, or homophobic utterances or for engaging in behavior that expresses the same kinds of discriminatory attitudes.[2] The stimulus for the regulations has been an apparent upsurge in racist, sexist, and homophobic incidents on college campuses over the past decade. The regulations that have actually been proposed or enacted vary widely in the scope of what they prohibit.

The rules at Stanford University are narrow in scope. They require that speech meet three conditions before it falls into the proscribed zone: the speaker must intend to insult or stigmatize another on the basis of certain characteristics such as race, gender, or sexual orientation; the speech must be addressed directly to those whom it is intended to stigmatize; and the speech must employ epithets or terms that similarly convey "visceral hate or contempt" for the people at whom it is directed.[3]

On the other hand, the rules of the University of Connecticut, in their original form, were relatively sweeping in scope. According to these rules, "Every member of the University is obligated to refrain from actions that intimidate, humiliate or demean persons or groups or that undermine their security or self-esteem." Explicitly mentioned as examples of proscribed speech were "making inconsiderate jokes . . . stereotyping the experiences, background, and skills of individuals, . . . imitating stereotypes in speech or mannerisms [and] attributing objections to any of the above actions to 'hypersensitivity' of the targeted individual or group."[4]

Even the narrower forms of hate-speech regulation, such as we find at Stanford, must be distinguished from a simple prohibition of verbal harassment. As commonly understood, harassment involves a pattern of conduct that is intended to annoy a person so much as to disrupt substantially her activities. No one questions the authority of universities to enact regulations that prohibit such conduct, whether the conduct be verbal or not. There are three principal differences between hate-speech rules and rules against harassment. First, hate-speech rules do not require a pattern of conduct: a single incident is sufficient to incur liability. Second, hate-speech rules describe the offending conduct in ways that refer to the moral and political viewpoint it expresses. The conduct is not simply annoying or disturbing; it is racist, sexist, or homophobic.

The third difference is tied closely to the second and is the most important one: rules against hate speech are not viewpoint-neutral. Such rules rest on the view that racism, sexism, and homophobia are morally wrong. The liberal principle of viewpoint-neutrality holds that those in authority should not be permitted to limit speech on the ground that it expresses a viewpoint that is wrong, evil, or otherwise deficient. Yet, hate-speech rules rest on precisely such a basis. Rules against harassment, on the other hand, are not viewpoint-based. Anyone in our society could accept the prohibition of harassment because it would not violate their normative political or moral beliefs to do so. The same cannot be said for hate-speech rules because they embody a view of race, gender, and homosexuality contrary to the normative viewpoints held by some people. . . .

. . . The fact is that any plausible justification of hate-speech regulation hinges on the premise that racism, sexism, and homophobia are wrong. Without that premise there would be no basis for arguing that the viewpoint-neutral proscription of verbal harassment is insufficient to protect the rights of minorities and women. The liberal who favors hate-speech regulations, no matter how narrowly drawn, must therefore be prepared to carve out an exception to the principle of viewpoint-neutrality.

THE HARMS OF HATE SPEECH

Many of the proponents of campus hate-speech regulation defend their position by arguing that hate speech causes serious harm to those who are the targets of such speech. Among the most basic of these harms are psychological ones. Even when it involves no direct threat of violence, hate speech can cause abiding feelings of fear, anxiety, and insecurity in those at whom it is targeted. As Mari Matsuda has argued, this is in part because many forms of such speech tacitly draw on a history of violence against certain groups.[5] The symbols and language of hate speech call up historical memories of violent persecution and may encourage fears of current violence. Moreover, hate speech can cause a variety of other harms, from feelings of isolation, to a loss of self-confidence, to physical problems associated with serious psychological disturbance.[6]

The question is whether or not the potential for inflicting these harms is sufficient ground for some sort of hate-speech regulation. As powerful as these appeals to the harms of hate speech are, there is a fundamental sticking point in accepting them as justification for regulation, from a liberal point of view. The basic problem is that the proposed justification sweeps too broadly for a liberal to countenance it. Forms of racist, sexist, or homophobic speech that the liberal is committed to protecting may cause precisely the kinds of harm that the proposed justification invokes.

The liberal will not accept the regulation of racist, sexist, or homophobic speech couched in a scientific, religious, philosophical, or political mode of discourse. The regulation of such speech would not merely carve out a minor exception to the principle of viewpoint-neutrality but would, rather, eviscerate it in a way unacceptable to any liberal. Yet, those forms of hate speech can surely cause in minorities the harms that are invoked to justify regulation: insecurity, anxiety, isolation, loss of self-confidence, and so on. Thus, the liberal must invoke something beyond these kinds of harm in order to justify any hate-speech regulation.

Liberals who favor regulation typically add to their argument the contention that the value to society of the hate speech they would proscribe is virtually nil, while scientific, religious, philosophical, and political forms of hate speech have at least some significant value. Thus, Mary Ellen Gale says that the forms she would prohibit "neither advance knowledge, seek truth, expose government abuses, initiate dialogue, encourage participation, further tolerance of divergent views, nor enhance the victim's individual dignity or self respect."[7] As an example of such worthless hate speech Gale cites an incident of white students writing a message on the mirror in the dorm room of blacks: "African monkeys, why don't you go back to the jungle."[8] But she would protect a great deal of racist or sexist speech, such as a meeting of neo-Nazi students at which swastikas are publicly displayed and speeches made that condemn the presence of Jews and blacks on campus.[9]

Although Gale ends up defending relatively narrow regulations, I believe liberals should be very hesitant to accept her argument for distinguishing regulable from nonregulable hate speech. One problem is that she omits from her list of the values that valuable speech serves one which liberals have long considered important, especially for speech that upsets and disturbs others. Such speech, it is argued, enables the speaker to "blow off steam" in a relatively nondestructive and nonviolent way. Calling particular blacks "African monkeys" might serve as a psychological substitute for harming them in a much more serious way, for example, by lynchings or beatings.

Gale could respond that slurring blacks might just as well serve as an encouragement and prelude to the more serious harms. But the same can be said of forms of hate speech that Gale would protect from regulation, for example, the speech at the neo-Nazi student meeting. Moreover, liberals should argue that it is the job of legal rules against assault, battery, conspiracy, rape, and so on to protect people from violence. It is, at best, highly speculative that hate speech on campus contributes to violence against minorities or women. And while the claim about blowing off steam is also a highly speculative one, the liberal tradition clearly puts a substantial burden of proof on those who would silence speech.

There is a more basic problem with any effort to draw the line between regulable and nonregulable hate speech by appealing to the value of speech. Such appeals invariably involve substantial departures from the principle of viewpoint-neutrality. There is no way to make differential judgments about the value of different types of hate speech without taking one or another moral and political viewpoint. . . .

I do not assume that the principle of viewpoint-neutrality is an absolute or ultimate one within the liberal framework. . . . Moreover, the viewpoint-neutrality principle itself rests on deeper liberal concerns which it is thought to serve. Ideally, a liberal argument for the regulation of hate speech would show that regulations can be developed that accommodate these deeper concerns and that simultaneously serve important liberal values. I believe that there is such a liberal argument. In order to show this, however, it is necessary to examine a kind of wrong committed by hate speakers that is quite different from the harmful psychological effects of their speech.

SUBORDINATION AND SPEECH ACTS

Some proponents of regulation claim that there is an especially close connection between hate speech and the subordination of minorities. Thus, Charles Lawrence contends, "all racist speech constructs the social reality that constrains the liberty of non-whites because of their race."[10] Along the same lines, Mari Matsuda claims, "racist speech is particularly harmful because it is a mechanism of subordination."[11]

The position of Lawrence and Matsuda can be clarified and elaborated using J. L. Austin's distinction between perlocutionary effects and illocutionary force.[12] The perlocutionary effects of an utterance consist of its causal effects on the hearer: infuriating her, persuading her, frightening her, and so on. The illocutionary force of an utterance consists of the kind of speech act one is performing in making the utterance: advising, warning, stating, claiming, arguing, and so on. Lawrence and Matsuda are not simply suggesting that the direct perlocutionary effects of racist speech constitute harm. Nor are they simply suggesting that hate speech can persuade listeners to accept beliefs that then motivate them to commit acts of harm against racial minorities. That again is a matter of the perlocutionary effects of hate speech. Rather, I believe that they are suggesting that hate speech can inflict a wrong in virtue of its illocutionary acts, the very speech acts performed in the utterances of such speech.

What exactly does this speech-act wrong amount to? My suggestion is that it is the wrong of treating a person as having inferior moral standing. In other words, hate speech involves the performance of a certain kind of illocutionary act, namely, the act of treating someone as a moral subordinate.

Treating persons as moral subordinates means treating them in a way that takes their interests to be intrinsically less important, and their lives inherently less valuable, than the interests and lives of those who belong to some reference group. There are many ways of treating people as moral subordinates that are natural as opposed to conventional: the status of these acts as acts of subordination depend solely on universal principles of morality and not on the conventions of a given society. Slavery and genocide, for example, treat people as having inferior moral standing simply in virtue of the affront of such practices to universal moral principles.

Other ways of treating people as moral subordinates have both natural and conventional elements. The practice of racial segregation is an example. It is subordinating because the conditions imposed on blacks by such treatment violate moral principles but also because the act of separation is a convention for putting the minority group in its (supposedly) proper, subordinate place.

I believe that the language of racist, sexist, and homophobic slurs and epithets provides wholly conventional ways of treating people as moral subordinates. Terms such as 'kike', 'faggot', 'spic', and 'nigger' are verbal instruments of subordination. They are used not only to express hatred or contempt for people but also to "put them in their place," that is, to treat them as having inferior moral standing.

It is commonly recognized that through language we can "put people down," to use the vernacular expression. There are many different modes of putting people down: putting them down as less intelligent or less clever or less articulate or less skillful. Putting people down in these ways is not identical to treating them as moral subordinates, and the ordinary put-down does not involve regarding someone as having inferior moral standing. The put-downs that are accomplished with the slurs and epithets of hate speech are different from the ordinary verbal put-down in that respect, even though both sorts of put-down are done through language.

I have contended that the primary verbal instruments for treating people as moral subordinates are the slurs and epithets of hate speech. In order to see this more clearly, consider the difference between derisively calling someone a "faggot" and saying to that person, with equal derision, "You are contemptible for being homosexual." Both utterances can treat the homosexual as a moral subordinate, but the former accomplishes it much more powerfully than the latter. This is, I believe, because the conventional rules of language make the epithet 'faggot' a term whose principal purpose is precisely to treat homosexuals as having inferior moral standing.

I do not believe that a clean and neat line can be drawn around those forms of hate speech that treat their targets as moral subordinates. Slurs and epithets are certainly used that way often, but not always, as is evidenced by the fact that sometimes victimized groups seize on the slurs that historically have subordinated them and seek to "transvalue" the terms. For example, homosexuals have done this with the term 'queer', seeking to turn it into a term of pride rather than one of subordination.

Hate speech in modes such as the scientific or philosophical typically would not involve illocutionary acts of moral subordination. This is because speech in those modes usually involves essentially different kinds of speech acts: describing, asserting, stating, arguing, and so forth. To assert or argue that blacks are genetically inferior to whites is not to perform a speech act that itself consists of treating blacks as inferior. Yet, language is often ambiguous and used for multiple purposes, and I would not rule out a priori that in certain contexts even scientific or philosophical hate speech is used in part to subordinate.

The absence of a neat and clean line around those forms of hate speech that subordinate through speech acts does not entail that it is futile to attempt to formulate regulations that target such hate speech. Rules and regulations rarely have an exact fit with what they aim to prevent: over- and underinclusiveness are pervasive in any system of rules that seeks to regulate conduct. The problem is to develop rules that have a reasonably good fit. Later I argue that there are hate-speech regulations that target subordinating hate speech reasonably well. But first I must argue that such speech commits a wrong that may be legitimately targeted by regulation.

SPEECH-ACT WRONG

I have argued that some forms of hate speech treat their targets as moral subordinates on account of race, gender, or sexual preference. Such treatment runs counter to the central liberal idea of persons as free and equal. To that extent, it constitutes a wrong, a speech-act wrong inflicted on those whom it addresses. However, it does not follow that it is a wrong that may be legitimately targeted by regulation. A liberal republic is not a republic of virtue in which the authorities prohibit every conceivable wrong. The liberal republic protects a substantial zone of liberty around the individual in which she is free from authoritative intrusion even to do some things that are wrong.

Yet, the wrongs of subordination based on such characteristics as race, gender, and sexual preference are not just any old wrongs. Historically, they are among the principal wrongs that have prevented—and continue to prevent—Western liberal democracies from living up to their ideals and principles. As such, these wrongs are especially appropriate targets of regulation in our liberal republic. Liberals recognize the special importance of combating such wrongs in their strong support for laws prohibiting discrimination in employment, housing, and public accommodations. And even if the regulation of speech-act subordination on campus is not regarded as mandatory for universities, it does seem that the choice of an institution to regulate that type of subordination on campus is at least justifiable within a liberal framework.

In opposition, it may be argued that subordination is a serious wrong that should be targeted but that the line should be drawn when it comes to subordination through speech. There, viewpoint-neutrality must govern. But I believe that the principle of viewpoint-neutrality must be understood as resting on deeper liberal concerns. Other things being equal, a departure from viewpoint-neutrality will be justified if it can accommodate these deeper concerns while at the same time serving the liberal principle of the equality of persons.

The concerns fall into three basic categories. First is the Millian idea that speech can promote individual development and contribute to the public political dialogue, even when it is wrong, misguided, or otherwise deficient. Second is the Madisonian reason that the authorities cannot be trusted with formulating and enforcing rules that silence certain views: they will be too tempted to abuse such rules in order to promote their own advantage or their own sectarian viewpoint. Third is the idea that any departures from viewpoint-neutrality might serve as precedents that could be seized upon by would-be censors with antiliberal agendas to further their broad efforts to silence speech and expression.

These concerns that underlie viewpoint-neutrality must be accommodated for hate-speech regulation to be justifiable from a liberal perspective. But that cannot be done in the abstract. It needs to be done in the context of a particular set of regulations. In the next section, I argue that there are regulations that target reasonably well those forms of hate speech that subordinate, and in the following section I argue that such regulations accommodate the concerns that underlie the liberal endorsement of the viewpoint-neutrality principle.

TARGETING SPEECH-ACT WRONG

If I am right in thinking that the slurs and epithets of hate speech are the principal instruments of the speech-act wrong of treating someone as a moral subordinate and that such a wrong is a legitimate target of regulation, then it will not be difficult to formulate rules that have a reasonably good fit with the wrong they legitimately seek to regulate. In general, what are needed are rules that prohibit speech that *(a)* employs slurs and epithets conventionally used to subordinate persons on account of their race, gender, religion, ethnicity, or sexual preference, *(b)* is addressed to particular persons, and *(c)* is expressed with the intention of degrading such persons on account of their race, gender, religion, ethnicity, or sexual preference. With some modification, this is essentially what one finds in the regulations drafted by Grey for Stanford.[13]

Restricting the prohibition to slurs and epithets addressed to specific persons will capture many speech-act wrongs of subordination. But it will not capture them all. Slurs and epithets are not necessary for such speech acts, as I conceded earlier. In addition, it may be possible to treat someone as a moral subordinate through a speech act, even though the utterance is not addressing that person. However, prohibiting more than slurs and epithets would run a high risk of serious overinclusiveness, capturing much speech that performs legitimate speech acts such as stating and arguing. And prohibiting all use of slurs and epithets, whatever the context, would mandate a degree of intrusiveness into the private lives of students that would be difficult for liberals to license.

The regulations should identify examples of the kinds of terms that count as epithets or slurs conventionally used to perform speech acts of subordination. This is required in order to give people sufficient fair warning. But because the terms of natural languages are not precise, univocal, and unchanging, it is not possible to give an exhaustive list, nor is it mandatory to try. Individuals who innocently use an epithet that conventionally subordinates can plead lack of the requisite intent.

The intent requirement is needed to accommodate cases in which an epithet or slur is not used with any intent to treat the addressee as a moral subordinate. These cases cover a wide range, including the efforts of some minorities to capture and transvalue terms historically used to subordinate them. There are several different ways in which the required intent could be described: the intent to stigmatize or to demean or to insult or to degrade and so on. I think that 'degrade' does the best job of capturing the idea of treating someone as a moral subordinate in language the average person will find familiar and understandable. 'Insult' does the poorest job and should be avoided. Insulting someone typically does not involve treating the person as a moral subordinate. Rather, it involves putting someone down in other ways: as less skillful, less intelligent, less clever, and the like.

The regulations at some universities extend beyond what I have defended and prohibit speech that demeans on the basis of physical appearance. I do not believe that such regulations can be justified within the liberal framework I have developed here. Speech can certainly be used to demean people based on physical appearance. 'Slob', 'dog', 'beast', 'pig': these are some examples of terms that are used in such verbal put-downs. But I do not believe that they are used to treat people as moral subordinates, and thus the terms do not inflict the kind of speech-act wrong that justifies the regulation of racist, sexist, or homophobic slurs and epithets.

It should not be surprising that terms which demean on the basis of appearance do not morally subordinate, since the belief that full human moral standing depends on good looks is one that few people, if any, hold.[14] The terms that put people down for their appearance are thus fundamentally different from racist, sexist, or homophobic slurs and epithets. The latter terms do reflect beliefs that are held by many about the lower moral standing of certain groups.

ACCOMMODATING LIBERAL CONCERNS

I have argued that regulations should target those forms of hate speech that inflict the speech-act wrong of subordination on their victims. This wrong is distinct from the psychological harm that hate speech causes. In targeting speech-act subordination, the aim of regulation is not to prohibit speech that has undesirable psychological effects on individuals but, rather, to prohibit speech that treats people as moral subordinates. To target speech that has undesirable psychological effects is invariably to target certain ideas, since it is through the communication of ideas that the psychological harm occurs. In contrast, targeting speech-act subordination does not target ideas. Any idea would be free from regulation as long as it was expressed through a speech act other than one which subordinates: stating, arguing, claiming, defending, and so on would all be free of regulation.

Because of these differences, regulations that target speech-act subordination can accommodate the liberal concerns underlying viewpoint-neutrality, while regulations that sweep more broadly cannot. Consider the important Millian idea that individual development requires that people be left free to say things that are wrong and to learn from their mistakes. Under the sort of regulation I endorse, people would be perfectly free to make racist, sexist, and homophobic assertions and arguments and to learn of the deficiencies of their views from the counterassertions and counterarguments of others. And the equally important Millian point that public dialogue gains even through the expression of false ideas is accommodated in a similar way. Whatever contribution a racist viewpoint can bring to public discussion can be made under regulations that only target speech-act subordination.

The liberal fear of trusting the authorities is somewhat more worrisome. Some liberals have argued that the authorities cannot be trusted with impartial enforcement of hate-speech regulations. Nadine Strossen, for example, claims that the hate-speech regulations at the University of Michigan have been applied in a biased manner, punishing the racist and homophobic speech of blacks but not of whites.[15] Still, it is not at all clear that the biased application of rules is any more of a problem with rules that are not viewpoint-neutral than with those that are. A neutral rule against harassment can also be enforced in a racially discriminatory manner. There is no reason to think a priori that narrowly drawn hate-speech rules would be any more liable to such abuse. Of course, if it did turn out that there was a pervasive problem with the biased enforcement of hate-speech rules, any sensible liberal would advocate rescinding them. But absent a good reason for thinking that this is likely to happen—not just that it could conceivably happen—the potential for abusive enforcement is no basis for rejecting the kind of regulation I have defended.

Still remaining is the problem of precedent: even narrowly drawn regulations targeting only speech-act subordination could be cited as precedent for more sweeping, antiliberal restrictions by those at other universities or in the community at large who are not committed to liberal values. In response to this concern, it should be argued that narrowly drawn rules will not serve well as precedents for would-be censors with antiliberal agendas. Those who wish to silence socialists, for example, on the ground that socialism is as discredited as racism will find scant precedential support from regulations that allow the expression of racist opinions as long as they are not couched in slurs and epithets directed at specific individuals.

There may be some precedent-setting risk in such narrow regulations. Those who wish to censor the arts, for example, might draw an analogy between the epithets that narrow hate-speech regulations proscribe and the "trash" they would proscribe: both forms of expression are indecent, ugly, and repulsive to the average American, or so the argument might go.

Yet, would-be art censors already have precedents at their disposal providing much closer analogies in antiobscenity laws. Hate-speech regulations are not likely to give would-be censors of the arts any additional ammunition. To this, a liberal opponent of any hate-speech regulation might reply that there is no reason to take the risk. But the response will be that there is a good reason, namely, to prevent the wrong of speech-act subordination that is inflicted by certain forms of hate speech.

CONCLUSIONS

There is a defensible liberal middle ground between those who oppose all campus hate-speech regulation and those who favor the sweeping regulation of such speech. But the best defense of this middle ground requires the recognition that speech acts of subordination are at the heart of the hate-speech issue. Some forms of hate speech do wrong to people by treating them as moral subordinates. This is the wrong that can and should be the target of campus hate-speech regulations.

NOTES

1 In a discussion of the strictly legal issues surrounding the regulation of campus hate speech, the distinction between private and public universities would be an important one. The philosophical considerations on which this article focuses, however, apply both to public and private institutions.

2 In this article I will focus on the restriction of racist (understood broadly to include anti-Semitic), sexist, and homophobic expression. In addition to such expression, regulations typically prohibit discriminatory utterances based on ethnicity, religion, and physical appearance. The argument I develop in favor of regulation applies noncontroversially to ethnicity and religion, as well as to race, gender, and sexual preference. But in a later section I argue against the prohibition of discriminatory remarks based on appearance. . . .

3 The full text of the Stanford regulations is in Thomas Grey, "Civil Rights v. Civil Liberties: The Case of Discriminatory Verbal Harassment," *Social Philosophy and Policy* 8 (1991): 106–7.

4 The University of Connecticut's original regulations are found in the pamphlet "Protect Campus Pluralism," published under the auspices of the Department of Student Affairs, the Dean of Students Office, and the Division of Student Affairs and Services. The regulations have since been rescinded in response to a legal challenge and replaced by ones similar to those in effect at Stanford. See *University of Connecticut Student Handbook* (Storrs: University of Connecticut, 1990–91), p. 62.

5 Mari Matsuda, "Legal Storytelling: Public Response to Racist Speech: Considering the Victim's Story," *Michigan Law Review* 87 (1989): 2329–34, 2352.

6 See Richard Delgado, "Words That Wound: A Tort Action for Racial Insults, Epithets and Name-Calling," *Harvard Civil Rights–Civil Liberties Law Review* 17 (1982): 137, 146.

7 Mary Ellen Gale, "Reimagining the First Amendment: Racist Speech and Equal Liberty," *St. John's Law Review* 65 (1991): 179–80.

8 Ibid., p. 176.

9 Ibid.

10 Charles Lawrence, "If He Hollers Let Him Go: Regulating Racist Speech on Campus," *Duke Law Journal* (1990), p. 444.

11 Matsuda, p. 2357.

12 J. L. Austin, *How to Do Things with Words* (New York: Oxford University Press, 1962), pp. 98 ff. . . .

13 Stanford describes the intent that is needed for a hate speaker to be liable as the intent to insult or stigmatize. My reservations about formulating the requisite intent in terms of 'insult' are given below.

14 Some people believe that being overweight is the result of a failure of self-control and thus a kind of moral failing. But that is quite different from thinking that the rights and interests of overweight people are morally less important than those of people who are not overweight. . . .

15 Nadine Strossen, "Regulating Racist Speech on Campus: A Modest Proposal?" *Duke Law Journal* (1990), pp. 557–58. . . .

QUESTIONS

1 How significant are the psychological harms produced by hate speech? Do these harms provide a sufficient basis for hate-speech regulation?

2 Does Altman provide an adequate theoretical basis for hate-speech regulation?

3 Do you agree with Altman that hate-speech regulation targeting the speech-act wrong of subordination can accommodate the liberal concerns underlying the principle of viewpoint-neutrality?

Opinion in *Corry v. Stanford University*

Judge Peter Stone

In this case, a group of Stanford University students challenged the constitutionality of the hate-speech regulations that were in effect at that university in the early 1990s. (An articulation of the Stanford regulations is provided in the last section of the introduction to this chapter.) In this excerpt from a California Superior Court opinion, Judge Stone finds that the Stanford regulations cannot survive First Amendment analysis and are unconstitutional for two reasons. First, in prohibiting speech more expansively than is allowable based on a properly understood fighting-words standard, the Stanford regulations are unconstitutionally overbroad. Second, even if the first problem could be avoided, the regulations embody a kind of content-based regulation that is incompatible with the First Amendment.

To summarize the parties' arguments, defendants in this case maintain that the type of speech that the speech code proscribes is not protected under the Constitution. Defendants argue that the speech code only proscribes "fighting words," which [is] constitutionally permissible under the case of *Chaplinsky v. New Hampshire* (1942).

Plaintiffs, on the other hand, maintain that this speech code is a violation of their First Amendment rights to free speech under the U.S. Constitution. Relying on the case of *R.A.V. v. City of St. Paul* (1992), plaintiffs argue that defendants' speech code seeks to prohibit speech on the basis of its content and therefore is constitutionally impermissible. . . .

I. THE CONSTITUTIONALITY OF DEFENDANTS' SPEECH CODE

A. Constitutionality under *Chaplinsky* and Later Line of Cases

Defendants argue that the speech code proscribes only gutter epithets that are fighting words, and that under *Chaplinsky v. New Hampshire* (1942) such words are not subject to constitutional protection. In *Chaplinsky,* the Supreme Court upheld a conviction under New Hampshire speech statute which prohibited offensive or annoying words on public streets. The Court, basing its decision on the state court's narrow interpretation of the statute, held that "fighting words," those words "which

California Superior Court, Santa Clara County (1995), no. 740309.

by their very utterance inflict injury or tend to incite an immediate breach of the peace," did not enjoy First Amendment protection.

The court reasoned that the statute had been appropriately applied to Mr. Chaplinsky, who had called a city official a "God-damned racketeer" and a "damned Fascist," since his words would have "likely provoked the average person to retaliate, and thereby cause a breach of the peace." In this case, defendants argue that their speech code comports with the standard set forth in *Chaplinsky,* since the speech code explicitly sets out the fighting words test in its regulations.

Defendants further argue that this speech code is "meant to insure that no idea as such is proscribed, and accordingly it does not prohibit the expression of any view, however racist, sexist, homophobic, or blasphemous in content." Rather, defendants state that the speech code "draws the line at fighting words. . . ." Such an argument is persuasive since vilifying a student with racial epithets, for example, would clearly have the effect of likely provoking the average person to retaliate and of inflicting injury by their very utterance. If phrases such as "God damned racketeer" and "damned Fascist" are "no essential part of any exposition of ideas . . . ," then certainly words which the defendants seek to proscribe (such as "damned nigger," etc.) should not enjoy constitutional protection.

Plaintiffs' gravamen, however, does not lie with any desire to vilify another student with "gutter epithets." Instead, it appears that plaintiffs' complaint rests on the argument that defendants' speech code, as drawn, goes beyond fighting words and, in effect, proscribes the expression of particular ideas and constitutionally protected speech. Plaintiffs partly base this claim on the rationale that the *Chaplinsky* holding has now been significantly narrowed to apply to only fighting words whose "utterance is likely to lead to immediate violence." Such a claim, if valid, would undermine the constitutionality of the speech code since, as plaintiffs argue, it prohibits "insults" and "offensive speech," not just "words that make people fight."

Plaintiffs' argument has merit. A review of authority reveals that there has been an apparent narrowing of the *Chaplinsky* doctrine. For example, in *Terminiello v. Chicago* (1949), the Supreme Court reversed petitioner's conviction under a breach of the peace ordinance which the trial court had interpreted to include speech which "stirs the public anger [or] invites dispute," as well as speech which creates a disturbance. Although the petitioner's criticism of political and racial groups had caused several disturbances among spectators, the court found that such words, "unless shown likely to produce a clear and present danger of serious substantive evil that rises far above public inconvenience, annoyance, or unrest," could not be proscribed.

In *Terminiello,* the Supreme Court reasoned that speech which "stirs the audience to anger" or "invites dispute" is protected under the First Amendment.

Additionally, in the case of *Gooding v. Wilson* (1972), the Supreme Court reversed petitioner's conviction under a Georgia abusive language statute after he had threatened and insulted two police officers. The Supreme Court found that even though the statute regulated only language which inflicts injury or affects the "sensibilities" of the hearer, it did not meet the requirements of the fighting words doctrine because it was not limited to words that "tend to cause an immediate breach of the peace." The Court found the statute was not limited to words that would have a direct tendency to cause acts of violence by the person to whom, individually, the remark was addressed.

Thereafter, in *Lewis v. City of New Orleans* (1974), the Supreme Court remanded a conviction under a Louisiana statute that banned the use of obscene language toward any police officer in the line of duty. Even though the state court held that the law prohibited only "fighting words," the Supreme Court found that, in light of *Gooding,* the statute was unconstitutionally overbroad since "obscene" and "opprobrious" words regulated under the statute "may well have conveyed anger and frustration without provoking a violent reaction from an officer."

More recently, in the case of *UWM Post v. Board of Regents of U. of Wisconsin* (1991), the Court stated that "since *Chaplinsky,* the Supreme Court has narrowed and clarified the scope of the fighting words doctrine . . . to include only words which tend to incite an immediate breach of the peace."[1] In addition to limiting the scope of the fighting words to words which tend to incite an immediate breach of the peace, it appears that a more stringent definition of "breach of the peace" has been set forth. Referring to the *Gooding* case, the Supreme Court stated that "in order to constitute fighting words, speech must not only breach decorum but also must tend to bring the addressee to fisticuffs." Consequently, in *UWM Post,* the Court found that since the elements of the *UWM* Rule did not require that "the regulated speech, by its very utterance, tend to incite violent reaction, the rule [went] beyond the . . . scope of the fighting words doctrine."

In sum, therefore, based upon the line of cases following *Chaplinsky,* it appears that the Court has, in effect, narrowed the *Chaplinsky* definition of fighting words to eliminate the "inflict injury" prong of the test. As such, under this narrowed version of *Chaplinsky,* defendants' speech code presumably proscribes more than "fighting words" as defined in subsequent case law. On its face, the speech code prohibits words which will not only cause people to react violently, but also cause them to feel insulted or stigmatized. As discussed above, however, defendants cannot proscribe speech that merely hurts the feelings of those who hear it.

The speech code also punishes words that "are commonly understood to convey" hatred and contempt on the basis of race, religion, etc. Clearly, this focuses upon the content of the words. All that is required under the speech code is that the words convey a message of hatred and contempt, not that they will likely cause an imminent breach of the peace. By proscribing certain words, without even considering their context, i.e., whether under a given situation there will be a breach of the peace, defendants' speech code fails to meet the "fighting words" standard as set forth under *Chaplinsky* and the later line of cases. As written, the speech code clearly punishes students for words which may not cause an imminent breach of the peace, but instead merely "conveys a message of hatred and contempt." To this extent, the speech code is overbroad since it is conceivable that a student could be punished for speech that did not (and would not) result in immediate violence. As a result, due to its overbreadth, defendants' speech code cannot pass constitutional scrutiny.

B.   Constitutionality under *R.A.V. v. City of St. Paul*

. . . Even assuming, arguendo, that all the expressions under the speech code are proscribable under the "fighting words" doctrine, under *R.A.V. v. City of St. Paul*

(1992), the speech code would still be unconstitutional if it proscribes speech on the basis of the content the speech addresses.

Plaintiffs claim this is exactly what defendants' speech code does. Plaintiffs argue that the speech code, similar to the ordinance in *R.A.V.,* is an impermissible content-based regulation, since it does not proscribe all fighting words, but only those that are based on sex, race, color, and the like. Plaintiffs state that such "hostility" or "favoritism" toward the underlying message . . . is unconstitutional. "The First Amendment forbids such selective incorporation." . . .

. . . In *R.A.V.,* the Supreme Court struck down a St. Paul "bias motivated hate crime" ordinance which made it a misdemeanor to place on private or public property a symbol which one knows, or has reasonable grounds to know, arouses anger in others on the basis of race, color, creed, religion or gender.

The majority accepted the Minnesota Supreme Court's construction of the ordinance as only applying to fighting words, an area of speech traditionally unprotected. Nevertheless, the Court found the ordinance unconstitutional since it did not proscribe all fighting words, but only those based on the categories listed in the ordinance.

The Court reasoned that such selectivity created the very real possibility that "the city was seeking to handicap the expression of particular ideas," and not fighting words in general. The Court did hold that the government could still prohibit fighting words so long as the proscription was unrelated to the distinct message contained in the expression. Thus, as the majority noted, libel could be proscribed, but not libel only critical of the government.

In the case at hand, a close examination of defendants' speech code reveals that plaintiffs' position is compelling. Similar to the ordinance in *R.A.V.,* defendants' speech code only proscribes a select class of fighting words: insults aimed at sex, race, color, handicap, sexual orientation, national or ethnic origin. Here, the same dangers the majority warned against exist. Defendants' speech code singles out a limited type of proscribable expression for a broad range of proscribable expression. Fighting words directed toward race and the like are punishable, yet those directed toward political affiliation, for example, are not. As plaintiffs note, "Insults, no matter how vicious or severe, are permissible unless they are addressed to one of the specified disfavored groups." Defendants, it would appear, have prohibited certain expression based on the underlying message. This is the type of content-based regulation the Court in *R.A.V.* found impermissible under the First Amendment. . . .

NOTE

1 It must be noted that the *Chaplinsky* court originally set out a two-part definition for fighting words: (1) words which by their very utterance inflict injury; and (2) words which by their very utterance tend to inflict an immediate breach of the peace.

QUESTIONS

1 If the Stanford hate-speech code had survived constitutional analysis, would you support the introduction of a similar code on your campus?
2 In view of the constitutional problems confronting campus hate-speech codes, what other strategies might colleges and universities employ to combat the use of hate speech on their campuses or otherwise minimize the damage it does?

SUGGESTED ADDITIONAL READINGS FOR CHAPTER 5

ALTMAN, ANDREW: "Speech Codes and Expressive Harm." In Hugh LaFollette, ed., *Ethics in Practice: An Anthology,* 2d ed. Oxford: Blackwell Publishing, 2002, pp. 376–385. Altman develops the concept of expressive harm in an effort to carry forward the case for campus speech codes.

BAIRD, ROBERT M., and STUART E. ROSENBAUM, eds.: *Pornography: Private Right or Public Menace?* rev. ed. Amherst, N.Y.: Prometheus, 1998. This anthology provides articles written from feminist, libertarian, and religious perspectives. It also includes a section on "the causal issue."

BERGER, FRED R., ed.: *Freedom of Expression.* Belmont, Calif.: Wadsworth, 1980. Several articles in this collection deal with the philosophical basis of the right of free expression. Other articles deal with more concrete freedom-of-expression issues.

GATES, HENRY LOUIS, JR., et al.: *Speaking of Race, Speaking of Sex: Hate Speech, Civil Rights, and Civil Liberties.* New York: New York University Press, 1994. The six authors who contribute articles to this collection are generally critical of proposals to regulate hate speech.

GRUEN, LORI: "Pornography and Censorship." In R. G. Frey and Christopher Heath Wellman, eds., *A Companion to Applied Ethics.* Oxford: Blackwell Publishing, 2003, pp. 154–166. Gruen examines two prominent arguments against pornography—that it causes harm and that it violates women's equality. She concludes that these arguments fail to justify the censorship of pornography.

HILL, JUDITH M.: "Pornography and Degradation." *Hypatia,* vol. 2, Summer 1987, pp. 39–54. Hill analyzes the concept of degradation and argues that the pornography industry degrades all women by perpetuating derogatory myths about them.

LEDERER, LAURA, ed.: *Take Back the Night: Women on Pornography.* New York: Morrow, 1980. This anthology provides an overall indictment of pornography from a feminist point of view.

MATSUDA, MARI J., CHARLES R. LAWRENCE III, RICHARD DELGADO, and KIMBERLE WILLIAMS CRENSHAW: *Words That Wound: Critical Race Theory, Assaultive Speech, and the First Amendment.* Boulder, Colo.: Westview Press, 1993. Each of the authors, all of whom are advocates for the regulation of racially abusive hate speech, contributes a long essay. The authors identify themselves as two African Americans, a Chicano, and an Asian American, and they say that the view they collectively defend is "grounded in our experiences as people of color."

RAUCH, JONATHAN: "In Defense of Prejudice: Why Incendiary Speech Must Be Protected." *Harper's Magazine,* vol. 290, May 1995, pp. 37–46. Rauch argues against societal efforts to suppress hate speech.

SHIELL, TIMOTHY C.: *Campus Hate Speech on Trial.* Lawrence: University Press of Kansas, 1998. Shiell surveys the arguments initially made for and against campus hate-speech codes, reviews the relevant legal cases, and explores the possibility of restricting campus hate speech on hostile environment harassment grounds.

SOBLE, ALAN: "Pornography: Defamation and the Endorsement of Degradation." *Social Theory and Practice,* vol. 11, Spring 1985, pp. 61–87. Soble critiques and rejects two arguments commonly made by feminists (e.g., Longino) against pornography. He finds unsound both (1) the argument that pornography defames women and (2) the argument that pornography endorses the degradation of women.

CHAPTER 6

Drug Control and Addiction

Millions of Americans smoke marijuana, imbibe various forms of alcohol, smoke tobacco cigarettes, and use other substances that can be widely classified as drugs. The personal, economic, and social costs of these activities are extremely high. Alcohol, for example, is involved in about half of all fatal car collisions and in a large number of cases of child and spousal abuse. Deaths and illnesses caused by smoking tobacco, as well as the related medical costs, are now a matter of public knowledge. However, both alcohol and tobacco are legal substances, whereas drugs such as marijuana, cocaine, crack, and heroin are illegal, and users of them can face many years in prison if caught. The costs of enforcing prohibitory laws and conducting the drug war are constantly escalating, thus adding to the exhorbitant costs associated with drug abuse.

In this chapter, we focus on the question of the morally legitimate role of government in respect to drug use. Is a government justified in adopting measures designed to prevent or discourage adults from using drugs?

SOME PRELIMINARY CLARIFICATIONS

Drugs, for the purposes of this chapter, can be broadly defined as psychoactive chemicals—chemicals that are transported to the brain via the bloodstream, influencing consciousness directly and significantly. By this definition, alcohol, nicotine, and caffeine—as well as currently illegal substances, such as heroin—are all drugs. Drugs can serve many purposes besides medical ones. They can be used for recreation—that is, to achieve or enhance pleasure. They also can be used instrumentally, as the caffeine in coffee is sometimes used to enhance work performance. Drugs might also be used in religious practices or to stimulate creativity.

Drug abuse is sometimes defined as any nonmedical use of a drug that carries a serious risk of significant harm to oneself or others. *Drug abuse,* in its ordinary usage, is a pejorative expression and is often applied to any use of drugs that is seen as objectionable. Thus, any use of illegal drugs, such as marijuana, is frequently considered drug abuse because it involves breaking the law, even though mild marijuana use may not be harmful. In contrast, alcohol consumption is typically considered a form of drug abuse only if it is excessive.

Drug abuse can take various forms. Misuse may be occasional. Think of someone who drinks too much at a party and causes an embarrassing scene. If a drug is used more and more frequently, however, the user may become drug dependent. The dependency may be physical, psychological, or both. Someone with a severe dependency who attempts to stop using the drug may experience physiological withdrawal symptoms. *Drug addiction,* the most serious form of drug abuse, is frequently understood as involving a high degree of physical and psychological dependency and severe withdrawal symptoms, as well as a strong tendency to relapse after withdrawal. However, the precise nature of drug addiction remains a controversial issue. In this chapter, Daniel Shapiro rejects what he labels the standard model of addiction and develops an alternative model.

Arguments against current drug laws often use the word *legalization* as a blanket term to cover very different suggestions for policy changes. In its strictest sense, *legalization* means having a free market in all drugs. This is the position espoused by Thomas Szasz in this chapter, although he would allow some restrictions on the sale of drugs to minors. Other legalization proposals are less sweeping. Some would allow the government, but only the government, to produce and sell drugs. Others would allow a private market in drugs but incorporate restrictions on advertising, dosage, and place of consumption.

Often those who argue for legalization, however, advocate less sweeping proposals. As Ethan Nadelmann, a proponent of legalization, points out in a related article in this chapter,

> Drugs are here to stay. The time has come to abandon the concept of a "drug-free society." We need to focus on learning to live with drugs in such a way that they do the least possible harm. . . .
>
> There is a wide range of choice in drug-policy options between the free-market approach favored by Milton Friedman and Thomas Szasz and the zero-tolerance approach of William Bennett. These options fall under the concept of harm reduction. That concept holds that drug policies need to focus on *reducing harm,* whether engendered by drugs or by the prohibition of drugs. And it holds that disease and death can be diminished even among people who can't, or won't, stop taking drugs.[1]

Harm-reduction policies may involve decriminalization and/or medicalization. Decriminalization policies, for example, might eliminate criminal sanctions for the possession of small amounts of drugs for personal use while still forbidding the manufacture, importation, and sale of currently illegal drugs. Medicalization policies might allow physicians to prescribe drugs that are currently illegal to addicts who are already drug dependent.

Harm-reduction policies may take other forms as well—such as developing needle exchange programs to prevent the spread of HIV infections, advocating responsible drug use rather than no drug use, and providing "low threshold" methadone maintenance without requiring counseling or regular attendance.

---

[1] Ethan Nadelmann, "The War on Drugs Is Lost," *National Review,* February 12, 1996, pp. 38–39.

THE LEGALIZATION ISSUE

The major arguments for prohibitory drug laws can be best understood by reference to one or more of the following three liberty-limiting principles—the harm
principle, the principle of legal paternalism, and the principle of legal moralism.
(These liberty-limiting principles are discussed in the introduction to Chapter 5.)
Thus, the main arguments for some form of legalization can also be understood by
reference to these principles.

Drug Laws, Legalization, and the Harm Principle

The harm principle allows interference with individual liberty in order to prevent
harm to others, but only in those cases in which coercive legislation causes less
harm than the harms that would occur in the absence of such legislation. The harm
principle is a relatively uncontroversial liberty-limiting principle. Thus, much of the
current debate regarding drug laws involves disputes about the harms caused by
drug abuse and addiction, the harms *prevented* by current drug laws, and the harms
caused by current policies. Many of those who argue for some form of legalization,
like Nadelmann in this chapter, maintain that the majority of the harms related to
drug abuse are caused by current drug policies. Among these harms, Nadelmann
identifies the following: the enormous financial costs of the drug war, the crimes
caused by addicts who need money to support their habits, the overloaded judicial
system, the costs of maintaining the ever increasing number of jail inmates who are
incarcerated on drug-related charges, police corruption, and the costs paid by innocent inner-city dwellers whose neighborhoods are dominated by those engaged in
illegal drug trading. In addition, he cites the costs incurred by illegal drug users
whose lives and health are at risk because there is no quality control over the drugs
they use, because shared needles can transmit HIV infections, and because the possibility of arrest under drug laws is a threat to their livelihoods.

Many of those who argue in support of current drug policies, such as Justice Jacob J.
Spiegel, who defends the constitutionality of Massachusetts's marijuana restrictions
in this chapter, focus on the prevention of harms perpetrated by drug abusers. Justice
Spiegel, for example, argues that antimarijuana laws are necessary to prevent harms
that some experts associate with marijuana use, such as psychotic breaks and automobile accidents caused by marijuana-smoking drivers. James Q. Wilson, also in this
chapter, focuses on users of crack cocaine. He maintains that crack users regularly
neglect their children, fail to provide for their spouses, and short-change their
employers as well as their coworkers because of their drug-induced lethargy. In
Wilson's view, the harms resulting from drug legalization would far outweigh the
harms caused by their prohibition. Without current drug laws, he maintains, drug
addiction would rise exponentially, as would the harms caused by addicts. Both
Nadelmann and Shapiro challenge that conclusion in this chapter.

Drug Laws, Legalization, and the Principle of Legal Paternalism

Those who want to retain current drug laws in order to prevent a possible rise in
addiction may be motivated by paternalistic reasons. If harm to others is the concern,

then the harm principle is the basis of the argument. If, however, the concern is with preventing potential addicts from engaging in risk-running, self-harming behavior, then the grounds are paternalistic, and the underlying idea is that interference with individual liberty is justified to prevent self-harm. When Justice Spiegel argues, for example, that current antimarijuana laws are justified insofar as they prevent psychotic breaks, he may simply be concerned with the harm to others that might be caused by a psychotic individual. In that case, his reasoning is related to the harm principle. If, however, he is concerned with preventing harm to the individual undergoing a psychotic break, then his reasoning is paternalistic. Thomas S. Szasz, in this chapter, rejects all paternalistically motivated laws, including drug laws, as unacceptable infringements on individual freedom.

The reasoning underlying antipaternalistic arguments for legalization can be summarized as follows. Adults have a right to self-determination (sometimes called a right of autonomy)—a right to live and act in accordance with their own aims and values, unless doing so violates others' rights. Some people value the pleasure they achieve by using recreational drugs and are willing to run the associated risks. Using these drugs does not, generally, dispose people to violate the rights of others—by committing crimes, for example. Heavily dependent and addicted drug users do sometimes fail to meet their obligations to others, but most drug users are neither heavily dependent nor addicted. Since adults do have a right to self-determination, they have a right to use drugs for recreation. However, individuals who commit crimes while under the influence of drugs should be held responsible for their actions and punished accordingly.

Philosophers who base their arguments for drug laws on paternalistic considerations often relate their reasoning to John Stuart Mill's argument against voluntary slavery. Despite his opposition to legal paternalism, Mill maintains that individuals cannot be allowed to sell themselves into voluntary slavery and argues as follows:

> . . . by selling himself for a slave, he abdicates his liberty; he foregoes any future use of it beyond that single act. He therefore defeats, in his own case, the very purpose which is the justification of allowing him to dispose of himself. . . . The principle of freedom cannot require that he should be free not to be free. It is not freedom, to be allowed to alienate his freedom. These reasons, the force of which is so conspicuous in this peculiar case, are evidently of far wider applications. . . .[2]

According to this line of reasoning, individuals must be protected against making and acting on a choice that will result in their forfeiting their freedom to make future choices. So, too, it can be argued, individuals must be protected from freely and voluntarily choosing to take drugs that will eventually result in addiction, and the concominant loss of autonomy (capacity for self-determination). In this chapter, Shapiro rejects this line of reasoning and challenges the underlying conception of addiction.

Somewhat implicit in the article by Robert E. Goodin included in this chapter, but explicitly developed by him in another article,[3] is his overall approach to the problem of the voluntariness of the choices made by addicted cigarette smokers.

---

[2]John Stuart Mill, *On Liberty* (New York: E. P. Dutton & Co., 1951), p. 213.
[3]Robert E. Goodin, "The Ethics of Smoking," *Ethics,* vol. 99, April 1989, pp. 579–587, 596–597.

In Goodin's view, addicted smokers lack free will with respect to the substance to which they are addicted and, hence, are not capable of giving their voluntary and informed consent to the continuation of the addictive behavior. Goodin's reasoning is based on his understanding of addiction (a conception challenged by Shapiro), as well as on a conception of autonomy and free will advanced by various philosophers who adopt a multitier approach to an agent's desires—an approach that distinguishes between first- and second-order desires and preferences.[4] First-order desires and preferences are those directed toward actions. Sally might have a desire to attend the Olympic Games in another country, for example. If she is able to act on this desire because nothing external prevents her from doing so— for example, tickets for the games are available, and there are no visa requirements that would prevent her traveling to the country where the games are taking place—she can accurately be described as performing free actions when she attends the games. Sally is doing what she wants to do. But a free action is not necessarily an autonomous one. Her action is autonomous only if her first-order desires are controlled by her second-order desires. For example, Sally might deplore the fact that her first-order desire to attend the Olympic Games is so strong that she has spent funds needed to pay overdue debts and has caused anguish to family members as a result, but she is still unable to resist the desire to attend. If Sally strongly desires not to be the kind of person who would give preference to attendance at athletic competitions over serious family considerations but cannot control her desire to attend the games, she is acting nonautonomously. Sally does not want to want what she wants to do. According to this view, whether an action is autonomous is a function of the relation between one's first- and second-order desires. Some philosophers identify second-order desires with a person's fundamental or settled aims and values—the aims and values with which the person identifies. Thus, Gerald Dworkin writes as follows:

> It is the attitude a person takes towards the influences motivating him which determines whether or not they are to be considered "his." Does he identify with them, assimilate them to himself, view himself as the kind of person who wishes to be motivated in these particular ways? If, on the contrary, a man resents his being motivated in certain ways, is alienated from those influences, resents acting in accordance with them, would prefer to be the kind of person who is motivated in different ways, then those influences, even though they may be causally effective, are not viewed as "his."[5]

According to this line of reasoning, addicted smokers are not acting autonomously when they act on their first-order desires to smoke if these desires are at odds with their settled aims and values. In that case, laws intended to prevent or discourage them from smoking need not factor out as violations of their right to self-determination. Goodin construes such laws as a very weak form of paternalism, since they do not

---

[4]See the following, for example: Gerald Dworkin, "Autonomy and Behavior Control," *Hastings Center Report,* vol. 6, February 1976, pp. 23–28 and Harry G. Frankfurt, "Freedom of the Will and the Concept of a Person," *Journal of Philosophy,* vol. 68, 1971, pp. 5–20.

[5]Dworkin, "Autonomy and Behavior Control," p. 25.

involve the imposition of others' values on the addict but, rather, help individuals to live in accordance with those values with which they themselves identify. Goodin's reasoning would support laws that prevent addicts from having access to drugs, whereas the earlier analogy between drug addiction and slavery would support laws prohibiting access to addictive drugs even to those who are not yet addicted. However, the cogency of both these arguments depends on an acceptance of the underlying conception of addiction.

Drug Laws, Legalization, and the Principle of Legal Moralism

A moral distinction is sometimes made between some psychoactive substances, such as cocaine and marijuana, on the one hand, and other psychoactive substances, such as tobacco and alcohol, on the other. The very use of the former for recreational purposes, or other nonmedicinal ends, is seen as immoral, whereas the same is not true of tobacco or alcohol use. Sometimes those who make this distinction believe that laws prohibiting the sale and use of drugs such as marijuana, crack, and heroin are justified because the very use of these drugs is immoral. The underlying reasoning here is based on the principle of legal moralism, which allows interferences with individual liberty in order to keep individuals from acting immorally. Aside from the problematic nature of the principle of legal moralism, such reasoning raises questions of consistency. Nadelmann denies, for example, that there are any morally significant differences between these two classes of psychoactive substances. It follows, for Nadelmann, that laws governing the sale and use of drugs that are currently illegal, on the one hand, and those governing the sale and use of tobacco and alcohol, on the other, are morally inconsistent. In contrast to Nadelmann, Wilson argues, specifically with respect to the difference between *nicotine* and cocaine, that there is a morally significant difference between these two substances. In his view, cocaine is debasing—that is, it destroys the user's essential humanity—whereas nicotine, even though it is harmful in other ways, does not. Although Wilson does not explicitly state that cocaine's power to effect such degradation makes its very use immoral, this seems to be the underlying idea. Thus, the reasoning Wilson advances to support the differential legal treatment of nicotine and cocaine seems to rely on the principle of legal moralism. But another thread in his reasoning seems to rely on the harm principle, since he expresses concern about the consequences for society if the degradation caused by cocaine becomes more commonplace. With respect to the differences between how the laws treat *alcohol* and cocaine, however, Wilson simply focuses on the harms that might result from the legalization of the latter. He grants that the harms resulting from alcohol are manifold. Nonetheless he does not want the laws to change. In his view, addiction to drugs such as cocaine would rise dramatically on legalization and would cause even greater harm than does current alcohol use.

Jane S. Zembaty

Opinion in *Commonwealth v. Joseph D. Leis*

Justice Jacob J. Spiegel

Six defendants, including Joseph D. Leis, were convicted for the unlawful possession of marijuana and for conspiracy to violate the Narcotic Drugs Law of Massachusetts. They were also indicted for illegal possession of marijuana with intent to sell it unlawfully. The defendants filed a motion with the Supreme Court of Massachusetts to dismiss the charges, on the grounds that the Commonwealth's statutory provisions regarding the possession, use, and sale of marijuana are unconstitutional. Ruling against the defendants, the Supreme Court of Massachusetts upheld the constitutionality of the Massachusetts laws.

In challenging the constitutionality of Massachusetts's marijuana laws, the defendants advanced two lines of argument in support of their claim that the laws are arbitrary, unreasonable, and irrational. First, they argued that the laws serve no legitimate state purpose because there is no evidence that the use of marijuana is a threat to the public health, safety, welfare, or morals. Second, they contended that the inclusion of marijuana among those substances defined as narcotic drugs is arbitrary for various reasons, including the exclusion from this classification of substances that are far more harmful. In rejecting their claims, Justice Spiegel maintains that, since the effects of marijuana and other illicit drugs are not known and subject to a great deal of dispute, it is legitimate for the state to treat these drugs differently than it treats alcohol and tobacco in its attempt to prevent some of the possible harms resulting from drug use.

1. The defendants allege that the Narcotic Drugs Law of the Commonwealth is "arbitrary and irrational and not suited to achieve any valid legislative end in that . . . it imposes harsh penalties upon mere possession of marihuana, or possession with intent to sell, or being present where marihuana is kept, without a showing that use of this substance poses a threat to the public health, safety, welfare or morals." They conclude that it therefore violates Part II, c. 1, § 1, art. 4, of the Constitution of the Commonwealth[1] and the Due Process Clause of the Fourteenth Amendment of the Constitution of the United States.[2] The defendants contend that the law, "as applied to marihuana, goes beyond the police power of the Commonwealth in that it is not and cannot be aimed at achieving any valid legislative end, namely protection of the health, safety, welfare and morals." They assert that it therefore violates, in addition to Part II, c. 1, § 1, art. 4, of the Constitution of the Commonwealth and the Due Process Clause of the Fourteenth Amendment of the Constitution of the United States, art. 7[3] and art. 1[4] of the Declaration of Rights of the Constitution of the Commonwealth.

The defendants first argue that the law is "irrational and unreasonable" because the Legislature did not thoroughly investigate the available scientific and medical evidence concerning marihuana when enacting and revising the law.

Supreme Judicial Court of Massachusetts (1969). 355 Mass. 189; 243 N.E.2d 898. Reprinted with permission of West Group.

We know of nothing that *compels* the Legislature to thoroughly investigate the available scientific and medical evidence when enacting a law. The test of whether an act of the Legislature is rational and reasonable is not whether the records of the Legislature contain a sufficient basis of fact to sustain that act. The Legislature is presumed to have acted rationally and reasonably. "Unless the act of the Legislature cannot be supported upon any rational basis of fact that reasonably can be conceived to sustain it, the court has no power to strike it down as violative of the Constitution."

The defendants then argue that the law is irrational and unreasonable and that it serves no legitimate State interest because there is no evidence that marihuana endangers the health, safety, welfare or morals of the community. They assert, inter alia, that there is no evidence to support the "allegations" that the smoking of marihuana causes psychotic reactions or "psychotic breaks" and that the use of marihuana leads to the use of more dangerous drugs. They summarily dispose of "[t]he charge that marihuana causes disorientation, psychomotor discoordination, excitement and confusion" as merely a statement that marihuana causes a state of intoxication if used to excess, and of the "charge" that marihuana causes automobile accidents as pure "speculation."

The testimony of the experts fully justifies the conclusion that marihuana is a "mind-altering" drug. There was evidence that the effect of such a drug is "a complex interaction between the physical or pharmacological properties of that drug . . . and most importantly the personality or character structure of the person consuming that drug, and . . . the social setting or context in which the drug is taken, including expectations, attitudes, et cetera." The smoking of marihuana may cause a state of euphoria and hallucinations or mental confusion and acute panic. It tends to exacerbate an underlying mental condition and to accentuate the smoker's basic personality makeup. When used by persons who have personality disorders or who are predisposed to "psychotic breaks," it may contribute to the onset of a "psychotic break."[5] The problem is magnified by the fact that persons having personality disorders and predispositions to "psychotic breaks" are more likely to experiment with marihuana and to become psychologically dependent upon it. Although the smoking of marihuana triggers only "acute [short-term] psychotic breaks" and does not apparently cause permanent psychotic injury or mental deterioration, an acute psychotic break, while it lasts, is as serious as a chronic mental disorder.

Essentially the experts do not point to any evidence of a direct, causal relationship between the smoking of marihuana and the use of more dangerous drugs. The studies that do exist discount the once prevalent belief that the smoking of marihuana inevitably leads to the use of more dangerous drugs. However, it is not necessary to show such a direct, causal relationship. There is considerable evidence that marihuana does lead some people to the use of more dangerous drugs. The progression from marihuana to heroin or LSD is a frequent sequence.

In an attempt to disprove the claim that the use of marihuana may cause automobile accidents, the defendants say that "no evidence [was] produced linking marihuana use with . . . [such] accidents." The evidence, however, showed there is no accurate, reliable scientific means of determining whether the operator of a motor vehicle has recently smoked marihuana. A person "high" on marihuana is unlikely to stagger or weave when he walks. While the smoking of marihuana may cause dilatation of the conjunctival blood vessels, there is recent evidence that it does not cause pupillary dilatation. The burning of marihuana does produce a recognizable odor, but that odor could be easily disguised. These properties of the drug undoubtedly account for the unavailability of statistical data. However, there is agreement among the experts that marihuana causes an alteration of sensory perception, a degree of psychomotor discoordination and an inability to concentrate. All of these effects of marihuana would interfere with the operation of a motor vehicle.

We do not think that the present unavailability of or inability to collect absolute, statistical and scientific proof that the smoking of marihuana (1) triggers "psychotic breaks," (2) leads to the use of more dangerous drugs and (3) causes automobile accidents prevents the Legislature from acting to prohibit its use. Surely the defendants would not contend, for example, that unless experiments absolutely establish that thalidomide causes birth defects the Legislature could not prevent the distribution of that drug. To prevent "psychotic breaks," to guard against the use of more dangerous drugs and to eliminate a cause of automobile accidents are valid State interests.

The defendants insist that the right to smoke marihuana is guaranteed by the Constitutions of the Commonwealth and of the United States and must be balanced against the interests of the State in prohibiting its use. No such right exists. It is not specifically preserved by either Constitution. The right to smoke marihuana is not "fundamental to the American scheme of justice . . . necessary to an Anglo-American regime of ordered liberty." It is not within a "zone of privacy" formed by "penumbras" of the First, Third, Fourth and Fifth Amendments and the Ninth Amendment of the Constitution of the United States. The defendants have no right, fundamental or otherwise, to become intoxicated by means of the smoking of marihuana.

We do not agree with the defendants that the Legislature is bound to adopt the "least restrictive alternative" that would fulfill its purpose of protecting the health, safety and welfare of the community. The least restrictive alternative doctrine does not apply to the instant case. It has been limited to regulations affecting interstate commerce. The Narcotic Drugs Law is not an economic regulation. It affects neither interstate commerce nor constitutionally sheltered activity.

In any event, there is ample justification for the Legislature to conclude that the total prohibition of marihuana is the "least restrictive alternative." The evidence indicates that the effects of smoking marihuana are unpredictable. No one can predict how a given person will react, or how such a person will react to the drug at any given time. There is no known means of determining whether a person has smoked marihuana, how much he has smoked or even how much causes intoxication. The difficulty of establishing the intoxication of the driver who is under the influence of marihuana renders G.L. c. 90, § 24(1) (a),[6] as amended through St.1963, c. 369, § 2, an insufficient safeguard with regard to the danger of automobile accidents.

2. The defendants maintain that the Narcotic Drugs Law "has singled out for prohibition and punishment possessors of and possessors of with intent to sell,

marihuana, while the laws permit the regulated use, sale and possession of substances far more harmful than marihuana . . . punish less harshly possession and sale of substances far more harmful than marihuana . . . and punish equally harshly substances far more harmful than marihuana." Therefore, they say that it violates art. 1 of the Declaration of Rights of the Constitution of the Commonwealth and the Equal Protection Clause of the Fourteenth Amendment of the Constitution of the United States.

The defendants argue that the inclusion of marihuana in the class of drugs defined by G.L. c. 94, § 197, to be "narcotic drugs" is arbitrary. This argument ignores "the rules by which this contention must be tested. . . . 1. The equal protection clause of the 14th Amendment does not take from the state the power to classify in the adoption of police laws, but admits of the exercise of a wide scope of discretion in that regard, and voids what is done only when it is without any reasonable basis, and therefore is purely arbitrary. 2. A classification having some reasonable basis does not offend against that clause merely because it is not made with mathematical nicety, or because in practice it results in some inequality. 3. When the classification in such a law is called in question, if any state of facts reasonably can be conceived that would sustain it, the existence of that state of facts at the time the law was enacted must be assumed. 4. One who assails the classification in such a law must carry the burden of showing that it does not rest upon any reasonable basis, but is essentially arbitrary."

"Narcotic drug" as defined in G.L. c. 94, § 197, as amended through St.1966, c. 71, §§ 1 and 2, includes "coca leaves, cocaine, alpha or beta eucaine . . . opium, morphine, heroin, codeine, apomorphine, isonipecaine, amidone, isoamidone, ketobemidone, peyote, LSD, psilocybin, D.M.T. . . . and cannabis (sometimes called marihuana . . .)." All of these substances are "mind-altering" drugs. The fact that some are more potent or more dangerous than others does not render the classification arbitrary. To some degree they are all capable of producing psychotic disorders, states of intoxication and psychological dependency, and consequently present some danger to the health and safety of the community. We do not think that the classification of marihuana with the others is arbitrary or irrational.

The defendants also contend that the noninclusion of other "mind-altering" drugs in G.L. c. 94, § 197, as amended through St.1966, c. 71, §§ 1 and 2, which are "acknowledged to be . . . more harmful" than marihuana, causes the law to "run afoul of the requirements of equal protection." They concede that the Legislature may select the kinds of behavior that it wishes to proscribe. They claim, however, that this "does not mean that a Legislature may actually proscribe behavior of one class of people (e. g., those who choose to obtain a mild state of intoxication with marihuana) and allow another class of people to freely indulge in behavior of an exactly similar nature (e. g., those who choose to obtain a mild state of intoxication with alcohol)."

We do not think that a statute which proscribes generally certain conduct can be said to be discriminatory simply because a certain group of persons tend to engage more often in that conduct than others. Such "de facto" discrimination does not violate the Equal Protection Clause. There are at least two distinctions between alcohol and the "mind-altering" intoxicants that are defined by the law to be narcotic drugs. First, alcohol is susceptible to a less restrictive alternative means of control. There are recognized, accurate means of determining its use and its abuse. Second, the effects of alcohol upon the user are known. We think that the Legislature is warranted in treating this known intoxicant differently from marihuana, LSD or heroin, the effects of which are largely still unknown and subject to extensive dispute. The Legislature is free to recognize degrees of harm and may confine its restrictions to instances where it determines the need for them is clearest. . . .

NOTES

1 "[F]ull power and authority are hereby given and granted to the said general court, from time to time, to make, ordain, and establish, all manner of wholesome and reasonable orders, laws, statutes, and ordinances, directions and instructions, either with penalties or without . . . as they shall judge to be for the good and welfare of this commonwealth, and for the government and ordering thereof, and of the subjects of the same."

2 "No state shall . . . deprive any person of life, liberty, or property, without due process of law."

3 "Government is instituted for the common good; for the protection, safety, prosperity and happiness of the people."

4 "All men are born free and equal, and have certain natural, essential, and unalienable rights; among which may be reckoned the right of enjoying and defending their lives and liberties; that of acquiring, possessing, and protecting property; in fine, that of seeking and obtaining their safety and happiness."

5 The defendants point to one witness at the hearing who denied that psychotic breaks triggered by marihuana exist and to another who considered the "so-called psychotic break" to be so rare as to be "non-existent." They overlook however other witnesses who testified that between one and ten percent of the population of the United States are susceptible to them. The credibility or reliability of these witnesses is not lessened by the fact they had not personally observed a substantial number of marihuana-induced "psychotic breaks." They were not testifying only with regard to their personal experiences and experiments but also with regard to information gathered from the vast amount of literature concerning marihuana. In addition, we note that the psychotic breaks triggered by marihuana are acute, and that it is unlikely that persons suffering from them would seek medical attention during the effects of the drug.

6 "Whoever . . . operates a motor vehicle while under the influence of . . . narcotic drugs, as defined in section one hundred and ninety-seven of chapter ninety-four . . . shall be punished by a fine of not less than thirty-five nor more than one thousand dollars, or by imprisonment for not less than two weeks nor more than two years, or both."

QUESTIONS

1 Is Justice Spiegel correct in concluding that the potential for harm stemming from marijuana use is sufficient to justify laws prohibiting its sale and use?

2 Is Justice Spiegel correct in concluding that the differences between marijuana and alcohol are sufficient to justify their different legal treatment?

3 Is the development of saliva-based drug tests that could be used on motorists to check for marijuana use, just as drunk-driving tests are currently used to determine alcohol use, relevant to Justice Spiegel's reasoning?

The Ethics of Addiction

Thomas S. Szasz

Szasz asserts a fundamental right to self-medication. He maintains that the harm principle is the only legitimate liberty-limiting principle and argues for free trade in all drugs, regardless of their possible dangerousness. In his view, currently illicit drugs should be treated as alcohol is treated. First, adults should be free to use and possess drugs, although their sale to minors should be prohibited. Second, those who break the law while under the influence of drugs should be held legally responsible for their actions.

PROPAGANDA TO JUSTIFY PROHIBITION

Like any social policy, our drug laws may be examined from two entirely different points of view: technical and moral. Our present inclination is either to ignore the moral perspective or to mistake the technical for the moral.

Since most of the propagandists against drug abuse seek to justify certain repressive policies because of the alleged dangerousness of various drugs, they often falsify the facts about the true pharmacological properties of the drugs they seek to prohibit. They do so for two reasons: first, because many substances in daily use are just as harmful as the substances they want to prohibit; second, because they realize that dangerousness alone is never a sufficiently persuasive argument to justify the prohibition of any drug, substance, or artifact. Accordingly, the more they ignore the moral dimensions of the problem, the more they must escalate their fraudulent claims about the dangers of drugs.

To be sure, some drugs are more dangerous than others. It is easier to kill one-self with heroin than with aspirin. But it is also easier to kill oneself by jumping off a high building than a low one. In the case of drugs, we regard their potentiality for self-injury as justification for their prohibition; in the case of buildings, we do not.

Furthermore, we systematically blur and confuse the two quite different ways in which narcotics may cause death: by a deliberate act of suicide or by accidental overdosage.

Every individual is capable of injuring or killing himself. This potentiality is a fundamental expression of human freedom. Self-destructive behavior may be regarded as sinful and penalized by means of informal sanctions. But it should not be regarded as a crime or (mental) disease, justifying or warranting the use of the police powers of the state for its control.

Therefore, it is absurd to deprive an adult of a drug (or of anything else) because he might use it to kill himself. To do so is to treat everyone the way institutional psychiatrists treat the so-called suicidal mental patient: they not only imprison such a person but take everything away from him—shoelaces, belts, razor blades, eating utensils, and so forth—until the "patient" lies naked on a mattress in a padded cell—lest he kill himself. The result is degrading tyrannization.

Death by accidental overdose is an altogether different matter. But can anyone doubt that this danger now looms so large precisely because the sale of narcotics and many other drugs is illegal? Those who buy illicit drugs cannot be sure what drug they are getting or how much of it. Free trade in drugs, with governmental action limited to safeguarding the purity of the product and the veracity of the labeling, would reduce the risk of accidental overdose with "dangerous drugs" to the same levels that prevail, and that we find acceptable, with respect to other chemical agents and physical artifacts that abound in our complex technological society.

This essay is not intended as an exposition on the pharmacological properties of narcotics and other mind-affecting drugs. However, I want to make it clear that in my view, *regardless* of their danger, all drugs should be "legalized" (a misleading term I employ reluctantly as a concession to common usage). Although I recognize that some drugs—notably heroin, the amphetamines, and LSD, among those now in vogue—may have undesirable or dangerous consequences, I favor free trade in drugs for the same reason the Founding Fathers favored free trade in ideas. In an open society, it is none of the government's business what idea a man puts into his mind; likewise, it should be none of the government's business what drug he puts into his body.

WITHDRAWAL PAINS FROM TRADITION

It is a fundamental characteristic of human beings that they get used to things: one becomes habituated, or "addicted," not only to narcotics, but to cigarettes, cocktails before dinner, orange juice for breakfast, comic strips, and so forth. It is similarly a fundamental characteristic of living organisms that they acquire increasing tolerance to various chemical agents and physical stimuli: the first cigarette may cause nothing but nausea and headache; a year later, smoking three packs a day may be pure joy. Both alcohol and opiates are "addictive" in the sense that the more regularly they are used, the more the user craves them and the greater his tolerance for them becomes. Yet none of this involves any mysterious process of "getting hooked." It is simply an aspect of the universal biological propensity for *learning,* which is especially well developed in man. The opiate habit, like the cigarette habit or food habit, can be broken—and without any medical assistance—provided the person wants to break it. Often he doesn't. And why, indeed, should he, if he has nothing better to do with his life? Or, as happens to be the case with morphine, if he can live an essentially normal life while under its influence?

Actually, opium is much less toxic than alcohol. Just as it is possible to be an "alcoholic" and work and be productive, so it is (or, rather, it used to be) possible to be an opium addict and work and be productive. According to a definitive study published by the American Medical Association in 1929, ". . . morphine addiction is not characterized by physical deterioration or impairment of physical fitness. . . . There is no evidence of change in the circulatory, hepatic, renal, or endocrine functions. When it is considered that these subjects had been addicted for at least five years, some of them for as long as twenty years, these negative observations are highly significant." In a 1928 study, Lawrence Kolb, an Assistant Surgeon General of the United States Public Health Service, found that of 119 persons addicted to opiates through medical practice, "90 had good industrial records and only 29 had poor ones. . . . Judged by the output of labor and their own statements, none of the normal persons had [his] efficiency reduced by opium. Twenty-two of them worked regularly while taking opium for twenty-five years or more; one of them, a woman aged 81 and still alert mentally, had taken 3 grains of morphine daily for 65 years. [The usual therapeutic dose is one-quarter grain, three to four grains being fatal for the nonaddict.] She gave birth to and raised six children, and managed her house-hold affairs with more than average efficiency. A widow, aged 66, had taken 17 grains of morphine daily for most of 37 years. She is alert mentally . . . does physical labor every day, and makes her own living."

I am not citing this evidence to recommend the opium habit. The point is that we must, in plain honesty, distinguish between pharmacological effects and personal inclinations. Some people take drugs to help them function and conform to social expectations; others take them for the very opposite reason, to ritualize their refusal to function and conform to social expectations. Much of the "drug abuse" we now witness—perhaps nearly all of it—is of the second type. But instead of acknowl-edging that "addicts" are unfit or unwilling to work and be "normal," we prefer to believe that they act as they do because certain drugs—especially heroin, LSD, and the amphetamines—make them "sick." If only we could get them "well," so runs this comforting view, they would become "productive" and "useful" citizens. To believe this is like believing that if an illiterate cigarette smoker would only stop smoking, he would become an Einstein. With a falsehood like this, one can go far. No wonder that politicians and psychiatrists love it. . . .

The fear that free trade in narcotics would result in vast masses of our popula-tion spending their days and nights smoking opium or mainlining heroin, rather than working and taking care of their responsibilities, is a bugaboo that does not deserve to be taken seriously. Habits of work and idleness are deep-seated cultural patterns. Free trade in abortions has not made an industrious people like the Japanese give up work for fornication. Nor would free trade in drugs convert such a people from hustlers to hippies. Indeed, I think the opposite might be the case: it is questionable whether, or for how long, a responsible people can tolerate being treated as totally irresponsible with respect to drugs and drug-taking. In other words, how long can we live with the inconsistency of being expected to be respon-sible for operating cars and computers, but not for operating our own bodies? . . .

THE RIGHT OF SELF-MEDICATION

Clearly, the argument that marijuana—or heroin, methadone, or morphine—is pro-hibited because it is addictive or dangerous cannot be supported by facts. For one thing, there are many drugs, from insulin to penicillin, that are neither addictive nor dangerous but are nevertheless also prohibited; they can be obtained only through a physician's prescription. For another, there are many things, from dynamite to guns, that are much more dangerous than narcotics (especially to others) but are not prohibited. As everyone knows, it is still possible in the United States to walk into a store and walk out with a shotgun. We enjoy this right not because we believe that guns are safe but because we believe even more strongly that civil liberties are precious. At the same time, it is not possible in the United States to walk into a store and walk out with a bottle of barbiturates, codeine, or other drugs.

I believe that just as we regard freedom of speech and religion as fundamental rights, so we should also regard freedom of self-medication as a fundamental right. Like most rights, the right of self-medication should apply only to adults; and it should not be an unqualified right. Since these are important qualifications, it is necessary to specify their precise range.

John Stuart Mill said (approximately) that a person's right to swing his arm ends where his neighbor's nose begins. And Oliver Wendell Holmes said that no one has a right to shout "Fire!" in a crowded theater. Similarly, the limiting condition with respect to self-medication should be the inflicting of actual (as against symbolic) harm on others.

Our present practices with respect to alcohol embody and reflect this individualistic ethic. We have the right to buy, possess, and consume alcoholic beverages. Regardless of how offensive drunkenness might be to a person, he cannot interfere with another person's "right" to become inebriated so long as that person drinks in the privacy of his own home or at some other appropriate location, and so long as he conducts himself in an otherwise law-abiding manner. In short, we have a right to be intoxicated—in private. Public intoxication is considered an offense to others and is therefore a violation of the criminal law. It makes sense that what is a "right" in one place may become, by virtue of its disruptive or disturbing effect on others, an offense somewhere else.

The right to self-medication should be hedged in by similar limits. Public intoxication, not only with alcohol but with any drug, should be an offense punishable by the criminal law. Furthermore, acts that may injure others—such as driving a car—should, when carried out in a drug-intoxicated state, be punished especially strictly and severely. The right to self-medication must thus entail unqualified responsibility for the effects of one's drug-intoxicated behavior on others. For unless we are willing to hold ourselves responsible for our own behavior, and hold others responsible for theirs, the liberty to use drugs (or to engage in other acts) degenerates into a license to hurt others.

Such, then, would be the situation of adults, if we regarded the freedom to take drugs as a fundamental right similar to the freedom to read and worship. What would be the situation of children? Since many people who are now said to be drug addicts or drug abusers are minors, it is especially important that we think clearly about this aspect of the problem.

I do not believe, and I do not advocate, that children should have a right to ingest, inject, or otherwise use any drug or substance they want. Children do not have the right to drive, drink, vote, marry, or make binding contracts. They acquire these rights at various ages, coming into their full possession at maturity, usually between the ages of eighteen and twenty-one. The right to self-medication should similarly be withheld until maturity.

In short, I suggest that "dangerous" drugs be treated, more or less, as alcohol is treated now. Neither the use of narcotics, nor their possession, should be prohibited, but only their sale to minors. Of course, this would result in the ready availability of all kinds of drugs among minors—though perhaps their availability would be no greater than it is now, but would only be more visible and hence more easily subject to proper controls. This arrangement would place responsibility for the use of all drugs by children where it belongs: on parents and their children. This is where the major responsibility rests for the use of alcohol. It is a tragic symptom of our refusal to take personal liberty and responsibility seriously that there appears to be no public desire to assume a similar stance toward other "dangerous" drugs.

Consider what would happen should a child bring a bottle of gin to school and get drunk there. Would the school authorities blame the local liquor stores as pushers? Or would they blame the parents and the child himself? There is liquor in practically every home in America and yet children rarely bring liquor to school. Whereas marijuana, Dexedrine, and heroin—substances children usually do not find at home and whose very possession is a criminal offense—frequently find their way into the school.

Our attitude toward sexual activity provides another model for our attitude toward drugs. Although we generally discourage children below a certain age from engaging in sexual activities with others, we do not prohibit such activities by law. What we do prohibit by law is the sexual seduction of children by adults. The "pharmacological seduction" of children by adults should be similarly punishable. In other words, adults who give or sell drugs to children should be regarded as offenders. Such a specific and limited prohibition—as against the kinds of general-ized prohibitions that we had under the Volstead Act or have now with respect to countless drugs—would be relatively easy to enforce. Moreover, it would probably be rarely violated, for there would be little psychological interest and no economic profit in doing so. . . .

LIFE, LIBERTY, AND THE PURSUIT OF HIGHS

Sooner or later we shall have to confront the basic moral dilemma underlying this problem: does a person have the right to take a drug, any drug—not because he needs it to cure an illness, but because he wants to take it?

The Declaration of Independence speaks of our inalienable right to "life, liberty, and the pursuit of happiness." How are we to interpret this? By asserting that we ought to be free to pursue happiness by playing golf or watching television, but not by drinking alcohol, or smoking marijuana, or ingesting pep pills?

The Constitution and the Bill of Rights are silent on the subject of drugs. This would seem to imply that the adult citizen has, or ought to have, the right to med-icate his own body as he sees fit. Were this not the case, why should there have been a need for a Constitutional Amendment to outlaw drinking? But if ingesting alcohol was, and is now again, a Constitutional right, is ingesting opium, or heroin, or barbiturates, or anything else, not also such a right? If it is, then the Harrison Narcotic Act is not only a bad law but is unconstitutional as well, because it prescribes in a legislative act what ought to be promulgated in a Constitutional Amendment.

The questions remain: as American citizens, should we have the right to take narcotics or other drugs? If we take drugs and conduct ourselves as responsible and law-abiding citizens, should we have a right to remain unmolested by the government? Lastly, if we take drugs and break the law, should we have a right to be treated as persons accused of crime, rather than as patients accused of mental illness?

These are fundamental questions that are conspicuous by their absence from all contemporary discussions of problems of drug addiction and drug abuse. The result is that instead of debating the use of drugs in moral and political terms, we define our task as the ostensibly narrow technical problem of protecting people from poisoning themselves with substances for whose use they cannot possibly assume responsibility. This, I think, best explains the frightening national consensus against personal responsibility for taking drugs and for one's conduct while under their influence. In 1965, for example, when President Johnson sought a bill imposing tight federal controls over pep pills and goof balls, the bill cleared the House by a unanimous vote, 402 to 0.

The failure of such measures to curb the "drug menace" has only served to inflame our legislators' enthusiasm for them. In October 1970 the Senate passed, again by a unanimous vote (54 to 0), "a major narcotics crackdown bill."

To me, unanimity on an issue as basic and complex as this means a complete evasion of the actual problem and an attempt to master it by attacking and overpowering a scapegoat—"dangerous drugs" and "drug abusers." There is an ominous resemblance between the unanimity with which all "reasonable" men—and especially politicians, physicians, and priests—formerly supported the protective measures of society against witches and Jews, and that with which they now support them against drug addicts and drug abusers.

After all is said and done, the issue comes down to whether we accept or reject the ethical principle John Stuart Mill so clearly enunciated: "The only purpose [he wrote in *On Liberty*] for which power can be rightfully exercised over any member of a civilized community, against his will, is to prevent harm to others. His own good, either physical or moral, is not a sufficient warrant. He cannot rightfully be compelled to do or forbear because it will make him happier, because in the opinions of others, to do so would be wise, or even right . . . In the part [of his conduct] which merely concerns himself, his independence is, of right, absolute. Over himself, over his own body and mind, the individual is sovereign."

By recognizing the problem of drug abuse for what it is—a moral and political question rather than a medical or therapeutic one—we can choose to maximize the sphere of action of the state at the expense of the individual, or of the individual at the expense of the state. In other words, we could commit ourselves to the view that the state, the representative of many, is more important than the individual; that it therefore has the right, indeed the duty, to regulate the life of the individual in the best interests of the group. Or we could commit ourselves to the view that individual dignity and liberty are the supreme values of life, and that the foremost duty of the state is to protect and promote these values.

In short, we must choose between the ethic of collectivism and individualism, and pay the price of either—or of both.

QUESTIONS

1 Do we have a moral right to decide for ourselves what drugs we will and will not use?
2 Does society have a right—contra Szasz—to protect individuals from engaging in seriously risky behavior that might have irrevocable consequences on their ability to make future decisions rationally?

Permissible Paternalism:
Saving Smokers from Themselves

Robert E. Goodin

Goodin argues in favor of some paternalistic public policies. Using smoking, which he considers an addiction, as an example, Goodin maintains that public paternalism is justified when its intent is to prevent decisions that involve high stakes, have far-reaching consequences, and are substantially irreversible. Arguing for what he identifies as a very weak form of paternalism, Goodin holds that public policies designed to deter individuals from acting on their preferences are justifiable only if they are grounded in their own deeper preferences. He sees smokers, for example, as paradigms of individuals who apparently "choose" to smoke while at the same time wishing to refrain from smoking.

Paternalism is desperately out of fashion. Nowadays notions of "children's rights" severely limit what even parents may do to their own offspring, in their children's interests but against their will. What public officials may properly do to adult citizens, in their interests but against their will, is presumably even more tightly circumscribed. So the project I have set for myself—carving out a substantial sphere of morally permissible paternalism—might seem simply preposterous in present political and philosophical circumstances.

Here I shall say no more about the paternalism of parents toward their own children. My focus will instead be upon ways in which certain public policies designed to promote people's interests might be morally justifiable even if those people were themselves opposed to such policies.

Neither shall I say much more about notions of rights. But in focusing upon people's interests rather than their rights, I shall arguably be sticking closely to the sorts of concerns that motivate rights theorists. Of course, what it is to have a right is itself philosophically disputed; and on at least one account (the so-called "interest theory") to have a right is nothing more than to have a legally protected interest. But on the rival account (the so-called "choice theory") the whole point of rights is

Originally published as "Permissible Paternalism: In Defense of the Nanny State," *The Responsive Community,* vol. 1 (Summer 1991), pp. 42–51. Reprinted here, as slightly revised by the author.

to have a legally protected choice. There, the point of having a right is that your choice in the matter will be respected, even if that choice actually runs contrary to your own best interests.

It is that understanding of rights which leads us to suppose that paternalism and rights are necessarily at odds, and there are strict limits in the extent to which we might reconcile the two positions. Still, there is some substantial scope for compromise between the two positions.

Those theorists who see rights as protecting people's choices rather than promoting their interests would be most at odds with paternalists who were proposing to impose upon people what is judged to be *objectively* good for them. That is to say, they would be most at odds if paternalists were proposing to impose upon people outcomes which are judged to be good for those people, whether or not there were any grounds for that conclusion in those people's own subjective judgments of their own good.

Rights theorists and paternalists would still be at odds, but less at odds, if paternalists refrained from talking about interests in so starkly objective a way. Then, just as rights command respect for people's choices, so too would paternalists be insisting that we respect choices that people themselves have or would have made. The two are not quite the same, to be sure, but they are much more nearly the same than the ordinary contrast between paternalists and rights theorists would seem to suggest.

That is precisely the sort of conciliatory gesture that I shall here be proposing. In paternalistically justifying some course of action on the grounds that it is in someone's interests, I shall always be searching for some warrant in that person's own value judgments for saying that it is in that person's interests.

"Some warrant" is a loose constraint, to be sure. Occasionally will we find genuine cases of what philosophers call "weakness of will": people being possessed of a powerful, conscious present desire to do something that they nonetheless just cannot bring themselves to do. Then public policy forcing them to realize their own desire, though arguably paternalistic, is transparently justifiable even in terms of people's own subjective values. More often, though, the subjective value to which we are appealing is one which is present only in an inchoate form, or will only arise later, or can be appreciated only in retrospect.

Paternalism is clearly paternalistic in imposing those more weakly-held subjective values upon people in preference to their more strongly held ones. But, equally clearly, it is less offensively paternalistic thanks to this crucial fact: at least it deals strictly in terms of values that are or will be subjectively present, at some point or another and to some extent or another, in the person concerned.

I. THE SCOPE OF PATERNALISM

When we are talking about public policies (and maybe even when we are talking of private, familial relations), paternalism surely can only be justified for the "big decisions" in people's lives. No one, except possibly parents and perhaps not even they, would propose to stop you from buying candy bars on a whim, under the influence of seductive advertising and at some marginal cost to your dental health.

So far as public policy is concerned, certainly, to be a fitting subject for public paternalism a decision must first of all involve high stakes. Life-and-death issues most conspicuously qualify. But so do those that substantially shape your subsequent life prospects. Decisions to drop out of school or to begin taking drugs involve high stakes of roughly that sort. If the decision is also substantially irreversible—returning to school is unlikely, the drug is addictive—then that further bolsters the case for paternalistic intervention.

The point in both cases is that people would not have a chance to benefit by learning from their mistakes. If the stakes are so high that losing the gamble once will kill you, then there is no opportunity for subsequent learning. Similarly, if the decision is irreversible, you might know better next time but be unable to benefit from your new wisdom.

II. EVALUATING PREFERENCES

The case for paternalism, as I have cast it, is that the public officials might better respect your own preferences than you would have done through your own actions. That is to say that public officials are engaged in evaluating your (surface) preferences, judging them according to some standard of your own (deeper) preferences. Public officials should refrain from paternalistic interference, and allow you to act without state interference, only if they are convinced that you are acting on:

- *relevant* preferences;
- *settled* preferences;
- *preferred* preferences; and, perhaps,
- *your own* preferences.

In what follows, I shall consider each of those requirements in turn. My running example will be the problem of smoking and policies to control it. Nothing turns on the peculiarities of that example, though. There are many others like it in relevant respects.

It often helps, in arguments like this, to apply generalities to particular cases. So, in what follows, I shall further focus in on the case of one particular smoker, Rose Cipollone. Her situation is nowise unique—in all the respects that matter here, she might be considered the prototypical smoker. All that makes her case special is that she (or more precisely her heir) was the first to win a court case against the tobacco companies whose products killed her.

In summarizing the evidence presented at that trial, the judge described the facts of the case as follows.

> Rose . . . Cipollone . . . began to smoke at age 16 . . . while she was still in high school. She testified that she began to smoke because she saw people smoking in the movies, in advertisements, and looked upon it as something "cool, glamorous and grown-up" to do. She began smoking Chesterfields . . . primarily because of advertising of "pretty girls and movie stars," and because Chesterfields were described . . . as "mild." . . .
>
> Mrs. Cipollone attempted to quit smoking while pregnant with her first child . . . , but even then she would sneak cigarettes. While she was in labor she smoked an entire pack of cigarettes, provided to her at her request by her doctor, and after the birth. . . .

she resumed smoking. She smoked a minimum of a pack a day and as much as two packs a day.

In 1955, she switched . . . to L&M cigarettes . . . because . . . she believed that the filter would trap whatever was "bad" for her in cigarette smoking. She relied upon advertisements which supported that contention. She . . . switched to Virginia Slims . . . because the cigarettes were glamorous and long, and were associated with beautiful women—and the liberated woman. . . .

Because she developed a smoker's cough and heard reports that smoking caused cancer, she tried to cut down her smoking. These attempts were unsuccessful. . . .

Mrs. Cipollone switched to lower tar and nicotine cigarettes based upon advertising from which she concluded that those cigarettes were safe or safer . . . [and] upon the recommendation of her family physician. In 1981 her cancer was diagnosed, and even though her doctors advised her to stop she was unable to do so. She even told her doctors and her husband that she had quit when she had not, and she continued to smoke until June of 1982 when her lung was removed. Even thereafter she smoked occasionally—in hiding. She stopped smoking in 1983 when her cancer had metastasized and she was diagnosed as fatally ill.

This sad history contains many of the features that I shall be arguing make paternalism most permissible.

Relevant Preferences

The case against paternalism consists in the simple proposition that, morally, we ought to respect people's own choices in matters that affect themselves and by-and-large only themselves. But there are many questions we first might legitimately ask about those preferences, without in any way questioning this fundamental principle of respecting people's autonomy.

One is simply whether the preferences in play are genuinely *relevant* to the decision at hand. Often they are not. Laymen often make purely factual mistakes in their means-ends reasoning. They think—or indeed, as in the case of Rose Cipollone, are led by false advertising to suppose—that an activity is safe when it is not. They think that an activity like smoking is glamorous, when the true facts of the matter are that smoking may well cause circulatory problems requiring the distinctly unglamorous amputation of an arm or leg.

When people make purely factual mistakes like that, we might legitimately override their surface preferences (the preference to smoke) in the name of their own deeper preferences (to stay alive and bodily intact). Public policies designed to prevent youngsters from taking up smoking when they want to, or to make it harder (more expensive or inconvenient) for existing smokers to continue smoking when they want to, may be paternalistic in the sense of running contrary to people's own manifest choices in the matter. But this overriding of their choices is grounded in their own deeper preferences, so such paternalism would be minimally offensive from a moral point of view.

Settled Preferences

We might ask, further, whether the preferences being manifested are "settled" preferences or whether they are merely transitory phases people are going through.

It may be morally permissible to let people commit euthanasia voluntarily, if we are sure they really want to die. But if we think that they may subsequently change their minds, then we have good grounds for supposing that we should stop them.

The same may well be true with smoking policy. While Rose Cipollone herself thought smoking was both glamorous and safe, youngsters beginning to smoke today typically know better. But many of them still say that they would prefer a shorter but more glamorous life, and that they are therefore more than happy to accept the risks that smoking entails. Say what they may at age sixteen, though, we cannot help supposing that they will think differently when pigeons eventually come home to roost. The risk-courting preferences of youth are a characteristic product of a peculiarly dare-devil phase that virtually all of them will, like their predecessors, certainly grow out of.

Insofar as people's preferences are not settled—insofar as they choose one option now, yet at some later time may wish that they had chosen another—we have another ground for permissible paternalism. Policy-makers dedicated to respecting people's own choices have, in effect, two of the person's own choices to choose between. How such conflicts should be settled is hard to say. We might weigh the strength or duration of the preferences, how well they fit with the person's other preferences, and so on.

Whatever else we do, though, we clearly ought not privilege one preference over another just because it got there first. Morally, it is permissible for policy-makers to ignore one of a person's present preferences (to smoke, for example) in deference to another that is virtually certain later to emerge (as was Rose Cipollone's wish to live, once she had cancer).

Preferred Preferences

A third case for permissible paternalism turns on the observation that people have not only multiple and conflicting preferences but also preferences for preferences. Rose Cipollone wanted to smoke. But, judging from her frequent (albeit failed) attempts to quit, she also wanted *not to want* to smoke.

In this respect, it might be said, Rose Cipollone's history is representative of smokers more generally. The US Surgeon General reports that some 90 percent of regular smokers have tried and failed to quit. That recidivism rate has led the World Health Organization to rank nicotine as an addictive substance on a par with heroin itself.

That classification is richly confirmed by the stories that smokers themselves tell about their failed attempts to quit. Rose Cipollone tried to quit while pregnant, only to end up smoking an entire pack in the delivery room. She tried to quit once her cancer was diagnosed, and once again after her lung was taken out, even then only to end up sneaking an occasional smoke.

In cases like this—where people want to stop some activity, try to stop it but find that they cannot stop—public policy that helps them do so can hardly be said to be paternalistic in any morally offensive respect. It overrides people's preferences, to be sure. But the preferences which it overrides are ones which people themselves wish they did not have.

The preferences which it respects—the preferences to stop smoking (like preferences of reformed alcoholics to stay off drink, or of the obese to lose weight)—are, in contrast, preferences that the people concerned themselves prefer. They would themselves rank those preferences above their own occasional inclinations to backslide. In helping them to implement their own preferred preferences, we are only respecting people's own priorities.

Finally, before automatically respecting people's choices, we ought to make sure that they are really their *own* choices. We respect people's choices because in that way we manifest respect for them as persons. But if the choices in question were literally someone else's—the results of a post-hypnotic suggestion, for example—then clearly there that logic would provide no reason for our respecting those preferences.

Some people say that the effects of advertising are rather like that. No doubt there is a certain informational content to advertising. But that is not all there is in it. When Rose Cipollone read the tar and nicotine content in advertisements, what she was getting was information. What she was getting when looking at the accompanying pictures of movie stars and glamorous, liberated women was something else altogether.

Using the power of subliminal suggestion, advertising implants preferences in people in a way that largely or wholly by-passes their judgment. Insofar as it does so, the resulting preferences are not authentically that person's own. And those implanted preferences are not entitled to the respect that is rightly reserved for a person's authentic preferences, in consequence.

Such thoughts might lead some to say that we should therefore ignore altogether advertising-induced preferences in framing our public policy. I demur. There is just too much force in the rejoinder that, "Wherever those preferences came from in the first instance, they are mine now." If we want our policies to respect people by (among other things) respecting their preferences, then we will have to respect all of those preferences with which people now associate themselves.

Even admitting the force of that rejoinder, though, there is much that still might be done to curb the preference-shaping activities of, for example, the tobacco industry. Even those who say "they're my preferences now" would presumably have preferred, ahead of time, to make up their own minds in the matter. So there we have a case, couched in terms of people's own (past) preferences, for severely restricting the advertising and promotion of products—especially ones which people will later regret having grown to like, but which they will later be unable to resist.

III. CONCLUSIONS

What, in practical policy terms, follows from all that? Well, in the case of smoking, which has served as my running example, we might ban the sale of tobacco altogether or turn it into a drug available only on prescription to registered users. Or, less dramatically, we might make cigarettes difficult and expensive to obtain—especially for youngsters, whose purchases are particularly price-sensitive. We might ban all promotional advertising of tobacco products, designed as it is to attract new users.

We might prohibit smoking in all offices, restaurants, and other public places, thus making it harder for smokers to find a place to partake and providing a further inducement for them to quit.

All of those policies would be good for smokers themselves. They would enjoy a longer life expectancy and a higher quality of life if they stopped smoking. But that is to talk the language of interests rather than of rights and choices. In those latter terms, all those policies clearly go against smokers' manifest preferences, in one sense or another. Smokers want to keep smoking. They do not want to pay more or drive further to get their cigarettes. They want to be able to take comfort in advertisements constantly telling them how glamorous their smoking is.

In other more important senses, though, such policies can be justified even in terms of the preferences of smokers themselves. They do not want to die, as a quarter of them eventually will (and ten to fifteen years before their time) of smoking-related diseases; it is only false beliefs or wishful thinking that make smokers think that continued smoking is consistent with that desire not to avoid a premature death. At the moment they may think that the benefits of smoking outweigh the costs, but they will almost certainly revise that view once those costs are eventually sheeted home. The vast majority of smokers would like to stop smoking but, being addicted, find it very hard now to do so.

Like Rose Cipollone, certainly in her dying days and intermittently even from her early adulthood, most smokers themselves would say that they would have been better off never starting. Many even agree that they would welcome anything (like a workplace ban on smoking) that might now make them stop. Given the internally conflicting preferences here in play, smokers also harbor at one and the same time preferences pointing in the opposite direction; that is what might make helping them to stop seem unacceptably paternalistic. But in terms of other of their preferences—and ones that deserve clear precedence, at that— doing so is perfectly well warranted.

Smoking is unusual, perhaps, in presenting a case for permissible paternalism on all four of the fronts here canvassed. Most activities might qualify under only one or two of the headings. However, that may well be enough. My point here is not that paternalism is always permissible but merely that it may always be.

In the discourse of liberal democracies, the charge of paternalism is typically taken to be a knock-down objection to any policy. If I am right, that knee-jerk response is wrong. When confronted with the charge of paternalism, it should always be open to us to say, "Sure, this proposal is paternalistic—but is the paternalism in view permissible or impermissible, good or bad?" More often than not, I think we will find, paternalism might prove perfectly defensible along the lines sketched here.

QUESTIONS

1 Are the long-term deleterious effects of cigarette smoking sufficient to justify laws prohibiting the sale and use of cigarettes? If yes, are the laws justified on the basis of paternalistic reasoning or on the basis of some other liberty-limiting principle?

2 Can a case be made for the claim that those who smoke marijuana are not acting on preferences that are relevant, settled, preferred, and their own?

The Case for Legalization

Ethan A. Nadelmann

Nadelmann, a proponent of the harm-reduction approach to legalization, maintains that current drug laws are responsible for much of what Americans identify as the drug problem. He first discusses some of the costs of prohibition, such as expensive drug-enforcement measures, drug-related crimes, and the harms done to millions of illicit drug users who run the risk of imprisonment and job loss. Many of these users also suffer physical harms from the drugs they use—harms that could be prevented if the production and sale of drugs were subject to government regulation. Second, Nadelmann criticizes our inconsistent moral attitudes regarding alcohol and tobacco, on the one hand, and drugs such as marijuana and cocaine, on the other. Nadelmann advances arguments against those whose support of the current drug laws is implicitly based on the principle of legal moralism. Believing wrongly that there is a morally significant difference between alcohol and tobacco use, on the one hand, and the use of substances such as cocaine and heroin, on the other, they support public policies that are morally inconsistent. He grants that the strongest moral justification for treating the currently illicit drugs differently is a paternalistic one—to prevent those who lack sufficient self-restraint from harming themselves if drugs were easily available. Noting, however, that any such harms prevented by current laws are far outweighed by the harms resulting from the laws themselves, he concludes that we must rethink our moral position when laws intended to serve a moral end inflict tremendous damage on innocent parties. Finally, Nadelmann discusses the benefits of legalization. While acknowledging that legalization is a risky policy, he notes the failure of current policies and advocates exploring other options.

What can be done about the "drug problem"? Despite frequent proclamations of war and dramatic increases in government funding and resources in recent years, there are many indications that the problem is not going away and may even be growing worse. . . .

THE COSTS OF PROHIBITION

The fact that drug-prohibition laws and policies cannot eradicate or even significantly reduce drug abuse is not necessarily a reason to repeal them. They do, after all, succeed in deterring many people from trying drugs, and they clearly reduce the availability and significantly increase the price of illegal drugs. These accomplishments alone might warrant retaining the drug laws, were it not for the fact that these same laws are also responsible for much of what Americans identify as the "drug problem." Here the analogies to alcohol and tobacco are worth noting. There is little question that we could reduce the health costs associated with use and abuse of alcohol and tobacco if we were to criminalize their production, sale, and possession.

Reprinted with permission of the author from *The Public Interest,* no. 92 (Summer 1988), pp. 3, 11–14, 20–25, 30–31. © 1988 by National Affairs, Inc.

But no one believes that we could eliminate their use and abuse, that we could create an "alcohol-free" or "tobacco-free" country. Nor do most Americans believe that criminalizing the alcohol and tobacco markets would be a good idea. Their opposition stems largely from two beliefs: that adult Americans have the right to choose what substances they will consume and what risks they will take; and that the costs of trying to coerce so many Americans to abstain from those substances would be enormous. It was the strength of these two beliefs that ultimately led to the repeal of Prohibition, and it is partly due to memories of that experience that criminalizing either alcohol or tobacco has little support today.

Consider the potential consequences of criminalizing the production, sale, and possession of all tobacco products. On the positive side, the number of people smoking tobacco would almost certainly decline, as would the health costs associated with tobacco consumption. Although the "forbidden fruit" syndrome would attract some people to cigarette smoking who would not otherwise have smoked, many more would likely be deterred by the criminal sanction, the moral standing of the law, the higher cost and unreliable quality of the illicit tobacco, and the difficulties involved in acquiring it. Nonsmokers would rarely if ever be bothered by the irritating habits of their fellow citizens. The anti-tobacco laws would discourage some people from ever starting to smoke, and would induce others to quit.

On the negative side, however, millions of Americans, including both tobacco addicts and recreational users, would no doubt defy the law, generating a massive underground market and billions in profits for organized criminals. Although some tobacco farmers would find other work, thousands more would become outlaws and continue to produce their crops covertly. Throughout Latin America, farmers and gangsters would rejoice at the opportunity to earn untold sums of gringo greenbacks, even as U.S. diplomats pressured foreign governments to cooperate with U.S. laws. Within the United States, government helicopters would spray herbicides on illicit tobacco fields; people would be rewarded by the government for informing on their tobacco-growing, -selling, and -smoking neighbors; urine tests would be employed to identify violators of the anti-tobacco laws; and a Tobacco Enforcement Administration (the T.E.A.) would employ undercover agents, informants, and wire-taps to uncover tobacco-law violators. Municipal, state, and federal judicial systems would be clogged with tobacco traffickers and "abusers." "Tobacco-related murders" would increase dramatically as criminal organizations competed with one another for turf and markets. Smoking would become an act of youthful rebellion, and no doubt some users would begin to experiment with more concentrated, potent, and dangerous forms of tobacco. Tobacco-related corruption would infect all levels of government, and respect for the law would decline noticeably. Government expenditures on tobacco-law enforcement would climb rapidly into the billions of dollars, even as budget balancers longingly recalled the almost ten billion dollars per year in tobacco taxes earned by the federal and state governments prior to prohibition. Finally, the State of North Carolina might even secede again from the Union.

This seemingly far-fetched tobacco-prohibition scenario is little more than an extrapolation based on the current situation with respect to marijuana, cocaine, and heroin. In many ways, our predicament resembles what actually happened during Prohibition. Prior to Prohibition, most Americans hoped that alcohol could be effectively banned by passing laws against its production and supply. During the early years of Prohibition, when drinking declined but millions of Americans nonetheless continued to drink, Prohibition's supporters placed their faith in tougher laws and more police and jails. After a few more years, however, increasing numbers of Americans began to realize that laws and policemen were unable to eliminate the smugglers, bootleggers, and illicit producers, as long as tens of millions of Americans continued to want to buy alcohol. At the same time, they saw that more laws and policemen seemed to generate more violence and corruption, more crowded courts and jails, wider disrespect for government and the law, and more power and profits for the gangsters. Repeal of Prohibition came to be seen not as a capitulation to Al Capone and his ilk, but as a means of both putting the bootleggers out of business and eliminating most of the costs associated with the prohibition laws.

Today, Americans are faced with a dilemma similar to that confronted by our forebears sixty years ago. Demand for illicit drugs shows some signs of abating, but no signs of declining significantly. Moreover, there are substantial reasons to doubt that tougher laws and policing have played an important role in reducing consumption. Supply, meanwhile, has not abated at all. Availability of illicit drugs, except for marijuana in some locales, remains high. Prices are dropping, even as potency increases. And the number of drug producers, smugglers, and dealers remains sizable, even as jails and prisons fill to overflowing. As was the case during Prohibition, the principal beneficiaries of current drug policies are the new and old organized-crime gangs. The principal victims, on the other hand, are not the drug dealers, but the tens of millions of Americans who are worse off in one way or another as a consequence of the existence and failure of the drug-prohibition laws.

All public policies create beneficiaries and victims, both intended and unintended. When a public policy results in a disproportionate magnitude of unintended victims, there is good reason to reevaluate the assumptions and design of the policy. In the case of drug-prohibition policies, the intended beneficiaries are those individuals who would become drug abusers but for the existence and enforcement of the drug laws. The intended victims are those who traffic in illicit drugs and suffer the legal consequences. The unintended beneficiaries, conversely, are the drug producers and traffickers who profit handsomely from the illegality of the market, while avoiding arrest by the authorities and the violence perpetrated by other criminals. The unintended victims of drug prohibition policies are rarely recognized as such, however. Viewed narrowly, they are the 30 million Americans who use illegal drugs, thereby risking loss of their jobs, imprisonment, and the damage done to health by ingesting illegally produced drugs; viewed broadly, they are all Americans, who pay the substantial costs of our present ill-considered policies, both as taxpayers and as the potential victims of crime. These unintended victims are generally thought to be victimized by the unintended beneficiaries (i.e., the drug dealers), when in fact it is the drug-prohibition policies themselves that are primarily responsible for their plight.

If law-enforcement efforts could succeed in significantly reducing either the supply of illicit drugs or the demand for them, we would probably have little need to seek alternative drug-control policies. But since those efforts have repeatedly failed to make much of a difference and show little indication of working better in the future, at this point we must focus greater attention on their costs. Unlike the demand and supply of illicit drugs, which have remained relatively indifferent to legislative initiatives, the costs of drug-enforcement measures can be affected— quite dramatically—by legislative measures. What tougher criminal sanctions and more police have failed to accomplish, in terms of reducing drug-related violence, corruption, death, and social decay, may well be better accomplished by legislative repeal of the drug laws, and adoption of less punitive but more effective measures to prevent and treat substance abuse. . . .

PHYSICAL AND MORAL COSTS

Perhaps the most paradoxical consequence of the drug laws is the tremendous harm they cause to the millions of drug users who have not been deterred from using illicit drugs in the first place. Nothing resembling an underground Food and Drug Administration has arisen to impose quality control on the illegal-drug market and provide users with accurate information on the drugs they consume. Imagine that Americans could not tell whether a bottle of wine contained 6 percent, 30 percent, or 90 percent alcohol, or whether an aspirin tablet contained 5 or 500 grams of aspirin. Imagine, too, that no controls existed to prevent winemakers from diluting their product with methanol and other dangerous impurities, and that vineyards and tobacco fields were fertilized with harmful substances by ignorant growers and sprayed with poisonous herbicides by government agents. Fewer people would use such substances, but more of those who did would get sick. Some would die.

The above scenario describes, of course, the current state of the illicit drug market. Many marijuana smokers are worse off for having smoked cannabis that was grown with dangerous fertilizers, sprayed with the herbicide paraquat, or mixed with more dangerous substances. Consumers of heroin and the various synthetic substances sold on the street face even severer consequences, including fatal overdoses and poisonings from unexpectedly potent or impure drug supplies. More often than not, the quality of a drug addict's life depends greatly upon his or her access to reliable supplies. Drug-enforcement operations that succeed in temporarily disrupting supply networks are thus a double-edged sword: they encourage some addicts to seek admission into drug-treatment programs, but they oblige others to seek out new and hence less reliable suppliers; the result is that more, not fewer, drug-related emergencies and deaths occur. . . .

Most Americans perceive the drug problem as a moral issue and draw a moral distinction between use of the illicit drugs and use of alcohol and tobacco. Yet when one subjects this distinction to reasoned analysis, it quickly disintegrates. The most consistent moral perspective of those who favor drug laws is that of the Mormons and the Puritans, who regard as immoral any intake of substances to alter one's state of consciousness or otherwise cause pleasure: they forbid not only the illicit drugs and alcohol, but also tobacco, caffeine, and even chocolate. The vast majority of Americans are hardly so consistent with respect to the propriety of their pleasures. Yet once one acknowledges that there is nothing immoral about drinking alcohol or smoking tobacco for non-medicinal purposes, it becomes difficult to condemn the consumption of marijuana, cocaine, and other substances on moral grounds. The "moral" condemnation of some substances and not others proves to be little more than a prejudice in favor of some drugs and against others.

The same false distinction is drawn with respect to those who provide the psychoactive substances to users and abusers alike. If degrees of immorality were measured by the levels of harm caused by one's products, the "traffickers" in tobacco and alcohol would be vilified as the most evil of all substance purveyors. That they are perceived instead as respected members of our community, while providers of the no more dangerous illicit substances are punished with long prison sentences, says much about the prejudices of most Americans with respect to psychoactive substances, but little about the morality or immorality of their activities. . . .

Although a valid moral distinction cannot be drawn between the licit and the illicit psychoactive substances, one can point to a different kind of moral justification for the drug laws: they arguably reflect a paternalistic obligation to protect those in danger of succumbing to their own weaknesses. If drugs were legally available, most people would either abstain from using them or would use them responsibly and in moderation. A minority without self-restraint, however, would end up harming themselves if the substances were more readily available. Therefore, the majority has a moral obligation to deny itself legal access to certain substances because of the plight of the minority. This obligation is presumably greatest when children are included among the minority.

At least in principle, this argument seems to provide the strongest moral justification for the drug laws. But ultimately the moral quality of laws must be judged not by how those laws are intended to work in principle, but by how they function in practice. When laws intended to serve a moral end inflict great damage on innocent parties, we must rethink our moral position.

Because drug-law violations do not create victims with an interest in notifying the police, drug-enforcement agents rely heavily on undercover operations, electronic surveillance, and information provided by informants. These techniques are indispensable to effective law enforcement, but they are also among the least palatable investigative methods employed by the police. The same is true of drug testing: it may be useful and even necessary for determining liability in accidents, but it also threatens and undermines the right of privacy to which many Americans believe they are entitled. There are good reasons for requiring that such measures be used sparingly.

Equally disturbing are the increasingly vocal calls for people to inform not only on drug dealers but also on neighbors, friends, and even family members who use illicit drugs. Government calls on people not only to "just say no," but also to report those who have not heeded the message. Intolerance of illicit-drug use and users is heralded not only as an indispensable ingredient in the war against drugs, but also as a mark of good citizenship. Certainly every society requires citizens to assist in the enforcement of criminal laws. But societies—particularly democratic and pluralistic ones—also rely strongly on an ethic of tolerance toward those who are different but do no harm to others. Overzealous enforcement of the drug laws risks undermining that ethic, and encouraging the creation of a society of informants.

This results in an immorality that is far more dangerous in its own way than that associated with the use of illicit drugs.

THE BENEFITS OF LEGALIZATION

Repealing the drug-prohibition laws promises tremendous advantages. Between reduced government expenditures on enforcing drug laws and new tax revenue from legal drug production and sales, public treasuries would enjoy a net benefit of at least ten billion dollars a year, and possibly much more. The quality of urban life would rise significantly. Homicide rates would decline. So would robbery and burglary rates. Organized criminal groups, particularly the newer ones that have yet to diversify out of drugs, would be dealt a devastating setback. The police, prosecutors, and courts would focus their resources on combatting the types of crimes that people cannot walk away from. More ghetto residents would turn their backs on criminal careers and seek out legitimate opportunities instead. And the health and quality of life of many drug users—and even drug abusers—would improve significantly.

All the benefits of legalization would be for naught, however, if millions more Americans were to become drug abusers. Our experience with alcohol and tobacco provides ample warnings. Today, alcohol is consumed by 140 million Americans and tobacco by 50 million. All of the health costs associated with abuse of the illicit drugs pale in comparison with those resulting from tobacco and alcohol abuse. In 1986, for example, alcohol was identified as a contributing factor in 10 percent of work-related injuries, 40 percent of suicide attempts, and about 40 percent of the approximately 46,000 annual traffic deaths in 1983. An estimated eighteen million Americans are reported to be either alcoholics or alcohol abusers. The total cost of alcohol abuse to American society is estimated at over 100 billion dollars annually. Alcohol has been identified as the direct cause of 80,000 to 100,000 deaths annually, and as a contributing factor in an additional 100,000 deaths. The health costs of tobacco use are of similar magnitude. In the United States alone, an estimated 320,000 people die prematurely each year as a consequence of their consumption of tobacco. By comparison, the National Council on Alcoholism reported that only 3,562 people were known to have died in 1985 from use of all illegal drugs combined. Even if we assume that thousands more deaths were related in one way or another to illicit drug abuse but not reported as such, we are still left with the conclusion that all of the health costs of marijuana, cocaine, and heroin combined amount to only a small fraction of those caused by tobacco and alcohol.

Most Americans are just beginning to recognize the extensive costs of alcohol and tobacco abuse. At the same time, they seem to believe that there is something fundamentally different about alcohol and tobacco that supports the legal distinction between those two substances, on the one hand, and the illicit ones, on the other. The most common distinction is based on the assumption that the illicit drugs are more dangerous than the licit ones. Cocaine, heroin, the various hallucinogens, and (to a lesser extent) marijuana are widely perceived as, in the words of the President's Commission on Organized Crime, "inherently destructive to mind and body." They are also believed to be more addictive and more likely to cause dangerous and violent behavior than alcohol and tobacco. All use of illicit drugs is therefore thought to be abusive; in other words, the distinction between use and abuse of psychoactive substances that most people recognize with respect to alcohol is not acknowledged with respect to the illicit substances.

Most Americans make the fallacious assumption that the government would not criminalize certain psychoactive substances if they were not in fact dangerous. They then jump to the conclusion that any use of those substances is a form of abuse. The government, in its effort to discourage people from using illicit drugs, has encouraged and perpetuated these misconceptions—not only in its rhetoric but also in its purportedly educational materials. Only by reading between the lines can one discern the fact that the vast majority of Americans who have used illicit drugs have done so in moderation, that relatively few have suffered negative short-term consequences, and that few are likely to suffer long-term harm. . . .

There is no question that legalization is a risky policy, since it may lead to an increase in the number of people who abuse drugs. But that is a risk—not a certainty. At the same time, current drug-control policies are failing, and new proposals promise only to be more costly and more repressive. We know that repealing the drug-prohibition laws would eliminate or greatly reduce many of the ills that people commonly identify as part and parcel of the "drug problem." Yet legalization is repeatedly and vociferously dismissed, without any attempt to evaluate it openly and objectively. The past twenty years have demonstrated that a drug policy shaped by exaggerated rhetoric designed to arouse fear has only led to our current disaster. Unless we are willing to honestly evaluate our options, including various legalization strategies, we will run a still greater risk: we may never find the best solution for our drug problems.

QUESTIONS

1 Which approach to legalization is morally preferable—Nadelmann's harm-reduction strategy or Szasz's more sweeping approach?
2 Does moral consistency require that we either (a) legally prohibit alcohol sale and use or (b) legalize the use of currently illicit drugs, such as marijuana and cocaine?

Against the Legalization of Drugs

James Q. Wilson

Wilson argues that crack-dependent people and heroin users cause all sorts of harm to others, such as producing crack-addicted babies and neglecting spouses and children. In his view, drug legalization would result in a sharp increase in

Reprinted with the permission of The American Enterprise Institute for Public Policy Research, Washington, D.C., from James Q. Wilson, *On Character* (1991), pp. 149–163.

drug use, a more widespread degradation of the human personality, and a greater rate of accidents and violence. Whereas Nadelmann stresses the benefits of legalization, Wilson stresses the benefits of the current system. Whereas Nadelmann sees our treatment of tobacco and alcohol, on the one hand, and currently illicit drugs, on the other, as morally inconsistent, Wilson advances reasons in support of this differential treatment.

In 1972 President Richard Nixon appointed me chairman of the National Advisory Council for Drug Abuse Prevention. Created by Congress, the council was charged with providing guidance on how best to coordinate the national war on drugs. (Yes, we called it a war then too.) In those days the drug we were chiefly concerned with was heroin. When I took office, heroin use had been increasing dramatically. Everybody was worried that this increase would continue. Such phrases as "heroin epidemic" were commonplace.

That same year the eminent economist Milton Friedman published an essay in *Newsweek* in which he called for legalizing heroin. His argument was on two grounds: as a matter of ethics the government has no right to tell people not to use heroin (or to drink or to commit suicide); as a matter of economics the prohibition of drug use imposes costs on society that far exceed the benefits. Others, such as the psychoanalyst Thomas Szasz, made the same argument. . . .

RELIVING THE PAST

Suppose we had taken Friedman's advice in 1972. What would have happened? We cannot be entirely certain, but at a minimum we would have placed the young heroin addicts (and, above all, the prospective addicts) in a different position from the one in which they actually found themselves. Heroin would have been legal. Its price would have been reduced by 95 percent (minus whatever we chose to recover in taxes). Now that it could have been sold by the same people who make aspirin, its quality would have been assured: no poisons, no adulterants. Sterile hypodermic needles would have been readily available at the neighborhood drugstore, probably at the same counter where the heroin was sold. No need to travel to big cities or unfamiliar neighborhoods—heroin could have been purchased anywhere, perhaps by mail order.

There would no longer have been any financial or medical reason to avoid heroin use. Anybody could have afforded it. We might have tried to prevent children from buying it, but as we have learned from our efforts to prevent minors from buying alcohol and tobacco, young people have a way of penetrating markets theoretically reserved for adults. Returning Vietnam veterans would have discovered that Omaha and Raleigh had been converted into the pharmaceutical equivalent of Saigon.

Under these circumstances can we doubt for a moment that heroin use would have grown exponentially? . . .

BACK TO THE FUTURE

Now cocaine, especially in its potent form, crack, is the focus of attention. Now as in 1972 the government is trying to reduce its use. Now as then some people are advocating legalization. Is there any more reason to yield to those arguments today than there was almost two decades ago?

I think not. If we had yielded in 1972, we almost certainly would have had today a permanent population of several million, not several hundred thousand, heroin addicts. If we yield now, we will have a far more serious problem with cocaine. . . .

Women are much more likely to use crack than heroin, and if they are pregnant, the effects on their babies are tragic. Douglas Besharov, who has been following the effects of drugs on infants for twenty years, writes that nothing he learned about heroin prepared him for the devastation of cocaine. Cocaine harms the fetus and can lead to physical deformities or neurological damage. Some crack babies have for all practical purposes suffered a disabling stroke while still in the womb. The long-term consequences of this brain damage are lowered cognitive ability and the onset of mood disorders. Besharov estimates that about 30,000 to 50,000 such babies are born every year, about 7,000 in New York City alone. There may be ways to treat such infants, but from everything we know, the treatment will be long, difficult, and expensive. Worse, the mothers who are most likely to produce crack babies are precisely the ones who, because of poverty or temperament, are least able and willing to obtain such treatment. In fact anecdotal evidence suggests that crack mothers are likely to abuse their infants.

The notion that abusing drugs such as cocaine is a victimless crime is not only absurd but dangerous. Even ignoring the fetal drug syndrome, crack-dependent people, like heroin addicts, are individuals who regularly victimize their children by neglect, their spouses by improvidence, their employers by lethargy, and their co-workers by carelessness. Society is not and could never be a collection of autonomous individuals. We all have a stake in ensuring that each of us displays a minimal level of dignity, responsibility, and empathy. We cannot of course coerce people into goodness, but we can and should insist that some standards must be met if society itself—on which the existence of the human personality depends—is to persist. Drawing the line that defines those standards is difficult and contentious, but if crack and heroin use does not fall below it, what does? . . .

BENEFITS OF ILLEGALITY

The advocates of legalization find nothing to be said in favor of the current system except, possibly, that it keeps the number of addicts smaller than it would otherwise be. In fact the benefits are more substantial than that.

First, treatment: all the talk about providing treatment on demand implies a demand for treatment. That is not quite right. Some drug-dependent people genuinely want treatment and will remain in it if offered; they should receive it. But far more want only short-term help after a bad crash; once stabilized and bathed, they are back on the street again, hustling. And even many of the addicts who enroll in a program and honestly want help drop out after a short while when they discover that help takes time and commitment. Drug-dependent people have short time horizons and a weak capacity for commitment. These two groups—those looking for a quick fix and those unable to stick with a long-term fix—are not easily helped. Even if we increase the number of treatment slots—as we should—we would have to do something to make treatment more effective.

One thing that can often make it more effective is compulsion. Douglas Anglin of UCLA, in common with many other researchers, has found that the longer one stays in a treatment program, the better the chances of a reduction in drug dependency. But he, again like most other researchers, has found that dropout rates are high. He has also found, however, that patients who enter treatment under legal compulsion stay in the program longer than those not subject to such pressure. His research on the California civil commitment program, for example, found that heroin users involved with its required drug-testing program had over the long term a lower rate of heroin use than similar addicts who were free of such constraints. If compulsion is a useful component of treatment for many addicts, it is not clear how compulsion could be achieved in a society in which purchasing, possessing, and using the drug were legal. It could be managed, I suppose, but I would not want to have to answer the challenge from the American Civil Liberties Union that it is wrong to compel a person to undergo treatment for consuming a legal commodity.

Next, education: we are now investing substantially in drug-education programs in the schools. Although we do not yet know for certain what will work, there are some promising leads. But I wonder how credible such programs would be if they were aimed at dissuading children from doing something perfectly legal. We could of course treat drug education like smoking education: inhaling crack and inhaling tobacco are both legal, but you should not do it because it is bad for you. That tobacco is bad for you is easily shown; the surgeon general has seen to that. But what do we say about crack? It is pleasurable, but devoting yourself to so much pleasure is not a good idea (though perfectly legal)? Unlike tobacco, cocaine will not give you cancer or emphysema, but it will lead you to neglect your duties to family, job, and neighborhood? Everybody is doing cocaine, but you should not?

Again it might be possible under a legalized regime to have effective drug-prevention programs, but their effectiveness would depend heavily on first having decided that cocaine use, like tobacco use, is purely a matter of practical consequences; no fundamental moral significance attaches to either. But if we believe—as I do—that dependency on certain mind-altering drugs is a moral issue and that their illegality rests in part on their immorality, then legalizing them undercuts, if it does not eliminate altogether, the moral message.

That message is at the root of the distinction we now make between nicotine and cocaine. Both are highly addictive; both have harmful physical effects. But we treat the two drugs differently, not simply because nicotine is so widely used as to be beyond the reach of effective prohibition but because its use does not destroy the user's essential humanity. Tobacco shortens one's life, cocaine debases it. Nicotine alters one's habits, cocaine alters one's soul. The heavy use of crack, unlike the heavy use of tobacco, corrodes those natural sentiments of sympathy and duty that constitute our human nature and make possible our social life. To say, as does Nadelmann, that distinguishing morally between tobacco and cocaine is "little more than a transient prejudice" is close to saying that morality itself is but a prejudice.

THE ALCOHOL PROBLEM

Now we have arrived where many arguments about legalizing drugs begin: is there any reason to treat heroin and cocaine differently from the way we treat alcohol?

There is no easy answer to that question because, as with so many human problems, one cannot decide simply on the basis either of moral principles or of individual consequences; one has to temper any policy by a common-sense judgment of what is possible. Alcohol, like heroin, cocaine, PCP, and marijuana, is a drug—that is, a mood-altering substance—and consumed to excess, it certainly has harmful consequences: auto accidents, barroom fights, bedroom shootings. It is also, for some people, addictive. We cannot confidently compare the addictive powers of these drugs, but the best evidence suggests that crack and heroin are much more addictive than alcohol.

Many people, Nadelmann included, argue that since the health and financial costs of alcohol abuse are so much higher than those of cocaine or heroin abuse, it is hypocritical folly to devote our efforts to preventing cocaine or drug use. But as Mark Kleiman of Harvard has pointed out, this comparison is quite misleading. What Nadelmann is doing is showing that a legalized drug (alcohol) produces greater social harm than illegal ones (cocaine and heroin). But of course. Suppose that in the 1920s we had made heroin and cocaine legal and alcohol illegal. Can anyone doubt that Nadelmann would now be writing that it is folly to continue our ban on alcohol because cocaine and heroin are so much more harmful?

And let there be no doubt about it—widespread heroin and cocaine use are associated with all manner of ills. Thomas Bewley found that the mortality rate of British heroin addicts in 1968 was twenty-eight times as high as the death rate of the same age group of nonaddicts. Even though in England at the time an addict could obtain free or low-cost heroin and clean needles from British clinics. Perform the following mental experiment: suppose we legalized heroin and cocaine in this country. In what proportion of auto fatalities would the state police report that the driver was nodding off on heroin or recklessly driving on a coke high? In what proportion of spouse assault and child abuse cases would the local police report that crack was involved? In what proportion of industrial accidents would safety investigators report that the forklift or drill-press operator was in a drug-induced stupor or frenzy? We do not know exactly what the proportion would be, but anyone who asserts that it would not be much higher than it is now would have to believe that these drugs have little appeal except when they are illegal. And that is nonsense.

An advocate of legalization might concede that social harm—perhaps harm equivalent to that already produced by alcohol—would follow from making cocaine and heroin generally available. But at least, he might add, we would have the problem out in the open, where it could be treated as a matter of public health. That is well and good if we knew how to treat—that is, cure—heroin and cocaine abuse. But we do not know how to do it for all the people who would need such help. We are having only limited success in coping with chronic alcoholics. Addictive behavior is immensely difficult to change, and the best methods for changing it—living in drug-free therapeutic communities, becoming faithful members of Alcoholics Anonymous or Narcotics Anonymous—require great personal commitment, a quality that is, alas, in short supply among the persons—young people, disadvantaged people—who are often most at risk for addiction.

Suppose that today we had not 15 million alcohol abusers but half a million. Suppose that we already knew what we have learned from our long experience with the widespread use of alcohol. Would we make whiskey legal? I do not know, but I suspect there would be a lively debate. The surgeon general would remind us of the risks alcohol poses to pregnant woman. The National Highway Traffic Safety Administration would point to the likelihood of more highway fatalities caused by drunk drivers. The Food and Drug Administration might find that there is a nontrivial increase in cancer associated with alcohol consumption. At the same time the police would report great difficulty in keeping illegal whiskey out of our cities, officers being corrupted by bootleggers, and alcohol addicts often resorting to crime to feed their habit. Libertarians for their part would argue that every citizen has a right to drink anything he wishes and that drinking is in any event a victimless crime.

However the debate might turn out, the central fact would be that the problem was still at that point a small one. The government cannot legislate away the addictive tendencies in all of us nor can it remove completely even the most dangerous addictive substances. But it can cope with harms when the harms are still manageable. . . .

IF I AM WRONG

No one can know what our society would be like if we changed the law to make access to cocaine, heroin, and PCP easier. I believe, for reasons given, that the result would be a sharp increase in use, a more widespread degradation of the human personality, and a greater rate of accidents and violence.

I may be wrong. If I am, then we will needlessly have incurred heavy costs in law enforcement and some forms of criminality. But if I am right, and the legalizers prevail anyway, then we will have consigned millions of people, hundreds of thousands of infants, and hundreds of neighborhoods to a life of oblivion and disease. To the lives and families destroyed by alcohol, we will have added countless more destroyed by cocaine, heroin, PCP, and whatever else a basement scientist can invent.

Human character is formed by society; indeed human character is inconceivable without society, and good character is less likely in a bad society. Will we, in the name of an abstract doctrine of radical individualism, and with the false comfort of suspect predictions, decide to take the chance that somehow individual decency can survive amid a more general level of degradation?

I think not. The American people are too wise for that, whatever the academic essayists and cocktail party pundits may say. But if Americans today are less wise than I suppose, then Americans at some future time will look back on us now and wonder, what kind of people were they that they could have done such a thing?

QUESTIONS

1 Are there good reasons to believe that legalizing currently illicit drugs will result in a serious increase in addiction?
2 Is Wilson correct in claiming that drugs such as cocaine and heroin are dehumanizing? What does it mean to be dehumanized?

Addiction and Drug Policy

Daniel Shapiro

Shapiro advances an argument to undercut the worry that legalizing cocaine and heroin would produce an explosion of addiction. He rejects what he calls the "standard view"—the view that these drugs are highly and inherently addictive due to the pharmacological effects they have on the brain. Shapiro proposes an alternative view of addiction, which focuses on the individual's mindset and social or cultural setting in explaining his or her use or abuse of drugs. Finally, Shapiro looks at cigarette smoking and examines the interaction among tobacco's pharmacological effects, the smoker's mindset, and the social setting.

Most people think that illegal drugs, such as cocaine and heroin, are highly addictive. Usually their addictiveness is explained by pharmacology: their chemical composition and its effects on the brain are such that, after a while, it's hard to stop using them. This view of drug addiction—I call it the standard view—underlies most opposition to legalizing cocaine and heroin. James Wilson's (1990) arguments are typical: legalization increases access, and increased access to addictive drugs increases addiction. The standard view also underlies the increasingly popular opinion, given a philosophical defense by Robert Goodin (1989), that cigarette smokers are addicts in the grip of a powerful drug.

However, the standard view is false: pharmacology, I shall argue, does not by itself do much to explain drug addiction. I will offer a different explanation of drug addiction and discuss its implications for the debate about drug legalization.

PROBLEMS WITH THE STANDARD VIEW

We label someone as a drug addict because of his behavior. A drug addict uses drugs repeatedly, compulsively, and wants to stop or cut back on his use but finds it's difficult to do so; at its worst, drug addiction dominates or crowds out other activities and concerns. The standard view attempts to explain this compulsive behavior by

This is a slightly revised version of the essay that appears in *Social Ethics,* 6th ed. Reprinted with permission of Daniel Shapiro from *Morality and Moral Controversies,* 7th ed. (Pearson Prentice-Hall, 2005), edited by John Arthur, pp. 515–521. The essay's addendum is omitted here. Copyright © 2003 by Daniel Shapiro.

the drug's effects on the brain. Repeated use of an addictive drug induces cravings and the user comes to need a substantial amount to get the effect she wants, i.e., develops tolerance. If the user tries to stop, she then suffers very disagreeable effects, called withdrawal symptoms. (For more detail on the standard view, see American Psychiatric Association 1994, 176–81.)

Cravings, tolerance, and withdrawal symptoms: do these explain drug addiction? A craving or strong desire to do something doesn't *make* one do something: one can act on a desire or ignore it *or* attempt to extinguish it. Tolerance explains why the user increases her intake to get the effect she wants, but that doesn't explain why she would find it difficult to *stop wanting* this effect. Thus, the key idea in the standard view is really withdrawal symptoms, because that is needed to explain the difficulty in extinguishing the desire to take the drug or to stop wanting the effects the drug produces. However, for this explanation to work, these symptoms have to be really bad, for if they aren't, why not just put up with them as a small price to pay for getting free of the drug? However, withdrawal symptoms aren't *that* bad. Heroin is considered terribly addictive, yet pharmacologists describe its withdrawal symptoms as like having a bad flu for about a week: typical withdrawal symptoms include fever, diarrhea, sneezing, muscle cramps, and vomiting (Kaplan 1983, 15, 19, 35). While a bad flu is quite unpleasant, it's not so bad that one has little choice but to take heroin rather than experience it. Indeed, most withdrawal symptoms for any drug cease within a few weeks, yet most heavy users who relapse do so after that period and few drug addicts report withdrawal symptoms as the reason for their relapse (Peele 1985, 19–20, 67; Schacter 1982, 436–44; Waldorf, Reinarman, and Murphy 1991, 241).

Thus, cravings, tolerance, and withdrawal symptoms cannot explain addiction. An additional problem for the standard view is that most drug users, whether they use legal or illegal drugs, do not become addicts, and few addicts remain so permanently. (Cigarette smokers are a partial exception, which I discuss later.) Anonymous surveys of drug users by the Substance Abuse and Mental Health Services Administration indicate that less than 10 percent of those who have tried powder cocaine use it monthly (National Household Survey of Drug Abuse 2001, tables H1 and H2). Furthermore, most monthly users are not addicts; a survey of young adults, for example (Johnston, O'Malley, and Bachman for the National Institute on Drug Abuse 1996, 84–5), found that less than 10 percent of monthly cocaine users used it daily. (Even a daily user need not be an addict; someone who drinks daily is not thereby an alcoholic.) The figures are not appreciably different for crack cocaine (Erickson, Smart, and Murray 1994, 167–74, 231–32, Morgan and Zimmer 1997, 142–44) and only slightly higher for heroin (Husak 1992, 125; Sullum 2003, 228). These surveys have been confirmed by longitudinal studies—studies of a set of users over time—which indicate that moderate and/or controlled use of these drugs is the norm, not the exception, and that even heavy users do not inevitably march to addiction, let alone remain permanent addicts (Waldorf, Reinarman, and Murphy 1991, Erickson, Smart, and Murray 1994; Zinberg 1984, 111–34, 152–71). The standard view has to explain the preeminence of controlled use by arguing that drug laws reduce access to illegal drugs. However, I argue below that even with easy access to drugs most people use them responsibly, and so something other than the law and pharmacology must explain patterns of drug use.

AN ALTERNATIVE VIEW

I will defend a view of addiction summed up by Norman Zinberg's book, *Drug, Set, and Setting* (1984). "Drug" means pharmacology; "set" means the individual's mindset, his personality, values, and expectations; and "setting" means the cultural or social surroundings of drug use. This should sound like common sense. Humans are interpretative animals, and so what results from drug use depends not just on the experience or effects produced by the drug but *also* on the interpretation of that experience or effects. And how one interprets or understands the experience depends on one's individuality and the cultural or social setting. I begin with setting. Hospital patients that get continuous and massive doses of narcotics rarely get addicted or crave the drugs after release from the hospital (Peele 1985, 17; Falk 1996, 9). The quantity and duration of their drug use pales in significance compared with the setting of their drug consumption: subsequent ill effects from the drug are rarely interpreted in terms of addiction. A study of Vietnam veterans, the largest study of untreated heroin users ever conducted, provides more dramatic evidence of the role of setting. Three-quarters of Vietnam vets who used heroin in Vietnam became addicted, but after coming home, only half of heroin users in Vietnam continued to use, and of those only 12 percent were addicts (Robins, Heltzer, Hesselbrock, and Wish 1980). Wilson also mentions this study and says that the change was because heroin is illegal in the U.S. (1990, 22), and while this undoubtedly played a role, so did the difference in social setting: Vietnam, with its absence of work and family, as well as loneliness and fear of death, helped to promote acceptance of heavy drug use.

Along the same lines, consider the effects of alcohol in different cultures. In Finland, for example, violence and alcohol are linked, for sometimes heavy drinkers end up in fights; in Greece, Italy, and other Mediterranean countries, however, where almost all drinking is moderate and controlled, there is no violence-alcohol link (Peele 1985, 25). Why the differences? Humans are social or cultural animals, not just products of their biochemistry, and this means, in part, that social norms or rules play a significant role in influencing behavior. In cultures where potentially intoxicating drugs such as alcohol are viewed as supplements or accompaniments to life, moderate and controlled use will be the norm—hence, even though Mediterranean cultures typically consume large amounts of alcohol, there is little alcoholism—while in cultures where alcohol is also viewed as a way of escaping one's problems, alcoholism will be more prevalent, which may explain the problem in Finland and some other Scandinavian cultures. In addition to cultural influences, most people learn to use alcohol responsibly by observing their parents. They see their parents drink at a ball game or to celebrate special occasions or with food at a meal, but rarely on an empty stomach; they learn it's wrong to be drunk at work, to drink and drive; they learn that uncontrolled behavior with alcohol is generally frowned upon; they absorb certain norms and values such as "know your limit," "don't drink alone," "don't drink in the morning," and so forth. They learn about rituals which reinforce moderation, such as the phrase "let's have a drink." These informal rules and rituals teach most people how to use alcohol responsibly (Zinberg 1987, 258–62).

While social controls are harder to develop with illicit drugs—accurate information is pretty scarce, and parents feel uncomfortable teaching their children about controlled use—even here sanctions and rituals promoting moderate use exist. For example, in a study of an eleven-year follow-up of an informal network of middle-class cocaine users largely connected through ties of friendship, most of whom were moderate users, the authors concluded that:

> Rather than cocaine overpowering user concerns with family, health, and career, we found that the high value most of our users placed upon family, health, and career achievement . . . mitigated against abuse and addiction. Such group norms and the informal social controls that seemed to stem from them (e.g., expressions of concern, warning about risks, the use of pejorative names like "coke hog," refusal to share with abusers) mediated the force of pharmacological, physiological, and psychological factors which can lead to addiction (Murphy 1989: 435).

Even many heavy cocaine users are able to prevent their use from becoming out of control (or out of control for significant periods of time) by regulating the time and circumstances of use (not using during work, never using too late at night, limiting use on weekdays), using with friends rather than alone, employing fixed rules (paying bills before spending money on cocaine), etc. (Waldorf, Reinarman, and Murphy 1991). Unsurprisingly, these studies of controlled cocaine use generally focus on middle-class users: their income and the psychological support of friends and family put them at less of a risk of ruining their lives by drug use than those with little income or hope (Peele 1991, 159–60).

I now examine the effects of set on drug use, that is, the effect of expectations, personality, and values. Expectations are important because drug use occurs in a pattern of ongoing activity, and one's interpretation of the drug's effects depends upon expectations of how those effects will fit into or alter those activities. Expectations explain the well-known placebo effect: if people consume something they mistakenly believe will stop or alleviate their pain, it often does. Along the same lines, in experiments with American college-age men, aggression and sexual arousal increased when these men were told they were drinking liquor, even though they were drinking 0 proof, while when drinking liquor and told they were not, they acted normally (Peele 1985, 17). The role of expectations also explains why many users of heroin, cocaine, and other psychoactive drugs do not like or even recognize the effects when they first take it and have to be taught to or learn how to appreciate the effects (Peele 1985, 13–14; Waldorf, Reinarman, and Murphy 1991, 264; Zinberg 1984, 117). The importance of expectations means that those users who view the drug as overpowering them will tend to find their lives dominated by the drug, while those who view it as an enhancement or a complement to certain experiences or activities will tend not to let drugs dominate or overpower their other interests (Peele 1991, 156–58, 169–70).

As for the individual's personality and values, the predictions of common sense are pretty much accurate. Psychologically healthy people are likely to engage in controlled, moderate drug use, or if they find themselves progressing to uncontrolled use, they tend to cut back. On other hand, drug addicts of all kinds tend to have more psychological problems before they started using illicit drugs (Peele 1991, 153–54, 157, Zinberg 1984, 74–76.) People who are motivated to control their own lives will tend to make drug use an accompaniment or an ingredient in their lives, not the dominant factor. Those who place a high value on responsibility, work, family, productivity, etc., will tend to fit drug use into their lives rather than letting it run their lives (Waldorf, Reinarman, and Murphy 1991, 267; Peele 1991, 160–66). That's why drug use of all kinds, licit or illicit, tends to taper off with age: keeping a job, raising a family, and so forth leave limited time or motivation for uncontrolled or near continuous drug use (Peele 1985, 15). And it's why it's not uncommon for addicts to explain their addiction by saying that they drifted into the addict's life; with little to compete with their drug use, or lacking motivation to substitute other activities or interests, drug use comes to dominate their lives (DeGrandpre and White 1996, 44–46). Those with richer lives, or who are motivated on an individual and/or cultural level to get richer lives, are less likely to succumb to addiction. To summarize: even with easy access to intoxicating drugs, most drug users don't become addicts, or if they do, don't remain addicts for that long, because most people have and are motivated to find better things to do with their lives. These better things result from their individual personality and values and their social or cultural setting.

CIGARETTE SMOKING AND THE ROLE OF PHARMACOLOGY

I've discussed how set and setting influence drug use, but where does pharmacology fit in? Its role is revealed by examining why it is much harder to stop smoking cigarettes—only half of smokers that try to stop smoking succeed in quitting—than to stop using other substances. (For more detail in what follows, see Shapiro 1994 and the references cited therein).

Smokers smoke to relax; to concentrate; to handle anxiety, stress, and difficult interpersonal situations; as a way of taking a break during the day; as a social lubricant; as a means of oral gratification—and this is a partial list. Since smoking is a means to or part of so many activities, situations, and moods, stopping smoking is a major life change and major life changes do not come easily. Part of the reason smoking is so integrated into people's lives is pharmacological. Nicotine's effects on the brain are mild and subtle: it doesn't disrupt your life. While addicts or heavy users of other drugs such as cocaine, heroin, or alcohol *also* use their drugs as a means to or part of a variety of activities, situations, and moods, most users of these drugs are not lifelong addicts or heavy users, because these drugs are not so mild and heavy use has a stronger tendency over time to disrupt people's lives.

The pharmacology of smoking, however, cannot be separated from its social setting. Smoking doesn't disrupt people's lives in part because it is legal. Even with increasing regulations, smokers still can smoke in a variety of situations (driving, walking on public streets, etc.), while one cannot use illegal drugs except in a furtive and secretive manner. Furthermore, the mild effects of nicotine are due to its mild potency—smokers can carefully control their nicotine intake, getting small doses throughout the day—and its mild potency is due partly to smoking being legal. Legal drugs tend to have milder potencies than illegal ones for two reasons. First, illegal markets create incentives for stronger potencies, as sellers will favor concentrated forms of a drug that can be easily concealed and give a big bang for the buck. Second, in legal markets different potencies of the same drug openly compete, and over time the weaker ones come to be preferred—consider the popularity of low tar/nicotine cigarettes and wine and beer over hard liquor.

Thus, pharmacology and setting interact: smoking is well integrated into people's lives because the nicotine in cigarettes has mild pharmacological effects and because smoking is legal, and nicotine has those mild effects in part because smoking is legal. Pharmacology also interacts with what I've been calling set. The harms of smoking are slow to occur, are cumulative, and largely affect one's health, not one's ability to perform normal activities (at least prior to getting seriously ill). Furthermore, to eliminate these harms requires complete smoking cessation; cutting back rarely suffices (even light smokers increase their chances of getting lung cancer, emphysema, and heart disease). Thus, quitting smoking requires strong motivation, since its bad effects are not immediate and it does not disrupt one's life. Add to this what I noted earlier, that stopping smoking means changing one's life, and it's unsurprising that many find it difficult to stop.

Thus, it is a mistake to argue, as Goodin did, that the difficulty in quitting is mainly explicable by the effects of nicotine. Smokers are addicted to smoking, an *activity,* and their being addicted to it is not reducible to their being addicted to a *drug.* If my explanation of the relative difficulty of quitting smoking is correct, then the standard view of an addictive drug is quite suspect. That view suggests that knowledge of a drug's pharmacology provides a basis for making reasonable predictions about a drug's addictiveness. However, understanding nicotine's effects upon the brain (which is what Goodin stressed in his explanation of smokers' addiction) does not tell us that it's hard to stop smoking; we only know that once we add information about set and setting. Generalizing from the case of smoking, all we can say is:

> The milder the effects upon the brain, the easier for adults to purchase, the more easily integrated into one's life, and the more the bad effects are cumulative, slow-acting and only reversible upon complete cessation, the more addictive the drug.

Besides being a mouthful, this understanding of drug addiction requires introducing the *interaction* of set and setting with pharmacology to explain the addictiveness potential of various drugs. It is simpler and less misleading to say that people tend to *addict themselves* to various substances (and activities), this tendency varying with various cultural and individual influences.

CONCLUSION

My argument undercuts the worry that legalizing cocaine and heroin will produce an explosion of addiction because people will have access to inherently and powerfully addictive drugs. The standard view that cocaine and heroin are inherently addictive is false, because no drug is *inherently* addictive. The desire of most people to lead responsible and productive lives in a social setting that rewards such desires is what controls and limits most drug use. Ironically, if cocaine and heroin in a legal market would be as disruptive as many drug prohibitionists fear, then that is an excellent reason why addiction would not explode under legalization—drug use that tends to thrive is drug use that is woven into, rather than disrupts, responsible people's lives. . . .

REFERENCES

American Psychiatric Association. 1994. *Diagnostic and Statistical Manual of Mental Disorders.* 4th ed. Washington, D.C.: American Psychiatric Association.

DeGrandpre, R., and E. White. 1996. "Drugs: In Care of the Self." *Common Knowledge* 3: 27–48.

Erickson. P., E. Edward, R. Smart, and G. Murray. 1994. *The Steel Drug: Crack and Cocaine in Perspective,* 2nd ed. New York: MacMillan.

Falk, J, 1996. "Environmental Factors in the Instigation and Maintenance of Drug Abuse." In W. Bickel and R. DeGrandpre, eds., *Drug Policy and Human Nature.* New York: Plenum Press.

Goodin, R. 1989. "The Ethics of Smoking." *Ethics* 99: 574–624.

Husak, D. 1992. *Drugs and Rights.* New York: Cambridge University Press.

Johnston. L. D., P. M. O'Malley, and J. G. Bachman. 1996. *Monitoring the Future Study, 1975–1994; National Survey Results on Drug Use.* Volume II: *College Students and Young Adults.* Rockville, Md.: National Institute on Drug Abuse.

Kaplan, J. 1983. *The Hardest Drug: Heroin and Public Policy.* Chicago: University of Chicago Press.

Morgan, J., and L. Zimmerman. 1997. "The Social Pharmacology of Smokeable Cocaine: Not All It's Cracked Up to Be." In C. Reinarman and H. Levine, eds., *Crack in America: Demon Drugs and Social Justice,* Berkeley: University of California Press.

Murphy, S., C. Reinarman, and D. Waldorf. 1989. "An 11 Year Follow-Up of a Network of Cocaine Users," *British Journal of Addiction* 84: 427–36.

Peele, S. 1985. *The Meaning of Addiction; Compulsive Experience and Its Interpretation.* Lexington, Mass.: D.C. Heath and Company.

Peele, S. 1991. *The Diseasing of America: Addiction Treatment Out of Control.* Boston: Houghton Mifflin Company.

Robins, L., J. Helzer. M. Hesselbrock, and E. Wish. 1980. "Vietnam Veterans Three Years After Vietnam: How Our Study Changed Our View of Heroin." In L. Brill and C. Winick, eds., *The Yearbook of Substance Use and Abuse.* Vol. 2. New York: Human Sciences Press.

Schacter, S. 1982. "Recidivism and Self-Cure of Smoking and Obesity." *American Psychologist* 37: 436–44.

Shapiro. D. 1994. "Smoking Tobacco: Irrationality, Addiction and Paternalism." *Public Affairs Quarterly* 8: 187–203.

Substance Abuse and Mental Health Services Administration. 2002. *Tables from the 2001 National Household Survey on Drug Abuse,* Department of Health and Human Services, available online at http://www.samhsa.gov/oas/NHSDA/2k1NHSDA/vol2/appendixh_l.htm.

Sullum. J. 2003. *Saying Yes: In Defense of Drug Use.* New York: Tarcher/Putnam.

Waldorf, D., C. Reinarman, and S. Murphy. 1991. *Cocaine Changes: The Experience of Using and Quitting.* Philadelphia: Temple University Press.

Wilson, J. 1990. "Against the Legalization of Drugs." *Commentary* 89: 21–28.

Zinberg, N. 1984. *Drug, Set, and Setting.* New Haven, Conn.: Yale University Press.

Zinberg, N. 1987. "The Use and Misuse of Intoxicants." In R. Hamowy, ed., *Dealing with Drugs.* Lexington, Mass.: D. C. Heath and Company.

QUESTIONS

1 Can Wilson's position on addiction be defended against Shapiro's critique of the standard view?

2 Taking into account the various arguments that can be made for and against drug legalization, what overall drug policy would you endorse?

SUGGESTED ADDITIONAL READINGS FOR CHAPTER 6

BELENKO, STEVEN R., ed: *Drugs and Drug Policy in America.* Westport, Conn.: Greenwood Press, 2000. This is an excellent documentary history of American drug policy. It combines explanatory commentary with a variety of original documents, including enacted laws and other government documents, court decisions, scholarly writings, and articles from the popular media.

BROCK, DAN: "The Use of Drugs for Pleasure." In Thomas H. Murray, Willard Gaylin, and Ruth Macklin, eds., *Feeling Good and Doing Better: Ethics and Nontherapeutic Drug Use.* Clifton. N J.: Humana Press, 1984, pp. 83–106. Brock argues in support of ethical hedonism, maintaining that the pleasure derived from drug use does not necessarily conflict with living the good life and may even be compatible with it.

DE MARNEFFE, PETER: "Do We Have a Right to Use Drugs?" *Public Affairs Quarterly.* vol. 10, July 1996, pp. 229–247. De Marneffe argues that there is no overriding moral reason why democratic governments should not enact and enforce some laws against drug sale and use.

DUKE, STEVEN B.: "Drug Prohibition: An Unnatural Disaster." *Connecticut Law Review,* vol. 27, Winter 1995, pp. 571–612. Duke argues that drug prohibition has far eclipsed alcohol prohibition as America's costliest and most catastrophic social program.

HUSAK, DOUGLAS N.: *Drugs and Rights.* New York: Cambridge University Press, 1992. Husak focuses on the moral rights of adult users of recreational drugs. Defending a moderate position on the issue, he develops criteria to be used in determining which drugs should be criminalized.

LOKEN, GREGORY A.: "The Importance of Being More Than Earnest: Why the Case for Drug Legalization Remains Unproven." *Connecticut Law Review,* vol. 27, Winter 1995, pp. 660–691. Loken rejects the view that drug prohibition is the cause of an increase in crime. He argues that the drug war has successfully reduced crime and that legalization would have disastrous consequences, especially for children.

MURRAY, THOMAS H.: "The Coercive Power of Drugs in Sports." *The Hastings Center Report,* vol. 13, August 1983, pp. 24–30. Murray argues against the use of drugs in sports. He offers arguments in support for sanctioning both competing athletes who take performance-enhancing drugs and their coaches.

ZIMMER, LYNN, and JOHN P. MORGAN: *Marijuana Myths, Marijuana Facts: A Review of the Scientific Evidence.* New York: The Lindesmith Center, 1997. Zimmer and Morgan review the scientific research on marijuana. They list numerous claims made about the harmful effects of marijuana, some of which are found in government documents as well as magazines and newspapers. They refute each claim, basing their refutations on relevant scientific research.

CHAPTER 7

Terrorism, Human Rights, and Civil Liberties

Although terrorism is not a new phenomenon, the September 11, 2001, attacks on the World Trade Center in New York and on the Pentagon in Washington brought terrorism home to Americans and exposed a vulnerability to new kinds of terrorist acts that had not been recognized before. The ensuing war on terrorism, proclaimed by President George W. Bush in response to these attacks, has resulted in wars in Afghanistan and Iraq and the internment of terrorist suspects at Guantánamo Bay. It has also had domestic consequences including the passage of the Patriot Act, which has given rise to a concern about possible infringements on civil liberties.

The conceptual and moral issues raised by terrorism and by the war on terrorism are complex. This chapter deals with only a few of these issues. What is terrorism? Are terrorist acts ever morally justified? Can we draw a morally principled distinction between terrorist acts and acts of war if both result in harm to individuals whom we might describe as civilians, noncombatants, or innocents? How do we reconcile the need to maintain national security, on the one hand, with the need to respect human rights and guarantee civil liberties on the other?

DEFINITIONS OF TERRORISM

How should we understand the word *terrorism*? Answers to this question are crucially intertwined with answers to questions related to the moral issues raised by terrorist acts and responses to them. Yet no definition of *terrorism* is universally accepted. Various U.S. government documents, for example, adopt different definitions. The United States State Department, in its *Patterns of Global Terrorism,* uses the following definition: "'terrorism' means premeditated, politically motivated violence perpetrated against noncombatant targets by subnational groups or clandestine agents, usually intended to influence an audience."[1] The FBI, using a definition from the Code of Federal Regulations,[2] states that terrorism is "the unlawful use of force and violence against persons or property to intimidate or coerce a government, the civilian population, or any segment thereof, in furtherance of political or social objectives."[3] Other government documents work with other definitions.

Among philosophers, disagreement is also widespread. The following two examples illustrate one of these points of disagreement. The definition of *terrorism* advanced by Stephen Nathanson in a reading in this chapter includes as a central element the killing or injuring of innocent people or the threat of such harms to them. By contrast, Virginia Held maintains that the targeting of "innocents," as in Nathanson's definition, or "noncombatants" as in the State Department's definition, is not an essential characteristic of terrorist acts. Held defines *terrorism* as "political violence that usually involves sudden attacks to spread fear to a wider group than those attacked, often doing so by targeting civilians."[4] In keeping with government definitions, such as those given above, as well as many philosophical ones not included here, it is conceptually impossible for states to perpetrate terrorist acts. In contrast, according to both Nathanson's and Held's definitions, it is conceptually possible for states as well as nonstate entities to be perpetrators of terrorism.

Discussions concerning the defining features of terrorism center on the attribution of the following characteristics to terrorist acts:

1 They involve the use of violence or the threat of violence.
2 They are politically motivated.
3 They are perpetrated by subnational groups or individuals.
4 They target innocents.

The first two features are usually accepted as stating essential characteristics of terrorism, although Alison M. Jaggar, in a reading in this chapter, rejects political motivation as an essential part of the definition of terrorism. But these two features are surely not sufficient to constitute terrorism. In respect to the violence requirement, think of someone angrily punching another person or someone tackling a man wielding a semiautomatic weapon in order to prevent harm to passersby. Although these are violent acts, it would be inappropriate to call them acts of terrorism. Thus terrorist acts can be seen as falling into a subcategory of violent acts, but we need other criteria to determine which acts qualify as terrorist.

The second feature, political motivation, does provide a plausible criterion for distinguishing terrorist acts from others involving violence. Politically motivated violence has been seen as a feature of terrorist acts ever since the word was first used in France to describe the reign of terror during the French Revolution. However, wars are also waged for political reasons. If there are important reasons for keeping terrorism and war in separate categories, then we need to find a criterion

---

[1]*Patterns of Global Terrorism,* May 2002 (http://www.state.gov).
[2]28 Code of Federal Regulations, Section 0.85.
[3]http://www.fbi.gov/publications/terror/terror2000_2001.pdf.
[4]Virginia Held, "Legitimate Authority in Non-State Groups Using Violence," *Journal of Social Philosophy,* vol. 36, no. 2, 2005:178.

that applies to the former but not the latter. Acceptance of the third feature would make that possible. If we limit the category of perpetrators of terrorism to subnationals or individuals, we shut out the possibility that states could be perpetrators of terrorism. But unless the distinction is rationally grounded, it seems arbitrary. Examples of state actions some label as terrorist abound in the literature. Think, for example, of the Russian destruction of Grozny during the Chechen war. It is not surprising, then, that there is so much disagreement about the third feature.

In contrast, it is easy to see why most framers of definitions of terrorism consider the fourth feature to be an essential element in terrorist acts. First, many acts commonly considered terrorist do target innocents. Second, the harming of innocents is sufficient to establish a presumption that these acts are morally wrong, giving us at the very least a prima facie moral basis for our condemnations of terrorism. Yet this criterion raises important questions. Who are the innocents? Infants and young children? Certainly. But what about voters who support a government that is performing acts of violence to which the terrorists may be reacting? What about civilian populations in wartime whose efforts on the home front make the continuation of wartime violence possible? In light of such difficulties, writers sometimes talk of *noncombatants* rather than *innocents*. Yet, this too raises difficulties. On this description, members of the military in wartime would be legitimate targets of violence while civilian officeholders who issue orders to military personnel would not. One suggested approach, discussed by Jaggar in this chapter, is to amend the fourth feature as follows: Terrorist acts target innocent civilians. Of course, on this view, there is still a problem of determining just who is and who is not an innocent civilian. After the bombing of the World Trade Center, defenders of the bombing claimed that the civilians who were killed and injured in that attack were not innocents because they were engaged in the kind of global business practices that were inimical to the terrorists. But even if that claim were true, it would not apply to others who were killed in the attack, such as restaurant employees.

Several writers have maintained that the fourth criterion, even as amended, is too restrictive. One reason given for that criticism is that in our ordinary ascriptions, we often describe as terrorist not only actions that primarily target innocent civilians but also actions whose primary targets have been members of the military. The attack on the *USS Cole* is one example; the September 11, 2001, attack on the Pentagon is another. One attempt to take account of this reasoning is seen in Held's definition above, which states that terrorist acts *often* target civilians.

CAN TERRORISM EVER BE MORALLY JUSTIFIED?

Many people believe that terrorism is always morally wrong. For them, the word *terrorism* functions like the word *murder*—just as any act of murder is wrong by definition, so, too, is any act of terrorism. On this approach, the possibility of justified terrorism is nonexistent. But on a wider understanding of terrorism, such as Held's above or Jaggar's in this chapter, the question is an intelligible one.

Attempts to provide a principled basis for either condemning all terrorist actions or leaving open the possibility that some terrorist acts may be morally justified frequently focus on the differences and similarities between war and terrorism. Those who use this approach often place their reasoning within the context of *just war theory,* which falls into two parts. The first part presents principles that are to be used to determine whether the war itself is just (*jus ad bellum* or "right to go to war"). The second presents principles to be used to determine whether the actions performed in the conduct of the war are just (*jus in bello* or "right conduct in war").

Just war theorists have given different accounts of the conditions that must hold before a nation has a right to go to war. The following statement is one way of capturing their central concerns. One nation (A) is justified in engaging in war with another nation (B) if and only if:

• A is attacked by B, or is attempting to help another nation C that has been attacked by B, or A or C are about to be attacked by B (*the just cause requirement*).

• The individuals in A who declare war on B are those members of A who have the legitimate authority to do so (*the legitimate authority requirement*).

• A's intentions in waging war are limited to repelling B's attack and establishing a fair peace (*the good intentions requirement*).

• A has a reasonable hope of successfully achieving the good it intends (*the reasonable hope of success requirement*).

• The good A can reasonably hope to achieve is proportional to the evils that can reasonably be expected to result from waging war (*the proportionality of just cause to means requirement*).

• A has exhausted all peaceful alternatives, and fighting the war is the last resort (*the last resort requirement*).

• A does not use or anticipate using immoral means in waging war (*the moral means requirement*).

In just war doctrine, two principles are central in determining what types of action are morally permissible in warfare:

1 *The principle of proportionality*—The level of force employed must be proportional to the good that the action is intended to achieve.

2 *The principle of discrimination*—Force should be used in a way that respects the difference between combatants and noncombatants.

The principle of discrimination is usually understood as prohibiting the direct intentional killing of *noncombatants.* In the conduct of wars, however, civilian deaths are sometimes unavoidable. Those who argue that some civilian deaths can be morally justified often invoke the *doctrine of double effect.* On this doctrine, civilian casualties are justifiable if their deaths, although foreseen, are not intended. (Some of the problems with the doctrine of double effect are discussed by Nathanson in this chapter.)

Moral evaluations of terrorism usually focus on the principle of discrimination. If the intentional infliction of harm on innocent civilians is an essential characteristic of terrorism, then, in the views of many, terrorism, which violates that principle, can never be morally justified. However, countless acts of war have targeted civilians. Think of the atomic bombing of Hiroshima or the bombing of Dresden in World War II. Such examples pose problems for those who would condemn all terrorism while refusing to condemn similar wartime actions. Stephen Nathanson, in this chapter, addresses the moral issues raised by this apparent discrepancy.

He suggests principles that could be used to distinguish between those wartime acts that are legitimate even when they harm innocent civilians, on the one hand, and illegitimate wartime acts and all terrorist acts, on the other. By contrast, Alison Jaggar, in this chapter, suggests that the principles used to determine whether a war is just (*jus ad bellum*) can also be used in judging the actions of terrorists, leaving open the possibility that some of the latter might be justified.

Most moral evaluations of terrorism focus on terrorist attacks and do not consider the reasons why terrorists employ such tactics. As we saw above, in evaluating wars as just or unjust, we ask not only if the means used in conducting the war were morally legitimate but also whether going to war was just in the first place. One of Jaggar's principles for evaluating terrorism is a version of the principle of last resort: Terrorist tactics must be a last resort. All other means of remedying the perceived injustice, including conventional warfare, must be unavailable or have failed.

In applying the principle of last resort, we would have to look at several factors. We would need to understand the causes that led to terrorism in order to determine if the cause is just. We would also have to look at what steps the group took to achieve its ends by other means. In doing this, we would need to determine what possibilities for peaceful resolution were available to it. This would require examining not only the acts of the terrorists but also those of the governments against which the terrorism is aimed. If actions by those governments were such as to make any peaceful resolutions impossible, then it seems as if the latter would bear some responsibility for the ensuing terrorism. Take, for example, the terrorism in South Africa that was directed against the policy of apartheid. If the government blocked every other avenue for achieving the end of apartheid, which involved gross violations of human rights, and left the groups fighting against it no other recourse, then the antiapartheid terrorist activities might be in keeping with the principle of last resort. Of course, there are other principles that would have to be satisfied as well.

SECURITY, HUMAN RIGHTS, AND CIVIL LIBERTIES

Time and again throughout its history, when the security of the United States has been seriously threatened, measures have been adopted that involved serious infringements on civil liberties and yet were upheld by the courts. In hindsight, government officials and others have often acknowledged that the infringements were unjust and that they played no essential role in achieving victory. A paradigm example of such misguided measures was the internment of Japanese and Japanese-Americans during World War II. Several challenges to the constitutionality of the infringements on the liberties and rights of Japanese and Japanese-Americans culminated in United States Supreme Court cases. In one such case, *Korematsu v. United States* (1944), the Court ruled against the challenger, Fred T. Korematsu, despite a great deal of disagreement among the justices. Excerpts from both the majority opinion written by Justice Black and a dissenting opinion written by Justice Murphy are reprinted in this chapter. Although in this and other cases, the Court upheld the constitutionality of the actions taken against Japanese-Americans, later presidents and a government-appointed commission appointed by Congress to investigate the treatment of Japanese-Americans during World War II acknowledged their wrongness. In 1988, President Reagan declared the Japanese internment a grave injustice. Korematsu himself was awarded the Presidential Medal of Freedom.

Once again, the United States is under serious threat of harm as illustrated by the attacks on September 11, 2001, as well as other terrorist threats. And once again infringements on civil liberties and violations of human rights are often held to be justified in the name of national security. Some of these measures are reflected in the U.S. treatment of prisoners held at Guantánamo Bay. Labeled as unlawful combatants, the detainees are said not to be entitled to the protections extended to prisoners of war by the Geneva Convention. At the same time, they are not considered to be criminals entitled to the legal protections built into the criminal justice system. In a reading in this chapter, David Luban discusses the moral issues raised by such imprisonments and argues that as long as it continues, "the war on terrorism" means the end of human rights for those "near enough to be touched by the fire of battle."

On the domestic front, various executive orders as well as the U.S.A. Patriot Act[5] are seen by many as a serious threat to civil liberties. Geoffrey R. Stone identifies the following as among the more questionable restrictions on freedom:

> . . . indefinite detention, with no access to judicial review, of more than a thousand noncitizens who were lawfully in the United States and had not been charged with any crime; blanket secrecy concerning the identity of these detainees; refusal to permit many of these detainees to communicate with an attorney; an unprecedented assertion of authority to eavesdrop on constitutionally protected attorney-client communications; secret deportation proceedings; the incarceration for more than two years of an American citizen, arrested on American soil, incommunicado, with no access to a lawyer, solely on the basis of an executive determination that he was an "enemy combatant"; significant new limitations on the scope of the Freedom of Information Act; expanded authority to conduct undercover infiltration and surveillance of political and religious groups; increased power to wiretap, engage in electronic eavesdropping, and covertly review Internet and e-mail communications; new power to secretly review banking, brokerage, and other financial records; and expanded authority to conduct clandestine physical searches.[6]

No one would deny that terrorism is currently a serious threat to the security of the United States and other countries throughout the world. Nor would anyone deny that governments have a responsibility to protect their people against such threats. But, as in other critical times, there is a risk that rights and civil liberties may be infringed upon unnecessarily in the interest of national security. Those who defend the most recent infringements on liberty frequently assert that there is a need to strike an appropriate balance between security and freedom. In one of this chapter's readings, Jeremy Waldron examines this assertion.

Jane S. Zembaty

---

[5]The U.S.A. Patriot Act (Uniting and Strengthening America by Providing Appropriate Tools Required to Intercept and Obstruct Terrorism) was enacted by Congress in 2001 and renewed, with some modifications, in 2006.

[6]Geoffrey R. Stone, *Perilous Times: Free Speech in Wartime* (New York: Norton, 2004), p. 552. Stone gives extensive documentation for these statements in endnotes on p. 689.

Can Terrorism Be Morally Justified?

Stephen Nathanson

In Nathanson's view, from a moral perspective, the central feature of terrorist acts is that they kill or injure innocent people or threaten them with serious harms. Since some violent acts committed in warfare also share this feature, Nathanson focuses on whether there can be a morally significant difference between acts of war and acts committed by terrorists. He examines, criticizes, and rejects several arguments that others have advanced to distinguish between legitimate acts of warfare and terrorist acts. In conclusion, Nathanson offers his "bend over backwards" rule as a principled basis for condemning terrorist acts, on the one hand, and for justifying legitimate acts of warfare, on the other. He also uses the rule to distinguish between morally unacceptable acts of warfare and legitimate ones.

Can terrorism be morally justified?

Even asking this question can seem like an insult—both to victims of terrorist actions and to moral common sense. One wants to say: if the murder of innocent people by terrorists is not clearly wrong, what is?

But the question is more complicated than it looks. We can see this by broadening our focus and considering some of the other beliefs held by people who condemn terrorism. Very few of us accept the pacifist view that all violence is wrong. Most of us believe that some acts of killing and injuring people are morally justified. Indeed, most of us think that war is sometimes justified, even though it involves organized, large-scale killing, injuring, and destruction and even though innocent civilians are usually among the victims of war. So, most of us believe that even the killing of innocent people is sometimes morally justified. It is this fact that makes the condemnation of terrorism morally problematic. We pick out terrorism for special condemnation because its victims are civilian, noncombatants rather than military or governmental officials, but we also believe that such killings are sometimes morally permissible. Seen in this broader context, judgments about terrorism often seem hypocritical.

Seen in a broader context, moral judgments of terrorism often seem hypocritical. They often presuppose self-serving definitions of "terrorism" that allow people to avoid labeling actions that they approve as instances of terrorism, even though these actions are indistinguishable from other acts that are branded with this negative label. On other occasions, moral judgments of terrorism rest on biased, uneven applications of moral principles to the actions of friends and foes. Principles that are cited to condemn the actions of foes are ignored when similar actions are committed by friends.

Reprinted with permission of the author from *Morality in Practice*, 7th ed. (Wadsworth, 2004), edited by James P. Sterba, pp. 602–610.

We need to ask then: Can people who believe that war is sometimes morally permissible consistently condemn terrorist violence? Or are such condemnations necessarily hypocritical and self-serving?

If we are to avoid hypocrisy, then we need both (a) a definition of terrorism that is neutral with respect to who commits the actions, and (b) moral judgments of terrorism that derive from the consistent, even-handed applications of moral criteria.

This paper aims to achieve both of these things. First, I begin with a definition of terrorism and then discuss why terrorism is always wrong. In addition, I want to show that the condemnation of terrorism does not come without other costs. A consistent approach to terrorism requires us to revise some common judgments about historical events and forces us to reconsider actions in which civilians are killed as "collateral damage" (i.e., side effects) of military attacks.

My aim, then, is to criticize both terrorist actions and a cluster of widespread moral views about violence and war. This cluster includes the following beliefs:

1 Terrorism is always immoral.

2 The allied bombing of cities in World War II was morally justified because of the importance of defeating Nazi Germany and Japan.

3 It is morally permissible to kill civilians in war if these killings are not intended.

The trouble with this cluster is that the first belief expresses an absolute prohibition of acts that kill innocent people while the last two are rather permissive. If we are to avoid inconsistency and hypocrisy, we must revise our views either (a) by accepting that terrorism is sometimes morally permissible, or (b) by judging that city bombings and many collateral damage killings are morally wrong. I will defend the second of these options.

DEFINING TERRORISM

I offer the following definition of terrorism to launch my discussion of the moral issues.[1] Terrorist acts have the following features:

1 They are acts of serious, deliberate violence or destruction.

2 They are generally committed by groups as part of a campaign to promote a political or social agenda.

3 They generally target limited numbers of people but aim to influence a larger group and/or the leaders who make decisions for the group.

4 They either kill or injure innocent people or pose a serious threat of such harms to them.

This definition helps in a number of ways. First, it helps us to distinguish acts of terrorism from other acts of violence. Nonviolent acts are not terrorist acts; nor are violent actions that are unrelated to a political or social agenda. Ironically, some terrible kinds of actions are not terrorist because they are too destructive. As condition 3 tells us, terrorism generally targets limited numbers of people in order to influence a larger group. Acts of genocide that aim to destroy a whole group are not acts of terrorism, but the reason why makes them only worse, not better.

Second, the definition helps us to identify the moral crux of the problem with terrorism. Condition 1 is not the problem because most of us believe that some acts of violence are morally justified. Condition 2 can't be the problem because anyone who believes in just causes of war must accept that some causes are so important that violence may be a legitimate way to promote them. Condition 3 is frequently met by permissible actions, as when we punish some criminals to deter other people from committing crimes. Condition 4 seems closer to what is essentially wrong with terrorism. If terrorism is always immoral, it is because it kills and injures innocent people.

As I have already noted, however, morally conscientious people sometimes want to justify acts that kill innocent people. If a blanket condemnation of terrorism is to be sustained, then we must either condemn all killings of innocent people, or we must find morally relevant differences between the killing of innocents by terrorists and the killing of innocents by others whose actions we find morally acceptable.

TERRORISM AND CITY BOMBING: THE SAME OR DIFFERENT?

Many people who condemn terrorism believe that city bombing in the war against Nazism was justified, even though the World War II bombing campaigns intentionally targeted cities and their inhabitants. This view is defended by some philosophical theorists, including Michael Walzer, in his book *Just and Unjust Wars* and G. Wallace in "Terrorism and the Argument from Analogy."[2] By considering these theorists, we can see if there are relevant differences that allow us to say that terrorism is always wrong but that the World War II bombings were morally justified.

One of the central aims of Michael Walzer's *Just and Unjust Wars* is to defend what he calls the "war convention," the principles that prohibit attacks on civilians in wartime. Walzer strongly affirms the principle of noncombatant immunity, calling it a "fundamental principle [that] underlies and shapes the judgments we make of wartime conduct." He writes:

> A legitimate act of war is one that does not violate the rights of the people against whom it is directed. . . . [N]o one can be threatened with war or warred against, unless through some act of his own he has surrendered or lost his rights.[3]

Unlike members of the military, civilians have not surrendered their rights in any way, and therefore, Walzer says, they may not be attacked.

Given Walzer's strong support for noncombatant immunity and his definition of terrorism as the "method of random murder of innocent people," it is no surprise that he condemns terrorism.[4] At one point, after describing a terrorist attack on an Algerian milk bar frequented by teenagers, he writes:

> Certainly, there are historical moments when armed struggle is necessary for the sake of human freedom. But if dignity and self-respect are to be the outcomes of that struggle, it cannot consist of terrorist attacks against children.[5]

Here and elsewhere, Walzer denounces terrorism because it targets innocent people.

Nonetheless, he claims that the aerial attacks on civilians by the British early in World War II were justified. In order to show why, he develops the concept of a "supreme emergency." Nazi Germany, he tells us, was no ordinary enemy; it was an "ultimate threat to everything decent in our lives."[6] Moreover, in 1940, the Nazi threat to Britain was imminent. German armies dominated Europe and sought to control the seas. Britain feared an imminent invasion by a country that threatened the basic values of civilization.

According to Walzer, the combination of the enormity and the imminence of the threat posed by Nazi Germany produced a supreme emergency, a situation in which the rules prohibiting attacks on civilians no longer held. If killing innocents was the only way to ward off this dreadful threat, then it was permissible. Since air attacks on German cities were the only means Britain had for inflicting harm on Germany, it was morally permissible for them to launch these attacks.

Walzer does not approve all of the city bombing that occurred in World War II. The emergency lasted, he thinks, only through 1942. After that, the threat diminished, and the constraints of the war convention should once again have been honored. In fact, the bombing of cities continued throughout the war, climaxing in massive attacks that killed hundreds of thousands of civilians: the bombing of Dresden, the fire bombings of Japanese cities by the United States, and the atomic bombings of Hiroshima and Nagasaki. According to Walzer, none of these later attacks were justified because the supreme emergency had passed.[7]

While Walzer's discussion begins with the special threat posed by Nazism, he believes that supreme emergencies can exist in more ordinary situations. In the end, he supports the view that if a single nation is faced by "a threat of enslavement or extermination[,]" then its "soldiers and statesmen [may] override the rights of innocent people for the sake of their own political community. . . ."[8] While he expresses this view with "hesitation and worry," he nevertheless broadens the reach of the concept of "supreme emergency" to include circumstances that arise in many wars.

The problem for Walzer is that his acceptance of the broad "supreme emergency" exception threatens to completely undermine the principle of noncombatant immunity that lies at the heart of his own view of the ethics of warfare. How can the principle of noncombatant immunity be fundamental if it can be overridden in some cases? Moreover, his condemnation of terrorism is weakened because it seems to be possible that people might resort to terrorism in cases that qualify as supreme emergencies, as when their own people are threatened by extermination or enslavement. Walzer's defense of the bombing of cities, then, seems to be inconsistent with his sweeping denunciation of terrorism.

WALLACE'S ARGUMENT FROM ANALOGY

While Walzer does not directly address the tension between the two parts of his view, G. Wallace explicitly tries to defend the view that terrorism is wrong and that the bombing of cities was justified. According to Wallace, the bombing campaign was justified because it satisfied all four of the following criteria:[9]

1 It was a measure of last resort.
2 It was an act of collective self-defense.
3 It was a reply in kind against a genocidal, racist aggressor.
4 It had some chance of success.

He then asks whether acts of terrorism might be justified by appeal to these very same criteria.

Wallace's answer is that terrorism cannot meet these criteria. Or, more specifically, he says that while any one of the criteria might be met by a terrorist act, all four of them cannot be satisfied. Why not? The problem is not with criteria 2 and 3; a community might well be oppressed by a brutal regime and might well be acting in its own defense. In these respects, its situation would be like that of Britain in 1940.

But, Wallace claims, conditions 1 and 4 cannot both be satisfied in this case. If the community has a good chance of success through the use of terrorism (thus satisfying condition 4), then other means of opposition might work as well, and terrorism will fail to be a last resort. Hence it will not meet condition 1. At the same time, if terrorist tactics are a last resort because all other means of opposition will fail, then the terrorist tactics are also likely to fail, in which case condition 4 is not met.

What Wallace has tried to show is that there are morally relevant differences between terrorism and the city bombings by Britain. Even if some of the criteria for justified attacks on civilians can be met by would-be terrorists, all of them cannot be. He concludes that "[E]ven if we allow that conditions (1) and (4) can be met separately, their joint satisfaction is impossible."[10]

Unfortunately, this comforting conclusion—that the British city bombing was justified but that terrorism cannot be—is extremely implausible. Both terrorism and city bombing involve the intentional killing of innocent human beings in order to promote an important political goal. Wallace acknowledges this but claims that the set of circumstances that justified city bombing could not possibly occur again so as to justify terrorism.

There is no basis for this claim, however. Wallace accepts that the right circumstances occurred in the past, and so he should acknowledge that it is at least possible for them to occur in the future. His conclusion ought to be that if city bombing was justifiable, then terrorism is in principle justifiable as well. For these reasons, I believe that Wallace, like Walzer, is logically committed to acknowledging the possibility of morally justified terrorism.

This is not a problem simply for these two authors. Since the historical memory of city bombing in the United States and Britain sees these as justifiable means of war, the dilemma facing these authors faces our own society. We condemn terrorists for intentionally killing innocent people while we think it was right to use tactics in our own wars that did the same. Either we must accept the view that terrorism can sometimes be justified, or we must come to see our own bombings of cities as violations of the prohibitions on killing civilians in wartime.[11]

TERRORISM, COLLATERAL DAMAGE, AND THE PRINCIPLE OF DOUBLE EFFECT

Many of us believe that wars are sometimes justified, but we also know that even if civilians are not intentionally killed, the deaths of civilians is a common feature of warfare. Indeed, during the twentieth century, civilian deaths became a larger and larger proportion of the total deaths caused by war. A person who believes that wars may be justified but that terrorism cannot be must explain how this can be.

One common approach focuses on the difference between intentionally killing civilians, as terrorists do, and unintentionally killing civilians, as sometimes happens in what we regard as legitimate acts of war. According to this approach, terrorism is wrong because it is intentional while so-called "collateral damage" killings and injuries are morally permissible because they are not intended.

This type of view is developed by Igor Primoratz in "The Morality of Terrorism."[12] Primoratz attempts to show why terrorism is morally wrong and how it differs from other acts of wartime killing that are morally permissible.

First, he makes it clear that, by definition, terrorism always involves the intentional killing of innocent people. He then offers a number of arguments to show why such killings are wrong. The first two have to do with the idea that persons are moral agents who are due a high level of respect and concern. He writes:

> [E]very human being is an individual, a person separate from other persons, with a unique, irreproducible thread of life and a value that is not commensurable with anything else.[13]

Given the incommensurable value of individual persons, it is wrong to try to calculate the worth of some hoped-for goal by comparison with the lives and deaths of individual people. This kind of calculation violates the ideal of giving individual lives our utmost respect and concern. Terrorists ignore this central moral ideal. They treat innocent people as political pawns, ignoring their individual worth and seeing their deaths simply as means toward achieving their goals.

In addition, Primoratz argues, terrorists ignore the moral relevance of guilt and innocence in their treatment of individuals. They attack people who have no responsibility for the alleged evils that the terrorists oppose and thus violate the principle that people should be treated in accord with what they deserve.

Terrorists, Primoratz tells us, also forsake the ideal of moral dialogue amongst equals. They not only decide who will live and who will die, but they feel no burden to justify their actions in ways that the victims might understand and accept. People who take moral ideals seriously engage in open discussion in order to justify their actions. They engage others in moral debate. Ideally, according to Primoratz, a moral person who harms others should try to act on reasons that are so compelling that they could be acknowledged by the victims. Terrorist acts cannot be justified to their victims, and terrorists are not even interested in trying to do so.[14]

Though these ideas are sketched out rather than fully developed, Primoratz successfully expresses some important moral values. Drawing on these values, he concludes that terrorism is incompatible with "some of the most basic moral beliefs many of us hold."[15]

Primoratz vs. Trotsky

Having tried to show why terrorism is wrong, Primoratz considers an objection put forward by Leon Trotsky, who defended terrorism as a revolutionary tactic. Trotsky claims that people who approve traditional war but condemn revolutionary violence are in a weak position because the differences between these are morally arbitrary. If wars that kill innocent people can be justified, Trotsky claims, then so can revolutions that kill innocent people.

Primoratz replies by arguing that there is an important moral difference between terrorism and some acts of war that kill innocent people. While he acknowledges that the "suffering of civilians . . . is surely inevitable not only in modern, but in almost all wars," Primoratz stresses that the moral evaluation of acts of killing requires that we "attend not only to the suffering inflicted, but also to the way it is inflicted."[16] By this, he means that we need, among other things, to see what the person who did the act intended.

To illustrate his point, he contrasts two cases of artillery attacks on a village. In the first case, the artillery attack is launched with the explicit goal of killing the civilian inhabitants of the village. The civilians are the target of the attack. This attack is the equivalent of terrorism since both intentionally target innocent people, and just like terrorism, it is immoral.

In a second case, the artillery attack is aimed at "soldiers stationed in the village." While the soldiers know that innocent people will be killed, that is not their aim.

> Had it been possible to attack the enemy unit without endangering the civilians in any way, they would certainly have done so. This was not possible, so they attacked although they knew that the attack would cause civilian casualties too; but they did their best to reduce those inevitable, but undesired consequences as much as possible.[17]

In this second case, the civilian deaths and injuries are collateral damage produced by an attack on a legitimate military target. That is the key difference between terrorism and legitimate acts of war. Terrorism is intentionally directed at civilians, while legitimate acts of war do not aim to kill or injure civilians, even when this is their effect.

Primoratz concludes that Trotsky and other defenders of terrorism are wrong when they equate war and terrorism. No doubt, the intentional killing of civilians does occur in war, and when it does, Primoratz would condemn it for the same reason he condemns terrorism. But if soldiers avoid the intentional killing of civilians, then their actions can be morally justified, even when civilians die as a result of what they do. As long as soldiers and revolutionaries avoid the intentional killing of innocent people, they will not be guilty of terrorist acts.

Problems with Primoratz's View

Primoratz's view has several attractive features. Nonetheless, it has serious weaknesses.

In stressing the role of intentions, Primoratz appeals to the same ideas expressed by what is called the "principle of double effect." According to this principle, we should evaluate actions by their intended goals rather than their actual consequences. An act that produces collateral damage deaths is an unintentional killing and hence is not wrong in the way that the same act would be if the civilians' deaths were intended.

While the principle of double effect is plausible in some cases, it is actually severely defective. To see this, suppose that the September 11 attackers had only intended to destroy the Pentagon and the World Trade Center and had no desire to kill anyone. Suppose that they knew, however, that thousands would die in the attack on the buildings. And suppose, following the attack, they said "We are not murderers. We did not mean to kill these people."

What would be our reaction? I very much doubt that we would think them less culpable. They could not successfully justify or excuse their actions by saying that although they foresaw the deaths of many people, these deaths were not part of their aim. We would certainly reject this defense. But if we would reject the appeal to double effect in this case, then we should do so in others.

In Primoratz's example, the artillery gunners attack the village with full knowledge of the high probability of civilian deaths. The artillery gunners know they will kill innocent people, perhaps even in large numbers, and they go ahead with the attack anyway. If it would not be enough for my imagined September 11 attackers to say that they did not intend to kill people, then it is not enough for Primoratz's imagined soldiers to say that they did not mean to kill the villagers when they knew full well that this would result from their actions.

If we accept Primoratz's defense of collateral damage killings, his argument against terrorism is in danger of collapsing because terrorists can use Primoratz's language to show that their actions, too, may be justifiable. If Primoratz succeeds in justifying the collateral damage killings and if the distinction between these killings and terrorism cannot rest solely on whether the killings are intentional, then the criteria that he uses may justify at least some terrorist acts. Like the soldiers in his example, the terrorists may believe that the need for a particular attack is "so strong and urgent that it prevailed over the prohibition of killing or maiming a comparatively small number of civilians." Consistency would require Primoratz to agree that the terrorist act was justified in this case.

Recall, too, Primoratz's claim that actions need to be capable of being justified to the victims themselves. Would the victims of the artillery attack accept the claim that the military urgency justified the "killing or maiming a comparatively small number of civilians?"[18] Why should they accept the sacrifice of their own lives on the basis of this reasoning?

In the end, then, Primoratz does not succeed in showing why terrorism is immoral while collateral damage killing can be morally justified. Like Wallace and Walzer, he has trouble squaring the principles that he uses to condemn terrorism with his own approval of attacks that produce foreseeable collateral damage deaths.

The problem revealed here is not merely a problem for a particular author. The view that collateral damage killings are permissible because they are unintended is a very widespread view. It is the view that United States officials appealed to when our bombings in Afghanistan produced thousands of civilian casualties.[19] Our government asserted that we did not intend these deaths to occur, that we were aiming at legitimate targets, and that the civilian deaths were merely collateral damage. Similar excuses are offered when civilians are killed by cluster bombs and land mines, weapons whose delayed detonations injure and kill people indiscriminately, often long after a particular attack is over.[20]

There are many cases in which people are morally responsible for harms that they do not intend to bring about, but if these harms can be foreseen, their claims that they "did not mean to do it" are not taken seriously. We use labels like "reckless disregard" for human life or "gross negligence" to signify that wrongs have been done, even though they were not deliberate. When such actions lead to serious injury and death, we condemn such actions from a moral point of view, just as we condemn terrorism. The principle of double effect does not show that these condemnations are mistaken. If we want to differentiate collateral damage killings from terrorism so as to be consistent in our moral judgments, we will need something better than the principle of double effect and the distinction between intended and unintended effects.

A SKETCH OF A DEFENSE

I want to conclude by sketching a better rationale for the view that terrorist attacks on civilians are always wrong but that some attacks that cause civilian deaths and injuries as unintended consequences are morally justified.

I have argued that a central problem with standard defenses of collateral damage killings is that they lean too heavily on the distinction between what is intended and what is foreseen. This distinction, when used with the doctrine of double effect, is too slippery and too permissive. As I noted above, it might provide an excuse for the September 11 attacks if (contrary to fact) the attackers were only targeting the World Trade Center *building* and the Pentagon *building* and did not actually aim to kill innocent civilians.

Michael Walzer makes a similar criticism of the double effect principle. "Simply not to intend the death of civilians is too easy," he writes. "What we look for in such cases is some sign of a positive commitment to save civilian lives."[21] Walzer calls his revised version the principle of "double intention." It requires military planners and soldiers to take positive steps to avoid or minimize these evils, even if these precautions increase the danger to military forces.

Walzer's rule is a step in the right direction, but we need to emphasize that the positive steps must be significant. They cannot be *pro forma* or minimal efforts. In order to show a proper respect for the victims of these attacks, serious efforts must be made to avoid death and injury to them. I suggest the following set of requirements for just, discriminate fighting, offering them as a sketch rather than a full account. The specifics might have to be amended, but the key point is that serious efforts must be made to avoid harm to civilians. Not intending harm is not enough. In addition, military planners must really exert themselves. They must, as we say, *bend over backwards* to avoid harm to civilians. For example, they must:

1 Target attacks as narrowly as possible on military resources;

2 Avoid targets where civilian deaths are extremely likely;

3 Avoid the use of inherently indiscriminate weapons (such as land mines and cluster bombs) and inherently indiscriminate strategies (such as high-altitude bombing of areas containing both civilian enclaves and military targets); and

4 Accept that when there are choices between damage to civilian lives and damage to military personnel, priority should be given to saving civilian lives.

If a group has a just cause for being at war and adheres to principles like these, then it could be said to be acknowledging the humanity and value of those who are harmed by its actions. While its attacks might expose innocent people to danger, its adherence to these principles would show that it was not indifferent to their well-being. In this way, it would show that its actions lack the features that make terrorism morally objectionable.

Why is this? Because the group is combining its legitimate effort to defend itself or others with serious efforts to avoid civilian casualties. The spirit of their effort is captured in the phrase I have already used: "bending over backwards." The "bend over backwards" ideal is superior to the principle of double effect in many ways. First, it goes beyond the weak rule of merely requiring that one not intend to kill civilians. Second, while the double effect rule's distinction between intended and unintended results permits all sorts of fudges and verbal tricks, the "bend over backwards" rule can be applied in a more objective and realistic way. It would be less likely to approve sham compliance than is the doctrine of double effect.

The "bend over backwards" rule might even satisfy Primoratz's requirement that acts of violence be justifiable to their victims. Of course, no actual victim is likely to look favorably on attacks by others that will result in the victim's death or serious injury. But suppose we could present the following situation to people who might be victims of an attack (a condition that most of us inhabit) and have them consider it from something like Rawls's veil of ignorance. We would ask them to consider the following situation:

- Group A is facing an attack by group B; if successful, the attack will lead to death or the severest oppression of group A.
- The only way that group A can defend itself is by using means that will cause death and injury to innocent members of group B.
- You are a member of one of the groups, but you do not know which one.

Would you approve of means of self-defense that will kill and injure innocent members of B in order to defend group A?

In this situation, people would not know whether they would be victims or beneficiaries of whatever policy is adopted. In this circumstance, I believe that they would reject a rule permitting either intentional or indiscriminate attacks on civilians. Thus, they would reject terrorism as a legitimate tactic, just as they would reject indiscriminate attacks that kill and injure civilians.

At the same time, I believe that they would approve a rule that combined a right of countries to defend themselves against aggression with the restrictions on means of fighting contained in the "bend over backwards" rule. This would have the following benefits. If one were a member of a group that had been attacked, one's group would have a right of self-defense. At the same time, if one were an innocent citizen in the aggressor country, the defenders would be required to take serious steps to avoid injury or death to you and other civilians.

If people generally could accept such a rule, then actions that adhere to that rule would be justifiable to potential victims as well as potential attackers. This would include actions that cause civilian casualties but that adhere to the "bend over backwards" principle.

I believe that this sort of approach achieves what nonpacifist critics of terrorism want to achieve. It provides a principled basis for condemning terrorism, no matter who it is carried out by, and a principled justification of warfare that is genuinely defensive. Moreover, the perspective is unified in a desirable way. Terrorist actions cannot be morally justified because the *intentional* targeting of civilians is the most obvious kind of violation of the "bend over backwards" rule.

At the same time that these principles allow for the condemnation of terrorism, they are immune to charges of hypocrisy because they provide a basis for criticizing not only terrorist acts but also the acts of any group that violates the "bend over backwards" rule, either by attacking civilians directly or by failing to take steps to avoid civilian deaths.

CONCLUSION

Can terrorism be morally justified? Of course not. But if condemnations of terrorism are to have moral credibility, they must rest on principles that constrain our own actions and determine our judgments of what we ourselves do and have done. To have moral credibility, opponents of terrorism must stand by the principles underlying their condemnations, apply their principles in an evenhanded way, and bend over backwards to avoid unintended harms to civilians. Only in this way can we begin inching back to a world in which those at war honor the moral rules that prohibit the taking of innocent human lives. As long as condemnations of terrorism are tainted by hypocrisy, moral judgments will only serve to inflame people's hostilities rather than reminding them to limit and avoid serious harms to one another.

NOTES

1 For development and defense of this definition, see my "Prerequisites for Morally Credible Condemnations of Terrorism," in William Crotty, ed., *The Politics of Terrorism: Consequences for an Open Society* (Boston: Northeastern University Press, 2003).

2 Michael Walzer. *Just and Unjust Wars* (New York: Basic Books, 1977); Gerry Wallace, "Terrorism and the Argument from Analogy," *Journal of Moral and Social Studies,* vol. 6 (1991), 149–160.

3 Walzer, 135.

4 Walzer, 197.

5 Walzer, 205.

6 Walzer, 253.

7 Kenneth Brown, "'Supreme Emergency': A Critique of Michael Walzer's Moral Justification for Allied Obliteration Bombing in World War II," *Manchester College Bulletin of the Peace Studies Institute,* 1983 (13, nos. 1–2), 6–15.

8 Walzer, 254.

9 Wallace, 155.

10 Wallace, 155–156.

11 See Rawls on city bombing and the atomic bombings in *The Law of Peoples* and *Collected Papers.*

12 Igor Primoratz, "The Morality of Terrorism?" *Journal of Applied Philosophy,* vol. 14 (1997), 222. Primoratz defends his definition of terrorism in "What Is Terrorism?" *Journal of Applied Philosophy,* vol. 7 (1990), 129–138. These subjects are also helpfully discussed in Haig Khatchadourian, "Terrorism and Morality," *Journal of Applied Philosophy,* vol. 5 (1988), 131–145.

13 Primoratz, 224.

14 For a similar idea, see Thomas Nagel, *Equality and Partiality* (New York: Oxford, 1991), 23. "[W]e are looking for principles to deal with conflict that can at some level be endorsed by everyone. . . ."

15 Primoratz, "The Morality of Terrorism," 225.

16 Primoratz, 227.

17 Primoratz, 227.

18 Primoratz, 228.

19 Marc Herold, an economist at the University of New Hampshire, studied foreign press reports and has concluded that over 3,500 Afghan civilians were killed in the first 2 months of U.S. attacks in Afghanistan (http://pubpages.unh.edu/~mwherold and http://www.media-alliance.org/article.php?story=20031108153733172). The *Boston Globe* estimated 1,000 civilian deaths, but their estimate is based on investigations at 14 sites, which they admit "represent only a small fraction of the total sites targeted by the 18,000 bombs, missiles, and ordnance fired by U.S. forces since October. . . ." See John Donnelly and Anthony Shadid, "Civilian toll in US raids put at 1,000," *Boston Globe*, Feb. 17, 2002, 1. For further information on attacks on civilian targets, see John Donnelly, "U.S. targeting of vehicles is detailed," *Boston Globe*, Feb. 19, 2002, 1.

20 According to Human Rights Watch, cluster bombs "have proven to be a serious and long-lasting threat to civilians, soldiers, peacekeepers, and even clearance experts." Human Rights Watch, "Cluster Bombs in Afghanistan," www.hrw.org/backgrounder/arms/cluster-bck1031.htm.

21 Walzer, 155–156.

QUESTIONS

1   Is Nathanson correct in holding that being part of a campaign to promote a political or social agenda is one of the defining features of terrorism?

2   Do you agree with Nathanson that it is possible to draw a principled distinction between (a) terrorist actions and (b) some acts of warfare that result in harm to innocent people?

What Is Terrorism, Why Is It Wrong, and Could It Ever Be Morally Permissible?

Alison M. Jaggar

Jaggar offers several criteria to be used in evaluating answers to questions about the meaning of terrorism and applies them when developing her account. Jaggar's definition of terrorism is very broad. It allows for the possibility of state terrorism. It also allows attacks on nonhuman targets—such as infrastructure,

Reprinted with permission of the publisher from *Journal of Social Philosophy,* vol. 36, no. 2 (Summer 2005), pp. 202, 205–209, 211–217. © 2005 Blackwell Publishing Inc.

businesses, or buildings of religious, political, or other symbolic significance—to count as instances of terrorism. On Jaggar's definition, it is conceptually possible for some acts of terrorism to be morally justified. However, in explaining why terrorism is morally reprehensible, Jaggar makes it clear that the burden of proof of justifying some specific act of terrorism is a heavy one. Jaggar concludes by suggesting conditions, grounded in just war theory, for determining whether an act of terrorism is morally justified.

In the liberal democracies of North America and the European Union, terrorism is almost universally condemned. Moreover, few wish to question the "moral clarity" that denies any "moral equivalence" between terrorists and those who fight them (Held 2004, 59–60). However, the seeming consensus on the moral reprehensibility of terrorism is undermined by substantial disagreement about just what terrorism is. The United Nations has long been unable to agree on workable criteria for terrorism—though it may now be moving to a new consensus—and even the various agencies of the U.S. government disagree with each other. The primary purpose of this paper is to propose an account of terrorism capable of facilitating a more productive moral debate. I conclude by opening—though certainly not closing—the question of when, if ever, terrorism might be morally permissible. . . .

WHAT IS TERRORISM?

. . . I should like to propose an . . . account of terrorism. In undertaking this task, I assume that a good account meets the following desiderata:

1 Conservatism. First, a good account disturbs existing usage as little as possible. Proposals to modify common interpretations of a term must be given a plausible and appropriate rationale.

2 Consistency and non-arbitrariness. One appropriate rationale for modifying existing usage is an argument that such a change will improve consistency. Proposals for expanding or limiting the ways in which a term is used often point to continuities or discontinuities between the proposed usage and the term's central and generally accepted meanings.

3 Precision. Another appropriate rationale for modifying a term's interpretation is an argument that such a modification would improve precision, helping differentiate among phenomena that may otherwise be confused. For instance, a good account of terrorism should facilitate understanding terrorism's relation to such phenomena as war, guerrilla war, crime, revenge, hostage taking, and so on. Although precision is desirable, definitions should not be sharpened to the point where they remove genuine uncertainties by *fiat*. Concepts are always somewhat fuzzy, especially morally laden concepts, and dispute over borderline cases can never be excluded completely.

4 Impartiality. Finally, any term that has a moral dimension should be interpreted in such a way as to resist moral arbitrariness and bias. A good account should be impartial in the sense of not begging disputed moral and political questions, leaving these open to be debated on their merits.

Webster's Dictionary defines "terrorism" as the use of terror and violence to intimidate and subjugate, especially as a political weapon or policy, and as the intimidation and subjugation so produced. This definition leaves open several disputed questions about terrorism, which I will discuss in turn, drawing on the desiderata identified above. The account that I end up proposing is more inclusive than that implied by much recent usage but I suggest that it is more consistent, precise and impartial.

The Purposes or Goals of Terrorism

It is generally agreed that the immediate purpose of terrorism is to create a climate of terror. Thus, acts of terror are often marked by a concern for symbolic and dramatic effect; tumbrils rolling toward the guillotine were a powerful spectacle. As the nineteenth century anarchists put it, terrorism is "propaganda by the deed."

Can anything be said about terrorism's longer-range goals? Webster's definition seems to require that terrorism be ideologically or politically motivated, a suggestion that accords with the original Jacobin case and with much common usage, including my own in earlier work (Jaggar 2003). Defining terrorism as politically motivated meets the desideratum of conservatism, but I now suggest that this requirement be dropped because retaining it violates the remaining desiderata. First, it is empirically arbitrary to deny that the deliberate creation of terror for reasons that are unprincipled or personally motivated is indeed terrorism; if gang violence or even domestic violence is otherwise indistinguishable from politically motivated violence, acknowledging either as terrorist consistently extends the term. Second, insisting that terrorism be politically motivated is incompatible with the desideratum of precision, because the distinction between personal and political is often unclear, both in principle and in practice. In principle, theorists such as feminists contest the distinction, speaking of the politics of personal life and arguing that domestic violence is sometimes a form of terrorism (Card 2003); in practice, personal and political motivations are often intertwined, as in the case of a strongman who seizes state power in order to enrich himself from the sale of its resources. Thus, requiring that terrorism be politically or ideologically motivated will frequently result in indeterminacy concerning whether or not specific threats or intimidation are terrorist. Third and finally, it is morally arbitrary to withhold the usually pejorative term "terrorism" from any violence intended to create a climate of terror.

Because terrorists employ means that are widely perceived as evil or crazy, their long-range goals are often dismissed as evil or crazy but ends can be distinguished conceptually from means; *ius ad bellum* is distinct from *ius in bello*. Although non-ideological forms of terrorism leave little space for raising questions of moral justification, the use of terrorism to promote political or ideological ends raises significant moral questions. If a definition of "terrorism" is to be impartial, it must separate the moral assessment of terrorists' ends from the moral assessment of the means they choose to promote them. Therefore, I propose an account of "terrorism" that leaves open the possibility that its goals may be political or personal, just or unjust, noble or base.

The Objects or Targets of Terrorism

Terrorism uses extreme fear to subjugate and intimidate. Carl Wellman notes that the direct target of terrorist violence or threats is usually its secondary rather than its primary target; the primary target is usually a wider population that the terrorists wish to intimidate (Wellman 1979).

Little philosophical discussion has occurred concerning the identity of terrorism's primary (though indirect) targets. If terrorism is understood as motivated exclusively [by] ideological or political goals, the primary targets of terrorism presumably must be those whom the terrorists can influence politically. However a more inclusive account, which allows for the possibility that terrorism might not be ideologically motivated, sets no *a priori* limit on the individuals or groups that might be terrorism's indirect (though primary) targets. They might be governments, populations, political factions, demographic groups (racial, caste, ethnic, religious, gender, sexual), gangs, families, or even individuals.

The identity of terrorism's direct (though secondary) targets has been discussed more explicitly and most accounts of terrorism stipulate that its direct targets be civilian. This is true of the definition accepted by the State Department of the United States and of the definition emerging in international law, though a few philosophers disagree.[1] I propose that the targets of terrorism be identified not as civilians *simpliciter* but instead as civilians who are innocent by Jeffrie Murphy's helpful definition of innocence in war. In Murphy's view, innocence in war does not mean overall legal or moral innocence; rather it means being a non-combatant. Murphy argues that combatants include all those engaged in the attempt to destroy you, whatever their place in the chain of command or responsibility; thus, they include not only frontline military personnel but also the civilians who issue orders to those personnel. This account assumes a context of war between states but it is also adaptable to situations of popular uprising against unpopular or colonial governments. Murphy recognizes that his account of combatant status does not eliminate borderline cases, such as workers in factories that make products both for daily life and for war, but he asserts that these are cases of genuine uncertainty, not to be resolved by definitional *fiat*.[2] His definition leaves open the possibility that armed adult settlers who colonize a territory already inhabited by others perhaps should be counted as combatants rather than innocent civilians.

In contemporary usage, terrorism includes attacks not only on human but also on non-human targets, such as infrastructure, businesses, homes, and buildings of religious, political, or other symbolic significance. Direct threats to such targets are often effective in causing terror; indeed, people's lives become impossible if enough of their infrastructure is damaged. For this reason, intentionally destroying water supplies and power sources or harming the natural environment, through means such as defoliation or uranium poisoning, is terrorist if those primarily affected are innocent civilians.

The Agents of Terrorism

The most significant shift in the usage of "terrorism" over the past two centuries has been the move away from recognizing states as possible agents of terrorism.

However, if our account of terrorism is not only to be compatible with the original usage but also to be consistent, precise, and impartial, the possibility of state terrorism should be acknowledged.

Outside the United States, most people are well aware that governments or states may create terror in many ways. Sometimes governments terrorize segments of their own populations by means of discriminatory law enforcement and even legislation; examples include officially sanctioned violence against Jews and gypsies and the regimes of racist apartheid in South Africa and gender apartheid in Afghanistan or Saudi Arabia. Sometimes governments terrorize their own populations covertly rather than overtly, using unofficial militias to assassinate political opponents or labor leaders. In the 1970s and 1980s, extra-judicial death squads linked with governments were common in several Latin American countries. Governments may also use terrorist tactics to intimidate foreign rather than local populations. In wartime, states may use terrorism against enemy populations; for instance, they may initiate campaigns of looting and rape or they may use weapons that predictably incur large civilian casualties. They may even order direct attacks on civilian targets; the United States bombing of Japan at the end of World War II was described routinely at the time as terror bombing. Finally, covert state terrorism, like overt terrorism, sometimes extends beyond a country's own borders. In the 1980s, the U.S. government supported the so-called "contras" (counter-revolutionaries) in Nicaragua, who sought to undermine the Sandinista government by attacking infrastructure such as farms and clinics.

Denying the possibility of state terrorism is not only incompatible with the original usage of the term; it is also inconsistent, arbitrary, and biased. State terrorism has always caused far more harm than non-state terrorism, since the resources available to states are typically far more powerful and destructive than those available to private individuals or small groups, and it should remain central in our understanding terrorism. Recognizing the possibility of state terrorism reduces the bias against the weak implicit in accounts that deny this possibility, while still leaving completely open the question of whether terrorism might ever be morally justified.

The Methods of Terrorism

Since terrorism intends to intimidate or subjugate, it is natural to question how it is distinguished from other forms of threat or coercion. Because terror is an extreme state of fear, induced by threats perceived as especially horrifying, minor threats or damage do not ordinarily count as terrorist. However, since different things horrify different people, terrorism cannot be identified by reference to any particular method of intimidation. Cruelty to animals, especially pets, might be enough to induce terror in some people; others may be terrified by the prospect of social humiliation. Terrorist practices are distinguished from more ordinary threats not because they involve any particular methods of producing fear, but instead because they are intended to create a state of fear that is acute and long-lasting enough to influence future behavior. This is why terrorist attacks are often spectacular and directed toward symbolic targets. Typically, they are not "one-off" threats or atrocities but instead parts of wider campaigns of intimidation or "reigns" of terror, intersecting with other forms of struggle and negotiation (Tilly 2004, 10).

Proposed Account of Terrorism

The preceding discussion suggests the following account of terrorism:

> Terrorism is the use of extreme threats or violence designed to intimidate or subjugate governments, groups, or individuals. It is a tactic of coercion intended to promote further ends that in themselves may be good, bad or indifferent. Terrorism may be practiced by governments or international bodies or forces, sub-state groups or even individuals. Its threats or violence are aimed directly or immediately at the bodies or belongings of innocent civilians but these are typically terrorists' secondary targets; the primary targets of terrorists are the governments, groups or individuals that they wish to intimidate.

This account is quite inclusive, categorizing as terrorist several classes of action excluded by other recent accounts, but it is also precise because it distinguishes terrorism conceptually from a number of other phenomena with which it is often conflated. . . .

SOME ADVANTAGES OF THE PROPOSED ACCOUNT OF TERRORISM

. . . Although the public image of terrorism has changed over two centuries, its moral connotations have not improved. Unlike war, which is generally regarded as sometimes justifiable and even glorious, terrorism is widely thought to be inexcusably wrong and it has been integrated into the lexicon of war in a way that aligns it with the negative side of many dichotomies that characterize this lexicon. The terrorist is contrasted with the true warrior, he fights for some ideology rather than to defend his country, his cause is illegitimate rather than legitimate, he is uncivilized rather than civilized, undisciplined rather than disciplined, a bandit, barbarian, or savage. Whereas the soldier is brave, the terrorist is cowardly; he uses means that are treacherous and dishonorable rather than open and honorable; he is not above resorting to weapons of mass destruction. He is not a warrior but a murderer. Because of its negative moral associations, terrorism is much more likely to be attributed to "them" rather than to "us." As Held puts it, what "they" do is terrorism and what "we" do is not (Held 2004, 65). If "we" do anything that looks at all like terrorism, we call ourselves "freedom fighters" or "martyrs," or "law enforcers."

Although I dispute many of the dichotomies that characterize the contemporary vocabulary of war and although I do not believe that it is always "they" rather than "we" who are terrorist, I share the view that terrorism is bad and my account illuminates why it is so morally repugnant.

First, terrorism is morally repugnant because terrorists engage in coercion and intimidation, which are regarded ordinarily as morally wrong. Moreover, terrorists seek to produce not mere anxiety or apprehension but rather widespread, acute and long-lasting fear and to do this they use threats or violence that are especially horrifying.

Second, terrorism is morally repugnant because terrorists harm or threaten those who have not harmed them and do not threaten them, people who can in no way be said to deserve the harm.

By clarifying these elements, the proposed definition explains the widespread belief that terrorism is morally wrong and shows why the burden of justifying it is heavy.

Although my proposed account does not present terrorism as morally neutral and indeed clarifies why it is morally reprehensible, it is nonetheless impartial in that it does not close disputed questions arbitrarily or by *fiat*. Instead, it offers criteria to address such questions. Thus, by leaving open the question of who may be agents of terrorism, excluding none by stipulation, it counters the moral bias of recent usage, which tends to obscure and so justify terrorist intimidation by official forces. . . . The account's willingness to recognize state terrorism also expands the universe of moral discourse by making it possible to look beyond specific incidents or practices, such as disappearances or torture, and enabling us to question whether social institutions might be systematically terrorist. It allows us to question whether trade sanctions or embargos against economically weak countries might sometimes be terrorist (Gordon 2002) and to envision the possibility that not only specific practices of law enforcement might be terrorist but also whole systems of legislation, such as those that mandate race or gender apartheid.

Finally, the account proposed does not constrain moral discourse by stipulating that terrorism can never be morally justified; instead, it allows important moral questions to remain open, while showing how difficult they are to answer.

IS TERRORISM EVER MORALLY PERMISSIBLE?

. . . Terrorism is certainly heinous but that something is heinous does not entail that it is prohibited in all circumstances; it merely entails that anyone wishing to argue its moral permissibility bears a heavy burden of proof. As the proposed definition brings out, terrorism involves threats and violence against innocent civilians, who are used as means to the ends of others. However, most people who believe that war is sometimes justified also believe that it is occasionally morally justified to threaten and knowingly harm innocent civilians and to use some people as means to others' ends; such thinking is inherent in the doctrine of double effect, for instance, as well as in the expression "necessary evil." In his doctrine of a "Supreme Emergency," Michael Walzer argues that very extreme circumstances may occasionally justify the use of horrifying means to achieve ends that have great moral significance (Walzer 1977).

Although war is bad, it is often justified by appeal to various just war principles. However these principles specifically prohibit terrorism because this deliberately targets or fails adequately to protect innocent civilians, and so violates non-combatant immunity or protection, one of the two fundamental criteria regulating the just use of force, *ius in bello*. Nevertheless, it is not inconceivable that very extreme circumstances might justify violating such immunity; for instance, R. M. Hare contends that at least some of the terrorism practiced by the European Resistance during World War II might have been morally justified (Hare 1979).

I cannot explore such questions here but I would like to end with a suggestion that may serve as a starting point for a more careful and comprehensive discussion. The suggestion is that the traditional *ius ad bellum* criteria defining the right to resort to force also suggest several necessary, and perhaps jointly sufficient, conditions for justifying terrorism. For instance:

1 Just cause. For terrorism to be morally permissible, a necessary though certainly not sufficient condition is that it must be intended to secure people's most basic rights.

2 Competent authority. Early versions of just war theory limited permissible uses of force to those authorized by public authorities, a statist bias that made it impossible to justify uprisings against those authorities. Current international law recognizes rebel movements as having "belligerent status" if they control their territory but even this might-makes-right criterion may be too stringent since many rebel movements, especially in their early stages, are too weak to control the territory in which they operate, at least by day (Lackey 1989, 29–31). The question of when terrorists may legitimately claim to represent some oppressed population is difficult to answer, both in principle and in practice, although some indication may be provided by the extent of popular protest or rejoicing over terrorist acts.

3 Right intention. For their conduct to have a chance of being justified, terrorists must be convinced that all of the conditions necessary to justifying a war must be met. If terrorists are able to choose whether or not to participate in terrorist activity while military personnel are conscripted, then their subjective beliefs are even more important to assessing the conduct of terrorists than to assessing the conduct of official military personnel.

4 Proportionality. The use of force is justified in traditional just war theory only if the overall good it achieves is greater than the harm it causes. Since terrorism is even more atrocious than war, for reasons given above, the cause of the terrorist must be overwhelming in its righteousness. Only massive and systematic violations of human rights, not small injustices, could ever begin to justify the adoption of terrorist tactics and use of these tactics must be kept to a minimum, in terms of both quantity and quality.

5 Last resort. Terrorist tactics must be a last resort. All other means of remedying the perceived injustice, including conventional warfare, must be unavailable or have failed.

6 Reasonable hope of success. Those waging a just war must have a reasonable hope of success in achieving their ends. Because terrorism is so reprehensible, it seems plausible to insist that terrorism can be justified only when the hope of success is much more certain than required to justify war.

7 The aim of peace. Like a just war, any justified terrorism should aim at a just peace.

Whether these (or any other) conditions for justifying terrorism are ever met in practice will always be a matter of dispute. However, dramatically accelerating political and economic inequality, on both a national and international level, is likely to encourage increasing numbers of people to believe more frequently that they are met. For instance, as Held notes, the growing asymmetry of warfare makes it increasingly difficult for forces on the weaker side to attack the actual combatants of powerful countries. (Held 2004, 61). Similarly, as poverty deepens and ever larger populations are politically marginalized in countries run by authoritarian and well-armed governments, increasing numbers of marginalized and impoverished people are likely to regard their cause as just and terrorism as their only option.

Finally, when anti-government terrorism occurs, we may ask whether it is ever morally justified for powerful governments to strike back with terrorist tactics. French argues that it may sometimes be morally justified for the weaker party in an asymmetric conflict to abandon conventional *ius in bello* restrictions on the conduct of warfare but that this party then cannot complain if the stronger side also abandons those restrictions. She contends, in other words, that both sides must be constrained by the same rules (French 2003). I agree that the conduct of all parties in any conflict should be constrained by the same moral principles but I do not think that these principles necessarily require that all sides face identical moral constraints on their conduct. A powerful government cannot justify its use of terrorism simply by noting that its weaker opponents employ this strategy. In order to justify its use of terrorism, the powerful government would have to show, among other things, that no other means of continuing the conflict were available to it and, in an asymmetrical conflict, it is much more likely that the weaker than the stronger side will be able to make this argument convincingly. Finally, the use of terrorism by a powerful government would undermine that government's claim to legitimacy because "official disregard" for human rights is more egregious than private violations of rights (Pogge 2002, chap. 2).

NOTES

1 Walzer (2002) contends that the targets of terrorism are civilian but Virginia Held refuses to limit "terrorism" to attacks on civilian targets, because she argues that this limitation is inconsistent with existing usage, which typically describes isolated attacks on military targets as terrorist. In addition, she contends that this limitation would put the burden of being a "legitimate target" exclusively on the ordinary soldiers and sailors who are the lowest levels of the military hierarchy (Held 2004, 63–66).
2 Murphy also suggests the moral principle that individuals should be assumed "noncombatant until proven otherwise" (Murphy 1985, 66).

REFERENCES

Card, Claudia. 2003. "Making War on Terrorism in Response to 9/11." In *Terrorism and International Justice,* ed. James P. Sterba. Oxford and New York: Oxford University Press.

French, Shannon E. 2003. "Murderers, Not Warriors: The Moral Distinction between Terrorists and Legitimate Fighters in Asymmetric Conflicts." In *Terrorism and International Justice,* ed. James P. Sterba. Oxford and New York: Oxford University Press.

Gordon, Joy. 2002. "Cool War. Economic Sanctions as a Weapon of Mass Destruction." In *Harper's Magazine* (November). Retrieved from http://harpers.org/CoolWar.html.

Hare, R. M. 1979. "On Terrorism." *Journal of Value Inquiry* 13: 240–49.

Held, Virginia. 2004. "Terrorism and War." *The Journal of Ethics* 8: 59–75.

Jaggar, Alison M. 2003. "Responding to the Evil of Terrorism." *Hypatia* 18:1 (Winter): 175–82.

Lackey, Douglas P. 1989. *The Ethics of War and Peace.* Englewood Cliffs, NJ: Prentice Hall.

Murphy, Jeffrie. 1985, "The Killing of the Innocent." In *The Ethics of War and Nuclear Deterrence,* ed. James P. Sterba. Belmont, CA: Wadsworth, 61–67.

Pogge, Thomas. 2002. *World Poverty and Human Rights.* Cambridge, UK: Polity Press; Malden, MA: Blackwell Publishers. Inc.

Tilly, Charles. 2004. "Terror, Terrorism, Terrorists." *Sociological Theory* 22:1 (March): 5–13.

Walzer, Michael. 1977. *Just and Unjust Wars: A Moral Argument with Historical Illustrations.* New York: Basic Books.

———. 2002. "Five Questions about Terrorism." *Dissent* 49: 5–10.

Wellman, Carl. 1979. "On Terrorism Itself." *Journal of Value Inquiry,* 13: 250–58.

QUESTIONS

1 Jaggar offers a very broad definition of terrorism. In her view, for example, even domestic violence could be construed as terrorism. Do you agree with her definition?

2 Do you agree with the criteria Jaggar offers for determining if an act of terrorism is morally justified? Why or why not?

The War on Terrorism and the End of Human Rights

David Luban

Luban distinguishes between two models of state action—the war model and the criminal law model—and explains the protections built into both. He argues that in its war on terrorism, the U.S. government has blurred the distinction between these models and adopted a hybrid war-law model in its treatment of terrorist suspects, thereby denying them the protections of both models. Luban then considers the arguments for and against the hybrid approach. Considering the ways in which the hybrid model depresses human rights from their peacetime standard to the war level, he expresses concern about the extent to which the war on terrorism means the end of human rights.

In the immediate aftermath of September 11, President Bush stated that the perpetrators of the deed would be brought to justice. Soon afterwards, the President announced that the United States would engage in a war on terrorism. The first of these statements adopts the familiar language of criminal law and criminal justice. It treats the September 11 attacks as horrific crimes—mass murders—and the

Reprinted with permission of Rowman & Littlefield Publishers from Verna V. Gehring, ed., *War After September 11* (2003), pp. 51–60.

government's mission as apprehending and punishing the surviving planners and conspirators for their roles in the crimes. The War on Terrorism is a different proposition, however, and a different model of governmental action—not law but war. Most obviously, it dramatically broadens the scope of action, because now terrorists who knew nothing about September 11 have been earmarked as enemies. But that is only the beginning.

THE HYBRID WAR-LAW APPROACH

The model of war offers much freer rein than that of law, and therein lies its appeal in the wake of 9/11. First, in war but not in law it is permissible to use lethal force on enemy troops regardless of their degree of personal involvement with the adversary. The conscripted cook is as legitimate a target as the enemy general. Second, in war but not in law "collateral damage," that is, foreseen but unintended killing of non-combatants, is permissible. (Police cannot blow up an apartment building full of people because a murderer is inside, but an air force can bomb the building if it contains a military target.) Third, the requirements of evidence and proof are drastically weaker in war than in criminal justice. Soldiers do not need proof beyond a reasonable doubt, or even proof by a preponderance of evidence, that someone is an enemy soldier before firing on him or capturing and imprisoning him. They don't need proof at all, merely plausible intelligence. Thus, the U.S. military remains regretful but unapologetic about its January 2002 attack on the Afghani town of Uruzgan, in which 21 innocent civilians were killed, based on faulty intelligence that they were al Qaeda fighters. Fourth, in war one can attack an enemy without concern over whether he has done anything. Legitimate targets are those who in the course of combat *might* harm us, not those who *have* harmed us. No doubt there are other significant differences as well. But the basic point should be clear: given Washington's mandate to eliminate the danger of future 9/11s, so far as humanly possible, the model of war offers important advantages over the model of law.

There are disadvantages as well. Most obviously, in war but not in law, fighting back is a *legitimate* response of the enemy. Second, when nations fight a war, other nations may opt for neutrality. Third, because fighting back is legitimate, in war the enemy soldier deserves special regard once he is rendered harmless through injury or surrender. It is impermissible to punish him for his role in fighting the war. Nor can he be harshly interrogated after he is captured. The Third Geneva Convention provides: "Prisoners of war who refuse to answer [questions] may not be threatened, insulted, or exposed to unpleasant or disadvantageous treatment of any kind." And, when the war concludes, the enemy soldier must be repatriated.

Here, however, Washington has different ideas, designed to eliminate these tactical disadvantages in the traditional war model. Washington regards international terrorism not only as a military adversary, but also as a criminal activity and criminal conspiracy. In the law model, criminals don't get to shoot back, and their acts of violence subject them to legitimate punishment. That is what we see in Washington's prosecution of the War on Terrorism. Captured terrorists may be tried before military or civilian tribunals, and shooting back at Americans, including

American troops, is a federal crime (for a statute under which John Walker Lindh was indicted criminalizes anyone regardless of nationality, who "outside the United States attempts to kill, or engages in a conspiracy to kill, a national of the United States" or "engages in physical violence with intent to cause serious bodily injury to a national of the United States; or with the result that serious bodily injury is caused to a national of the United States"). Furthermore, the U.S. may rightly demand that other countries not be neutral about murder and terrorism. Unlike the war model, a nation may insist that those who are not with us in fighting murder and terror are against us, because by not joining our operations they are providing a safe haven for terrorists or their bank accounts. By selectively combining elements of the war model and elements of the law model, Washington is able to maximize its own ability to mobilize lethal force against terrorists while eliminating most traditional rights of a military adversary, as well as the rights of innocent bystanders caught in the crossfire.

A LIMBO OF RIGHTLESSNESS

The legal status of al Qaeda suspects imprisoned at the Guantanamo Bay Naval Base in Cuba is emblematic of this hybrid war-law approach to the threat of terrorism. In line with the war model, they lack the usual rights of criminal suspects—the presumption of innocence, the right to a hearing to determine guilt, the opportunity to prove that the authorities have grabbed the wrong man. But, in line with the law model, they are considered *unlawful* combatants. Because they are not uniformed forces, they lack the rights of prisoners of war and are liable to criminal punishment. Initially, the American government declared that the Guantanamo Bay prisoners have no rights under the Geneva Conventions. In the face of international protests, Washington quickly backpedaled and announced that the Guantanamo Bay prisoners would indeed be treated as decently as POWs—but it also made clear that the prisoners have no right to such treatment. Neither criminal suspects nor POWs, neither fish nor fowl, they inhabit a limbo of rightlessness. Secretary of Defense Rumsfeld's assertion that the U.S. may continue to detain them even if they are acquitted by a military tribunal dramatizes the point.

To understand how extraordinary their status is, consider an analogy. Suppose that Washington declares a War on Organized Crime. Troops are dispatched to Sicily and a number of Mafiosi are seized, brought to Guantanamo Bay, and imprisoned without a hearing for the indefinite future, maybe the rest of their lives. They are accused of no crimes, because their capture is based not on what they have done but on what they might do. After all, to become "made" they took oaths of obedience to the bad guys. Seizing them accords with the war model: they are enemy foot soldiers. But they are foot soldiers out of uniform; they lack a "fixed distinctive emblem," in the words of The Hague Convention. That makes them unlawful combatants, so they lack the rights of POWs. They may object that it is only a unilateral declaration by the American President that has turned them into combatants in the first place—he called it a war, they didn't—and that, since they do not regard themselves as literal foot soldiers it never occurred to them to wear a fixed distinctive emblem. They have a point. It seems too easy for the President to divest anyone in the world of rights and liberty simply by announcing that the U.S. is at war with them and then declaring them unlawful combatants if they resist. But, in the hybrid war-law model, they protest in vain.

Consider another example. In January 2002, U.S. forces in Bosnia seized five Algerians and a Yemeni suspected of al Qaeda connections and took them to Guantanamo Bay. The six had been jailed in Bosnia, but a Bosnian court released them for lack of evidence, and the Bosnian Human Rights Chamber issued an injunction that four of them be allowed to remain in the country pending further legal proceedings. The Human Rights Chamber, ironically, was created under U.S. auspices in the Dayton peace accords, and it was designed specifically to protect against treatment like this. Ruth Wedgwood, a well-known international law scholar at Yale and a member of the Council on Foreign Relations, defended the Bosnian seizure in war-model terms. "I think we would simply argue this was a matter of self-defense. One of the fundamental rules of military law is that you have a right ultimately to act in self-defense. And if these folks were actively plotting to blow up the U.S. embassy, they should be considered combatants and captured as combatants in a war." Notice that Professor Wedgwood argues in terms of what the men seized in Bosnia were *planning to do,* not what they *did*; notice as well that the decision of the Bosnian court that there was insufficient evidence does not matter. These are characteristics of the war model.

More recently, two American citizens alleged to be al Qaeda operatives (Jose Padilla, a.k.a. Abdullah al Muhajir, and Yasser Esam Hamdi) have been held in American military prisons, with no crimes charged, no opportunity to consult counsel, and no hearing. The President described Padilla as "a bad man" who aimed to build a nuclear "dirty" bomb and use it against America; and the Justice Department has classified both men as "enemy combatants" who may be held indefinitely. Yet, as military law expert Gary Solis points out, "Until now, as used by the attorney general, the term 'enemy combatant' appeared nowhere in U.S. criminal law, international law or in the law of war." The phrase comes from the 1942 Supreme Court case *Ex parte Quirin,* but all the Court says there is that "an enemy combatant who without uniform comes secretly through the lines for the purpose of waging war by destruction of life or property" would "not . . . be entitled to the status of prisoner of war, but . . . [they would] be offenders against the law of war subject to trial and punishment by military tribunals." For the Court, in other words, the status of a person as a non-uniformed enemy combatant makes him a criminal rather than a warrior, and determines *where* he is tried (in a military, rather than a civilian, tribunal) but not *whether* he is tried. Far from authorizing open-ended confinement, *Ex parte Quirin* presupposes that criminals are entitled to hearings: without a hearing how can suspects prove that the government made a mistake? *Quirin* embeds the concept of "enemy combatant" firmly in the law model. In the war model, by contrast, POWs may be detained without a hearing until hostilities are over. But POWs were captured in uniform, and only their undoubted identity as enemy soldiers justifies such open-ended custody. Apparently, Hamdi and Padilla will get the worst of both models—open-ended custody with no trial, like POWs, but no certainty beyond the U.S. government's say-so that they really are "bad men." This is the hybrid war-law model. It combines the *Quirin* category of "enemy combatant without uniform," used in the law model to justify a military trial, with the war model's practice of indefinite confinement with no trial at all.

THE CASE FOR THE HYBRID APPROACH

Is there any justification for the hybrid war-law model, which so drastically diminishes the rights of the enemy? An argument can be offered along the following lines. In ordinary cases of war among states, enemy soldiers may well be morally and politically innocent. Many of them are conscripts, and those who aren't do not necessarily endorse the state policies they are fighting to defend. But enemy soldiers in the War on Terrorism are, by definition, those who have embarked on a path of terrorism. They are neither morally nor politically innocent. Their sworn aim— "Death to America!"—is to create more 9/11s. In this respect, they are much more akin to criminal conspirators than to conscript soldiers. Terrorists will fight as soldiers when they must, and metamorphose into mass murderers when they can.

Furthermore, suicide terrorists pose a special, unique danger. Ordinary criminals do not target innocent bystanders. They may be willing to kill them if necessary, but bystanders enjoy at least some measure of security because they are not primary targets. Not so with terrorists, who aim to kill as many innocent people as possible. Likewise, innocent bystanders are protected from ordinary criminals by whatever deterrent force the threat of punishment and the risk of getting killed in the act of committing a crime offer. For a suicide bomber, neither of these threats is a deterrent at all—after all, for the suicide bomber one of the hallmarks of a *successful* operation is that he winds up dead at day's end. Given the unique and heightened danger that suicide terrorists pose, a stronger response that grants potential terrorists fewer rights may be justified. Add to this the danger that terrorists may come to possess weapons of mass destruction, including nuclear devices in suitcases. Under circumstances of such dire menace, it is appropriate to treat terrorists as though they embody the most dangerous aspects of both warriors and criminals. That is the basis of the hybrid war-law model.

THE CASE AGAINST EXPEDIENCY

The argument against the hybrid war-law model is equally clear. The U.S. has simply chosen the bits of the law model and the bits of the war model that are most convenient for American interests, and ignored the rest. The model abolishes the rights of potential enemies (and their innocent shields) by fiat—not for reasons of moral or legal principle, but solely because the U.S. does not want them to have rights. The more rights they have, the more risk they pose. But Americans' urgent desire to minimize our risks doesn't make other people's rights disappear. Calling our policy a War on Terrorism obscures this point.

The theoretical basis of the objection is that the law model and the war model each comes as a package, with a kind of intellectual integrity. The law model grows out of relationships within states, while the war model arises from relationships between states. The law model imputes a ground-level community of values to those subject to the law—paradigmatically, citizens of a state, but also visitors and foreigners who choose to engage in conduct that affects a state. Only because law imputes shared basic values to the community can a state condemn the conduct of criminals and inflict punishment on them. Criminals deserve condemnation and punishment because their conduct violates norms that we are entitled to count on their sharing. But, for the same reason—the imputed community of values—those subject to the law ordinarily enjoy a presumption of innocence and an expectation of safety. The government cannot simply grab them and confine them without making sure they have broken the law, nor can it condemn them without due process for ensuring that it has the right person, nor can it knowingly place bystanders in mortal peril in the course of fighting crime. They are our fellows, and the community should protect them just as it protects us. The same imputed community of values that justifies condemnation and punishment creates rights to due care and due process.

War is different. War is the ultimate acknowledgment that human beings do not live in a single community with shared norms. If their norms conflict enough, communities pose a physical danger to each other, and nothing can safeguard a community against its enemies except force of arms. That makes enemy soldiers legitimate targets; but it makes our soldiers legitimate targets as well, and, once the enemy no longer poses a danger, he should be immune from punishment, because if he has fought cleanly he has violated no norms that we are entitled to presume he honors. Our norms are, after all, *our* norms, not his.

Because the law model and war model come as conceptual packages, it is unprincipled to wrench them apart and recombine them simply because it is in America's interest to do so. To declare that Americans can fight enemies with the latitude of warriors, but if the enemies fight back they are not warriors but criminals, amounts to a kind of heads-I-win-tails-you-lose international morality in which whatever it takes to reduce American risk, no matter what the cost to others, turns out to be justified. This, in brief, is the criticism of the hybrid war-law model.

To be sure, the law model could be made to incorporate the war model merely by rewriting a handful of statutes. Congress could enact laws permitting imprisonment or execution of persons who pose a significant threat of terrorism whether or not they have already done anything wrong. The standard of evidence could be set low and the requirement of a hearing eliminated. Finally, Congress could authorize the use of lethal force against terrorists regardless of the danger to innocent bystanders, and it could immunize officials from lawsuits or prosecution by victims of collateral damage. Such statutes would violate the Constitution, but the Constitution could be amended to incorporate anti-terrorist exceptions to the Fourth, Fifth, and Sixth Amendments. In the end, we would have a system of law that includes all the essential features of the war model.

It would, however, be a system that imprisons people for their intentions rather than their actions, and that offers the innocent few protections against mistaken detention or inadvertent death through collateral damage. Gone are the principles that people should never be punished for their thoughts, only for their deeds, and that innocent people must be protected rather than injured by their own government. In that sense, at any rate, repackaging war as law seems merely cosmetic, because it replaces the ideal of law as a protector of rights with the more problematic goal of protecting some innocent people by sacrificing others. The hypothetical legislation incorporates war into law only by making law as partisan and ruthless as war. It no longer resembles law as Americans generally understand it.

THE THREAT TO INTERNATIONAL HUMAN RIGHTS

In the War on Terrorism, what becomes of international human rights? It seems beyond dispute that the war model poses a threat to international human rights, because honoring human rights is neither practically possible nor theoretically required during war. Combatants are legitimate targets; non-combatants maimed by accident or mistake are regarded as collateral damage rather than victims of atrocities; cases of mistaken identity get killed or confined without a hearing because combat conditions preclude due process. To be sure, the laws of war specify minimum human rights, but these are far less robust than rights in peacetime—and the hybrid war-law model reduces this schedule of rights even further by classifying the enemy as unlawful combatants.

One striking example of the erosion of human rights is tolerance of torture. It should be recalled that a 1995 al Qaeda plot to bomb eleven U.S. airliners was thwarted by information tortured out of a Pakistani suspect by the Philippine police—an eerie real-life version of the familiar philosophical thought-experiment. The *Washington Post* reports that since September 11 the U.S. has engaged in the summary transfer of dozens of terrorism suspects to countries where they will be interrogated under torture. But it isn't just the United States that has proven willing to tolerate torture for security reasons. Last December, the Swedish government snatched a suspected Islamic extremist to whom it had previously granted political asylum, and the same day had him transferred to Egypt, where Amnesty International reports that he has been tortured to the point where he walks only with difficulty. Sweden is not, to say the least, a traditionally hard-line nation on human rights issues. None of this international transportation is lawful—indeed, it violates international treaty obligations under the Convention against Torture that in the U.S. have constitutional status as "supreme Law of the Land"—but that may not matter under the war model, in which even constitutional rights may be abrogated.

It is natural to suggest that this suspension of human rights is an exceptional emergency measure to deal with an unprecedented threat. This raises the question of how long human rights will remain suspended. When will the war be over?

Here, the chief problem is that the War on Terrorism is not like any other kind of war. The enemy, Terrorism, is not a territorial state or nation or government. There is no opposite number to negotiate with. There is no one on the other side to call a truce or declare a ceasefire, no one among the enemy authorized to surrender. In traditional wars among states, the war aim is, as Clausewitz argued, to impose one state's political will on another's. The *aim* of the war is not to kill the enemy— killing the enemy is the *means* used to achieve the real end, which is to force capitulation. In the War on Terrorism, no capitulation is possible. That means that the real aim of the war is, quite simply, to kill or capture all of the terrorists—to keep on killing and killing, capturing and capturing, until they are all gone.

Of course, no one expects that terrorism will ever disappear completely. Everyone understands that new anti-American extremists, new terrorists, will always arise and always be available for recruitment and deployment. Everyone understands that even if al Qaeda is destroyed or decapitated, other groups, with other leaders, will arise in its place. It follows, then, that the War on Terrorism will be a war that can only be abandoned, never concluded. The War has no natural resting point, no moment of victory or finality. It requires a mission of killing and capturing, in territories all over the globe, that will go on in perpetuity. It follows as well that the suspension of human rights implicit in the hybrid war-law model is not temporary but permanent.

Perhaps with this fear in mind, Congressional authorization of President Bush's military campaign limits its scope to those responsible for September 11 and their sponsors. But the War on Terrorism has taken on a life of its own that makes the Congressional authorization little more than a technicality. Because of the threat of nuclear terror, the American leadership actively debates a war on Iraq regardless of whether Iraq was implicated in September 11; and the President's yoking of Iraq, Iran, and North Korea into a single axis of evil because they back terror suggests that the War on Terrorism might eventually encompass all these nations. If the U.S. ever unearths tangible evidence that any of these countries is harboring or abetting terrorists with weapons of mass destruction, there can be little doubt that Congress will support military action. So too, Russia invokes the American War on Terrorism to justify its attacks on Chechen rebels, China uses it to deflect criticisms of its campaign against Uighur separatists, and Israeli Prime Minister Sharon explicitly links military actions against Palestinian insurgents to the American War on Terrorism. No doubt there is political opportunism at work in some or all of these efforts to piggy-back onto America's campaign, but the opportunity would not exist if "War on Terrorism" were merely the code-name of a discrete, neatly-boxed American operation. Instead, the War on Terrorism has become a model of politics, a world-view with its own distinctive premises and consequences. As I have argued, it includes a new model of state action, the hybrid war-law model, which depresses human rights from their peace-time standard to the war-time standard, and indeed even further. So long as it continues, the War on Terrorism means the end of human rights, at least for those near enough to be touched by the fire of battle.

QUESTIONS

1 Is the hybrid approach a morally acceptable way of dealing with terrorist suspects? Why or why not?

2 Do you agree with Luban that the continuation of the "War on Terrorism" means the end of human rights for "those near enough to be touched by the fire of battle?"

Majority Opinion in *Korematsu v. United States*

Justice Hugo Lafayette Black

On December 7, 1941, the Japanese bombed Pearl Harbor. On February 19, 1942, in the interest of preventing acts of espionage and sabotage, President Franklin D. Roosevelt signed Executive Order 9066, which authorized certain military commanders to prescribe military areas and define their extent. On February 20, 1942, Lieutenant General DeWitt was made military commander of the Western Defense Command, covering the westernmost states of the United States, about one-fourth of the total area of the nation. On March 21, 1942, Congress passed an act making it a misdemeanor to enter, remain in, leave, or commit any act in any military area or military zone prescribed by any military commander contrary to the restrictions issued by the military. Subsequently, General DeWitt instituted a curfew for certain areas under his command that required all persons of Japanese ancestry to remain in their residences between 8 P.M. and 6 A.M. The curfew order was challenged by Gordon Hirabayashi in *Hirabayashi v. United States* (1943). The United States Supreme Court upheld Hirabayashi's conviction for violating the curfew.

In May 1942, General DeWitt issued Civilian Exclusion Order No. 34, which provided that after noon, May 8, 1942, all persons of Japanese ancestry, both alien and nonalien, were to be excluded from an area that included the county of Alameda. Residents of Japanese ancestry like Fred T. Korematsu, were required to go to an assembly center. Of the 120,000 individuals of Japanese descent forced to leave their homes and subsequently sent to internment camps, two-thirds were American citizens.

Fred T. Korematsu was a native-born citizen of the United States. He was convicted of refusing to report to the authorities for eventual internment. Korematsu appealed to the United States Supreme Court. The Court refused to overturn the military judgment although there were very strong disagreements among the justices, three of whom wrote dissenting opinions. Justice Black delivered the opinion of the Court.

Justice Black avers that the principles used in the Court's reasoning in *Hirabayashi* also apply in *Korematsu.* In *Hirabayashi,* the curfew was seen as a legitimate exercise of the government's power to act in ways necessary to prevent espionage and sabotage in an area threatened by Japanese attack. Similarly, Black upholds the military judgment that the exclusion order was a military necessity because of the threat of harm posed by disloyal Japanese and Japanese-Americans and the impossibility of immediately segregating those who were loyal from those who were not.

It should be noted, to begin with, that all legal restrictions which curtail the civil rights of a single racial group are immediately suspect. That is not to say that all such restrictions are unconstitutional. It is to say that courts must subject them to the most rigid scrutiny. Pressing public necessity may sometimes justify the existence of such restrictions; racial antagonism never can.

United States Supreme Court. 323 U.S. 214 (1944).

In the instant case prosecution of the petitioner was begun by information charging violation of an Act of Congress, of March 21,1942, 56 Stat. 173, which provides that

> . . . whoever shall enter, remain in, leave, or commit any act in any military area or military zone prescribed, under the authority of an Executive order of the President, by the Secretary of War, or by any military commander designated by the Secretary of War, contrary to the restrictions applicable to any such area or zone or contrary to the order of the Secretary of War or any such military commander, shall, if it appears that he knew or should have known of the existence and extent of the restrictions or order and that his act was in violation thereof, be guilty of a misdemeanor and upon conviction shall be liable to a fine of not to exceed $5,000 or to imprisonment for not more than one year, or both, for each offense.

Exclusion Order No. 34, which the petitioner knowingly and admittedly violated, was one of a number of military orders and proclamations, all of which were substantially based upon Executive Order No. 9066, 7 Fed. Reg. 1407. That order, issued after we were at war with Japan, declared that "the successful prosecution of the war requires every possible protection against espionage and against sabotage to national-defense material, national-defense premises, and national-defense utilities. . . ."

One of the series of orders and proclamations, a curfew order, which like the exclusion order here was promulgated pursuant to Executive Order 9066, subjected all persons of Japanese ancestry in prescribed West Coast military areas to remain in their residences from 8 P.M. to 6 A.M. As is the case with the exclusion order here, that prior curfew order was designed as a "protection against espionage and against sabotage." In *Hirabayashi* v. *United States,* we sustained a conviction obtained for violation of the curfew order. The *Hirabayashi* conviction and this one thus rest on the same 1942 Congressional Act and the same basic executive and military orders, all of which orders were aimed at the twin dangers of espionage and sabotage.

The 1942 Act was attacked in the *Hirabayashi* case as an unconstitutional delegation of power; it was contended that the curfew order and other orders on which it rested were beyond the war powers of the Congress, the military authorities and of the President, as Commander in Chief of the Army; and finally that to apply the curfew order against none but citizens of Japanese ancestry amounted to a constitutionally prohibited discrimination solely on account of race. To these questions, we gave the serious consideration which their importance justified. We upheld the curfew order as an exercise of the power of the government to take steps necessary to prevent espionage and sabotage in an area threatened by Japanese attack.

In the light of the principles we announced in the *Hirabayashi* case, we are unable to conclude that it was beyond the war power of Congress and the Executive to exclude those of Japanese ancestry from the West Coast war area at the time they did. True, exclusion from the area in which one's home is located is a far greater deprivation than constant confinement to the home from 8 P.M. to 6 A.M. Nothing short of apprehension by the proper military authorities of the gravest imminent danger to the public safety can constitutionally justify either. But exclusion from a threatened area, no less than curfew, has a definite and close relationship to the prevention of espionage and sabotage. The military authorities, charged with the primary responsibility of defending our shores, concluded that curfew provided inadequate protection and ordered exclusion. They did so, as pointed out in our *Hirabayashi* opinion, in accordance with Congressional authority to the military to say who should, and who should not, remain in the threatened areas.

In this case the petitioner challenges the assumptions upon which we rested our conclusions in the *Hirabayashi* case. He also urges that by May 1942, when Order No. 34 was promulgated, all danger of Japanese invasion of the West Coast had disappeared. After careful consideration of these contentions we are compelled to reject them.

Here, as in the *Hirabayashi* case, ". . . we cannot reject as unfounded the judgment of the military authorities and of Congress that there were disloyal members of that population, whose number and strength could not be precisely and quickly ascertained. We cannot say that the war-making branches of the Government did not have ground for believing that in a critical hour such persons could not readily be isolated and separately dealt with, and constituted a menace to the national defense and safety, which demanded that prompt and adequate measures be taken to guard against it."

Like curfew, exclusion of those of Japanese origin was deemed necessary because of the presence of an unascertained number of disloyal members of the group, most of whom we have no doubt were loyal to this country. It was because we could not reject the finding of the military authorities that it was impossible to bring about an immediate segregation of the disloyal from the loyal that we sustained the validity of the curfew order as applying to the whole group. In the instant case, temporary exclusion of the entire group was rested by the military on the same ground. The judgment that exclusion of the whole group was for the same reason a military imperative answers the contention that the exclusion was in the nature of group punishment based on antagonism to those of Japanese origin. That there were members of the group who retained loyalties to Japan has been confirmed by investigations made subsequent to the exclusion. Approximately five thousand American citizens of Japanese ancestry refused to swear unqualified allegiance to the United States and to renounce allegiance to the Japanese Emperor, and several thousand evacuees requested repatriation to Japan.

We uphold the exclusion order as of the time it was made and when the petitioner violated it. Cf. *Chastleton Corporation v. Sinclair, Block v. Hirsh.* In doing so, we are not unmindful of the hardships imposed by it upon a large group of American citizens. Cf. *Ex parte Kawato.* But hardships are part of war, and war is an aggregation of hardships. All citizens alike, both in and out of uniform, feel the impact of war in greater or lesser measure. Citizenship has its responsibilities as well as its privileges, and in time of war the burden is always heavier. Compulsory exclusion of large groups of citizens from their homes, except under circumstances of direst emergency and peril, is inconsistent with our basic governmental institutions. But when under conditions of modern warfare our shores are threatened by hostile forces, the power to protect must be commensurate with the threatened danger. . . .

It is said that we are dealing here with the case of imprisonment of a citizen in a concentration camp solely because of his ancestry, without evidence or inquiry concerning his loyalty and good disposition towards the United States. Our task would be simple, our duty clear, were this a case involving the imprisonment of a loyal citizen in a concentration camp because of racial prejudice. Regardless of the true nature of the assembly and relocation centers—and we deem it unjustifiable to call them concentration camps with all the ugly connotations that term implies—we are dealing specifically with nothing but an exclusion order. To cast this case into outlines of racial prejudice, without reference to the real military dangers which were presented, merely confuses the issue. Korematsu was not excluded from the Military Area because of hostility to him or his race. He *was* excluded because we are at war with the Japanese Empire, because the properly constituted military authorities feared an invasion of our West Coast and felt constrained to take proper security measures, because they decided that the military urgency of the situation demanded that all citizens of Japanese ancestry be segregated from the West Coast temporarily, and finally, because Congress, reposing its confidence in this time of war in our military leaders—as inevitably it must—determined that they should have the power to do just this. There was evidence of disloyalty on the part of some, the military authorities considered that the need for action was great, and time was short. We cannot—by availing ourselves of the calm perspective of hindsight—now say that at that time these actions were unjustified.

Affirmed.

QUESTIONS

1 In the past, in times of crisis, the United States has adopted measures—later recognized as morally wrong—that curtailed civil liberties in the interest of security. Does the current American response to terrorism involve a morally unacceptable curtailment of liberties? Why or why not?

2 Japanese-Americans who were interned during World War II have received some compensation from the government. Should individuals who were interned at Guantanamo Bay for a long period of time and later released with no charges made against them be compensated?

Dissenting Opinion in *Korematsu v. United States*

Justice Frank Murphy

Justice Murphy maintains that before individuals can be validly deprived of any of their constitutional rights on a plea of military necessity, the deprivation must be reasonably related to a public danger that is so immediate, imminent, and impending that it precludes any delays caused by the intervention of ordinary constitutional processes to alleviate the danger. In his view, Exclusion Order No. 34, which bans all

United States Supreme Court. 323 U.S. 214 (1944).

persons of Japanese ancestry from restricted areas of the Pacific Coast, does not meet the reasonability test. The order cannot be reasonable because it rests on false cultural and social assumptions regarding all Japanese and Japanese-Americans. Murphy notes that no attempts were made to treat persons of Japanese ancestry on an individual basis to differentiate those who were loyal to the United States from those who were not. He rejects what he sees as the legalization of racism.

This exclusion of "all persons of Japanese ancestry, both alien and non-alien," from the Pacific Coast area on a plea of military necessity in the absence of martial law ought not to be approved. Such exclusion goes over "the very brink of constitutional power" and falls into the ugly abyss of racism.

In dealing with matters relating to the prosecution and progress of a war, we must accord great respect and consideration to the judgments of the military authorities who are on the scene and who have full knowledge of the military facts. The scope of their discretion must, as a matter of necessity and common sense, be wide. And their judgments ought not to be overruled lightly by those whose training and duties ill-equip them to deal intelligently with matters so vital to the physical security of the nation.

At the same time, however, it is essential that there be definite limits to military discretion, especially where martial law has not been declared. Individuals must not be left impoverished of their constitutional rights on a plea of military necessity that has neither substance nor support. Thus, like other claims conflicting with the asserted constitutional rights of the individual, the military claim must subject itself to the judicial process of having its reasonableness determined and its conflicts with other interests reconciled. "What are the allowable limits of military discretion, and whether or not they have been overstepped in a particular case, are judicial questions." *Sterling v. Constantin*.

The judicial test of whether the Government, on a plea of military necessity, can validly deprive an individual of any of his constitutional rights is whether the deprivation is reasonably related to a public danger that is so "immediate, imminent, and impending" as not to admit of delay and not to permit the intervention of ordinary constitutional processes to alleviate the danger. *United States v. Russell, Mitchell v. Harmony, Raymond v. Thomas*. Civilian Exclusion Order No. 34, banishing from a prescribed area of the Pacific Coast "all persons of Japanese ancestry, both alien and non-alien," clearly does not meet that test. Being an obvious racial discrimination, the order deprives all those within its scope of the equal protection of the laws as guaranteed by the Fifth Amendment. It further deprives these individuals of their constitutional rights to live and work where they will, to establish a home where they choose and to move about freely. In excommunicating them without benefit of hearings, this order also deprives them of all their constitutional rights to procedural due process. Yet no reasonable relation to an "immediate, imminent, and impending" public danger is evident to support this racial restriction which is one of the most sweeping and complete deprivations of constitutional rights in the history of this nation in the absence of martial law.

It must be conceded that the military and naval situation in the spring of 1942 was such as to generate a very real fear of invasion of the Pacific Coast, accompanied by fears of sabotage and espionage in that area. The military command was therefore justified in adopting all reasonable means necessary to combat these dangers. In adjudging the military action taken in light of the then apparent dangers, we must not erect too high or too meticulous standards; it is necessary only that the action have some reasonable relation to the removal of the dangers of invasion, sabotage and espionage. But the exclusion, either temporarily or permanently, of all persons with Japanese blood in their veins has no such reasonable relation. And that relation is lacking because the exclusion order necessarily must rely for its reasonableness upon the assumption that *all* persons of Japanese ancestry may have a dangerous tendency to commit sabotage and espionage and to aid our Japanese enemy in other ways. It is difficult to believe that reason, logic or experience could be marshalled in support of such an assumption.

That this forced exclusion was the result in good measure of this erroneous assumption of racial guilt rather than bona fide military necessity is evidenced by the Commanding General's Final Report on the evacuation from the Pacific Coast area.[1] In it he refers to all individuals of Japanese descent as "subversive," as belonging to "an enemy race" whose "racial strains are undiluted," and as constituting "over 112,000 potential enemies . . . at large today" along the Pacific Coast. In support of this blanket condemnation of all persons of Japanese descent, however, no reliable evidence is cited to show that such individuals were generally disloyal, or had generally so conducted themselves in this area as to constitute a special menace to defense installations or war industries, or had otherwise by their behavior furnished reasonable ground for their exclusion as a group.

Justification for the exclusion is sought, instead, mainly upon questionable racial and sociological grounds not ordinarily within the realm of expert military judgment, supplemented by certain semi-military conclusions drawn from an unwarranted use of circumstantial evidence. Individuals of Japanese ancestry are condemned because they are said to be "a large, unassimilated, tightly knit racial group, bound to an enemy nation by strong ties of race, culture, custom and religion." They are claimed to be given to "emperor worshipping ceremonies" and to "dual citizenship." Japanese language schools and allegedly pro-Japanese organizations are cited as evidence of possible group disloyalty, together with facts as to certain persons being educated and residing at length in Japan. It is intimated that many of these individuals deliberately resided "adjacent to strategic points," thus enabling them "to carry into execution a tremendous program of sabotage on a mass scale should any considerable number of them have been inclined to do so." The need for protective custody is also asserted. The report refers without identity to "numerous incidents of violence" as well as to other admittedly unverified or cumulative incidents. From this, plus certain other events not shown to have been connected with the Japanese Americans, it is concluded that the "situation was fraught with danger to the Japanese population itself" and that the general public "was ready to take matters into its own hands." Finally, it is intimated, though not directly charged or proved, that persons of Japanese ancestry were responsible for three minor isolated shellings and bombings of the Pacific Coast area, as well as for unidentified radio transmissions and night signalling.

The main reasons relied upon by those responsible for the forced evacuation, therefore, do not prove a reasonable relation between the group characteristics of

Japanese Americans and the dangers of invasion, sabotage and espionage. The reasons appear, instead, to be largely an accumulation of much of the misinformation, half-truths and insinuations that for years have been directed against Japanese Americans by people with racial and economic prejudices—the same people who have been among the foremost advocates of the evacuation. A military judgment based upon such racial and sociological considerations is not entitled to the great weight ordinarily given the judgments based upon strictly military considerations. Especially is this so when every charge relative to race, religion, culture, geographical location, and legal and economic status has been substantially discredited by independent studies made by experts in these matters.

The military necessity which is essential to the validity of the evacuation order thus resolves itself into a few intimations that certain individuals actively aided the enemy, from which it is inferred that the entire group of Japanese Americans could not be trusted to be or remain loyal to the United States. No one denies, of course, that there were some disloyal persons of Japanese descent on the Pacific Coast who did all in their power to aid their ancestral land. Similar disloyal activities have been engaged in by many persons of German, Italian and even more pioneer stock in our country. But to infer that examples of individual disloyalty prove group disloyalty and justify discriminatory action against the entire group is to deny that under our system of law individual guilt is the sole basis for deprivation of rights. Moreover, this inference, which is at the very heart of the evacuation orders, has been used in support of the abhorrent and despicable treatment of minority groups by the dictatorial tyrannies which this nation is now pledged to destroy. To give constitutional sanction to that inference in this case, however well-intentioned may have been the military command on the Pacific Coast, is to adopt one of the cruelest of the rationales used by our enemies to destroy the dignity of the individual and to encourage and open the door to discriminatory actions against other minority groups in the passions of tomorrow.

No adequate reason is given for the failure to treat these Japanese Americans on an individual basis by holding investigations and hearings to separate the loyal from the disloyal, as was done in the case of persons of German and Italian ancestry. See House Report No. 2124 (77th Cong., 2d Sess.) 247–52. It is asserted merely that the loyalties of this group "were unknown and time was of the essence." Yet nearly four months elapsed after Pearl Harbor before the first exclusion order was issued; nearly eight months went by until the last order was issued; and the last of these "subversive" persons was not actually removed until almost eleven months had elapsed. Leisure and deliberation seem to have been more of the essence than speed. And the fact that conditions were not such as to warrant a declaration of martial law adds strength to the belief that the factors of time and military necessity were not as urgent as they have been represented to be.

Moreover, there was no adequate proof that the Federal Bureau of Investigation and the military and naval intelligence services did not have the espionage and sabotage situation well in hand during this long period. Nor is there any denial of the fact that not one person of Japanese ancestry was accused or convicted of espionage or sabotage after Pearl Harbor while they were still free, a fact which is some evidence of the loyalty of the vast majority of these individuals and of the effectiveness of the established methods of combatting these evils. It seems incredible that under these circumstances it would have been impossible to hold loyalty hearings for the mere 112,000 persons involved—or at least for the 70,000 American citizens—especially when a large part of this number represented children and elderly men and women. Any inconvenience that may have accompanied an attempt to conform to procedural due process cannot be said to justify violations of constitutional rights of individuals.

I dissent, therefore, from this legalization of racism. Racial discrimination in any form and in any degree has no justifiable part whatever in our democratic way of life. It is unattractive in any setting but it is utterly revolting among a free people who have embraced the principles set forth in the Constitution of the United States. All residents of this nation are kin in some way by blood or culture to a foreign land. Yet they are primarily and necessarily a part of the new and distinct civilization of the United States. They must accordingly be treated at all times as the heirs of the American experiment and as entitled to all the rights and freedoms guaranteed by the Constitution.

NOTE

1 Final Report, Japanese Evacuation from the West Coast, 1942, by Lt. Gen. J. L. DeWitt. This report is dated June 5, 1943, but was not made public until January, 1944. [All subsequent references in Justice Murphy's opinion to claims regarding racial and cultural characterizations of Japanese people are from this report.]

QUESTIONS

1 Is Murphy's reasonability test defensible?
2 To what extent are civil liberties presently being infringed upon in the interest of combating terrorism? Could these infringements pass Justice Murphy's reasonability test?

Security and Liberty: The Image of Balance

Jeremy Waldron

Waldron examines the following proposition: "a change in the scale and nature of the harms that threaten us explains and justifies a change in our scheme of civil liberties; and that process is best understood in terms of 'striking a new balance between liberty and security.'" His examination falls into three parts. First, he looks at what it would mean to take the idea of striking a new balance more or less

Reprinted with permission of the publisher from *The Journal of Political Philosophy,* vol. 11, no. 2 (2003), pp. 191–195, 200–208, 210. © 2003 Blackwell Publishing Ltd.

literally. Second, he looks at the issues raised by the distribution of the proposed changes in liberty and security, which limit the liberties of some minorities more than those of other members of society. Finally, he discusses the unintended effects of giving the government powers that had previously been denied to it.

I.

There seems to be general acceptance in the wake of the terrorist attacks of September 11, 2001 that some adjustment in our scheme of civil liberties is inevitable. This is partly the product of political defeatism: the state is always looking to limit liberty, and a terrorist emergency provides a fine opportunity. People become more than usually deferential to the demands of their rulers in these circumstances and more than usually fearful that if they criticize the proposed adjustments they will be reproached for being insufficiently patriotic. There is also little likelihood that reductions in civil liberties will be opposed by the courts. Even in countries like the United States with strong judicial review, the courts have proved reluctant to oppose reductions in civil liberties in times of war or war-like emergency. . . .

Political realism aside, there is also a sense that some curtailment of liberty might be *appropriate* in the wake of the terrorist attacks, and that it might be *unreasonable* to insist on the same restrictions on state action after September 11 as we insisted on before September 11.

A common suggestion invites us to think about this in terms of the idea of *balance*. According to this suggestion, it is *always* necessary—even in normal circumstances—to balance liberty against security. We always have to strike a balance between the individual's liberty to do as he pleases and society's need for protection against the harm that may accrue from some of the things it might please an individual to do. The former surely, cannot be comprehensive even under the most favorable circumstances—nobody argues for anarchy—and the latter has to be given some weight in determining how much liberty people should have. So there is always a balance to be struck. And—the suggestion continues—that balance is bound to change (and it is appropriate that it should change) as the threat to security becomes graver or more imminent. One newspaper columnist, Nicholas Kristoff, put it this way:

> [T]errorist incidents in the 1970s (such as at the Munich Olympics) had maximum death tolls of about a dozen; attacks in the 1980s and 1990s raised the scale (as in the Air India and Pan Am 103 bombings) to the hundreds; 9/11 lifted the toll into the thousands; and terrorists are now nosing around weapons of mass destruction that could kill hundreds of thousands. As risks change, we who care about civil liberties need to realign balances between security and freedom. It is a wrenching, odious task, but we liberals need to learn from 9/11 just as much as the FBI does.[1]

This is the proposition I want to examine: a change in the scale and nature of the harms that threaten us explains and justifies a change in our scheme of civil liberties; and that process is best understood in terms of "striking a new balance between liberty and security."

II.

The idea of striking a new balance can be interpreted more or less literally. We know the language of balance is used in morality and politics when there are things to be said on both sides of an issue, values that pull us in opposite directions. But what does it mean to say that we confront this array of values or reasons by *balancing* the competing considerations? And what are we implying when we say the balance has shifted? Is it just a matter of our having thought of a new reason, or of new facts having given rise to new reasons, which weigh more on one side than the other? That we can make sense of: there is now (say, since September 11, 2001) something new to be said on one side of a familiar debate and nothing new to be said on the other. But "balance" also has connotations of quantity and precision, as when we use it to describe the reconciliation of a set of accounts or the relative weight of two quantities of metal. Where is the warrant for our reliance on this quantitative imagery when we say that the new consideration not only adds something to the debate but "outweighs" all considerations on the other side?

Here is one possibility. We know that liberty is in some respects a matter of more or less. For example: I can range more or less widely without restrictions on my travel; or I may be permitted to come closer to or be kept back from important public sites or important public officials. So we may be able to make at least ordinal comparisons between different quantities of liberty L_x and L_y (for example, between one person's liberty and another's, or between my liberty one day and my liberty the following day). And security may be conceived quantitatively, too, in terms of the extent of risk (R) faced by a person (where R equals the magnitude of a possible harm times the probability of its occurrence): we might say that a person is less secure the greater R is with regard to that person. With this primitive apparatus, we might then be able to express the idea of the security cost to a person A of another person B having a certain amount of liberty. The security cost to A of B's having a higher amount of liberty L_y rather than a lower amount L_x is the difference between two risks, the higher risk (let us call it R_n) to A from B's having the greater liberty (L_y) and the lower risk (R_m) to A of B's having the lesser liberty (L_x).

Now, if we assume (for the sake of argument) that the balance between security and liberty was exactly right on September 10, 2001, then maybe what happened the following day was that we became aware (or it became the case) that the risks of ceding a given amount of liberty were greater than we thought. Even on September 10, we knew that any amount of liberty carried with it a certain risk of harm. But we were prepared to accept a certain risk—say, R_n rather than a lower risk R_m—because any attempt to secure R_m would mean giving up something we valued at least as much as that extra security, namely, a certain degree of liberty: on September 10, we thought that to secure R_m we would have to diminish individual liberty from L_y to L_x; and we were not prepared to do that. However even on September 10 we were not prepared to cede a greater degree of liberty than L_y— say L_z—because we knew that that would carry a risk of harm greater than R_n. And we were not prepared to accept a greater risk than R_n. However, it now turns out (in light of the events of September 11) that the cost of L_y (which we *were* prepared to concede) is much greater than we thought—say, R_o rather than R_n. Since we were prepared on September 10 to give up any degree of liberty that would pose a risk greater than R_n, consistency indicates that now we are going to have to settle for an amount of liberty much less than L_y—say, L_x—on September 12. That I think is what the case for "striking a new balance" is supposed to amount to. We have an idea of the maximum risk we are prepared to bear as a result of people's liberty, and we adjust their liberties downwards when it appears that the risk associated with a given quantum of liberty is greater than we thought (or greater than it used to be).

Of course it is possible that we could make the adjustment in the other direction. Instead of beginning with an idea of the maximum risk, R_n, we were prepared to bear as a result of people's liberty, we might begin with an idea of the minimum liberty, L_y, we were prepared to accept. The recalculation after September 11 would then require us not to accept less liberty but to brave a higher risk for the sake of the liberty we cherish. The appropriate changes in public policy, then, would be calls to greater courage, rather than diminutions of liberty. Most probably we work at the matter from both ends, and perhaps this is where talk of "balance" really comes into its own. Our liberties are not untouched. There has been a downward adjustment, to help address some of the graver risks. But even with the adjustments in civil liberties that have been put in place (and are likely to be put in place) since September 11, no one feels as secure as before: so everyone has to be a little braver for the sake of the modicum of liberty that is left.

III.

Readers may think all this is over-fussy. Surely everyone knows what we mean when we talk about the balance between liberty and security, and surely it is obvious that some adjustment has to be made after it becomes evident that terrorists can take advantage of our traditional liberties to commit murder on such a scale. Does it really need to be spelled out with this sort of algebra? Well, I think we *do* need to subject the balancing rhetoric to careful analytic scrutiny, and this for [at least two reasons]: . . .

(i) *Difficulties with distribution.* Though we may talk of balancing our liberties against our security, we need to pay some attention to the fact that the real diminution in liberty may affect some people more than others. So, as well as the objection to consequentialism, justice requires that we pay special attention to the distributive character of the changes that are proposed and to the possibility that the change involves, in effect, a proposal to trade off the liberties of a few against the security of the majority.

(ii) *Unintended effects.* When liberty is conceived as *negative* liberty, a reduction in liberty is achieved by enhancing the power of the state. This is done so that the enhanced power can be used to combat terrorism. But it would be naive to assume that this is the only thing that that enhanced power can be used for. We need to consider the possibility that diminishing liberty might also diminish security against the state, even as it enhances security against terrorism. . . .

I will discuss [each of] these concerns . . . in more detail in Sections IV . . . [and V] of this article, and I will try to show how they might apply to various issues of civil liberty.

As we pursue that discussion, we will need to bear in mind that the class of civil liberties at stake here is not necessarily a homogenous class of rights, principles, or guarantees. The term "civil liberties" represents a variety of concerns about the impact of governmental powers upon individual freedom. Because the issue of a change in the "balance" between civil liberties and security plays out slightly differently for different kinds of concern, let me briefly set out some distinctions.

(a) In its most straightforward meaning, "civil liberties" refers to certain freedoms understood as actions that individuals might wish to perform, which (it is thought) the state should not restrict. Free speech, religious freedom, freedom of travel fall into this category.

(b) We also use the phrase "civil liberties" to refer to more diffuse concerns about government power, which are not necessarily driven by any sense of a privileged type of action which individuals should be left free to perform. For example, the government's ability to listen in on telephone conversations is a civil liberties concern, even though the "liberty" in question—sometimes referred to as "privacy"—does not amount to very much more than the condition of not being subjected to this scrutiny.

(c) Sometimes "civil liberties" refers to procedural rights and powers which we think individuals should have when the state detains them or brings charges against them or plans to punish them. These are rights like the right not to be detained without trial, the right to a fair trial process, the right to counsel, etc.

This short list is by no means complete. A comprehensive account would also say something about (d) the rights associated with democracy and civic participation. Fortunately these rights have not been an issue in the current crisis. So for the rest of the article, I will focus mainly on (a), (b), and (c) and consider how the concerns I have outlined . . . apply to them.

IV.

My [first] point is this: in order to evaluate the balancing argument, we have to ask tough questions about the *distribution* of the various changes envisaged in liberty and security. It is tempting to read the argument set out in Section II in terms of a diminution in liberty for everyone—everyone's liberty is reduced from L_y to L_x—in order to secure the same amount of security for everyone. But often it does not work out that way.

The perpetrators of the September 11 attacks were foreigners, members of a foreign organization, and the U.S. government has taken that as grounds for drawing some quite sharp distinctions in its subsequent legislation between the protections accorded to the civil liberties of Americans and the protections accorded to others who are legally in the United States. Section 214 of the USA Patriot Act, for example, alters existing legislation concerning wire-tapping so that "investigation of a United States person is not conducted solely upon the basis of activities protected by the first amendment to the Constitution." (The class of "United States persons" includes American citizens and legally admitted permanent residents; but it does not include non-resident aliens legally present in the United States.) More importantly perhaps, the perpetrators of the September 11 attacks were not just non-residents but also members of a fairly visible ethnic group: and their actions mean that everyone (whether a United States person or not) who looks or dresses or speaks in any way like them is likely to face much greater levels of suspicion. Most of the changes in civil liberties are aimed specifically at suspected perpetrators or accomplices or persons who might be thought to have information about past or future terrorist actions, and most Americans assume that persons in these categories will look quite different from themselves.

True—as a legalistic matter, the changes in civil liberties may be formulated innocuously enough—"Anyone who is officially suspected of doing A or knowing B will have his or her liberty reduced from L_y to L_x,"—and the "anyone" term seems universalizable. However, we must avoid a certain childish formalism in making the claim that civil liberties are diminished equally for everyone. As Ronald Dworkin points out,

> None of the administration's decisions and proposals will affect more than a tiny number of American citizens: almost none of us will be indefinitely detained for minor violations or offenses, or have our houses searched without our knowledge, or find ourselves brought before military tribunals on grave charges carrying the death penalty. Most of us pay almost nothing in personal freedom when such measures are used against those the President suspects of terrorism.[2]

So perhaps the balance we ought to be discussing is not so much a balance between one thing we all like (liberty) and another thing we all like (security). It is more like the balance that is sometimes referred to when we say we should balance the interests of a dissident individual or minority against the interests of the community as a whole.

Ronald Dworkin has argued in a number of places that there is some confusion in the idea of a balance of interests between the individual and the community: "The interests of each individual are already balanced into the interests of the community as a whole, and the idea of a further balance, between their separate interests and the results of the first balance, is itself therefore mysterious."[3] But confusion is not the problem; the problem is moral, not logical. There are in fact two ways of parsing the idea of a balance between the interests of an individual and the interests of the community in the present context, neither of them reassuring.

First, talk of balancing the interests of the individual against the interests of the community may be a way of indicating that "the individual" in question is not really thought of as a member of the community at all: he is an alien, a foreigner, and so his interests have *not* already been counted in "the interests of the community." Alternatively, if we say that his interests *are* already counted in the interests of the community—for example, because he too is more secure from being blown up, as a result of what we do to the liberties of suspicious characters (like him)—we may mean to indicate that a balance must be struck between (i) what *justice* requires in the way of respect for his interests and (ii) what would best promote the aggregate interests—his included—calculated in a way that is indifferent to justice.

This second account is quite complicated, so let me explain it a little further. We know that "the interest of the community" is often calculated in a way that sidelines issues of justice and distribution: utilitarians do this all the time. To take a very crude example: suppose that a choice between two policies (I and II) offers the following pay-offs to three individuals:

	I	*II*
A	20	30
B	20	10
C	20	30

Plainly policy II best promotes the interests of the community (comprising A, B, and C) in an aggregate sense: the total pay-off is higher and so is the average. But someone who believes this may also acknowledge that the outcome of policy I is more fair; and let us assume for the sake argument that they are right. Now, since fairness is concerned particularly with what happens to individuals (rather than to arithmetical totals), and since A and C are both better off as individuals under the less fair policy, a concern about fairness and about the issue of sacrificing fairness to aggregate utility is likely to focus particularly on B. It would not be surprising if this concern were *abbreviated* as a concern about the balance between B's interests and the aggregate interests of the community, even though B's interests are actually counted in the aggregate interests of the community. Another way of putting it would be to say that the real issue is the relation between a concern for justice, on the one hand, and the prospect of gains (to some or to the aggregate) from ignoring justice, on the other.

Talk of "balance" here is quite insidious. Although it all sounds very moderate, the implication is that we should have *some* concern for justice but not too much: a proper sense of balance requires us to give up on justice when the costs of pursuing it (to those who would benefit from injustice) become too high. Now A and C might not think this in the choice between policy I and policy II above: there the cost to them of justice is not very great. But if we imagine that a new set of policy choices presents itself (say, on September 11), which greatly increases what A and C have to lose from sticking with justice—

	III	*IV*
A	10	30
B	10	5
C	10	30

—then we might be tempted to talk about "adjusting the balance" between justice and utility. After all, it is one thing to require A and C each to give up ten units of goodies for the sake of justice in the choice between I and II; it is quite another thing—and the afficionado of balance may say it is quite unreasonable—to expect them to give up twice that in the choice between III and IV.

I have put this provocatively—with what I hope is an ill-concealed sneer of outrage at the idea of "striking a new balance" between the demands of justice on the one hand, and what most members of a society could get for themselves if they were allowed to arrange their society unjustly on the other. But mainly what I am trying to establish is the need for care with the idea of balancing. If security-gains for most people are being balanced against liberty-losses for a few, then we need to pay attention to the few/most dimension of the balance, not just the liberty/security dimension. Given that the few/most dimension presents an issue of justice, it is by no means clear—I think it is clearly false—that simply adding something to the "most" side of the balance is sufficient by itself to justify taking something away from the "few".

Someone may respond by observing that the "few" in our present case are terrorists or persons suspected of participation or complicity in terrorism. No one believes that criminals should have the same rights as the rest of us, and even those who are suspected but not convicted of criminal activity have lesser rights even in ordinary times: they may be held pending trial, or required to surrender their passports, etc. The point may be accepted, but the issue is whether we should now make some additional downward adjustments to the scheme that already puts criminal suspects in a special position of more restricted liberty. The civil liberties in category (c) define the procedures and protections that are offered to those suspected of ordinary crimes, from the trivial to the heinous. Is there a good reason for changing these, in the light of the events of September 11?

Ronald Dworkin observes a temptation to think that the extraordinary gravity of the crimes that were committed on September 11 (or that terrorists are presently conspiring to commit) is itself a reason for diminishing the protections afforded to those who are charged with such offenses. But, as he said, that makes no sense: "If they are innocent, the injustice of convicting and punishing them is at least as great as the injustice in convicting some other innocent person for a less serious crime."[4] The "civil liberties" in category (c) are oriented in large part towards preventing such injustice, and the case for respecting them increases rather than diminishes the greater the crime that the suspect stands accused of. (This is because category (c) liberties are designed to protect people against condemnation and punishment, and both will be greater the more serious the charge.)

Can it not also be said, though, that the greater the crime the greater the dangers of a wrongful acquittal? It is not true in all cases, but it may be true with terrorists. Michael Dorf put the point this way:

> The traditional way we balance these things is with the maxim, "It's better that 10 guilty men go free than one innocent man be in jail." I think people are a little nervous about applying that maxim where the 10 guilty men who are going to go free could have biological weapons.[5]

The implicit suggestion that the 1:10 ratio needs to be adjusted in light of the greater damage that the ten may do sounds reasonable enough. But we must not give the impression that it is only a matter of striking a different balance between this one (innocent) suspect and these ten (guilty) ones. That is not who the balance is between. We are not balancing the rights of the innocent against the rights of the guilty. We are balancing the interests in life or liberty of the one innocent man against the security interests of those of the rest of us (nonsuspects) that will be served if the ten guilty men are convicted by the procedures that lead to the wrongful conviction of the innocent.

The innocent man is being put to death or imprisoned, and his reputation drastically and wrongly besmirched, so that *we* may be safer. It may not be done intentionally, but the gist of the proposal is that it is something we are entitled to be reckless about. There was a way of taking care that it should not happen (or that it should happen less often)—that is what the civil liberties safeguards represent—but for our own benefit we have decided to take less care.

James Fitzjames Stephen remarked, in connection with this business of trading off a certain number of guilty acquittals against innocent convictions that "[e]very-thing depends on what the guilty men have been doing, and something depends on the way in which the innocent man came to be suspected."[6] The first point is like Dorf's. But Stephen's second point is relevant too. If the innocent persons who are sacrificed to security in this way are sacrificed because it was in the circumstances perfectly reasonable to suspect them of terrorist offenses (though, as it turned out, mistaken)—that is one thing. But if they were suspected in the first place because of appearance, ethnicity, or religion, and if the changes in the scheme of civil liberties facilitated suspicion on just that basis, and removed some of the safeguards that would prevent or mitigate that sort of suspicion—then, that is quite another thing. The injustice associated with the reckless conviction of one innocent man for the sake of the greater good becomes particularly acute—and the "balancing" talk that underwrites it becomes particularly objectionable—when it is associated with ethnic or religious prejudice. At that stage, our worrying has to go beyond the issue of individual costs and benefits and look to the moral corruption of the system as a whole.

[V.]

A [second] reason for taking care with balancing arguments is that one of the terms—"liberty"—is a relational term, so that it has ramifications for both sides of the balance.

When liberty is understood (as it usually is) in a negative sense, it is something that cannot be reduced without increasing something else, namely the powers and means and mechanisms that obstruct or punish the ability of individuals to do what they want. Reducing liberty may prevent an action taking place which would otherwise pose a risk of harm. But it necessarily also increases the power of the state, and there is a corresponding risk that this enhanced power may also be used to cause harm.

It is important not to lose sight of this possibility. The protection of civil liberties is not just a matter of (a) cherishing certain freedoms that we particularly value. It is also a matter of suspicion of power, an apprehension that power given to the state is seldom ever used only for the purposes for which it is given, but is always and endemically liable to abuse. Category (b) of our civil liberties concerns picks this up precisely. Whether there is a freedom at stake or not, there are certain powers which we have traditionally thought it better that the state should not have.

Another way of putting this is to say that a commitment to civil liberties is born in part of a "liberalism of fear" (to use Judith Shklar's phrase),[7] that is, an apprehension about what may be done to us using the overwhelming means of force available to the state. True, the events of September 11 have heightened our fear of the worst that can be done to us by individuals and groups other than the state. And an increase in the power of the state may be necessary to prevent or diminish the prospect of that horror. *But the existence of a threat from terrorist attack does not diminish the threat that liberals have traditionally apprehended from the state.* The former complements the latter; it does not diminish it, and it may enhance it. In this regard Shklar notes that the liberalism of fear owes a lot to the political philosophy of John Locke.[8] It will not do, said Locke, in justifying strong unconstrained government, to point to the perils that it might protect us from: "This is to think, that Men are so foolish, that they take care to avoid what Mischiefs may be done them by *Pole-Cats,* or *Foxes,* but are content, nay think it Safety, to be devoured by *Lions*."[9] We have to worry that the very means given to the government to combat our enemies will be used by the government against *its* enemies—and although these those two classes "enemies of the people" and "enemies of the state" overlap, they are not necessarily co-extensive.

Nowhere is this point clearer than in our apprehensions about the use of torture. We all hope and pray that our government will not have resort to this expedient, although there have been suggestions from hitherto respectable civil libertarians that it should do so. There are official assurances that its use is out of the question, though that has to be balanced against the depressing precedent of two of our closest allies in the war against terrorism—the United Kingdom and Israel—having resorted in recent memory to methods very close to torture in dealing with their own terrorist emergencies. And even if we could rely on the official assurances that torture will not be used—and to do so we would want governments that have been rather less mendacious than ours have been about their support for such practices by other regimes in the past—it is worth pondering why this expedient is unthinkable and what that should tell us about other areas where we are less reluctant to sacrifice civil liberties.

On the face of it, the prohibition against torture should be exactly the sort of thing that gives way in the present atmosphere of adjusting the balance between liberty and security. What we are desperate for in the war against terrorism is information—who is planning what—and torture is supposed to be an effective way of securing information. Philosophy classes studying consequentialism thrive on hypotheticals involving scenarios of grotesque disproportion between the pain that a torturer might inflict on an informant and the pain that might be averted by timely use of the information extracted from him: a little bit of pain from the electrodes for him versus five hundred thousand people saved from nuclear incineration. But now the hypotheticals are beginning to look a little less fantastic. Alan Dershowitz asks: what if on September 11 law enforcement officials had "arrested terrorists boarding one of the planes and learned that other planes, then airborne, were heading towards unknown occupied buildings"? Would they not have been justified in torturing the terrorists in their custody—just enough to get the information that would allow the target buildings to be evacuated?[10] How could anyone object to the use of torture if it were dedicated specifically to saving thousands of lives in a case like this?

The answer comes from Henry Shue: "I can see no way to deny the permissibility of torture in a case *just like this.*"[11] But few cases are *just like this:* few have the certainty

11 Henry Shue, "Torture," *Philosophy and Public Affairs,* 7 (1978), 124, at p. 141.
12 Ibid., p. 142.
13 Ibid., p. 143.
14 The formulations in this paragraph are adapted from Shklar; "Liberalism of fear," p. 27.
15 I infer this from the recent case of Jose Padilla, held for having talked about the possibility of detonating a radiological bomb in Washington D.C. See Benjamin Weiser with Dana Canedy, "Traces of terror: the bomb plot," *New York Times,* June 12, 2002, p. A24.

QUESTIONS

1 If laws passed in the interest of security do, in effect, trade off the liberties of a few to safeguard the security of the majority, are such laws morally justifiable? Why or why not?
2 Which civil liberties, if any, should we be willing to give up in the interests of security? What risks would we run if those liberties were curtailed?

SUGGESTED ADDITIONAL READINGS FOR CHAPTER 7

COADY, C. A. J.: "Terrorism and Innocence." *The Journal of Ethics,* vol. 8, March 2004, pp. 37–58. Beginning with a discussion of different definitions of terrorism, Coady advances his own tactical definition. He then focuses on explicating the concept of innocents in definitions of terrorism, unpacking it in terms of noncombatants.

CORLETT, J. ANGELO: *Terrorism: A Philosophical Analysis.* Dordrecht: Kluwer Academic Publishers, 2003. Corlett's analysis covers terrorism and related concepts such as the obligation to obey the law, pacifism, civil disobedience, nonviolent direct action, political violence, revolution, and assassination.

CROTTY, WILLIAM, ed.: *The Politics of Terror: The U.S. Response to 9/11.* Boston: Northeastern University Press, 2003. The primary question addressed in this anthology is, Following 9/11, how can the U.S. strike a balance between national security and civil liberties? The book is divided into four major sections: moral dilemmas, the public response, civil liberties, and institutions and public policy.

DARMER, KATHERINE B., ROBERT M. BAIRD, and STUART E. ROSENBAUM, eds.: *Civil Liberties vs. National Security in a Post-9/11 World.* Amherst, N.Y.: Prometheus Books, 2004. This informative book is divided into six sections: the history of civil liberty issues in wartime, domestic surveillance and the U.S.A. Patriot Act, racial profiling, the use of torture in confessions, the designation of "enemy combatants," plus some recent developments such as the Abu Ghraib prison scandal.

HELD, VIRGINIA: "Terrorism and War." *The Journal of Ethics,* vol. 8, March 2004, pp. 59–75. Held compares terrorism to small wars and argues that just as some wars are less unjustifiable than others, so, too with terrorism. She maintains that we need to make comparable judgments, morally evaluating not simply the actions of terrorists who are seeking change but also the violent actions adopted by governments in order to prevent the changes.

KATCHADOURIAN, HAIG: *Terrorism and Morality.* New York: Peter Lang, 1998. After defining terrorism, Katchadourian argues that all forms of terrorism, even those designed to bring about a moral good, are always wrong because they deprive those who are terrorized of their basic humanity.

STERBA, JAMES P.: *Terrorism and International Justice,* New York: Oxford University Press, 2003. Although some of the articles in this anthology are written by members of other professions, the majority of the writers are philosophers. The articles explore answers to questions such as the following: Is terrorism always wrong, or are there morally justified acts of terrorism? Is war a morally defensible response to the terrorism of 9/11? Do failures of international justice motivate acts of terrorism?

STONE, GEOFFREY R.: *Perilous Times: Free Speech in Wartime.* New York: Norton, 2004. In his exploration of civil liberties in wartime, Stone provides an in-depth constitutional analysis as well as an account of the historical events that gave rise to attempts to curtail free speech. This excellent and informative book begins with the Sedition Act of 1798 and ends with the war on terrorism.

WALZER, MICHAEL: *Just and Unjust Wars: A Moral Argument with Historical Illustrations.* New York: Basic Books, 1977. After developing and defending just war theory, Walzer applies it to various wars including World War II and the war in Vietnam.

CHAPTER 8

Social and Economic Justice

Some people maintain that governmental domestic welfare programs are unjust because the government has no right to tax those who are relatively well off in order to provide funds for those in need. Others argue that it is unjust not to provide government aid to those who lack adequate food, clothing, and shelter. Some people argue that it is the government's role to promote gender equity; others disagree. Disagreements about issues such as these stem in large measure from different conceptions of justice and divergent views on a closely related issue—the morally correct role of government in economic activity. Thus, one of the concerns in this chapter is with the nature of justice and the closely related issue of the role that the government should play in a just society. In addition, some theorists argue that we cannot completely understand injustice without understanding the concept of oppression and the ways that oppressive social structures are inimical to justice. Hence, another concern in this chapter is the nature of oppression.

LIBERTY, EQUALITY, AND CONCEPTIONS OF JUSTICE

Two moral ideals, liberty and equality, are of key importance in conceptions of justice in general and economic justice in particular. A *libertarian* or *individualist* conception of justice holds liberty to be the ultimate moral ideal. A *socialist* conception of justice takes social equality to be the ultimate ideal; and a *liberal* conception of justice tries to combine both equality and liberty into one ultimate moral ideal.

The Libertarian Conception of Justice

For the libertarian, a society is just when individual liberty is maximized. To understand the libertarian position on liberty, it is necessary to see that liberty is not synonymous with freedom. Freedom is the broader category; liberty is one aspect of freedom. If freedom is understood as the overall absence of constraint,

liberty can be understood as the absence of a specific kind of constraint—
coercion, the forceful and deliberate interference by human beings in the affairs of
other human beings. Coercion can take two forms—either the direct use of physical force or the threat of harm, backed up by enforcement power. An example will
illustrate why liberty is not synonymous with freedom. In some countries, citizens
need a government permit to live and work in certain cities. Thus, their freedom,
more specifically their liberty to live and work in those cities, is restricted by coercion, the threat of harm should they disobey the rules. In the United States, citizens do not need such permits. There are no laws that threaten them with harm
should they choose to move to New York City or Los Angeles. But not everyone
who wants to do so is free to go to live and work in either city. All kinds of constraints may prevent it. Individuals may not have the money for transportation, for
example, and this lack may limit their freedom to do what they wish to do. The
jobs they are capable of doing may not be available, and this lack, too, may prevent them from moving to the city of their choice. Thus, individual freedom may
be limited in many ways. It is important to see that when libertarians advocate the
maximization of liberty, they are not concerned with maximizing freedom in general. Their focus is on minimizing coercion, especially on minimizing the coercive
interferences of governments.

In a libertarian view, individuals have certain moral rights to life, liberty, and
property, which any just society must recognize and respect. These rights are
sometimes described as warnings against interference: If A has a right to X, no one
should prevent A from pursuing X or deprive A of X, since A is entitled to it.
According to a libertarian, the sole function of the government is to protect the
individual's life, liberty, and property against force and fraud. Everything else in
society is a matter of individual responsibility, decision, and action. Providing for
the welfare of those who cannot or will not provide for themselves is not a morally
justifiable function of government. To make such provisions, the government
would have to take from some against their will in order to give to others. This is
perceived as an unjustifiable coercive limitation on individual liberty. Individuals
own their own bodies (or lives) and, therefore, the labor they exert. It follows, for
the libertarian, that individuals have the right to whatever income or wealth their
labor can earn in a free marketplace. Taxing some to give to others is analogous to
robbery. John Hospers, who defends a libertarian position in this chapter, argues
that laws requiring people to help one another (e.g., via welfare payments) rob
Peter to pay Paul.

Libertarians consider *laissez-faire capitalism* to be the only just economic system, because it is based on individual rights. Capitalism is an economic system
based on the private ownership of the means of production, the means whereby
consumer goods and services are produced (for example, land used to produce food
crops, as well as factories and equipment used to manufacture goods). Under
laissez-faire capitalism, all the means of production are privately owned, and there
is a totally *free market.* In a free market system, the economy is uncontrolled and
unregulated by any governmental actions or policies. Income is distributed and production is guided through the operation of markets. The government's only role in
the economic sphere is to protect individuals against force and fraud.

The Socialist Conception of Justice

A direct challenge to libertarians comes from those who defend a socialist conception of justice. There are many varieties of socialism. However, there are two common elements in socialist thought: (1) a commitment to the public ownership of the means of production and (2) a commitment to the ideal of equality. Equality is a complex ideal, including both the conception of moral equality and the conception of equality of condition. Moral equality is the belief that everyone's life matters equally. Equality of condition includes such ideals as equality of opportunity, the equal satisfaction of needs, and other factors that foster greater social equality. Since equality of condition is a central ideal, limitations on individual liberty, specifically on certain economic liberties, are seen as justified when they are necessary to promote equality.

Socialists attack libertarian views on the primacy of liberty, in at least three ways. *First,* they offer defenses of their ideal of social equality. These take various forms and will not concern us here. *Second,* they point out the meaninglessness of libertarian rights to those who lack adequate food, shelter, health care, and so on. For those who lack the money to buy the food and health care needed to sustain life, the libertarian right to life is an empty sham. The rights of liberty, such as the right to freedom of speech, are a joke to those who cannot exercise them because of economic considerations. *Third,* some defenders of socialism, such as Kai Nielsen in this chapter, argue that most people will have much more freedom in a socialist system than in a libertarian one because they will have more control over their economic lives. The freedom that the socialist wants to maximize, however, requires a society in which individuals have the greatest possible range of choices and not simply one in which government interference is minimal. It is important to recognize the difference between the socialist's conception of freedom and the libertarian's conception of liberty. Whereas libertarians stress liberty—understood as freedom from coercion, especially from government interference—socialists stress freedom from want. Whereas libertarians stress negative rights (rights not to be interfered with), socialists stress positive rights—rights *to* food, health care, productive work, and so on. Whereas libertarians criticize socialism for the limitations it imposes on liberty, socialists criticize libertarianism for allowing gross inequalities among those who are *moral equals.*

The Liberal Conception of Justice

Like the socialist, the liberal[1] rejects the libertarian conception of justice. Socialists and liberals agree in recognizing the extent to which economic constraints in industrial and technologically advanced societies effectively limit the exercise of libertarian rights by those lacking economic power. Unlike the socialist, however, the liberal considers some of the libertarian's negative rights extremely important and advocates social institutions that do two important things: (1) ensure certain basic liberties for all (e.g., freedom of speech), not allowing these liberties to be set aside

[1]There is a great deal of disagreement about the correct characterization of liberalism. The presentation here encapsulates one prominent way of understanding the term. For a different approach see Ronald Dworkin, "Liberalism," in *A Matter of Principle* (Cambridge, Mass.: Harvard University Press, 1985), pp. 181–204.

to promote other goals, such as social or economic equality, and (2) provide for the economic needs of the disadvantaged members of society. Like the socialists, liberals see equality as an important value, but they do not oppose all social and economic inequalities. Rather, they are committed to a principle of *basic worth*—all individuals are entitled to equal concern for their interests in the design of the basic institutions of their society. Moreover, all individuals also have the right to be equally respected in their desire to lead their lives on their own terms.

Liberals disagree among themselves, however, concerning the morally acceptable extent of social and economic inequalities and their correct justification. A utilitarian liberal might hold that inequalities are justified to the extent that allowing them maximizes the total amount of good in a society. If, for example, increased productivity depends on giving workers a significantly higher income than that given to welfare recipients, and if such incentive-stimulated productivity increases the total amount of good in a society, then the inequalities between the assembly-line workers and the welfare recipient would be justified for the utilitarian. A different approach is taken by John Rawls, who is considered a liberal egalitarian. He maintains that social and economic inequalities are justified only if they are compatible with fair equality of opportunity and contribute to raising the position of the least advantaged in society. Rawls's view is expressed in *the difference principle,* which asserts that social and economic inequalities are to be arranged so that they are both (a) reasonably expected to be to everyone's advantage, especially to the advantage of the least advantaged, and (b) attached to positions and offices open to all.[2]

In one of this chapter's readings, Howard McGary, arguing from a liberal perspective, maintains that some of our society's basic institutions are unjust with respect to a group of people who could be considered among the least advantaged in our society—the African-American underclass. He points, for example, to the inadequacies of the current health-care system and to an economic system that effectively denies members of the underclass any real equality of opportunity to obtain work that is satisfying and that draws on their abilities and talents.

The socioeconomic system that best coheres with the liberal conception of justice is *welfare-state capitalism.* In welfare-state capitalism, as in any form of capitalism, the means of production are, for the most part, privately owned. However, under welfare-state capitalism, the state plays an important role in protecting and promoting the economic and social well-being of its citizens. Under welfare-state capitalism, for example, the state bears the responsibility for protecting workers against the power of the capitalists. Laws that mandate a minimum wage are an example of this sort of protection, as are laws that require humane and safe working conditions. The government also bears the responsibility for structuring social reality in such a way that those who are unable to provide themselves with the necessities of life have their needs met. Thus, in accordance with the liberal conception of justice, raising money through taxation in order to provide funds for programs designed to help the needy attain food, clothing, shelter, and medical care is considered a morally legitimate (in fact, a morally required) state activity. Lessening social and economic inequalities is also seen as a legitimate goal in welfare-state capitalism.

[2]John Rawls, *A Theory of Justice* (Cambridge, Mass.: Harvard University Press), pp. 60, 302.

In one of this chapter's readings, Nancy Fraser argues that we need a new vision of the welfare state for the postindustrial age. In her view, the ideal underlying welfare programs during the industrial age was the now-outdated family-wage model premised on a nuclear family headed by a male breadwinner who would be paid a "family wage"—one sufficient to meet the needs of all the family members. Welfare programs that were geared to this model provided various forms of social insurance to cover the loss of the breadwinner's earnings, such as disability and unemployment insurance. They also provided aid to families without such breadwinners through welfare programs such as the now discarded Aid to Families with Dependent Children (AFDC). Fraser, writing from a feminist perspective, presents and evaluates three different visions of the postindustrial welfare state, each of which includes a commitment to gender equity.

OPPRESSION AND INJUSTICE

Much of the discussion of injustice in the United States is formulated in the language and within the framework of liberalism. However, some would argue that the categories of liberalism are inadequate tools for analyzing and evaluating the failure of our current social structures and practices to accord with justice. According to this line of reasoning, one of the categories that must be used when attempting to identify systematic injustices in our society is the category of oppression.

As normally understood, *oppression* is not a value-neutral term. To say that one person oppresses another or that an institution systematically oppresses some people is to express a criticism of the oppressor or institutional practice. Of course, not every constraint or limitation can correctly be described as oppressive. Chapter 5, for example, presents arguments regarding justifiable limitations on individual freedom. When laws are passed threatening individuals with harm if they harm others, those laws can be seen as constraining. But it would be a mistake to claim that the very existence of such laws is a form of oppression. Parents limit their children's freedom in all sorts of ways for their own good, but requiring their children to do a reasonable amount of schoolwork instead of playing video games all the time can hardly be seen as a form of oppression. Thus, whatever oppression is, it cannot be identified simply with constraints or limitations imposed on individuals by either other individuals or social structures.

Traditionally, oppression has been understood as the abuse of power by a ruling group and, hence, has been treated as synonymous with tyranny or despotism. On this understanding of oppression, a powerful group deliberately adopts policies intended to subjugate another group. The now disbanded system of apartheid in South Africa provides one example of this kind of oppression. But oppression, as it is understood by many writers today, need not involve the conscious and intentional subjugation of one group by another. The focus of these writers is on the way that economic, political, and cultural institutions systematically function to disadvantage certain groups even in well-intentioned societies. According to this view of oppression, all oppression involves two characteristics. First, a person is not oppressed as *a particular individual* but as *a member of a specific group*. Thus, one's oppressive treatment is due not to one's personal characteristics but to the characteristics attributed to one's group. Second, oppression is systematic. As Kenneth Clatterbaugh explains,

> Oppression of a group is systematic; that is, it exists throughout a society, usually over a substantial period of time, and the institutions of society interlock and reinforce each other in ways that create and maintain the oppression. For example, oppressed groups may be denied access to valuable resources of the society and in turn their lack of such resources may be used as evidence that they should continue to be denied access. Thus, the practice feeds the justification and the justification supports the practice.[3]

Iris M. Young maintains in this chapter that it is not possible to give a general definition of oppression. She grants that all oppressed people have something in common: They all suffer some inhibition of their ability to develop and exercise their capacities and express their needs, thoughts, and feelings. Beyond this, however, we cannot identify an attribute or a set of attributes that all oppressed people have in common. Rather, there are different forms of oppression: exploitation, marginalization, powerlessness, cultural imperialism, and systematic violence. The first three involve relations of power and oppression that result from the social division of labor. (Young's discussion of exploitation is particularly relevant to Nielsen's criticisms of capitalism in this chapter.) Cultural imperialism involves the acceptance of one group's experiences, values, goals, and achievements as universal. These norms are then used in judging members of other groups as deviant and inferior. Finally, systematic violence against individuals because of their group membership is seen as a form of oppression. Members of such groups share the knowledge that they may be victims of violence solely on the basis of their group identity. Young brings out the ways that these forms of oppression intersect, so that some groups can be judged to be more oppressed than others even though no one definition of oppression is possible.

Jane S. Zembaty

[3]Kenneth Clatterbaugh, "The Oppression Debate in Sexual Politics," in Larry May and Robert A. Strikwerda, eds., *Rethinking Masculinity* (Lanham, Md.: Rowman and Littlefield, 1992), p. 171.

What Libertarianism Is

John Hospers

Hospers defends two ideas central to libertarianism: (1) Individuals own their own lives. They, therefore, have the right to act as they choose unless their actions interfere with the liberty of others to act as they choose. (2) The only appropriate function of government is to protect human rights, understood as negative rights (i.e., rights of noninterference).

Reprinted with permission of Nelson-Hall Inc., Publishers, from Tibor R. Machan, ed., *The Libertarian Alternative* (1974).

The political philosophy that is called libertarianism (from the Latin *libertas,* liberty) is the doctrine that every person is the owner of his own life, and that no one is the owner of anyone else's life; and that consequently every human being has the right to act in accordance with his own choices, unless those actions infringe on the equal liberty of other human beings to act in accordance with *their* choices.

There are several other ways of stating the same libertarian thesis:

1 *No one is anyone else's master, and no one is anyone else's slave.* Since I am the one to decide how my life is to be conducted, just as you decide about yours, I have no right (even if I had the power) to make you my slave and be your master, nor have you the right to become the master by enslaving me. Slavery is *forced* servitude, and since no one owns the life of anyone else, no one has the right to enslave another. Political theories past and present have traditionally been concerned with who should be the master (usually the king, the dictator, or government bureaucracy) and who should be the slaves, and what the extent of the slavery should be. Libertarianism holds that no one has the right to use force to enslave the life of another, or any portion or aspect of that life.

2 *Other men's lives are not yours to dispose of.* I enjoy seeing operas; but operas are expensive to produce. Opera-lovers often say, "The state (or the city, etc.) should subsidize opera, so that we can all see it. Also it would be for people's betterment, cultural benefit, etc." But what they are advocating is nothing more or less than legalized plunder. They can't pay for the productions themselves, and yet they want to see opera, which involves a large number of people and their labor; so what they are saying in effect is, "Get the money through legalized force. Take a little bit more out of every worker's paycheck every week to pay for the operas we want to see." But I have no right to take by force from the workers' pockets to pay for what I want.

Perhaps it would be better if he *did* go to see opera—then I should try to convince him to go voluntarily. But to take the money from him forcibly, because in my opinion it would be good for *him,* is still seizure of his earnings, which is plunder.

Besides, if I have the right to force him to help pay for my pet projects, hasn't he equally the right to force me to help pay for his? Perhaps he in turn wants the government to subsidize rock-and-roll, or his new car, or a house in the country? If I have the right to milk him, why hasn't he the right to milk me? If I can be a moral cannibal, why can't he too?

We should beware of the inventors of utopias. They would remake the world according to their vision—with the lives and fruits of the labor of *other* human beings. Is it someone's utopian vision that others should build pyramids to beautify the landscape? Very well, then other men should provide the labor; and if he is in a position of political power, and he can't get men to do it voluntarily, then he must *compel* them to "cooperate"—i.e. he must enslave them.

A hundred men might gain great pleasure from beating up or killing just one insignificant human being; but other men's lives are not theirs to dispose of. "In order to achieve the worthy goals of the next five-year-plan, we must forcibly collectivize the peasants . . ."; but other men's lives are not theirs to dispose of. Do you want to occupy, rent-free, the mansion that another man has worked for twenty years to buy? But other men's lives are not yours to dispose of. Do you want operas so badly that everyone is forced to work harder to pay for their subsidization through taxes? But other men's lives are not yours to dispose of. Do you want to have free medical care at the expense of other people, whether they wish to provide it or not? But this would require them to work longer for you whether they want to or not, and other men's lives are not yours to dispose of.

> The freedom to engage in any type of enterprise, to produce, to own and control property, to buy and sell on the free market, is derived from the rights to life, liberty, and property . . . which are stated in the Declaration of Independence . . . [but] when a government guarantees a "right" to an education or parity on farm products or a guaranteed annual income, it is staking a claim on the property of one group of citizens for the sake of another group. In short, it is violating one of the fundamental rights it was instituted to protect.[1]

3 *No human being should be a nonvoluntary mortgage on the life of another.* I cannot claim your life, your work, or the products of your effort as mine. The fruit of one man's labor should not be fair game for every freeloader who comes along and demands it as his own. The orchard that has been carefully grown, nurtured, and harvested by its owner should not be ripe for the plucking for any bypasser who has a yen for the ripe fruit. The wealth that some men have produced should not be fair game for looting by government, to be used for whatever purposes its representatives determine, no matter what their motives in so doing may be. The theft of your money by a robber is not justified by the fact that he used it to help his injured mother.

It will already be evident that libertarian doctrine is embedded in a view of the rights of man. Each human being has the right to live his life as he chooses, compatibly with the equal right of all other human beings to live their lives as they choose.

All man's rights are implicit in the above statement. Each man has the right to life; any attempt by others to take it away from him, or even to injure him, violates this right, through the use of coercion against him. Each man has the right to liberty: to conduct his life in accordance with the alternatives open to him without coercive action by others. And every man has the right to property: to work to sustain his life (and the lives of whichever others he chooses to sustain, such as his family) and to retain the fruits of his labor.

People often defend the rights of life and liberty but denigrate property rights, and yet the right to property is as basic as the other two; indeed, without property rights no other rights are possible. Depriving you of property is depriving you of the means by which you live.

> . . . All that which an individual possesses by right (including his life and property) are morally his to use, dispose of and even destroy, as he sees fit. If I own my life, then it follows that I am free to associate with whom I please and not to associate with whom I please. If I own my knowledge and services, it follows that I may ask any compensation I wish for providing them for another, or I may abstain from providing them at all, if I so choose. If I own my house, it follows that I may decorate it as I please and live in it with whom I please. If I control my own business, it follows that I may charge what I please

for my products or services, hire whom I please and not hire whom I please. All that which I own in fact, I may dispose of as I choose to in reality. For anyone to attempt to limit my freedom to do so is to violate my rights.

Where do my rights end? Where yours begin. I may do anything I wish with my own life, liberty and property without your consent; but I may do nothing with your life, liberty and property without your consent. If we recognize the principle of man's rights, it follows that the individual is sovereign of the domain of his own life and property, and is sovereign of no other domain. To attempt to interfere forcibly with another's use, disposal or destruction of his own property is to initiate force against him and to violate his rights.

I have no right to decide how *you* should spend your time or your money. I can make that decision for myself, but not for you, my neighbor. I may deplore your choice of life-style, and I may talk with you about it provided you are willing to listen to me. But I have no right to use force to change it. Nor have I the right to decide how you should spend the money you have earned. I may appeal to you to give it to the Red Cross, and you may prefer to go to prizefights. But that is your decision, and however much I may chafe about it I do not have the right to interfere forcibly with it, for example by robbing you in order to use the money in accordance with *my* choices. (If I have the right to rob you, have you also the right to rob me?)

When I claim a right, I carve out a niche, as it were, in my life, saying in effect, "This activity I must be able to perform without interference from others. For you and everyone else, this is off limits." And so I put up a "no trespassing" sign, which marks off the area of my right. Each individual's right is his "no trespassing" sign in relation to me and others. I may not encroach upon his domain any more than he upon mine, without my consent. Every right entails a duty, true—but the duty is only that of *forbearance*—that is, of *refraining* from violating the other person's right. If you have a right to life, I have no right to take your life; if you have a right to the products of your labor (property), I have no right to take it from you without your consent. The non-violation of these rights will not guarantee you protection against natural catastrophes such as floods and earthquakes, but it will protect you against the aggressive activities *of other men*. And rights, after all, have to do with one's relations to other human beings, not with one's relations to physical nature.

Nor were these rights created by government; governments—some governments, obviously not all—*recognize* and *protect* the rights that individuals already have. Governments regularly forbid homicide and theft; and, at a more advanced stage, protect individuals against such things as libel and breach of contract. . . .

Government is the most dangerous institution known to man. Throughout history it has violated the rights of men more than any individual or group of individuals could do: it has killed people, enslaved them, sent them to forced labor and concentration camps, and regularly robbed and pillaged them of the fruits of their expended labor. Unlike individual criminals, government has the power to arrest and try; unlike individual criminals, it can surround and encompass a person totally, dominating every aspect of one's life, so that one has no recourse from it but to leave the country (and in totalitarian nations even that is prohibited). Government throughout history has a much sorrier record than any individual, even that of a ruthless mass murderer. The signs we see on bumper stickers are chillingly accurate: "Beware: the Government is Armed and Dangerous."

The only proper role of government, according to libertarians, is that of the protector of the citizen against aggression by other individuals. The government, of course, should never initiate aggression; its proper role is as the embodiment of the *retaliatory* use of force against anyone who initiates its use.

If each individual had constantly to defend himself against possible aggressors, he would have to spend a considerable portion of his life in target practice, karate exercises, and other means of self-defenses, and even so he would probably be helpless against groups of individuals who might try to kill, maim, or rob him. He would have little time for cultivating those qualities which are essential to civilized life, nor would improvements in science, medicine, and the arts be likely to occur. The function of government is to take this responsibility off his shoulders: the government undertakes to defend him against aggressors and to punish them if they attack him. When the government is effective in doing this, it enables the citizen to go about his business unmolested and without constant fear for his life. To do this, of course, government must have physical power—the police, to protect the citizen from aggression within its borders, and the armed forces, to protect him from aggressors outside. Beyond that, the government should not intrude upon his life, either to run his business, or adjust his daily activities, or prescribe his personal moral code.

Government, then, undertakes to be the individual's protector; but historically governments have gone far beyond this function. Since they already have the physical power, they have not hesitated to use it for purposes far beyond that which was entrusted to them in the first place. Undertaking initially to protect its citizens against aggression, it has often itself become an aggressor—a far greater aggressor, indeed, than the criminals against whom it was supposed to protect its citizens. Governments have done what no private citizen can do: arrest and imprison individuals without a trial and send them to slave labor camps. Government must have power in order to be effective—and yet the very means by which alone it can be effective make it vulnerable to the abuse of power, leading to managing the lives of individuals and even inflicting terror upon them.

What then should be the function of government? In a word, the *protection of human rights*.

1 *The right to life:* libertarians support all such legislation as will protect human beings against the use of force by others, for example, laws against killing, attempted killing, maiming, beating, and all kinds of physical violence.

2 *The right to liberty:* there should be no laws compromising in any way freedom of speech, of the press, and of peaceable assembly. There should be no censorship of ideas, books, films, or of anything else by government.

3 *The right to property:* libertarians support legislation that protects the property rights of individuals against confiscation, nationalization, eminent domain, robbery, trespass, fraud and misrepresentation, patent and copyright, libel and slander.

Someone has violently assaulted you. Should he be legally liable? Of course. He has violated one of your rights. He has knowingly injured you, and since he has initiated aggression against you he should be made to expiate.

Someone has negligently left his bicycle on the sidewalk where you trip over it in the dark and injure yourself. He didn't do it intentionally; he didn't mean you any harm. Should he be legally liable? Of course; he has, however unwittingly, injured you, and since the injury is caused by him and you are the victim, he should pay.

Someone across the street is unemployed. Should you be taxed extra to pay for his expenses? Not at all. You have not injured him, you are not responsible for the fact that he is unemployed (unless you are a senator or bureaucrat who agitated for further curtailing of business, which legislation passed, with the result that your neighbor was laid off by the curtailed business). You may voluntarily wish to help him out, or better still, try to get him a job to put him on his feet again; but since you have initiated no aggressive act against him, and neither purposely nor accidentally injured him in any way, you should not be legally penalized for the fact of his unemployment. (Actually, it is just such penalties that increase unemployment.)

One man, A, works hard for years and finally earns a high salary as a professional man. A second man, B, prefers not to work at all, and to spend wastefully what money he has (through inheritance), so that after a year or two he has nothing left. At the end of this time he has a long siege of illness and lots of medical bills to pay. He demands that the bills be paid by the government—that is, by the taxpayers of the land, including Mr. A.

But of course B has no such right. He chose to lead his life in a certain way—that was his voluntary decision. One consequence of that choice is that he must depend on charity in case of later need. Mr. A chose not to live that way. (And if everyone lived like Mr. B, on whom would he depend in case of later need?) Each has a right to live in the way he pleases, but each must live with the consequences of his own decision (which, as always, fall primarily on himself). He cannot, in time of need, claim A's beneficence as his right. . . .

Laws may be classified into three types: (1) laws protecting individuals against themselves, such as laws against fornication and other sexual behavior, alcohol, and drugs; (2) laws protecting individuals against aggressions by other individuals, such as laws against murder, robbery, and fraud; (3) laws requiring people to help one another; for example, all laws which rob Peter to pay Paul, such as welfare.

Libertarians reject the first class of laws totally. Behavior which harms no one else is strictly the individual's own affair. Thus, there should be no laws against becoming intoxicated, since whether or not to become intoxicated is the individual's own decision; but there should be laws against driving while intoxicated, since the drunken driver is a threat to every other motorist on the highway (drunken driving falls into type 2). Similarly, there should be no laws against drugs (except the prohibition of sale of drugs to minors) as long as the taking of these drugs poses no threat to anyone else. Drug addiction is a psychological problem to which no present solution exists. Most of the social harm caused by addicts,

other than to themselves, is the result of thefts which they perform in order to continue their habit—and then the *legal* crime is the theft, not the addiction. The
actual cost of heroin is about ten cents a shot; if it were legalized, the enormous
traffic in illegal sale and purchase of it would stop, as well as the accompanying
proselytization to get new addicts (to make more money for the pusher) and the
thefts performed by addicts who often require eighty dollars a day just to keep up
the habit. Addiction would not stop, but the crimes would: it is estimated that
75 percent of the burglaries in New York City today are performed by addicts, and
all these crimes would be wiped out at one stroke through the legalization of
drugs. (Only when the taking of drugs could be shown to constitute a threat to
others, should it be prohibited by law. It is only laws protecting people against
themselves that libertarians oppose.)

Laws should be limited to the second class only: aggression by individuals
against other individuals. These are laws whose function is to protect human beings
against encroachment by others; and this, as we have seen, is (according to libertarianism) the sole function of government.

Libertarians also reject the third class of laws totally: no one should be forced by
law to help others, not even to tell them the time of day if requested, and certainly not
to give them a portion of one's weekly paycheck. Governments, in the guise of human-
itarianism, have given to some by taking from others (charging a "handling fee" in the
process, which, because of the government's waste and inefficiency, sometimes is several hundred percent). And in so doing they have decreased incentive, violated the
rights of individuals, and lowered the standard of living of almost everyone.

All such laws constitute what libertarians call *moral cannibalism.* A cannibal in
the physical sense is a person who lives off the flesh of other human beings. A
moral cannibal is one who believes he has a right to live off the "spirit" of other
human beings—who believes that he has a moral claim on the productive capacity,
time, and effort expended by others.

It has become fashionable to claim virtually everything that one needs or desires
as one's *right.* Thus, many people claim that they have a right to a job, the right to
free medical care, to free food and clothing, to a decent home, and so on. Now if
one asks, apart from any specific context, whether it would be desirable if everyone
had these things, one might well say yes. But there is a gimmick attached to each
of them: *At whose expense?* Jobs, medical care, education, and so on, don't grow
on trees. These are goods and services *produced only by men.* Who, then, is to provide them, and under what conditions?

If you have a right to a job, who is to supply it? Must an employer supply it even if
he doesn't want to hire you? What if you are unemployable, or incurably lazy? (If you
say "the government must supply it," does that mean that a job must be created for you
which no employer needs done, and that you must be kept in it regardless of how much
or little you work?) If the employer is forced to supply it at his expense even if he
doesn't need you, then isn't *he* being enslaved to that extent? What ever happened to
his right to conduct his life and his affairs in accordance with his choices?

If you have a right to free medical care, then, since medical care doesn't exist
in nature as wild apples do, some people will have to supply it to you for free:
that is, they will have to spend their time and money and energy taking care of

you whether they want to or not. What ever happened to *their* right to conduct their lives as they see fit? Or do you have a right to violate theirs? Can there be a right to violate rights?

All those who demand this or that as a "free service" are consciously or unconsciously evading the fact that there is in reality no such thing as free services. All man-made goods and services are the result of human expenditure of time and effort. There is no such thing as "something for nothing" in this world. If you demand something free, you are demanding that other men give their time and effort to you without compensation. If they voluntarily choose to do this, there is no problem; but if you demand that they be *forced* to do it, you are interfering with their right not to do it if they so choose. "Swimming in this pool ought to be free!" says the indignant passerby. What he means is that others should build a pool, others should provide the materials, and still others should run it and keep it in functioning order, so that *he* can use it without fee. But what right has he to the expenditure of *their* time and effort? To expect something "for free" is to expect it *to be paid for by others* whether they choose to or not.

Many questions, particularly about economic matters, will be generated by the libertarian account of human rights and the role of government. Should government have no role in assisting the needy, in providing social security, in legislating minimum wages, in fixing prices and putting a ceiling on rents, in curbing monopolies, in erecting tariffs, in guaranteeing jobs, in managing the money supply? To these and all similar questions the libertarian answers with an unequivocal no.

"But then you'd let people go hungry!" comes the rejoinder. This, the libertarian insists, is precisely what would not happen; with the restrictions removed, the economy would flourish as never before. With the controls taken off business, existing enterprises would expand and new ones would spring into existence satisfying more and more consumer needs; millions more people would be gainfully employed instead of subsisting on welfare, and all kinds of research and production, released from the stranglehold of government, would proliferate, fulfilling man's needs and desires as never before. It has always been so whenever government has permitted men to be free traders on a free market. But *why* this is so, and how the free market is the best solution to all problems relating to the material aspect of man's life, is another and far longer story. . . .

NOTE

1 William W. Bayes, "What Is Property?" *The Freeman,* July 1970, p. 348.

QUESTIONS

1 Some libertarians argue that, from a moral standpoint, there is no difference between the actions of an ordinary thief and those of a government when it seizes money from some in order to support others. They assume that, if the former are wrong, then so are the latter. Are they correct?

2 Do you agree that the government should have no role in assisting the needy? What reasons can you advance to defend your answer?

A Moral Case for Socialism

Kai Nielsen

Nielsen puts forth a moral case for socialism. He identifies and explicates a cluster of values that are basic to our culture—freedom and autonomy, equality, justice, rights, and democracy—and then compares "pure socialism" and "pure capitalism" in respect to these values. Nielsen concludes that a socialist system is much more likely to exemplify our basic values than is a capitalist system.

I

In North America socialism gets a bad press. It is under criticism for its alleged economic inefficiency and for its moral and human inadequacy. I want here to address the latter issue. Looking at capitalism and socialism, I want to consider, against the grain of our culture, what kind of moral case can be made for socialism.

The first thing to do, given the extensive, and, I would add, inexcusably extensive, confusions about this, is to say what socialism and capitalism are. That done I will then, appealing to a cluster of values which are basic in our culture, concerning which there is a considerable and indeed a reflective consensus, examine how capitalism and socialism fare with respect to these values. Given that people generally, at least in Western societies, would want it to be the case that these values have a stable exemplification in our social lives, it is appropriate to ask the question: which of these social systems is more likely stably to exemplify them? I shall argue, facing the gamut of a careful comparison in the light of these values, that, everything considered, socialism comes out better than capitalism. And this, if right, would give us good reason for believing that socialism is preferable—indeed morally preferable—to capitalism if it also turns out to be a feasible socio-economic system.

What, then, are socialism and capitalism? Put most succinctly, capitalism requires the existence of private *productive* property (private ownership of the means of production) while socialism works toward its abolition. What is essential for socialism is public ownership and control of the means of production and public ownership means just what it says: *ownership by the public.* Under capitalism there is a domain of private property rights in the means of production which are not subject to political determination. That is, even where the political domain is a democratic one, they are not subject to determination by the public; only an individual or a set of individuals who own that property can make the final determination of what is to be done with that property. These individuals make the determination and not citizens at large, as under socialism. In fully developed socialism, by contrast, there is, with respect to productive property, no domain which is not subject to political determination by the public, namely by the citizenry at large. Thus, where this public ownership and control is genuine, and not a mask for control by an elite of state bureaucrats, it will mean genuine popular and democratic control over productive

Reprinted with permission from *Critical Review,* vol. 3, Summer/Fall 1989, pp. 542–552.

property. What socialism is *not* is *state* ownership in the absence of, at the very least, popular sovereignty, i.e., genuine popular control over the state apparatus including any economic functions it might have.

The property that is owned in common under socialism is the means of existence—the productive property in the society. Socialism does not proscribe the ownership of private personal property, such as houses, cars, television sets and the like. It only proscribes the private ownership of the means of production.

The above characterizations catch the minimal core of socialism and capitalism, what used to be called the essence of those concepts. But beyond these core features, it is well, in helping us to make our comparison, to see some other important features which characteristically go with capitalism and socialism. Minimally, capitalism is private ownership of the means of production but it is also, at least characteristically, a social system in which a class of capitalists owns and controls the means of production and hires workers who, owning little or no means of production, sell their labor-power to some capitalist or other for a wage. This means that a capitalist society will be a class society in which there will be two principal classes: capitalists and workers. Socialism by contrast is a social system in which every able-bodied person is, was or will be a worker. These workers commonly own and control the means of production (this is the characteristic form of public ownership). Thus in socialism we have, in a perfectly literal sense, a classless society for there is no division between human beings along class lines.

There are both pure and impure forms of capitalism and socialism. The pure form of capitalism is competitive capitalism, the capitalism that Milton Friedman would tell us is the real capitalism while, he would add, the impure form is monopoly or corporate capitalism. Similarly the pure form of socialism is democratic socialism, with firm workers' control of the means of production and an industrial as well as a political democracy, while the impure form is state bureaucratic socialism.

Now it is a noteworthy fact that, to understate it, actually existing capitalisms and actually existing socialisms tend to be the impure forms. Many partisans of capitalism lament the fact that the actually existing capitalisms overwhelmingly tend to be forms of corporate capitalism where the state massively intervenes in the running of the economy. It is unclear whether anything like a fully competitive capitalism actually exists—perhaps Hong Kong approximates it—and it is also unclear whether many of the actual players in the major capitalist societies (the existing capitalists and their managers) want or even expect that it is possible to have laissez-faire capitalism again (if indeed we ever had it). Some capitalist societies are further down the corporate road than other societies, but they are all forms of corporate, perhaps in some instances even monopoly, capitalism. Competitive capitalism seems to be more of a libertarian dream than a sociological reality or even something desired by many informed and tough-minded members of the capitalist class. Socialism has had a similar fate. Its historical exemplifications tend to be of the impure forms, namely the bureaucratic state socialisms. Yugoslavia is perhaps to socialism what Hong Kong is to capitalism. It is a candidate for what might count as an exemplification, or at least a near approximation, of the pure form.

This paucity of exemplifications of pure forms of either capitalism or socialism raises the question of whether the pure forms are at best unstable social systems and at worst merely utopian ideals. I shall not try directly to settle that issue here. What I shall do instead is to compare *models* with *models*. In asking about the moral case for socialism, I shall compare forms that a not inconsiderable number of the theoretical protagonists of each take to be pure forms but which are still, they believe, historically feasible. But I will also be concerned to ask whether these models—these pure forms—can reasonably be expected to come to have a home. If they are not historically feasible models, then, even if we can make a good theoretical moral case for them, we will have hardly provided a good moral case for socialism or capitalism. To avoid bad utopianism we must be talking about forms which could be on the historical agenda. (I plainly here do not take "bad utopianism" to be pleonastic.)

II

Setting aside for the time being the feasibility question, let us compare the pure forms of capitalism and socialism—that is to say, competitive capitalism and dem-ocratic socialism—as to how they stand with respect to sustaining and furthering the values of freedom and autonomy, equality, justice, rights and democracy. My argument shall be that socialism comes out better with respect to those values.

Let us first look at freedom and autonomy. An autonomous person is a person who is able to set her ends for herself and in optimal circumstances is able to pur-sue those ends. But freedom does not only mean being autonomous; it also means the absence of unjustified political and social interference in the pursuit of one's ends. Some might even say that it is just the absence of interference with one's ends. Still it is self-direction—autonomy—not non-interference which is *intrinsically* desirable. Non-interference is only valuable where it is an aid to our being able to do what we want and where we are sufficiently autonomous to have some control over our wants.

How do capitalism and socialism fare in providing the social conditions which will help or impede the flourishing of autonomy? Which model society would make for the greater flourishing of autonomy? My argument is (a) that democratic social-ism makes it possible for more people to be more fully autonomous than would be autonomous under capitalism; and (b) that democratic socialism also interferes less in people's exercise of their autonomy than any form of capitalism. All societies limit liberty by interfering with people doing what they want to do in some ways, but the restrictions are more extensive, deeper and more undermining of autonomy in capitalism than in democratic socialism. Where there is private ownership of pro-ductive property, which, remember, is private ownership of the means of life, it can-not help but be the case that a few (the owning and controlling capitalist class) will have, along with the managers beholden to them, except in periods of revolution-ary turmoil, a firm control, indeed a domination, over the vast majority of people in the society. The capitalist class with the help of their managers determines whether workers (taken now as individuals) can work, how they work, on what they work, the conditions under which they work and what is done with what they produce (where they are producers) and what use is made of their skills and the like. As we move to welfare state capitalism—a compromise still favoring capital which emerged out of long and bitter class struggles—the state places some restrictions on some of these powers of capital. Hours, working conditions and the like are controlled in certain ways. Yet whether workers work and continue to work, how they work and on what, what is done with what they produce, and the rationale for their work are not determined by the workers themselves but by the owners of capital and their managers; this means a very considerable limitation on the autonomy and freedom of workers. Since workers are the great majority, such socio-economic relations place a very considerable limitation on human freedom and indeed on the very most important freedom that people have, namely their being able to live in a self-directed manner, when compared with the industrial democracy of democratic socialism. Under capitalist arrangements it simply cannot fail to be the case that a very large number of people will lose control over a very central set of facets of their lives, namely central aspects of their work and indeed in many instances, over their very chance to be able to work.

Socialism would indeed prohibit capitalist acts between consenting adults; the capitalist class would lose its freedom to buy and sell and to control the labor market. There should be no blinking at the fact that socialist social relations would impose some limitations on freedom, for there is, and indeed can be, no society without norms and some sanctions. In any society you like there will be some things you are at liberty to do and some things that you may not do. However, democratic socialism must bring with it an industrial democracy where workers by various democratic procedures would determine how they are to work, on what they are to work, the hours of their work, under what conditions they are to work (insofar as this is alterable by human effort at all), what they will produce and how much, and what is to be done with what they produce. Since, instead of there being "private ownership of the means of production," there is in a genuinely socialist society "public ownership of the means of production," the means of life are owned by everyone and thus each person has a *right* to work: she has, that is, a right to the means of life. It is no longer the private preserve of an individual owner of capital but it is owned in common by us all. This means that each of us has an equal right to the means of life. Members of the capitalist class would have a few of their liberties restricted, but these are linked with owning and controlling capital and are not the important civil and political liberties that we all rightly cherish. Moreover, the limitation of the capitalist liberties to buy and sell and the like would make for a more extensive liberty for many, many more people.

One cannot respond to the above by saying that workers are free to leave the working class and become capitalists or at least petty bourgeoisie. They may indeed all in theory, taken *individually,* be free to leave the working class, but if many in fact try to leave, the exits will very quickly become blocked. Individuals are only free on the condition that the great mass of people, taken collectively, are not. We could not have capitalism without a working class and the working class is not free within the capitalist system to cease being wage laborers. We cannot all be capitalists. A people's capitalism is nonsense. Though a petty commodity production system (the family farm writ large) is a logical possibility, it is hardly a stable empirical possibility and, what is most important for the present discussion, such a system would not be a capitalist system. Under capitalism, most of us, if we are to find any work at all, will just have to sell (or *perhaps* "rent" is the better word) our labor-power as a commodity. Whether you sell or rent your labor power or, where it is provided, you go on welfare, you will not have much control over areas very crucial to your life. If these are the only feasible alternatives facing the working class, working class autonomy is very limited indeed. But these are the only alternatives under capitalism.

Capitalist acts between consenting adults, if they become sufficiently widespread, lead to severe imbalances in power. These imbalances in power tend to undermine autonomy by creating differentials in wealth and control between workers and capitalists. Such imbalances are the name of the game for capitalism. Even if we (perversely I believe) call a system of petty commodity production capitalism, we still must say that such a socio-economic system is inherently unstable. Certain individuals would win out in this exchanging of commodities and in fairly quick order it would lead to a class system and the imbalances of power—the domination of the many by the few—that I take to be definitive of capitalism. By abolishing capitalist acts between consenting adults, then (but leaving personal property and civil and political liberties untouched), socialism protects more extensive freedoms for more people and in far more important areas of their lives.

III

So democratic socialism does better regarding the value that epitomizes capitalist pride (*hubris,* would, I think, be a better term), namely autonomy. It also does better, I shall now argue, than capitalism with respect to another of our basic values, namely democracy. Since this is almost a corollary of what I have said about autonomy I can afford to be briefer. In capitalist societies, democracy must simply be *political* democracy. There can in the nature of the case be no genuine or thorough workplace democracy. When we enter the sphere of production, capitalists and not workers own, and therefore at least ultimately control, the means of production. While capitalism, as in some workplaces in West Germany and Sweden, sometimes can be pressured into allowing an ameliorative measure of worker control, once ownership rights are given up, we no longer have private productive property but public productive property (and in that way social ownership): capitalism is given up and we have socialism. However, where worker control is restricted to a few firms, we do not yet have socialism. What makes a system socialist or capitalist depends on what happens across the whole society, not just in isolated firms. Moreover, managers can become very important within capitalist firms, but as long as ownership, including the ability to close the place down and liquidate the business, rests in the hands of capitalists we can have no genuine workplace democracy. Socialism, in its pure form, carries with it, in a way capitalism in any form cannot, workplace democracy. (That some of the existing socialisms are anything but pure does not belie this.)

Similarly, whatever may be said of existing socialisms or at least of some existing socialisms, it is not the case that there is anything in the very idea of socialism that militates against political as well as industrial democracy. Socialists are indeed justly suspicious of some of the tricks played by parliamentary democracy in bourgeois countries, aware of its not infrequent hypocrisy and the limitations of its stress on purely legal and formal political rights and liberties. Socialists are also, without at all wishing to throw the baby out with the bath water, rightly suspicious of any simple reliance on majority rule, unsupplemented by other democratic procedures and safeguards. But there is nothing in socialist theory that would set it against political democracy and the protection of political and civil rights; indeed there is much in socialism that favors them, namely its stress on both autonomy and equality.

The fact that political democracy came into being and achieved stability within capitalist societies may prove something about conditions necessary for its coming into being, but it says nothing about capitalism being necessary for sustaining it. In Chile, South Africa and Nazi Germany, indeed, capitalism has flourished without the protection of civil and political rights or anything like a respect for the democratic tradition. There is nothing structural in socialism that would prevent it from continuing those democratic traditions or cherishing those political and civil rights. That something came about under certain conditions does not establish that these conditions are necessary for its continued existence. That men initially took an interest in chess does not establish that women cannot quite naturally take an interest in it as well. When capitalist societies with long-flourishing democratic traditions move to socialism there is no reason at all to believe that they will not continue to be democratic. (Where societies previously had no democratic tradition or only a very weak one, matters are more problematic.)

IV

I now want to turn to a third basic value, equality. In societies across the political spectrum, *moral* equality (the belief that everyone's life matters equally) is an accepted value. Or, to be somewhat cynical about the matter, at least lip service is paid to it. But even this lip service is the compliment that vice pays to virtue. That is to say, such a belief is a deeply held considered conviction in modernized societies, though it has not been at all times and is not today a value held in all societies. This is most evident concerning moral equality.

While this value is genuinely held by the vast majority of people in capitalist societies, it can hardly be an effective or functional working norm where there is such a diminishment of autonomy as we have seen obtains unavoidably in such societies. Self-respect is deeply threatened where so many people lack effective control over their own lives, where there are structures of domination, where there is alienated labor, where great power differentials and differences in wealth make for very different (and often very bleak) life chances. For not inconsiderable numbers, in fact, it is difficult to maintain self-respect under such conditions unless they are actively struggling against the system. And, given present conditions, fighting the system, particularly in societies such as the United States, may well be felt to be a hopeless task. Under such conditions any real equality of opportunity is out of the question. And the circumstances are such, in spite of what is often said about these states, that equality of condition is an even more remote possibility. But without at least some of these things moral equality cannot even be approximated. Indeed, even to speak of it sounds like an obscene joke given the social realities of our lives.

Although under welfare-state capitalism some of the worst inequalities of capitalism are ameliorated, workers still lack effective control over their work, with repercussions in political and public life as well. Differentials of wealth cannot but give rise to differentials in power and control in politics, in the media, in education, in the direction of social life and in what options get seriously debated. The life chances of workers and those not even lucky enough to be workers (whose ranks are growing and will continue to grow under capitalism) are impoverished compared to the life chances of members of the capitalist class and its docile professional support stratum.

None of these equality-undermining features would obtain under democratic socialism. Such societies would, for starters, be classless, eliminating the power and control differentials that go with the class system of capitalism. In addition to political democracy, industrial democracy and all the egalitarian and participatory control that goes with that would, in turn, reinforce moral equality. Indeed it would make it possible where before it was impossible. There would be a commitment under democratic socialism to attaining or at least approximating, as far as it is feasible, equality of condition; and this, where approximated, would help make for real equality of opportunity, making equal life chances something less utopian than it must be under capitalism.

In fine, the very things, as we have seen, that make for greater autonomy under socialism than under capitalism, would, in being more equally distributed, make for greater equality of condition, greater equality of opportunity and greater moral equality in a democratic socialist society than in a capitalist one. These values are values commonly shared by both capitalistically inclined people and those who are socialistically inclined. What the former do not see is that in modern industrial societies, democratic socialism can better deliver these goods than even progressive capitalism.

There is, without doubt, legitimate worry about bureaucratic control under socialism. But that is a worry under any historically feasible capitalism as well, and it is anything but clear that state bureaucracies are worse than great corporate bureaucracies. Indeed, if socialist bureaucrats were, as the socialist system requires, really committed to production for needs and to achieving equality of condition, they might, bad as they are, be the lesser of two evils. But in any event democratic socialism is not bureaucratic state socialism, and there is no structural reason to believe that it must—if it arises in a society with skilled workers committed to democracy—give rise to bureaucratic state socialism. There will, inescapably, be some bureaucracy, but in a democratic socialist society it must and indeed will be controlled. This is not merely a matter of optimism about the will of socialists, for there are more mechanisms for democratic control of bureaucracy within a democratic socialism that is both a political and an industrial democracy, than there can be under even the most benign capitalist democracies—democracies which for structural reasons can never be industrial democracies. If, all that notwithstanding, bureaucratic creepage is inescapable in modern societies, then that is just as much a problem for capitalism as for socialism.

The underlying rationale for production under capitalism is profit and capital accumulation. Capitalism is indeed a marvelous engine for building up the productive forces (though clearly at the expense of considerations of equality and autonomy). We might look on it, going back to earlier historical times, as something like a forced march to develop the productive forces. But now that the productive forces in advanced capitalist societies are wondrously developed, we are in a position to direct them to far more humane and more equitable uses under a socio-economic system whose rationale for production is to meet human needs (the needs of every-one as far as this is possible). This egalitarian thrust, together with the socialists' commitment to attaining, as far as that is possible, equality of condition, makes it clear that socialism will produce more equality than capitalism.

V

In talking about autonomy, democracy and equality, we have, in effect, already been talking about justice. A society or set of institutions that does better in these respects than another society will be a more just society than the other society.

Fairness is a less fancy name for justice. If we compare two societies and the first is more democratic than the second; there is more autonomy in the first society than in the second; there are more nearly equal life chances in the first society than in the second and thus greater equality of opportunity; if, without sacrifice of auton-omy, there is more equality of condition in the first society than in the second; and if there is more moral equality in the first society than in the second, then we can-not but conclude that the first society is a society with more fairness than the sec-ond and, thus, that it is the more just society. But this is exactly how socialism comes out vis-á-vis even the best form of capitalism.

A society which undermines autonomy, heels in democracy (where democracy is not violating rights), makes equality impossible to achieve and violates rights cannot be a just society. If, as I contend, that is what capitalism does, and cannot help doing, then a capitalist society cannot be a just society. Democratic socialism, by contrast, does not need to do any of those things, and we can predict that it would not, for there are no structural imperatives in democratic socialism to do so and there are deep sentiments in that tradition urging us not to do so. I do not for a moment deny that there are similar sentiments for autonomy and democracy in cap-italist societies, but the logic of capitalism, the underlying structures of capitalist societies—even the best of capitalist societies—frustrate the realization of the states of affairs at which those sympathies aim. A radical democrat with a commit-ment to human rights, to human autonomy and moral equality and fair equality of opportunity ought to be a democratic socialist and a firm opponent of capitalism—even a capitalism with a human face.

QUESTIONS

1 Does Nielsen provide good arguments in support of his claim that a socialist system makes it possible for more people to be more fully autonomous than does a capitalist sys-tem?

2 What arguments, if any, could Hospers offer to refute Nielsen's claim that a socialist system is more democratic than a capitalist system?

Five Faces of Oppression

Iris M. Young

In Young's view, all oppressed people have something in common: They all suffer some inhibition of their ability to develop and exercise their capacities and express their needs, thoughts, and feelings. However, no one set of criteria can be used to describe the condition of all those who are oppressed. Rather, oppression takes multiple forms: exploitation, marginalization, powerlessness, cultural imperialism, and systematic violence. In Young's view, the presence of even one of these five conditions is sufficient for calling a group oppressed.

Many people in the United States would not choose the term "oppression" to name injustice in our society. For contemporary emancipatory social movements, on the other hand—socialists, radical feminists, American Indian activists, Black activists, gay and lesbian activists—oppression is a central category of political discourse. Entering the political discourse in which oppression is a central category involves adopting a general mode of analyzing and evaluating social structures and practices which is incommensurate with the language of liberal individualism that dominates political discourse in the United States.

A major political project for those of us who identify with at least one of these movements must thus be to persuade people that the discourse of oppression makes sense of much of our social experience. We are ill prepared for this task, however, because we have no clear account of the meaning of oppression. While we find the term used often in the diverse philosophical and theoretical literature spawned by radical social movements in the United States, we find little direct discussion of the meaning of the concept as used by these movements.

In this [essay] I offer some explication of the concept of oppression as I understand its use by new social movements in the United States since the 1960s. My starting point is reflection on the conditions of the groups said by these movements to be oppressed: among others women, Blacks, Chicanos, Puerto Ricans and other Spanish-speaking Americans, American Indians, Jews, lesbians, gay men, Arabs, Asians, old people, working-class people, and the physically and mentally disabled. I aim to systematize the meaning of the concept of oppression as used by these diverse political movements, and to provide normative argument to clarify the wrongs the term names.

Obviously the above-named groups are not oppressed to the same extent or in the same ways. In the most general sense, all oppressed people suffer some inhibition of their ability to develop and exercise their capacities and express their needs, thoughts, and feelings. In that abstract sense all oppressed people face a common condition. Beyond that, in any more specific sense, it is not possible to define a single set of criteria that describe the condition of oppression of the above groups.

Consequently, attempts by theorists and activists to discover a common description or the essential causes of the oppression of all these groups have frequently led to fruitless disputes about whose oppression is more fundamental or more grave. The contexts in which members of these groups use the term oppression to describe the injustices of their situation suggest that oppression names in fact a family of concepts and conditions, which I divide into five categories: exploitation, marginalization, powerlessness, cultural imperialism, and violence. . . .

THE FACES OF OPPRESSION

Exploitation

The central function of Marx's theory of exploitation is to explain how class structure can exist in the absence of legally and normatively sanctioned class distinctions. In precapitalist societies domination is overt and accomplished through directly political means. In both slave society and feudal society the right to appropriate the product of the labor of others partly defines class privilege, and these societies legitimate class distinctions with ideologies of natural superiority and inferiority.

Capitalist society, on the other hand, removes traditional juridically enforced class distinctions and promotes a belief in the legal freedom of persons. Workers freely contract with employers and receive a wage; no formal mechanisms of law or custom force them to work for that employer or any employer. Thus the mystery of capitalism arises: when everyone is formally free, how can there be class domination? Why do class distinctions persist between the wealthy, who own the means of production, and the mass of people, who work for them? The theory of exploitation answers this question.

Profit, the basis of capitalist power and wealth, is a mystery if we assume that in the market goods exchange at their values. The labor theory of value dispels this mystery. Every commodity's value is a function of the labor time necessary for its production. Labor power is the one commodity which in the process of being consumed produces new value. Profit comes from the difference between the value of the labor performed and the value of the capacity to labor which the capitalist purchases. Profit is possible only because the owner of capital appropriates any realized surplus value. . . .

Marx's theory of exploitation lacks an explicitly normative meaning, even though the judgment that workers are exploited clearly has normative as well as descriptive power in that theory. C. B. Macpherson (1973, chap. 3) reconstructs this theory of exploitation in a more explicitly normative form. The injustice of capitalist society consists in the fact that some people exercise their capacities under the control, according to the purposes, and for the benefit of other people. Through private ownership of the means of production, and through markets that allocate labor and the ability to buy goods, capitalism systematically transfers the powers of some persons to others, thereby augmenting the power of the latter. In this process of the transfer of powers, according to Macpherson, the capitalist class acquires and maintains an ability to extract benefits from workers. Not only are powers transferred from workers to capitalists, but also the powers of workers diminish by more than the amount of transfer, because workers suffer material deprivation and a loss of control, and hence are deprived of important elements of self-respect. Justice, then, requires eliminating the institutional forms that enable and enforce this process of transference and replacing them with institutional forms that enable all to develop and use their capacities in a way that does not inhibit, but rather can enhance, similar development and use in others.

The central insight expressed in the concept of exploitation, then, is that this oppression occurs through a steady process of the transfer of the results of the labor of one social group to benefit another. The injustice of class division does not consist only in the distributive fact that some people have great wealth while most people have little. Exploitation enacts a structural relation between social groups. Social rules about what work is, who does what for whom, how work is compensated, and the social process by which the results of work are appropriated operate to enact relations of power and inequality. These relations are produced and reproduced through a systematic process in which the energies of the have-nots are continuously expended to maintain and augment the power, status, and wealth of the haves. . . .

Feminists have had little difficulty showing that women's oppression consists partly in a systematic and unreciprocated transfer of powers from women to men. Women's oppression consists not merely in an inequality of status, power, and wealth resulting from men's excluding them from privileged activities. The freedom, power, status, and self-realization of men is possible precisely because women work for them. Gender exploitation has two aspects, transfer of the fruits of material labor to men and transfer of nurturing and sexual energies to men.

Christine Delphy (1984), for example, describes marriage as a class relation in which women's labor benefits men without comparable remuneration. She makes it clear that the exploitation consists not in the sort of work that women do in the home, for this might include various kinds of tasks, but in the fact that they perform tasks for someone on whom they are dependent. Thus, for example, in most systems of agricultural production in the world, men take to market the goods women have produced, and more often than not men receive the status and often the entire income from this labor.

With the concept of sex-affective production, Ann Ferguson (1984; 1989, chap. 4) identifies another form of the transference of women's energies to men. Women provide men and children with emotional care and provide men with sexual satisfaction, and as a group receive relatively little of either from men. The gender socialization of women makes us tend to be more attentive to interactive dynamics than men, and makes women good at providing empathy and support for people's feelings and at smoothing over interactive tensions. Both men and women look to women as nurturers of their personal lives, and women frequently complain that when they look to men for emotional support they do not receive it. The norms of heterosexuality, moreover, are oriented around male pleasure, and consequently many women receive little satisfaction from their sexual interaction with men.

Most feminist theories of gender exploitation have concentrated on the institutional structure of the patriarchal family. Recently, however, feminists have begun to explore relations of gender exploitation enacted in the contemporary workplace and through the state. Carol Brown argues that as men have removed themselves from responsibility for children, many women have become dependent on the state for subsistence as they continue to bear nearly total responsibility for childrearing (Brown, 1981). This creates a new system of the exploitation of women's domestic labor mediated by state institutions, which she calls public patriarchy.

In twentieth-century capitalist economies the workplaces that women have been entering in increasing numbers serve as another important site of gender exploitation. David Alexander (1987) argues that typically feminine jobs involve gender-based tasks requiring sexual labor, nurturing, caring for others' bodies, or smoothing over workplace tensions. In these ways women's energies are expended in jobs that enhance the status of, please, or comfort others, usually men; and these gender-based labors of waitresses, clerical workers, nurses, and other caretakers often go unnoticed and undercompensated.

To summarize, women are exploited in the Marxist sense to the degree that they are wage workers. Some have argued that women's domestic labor also represents a form of capitalist class exploitation insofar as it is labor covered by the wages a family receives. As a group, however, women undergo specific forms of gender exploitation in which their energies and power are expended, often unnoticed and unacknowledged, usually to benefit men by releasing them for more important and creative work, enhancing their status or the environment around them, or providing them with sexual or emotional service.

Race is a structure of oppression at least as basic as class or gender. Are there, then, racially specific forms of exploitation? There is no doubt that racialized groups in the United States, especially Blacks and Latinos, are oppressed through capitalist superexploitation resulting from a segmented labor market that tends to reserve skilled, high-paying, unionized jobs for whites. There is wide disagreement about whether such superexploitation benefits whites as a group or only benefits the capitalist class and I do not intend to enter into that dispute here.

However one answers the question about capitalist superexploitation of racialized groups, is it possible to conceptualize a form of exploitation that is racially specific on analogy with the gender-specific forms just discussed? I suggest that the category of *menial* labor might supply a means for such conceptualization. In its derivation "menial" designates the labor of servants. Wherever there is racism, there is the assumption, more or less enforced, that members of the oppressed racial groups are or ought to be servants of those, or some of those, in the privileged group. In most white racist societies this means that many white people have dark- or yellow-skinned domestic servants, and in the United States today there remains significant racial structuring of private household service. But in the United States today much service labor has gone public: anyone who goes to a good hotel or a good restaurant can have servants. Servants often attend the daily—and nightly—activities of business executives, government officials, and other high-status professionals. In our society there remains strong cultural pressure to fill servant jobs—bellhop, porter, chambermaid, busboy, and so on—with Black and Latino workers. These jobs entail a transfer of energies whereby the servers enhance the status of the served.

Menial labor usually refers not only to service, however, but also to any servile, unskilled, low-paying work lacking in autonomy, in which a person is subject to taking orders from many people. Menial work tends to be auxiliary work, instrumental to the work of others, where those others receive primary recognition for doing the job. Laborers on a construction site, for example, are at the beck and call of welders, electricians, carpenters, and other skilled workers, who receive recognition for the job done. In the United States explicit racial discrimination once reserved menial work for Blacks, Chicanos, American Indians, and Chinese, and menial work still tends to be linked to Black and Latino workers. I offer this category of menial labor as a form of racially specific exploitation, as a provisional category in need of exploration. . . .

Marginalization

Increasingly in the United States racial oppression occurs in the form of marginalization rather than exploitation. Marginals are people the system of labor cannot or will not use. Not only in Third World capitalist countries, but also in most Western capitalist societies, there is a growing underclass of people permanently confined to lives of social marginality, most of whom are racially marked—Blacks or Indians in Latin America, and Blacks, East Indians, Eastern Europeans, or North Africans in Europe.

Marginalization is by no means the fate only of racially marked groups, however. In the United States a shamefully large proportion of the population is marginal: old people, and increasingly people who are not very old but get laid off from their jobs and cannot find new work; young people, especially Black or Latino, who cannot find first or second jobs; many single mothers and their children; other people involuntarily unemployed; many mentally and physically disabled people; American Indians, especially those on reservations.

Marginalization is perhaps the most dangerous form of oppression. A whole category of people is expelled from useful participation in social life and thus potentially subjected to severe material deprivation and even extermination. The material deprivation marginalization often causes is certainly unjust, especially in a society where others have plenty. Contemporary advanced capitalist societies have in principle acknowledged the injustice of material deprivation caused by marginalization, and have taken some steps to address it by providing welfare payments and services. The continuance of this welfare state is by no means assured, and in most welfare state societies, especially the United States, welfare redistributions do not eliminate large-scale suffering and deprivation.

Material deprivation, which can be addressed by redistributive social policies, is not, however, the extent of the harm caused by marginalization. Two categories of injustice beyond distribution are associated with marginality in advanced capitalist societies. First, the provision of welfare itself produces new injustice by depriving those dependent on it of rights and freedoms that others have. Second, even when material deprivation is somewhat mitigated by the welfare state, marginalization is unjust because it blocks the opportunity to exercise capacities in socially defined and recognized ways. I shall explicate each of these in turn.

Liberalism has traditionally asserted the right of all rational autonomous agents to equal citizenship. Early bourgeois liberalism explicitly excluded from citizenship all those whose reason was questionable or not fully developed, and all those not independent. Thus poor people, women, the mad and the feebleminded, and children were explicitly excluded from citizenship, and many of these were housed in institutions modeled on the modern prison: poorhouses, insane asylums, schools.

Today the exclusion of dependent persons from equal citizenship rights is only barely hidden beneath the surface. Because they depend on bureaucratic institutions for support or services, the old, the poor, and the mentally or physically disabled are subject to patronizing, punitive, demeaning, and arbitrary treatment by the policies and people associated with welfare bureaucracies. Being a dependent in our society implies being legitimately subject to the often arbitrary and invasive authority of social service providers and other public and private administrators, who enforce rules with which the marginal must comply, and otherwise exercise power over the conditions of their lives. In meeting needs of the marginalized, often with the aid of social scientific disciplines, welfare agencies also construct the needs themselves. Medical and social service professionals know what is good for those they serve, and the marginals and dependents themselves do not have the right to claim to know what is good for them. Dependency in our society thus implies, as it has in all liberal societies, a sufficient warrant to suspend basic rights to privacy, respect, and individual choice.

Although dependency produces conditions of injustice in our society, dependency in itself need not be oppressive. One cannot imagine a society in which some people would not need to be dependent on others at least some of the time: children, sick people, women recovering from childbirth, old people who have become frail, depressed or otherwise emotionally needy persons, have the moral right to depend on others for subsistence and support.

An important contribution of feminist moral theory has been to question the deeply held assumption that moral agency and full citizenship require that a person be autonomous and independent. Feminists have exposed this assumption as inappropriately individualistic and derived from a specifically male experience of social relations, which values competition and solitary achievement. Female experience of social relations, arising both from women's typical domestic care responsibilities and from the kinds of paid work that many women do, tends to recognize dependence as a basic human condition. Whereas on the autonomy model a just society would as much as possible give people the opportunity to be independent, the feminist model envisions justice as according respect and participation in decisionmaking to those who are dependent as well as to those who are independent. Dependency should not be a reason to be deprived of choice and respect, and much of the oppression many marginals experience would be lessened if a less individualistic model of rights prevailed.

Marginalization does not cease to be oppressive when one has shelter and food. Many old people, for example, have sufficient means to live comfortably but remain oppressed in their marginal status. Even if marginals were provided a comfortable material life within institutions that respected their freedom and dignity, injustices of marginality would remain in the form of uselessness, boredom, and lack of self-respect. Most of our society's productive and recognized activities take place in contexts of organized social cooperation, and social structures and processes that close persons out of participation in such social cooperation are unjust. Thus while marginalization definitely entails serious issues of distributive justice, it also involves the deprivation of cultural, practical, and institutionalized conditions for exercising capacities in a context of recognition and interaction. . . .

Powerlessness

As I have indicated, the Marxist idea of class is important because it helps reveal the structure of exploitation: that some people have their power and wealth because they profit from the labor of others. For this reason I reject the claim some make that a traditional class exploitation model fails to capture the structure of contemporary society. It remains the case that the labor of most people in the society augments the power of relatively few. Despite their differences from nonprofessional workers, most professional workers are still not members of the capitalist class. Professional labor either involves exploitative transfers to capitalists or supplies important conditions for such transfers. Professional workers are in an ambiguous class position, it is true, because . . . they also benefit from the exploitation of nonprofessional workers.

While it is false to claim that a division between capitalist and working classes no longer describes our society, it is also false to say that class relations have remained unaltered since the nineteenth century. An adequate conception of oppression cannot ignore the experience of social division reflected in the colloquial distinction between the "middle class" and the "working class," a division structured by the social division of labor between professionals and nonprofessionals. Professionals are privileged in relation to nonprofessionals, by virtue of their position in the division of labor and the status it carries. Nonprofessionals suffer a form of oppression in addition to exploitation, which I call powerlessness.

In the United States, as in other advanced capitalist countries, most workplaces are not organized democratically, direct participation in public policy decisions is rare, and policy implementation is for the most part hierarchical, imposing rules on bureaucrats and citizens. Thus most people in these societies do not regularly participate in making decisions that affect the conditions of their lives and actions, and in this sense most people lack significant power. At the same time, domination in modern society is enacted through the widely dispersed powers of many agents mediating the decisions of others. To that extent many people have some power in relation to others, even though they lack the power to decide policies or results. The powerless are those who lack authority or power even in this mediated sense, those over whom power is exercised without their exercising it; the powerless are situated so that they must take orders and rarely have the right to give them. Powerlessness also designates a position in the division of labor and the concomitant social position that allows persons little opportunity to develop and exercise skills. The powerless have little or no work autonomy, exercise little creativity or judgment in their work, have no technical expertise or authority, express themselves awkwardly, especially in public or bureaucratic settings, and do not command respect. Powerlessness names the oppressive situations Sennett and Cobb (1972) describe in their famous study of working-class men.

This powerless status is perhaps best described negatively: the powerless lack the authority, status, and sense of self that professionals tend to have. The status privilege of professionals has three aspects, the lack of which produces oppression for nonprofessionals.

First, acquiring and practicing a profession has an expansive, progressive character. Being professional usually requires a college education and the acquisition of a specialized knowledge that entails working with symbols and concepts. Professionals experience progress first in acquiring the expertise, and then in the course of professional advancement and rise in status. The life of the nonprofessional by comparison is powerless in the sense that it lacks this orientation toward the progressive development of capacities and avenues for recognition.

Second, while many professionals have supervisors and cannot directly influence many decisions or the actions of many people, most nevertheless have considerable day-to-day work autonomy. Professionals usually have some authority over others, moreover—either over workers they supervise, or over auxiliaries, or over clients. Nonprofessionals, on the other hand, lack autonomy, and in both their working and their consumer-client lives often stand under the authority of professionals.

Though based on a division of labor between "mental" and "manual" work, the distinction between "middle class" and "working class" designates a division not only in working life, but also in nearly all aspects of social life. Professionals and nonprofessionals belong to different cultures in the United States. The two groups tend to live in segregated neighborhoods or even different towns, a process itself mediated by planners, zoning officials, and real estate people. The groups tend to have different tastes in food, decor, clothes, music, and vacations, and often different health and educational needs. Members of each group socialize for the most part with others in the same status group. While there is some intergroup mobility between generations, for the most part the children of professionals become professionals and the children of nonprofessionals do not.

Thus, third, the privileges of the professional extend beyond the workplace to a whole way of life. I call this way of life "respectability." To treat people with respect is to be prepared to listen to what they have to say or to do what they request because they have some authority, expertise, or influence. The norms of respectability in our society are associated specifically with professional culture. Professional dress, speech, tastes, demeanor, all connote respectability. Generally professionals expect and receive respect from others. In restaurants, banks, hotels, real estate offices, and many other such public places, as well as in the media, professionals typically receive more respectful treatment than nonprofessionals. For this reason nonprofessionals seeking a loan or a job, or to buy a house or a car, will often try to look "professional" and "respectable" in those settings.

The privilege of this professional respectability appears starkly in the dynamics of racism and sexism. In daily interchange women and men of color must prove their respectability. At first they are often not treated by strangers with respectful distance or deference. Once people discover that this woman or that Puerto Rican man is a college teacher or a business executive, however, they often behave more respectfully toward her or him. Working-class white men, on the other hand, are often treated with respect until their working-class status is revealed. . . .

Cultural Imperialism

Exploitation, marginalization, and powerlessness all refer to relations of power and oppression that occur by virtue of the social division of labor—who works for whom, who does not work, and how the content of work defines one institutional position relative to others. These three categories refer to structural and institutional relations that delimit people's material lives, including but not restricted to the resources they have access to and the concrete opportunities they have or do not have to develop and exercise their capacities. These kinds of oppression are a matter of concrete power in relation to others—of who benefits from whom, and who is dispensable.

Recent theorists of movements of group liberation, notably feminist and Black liberation theorists, have also given prominence to a rather different form of oppression, which following Lugones and Spelman (1983) I shall call cultural imperialism. To experience cultural imperialism means to experience how the dominant meanings of a society render the particular perspective of one's own group invisible at the same time as they stereotype one's group and mark it out as the Other.

Cultural imperialism involves the universalization of a dominant group's experience and culture, and its establishment as the norm. Some groups have exclusive or primary access to what Nancy Fraser (1987) calls the means of interpretation and communication in a society. As a consequence, the dominant cultural products of the society, that is, those most widely disseminated, express the experience, values, goals, and achievements of these groups. Often without noticing they do so, the dominant groups project their own experience as representative of humanity as such. Cultural products also express the dominant group's perspective on and interpretation of events and elements in the society, including other groups in the society, insofar as they attain cultural status at all.

An encounter with other groups, however, can challenge the dominant group's claim to universality. The dominant group reinforces its position by bringing the other groups under the measure of its dominant norms. Consequently, the difference of women from men, American Indians or Africans from Europeans, Jews from Christians, homosexuals from heterosexuals, workers from professionals, becomes reconstructed largely as deviance and inferiority. Since only the dominant group's cultural expressions receive wide dissemination, their cultural expressions become the normal, or the universal, and thereby the unremarkable. Given the normality of its own cultural expressions and identity, the dominant group constructs the differences which some groups exhibit as lack and negation. These groups become marked as Other.

The culturally dominated undergo a paradoxical oppression, in that they are both marked out by stereotypes and at the same time rendered invisible. As remarkable, deviant beings, the culturally imperialized are stamped with an essence. The stereotypes confine them to a nature which is often attached in some way to their bodies, and which thus cannot easily be denied. These stereotypes so permeate the society that they are not noticed as contestable. Just as everyone knows that the earth goes around the sun, so everyone knows that gay people are promiscuous, that Indians are alcoholics, and that women are good with children. White males, on the other hand, insofar as they escape group marking, can be individuals.

Those living under cultural imperialism find themselves defined from the outside, positioned, placed, by a network of dominant meanings they experience as arising from elsewhere, from those with whom they do not identify and who do not identify with them. Consequently, the dominant culture's stereotyped and inferiorized images of the group must be internalized by group members at least to the extent that they are forced to react to behavior of others influenced by those images. This creates for the culturally oppressed the experience that W.E.B. Du Bois called "double consciousness"—"this sense of always looking at one's self through the eyes of others, of measuring one's soul by the tape of a world that looks on in amused contempt and pity" (Du Bois, 1969 [1903], p. 45). Double consciousness arises when the oppressed subject refuses to coincide with these devalued, objectified, stereotyped visions of herself or himself. While the subject desires recognition as human, capable of activity, full of hope and possibility, she receives from the dominant culture only the judgment that she is different, marked, or inferior.

The group defined by the dominant culture as deviant, as a stereotyped Other, *is* culturally different from the dominant group, because the status of Otherness creates specific experiences not shared by the dominant group, and because culturally oppressed groups also are often socially segregated and occupy specific positions in the social division of labor. Members of such groups express their specific group experiences and interpretations of the world to one another, developing and perpetuating their own culture. Double consciousness, then, occurs because one finds one's being defined by two cultures: a dominant and a subordinate culture. Because they can affirm and recognize one another as sharing similar experiences and perspectives on social life, people in culturally imperialized groups can often maintain a sense of positive subjectivity.

Cultural imperialism involves the paradox of experiencing oneself as invisible at the same time that one is marked out as different. The invisibility comes about when dominant groups fail to recognize the perspective embodied in their cultural expressions as a perspective. These dominant cultural expressions often simply have little place for the experience of other groups, at most only mentioning or referring to them in stereotyped or marginalized ways. This, then, is the injustice of cultural imperialism: that the oppressed group's own experience and interpretation of social life finds little expression that touches the dominant culture, while that same culture imposes on the oppressed group its experience and interpretation of social life. . . .

Violence

Finally, many groups suffer the oppression of systematic violence. Members of some groups live with the knowledge that they must fear random, unprovoked attacks on their persons or property, which have no motive but to damage, humiliate, or destroy the person. In American society women, Blacks, Asians, Arabs, gay men, and lesbians live under such threats of violence, and in at least some regions Jews, Puerto Ricans, Chicanos, and other Spanish-speaking Americans must fear such violence as well. Physical violence against these groups is shockingly frequent. Rape Crisis Center networks estimate that more than one-third of all American women experience an attempted or successful sexual assault in their lifetimes. Manning Marable (1984, pp. 238–41) catalogues a large number of incidents of racist violence and terror against Blacks in the United States between 1980 and 1982. He cites dozens of incidents of the severe beating, killing, or rape of Blacks by police officers on duty, in which the police involved were acquitted of any wrongdoing. In 1981, moreover, there were at least five hundred documented cases of random white teenage violence against Blacks. Violence against gay men and lesbians is not only common, but has been increasing in the last five years. While the frequency of physical attack on members of these and other racially or sexually marked groups is very disturbing, I also include in this category less severe incidents of harrassment, intimidation, or ridicule simply for the purpose of degrading, humiliating, or stigmatizing group members.

Given the frequency of such violence in our society, why are theories of justice usually silent about it? I think the reason is that theorists do not typically take such incidents of violence and harrassment as matters of social injustice. No moral theorist would deny that such acts are very wrong. But unless all immoralities are injustices, they might wonder, why should such acts be interpreted as symptoms of social injustice? Acts of violence or petty harrassment are committed by particular individuals, often extremists, deviants, or the mentally unsound. How then can they be said to involve the sorts of institutional issues I have said are properly the subject of justice?

What makes violence a face of oppression is less the particular acts themselves, though these are often utterly horrible, than the social context surrounding them, which makes them possible and even acceptable. What makes violence a phenomenon of social injustice, and not merely an individual moral wrong, is its systemic character, its existence as a social practice.

Violence is systemic because it is directed at members of a group simply because they are members of that group. Any woman, for example, has a reason to fear rape. Regardless of what a Black man has done to escape the oppressions of marginality or powerlessness, he lives knowing he is subject to attack or harrassment. The oppression of violence consists not only in direct victimization, but in the daily knowledge shared by all members of oppressed groups that they are *liable* to violation, solely on account of their group identity. Just living under such a threat of attack on oneself or family or friends deprives the oppressed of freedom and dignity, and needlessly expends their energy.

Violence is a social practice. It is a social given that everyone knows happens and will happen again. It is always at the horizon of social imagination, even for those who do not perpetrate it. According to the prevailing social logic, some circumstances make such violence more "called for" than others. The idea of rape will occur to many men who pick up a hitchhiking woman; the idea of hounding or teasing a gay man on their dorm floor will occur to many straight male college students. Often several persons inflict the violence together, especially in all-male groupings. Sometimes violators set out looking for people to beat up, rape, or taunt. This rule-bound, social, and often premeditated character makes violence against groups a social practice.

Group violence approaches legitimacy, moreover, in the sense that it is tolerated. Often third parties find it unsurprising because it happens frequently and lies as a constant possibility at the horizon of the social imagination. Even when they are caught, those who perpetrate acts of group-directed violence or harrassment often receive light or no punishment. To that extent society renders their acts acceptable.

An important aspect of random, systemic violence is its irrationality. Xenophobic violence differs from the violence of states or ruling-class repression. Repressive violence has a rational, albeit evil, motive: rulers use it as a coercive tool to maintain their power. Many accounts of racist, sexist, or homophobic violence attempt to explain its motivation as a desire to maintain group privilege or domination. I do not doubt that fear of violence often functions to keep oppressed groups subordinate, but I do not think xenophobic violence is rationally motivated in the way that, for example, violence against strikers is.

On the contrary, the violation of rape, beating, killing, and harrassment of women, people of color, gays, and other marked groups is motivated by fear or hatred of those groups. Sometimes the motive may be a simple will to power, to victimize those marked as vulnerable by the very social fact that they are subject to violence. If so, this motive is secondary in the sense that it depends on a social practice of group violence. Violence-causing fear or hatred of the other at least partly involves insecurities on the part of the violators; its irrationality suggests that unconscious processes are at work. . . .

Cultural imperialism, moreover, itself intersects with violence. The culturally imperialized may reject the dominant meanings and attempt to assert their own subjectivity, or the fact of their cultural difference may put the lie to the dominant culture's implicit claim to universality. The dissonance generated by such a challenge to the hegemonic cultural meanings can also be a source of irrational violence. . . .

APPLYING THE CRITERIA

Social theories that construct oppression as a unified phenomenon usually either leave out groups that even the theorists think are oppressed, or leave out important ways in which groups are oppressed. Black liberation theorists and feminist theorists have argued persuasively, for example, that Marxism's reduction of all oppressions to class oppression leaves out much about the specific oppression of Blacks and women. By pluralizing the category of oppression in the way explained in this [essay,] social theory can avoid the exclusive and oversimplifying effects of such reductionism.

I have avoided pluralizing the category in the way some others have done, by constructing an account of separate systems of oppression for each oppressed group: racism, sexism, classism, heterosexism, ageism, and so on. There is a double problem with considering each group's oppression a unified and distinct structure or system. On the one hand, this way of conceiving oppression fails to accommodate the similarities and overlaps in the oppressions of different groups. On the other hand, it falsely represents the situation of all group members as the same.

I have arrived at the five faces of oppression—exploitation, marginalization, powerlessness, cultural imperialism, and violence—as the best way to avoid such exclusions and reductions. They function as criteria for determining whether individuals and groups are oppressed, rather than as a full theory of oppression. I believe that these criteria are objective. They provide a means of refuting some people's belief that their group is oppressed when it is not, as well as a means of persuading others that a group is oppressed when they doubt it. Each criterion can be operationalized; each can be applied through the assessment of observable behavior, status relationships, distributions, texts and other cultural artifacts. I have no illusions that such assessments can be value-neutral. But these criteria can nevertheless serve as means of evaluating claims that a group is oppressed, or adjudicating disputes about whether or how a group is oppressed.

The presence of any of these five conditions is sufficient for calling a group oppressed. But different group oppressions exhibit different combinations of these forms, as do different individuals in the groups. Nearly all, if not all, groups said by contemporary social movements to be oppressed suffer cultural imperialism. The other oppressions they experience vary. Working-class people are exploited and powerless, for example, but if employed and white do not experience marginalization and violence. Gay men, on the other hand, are not qua gay exploited or powerless, but they experience severe cultural imperialism and violence. Similarly, Jews and Arabs as groups are victims of cultural imperialism and violence, though many members of these groups also suffer exploitation or powerlessness. Old people are oppressed by marginalization and cultural imperialism, and this is also true of physically and mentally disabled people. As a group women are subject to gender-based exploitation, powerlessness, cultural imperialism, and violence. Racism in the United States condemns many Blacks and Latinos to marginalization, and puts many more at risk, even though many members of these groups escape that condition; members of these groups often suffer all five forms of oppression.

Applying these five criteria to the situation of groups makes it possible to compare oppressions without reducing them to a common essence or claiming that one is more fundamental than another. One can compare the ways in which a particular form of oppression appears in different groups. For example, while the operations of cultural imperialism are often experienced in similar fashion by different groups, there are also important differences. One can compare the combinations of oppressions groups experience, or the intensity of those oppressions. Thus with these criteria one can plausibly claim that one group is more oppressed than another without reducing all oppressions to a single scale. . . .

REFERENCES

Alexander, David. 1987. "Gendered Job Traits and Women's Occupations." Ph.D. dissertation, Economics, University of Massachusetts.

Brown, Carol. 1981. "Mothers, Fathers and Children: From Private to Public Patriarchy." In Lydia Sargent, ed., *Women and Revolution*. Boston: South End.

Delphy, Christine. 1984. *Close to Home: A Materialist Analysis of Women's Oppression*. Amherst: University of Massachusetts Press.

Du Bois, W.E.B. 1969 [1903]. *The Souls of Black Folk*. New York: New American Library.

Ferguson, Ann. 1984. "On Conceiving Motherhood and Sexuality: A Feminist Materialist Approach." In Joyce Trebilcot, ed., *Mothering: Essays in Feminist Theory*. Totowa, N.J.: Rowman and Allanheld.

———. 1989. *Blood at the Root*. London: Pandora.

Fraser, Nancy. 1987. "Social Movements vs. Disciplinary Bureaucracies: The Discourse of Social Needs." CHS Occasional Paper No. 8. Center for Humanistic Studies, University of Minnesota.

Lugones, Maria C., and Elizabeth V. Spelman. 1983. "Have We Got a Theory for You! Feminist Theory, Cultural Imperialism and the Demand for 'the Woman's Voice.'" *Women's Studies International Forum* 6:573–81.

Macpherson, C. B. 1973. *Democratic Theory: Essays in Retrieval*. Oxford: Oxford University Press.

Marable, Manning. 1984. *Race, Reform and Rebellion: The Second Reconstruction in Black America, 1945–82*. Jackson: University Press of Mississippi.

Sennett, Richard, and Jonathan Cobb. 1972. *The Hidden Injuries of Class*. New York: Vintage.

QUESTIONS

1 How do stereotypes reinforce oppression?
2 Is marginalization the most dangerous form of oppression?
3 Can social institutions that systematically oppress members of some groups be considered just?

The African-American Underclass and the Question of Values

Howard McGary

McGary addresses the question: Why are members of the underclass locked into their underclass status? In his view, a correct response requires understanding both (1) the mindset of members of the underclass and (2) the effect that the unjust design of the basic structure of society has on their mindset. McGary begins by discussing the views of liberal theorists, such as John Rawls, on the meaning of *full citizenship* and explains the kinds of things that can count as evidence that one has full citizenship. He then advances arguments to support the claim that members of the underclass have good reason to doubt that they have full citizenship and explains how having reasonable doubts about their political status can affect the mindset, and hence the motivation, of members of the underclass.

Reprinted from Howard McGary, *Race and Social Justice* (Blackwell, 1999), pp. 62–78. Originally from *The Underclass Question,* edited by Bill E. Lawson. Reprinted by permission of Temple University Press. © 1992 by Temple University. All Rights Reserved.

The African-American underclass is said to be poor, badly educated, directly related to crime either as perpetrators or victims, and typically young. Data indicate that, unlike the African-American urban poor in the recent past, the underclass also appears to be locked into a cycle of poverty. If these data are accurate, then the crucial question is "Why are members of the underclass locked into their underclass status?" A debate rages between conservatives and liberals about how to answer this question. Conservatives maintain that the key to solving the problem is altering the values of the African-American underclass so that it might better participate in the capitalist market economy. Conservatives also typically add that the state should eliminate many of the burdensome regulations that they believe work to the detriment of people at the bottom rungs of the socioeconomic ladder, for example, minimum wage laws. Liberals, on the other hand, assert that the state must play an active role in solving the problems of the African-American underclass. The state, in their view, should create laws and programs that provide state funds to educate and house those who are said to be locked into the African-American underclass.

The dispute between conservatives and liberals over the African-American underclass often occurs in the political arena, but it occurs in academic circles as well. William Julius Wilson in his book *The Truly Disadvantaged*[1] argues that liberals have failed to keep up their side of the debate in the dispute over the African-American underclass. He attributes this to a reluctance by liberals to examine some of the controversial data about members of the African-American underclass. Wilson believes that the sensitive nature of these data causes liberals to believe that if they examine the data they will be accused of "blaming the victims." They also fear that focusing on the inadequacies of this class will allow some to intensify the racism that exists in American society. Refusing to focus on the personal shortcomings of the members of the underclass, the liberals find fault instead with the design of social institutions.

In my view, both the conservative and liberal solutions involve doctrinaire commitments that blind each approach to the virtues of the other's solution. Conservatives are right to focus on the mindset of members of the underclass, and liberals are correct when they maintain that we must focus on the social structure, but what they both fail to appreciate is just how much the design of social institutions influences the way people think. I argue that members of the underclass do suffer from an understandable but crippling resentment that is fostered by the unjust design of the basic structure of society.

My aim in this discussion is modest. I wish to suggest a possible reason why both conservatives and liberals miss the point. In doing so, I take it as a postulate that it is possible to solve the problems of the African-American underclass without rejecting the capitalist mode of production. This is a big assumption, but one that conservatives and liberals usually accept. First, I describe what prominent liberal theorists have meant by full citizenship, especially in modern democratic societies. Second, I explain the kinds of things that can count as evidence that one has full citizenship. Third, I argue that members of the African-American underclass have good reason to doubt that they have full citizenship. I conclude by showing what effects having reasonable doubts about one's political status can have on people considered to be in the "underclass." . . .

THE NATURE OF FULL CITIZENSHIP

Individuals join together to form civil society for a variety of reasons, many of which have been discussed by political theorists. Some say that the only valid ground for state authority is the protection of the individual. Others maintain that it is for the promotion of the interests of those who form the social union. Those of a more collectivist sort claim that the promotion of the common good is the basis for civil society. I do not want to enter into this debate. My point is that in the liberal tradition a person who is said to be a citizen has the same basic rights as any other citizen. Of course, this does not mean everyone within the liberal tradition has defined the consequences of equal citizenship in the same way. For instance, some have been strong supporters of individual rights, while others have focused on the common good and have supported the rights of individuals only when doing so promotes the common good. However, the US Constitution vests rights in individuals, and modern theorists—be they contractarians, human rights theorists, or utilitarians—have been leery of any proposal that denies equal protection under the law to any citizen.

As Ronald Dworkin has said, equal citizenship requires each citizen to be treated with "equal concern and respect."[2] The belief that one is treated with equal concern and respect has an important impact on one's self-concept and plays a vital role in the formula for flourishing in a social context. By flourishing, I have in mind being able to construct one's life plan consistent with one's abilities and talents. Citizenship, in the liberal tradition, is thought to provide one with the opportunity to flourish by arranging society, such that its basic structure does not unfairly inhibit or prohibit one's pursuit of a chosen plan of life. The belief that one has a full citizenship also allows one to feel comfortable in supporting and defending what John Rawls has called the "basic structure of society." By basic structure Rawls means "the way in which the major social institutions distribute fundamental rights and duties and determine the division of advantages from social cooperation." Rawls goes on to define major social institutions as "the political constitution and the principal economic and social arrangements." The major institutions "define people's rights and duties and influence their life prospects."[3] Full citizenship certainly does not entail that one will get whatever one wants, but it does say that one will have the opportunity to satisfy one's needs and desires. When these things cannot be satisfied, it cannot be blamed on the basic structure of society.

According to this view, citizens are competitors in a game of life in which rules are not rigged in favor of any of the competitors. However, this view does not assume that people cannot be treated unfairly because of the unjust actions of individuals; it is clearly understood that the unfairness is not the result of the design of the basic structure of society. Persons who feel that they are full citizens believe that their rights are recognized and protected and that their failings can be traced to some personal shortcoming, individual act of injustice, or poor fate, but not to the design of the basic structure of society.

EVIDENCE OF FULL CITIZENSHIP

What things count as evidence in modern liberal democratic societies that one has full citizenship? The following list is not all-inclusive, but it does include many important indicators of full citizenship. Citizens have the right to participate in the political process. They have the right to earn a living without being forced to engage in activities that are degrading or exploitative. Citizens are not denied opportunities simply because of their race, sex, or religious affiliations. Citizens also have legal due process. Notice that I have not included in this list a right to a certain income. Liberals have disagreed over whether citizens' basic rights include welfare rights. However, citizens who languish in a permanent condition of poverty in a society that has plenty have to wonder about their equal citizenship status.

Having the secure conviction that one has the aforementioned rights and opportunities helps to foster the belief that one can succeed, but just as important, it allows one to believe that one is a legitimate member of a social community, and that the community interprets the common good in a manner that is consistent with one's own good. Of course, this does not mean that everything always goes one's way. Nor does it mean that some individuals cannot have more of societal good than others. However, to use Rawlsian terminology, it does mean that even the least-advantaged members of society will have a secure conviction that the basic structure of society is just.

LAZINESS AND THE AFRICAN-AMERICAN UNDERCLASS

Wilson and others have defined the African-American underclass as young, poorly educated, intimately connected to crime either as perpetrators or as victims, and locked into a cycle of poverty. The important question is "Why is a certain segment of society plagued by these problems?" I said that both conservatives and liberals have their fingers on part of the answer. The liberals are correct in maintaining that there is still work to be done to guarantee equal opportunity to certain groups, particularly African-Americans. They are also correct in contending that the state must play some active role in this process. For example, because of their race African-Americans are still severely restricted when it comes to finding decent, inexpensive housing. This is true even for African-Americans who have been able to acquire middle-class status, but it is an especially acute problem for African-Americans who are members of the lower classes. A persistent worry for these people is finding and keeping a place to live. As psychological studies have shown, this type of insecurity is very debilitating, especially for the young.

Conservatives, of course, argue that we have equal housing legislation on the books, so adding additional legislation will not solve the problem. Conservatives may be right that equal housing laws are on the books, but they are wrong if they mean that these laws are being enforced. In fact, during the Reagan years in which we have seen the emergence of the African-American underclass, the enforcement of equal housing laws has been virtually nonexistent. Therefore, I think the liberals are right that there is more work for the state to do, even if it is primarily the enforcement of civil rights laws already on the books.

But liberals may be wrong if they believe that at this point in the process enforcement of civil rights laws will solve the problems facing the underclass. Of course, few liberals have said that legislation alone will solve the problems. This is just a caricature of the liberal view advanced by some conservatives. However, I think it is fair to say that liberals have been reluctant publicly to declare that something about the people who make up the underclass may contribute to their underclass status.

Here we can learn from the conservatives, but they are not the only people who have asked African-Americans to examine themselves for a solution to their predicament. Black Muslims, for example, have consistently urged African-Americans to examine their commitments, habits, and values and to fashion their own remedy to their problems rather than waiting for whites to solve them. But, unlike the conservatives, the Muslims are quick to warn that the initial cause of African-American problems is white people. Black Muslims have attempted to provide an economic and social structure for African-Americans to enhance their self-esteem while providing them with the necessary resources for putting their life plans into action. Booker T. Washington also asked African-Americans to do some critical self-evaluation before fashioning their own programs for economic and social improvement.[4]

Clearly there has been progress over the years when it comes to race relations, and it is probably true that the significance of race is declining; nonetheless, race is still an important defining characteristic of people in our society. It is my contention that African-Americans in the underclass have been placed in an untenable position that makes it extremely difficult for them to evaluate their personal successes and failures. They have been told that racism no longer exists, and wealthy and middle-class African-Americans are pointed to as support for this claim. So, when poor African-Americans fail, people are quick to say that it is because of personal shortcomings and not systemic failings. Some African-American scholars have recently claimed that the values of the African-American underclass are the source of its predicament. In other words, opportunities exist for these poor African-Americans, but the members of the underclass fail to take advantage of these opportunities because they are lazy, undisciplined, and too prone to satisfying their immediate desires. This view has become quite popular in some quarters.

Let us now examine this harsh critique of members of the African-American underclass. Being lazy means being resistant to work or disposed to idleness. Are all or most members of the African-American underclass lazy? I think not. First, it is not at all clear that African-Americans in the underclass are resistant to work. In order for someone to be properly described as being lazy, there must be a genuine opportunity for that person to engage in meaningful and nonexploitative work. For example, it would be wrong to call slaves lazy because they refused to work in the slavemaster's cotton fields. And it would be wrong to label as lazy someone who refused to prostitute his or her body for a wage. One thing is certainly clear. African-Americans in the underclass are not turning down good-paying, safe, and non-dead-end jobs. It is questionable whether enough gainful employment exists to successfully integrate members of the underclass into the broader economy. In fact, some economists have argued that integration of the underclass would require a rapid growth of the economy. There is no guarantee that such growth will occur. Another question is whether it is rational for mothers heading single-family households to accept jobs that do not have health plans and child care services. Given the tremendous costs of health care and child care, the welfare system may be the only viable alternative for many underclass families. But what about those women who do work their way off the welfare rolls? Typically, these are people who have families to draw upon. Of course, a few women manage to secure low-paying entry-level jobs that do provide some modest health coverage; however, such jobs are the exception rather than the rule.

Those who criticize the members of the African-American underclass for lacking in values will sometimes admit that members of the African-American underclass face harsh conditions, but they quickly add that these persons have to be tough and do those things that will allow them to flourish. But is it fair to expect members of the African-American underclass to fight through these adversities? I do not deny that some do, but should this be expected of all members of this group? For example, suppose a person loses both legs because of some unjust act, and that the injustice goes uncompensated. Suppose further that this person goes on to accomplish a great deal in spite of her handicap. Should anyone in her circumstances be expected to act as she does? I think not. This person receives high praise because she stands apart from the norm. If her accomplishments were what the average person could be expected to do, then we would not hold her in such high regard. So, it would seem to be wrong or at least insensitive to condemn people for not being exceptional at overcoming serious adversities. However, I think this is just what is being expected of members of the African-American underclass.

I have attempted thus far to cast doubt on the claim that most members of the African-American underclass are lazy. Now I would like to buttress my rejection of this claim by looking carefully at the claim that members of this class are poorly motivated due to laziness. Such a view overlooks the relationship between being motivated and having the secure conviction that the rules or structure of society are not stacked against one. Living in a society in which one has good reason to believe that the basic structure is just does a lot for enhancing or at least sustaining one's motivational level. Members of the underclass lack good evidence that they live in such a society. When they look around their community, they see that its members lack the material things and opportunities that many other communities take for granted. This is especially devastating when we note that a large segment of the underclass are children. It is extremely difficult for children to understand that they must use modest opportunities and resources to fight against awful odds if they are to succeed, especially when they know that children in other communities do not face such an uphill struggle. They often see this as too much to ask of them, and this belief works against their being highly motivated. Is this a reasonable conclusion? I think so.

Rawls has persuasively argued that people do not deserve the benefits that result from the luck of the natural lottery. Therefore, children in the African-American underclass do not deserve to be poor, nor do children born into affluent families deserve to be rich. The large number of children in the African-American underclass have a good reason for thinking that their situation is not something that they deserve. They are born into poor families and must work harder than people from more affluent families if they are to succeed. These beliefs have a negative impact on their motivational levels.

If what I have argued for so far is sound, then we have several reasons for doubting that members of the African-American underclass are lazy. Similar arguments would also seem to apply to the criticism that members of the African-American underclass are undisciplined and unable to defer gratification. Being disciplined and deferring gratification both depend upon having good evidence that the cards are not stacked against one. Exit studies for female and African-American students who have dropped out of graduate programs point to the difficulty of being disciplined when the environment in which one must operate is tainted by racism or sexism. Students in these studies report that it is difficult to separate their inadequacies from biased or unfair expectations. This uncertainty serves to impact negatively on their ability to gain strength through training. While in the process of growing and acquiring new skills, a time that is generally filled with self-doubt, they find it extremely taxing to separate the anguish and paranoia associated with a rigorous graduate program from the subtle forms of racism and sexism that still exist in institutions of higher learning. The underclass faces the same problem, but in more drastic circumstances. So, one should be cautious in such circumstances in condemning those who must deal with covert racism as suffering from a lack of discipline.

Of course, one could object that my argument is unsound because African-Americans in the past had to deal with racism and its effects, but nonetheless they were motivated to succeed and clearly did not suffer from "poor" values. However, such a response does not succeed when examined closely. First, the claim that African-Americans suffer because of poor values has existed since slavery. In fact, it was even offered as a justification for slavery. So, the idea that the downtrodden position of underclass African-Americans can be attributed to their poor values or lack of values is not new. What is new, though, is that we now have a chorus of African-American voices singing this tune. Unlike in the past, the increase in violent crime and the drug problem have caused many, including African-Americans, to search frantically for answers that may help to eliminate social problems that touch all of our lives. However, many critics might agree that the appeal to poor values was once a smoke screen, but that now this position has credibility.

Another explanation exists for why the effects of racism severely hamper members of the African-American underclass to a degree not experienced by blacks up until the 1960s. Several commentators, discussing the impact of integration on African-American communities in the United States, have pointed out that middle-class African-Americans have left these communities and taken with them the tax base and many of the things associated with stable communities. Large, urban African-American communities are now pretty much populated by people from the bottom rung of the economic ladder. Major institutions in these communities have been either destroyed or severely weakened by the flight of the black middle class. One consequence of this flight is that people do not have the resources at their disposal to address many day-to-day problems. This may seem like a small point, but I assure you that it is not. It is one thing for a person from the outside to say that you can make it and another for someone who is struggling with the inadequate resources to do so. At one time, "making it" meant rising to the top in one's community; and as individuals progressed, so did the community. However, since the integration movement, "making it" has meant escaping from one's community. This has the consequence of intensifying any antagonisms that exist between poor African-Americans and those who are better-off. Members of the so-called African-American underclass now face a society in which the basic structure is not just, intense competition for scarce resources, and abandonment by those best able to help ward off the effects of living in a society that is still plagued by racism.

Some may find my conclusion about laziness and the African-American underclass disturbing because they believe that it provides a convenient rationale for underclass African-Americans to acquiesce in their downtrodden position. Others may conclude that it supports the more disturbing position that African-Americans (especially healthy black males) should be excused for failing to do what is necessary in order to provide for their families. However, neither of these things follow from anything that I have said. It is not my contention that African-Americans should not go beyond what is expected of whites if they are to overcome the adversities that are so much a part of their daily lives. What I do say, however, is that those who cannot muster this strength should not be described as lazy. Many people in the African-American underclass are putting forth a gallant effort against bad odds to secure a living for their families. We must draw a line between what people are required to do as a matter of moral duty and supererogatory acts. People should not have to sacrifice their sense of self completely, even if doing so would serve some noble end, such as providing for the well-being of one's family. Of course, the morally good person is willing to make some sacrifice; however, at some point we must draw the line. When we fail to do so, then we are too willing to accept false accusations, such as that all the members of the African-American underclass are lazy, because such accusations wrongly shift the focus from institutional design and social structure to the individual.

The line of argument advanced here does not deny that some members of the underclass are lazy. However, all classes within our society have some lazy members. But for the argument, that attributes underclass status to laziness, to succeed it must be the case that all, many, or most of the African-American underclass is lazy. There is no evidence available to support this strong evaluative claim. . . .

. . . When African-American conservatives talk about opportunities, they typically mean that there are jobs available. They claim that certain jobs are crying out to be filled, particularly jobs requiring highly specialized skills or those in the service industries that require minimal skills. This may be true, but a further question has to be asked: If employers are in such desperate need of these employees, why are they not doing more to train and recruit these people? Their lack of effort in these areas may cast some doubt on how desperate they are to fill these jobs.

However, putting this issue aside, there is a more fundamental problem with the contention by African-American conservatives that ample opportunities exist for those who are willing to work. As we know, being positioned to take advantage of opportunities is conditioned by a number of things, for example, being properly educated or trained and having a work ethic. But several other things impinge on these two factors, for example, health care. All too often members of the underclass lack proper health care—not just health care in the narrow sense of being able to go to a doctor when one is very sick, but health care to the extent that pregnant women in this class can receive the proper prenatal care that is so crucial in preventing infants from experiencing physical and mental problems that will hamper their ability to learn. We also have to focus on environmental impediments such as the disproportionate number of persons from the underclass who are exposed to lead contamination, which can have disastrous effects on a developing child's ability to learn.

What these conservatives fail to see is that legitimate opportunities must be understood as more than whether or not there are jobs available. For example, in a number of large cities, such as Milwaukee, a number of jobs that underclass residents are qualified to fill have moved out of the inner cities to the suburbs, making transportation a major obstacle for people who would like to fill these positions. Furthermore, the cost of housing in the suburbs and housing discrimination prevent them from moving to where the jobs are. Once we see the obstacles that stand in the way of people who have few resources at their disposal, people who appear to lack motivation in the face of opportunity might really require motivational levels that would far exceed those of persons who we think are our most productive and successful citizens.

In light of this, is "lazy" or some other derogatory term the proper way to characterize members of the underclass? I think not. A number of people, including some liberals, are uneasy with my answer. They worry that such a response is a way of coddling people, of encouraging people to acquiesce in their misery. Very often these people will respond, "Surely you are not encouraging members of the underclass to prefer public assistance to earning their own living?" Nothing that I have said so far commits me to the view that members of the underclass should not attempt to help themselves. What I have tried to point out are some of the difficulties they encounter in trying to do so. However, if this question is posed to a member of the underclass who has had her motivational level damaged by racial discrimination and injustice, it is not clear that it would be unreasonable or immoral for such a person to prefer public assistance (which includes medical benefits) to a menial, low-paying, dead-end job without medical benefits. At first, this seems ridiculous because the model job we tend to use when analyzing such cases is one that draws on our abilities and talents in ways that we consider to be interesting or, if not, at least compensates such that the job is desirable even if it is uninteresting. If the job is low-paying and uninteresting, we might see it as a viable opportunity if it leads to a job that pays well or does draw on our abilities and talents in interesting ways. However, the question we must ask is, "Are members of the underclass being offered jobs that satisfy these conditions?" If the answer is yes, then clearly they should prefer working to public assistance. If the answer is no, I do not think that it is clearly rational to prefer a low-paying, uninteresting, dead-end job without medical benefits to public assistance that would provide one with the same income plus medical care.

Of course my critics would argue that I have excluded an important consideration, namely, the joy and satisfaction that a person receives from being self-reliant. In fact, Booker T. Washington, who some see as the father of the African-American conservative position, stressed the value of self-help in his famous "Atlanta Exposition Address." In this speech, Washington urged African-Americans to "Cast down your buckets where you are."[5] By this he meant that African-Americans should take any job, no matter how menial, as a first step on the road toward advancement. Clearly, self-reliance in most cases is a good thing, but even good things can be taken too far. It is clear that in some cases self-reliance can clash with rationality. Are the members of the underclass asked to be self-reliant at the expense of rationality?

Unfortunately, I think that in a large number of cases it is irrational for members of the underclass to choose self-reliance over public assistance. As I said earlier, adequate health care is an important component of any realistic appraisal of the opportunities available to members of the underclass. The United States is one of very few countries that do not provide some form of national health care. Health care in the United States is tied to certain jobs in the form of employee medical benefits. Given the high costs of medical care and the medical problems that correlate highly with poor people, adequate health care has to be a weighty consideration in the deliberations of members of the African-American underclass. Surely self-reliance ought to be given some weight by members of this class, but even if it is, it will lose out in their deliberations because being self-reliant would have the undesirable consequence of denying them adequate health care. In order to make self-reliance a rational choice for members of this group, there would have to be structural changes in the current welfare and health care systems.

To think that we can eliminate the problems faced by members of the underclass without altering some of our basic institutions and social policies is to look at the problem through rose-colored glasses.

NOTES

1 William Julius Wilson, *The Truly Disadvantaged* (Chicago: University of Chicago Press, 1987).
2 Ronald Dworkin, *Taking Rights Seriously* (Cambridge, MA: Harvard University Press, 1977), 180–3.
3 John Rawls, *A Theory of Justice* (Cambridge, MA: Harvard University Press, 1971), sec. 2, 7–11.
4 Booker T. Washington, "The Intellectuals and the Boston Mob," in *Negro Social and Political Thought, 1850–1920*, ed. Howard Brotz (New York: Basic Books, 1966).
5 Booker T. Washington, "Atlanta Exposition Address," in *Negro Social and Political Thought, 1850–1920*, 357.

QUESTIONS

1 According to McGary, those who are full citizens have a right to earn a living without being forced to engage in activities that are degrading or exploitative. Does a capitalist system necessarily involve exploitation? If so, does it follow that many (most) workers in our society are denied the rights of full citizens?
2 Do any of Young's five forms of oppression apply to the African-American underclass as it is described by McGary? Is there another form of oppression that would better describe the experiences of this underclass?

After the Family Wage: A Postindustrial Thought Experiment

Nancy Fraser

Fraser maintains that we are in a postindustrial age that calls for a new vision of the welfare state, a vision that will incorporate gender equity as one of its goals. Fraser first presents seven normative principles, each of which she sees as an essential element in gender equity: (1) the antipoverty principle, (2) the antiexploitation principle, (3) the income-equality principle, (4) the leisure-time-equality principle, (5) the equality-of-respect principle, (6) the antimarginalization principle, and (7) the antiandrocentrism principle. Fraser then evaluates two feminist visions of a postindustrial state—the Universal Breadwinner model and the Caregiver Parity model—before presenting, evaluating, and ultimately recommending a third feminist vision—the Universal Caregiver model.

The current crisis of the welfare state has many roots—global economic trends, massive movements of refugees and immigrants, popular hostility to taxes, the weakening of trade unions and labor parties, the rise of national and "racial"-ethnic antagonisms, the decline of solidaristic ideologies, and the collapse of state socialism. One absolutely crucial factor, however, is the crumbling of the old gender order. Existing welfare states are premised on assumptions about gender that are increasingly out of phase with many people's lives and self-understandings. They therefore do not provide adequate social protections, especially for women and children.

The gender order that is now disappearing descends from the industrial era of capitalism and reflects the social world of its origin. It was centered on the ideal of *the family wage.* In this world people were supposed to be organized into heterosexual, male-headed nuclear families, which lived principally from the man's labor-market earnings. The male head of the household would be paid a family wage, sufficient to support children and a full-time wife-and-mother, who performed domestic labor without pay. Of course, countless lives never fit this pattern. Still, it provided the normative picture of a proper family.

The family-wage ideal was inscribed in the structure of most industrial-era welfare states. That structure had three tiers, with social-insurance programs occupying the first rank. Designed to protect people from the vagaries of the labor market (and to protect the economy from shortages of demand), these programs replaced the breadwinner's wage in case of sickness, disability, unemployment, or old age. Many countries also featured a second tier of programs, providing direct support for full-time female homemaking and mothering. A third tier served the "residuum." Largely a holdover from traditional poor relief, public assistance programs provided paltry,

From Nancy Fraser, *Justice Interruptus: Critical Reflection on the "Postsocialist" Condition,* Chapter 2. Copyright © 1997. Reproduced by permission of the author and Routledge/Taylor & Francis Group, LLC.

stigmatized, means-tested aid to needy people who had no claim to honorable support because they did not fit the family-wage scenario.

Today, however, the family-wage assumption is no longer tenable—either empirically or normatively. We are currently experiencing the death throes of the old, industrial gender order with the transition to a new, *postindustrial* phase of capitalism. The crisis of the welfare state is bound up with these epochal changes. It is rooted in part in the collapse of the world of the family wage, and of its central assumptions about labor markets and families. . . .

What, then, should a postindustrial welfare state look like? Conservatives have lately had a lot to say about "restructuring the welfare state," but their vision is counterhistorical and contradictory; they seek to reinstate the male breadwinner/female homemaker family for the middle class, while demanding that poor single mothers "work." Neoliberal policies have recently been instituted in the United States but they, too, are inadequate in the current context. Punitive, androcentric, and obsessed with employment despite the absence of good jobs, they are unable to provide security in a postindustrial world. Both these approaches ignore one crucial thing: a postindustrial welfare state, like its industrial predecessor, must support a gender order. But the only kind of gender order that can be acceptable today is one premised on *gender equity*.

Feminists, therefore, are in a good position to generate an emancipatory vision for the coming period. They, more than anyone, appreciate the importance of gender relations to the current crisis of the industrial welfare state and the centrality of gender equity to any satisfactory resolution. Feminists also appreciate the importance of carework for human well-being and the effects of its social organization on women's standing. They are attuned, finally, to potential conflicts of interest within families and to the inadequacy of androcentric definitions of work.

To date, however, feminists have tended to shy away from systematic reconstructive thinking about the welfare state. Nor have we yet developed a satisfactory account of gender equity that can inform an emancipatory vision. We need now to undertake such thinking. We should ask: What new, postindustrial gender order should replace the family wage? And what sort of welfare state can best support such a new gender order? What account of gender equity best captures our highest aspirations? And what vision of social welfare comes closest to embodying it?

Two different sorts of answers are currently conceivable, I think, both of which qualify as feminist. The first I call the Universal Breadwinner model. It is the vision implicit in the current political practice of most U.S. feminists and liberals. It aims to foster gender equity by promoting women's employment; the centerpiece of this model is state provision of employment-enabling services such as day care. The second possible answer I call the Caregiver Parity model. It is the vision implicit in the current political practice of most Western European feminists and social democrats. It aims to promote gender equity chiefly by supporting informal carework; the centerpiece of this model is state provision of caregiver allowances.

Which of these two approaches should command our loyalties in the coming period? Which expresses the most attractive vision of a postindustrial gender order? Which best embodies the ideal of gender equity?

In this chapter, I outline a framework for thinking systematically about these questions. I analyze highly idealized versions of Universal Breadwinner and

Caregiver Parity in the manner of a thought experiment. I postulate, contrary to fact, a world in which both these models are feasible in that their economic and political preconditions are in place. Assuming very favorable conditions, then, I assess the respective strengths and weaknesses of each. . . .

GENDER EQUITY: A COMPLEX CONCEPTION

To evaluate alternative visions of a postindustrial welfare state, we need some normative criteria. Gender equity, I have said, is one indispensable standard. But of what precisely does it consist? . . .

I propose we reconceptualize gender equity as a complex, not a simple, idea. This means breaking with the assumption that gender equity can be identified with any single value or norm, whether it be equality, difference, or something else. Instead, we should treat it as a complex notion comprising a plurality of distinct normative principles. . . .

In what follows, I assume that gender equity is complex in this way. And I propose an account of it that is designed for the specific purpose of evaluating alternative pictures of a postindustrial welfare state. For issues other than welfare, a somewhat different package of norms might be called for. Nevertheless, I believe that the general idea of treating gender equity as a complex conception is widely applicable. The analysis here may serve as a paradigm case demonstrating the usefulness of this approach.

For this particular thought experiment, in any case, I unpack the idea of gender equity as a compound of seven distinct normative principles. Let me enumerate them one by one.

1 *The Antipoverty Principle.* The first and most obvious objective of social-welfare provision is to prevent poverty. Preventing poverty is crucial to achieving gender equity now, after the family wage, given the high rates of poverty in solo-mother families and the vastly increased likelihood that U.S. women and children will live in such families. If it accomplishes nothing else, a welfare state should at least relieve suffering by meeting otherwise unmet basic needs. Arrangements, such as those in the United States, that leave women, children, and men in poverty, are unacceptable according to this criterion. Any postindustrial welfare state that prevented such poverty would constitute a major advance. So far, however, this does not say enough. The antipoverty principle might be satisfied in a variety of different ways, not all of which are acceptable. Some ways, such as the provision of targeted, isolating, and stigmatized poor relief for solo-mother families, fail to respect several of the following normative principles, which are also essential to gender equity in social welfare.

2 *The Antiexploitation Principle.* Antipoverty measures are important not only in themselves but also as a means to another basic objective: preventing exploitation of vulnerable people. This principle, too, is central to achieving gender equity after the family wage. Needy women with no other way to feed themselves and their children, for example, are liable to exploitation—by abusive husbands, by sweatshop foremen, and by pimps. In guaranteeing relief of poverty, then, welfare provision should also aim to mitigate exploitable dependency. The availability of an alternative source of income enhances the bargaining position of subordinates in unequal relationships. The nonemployed wife who knows she can support herself and her children outside her marriage has more leverage within it; her "voice" is enhanced as her possibilities of "exit" increase. The same holds for the low-paid nursing-home attendant in relation to her boss. For welfare measures to have this effect, however, support must be provided as a matter of right. When receipt of aid is highly stigmatized or discretionary, the anti-exploitation principle is not satisfied. At best the claimant would trade exploitable dependence on a husband or a boss for exploitable dependence on a caseworker's whim. The goal should be to prevent at least three kinds of exploitable dependencies: exploitable dependence on an individual family member, such as a husband or an adult child; exploitable dependence on employers and supervisors; and exploitable dependence on the personal whims of state officials. Rather than shuttle people back and forth among these exploitable dependencies, an adequate approach must prevent all three simultaneously. This principle rules out arrangements that channel a homemaker's benefits through her husband. It is likewise incompatible with arrangements that provide essential goods, such as health insurance, only in forms linked conditionally to scarce employment. . . .

3 *The Income-Equality Principle.* One form of equality that is crucial to gender equity concerns the distribution of real per capita income. This sort of equality is highly pressing now, after the family wage, when U.S. women's earnings are approximately 70 percent of men's, when much of women's labor is not compensated at all, and when many women suffer from "hidden poverty" due to unequal distribution within families. As I interpret it, the principle of income equality does not require absolute leveling, but it does rule out arrangements that reduce women's incomes after divorce by nearly half, while men's incomes nearly double. It likewise rules out unequal pay for equal work and the wholesale undervaluation of women's labor and skills. The income-equality principle requires a substantial reduction in the vast discrepancy between men's and women's incomes. In so doing, it tends, as well, to help equalize the life-chances of children in that a majority of U.S. children are currently likely to live at some point in solo-mother families.

4 *The Leisure-Time-Equality Principle.* Another kind of equality that is crucial to gender equity concerns the distribution of leisure time. This sort of equality is highly pressing now, after the family wage, when many women, but only a few men, do both paid work and unpaid primary carework and when women suffer disproportionately from "time poverty." . . . The leisure-time-equality principle rules out welfare arrangements that would equalize incomes while requiring a double shift of work from women but only a single shift from men. It likewise rules out arrangements that would require women, but not men, to do either the "work of claiming" or the time-consuming "patchwork" of piecing together income from several sources and of coordinating services from different agencies and associations.

5 *The Equality-of-Respect Principle.* Equality of respect is also crucial to gender equity. This kind of equality is especially pressing now, after the family wage, when postindustrial culture routinely represents women as sexual objects for the pleasure of male subjects. The principle of equal respect rules out social arrangements that objectify and deprecate women—even if those arrangements prevent poverty and exploitation, and even if in addition they equalize income and leisure time. It is incompatible with welfare programs that trivialize women's activities and ignore women's contributions—hence with "welfare reforms" in the United States that assume AFDC claimants do not "work." Equality of respect requires recognition of women's personhood and recognition of women's work. . . .

6 *The Antimarginalization Principle.* A welfare state could satisfy all the preceding principles and still function to marginalize women. By limiting support to generous mothers' pensions, for example, it could render women independent, well provided for, well rested, and respected but enclaved in a separate domestic sphere, removed from the life of the larger society. Such a welfare state would be unacceptable. Social policy should promote women's full participation on a par with men in all areas of social life—in employment, in politics, in the associational life of civil society. The antimarginalization principle requires provision of the necessary conditions for women's participation, including day care, elder care, and provision for breast-feeding in public. It also requires the dismantling of masculinist work cultures and woman-hostile political environments. . . .

7 *The Antiandrocentrism Principle.* A welfare state that satisfied many of the foregoing principles could still entrench some obnoxious gender norms. It could assume the androcentric view that men's current life patterns represent the human norm and that women ought to assimilate to them. (This is the real issue behind the previously noted worry about equality.) Such a welfare state is unacceptable. Social policy should not require women to become like men nor to fit into institutions designed for men, in order to enjoy comparable levels of well-being. Policy should aim instead to restructure androcentric institutions so as to welcome human beings who can give birth and who often care for relatives and friends, treating them not as exceptions but as ideal-typical participants. The antiandrocentrism principle requires decentering masculinist norms—in part by revaluing practices and traits that are currently undervalued because they are associated with women. It entails changing men as well as changing women.

Here, then, is an account of gender equity in social welfare. On this account, gender equity is a complex idea comprising seven distinct normative principles, each of which is necessary and essential. No postindustrial welfare state can realize gender equity unless it satisfies them all. . . .

THE UNIVERSAL BREADWINNER MODEL

In one vision of postindustrial society, the age of the family wage would give way to the age of the Universal Breadwinner. This is the vision implicit in the current political practice of most U.S. feminists and liberals. (It was also assumed in the former communist countries!) It aims to achieve gender equity principally by promoting women's employment. The point is to enable women to support themselves and their families through their own wage-earning. The breadwinner role is to be universalized, in sum, so that women, too, can be citizen-workers.

Universal Breadwinner is a very ambitious postindustrial scenario, requiring major new programs and policies. One crucial element is a set of employment-enabling services, such as day care and elder care, aimed at freeing women from unpaid responsibilities so they could take full-time employment on terms comparable to men. Another essential element is a set of workplace reforms aimed at removing equal-opportunity obstacles, such as sex discrimination and sexual harassment. Reforming the workplace requires reforming the culture, however—eliminating sexist stereotypes and breaking the cultural association of breadwinning with masculinity. Also required are policies to help change socialization, so as, first, to reorient women's aspirations toward employment and away from domesticity, and second, to reorient men's expectations toward acceptance of women's new role. None of this would work, however, without one additional ingredient: macroeconomic policies to create full-time, high-paying, permanent jobs for women. These would have to be true breadwinner jobs in the primary labor force, carrying full, first-class social-insurance entitlements. Social insurance, finally, is central to Universal Breadwinner. The aim here is to bring women up to parity with men in an institution that has traditionally disadvantaged them.

How would this model organize carework? The bulk of such work would be shifted from the family to the market and the state, where it would be performed by employees for pay. Who, then, are these employees likely to be? In many countries today, including the United States, paid institutional carework is poorly remunerated, feminized, and largely racialized and/or performed by immigrants. But such arrangements are precluded in this model. If the model is to succeed in enabling *all* women to be breadwinners, it must upgrade the status and pay attached to carework employment, making it, too, into primary-labor-force work. Universal Breadwinner, then, is necessarily committed to a policy of "comparable worth"; it must redress the widespread undervaluation of skills and jobs currently coded as feminine and/or "nonwhite," and it must remunerate such jobs with breadwinner-level pay.

Universal Breadwinner would link many benefits to employment and distribute them through social insurance, with levels varying according to earnings. In this respect, the model resembles the industrial-era welfare state. The difference is that many more women would be covered on the basis of their own employment records. And many more women's employment records would look considerably more like men's.

Not all adults can be employed, however. Some will be unable to work for medical reasons, including some adults not previously employed. Others will be unable to get jobs. Some, finally, will have carework responsibilities that they are unable or unwilling to shift elsewhere. Most of these last will be women. To provide for these people, Universal Breadwinner must include a residual tier of social welfare that provides need-based, means-tested wage replacements.

Universal Breadwinner is far removed from present realities. It requires massive creation of primary-labor-force jobs—jobs sufficient to support a family single-handedly. That, of course, is wildly askew of current postindustrial trends, which generate jobs not for breadwinners but for "disposable workers." Let us assume for the sake of the thought experiment, however, that its conditions of possibility could be met. And let us consider whether the resulting postindustrial welfare state could claim title to gender equity.

1 *Antipoverty*. We can acknowledge straight off that Universal Breadwinner would do a good job of preventing poverty. A policy that created secure breadwinner-quality jobs for all employable women and men—while providing the services that would enable women to take such jobs—would keep most families out of poverty. And generous levels of residual support would keep the rest out of poverty through transfers.

2 *Antiexploitation*. The model should also succeed in preventing exploitable dependency for most women. Women with secure breadwinner jobs are able to exit unsatisfactory relations with men. And those who do not have such jobs but know they can get them will also be less vulnerable to exploitation. Failing that, the residual system of income support provides backup protection against exploitable dependency—assuming that it is generous, nondiscretionary, and honorable.

3 *Income equality*. Universal Breadwinner is only fair, however, at achieving income equality. Granted, secure breadwinner jobs for women—plus the services that would enable women to take them—would narrow the gender wage gap. Reduced inequality in earnings, moreover, translates into reduced inequality in social-insurance benefits. And the availability of exit options from marriage should encourage a more equitable distribution of resources within it. But the model is not otherwise egalitarian. It contains a basic social fault line dividing breadwinners from others, to the considerable disadvantage of the others—most of whom would be women. Apart from comparable worth, moreover, it does not reduce pay inequality among breadwinner jobs. To be sure, the model reduces the weight of gender in assigning individuals to unequally compensated breadwinner jobs, but it thereby increases the weight of other variables, presumably class, education, "race"-ethnicity, and age. Women—and men—who are disadvantaged in relation to those axes of social differentiation will earn less than those who are not.

4 *Leisure-time equality*. The model is quite poor, moreover, with respect to equality of leisure time, as we know from the communist experience. It assumes that all of women's current domestic and carework responsibilities can be shifted to the market and/or the state. But that assumption is patently unrealistic. Some things, such as childbearing, attending to family emergencies, and much parenting work, cannot be shifted—short of universal surrogacy and other presumably undesirable arrangements. Other things, such as cooking and (some) housekeeping, could—provided we were prepared to accept collective living arrangements or high levels of commodification. Even those tasks that are shifted, finally, do not disappear without a trace but give rise to burdensome new tasks of coordination. Women's chances for equal leisure, then, depend on whether men can be induced to do their fair share of this work. On this, the model does not inspire confidence. Not only does it offer no disincentives to free-riding, but in valorizing paid work, it implicitly devalues unpaid work, thereby fueling the motivation to shirk. Women without partners would in any case be on their own. And those in lower-income households would be less able to purchase replacement services. Employed women would have a second shift on this model, then, albeit a less burdensome one than some have now; and there would be many more women employed full-time. Universal Breadwinner, in sum, is not likely to deliver equal leisure. Anyone who does not free-ride in this possible postindustrial world is likely to be harried and tired.

5 *Equality of respect.* The model is only fair, moreover, at delivering equality of respect. Because it holds men and women to the single standard of the citizen-worker, its only chance of eliminating the gender respect gap is to admit women to that status on the same terms as men. This, however, is unlikely to occur. A more likely outcome is that women would retain more connection to reproduction and domesticity than men, thus appearing as breadwinners manqué. In addition, the model is likely to generate another kind of respect gap. By putting a high premium on breadwinner status, it invites disrespect for others. Participants in the means-tested residual system will be liable to stigmatization, and most of these will be women. Any employment-centered model, even a feminist one, has a hard time constructing an honorable status for those it defines as "nonworkers."

6 *Antimarginalization.* This model is also only fair at combating women's marginalization. Granted, it promotes women's participation in employment, but its definition of participation is narrow. Expecting full-time employment of all who are able, the model may actually impede participation in politics and civil society. Certainly, it does nothing to promote women's participation in those arenas. It fights women's marginalization, then, in a one-sided, "workerist" way.

7 *Antiandrocentrism.* Last, the model performs poorly in overcoming androcentrism. It valorizes men's traditional sphere—employment—and simply tries to help women fit in. Traditionally female carework, in contrast, is treated instrumentally; it is what must be sloughed off in order to become a breadwinner. It is not itself accorded social value. The ideal-typical citizen here is the breadwinner, now nominally gender-neutral. But the content of the status is implicitly masculine; it is the male half of the old breadwinner/homemaker couple, now universalized and required of everyone. The female half of the couple has simply disappeared. None of her distinctive virtues and capacities has been preserved for women, let alone universalized to men. The model is androcentric.

We can summarize the merits of Universal Breadwinner in Figure 2.1. Not surprisingly, Universal Breadwinner delivers the best outcomes to women whose lives most closely resemble the male half of the old family-wage ideal couple. It is especially good to childless women and to women without other major domestic

Fig. 2.1

Principle	Universal Breadwinner
Antipoverty	good
Antiexploitation	good
Income equality	fair
Leisure-time equality	poor
Equality of respect	fair
Antimarginalization	fair
Antiandrocentrism	poor

responsibilities that cannot easily be shifted to social services. But for those women, as well as for others, it falls short of full gender equity.

THE CAREGIVER PARITY MODEL

In a second vision of postindustrial society, the era of the family wage would give way to the era of Caregiver Parity. This is the picture implicit in the political practice of most Western European feminists and social democrats. It aims to promote gender equity principally by supporting informal carework. The point is to enable women with significant domestic responsibilities to support themselves and their families either through carework alone or through carework plus part-time employment. (Women without significant domestic responsibilities would presumably support themselves through employment.) The aim is not to make women's lives the same as men's but, rather, to "make difference costless." Thus, childbearing, child rearing, and informal domestic labor are to be elevated to parity with formal paid labor. The caregiver role is to be put on a par with the breadwinner role—so that women and men can enjoy equivalent levels of dignity and well-being.

Caregiver Parity is also extremely ambitious. On this model, many (though not all) women will follow the current U.S. female practice of alternating spells of full-time employment, spells of full-time carework, and spells that combine part-time carework with part-time employment. The aim is to make such a life-pattern costless. To this end, several major new programs are necessary. One is a program of caregiver allowances to compensate childbearing, child rearing, housework, and other forms of socially necessary domestic labor; the allowances must be sufficiently generous at the full-time rate to support a family—hence equivalent to a breadwinner wage. Also required is a program of workplace reforms. These must facilitate the possibility of combining supported carework with part-time employment and of making transitions between different life-states. The key here is flexibility. One obvious necessity is a generous program of mandated pregnancy and family leaves so that caregivers can exit and enter employment without losing security or seniority. Another is a program of retraining and job search for those not returning to old jobs. Also essential is mandated flextime so that caregivers can shift their hours to accommodate their carework responsibilities, including shifts between full- and part-time employment. Finally, in the wake of all this flexibility, there must be programs to ensure continuity of all the basic social-welfare benefits, including health, unemployment, disability, and retirement insurance.

This model organizes carework very differently from Universal Breadwinner. Whereas that approach shifted carework to the market and the state, this one keeps the bulk of such work in the household and supports it with public funds. Caregiver Parity's social-insurance system also differs sharply. To assure continuous coverage for people alternating between carework and employment, benefits attached to both must be integrated in a single system. In this system, part-time jobs and supported carework must be covered on the same basis as full-time jobs. Thus, a woman finishing a spell of supported carework would be eligible for unemployment insurance benefits on the same basis as a recently laid off employee in the event she could not find a suitable job. And a supported careworker who became disabled would receive disability payments on the same basis as a disabled employee. Years of supported carework would count on a par with years of employment toward eligibility for retirement pensions. Benefit levels would be fixed in ways that treat carework and employment equivalently.

Caregiver Parity also requires another, residual tier of social welfare. Some adults will be unable to do either carework or waged work, including some adults without prior work records of either type. Most of these people will probably be men. To provide for them, the model must offer means-tested wage-and-allowance replacements. Caregiver Parity's residual tier should be smaller than Universal Breadwinner's, however; nearly all adults should be covered in the integrated breadwinner-caregiver system of social insurance.

Caregiver Parity, too, is far removed from current U.S. arrangements. It requires large outlays of public funds to pay caregiver allowances, hence major structural tax reform and a sea change in political culture. Let us assume for the sake of the thought experiment, however, that its conditions of possibility could be met. And let us consider whether the resulting postindustrial welfare state could claim title to gender equity.

1 *Antipoverty.* Caregiver Parity would do a good job of preventing poverty—including for those women and children who are currently most vulnerable. Sufficiently generous allowances would keep solo-mother families out of poverty during spells of full-time carework. And a combination of allowances and wages would do the same during spells of part-time supported carework and part-time employment. Since each of these options would carry the basic social-insurance package, moreover, women with "feminine" work patterns would have considerable security.

2 *Antiexploitation.* Caregiver Parity should also succeed in preventing exploitation for most women, including for those who are most vulnerable today. By providing income directly to nonemployed wives, it reduces their economic dependence on husbands. It also provides economic security to single women with children, reducing their liability to exploitation by employers. Insofar as caregiver allowances are honorable and nondiscretionary, finally, recipients are not subject to caseworkers' whims.

3 *Income equality.* Caregiver Parity performs quite poorly, however, with respect to income equality, as we know from the Nordic experience. Although the system of allowances-plus-wages provides the equivalent of a basic minimum breadwinner wage, it also institutes a "mommy track" in employment—a market in flexible, noncontinuous full- and/or part-time jobs. Most of these jobs will pay considerably less even at the full-time rate than comparable breadwinner-track jobs. Two-partner families will have an economic incentive to keep one partner on the breadwinner track rather than to share spells of carework between them, and given current labor markets, making the breadwinner the man will be most advantageous for heterosexual couples. Given current culture and socialization, moreover, men are generally unlikely to choose the mommy track in the same proportions as women. So the two employment tracks will carry traditional gender associations. Those associations are likely in turn to produce discrimination against women in the breadwinner track. Caregiver Parity may make difference cost less, then, but it will not make difference costless.

4 *Leisure-time equality.* Caregiver Parity does somewhat better, however, with respect to equality of leisure time. It makes it possible for all women to avoid the double shift, if they choose, by opting for full- or part-time supported carework at various stages in their lives. (Currently, this choice is available only to a small percentage of privileged U.S. women.) We just saw, however, that this choice is not truly costless. Some women with families will not want to forego the benefits of breadwinner-track employment and will try to combine it with carework. Those not partnered with someone on the caregiver track will be significantly disadvantaged with respect to leisure time, and probably in their employment as well. Men, in contrast, will largely be insulated from this dilemma. On leisure time, then, the model is only fair.

5 *Equality of respect.* Caregiver Parity is also only fair at promoting equality of respect. Unlike Universal Breadwinner, it offers two different routes to that end. Theoretically, citizen-workers and citizen-caregivers are statuses of equivalent dignity. But are they really on a par with each other? Caregiving is certainly treated more respectfully in this model than in current U.S. society, but it remains associated with femininity. Breadwinning likewise remains associated with masculinity. Given those traditional gender associations, plus the economic differential between the two lifestyles, caregiving is unlikely to attain true parity with breadwinning. In general, it is hard to imagine how "separate but equal" gender roles could provide genuine equality of respect today.

6 *Antimarginalization.* Caregiver Parity performs poorly, moreover, in preventing women's marginalization. By supporting women's informal carework, it reinforces the view of such work as women's work and consolidates the gender division of domestic labor. By consolidating dual labor markets for breadwinners and caregivers, moreover, the model marginalizes women within the employment sector. By reinforcing the association of caregiving with femininity, finally, it may also impede women's participation in other spheres of life, such as politics and civil society.

7 *Antiandrocentrism.* Yet Caregiver Parity is better than Universal Breadwinner at combating androcentrism. It treats caregiving as intrinsically valuable, not as a mere obstacle to employment, thus challenging the view that only men's traditional activities are fully human. It also accommodates "feminine" life-patterns, thereby rejecting the demand that women assimilate to "masculine" patterns. But the model still leaves something to be desired. Caregiver Parity stops short of affirming the universal value of activities and life-patterns associated with women. It does not value caregiving enough to demand that men do it, too; it does not ask men to change. Thus, Caregiver Parity represents only one-half of a full-scale challenge to androcentrism. Here, too, its performance is only fair.

Caregiver Parity's strengths and weaknesses are summarized in Figure 2.2. In general, Caregiver Parity improves the lot of women with significant carework responsibilities, but for those women, as well as for others, it fails to deliver full gender equity.

TOWARD A UNIVERSAL CAREGIVER MODEL

Both Universal Breadwinner and Caregiver Parity are highly utopian visions of a postindustrial welfare state. Either would represent a major improvement over current U.S. arrangements, yet neither is likely to be realized soon. Both models assume background preconditions that are strikingly absent today. Both presuppose major political-economic restructuring, including significant public control over

Fig. 2.2

Principle	Caregiver Parity
Antipoverty	good
Antiexploitation	good
Income equality	poor
Leisure-time equality	fair
Equality of respect	fair
Antimarginalization	poor
Antiandrocentrism	fair

corporations, the capacity to direct investment to create high-quality permanent jobs, and the ability to tax profits *and wealth* at rates sufficient to fund expanded high-quality social programs. Both models also assume broad popular support for a postindustrial welfare state that is committed to gender equity.

If both models are utopian in this sense, neither is utopian enough. Neither Universal Breadwinner nor Caregiver Parity can actually make good on its promise of gender equity—even under very favorable conditions. Although both are good at preventing women's poverty and exploitation, both are only fair at redressing inequality of respect: Universal Breadwinner holds women to the same standard as men, while constructing arrangements that prevent them from meeting it fully; Caregiver Parity, in contrast, sets up a double standard to accommodate gender difference, while institutionalizing policies that fail to assure equivalent respect for "feminine" activities and life-patterns. When we turn to the remaining principles, moreover, the two models' strengths and weaknesses diverge. Universal Breadwinner fails especially to promote equality of leisure time and to combat androcentrism, while Caregiver Parity fails especially to promote income equality and to prevent women's marginalization. Neither model, in addition, promotes women's full participation on a par with men in politics and civil society. And neither values female-associated practices enough to ask men to do them too; neither asks men to change. (The relative merits of Universal Breadwinner and Caregiver Parity are summarized in Figure 2.3.) Neither model, in sum, provides everything feminists want. Even in a highly idealized form neither delivers full gender equity.

If these were the only possibilities, we would face a very difficult set of trade-offs. Suppose, however, we reject this Hobson's choice and try to develop a third alternative. The trick is to envision a postindustrial welfare state that combines the best of Universal Breadwinner with the best of Caregiver Parity, while jettisoning the worst features of each. What third alternative is possible?

So far we have examined—and found wanting—two initially plausible approaches: one aiming to make women more like men are now; the other leaving men and women pretty much unchanged, while aiming to make women's difference costless. A third possibility is to *induce men to become more like most women are now,* namely, people who do primary carework.

Fig. 2.3

Principle	Universal Breadwinner	Caregiver Parity
Antipoverty	good	good
Antiexploitation	good	good
Income equality	fair	poor
Leisure-time equality	poor	fair
Equality of respect	fair	fair
Antimarginalization	fair	poor
Antiandrocentrism	poor	fair

Consider the effects of this one change on the models we have just examined. If men were to do their fair share of carework, Universal Breadwinner would come much closer to equalizing leisure time and eliminating androcentrism, and Caregiver Parity would do a much better job of equalizing income and reducing women's marginalization. Both models, in addition, would tend to promote equality of respect. If men were to become more like women are now, in sum, both models would begin to approach gender equity.

The key to achieving gender equity in a postindustrial welfare state, then, is to make women's current life-patterns the norm for everyone. Women today often combine breadwinning and caregiving, albeit with great difficulty and strain. A postindustrial welfare state must ensure that men do the same, while redesigning institutions so as to eliminate the difficulty and strain. We might call this vision *Universal Caregiver.*

What, then, might such a welfare state look like? Unlike Caregiver Parity, its employment sector would not be divided into two different tracks; all jobs would be designed for workers who are caregivers, too; all would have a shorter work-week than full-time jobs have now; and all would have the support of employment-enabling services. Unlike Universal Breadwinner, however, employees would not be assumed to shift all carework to social services. Some informal carework would be publicly supported and integrated on a par with paid work in a single social-insurance system. Some would be performed in households by relatives and friends, but such households would not necessarily be heterosexual nuclear families. Other supported carework would be located outside households altogether—in civil society. In state-funded but locally organized institutions, childless adults, older people, and others without kin-based responsibilities would join parents and others in democratic, self-managed carework activities.

A Universal Caregiver welfare state would promote gender equity by effectively dismantling the gendered opposition between breadwinning and caregiving. It would integrate activities that are currently separated from one another, eliminate their gender-coding, and encourage men to perform them too. This, however, is tantamount to a wholesale restructuring of the institution of gender. The construction of breadwinning and caregiving as separate roles, coded masculine and feminine respectively, is a principal undergirding of the current gender order. To dismantle those roles and their cultural coding is in effect to overturn that order. It means subverting the existing gender division of labor and reducing the salience of gender as a structural principle of social organization. At the limit, it suggests deconstructing gender. By deconstructing the opposition between breadwinning and caregiving, moreover, Universal Caregiver would simultaneously deconstruct the associated opposition between bureaucratized public institutional settings and intimate private domestic settings. Treating civil society as an additional site for carework, it would overcome both the "workerism" of Universal Breadwinner and the domestic privatism of Caregiver Parity. Thus, Universal Caregiver promises expansive new possibilities for enriching the substance of social life and for promoting equal participation.

Only by embracing the Universal Caregiver vision, moreover, can we mitigate potential conflicts among our seven component principles of gender equity and minimize the need for trade-offs. Rejecting this approach, in contrast, makes such conflicts, and hence trade-offs, more likely. *Achieving gender equity in a postindustrial welfare state, then, requires deconstructing gender.*

Much more work needs to be done to develop this third—Universal Caregiver—vision of a postindustrial welfare state. A key is to develop policies that discourage free-riding. *Contra* conservatives, the real free-riders in the current system are not poor solo mothers who shirk employment. Instead, they are men of all classes who shirk carework and domestic labor, as well as corporations who free-ride on the labor of working people, both underpaid and unpaid.

A good statement of the Universal Caregiver vision comes from the Swedish Ministry of Labor: "To make it possible for both men and women to combine parenthood and gainful employment, a new view of the male role and a radical change in the organization of working life are required."[1] The trick is to imagine a social world in which citizens' lives integrate wage earning, caregiving, community activism, political participation, and involvement in the associational life of civil society—while also leaving time for some fun. This world is not likely to come into being in the immediate future, but it is the only imaginable postindustrial world that promises true gender equity. And unless we are guided by this vision now, we will never get any closer to achieving it.

NOTE

1 Quoted in Ruth Lister, "Women, Economic Dependency, and Citizenship," *Journal of Social Policy* 19, no. 4 (1990), p. 463.

QUESTIONS

1 In a just society, should the government play a significant role in promoting gender equity?
2 Should any of the three visions presented by Fraser be a guiding ideal in formulating policy decisions in a just society?

SUGGESTED ADDITIONAL READINGS FOR CHAPTER 8

CHRISTMAN, JOHN: "Autonomy, Independence, and Poverty-Related Welfare Programs." *Public Affairs Quarterly,* vol. 12, 1998, pp. 383–405. Christman argues that, insofar as autonomy is the justifying goal of welfare programs for the poor, these programs will fail unless provisions are made to guarantee the material conditions necessary for autonomous choice *prior to,* and independent of, labor force participation. He then advances a critical examination of recent U.S. programs whose aim is to reduce welfare dependency.

FRIEDMAN, MILTON: *Capitalism and Freedom.* Chicago: University of Chicago Press, 1962. For Friedman, an economist and libertarian, the ethical principle governing the distribution of income in a free society is "to each according to what he or the instruments he owns produces." He sees economic freedom as a necessary condition for political freedom.

GINSBERG, LEON: *Conservative Social Welfare Policy: A Description and Analysis.* Chicago: Nelson-Hall, 1998. Ginsberg analyzes conservative and neoconservative perspectives on social welfare. His account includes a description of the history of social welfare, as well as an examination of the role that American business and economics have played in shaping social policy.

GOVIER, TRUDY: "The Right to Eat and the Duty to Work." *Philosophy of the Social Sciences,* vol. 5, 1975, pp. 125–143. Govier identifies three possible positions on welfare: individualist, puritan, and permissive. Evaluating each from both a utilitarian and justice standpoint, she argues that the permissive position is morally superior to the others.

HARRINGTON, MICHAEL: *Socialism.* New York: Saturday Review Press, 1970, 1972. Harrington explores various "socialisms"—positions that he considers antisocialist. He presents his account of socialism as a possible alternative to both communism and the welfare state.

HASLETT, D. W.: "Is Inheritance Justified?" *Philosophy and Public Affairs,* vol. 15, Spring 1986, pp. 122–155. Haslett addresses the following question: Should property rights incorporate the practice of inheritance as it exists in the United States today? Giving a negative response, be argues that the inheritance of wealth is inconsistent with the fundamental values that underlie capitalism.

KYMLICKA, WILL: *Contemporary Political Philosophy.* Oxford: Oxford University Press, 1990. Kymlicka discusses the competing views of justice and community advanced by the major schools in contemporary political theory.

LAWSON, BILL E., ed.: *The Underclass Question.* Philadelphia: Temple University Press, 1992. This set of articles explores various philosophical questions raised by the recent growth of an economically and politically disadvantaged black group at a time when the black middle class is expanding.

NIELSEN, KAI: *Equality and Liberty: A Defense of Radical Egalitarianism.* Totowa, N.J.: Rowman & Littlefield, 1984. Nielsen defends the egalitarian ideal that is at the basis of socialist thinking.

NOZICK, ROBERT: *Anarchy, State, and Utopia.* New York: Basic, 1974. This book has engendered a great deal of discussion among philosophers concerned with distributive justice. Nozick, who endorses the libertarian conception of justice, holds the libertarian ideal to be exemplified by the principle "from each as he chooses, to each as he is chosen."

OKIN, SUSAN MOLLER: *Justice. Gender, and the Family.* New York: Basic, 1989. Okin argues that, without a just family structure, there will not be a just society. She criticizes various contemporary Anglo-American theories of justice, such as those of Robert Nozick and John Rawls, for their androcentrism. However, Okin finds Rawls's veil of ignorance useful in developing a theory of justice within the family.

RAWLS, JOHN: *A Theory of Justice,* rev. ed. Cambridge, Mass.: Harvard University Press, 1999. In his seminal work, *A Theory of Justice,* published in 1971, Rawls presents his theory of justice *as* fairness. In this revised edition, Rawls attempts to clear up a number of difficulties he and others have found in the original book.

CHAPTER 9

World Hunger and Poverty

Widespread hunger and poverty are undeniable facts in the world today. Famines are commonplace in Africa and Southeast Asia, and, for many people in very diverse places on the globe, malnutrition is an everyday fact of life. According to the United Nation's *Human Development Report 2005,* over a billion people in the world survive on less than one dollar a day while another 1.5 billion people live on between one and two dollars a day. There is a close link between poverty and hunger. "More than 850 million people, including one in three preschool children, are trapped in a vicious cycle of malnutrition and its effects."[1] Very few of the victims of famine and malnutrition actually "die of hunger." More commonly, they die of illnesses, such as flu and intestinal problems, which they could have survived if they had not been weakened by hunger. The victims are often very old or very young. Aftereffects for those who survive are often tragic and long-lasting. A large number of children are stunted in growth and suffer incapacitating brain damage as a result of malnutrition. Whole populations are permanently weakened, listless, and lethargic, lacking the energy for any economic advances that might help prevent future famines. At the same time, globalization, with its massive flow of money and technology across territorial boundaries, is changing economic conditions in many developing nations, benefiting some members of these nations but impoverishing others. One of the results of globalization is the proliferation in developing countries of so-called sweatshops that produce goods sold primarily in affluent countries. These places are called sweatshops because the workers are very poorly paid and work under conditions that are considered inhumane by Western ethical standards.

The moral issues raised by ongoing world hunger and poverty are many and complex. In this chapter we focus on only three questions regarding the responsibilities of affluent countries and of individuals who live in those countries. First, what should affluent nations do to prevent and alleviate devastating hunger,

---

[1]"The State of Human Development" in *Human Development Report 2005,* http://hdr.undp.org/reports/global/2005, chap. 1, p. 24.

malnutrition, and poverty in developing countries? Second, what are the moral obligations of individuals in affluent nations with respect to world hunger and poverty? Third, what ethical standards should individuals in affluent nations use when deciding whether to buy goods produced in international sweatshops?

THE MORAL OBLIGATIONS OF AFFLUENT NATIONS AND THE CAUSES OF WORLD HUNGER AND POVERTY

As many of the readings in this chapter show, answers to questions concerning the moral obligations of more affluent nations with regard to world hunger and poverty are intertwined with answers to questions concerning the *causes* of world hunger and poverty. Four major approaches to answering these questions are discussed below.

The Neo-Malthusian Approach

The first approach taken regarding the causes of world hunger and poverty is offered by people labeled "neo-Malthusians." Following Thomas Robert Malthus (1766–1834), they identify the cause as *overpopulation*. According to Malthus, unrestricted population growth necessarily outstrips economic growth, especially the growth in food supplies. This, in turn, *necessarily* results in famines. Uncontrolled fertility is the cause of poverty, and poverty is the cause of the miseries of the poor, including starvation. It has been shown that Malthus was wrong in certain respects, since in many countries the economic growth rate, including the growth in food supplies, has far outstripped the population growth rate. But contemporary neo-Malthusians hold that, in the long run, economic growth rate cannot be sustained. Having identified overpopulation as *the cause* of scarcity, neo-Malthusians locate the solution to problems of world hunger in population control. Optimistic neo-Malthusians hold that birth-control measures can eventually succeed in curbing population growth sufficiently to avert future famines. Pessimistic neo-Malthusians hold that serious political and psychological obstacles to planned population-control measures make famine inevitable in some countries. They predict that these famines will in turn effectively curb unsustainable population growth unless those in more affluent countries intervene.

Some pessimistic neo-Malthusians, including Garrett Hardin in this chapter, use their Malthusian analyses of world hunger to support claims about what more affluent individuals and nations *ought* to do regarding the needs of potential famine victims. Using a lifeboat metaphor, Hardin compares nations to boats and maintains that many countries have outstripped their "carrying capacity." He advances a consequentialist argument to support his claim that the affluent *ought not* help those in the overpopulating countries. In Hardin's view, the long-range effects of food aid will be not only harmful but disastrous for everyone. These effects will be disastrous for countries whose fertility rates remain uncontrolled by either human planning or nature because, sooner or later, future generations in these countries will suffer massive starvation and profound misery. They will also be disastrous for affluent countries that will use up their resources to help overpopulating countries. Hardin even suggests that the very survival of human beings is at risk. He maintains that if giving food to *any* overpopulated country does more harm than good, that food should not be given.

A Contra Neo-Malthusian Approach

The second approach taken regarding the causes of world hunger and poverty focuses on identifying the causes of high fertility rates among the poor in developing countries. Only if we understand *why* the poor have high rates of reproduction can we help instigate and support social practices that will tend to end the cycle of poverty, high birth rates, and starvation. Against the pessimistic neo-Malthusians, proponents of this approach argue that famines and malnutrition are not inevitable. Against the optimistic neo-Malthusians, they argue that planned birth-control practices backed by government policies are not the solution. Ironically, the major factors influencing high fertility rates are identified as hunger and poverty. On this analysis, eradicating famine and malnutrition requires social and economic changes in the developing countries themselves, changes that would eliminate some of the gross inequalities of wealth and property in these countries. Without the recommended changes, it is argued, economic growth, including growth in the food supply, will not take place, population growth will not be slowed, and the tragic cycle will be repeated indefinitely. Amartya Sen, for example, argues in this chapter that the primary cause of famine, hunger, and high population growth is a system of entitlements, which leaves some people without the entitlements to obtain the necessities of life. In his view, eradicating hunger and famine would require the development of policies that would give entitlements to those who are deprived, perhaps by reducing the entitlements of the more prosperous groups.

The Interconnectedness or Interaction Approach

The third approach taken to the causes of world hunger and poverty focuses on the interconnections and interactions among nations—interconnections and interactions that are especially significant given the rapid increase in globalization. These interconnections and interactions can be seen as seriously undermining Hardin's lifeboat metaphor. Those who take this approach frequently argue that affluent nations are often causally responsible for the hunger and poverty in poorer countries since, for example, they adopt practices that prevent some of the poorest countries from increasing their own food supply. The identified culprits include multinational agribusinesses based in Western societies. It is charged that these multinationals have shifted the production of luxury items for the Western market from the highly industrialized countries to underdeveloped ones, where cheap land and labor are available. As a result, the land in needy, underdeveloped countries is used to produce cash crops—crops that can be sold to members of the more affluent countries—while the food that is needed for the home market remains unproduced.

In addition, it is argued that the international economic order favors the affluent, industrialized nations and is shaped by their needs. It is the affluent, industrialized societies that largely determine the prices for both the manufactured goods developing nations must import and the agricultural products the needy countries export. To the extent that the practices of those in affluent societies work against the potential self-sufficiency and real economic growth of developing countries, they help create and perpetuate the cycle of poverty, high fertility rates, and hunger. Thomas Pogge, in this chapter, argues in this vein and uses the WTO (World Trade Organization) to exemplify the ways that affluent nations disadvantage impoverished developing ones.

The WTO, created in 1995, is an international organization with 148 member countries that serves as a forum for negotiating international trade agreements. It is also the monitoring and regulating body for enforcing these agreements.[2] Supporters of the WTO argue that by expanding world trade, the WTO helps to raise living standards around the world. Critics, like Pogge, point out that developing countries are at a disadvantage in the WTO decision-making processes because they lack the expertise and staffing capabilities of affluent countries. They are also adversely affected by many of the decisions made. Affluent nations, for example, are especially protectionist in sectors where developing countries are in a good position to compete—agriculture, textiles, and clothing—leading to tariff decisions that adversely affect developing nations. In Pogge's view, one of the reasons why affluent nations have a moral obligation to alleviate poverty in the world is that, through the WTO, they continue to support a world order that disadvantages poorer countries and makes it more difficult for them to eliminate poverty and hunger.

The United Nations' member states have made a commitment to alleviate extreme poverty in the world. In the *United Nations Millennium Declaration (2000),* the UN's 191 member states agreed on a set of goals to be met by 2015. The first and primary goal is "to halve, by the year 2015, the proportion of the world's people whose income is less than one dollar a day and the proportion of people who suffer from hunger."[3] Pogge, in a longer version of the article reprinted in this chapter,[4] analyzes the UN's interpretation of this goal and finds the resulting actual commitment to be inadequate.

Pogge reasons as follows. In 2000, the total human population was 6,070.6 million; 1,094 million were reported to be living below one dollar per day (considered extreme poverty). Thus, in 2000, 18.02 percent of the people in the world were living in extreme poverty. If the goal is to halve that proportion, then it would seem that the goal is that by 2015 no more than 9.01 percent of people would be living in extreme poverty. Given an expected human population of 7,197 million in 2015, the implied goal would seem to be to reduce the number of extremely poor people to 648.5 million by 2015.[5] However, Pogge argues, in reality the planned poverty

---

[2]http://www.wto.org.
[3]*United Nations Millennium Declaration (2000),* http://www.undp.org.in.
[4]Thomas Pogge, "The First United Nations Millennium Development Goal: A Cause for Celebration?" *Journal of Human Development,* vol. 5, November 2004, pp. 377–397.
[5]Ibid., p. 378.

reduction is much less than that, largely because the UN's interpretation of the goal uses 1990 rather than 2000 as the baseline, understanding its goal to be that the proportion of extremely poor people in 2015 should be no more than one-half of what it was in 1990.[6] In 1990, the number of people reported to be living in extreme poverty was 1,218.5 million or 23.15 percent of the total human population at that time. Halving this percentage would commit world governments to a goal of no more than 11.575 percent of the human population living in extreme poverty in 2015. Given a projected world population of 7,197 million in 2015, this would still leave 833 million living on less than one dollar per day. Pogge goes on to point out other aspects of the UN's interpretation that result in an even less ambitious goal—to cut the number of people living in extreme poverty in 2015 to 883.5 million, or 12.276 percent of the projected 2015 population. This is only 19 percent less than the 1,094 million living on less than one dollar per day in 2000. For Pogge, this is morally reprehensible. (Pogge also rejects the view that any more ambitious goal would be too costly.)

Yet, according to the *Human Development Report 2005,* it is doubtful that even this goal will be met. One of the problems has already been noted above—international trade policies. As the 2005 report states,

> Rich country trade policies continue to deny poor countries and poor people a fair share of global prosperity—and they fly in the face of the Millennium Declaration. More than aid, trade has the potential to increase the share of the world's poorest countries and people in global prosperity. Limiting that potential through unfair trade policies is inconsistent with a commitment to the MDGs [millennium development goals]. More than that, it is unjust and hypocritical.[7]

The Socialist Approach

The fourth approach, taken by Marxists and other socialists, incorporates some of the elements already discussed above. (Socialism is discussed in the introduction to Chapter 8 and in a reading by Kai Nielsen in that chapter.) Socialists reject both the contention that overpopulation is the cause of scarcity in the world and the contention that the requisite economic growth is impossible. They identify capitalism as the major cause of worldwide scarcity. Agreeing with the kinds of claims just discussed concerning the negative impact of multinational corporations on the economic growth of developing countries, they see a socialist economic system as the only solution to the problem of world hunger and poverty.[8]

---

[6]The problem is that the UN's formulation of the goal specifies the year 2015 as the end of the plan period but does not specify a baseline year. One might naturally assume that the missing baseline year is the year 2000 in which the MDGs (millennium development goals) were adopted. But the UN actually uses 1990, which makes a significant difference in determining just what the actual goal is (pp. 378–379).

[7]"Overview," *Human Development Report 2005,* p. 3.

[8]See, for example, Kai Nielsen, "Global Justice, Capitalism and the Third World," in Robin Attfield and Barry Wilins, eds., *International Justice and the Third World* (New York: Routledge, 1992), pp. 17–34.

THE MORAL OBLIGATIONS OF INDIVIDUALS

What moral obligations do individuals who live in affluent nations have toward those in impoverished developing nations? With respect to famine and poverty, as the above discussion shows, answers to this question may depend on what we take to be a correct analysis of the causes of famine and poverty in the world. But, if we set aside the kind of factual questions discussed earlier, we can still ask questions about the basis of a possible *moral obligation* that we as individuals might have to prevent starvation and malnutrition among the needy. In this chapter, Peter Singer, a utilitarian, argues for such a moral obligation. Utilitarianism holds that an action or a practice is morally correct only if it is likely to produce the greatest balance of good over evil, everyone considered. Proceeding in a utilitarian spirit, Singer argues for an obligation to famine victims on the basis of the following principle: Persons are morally required to prevent something bad from happening if they can do so "without sacrificing anything of comparable moral importance." In Singer's view, even a weaker version of this principle is sufficient to establish a moral obligation to aid the victims of severe famines.

But famines are not the only events in developing countries calling for a moral response. International sweatshops have also caused a great deal of moral concern. The term *sweatshops* may be understood in various ways. However, as Matt Zwolinski points out in this chapter, in the historical and social context in which the term arose, sweatshops were seen as places where the basic rights of employees were violated, or simple standards of decency were not observed. On this understanding of the term, reference to a place of employment as a "sweatshop" entails a moral judgment of condemnation.

Sweatshops in the developing world have been both defended and criticized. Defenders, such as Max Borders in this chapter, see these places as providing employment not otherwise available and as a first step toward economic prosperity. Critics have a different view, claiming that Western corporations can afford to pay "living wages," even when that is not the norm in a society, and that anything else is exploitation. They also point to various abuses and abysmal working conditions in these places. These critics include student activists on university campuses who have raised questions about where goods sold in university shops have been produced. One student group, United Trauma Relief, which was founded at the Massachusetts Institute of Technology (MIT), formulated the consensus statement reprinted in this chapter that first identifies and then rebuts claims made by defenders of sweatshops. Zwolinski takes an intermediate approach. After defining sweatshops, Zwolinski addresses two moral questions with respect to them. The first focuses on whether Western companies that use sweatshop manufacturers are acting in a morally reprehensible manner. The second deals with our individual responsibilities regarding the purchase of items produced in sweatshops. In both cases, Zwolinski's responses are cautious. His concern is that we make informed decisions and act in ways that will actually benefit those employed in sweatshops and not cause them further harm.

Jane S. Zembaty

Famine, Affluence, and Morality

Peter Singer

Singer expresses concern over the fact that, whereas members of the more affluent nations spend money on trivia, people in the needier nations are starving. He argues that it is morally wrong not to prevent suffering whenever one can do so without sacrificing anything of comparable moral importance. Giving aid to the victims of famine can prevent such suffering. Even if giving requires a drastic reduction in the standard of living of the members of the more affluent societies, the latter are morally required to meet at least the basic need for food of people who will otherwise starve to death.

As I write this, in November 1971, people are dying in East Bengal from lack of food, shelter, and medical care. The suffering and death that are occurring there now are not inevitable, not unavoidable in any fatalistic sense of the term. Constant poverty, a cyclone, and a civil war have turned at least nine million people into destitute refugees; nevertheless, it is not beyond the capacity of the richer nations to give enough assistance to reduce any further suffering to very small proportions. The decisions and actions of human beings can prevent this kind of suffering. Unfortunately, human beings have not made the necessary decisions. At the individual level, people have, with very few exceptions, not responded to the situation in any significant way. Generally speaking, people have not given large sums to relief funds; they have not written to their parliamentary representatives demanding increased government assistance; they have not demonstrated in the streets, held symbolic fasts, or done anything else directed toward providing the refugees with the means to satisfy their essential needs. At the government level, no government has given the sort of massive aid that would enable the refugees to survive for more than a few days. Britain, for instance, has given rather more than most countries. It has, to date, given £14,750,000. For comparative purposes, Britain's share of the nonrecoverable development costs of the Anglo-French Concorde project is already in excess of £275,000,000, and on present estimates will reach £440,000,000. The implication is that the British government values a supersonic transport more than thirty times as highly as it values the lives of the nine million refugees. Australia is another country which, on a per capita basis, is well up in the "aid to Bengal" table. Australia's aid, however, amounts to less than one-twelfth of the cost of Sydney's new opera house. The total amount given, from all sources, now stands at about £65,000,000. The estimated cost of keeping the refugees alive for one year is £464,000,000. Most of the refugees have now been in the camps for more than six months. The World Bank has said that India needs a minimum of £300,000,000 in assistance from other countries before the end of the year. It seems obvious that assistance on this scale will not be forthcoming. India will be forced to choose between letting the refugees starve or diverting funds from her own development program, which will mean that more of her own people will starve in the future.[1]

These are the essential facts about the present situation in Bengal. So far as it concerns us here, there is nothing unique about this situation except its magnitude. The Bengal emergency is just the latest and most acute of a series of major emergencies in various parts of the world, arising both from natural and from man-made causes. There are also many parts of the world in which people die from malnutrition and lack of food independent of any special emergency. I take Bengal as my example only because it is the present concern, and because the size of the problem has ensured that it has been given adequate publicity. Neither individuals nor governments can claim to be unaware of what is happening there.

What are the moral implications of a situation like this? In what follows, I shall argue that the way people in relatively affluent countries react to a situation like that in Bengal cannot be justified; indeed, the whole way we look at moral issues—our moral conceptual scheme—needs to be altered, and with it, the way of life that has come to be taken for granted in our society.

In arguing for this conclusion I will not, of course, claim to be morally neutral. I shall, however, try to argue for the moral position that I take, so that anyone who accepts certain assumptions, to be made explicit, will, I hope, accept my conclusion.

I begin with the assumption that suffering and death from lack of food, shelter, and medical care are bad. I think most people will agree about this, although one may reach the same view by different routes. I shall not argue for this view. People can hold all sorts of eccentric positions, and perhaps from some of them it would not follow that death by starvation is in itself bad. It is difficult, perhaps impossible, to refute such positions, and so for brevity I will henceforth take this assumption as accepted. Those who disagree need read no further.

My next point is this: if it is in our power to prevent something bad from happening, without thereby sacrificing anything of comparable moral importance, we ought, morally, to do it. By "without sacrificing anything of comparable moral importance" I mean without causing anything else comparably bad to happen, or doing something that is wrong in itself, or failing to promote some moral good, comparable in significance to the bad thing that we can prevent. This principle seems almost as uncontroversial as the last one. It requires us only to prevent what is bad, and not to promote what is good, and it requires this of us only when we can do it without sacrificing anything that is, from the moral point of view, comparably important. I could even, as far as the application of my argument to the Bengal emergency is concerned, qualify the point so as to make it: if it is in our power to prevent something very bad from happening, without thereby sacrificing anything morally significant, we ought, morally, to do it. An application of this principle would be as follows: if I am walking past a shallow pond and see a child drowning in it, I ought to wade in and pull the child out. This will mean getting my clothes muddy, but this is insignificant, while the death of the child would presumably be a very bad thing.

The uncontroversial appearance of the principle just stated is deceptive. If it were acted upon, even in its qualified form, our lives, our society, and our world would be fundamentally changed. For the principle takes, firstly, no account of proximity or distance. It makes no moral difference whether the person I can help is a neighbor's child ten yards from me or a Bengali whose name I shall never know, ten thousand miles away. Secondly, the principle makes no distinction between cases in which I am the only person who could possibly do anything and cases in which I am just one among millions in the same position.

I do not think I need to say much in defense of the refusal to take proximity and distance into account. The fact that a person is physically near to us, so that we have personal contact with him, may make it more likely that we *shall* assist him, but this does not show that we *ought* to help him rather than another who happens to be further away. If we accept any principle of impartiality, universalizability, equality, or whatever, we cannot discriminate against someone merely because he is far away from us (or we are far away from him). Admittedly, it is possible that we are in a better position to judge what needs to be done to help a person near to us than one far away, and perhaps also to provide the assistance we judge to be necessary. If this were the case, it would be a reason for helping those near to us first. This may once have been a justification for being more concerned with the poor in one's own town than with famine victims in India. Unfortunately for those who like to keep their moral responsibilities limited, instant communication and swift transportation have changed the situation. From the moral point of view, the development of the world into a "global village" has made an important, though still unrecognized, difference to our moral situation. Expert observers and supervisors, sent out by famine relief organizations or permanently stationed in famine-prone areas, can direct our aid to a refugee in Bengal almost as effectively as we could get it to someone in our own block. There would seem, therefore, to be no possible justification for discriminating on geographical grounds.

There may be a greater need to defend the second implication of my principle—that the fact that there are millions of other people in the same position, in respect to the Bengali refugees, as I am, does not make the situation significantly different from a situation in which I am the only person who can prevent something very bad from occurring. Again, of course, I admit that there is a psychological difference between the cases; one feels less guilty about doing nothing if one can point to others, similarly placed, who have also done nothing. Yet this can make no real difference to our moral obligations. Should I consider that I am less obliged to pull the drowning child out of the pond if on looking around I see other people, no further away than I am, who have also noticed the child but are doing nothing? One has only to ask this question to see the absurdity of the view that numbers lessen obligation. It is a view that is an ideal excuse for inactivity; unfortunately most of the major evils—poverty, overpopulation, pollution—are problems in which everyone is almost equally involved.

The view that numbers do make a difference can be made plausible if stated in this way: if everyone in circumstances like mine gave £5 to the Bengal Relief Fund, there would be enough to provide food, shelter, and medical care for the refugees; there is no reason why I should give more than anyone else in the same circumstances as I am; therefore I have no obligation to give more than £5. Each premise in this argument is true, and the argument looks sound. It may convince us, unless we notice that it is based on a hypothetical premise, although the conclusion is not stated hypothetically. The argument would be sound if the conclusion were: if everyone in circumstances like mine were to give £5, I would have no obligation to give more than £5. If the conclusion were so stated, however, it would be obvious that the argument has no bearing on a situation in which it is not the case that every-one else gives £5. This, of course, is the actual situation. It is more or less certain that not everyone in circumstances like mine will give £5. So there will not be enough to provide the needed food, shelter, and medical care. Therefore by giving more than £5 I will prevent more suffering than I would if I gave just £5.

It might be thought that this argument has an absurd consequence. Since the situation appears to be that very few people are likely to give substantial amounts, it follows that I and everyone else in similar circumstances ought to give as much as possible, that is, at least up to the point at which by giving more one would begin to cause serious suffering for oneself and one's dependents—perhaps even beyond this point to the point of marginal utility, at which by giving more one would cause oneself and one's dependents as much suffering as one would prevent in Bengal. If everyone does this, however, there will be more than can be used for the benefit of the refugees, and some of the sacrifice will have been unnecessary. Thus, if everyone does what he ought to do, the result will not be as good as it would be if everyone did a little less than he ought to do, or if only some do all that they ought to do.

The paradox here arises only if we assume that the actions in question—sending money to the relief funds—are performed more or less simultaneously, and are also unexpected. For if it is to be expected that everyone is going to contribute some-thing, then clearly each is not obliged to give as much as he would have been obliged to had others not been giving too. And if everyone is not acting more or less simultaneously, then those giving later will know how much more is needed, and will have no obligation to give more than is necessary to reach this amount. To say this is not to deny the principle that people in the same circumstances have the same obligations, but to point out that the fact that others have given, or may be expected to give, is a relevant circumstance: those giving after it has become known that many others are giving and those giving before are not in the same circumstances. So the seemingly absurd consequence of the principle I have put forward can occur only if people are in error about the actual circumstances—that is, if they think they are giving when others are not, but in fact they are giving when others are. The result of everyone doing what he really ought to do cannot be worse than the result of everyone doing less than he ought to do, although the result of everyone doing what he reasonably believes he ought to do could be.

If my argument so far has been sound, neither our distance from a preventable evil nor the number of other people who, in respect to that evil, are in the same sit-uation as we are, lessens our obligation to mitigate or prevent that evil. I shall there-fore take as established the principle I asserted earlier. As I have already said, I need to assert it only in its qualified form: if it is in our power to prevent something very bad from happening, without thereby sacrificing anything else morally significant, we ought, morally, to do it.

The outcome of this argument is that our traditional moral categories are upset. The traditional distinction between duty and charity cannot be drawn, or at least, not in the place we normally draw it. Giving money to the Bengal Relief Fund is regarded as an act of charity in our society. The bodies which collect money are known as "charities." These organizations see themselves in this way—if you send them a check, you will be thanked for your "generosity." Because giving money is regarded as an act of charity, it is not thought that there is anything wrong with not giving. The charitable man may be praised, but the man who is not charitable is not condemned. People do not feel in any way ashamed or guilty about spending money on new clothes or a new car instead of giving it to famine relief. (Indeed, the alternative does not occur to them.) This way of looking at the matter cannot be justified. When we buy new clothes not to keep ourselves warm but to look "well-dressed" we are not providing for any important need. We would not be sacrificing anything significant if we were to continue to wear our old clothes, and give the money to famine relief. By doing so, we would be preventing another person from starving. It follows from what I have said earlier that we ought to give money away, rather than spend it on clothes which we do not need to keep us warm. To do so is not charitable, or generous. Nor is it the kind of act which philosophers and theologians have called "supererogatory"—an act which it would be good to do, but not wrong not to do. On the contrary, we ought to give the money away, and it is wrong not to do so.

I am not maintaining that there are no acts which are charitable, or that there are no acts which it would be good to do but not wrong not to do. It may be possible to redraw the distinction between duty and charity in some other place. All I am arguing here is that the present way of drawing the distinction, which makes it an act of charity for a man living at the level of affluence which most people in the "developed nations" enjoy to give money to save someone else from starvation, cannot be supported. It is beyond the scope of my argument to consider whether the distinction should be redrawn or abolished altogether. There would be many other possible ways of drawing the distinction—for instance, one might decide that it is good to make other people as happy as possible, but not wrong not to do so.

Despite the limited nature of the revision in our moral conceptual scheme which I am proposing, the revision would, given the extent of both affluence and famine in the world today, have radical implications. These implications may lead to further objections, distinct from those I have already considered. I shall discuss two of these.

One objection to the position I have taken might be simply that it is too drastic a revision of our moral scheme. People do not ordinarily judge in the way I have suggested they should. Most people reserve their moral condemnation for those who violate some moral norm, such as the norm against taking another person's property. They do not condemn those who indulge in luxury instead of giving to famine relief. But given that I did not set out to present a morally neutral description of the way people make moral judgments, the way people do in fact judge has nothing to do with the validity of my conclusion. My conclusion follows from the principle which I advanced earlier, and unless that principle is rejected, or the arguments shown to be unsound, I think the conclusion must stand, however strange it appears. . . .

The second objection to my attack on the present distinction between duty and charity is one which has from time to time been made against utilitarianism. It follows from some forms of utilitarian theory that we all ought, morally, to be working full time to increase the balance of happiness over misery. The position I have taken here would not lead to this conclusion in all circumstances, for if there were no bad occurrences that we could prevent without sacrificing something of comparable moral importance, my argument would have no application. Given the present conditions in many parts of the world, however, it does follow from my argument that we ought, morally, to be working full time to relieve great suffering of the sort that occurs as a result of famine or other disasters. Of course, mitigating circumstances can be adduced—for instance, that if we wear ourselves out through overwork, we shall be less effective than we would otherwise have been. Nevertheless, when all considerations of this sort have been taken into account, the conclusion remains: we ought to be preventing as much suffering as we can without sacrificing something else of comparable moral importance. This conclusion is one which we may be reluctant to face. I cannot see, though, why it should be regarded as a criticism of the position for which I have argued, rather than a criticism of our ordinary standards of behavior. Since most people are self-interested to some degree, very few of us are likely to do everything that we ought to do. It would, however, hardly be honest to take this as evidence that it is not the case that we ought to do it. . . .

The conclusion reached earlier [raises] the question of just how much we all ought to be giving away. One possibility, which has already been mentioned, is that we ought to give until we reach the level of marginal utility—that is, the level at which, by giving more, I would cause as much suffering to myself or my dependents as I would relieve by my gift. This would mean, of course, that one would reduce oneself to very near the material circumstances of a Bengali refugee. It will be recalled that earlier I put forward both a strong and a moderate version of the principle of preventing bad occurrences. The strong version, which required us to prevent bad things from happening unless in doing so we would be sacrificing something of a comparable moral significance, does seem to require reducing ourselves to the level of marginal utility. I should also say that the strong version seems to me to be the correct one. I proposed the more moderate version—that we should prevent bad occurrences unless, to do so, we had to sacrifice something morally significant—only in order to show that even on this surely undeniable principle, a great change in our way of life is required. On the more moderate principle, it may not follow that we ought to reduce ourselves to the level of marginal utility, for one might hold that to reduce oneself and one's family to this level is to cause something significantly bad to happen. Whether this is so I shall not discuss, since, as I have said, I can see no good reason for holding the moderate version of the principle rather than the strong version. Even if we accepted the principle only in its moderate form, however, it should be clear that we would have to give away enough to ensure that the consumer society, dependent as it is on people spending on trivia rather than giving to famine relief, would slow down and perhaps disappear entirely. There are several reasons why this would be desirable in itself. The value and necessity of economic growth are now being questioned not only by conservationists, but by economists as well.[2] There is no doubt, too, that the consumer society has had a distorting effect on the goals and purposes of its members. Yet looking at the matter purely from the point of view of overseas aid, there must be a limit to the extent to which we should deliberately slow down our economy; for it might be the case that if we gave away, say, forty percent of our Gross National Product, we would slow down the economy so much that in absolute terms we would be giving less than if we gave twenty-five percent of the much larger GNP that we would have if we limited our contribution to this smaller percentage.

I mention this only as an indication of the sort of factor that one would have to take into account in working out an ideal. Since Western societies generally consider one percent of the GNP an acceptable level for overseas aid, the matter is entirely academic. Nor does it affect the question of how much an individual should give in a society in which very few are giving substantial amounts.

It is sometimes said, though less often now than it used to be, that philosophers have no special role to play in public affairs, since most public issues depend primarily on an assessment of facts. On questions of fact, it is said, philosophers as such have no special expertise, and so it has been possible to engage in philosophy without committing oneself to any position on major public issues. No doubt there are some issues of social policy and foreign policy about which it can truly be said that a really expert assessment of the facts is required before taking sides or acting, but the issue of famine is surely not one of these. The facts about the existence of suffering are beyond dispute. Nor, I think, is it disputed that we can do something about it, either through orthodox methods of famine relief or through population control or both. This is therefore an issue on which philosophers are competent to take a position. The issue is one which faces everyone who has more money than he needs to support himself and his dependents, or who is in a position to take some sort of political action. These categories must include practically every teacher and student of philosophy in the universities of the Western world. If philosophy is to deal with matters that are relevant to both teachers and students, this is an issue that philosophers should discuss.

Discussion, though, is not enough. What is the point of relating philosophy to public (and personal) affairs if we do not take our conclusions seriously? In this instance, taking our conclusion seriously means acting upon it. The philosopher will not find it any easier than anyone else to alter his attitudes and way of life to the extent that, if I am right, is involved in doing everything that we ought to be doing. At the very least, though, one can make a start. The philosopher who does so will have to sacrifice some of the benefits of the consumer society, but he can find compensation in the satisfaction of a way of life in which theory and practice, if not yet in harmony, are at least coming together.

NOTES

1 There was also a third possibility: that India would go to war to enable the refugees to return to their lands. Since I wrote this paper, India has taken this way out. The situation is no longer that described above, but this does not affect my argument, as the next paragraph indicates.
2 See, for instance, John Kenneth Galbraith, *The New Industrial State* (Boston, 1967); and E. J. Mishan, *The Costs of Economic Growth* (London, 1967).

QUESTIONS

1 Think about the following claim: Contributing to famine relief is not a moral obligation that we must perform if we are to act in a morally correct way, but an act of charity that we may or may not perform. Can you offer any arguments to defend it?
2 Singer says, "We ought to be preventing as much suffering as we can without sacrificing something else of comparable moral importance." What moral considerations would outweigh the obligation Singer claims we have to aid famine victims?

Living on a Lifeboat

Garrett Hardin

Using the metaphor of a lifeboat, Hardin argues that the time may have come to refuse to give aid in the form of food to needy countries that do not accept the responsibility for limiting their population growth. He maintains that adherence to the principle "from each according to his ability; to each according to his need" will have strong adverse effects. Bolstered by our aid, needy countries will continue their irresponsible policies in regard to food production and population growth. Furthermore, the food we supply will enable these populations to continue to increase. This, in the long run, jeopardizes human survival.

No generation has viewed the problem of the survival of the human species as seriously as we have. Inevitably, we have entered this world of concern through the door of metaphor. Environmentalists have emphasized the image of the earth as a spaceship—Spaceship Earth. Kenneth Boulding (1966) is the principal architect of this metaphor. It is time, he says, that we replace the wasteful "cowboy economy" of the past with the frugal "spaceship economy" required for continued survival in the limited world we now see ours to be. The metaphor is notably useful in justifying pollution control measures.

Unfortunately, the image of a spaceship is also used to promote measures that are suicidal. One of these is a generous immigration policy, which is only a particular instance of a class of policies that are in error because they lead to the tragedy of the commons (Hardin 1968). These suicidal policies are attractive because they mesh with what we unthinkingly take to be the ideals of "the best people." What is missing in the idealistic view is an insistence that rights and responsibilities must go together. The "generous" attitude of all too many people results in asserting inalienable rights while ignoring or denying matching responsibilities.

For the metaphor of a spaceship to be correct the aggregate of people on board would have to be under unitary sovereign control (Ophuls 1974). A true ship always has a captain. It is conceivable that a ship could be run by a committee. But it could not possibly survive if its course were determined by bickering tribes that claimed rights without responsibilities.

What about Spaceship Earth? It certainly has no captain, and no executive committee. The United Nations is a toothless tiger, because the signatories of its charter wanted it that way. The spaceship metaphor is used only to justify spaceship demands on common resources without acknowledging corresponding spaceship responsibilities.

An understandable fear of decisive action leads people to embrace "incrementalism"—moving toward reform in tiny stages. As we shall see, this strategy is counterproductive in the area discussed here if it means accepting rights before responsibilities. Where human survival is at stake, the acceptance of responsibilities is a precondition to the acceptance of rights, if the two cannot be introduced simultaneously.

LIFEBOAT ETHICS

Before taking up certain substantive issues let us look at an alternative metaphor, that of a lifeboat. In developing some relevant examples the following numerical values are assumed. Approximately two-thirds of the world is desperately poor, and only one-third is comparatively rich. The people in poor countries have an average per capita GNP (Gross National Product) of about $200 per year; the rich, of about $3,000. (For the United States it is nearly $5,000 per year.) Metaphorically, each rich nation amounts to a lifeboat full of comparatively rich people. The poor of the world are in other, much more crowded lifeboats. Continuously, so to speak, the poor fall out of their lifeboats and swim for a while in the water outside, hoping to be admitted to a rich lifeboat, or in some other way to benefit from the "goodies" on board. What should the passengers on a rich lifeboat do? This is the central problem of "the ethics of a lifeboat."

First we must acknowledge that each lifeboat is effectively limited in capacity. The land of every nation has a limited carrying capacity. The exact limit is a matter for argument, but the energy crunch is convincing more people every day that we have already exceeded the carrying capacity of the land. We have been living on "capital"—stored petroleum and coal—and soon we must live on income alone.

Let us look at only one lifeboat—ours. The ethical problem is the same for all, and is as follows. Here we sit, say 50 people in a lifeboat. To be generous, let us assume our boat has a capacity of 10 more, making 60. (This, however, is to violate the engineering principle of the "safety factor." A new plant disease or a bad change in the weather may decimate our population if we don't preserve some excess capacity as a safety factor.)

The 50 of us in the lifeboat see 100 others swimming in the water outside, asking for admission to the boat, or for handouts. How shall we respond to their calls? There are several possibilities.

One. We may be tempted to try to live by the Christian ideal of being "our brother's keeper," or by the Marxian ideal (Marx 1875) of "from each according to his abilities, to each according to his needs." Since the needs of all are the same, we take all the needy into our boat, making a total of 150 in a boat with a capacity of 60. The boat is swamped, and everyone drowns. Complete justice, complete catastrophe.

Two. Since the boat has an unused excess capacity of 10, we admit just 10 more to it. This has the disadvantage of getting rid of the safety factor, for which action we will sooner or later pay dearly. Moreover, *which* 10 do we let in? "First come, first served?" The best 10? The neediest 10? How do we *discriminate*? And what do we say to the 90 who are excluded?

Three. Admit no more to the boat and preserve the small safety factor. Survival of the people in the lifeboat is then possible (though we shall have to be on our guard against boarding parties).

The last solution is abhorrent to many people. It is unjust, they say. Let us grant that it is.

"I feel guilty about my good luck," say some. The reply to this is simple: *Get out and yield your place to others.* Such a selfless action might satisfy the conscience of those who are addicted to guilt but it would not change the ethics of the lifeboat. The needy person to whom a guilt-addict yields his place will not himself feel guilty about his sudden good luck. (If he did he would not climb aboard.) The net result of conscience-stricken people relinquishing their unjustly held positions is the elimination of their kind of conscience from the lifeboat. The lifeboat, as it were, purifies itself of guilt. The ethics of the lifeboat persist, unchanged by such momentary aberrations.

This then is the basic metaphor within which we must work out our solutions. Let us enrich the image step by step with substantive additions from the real world.

REPRODUCTION

The harsh characteristics of lifeboat ethics are heightened by reproduction, particularly by reproductive differences. The people inside the lifeboats of the wealthy nations are doubling in numbers every 87 years; those outside are doubling every 35 years, on the average. And the relative difference in prosperity is becoming greater.

Let us, for a while, think primarily of the U.S. lifeboat. As of 1973 the United States had a population of 210 million people, who were increasing by 0.8% per year, that is, doubling in number every 87 years.

Although the citizens of rich nations are outnumbered two to one by the poor, let us imagine an equal number of poor people outside our lifeboat—a mere 210 million poor people reproducing at a quite different rate. If we imagine these to be the combined populations of Colombia, Venezuela, Ecuador, Morocco, Thailand, Pakistan, and the Philippines, the average rate of increase of the people "outside" is 3.3% per year. The doubling time of this population is 21 years.

Suppose that all these countries, and the United States, agreed to live by the Marxian ideal, "to each according to his needs," the ideal of most Christians as well. Needs, of course, are determined by population size, which is affected by reproduction. Every nation regards its rate of reproduction as a sovereign right. If our lifeboat were big enough in the beginning it might be possible to live *for a while* by Christian-Marxian ideals. *Might.*

Initially, in the model given, the ratio of non-Americans to Americans would be one to one. But consider what the ratio would be 87 years later. By this time Americans would have doubled to a population of 420 million. The other group (doubling every 21 years) would now have swollen to 3,540 million. Each American would have more than eight people to share with. How could the lifeboat possibly keep afloat?

All this involves extrapolation of current trends into the future, and is consequently suspect. Trends may change. Granted: but the change will not necessarily be favorable. If—as seems likely—the rate of population increase falls faster in the ethnic group presently inside the lifeboat than it does among those now outside, the future will turn out to be even worse than mathematics predicts, and sharing will be even more suicidal.

RUIN IN THE COMMONS

The fundamental error of the sharing ethics is that it leads to the tragedy of the commons. Under a system of private property the man (or group of men) who own property recognize their responsibility to care for it, for if they don't they will eventually suffer. A farmer, for instance, if he is intelligent, will allow no more cattle in a pasture than its carrying capacity justifies. If he overloads the pasture, weeds take over, erosion sets in, and the owner loses in the long run.

But if a pasture is run as a commons open to all, the right of each to use it is not matched by an operational responsibility to take care of it. It is no use asking independent herdsmen in a commons to act responsibly, for they dare not. The considerate herdsman who refrains from overloading the commons suffers more than a selfish one who says his needs are greater. (As Leo Durocher says, "Nice guys finish last.") Christian-Marxian idealism is counterproductive. That it *sounds* nice is no excuse. With distribution systems, as with individual morality, good intentions are no substitute for good performance.

A social system is stable only if it is insensitive to errors. To the Christian-Marxian idealist a selfish person is a sort of "error." Prosperity in the system of the commons cannot survive errors. If *everyone* would only restrain himself, all would be well; but it takes *only one less than everyone* to ruin a system of voluntary restraint. In a crowded world of less than perfect human beings—and we will never know any other—mutual ruin is inevitable in the commons. This is the core of the tragedy of the commons. . . .

WORLD FOOD BANKS

In the international arena we have recently heard a proposal to create a new commons, namely an international depository of food reserves to which nations will contribute according to their abilities, and from which nations may draw according to their needs. Nobel laureate Norman Borlaug has lent the prestige of his name to this proposal.

A world food bank appeals powerfully to our humanitarian impulses. We remember John Donne's celebrated line, "Any man's death diminishes me." But before we rush out to see for whom the bell tolls let us recognize where the greatest political push for international granaries comes from, lest we be disillusioned later. Our experience with Public Law 480 clearly reveals the answer. This was the law that moved billions of dollars worth of U.S. grain to food-short, population-long countries during the past two decades. When P.L. 480 first came into being, a headline in the business magazine *Forbes* (Paddock 1970) revealed the power behind it: "Feeding the World's Hungry Millions: How it will mean billions for U.S. business."

And indeed it did. In the years 1960 to 1970 a total of $7.9 billion was spent on the "Food for Peace" program, as P.L. 480 was called. During the years of 1948 to 1970 an additional $49.9 billion were extracted from American taxpayers to pay for other economic aid programs, some of which went for food and food-producing machinery. (This figure does *not* include military aid.) That P.L. 480 was a give-away program was concealed. Recipient countries went through the motions of paying for P.L. 480 food—with IOU's. In December 1973 the charade was brought to an end as far as India was concerned when the United States "forgave" India's $3.2 billion debt (Anonymous 1974). Public announcement of the cancellation of the debt was delayed for two months: one wonders why. . . .

What happens if some organizations budget for emergencies and others do not? If each organization is solely responsible for its own well-being, poorly managed ones will suffer. But they should be able to learn from experience. They have a chance to mend their ways and learn to budget for infrequent but certain emergencies. The weather, for instance, always varies and periodic crop failures are certain. A wise and competent government saves out of the production of the good years in anticipation of bad years that are sure to come. This is not a new idea. The Bible tells us that Joseph taught this policy to Pharaoh in Egypt more than 2,000 years ago. Yet it is literally true that the vast majority of the governments of the world today have no such policy. They lack either the wisdom or the competence, or both. Far more difficult than the transfer of wealth from one country to another is the transfer of wisdom between sovereign powers or between generations.

"But it isn't their fault! How can we blame the poor people who are caught in an emergency? Why must we punish them?" The concepts of blame and punishment are irrelevant. The question is, what are the operational consequences of establishing a world food bank? If it is open to every country every time a need develops, slovenly rulers will not be motivated to take Joseph's advice. Why should they? Others will bail them out whenever they are in trouble.

Some countries will make deposits in the world food bank and others will withdraw from it: there will be almost no overlap. Calling such a depository-transfer unit a "bank" is stretching the metaphor of *bank* beyond its elastic limits. The proposers, of course, never call attention to the metaphorical nature of the word they use.

THE RATCHET EFFECT

An "international food bank" is really, then, not a true bank but a disguised one-way transfer device for moving wealth from rich countries to poor. In the absence of such a bank, in a world inhabited by individually responsible sovereign nations, the population of each nation would repeatedly go through a cycle of the sort shown in Figure 1. P_2 is greater than P_1, either in absolute numbers or because a

Fig. 1

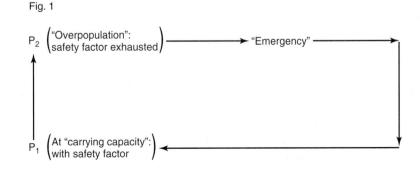

deterioration of the food supply has removed the safety factor and produced a dangerously low ratio of resources to population. P_2 may be said to represent a state of overpopulation, which becomes obvious upon the appearance of an "accident," e.g., a crop failure. If the "emergency" is not met by outside help, the population drops back to the "normal" level—the "carrying capacity" of the environment—or even below. In the absence of population control by a sovereign, sooner or later the population grows to P_2 again and the cycle repeats. The long-term population curve (Hardin 1966) is an irregularly fluctuating one, equilibrating more or less about the carrying capacity.

A demographic cycle of this sort obviously involves great suffering in the restrictive phase, but such a cycle is normal to any independent country with inadequate population control. The third century theologian Tertullian (Hardin 1969) expressed what must have been the recognition of many wise men when he wrote: "The scourges of pestilence, famine, wars, and earthquakes have come to be regarded as a blessing to overcrowded nations, since they serve to prune away the luxuriant growth of the human race."

Only under a strong and farsighted sovereign—which theoretically could be the people themselves, democratically organized—can a population equilibrate at some set point below the carrying capacity, thus avoiding the pains normally caused by periodic and unavoidable disasters. For this happy state to be achieved it is necessary that those in power be able to contemplate with equanimity the "waste" of surplus food in times of bountiful harvests. It is essential that those in power resist the temptation to convert extra food into extra babies. On the public relations level it is necessary that the phrase "surplus food" be replaced by "safety factor."

But wise sovereigns seem not to exist in the poor world today. The most anguishing problems are created by poor countries that are governed by rulers insufficiently wise and powerful. If such countries can draw on a world food bank in times of "emergency," the population *cycle* of Figure 1 will be replaced by the population *escalator* of Figure 2. The input of food from a food bank acts as the pawl of a ratchet, preventing the population from retracing its steps to a lower level. Reproduction pushes the population upward, inputs from the world bank prevent its moving downward. Population size escalates, as does the absolute magnitude of "accidents" and "emergencies." The process is brought to an end only by the total collapse of the whole system, producing a catastrophe of scarcely imaginable proportions.

Such are the implications of the well-meant sharing of food in a world of irresponsible reproduction. . . .

To be generous with one's own possessions is one thing; to be generous with posterity's is quite another. This, I think, is the point that must be gotten across to those who would, from a commendable love of distributive justice, institute a ruinous system of the commons. . . .

If the argument of this essay is correct, so long as there is no true world government to control reproduction everywhere it is impossible to survive in dignity if we are to be guided by Spaceship ethics. Without a world government that is sovereign in reproductive matters mankind lives, in fact, on a number of sovereign lifeboats.

Fig. 2

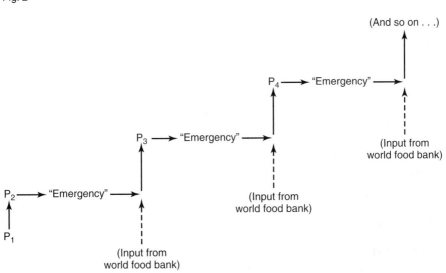

For the foreseeable future survival demands that we govern our actions by the ethics of a lifeboat. Posterity will be ill served if we do not.

REFERENCES

Anonymous. 1974. *Wall Street Journal,* 19 Feb.

Boulding, K. 1966. The economics of the coming spaceship earth. In H. Jarrett, ed. *Environmental Quality in a Growing Economy.* Johns Hopkins Press, Baltimore.

Hardin, G. 1966. Chap. 9 in *Biology: Its Principles and Implications,* 2nd ed. Freeman, San Francisco.

———. 1968. The tragedy of the commons. *Science* 162: 1243–1248.

———. 1969. Page 18 in *Population, Evolution, and Birth Control,* 2nd ed. Freeman, San Francisco.

Marx, K. 1875. *Critique of the Gotha program.* Page 388 in R. C. Tucker, ed. *The Marx-Engels Reader,* Norton, N.Y., 1972.

Ophuls, W. 1974. The scarcity society. *Harpers* 248 (1487): 47–52.

Paddock, W. C. 1970. How green is the green revolution? *Bioscience* 20: 897–902.

QUESTIONS

1 What evidence is available to support the claim that the resources of the world will not be able to save all the poor countries? If it cannot be conclusively proved that all the poor countries cannot be saved, can a moral justification be given for refusing to aid famine victims in all those countries?

2 Suppose that it is highly unlikely that all the nations in the world can be saved. Which would be the better moral choice: (1) to deliberately cut off aid to those least likely to survive in order to ensure the survival of the others or (2) to continue our aid, despite our awareness of the consequences that will probably follow?

Property and Hunger

Amartya Sen

Sen's article falls into three parts. First, he discusses property rights. He argues for the importance of incorporating empirical realities, especially economic ones, into the moral analyses of property rights. Property rights may have consequences that call for moral assessment. If a set of property rights leads to hunger and starvation, for example, then the moral approval of these property rights is severely compromised. Second, in Sen's view, famines are best understood in terms of the entitlement systems that leave many people without the entitlements that would give them the resources to acquire necessities, such as food. Public policies, such as a guaranteed minimum moral entitlement, could be designed to increase the entitlements of the deprived groups in order to prevent famine and starvation. But, as long as property rights are seen as inviolate, such public policies will be seen as morally unacceptable to the extent that they require that the property rights and related entitlements of those who are better off are violated. Third, Sen argues for the institutionalization of a moral right not to be hungry.

. . . [T]he claims of property rights, which some would defend and some . . . would dispute, are not just matters of basic moral belief that could not possibly be influenced one way or the other by any empirical arguments. They call for sensitive moral analysis responsive to empirical realities, including economic ones.

Moral claims based on intrinsically valuable rights are often used in political and social arguments. Rights related to ownership have been invoked for ages. But there are also other types of rights which have been seen as "inherent and inalienable," and the American Declaration of Independence refers to "certain unalienable rights," among which are "life, liberty and the pursuit of happiness." The Indian constitution talks even of "the right to an adequate means of livelihood."[1] The "right not to be hungry" has often been invoked in recent discussions on the obligation to help the famished.

RIGHTS: INSTRUMENTS, CONSTRAINTS, OR GOALS?

Rights can be taken to be morally important in three different ways. First, they can be considered to be valuable *instruments* to achieve other goals. This is the "instrumental view," and is well illustrated by the utilitarian approach to rights. Rights are, in that view, of no intrinsic importance. Violation of rights is not in itself a bad thing, nor fulfillment intrinsically good. But the acceptance of rights promotes, in this view, things that are ultimately important, to wit, utility. Jeremy Bentham rejected "natural rights" as "simple nonsense," and "natural and imprescriptible rights" as

From *Economics and Philosophy,* vol. 4, no. 1 (1988), pp. 57–68. Copyright © Cambridge University Press. Reprinted with the permission of Cambridge University Press.

"rhetorical nonsense, nonsense upon stilts." But he attached great importance to rights as instruments valuable to the promotion of a good society, and devoted much energy to the attempt to reform appropriately the actual system of rights.

The second view may be called the "constraint view," and it takes the form of seeing rights as *constraints* on what others can or cannot do. In this view rights *are* intrinsically important. However, they don't figure in moral accounting as goals to be generally promoted, but only as constraints that others must obey. As Robert Nozick has put it in a powerful exposition of this "constraint view": "Individuals have rights, and there are things no person or group may do to them (without violating their rights)." Rights "set the constraints within which a social choice is to be made, by excluding certain alternatives, fixing others, and so on."[2]

The third approach is to see fulfillments of rights as goals to be pursued. This "goal view" differs from the instrumental view in regarding rights to be intrinsically important, and it differs from the constraint view in seeing the fulfillment of rights as goals to be generally promoted, rather than taking them as demanding only (and exactly) that we refrain from violating the rights of others. In the "constraint view" there is no duty to help anyone with his or her rights (merely not to hinder), and also in the "instrumental view" there is no duty, in fact, to help unless the right fulfillment will also promote some other goal such as utility. The "goal view" integrates the valuation of rights—their fulfillment and violation—in overall moral accounting, and yields a wider sphere of influence of rights in morality.

I have argued elsewhere that the goal view has advantages that the other two approaches do not share, in particular, the ability to accommodate integrated moral accounting including inter alia the intrinsic importance of a class of fundamental rights. I shall not repeat that argument here. But there is an interesting question of dual roles of rights in the sense that some rights may be *both* intrinsically important and instrumentally valuable. For example, the right to be free from hunger could—not implausibly—be regarded as being valuable in itself as well as serving as a good instrument to promote other goals such as security, longevity or utility. If so, both the goal view and the instrumental view would have to be simultaneously deployed to get a comprehensive assessment of such a right. . . .

The instrumental aspect is an inescapable feature of every right, since irrespective of whether a certain right is intrinsically valuable or not, its acceptance will certainly have other consequences as well, and these, too, have to be assessed along with the intrinsic value of rights (if any). A right that is regarded as quite valuable in itself may nevertheless be judged to be morally rejectable if it leads to disastrous consequences. This is a case of the rights playing a *negative* instrumental role. It is, of course, also possible that the instrumental argument will *bolster* the intrinsic claims of a right to be taken seriously. . . .

There are two general conclusions to draw, at this stage, from this very preliminary discussion. First, we must distinguish between (1) the intrinsic value of a right, and (2) the overall value of a right taking note inter alia of its intrinsic importance (if any). The acceptance of the intrinsic importance of any right is no guarantee that its overall moral valuation must be favorable. Second, no moral assessment of a right can be independent of its likely consequences. The need for empirical assessment of the effects of accepting any right cannot be escaped. Empirical arguments are quite central to moral philosophy.

PROPERTY AND DEPRIVATION

The right to hold, use and bequeath property that one has legitimately acquired is often taken to be inherently valuable. In fact, however, many of its defenses seem to be actually of the instrumental type, e.g., arguing that property rights make people more free to choose one kind of a life rather than another. But even if we do accept that property rights may have some intrinsic value, this does not in any way amount to an overall justification of property rights, since property rights may have consequences which themselves will require assessment. Indeed, the causation of hunger as well as its prevention may materially depend on how property rights are structured. If a set of property rights leads, say, to starvation, as it well might, then the moral approval of these rights would certainly be compromised severely. In general, the need for consequential analysis of property rights is inescapable whether or not such rights are seen as having any intrinsic value. . . .

. . . I have tried to argue elsewhere . . . that famines are, in fact, best explained in terms of failures of entitlement systems. The entitlements here refer, of course, to legal rights and to practical possibilities, rather than to moral status, but the laws and actual operation of private ownership economies have many features in common with the moral system of entitlements analyzed by Nozick and others.

The entitlement approach to famines need not, of course, be confined to private ownership economies, and entitlement failures of other systems can also be fruitfully studied to examine famines and hunger. In the specific context of private ownership economies, the entitlements are substantially analyzable in terms, respectively, of what may be called "endowments" and "exchange entitlements." A person's endowment refers to what he or she initially owns (including the person's own labor power), and the exchange entitlement mapping tells us what the person can obtain through exchanging what he or she owns, either by production (exchange with nature), or by trade (exchange with others), or a mixture of the two. A person has to starve if neither the endowments, nor what can be obtained through exchange, yields an adequate amount of food.

If starvation and hunger are seen in terms of failures of entitlements, then it becomes immediately clear that the total availability of food in a country is only one of several variables that are relevant. Many famines occur without any decline in the availability of food. For example, in the Great Bengal famine of 1943, the total food availability in Bengal was not particularly bad (considerably higher than two years earlier when there was no famine), and yet three million people died, in a famine mainly affecting the rural areas, through rather violent shifts in the relative purchasing powers of different groups, hitting the rural laborers the hardest. The Ethiopian famine of 1973 took place in a year of average per capita food availability, but the cultivators and other occupation groups in the province of Wollo had lost their means of subsistence (through loss of crops and a decline of economic activity, related to a local drought) and had no means of commanding food from elsewhere in the country. Indeed, some food moved *out* of Wollo to more prosperous people in other parts of Ethiopia, repeating a pattern of contrary movement of food that was widely observed during the Irish famines of the 1840s (with food moving out of famine-stricken Ireland to prosperous England which had greater power in the battle for entitlements). The Bangladesh famine of 1974 took place in a year of *peak* food availability, but several occupation groups had lost their entitlement to food through loss of employment and other economic changes (including inflationary pressures causing prices to outrun wages). Other examples of famines without significant (or any) decline in food availability can be found, and there is nothing particularly surprising about this fact once it is recognized that the availability of food is only one influence among many on the entitlement of each occupation group. Even when a famine *is* associated with a decline of food availability, the entitlement changes have to be studied to understand the particular nature of the famine, e.g., why one occupation group is hit but not another. The causation of starvation can be sensibly sought in failures of entitlements of the respective groups.

The causal analysis of famines in terms of entitlements also points to possible public policies of prevention. The main economic strategy would have to take the form of increasing the entitlements of the deprived groups, and in general, of guaranteeing minimum entitlements for everyone, paying particular attention to the vulnerable groups. This can, in the long run, be done in many different ways, involving both economic growth (including growth of food output) and distributional adjustments. Some of these policies may, however, require that the property rights and the corresponding entitlements of the more prosperous groups be violated. The problem, in fact, is particularly acute in the short run, since it may not be possible to engineer rapid economic growth instantly. Then the burden of raising entitlements of the groups in distress would largely have to fall on reducing the entitlements of others more favorably placed. Transfers of income or commodities through various public policies may well be effective in quashing a famine (as the experience of famine relief in different countries has shown), but it may require substantial government intervention in the entitlements of the more prosperous groups.

There is, however, no great moral dilemma in this if property rights are treated as purely *instrumental*. If the goals of relief of hunger and poverty are sufficiently powerful, then it would be just right to violate whatever property rights come in the way, since—in this view—property rights have no intrinsic status. On the other hand, if property rights are taken to be morally inviolable irrespective of their consequences, then it will follow that these policies cannot be morally acceptable even though they might save thousands, or even millions, from dying. The inflexible moral "constraint" of respecting people's legitimately acquired entitlements would rule out such policies.

In fact this type of problem presents a reductio ad absurdum of the moral validity of constraint-based entitlement systems. However, while the conclusions to be derived from that approach might well be "absurd," the situation postulated is not an imaginary one at all. It is based on studies of actual famines and the role of entitlement failures in the causation of mass starvation. If there is an embarrassment here, it belongs solidly to the consequence-independent way of seeing rights.

I should add that this dilemma does not arise from regarding property rights to be of intrinsic value, which can be criticized on other grounds, but not this one. Even if property rights *are* of intrinsic value, their violation may be justified on grounds of the favorable consequences of that violation. A right, as was mentioned earlier, may be intrinsically valuable and still be justly violated taking everything into account. The "absurdum" does not belong to attaching intrinsic value to property rights, but to regarding these rights as simply acceptable, regardless of their consequences. A moral system that values both property rights and other goals—such as avoiding famines and starvation, or fulfilling people's right not to be hungry—can, on the one hand, give property rights intrinsic importance, and on the other, recommend the violation of property rights when that leads to better overall consequences (*including* the disvalue of rights violation).

The issue here is not the valuing of property rights, but their alleged inviolability. There is no dilemma here either for the purely instrumental view of property rights or for treating the fulfillment of property rights as one goal among many, but specifically for consequence-independent assertions of property rights and for the corresponding constraint-based approaches to moral entitlement of ownership.

That property and hunger are closely related cannot possibly come as a great surprise. Hunger is primarily associated with not owning enough food and thus property rights over food are immediately and directly involved. Fights over that property right can be a major part of the reality of a poor country, and any system of moral assessment has to take note of that phenomenon. The tendency to see hunger in purely technocratic terms of food output and availability may help to hide the crucial role of entitlements in the genesis of hunger, but a fuller economic analysis cannot overlook that crucial role. Since property rights over food are derived from property rights over other goods and resources (through production and trade), the entire system of rights of acquisition and transfer is implicated in the emergence and survival of hunger and starvation.

THE RIGHT NOT TO BE HUNGRY

Property rights have been championed for a long time. In contrast, the assertion of "the right not to be hungry" is a comparatively recent phenomenon. While this right is much invoked in political debates, there is a good deal of skepticism about treating this as truly a right in any substantial way. It is often asserted that this concept of "right not to be hungry" stands essentially for nothing at all ("simple nonsense," as Bentham called "natural rights" in general). That piece of sophisticated cynicism reveals not so much a penetrating insight into the practical affairs of the world, but a refusal to investigate what people mean when they assert the existence of rights that, for the bulk of humanity, are not in fact guaranteed by the existing institutional arrangements.

The right not to be hungry is not asserted as a recognition of an institutional right that already exists, as the right to property typically is. The assertion is primarily a moral claim as to what should be valued, and what institutional structure we should aim for, and try to guarantee if feasible. It can also be seen in terms of Ronald Dworkin's category of "background rights—rights that provide a justification for political decisions by society in abstract."[3] This interpretation serves as the basis for a reason to change the existing institutional structure and state policy.

It is broadly in this form that the right to "an adequate means of livelihood" is referred to in the Constitution of India: "The state shall, in particular, direct its policy towards securing . . . that the citizens, men and women equally, have the right to an adequate means of livelihood." This does not, of course, offer to each citizen a guaranteed right to an adequate livelihood, but the state is asked to take steps such that this right could become realizable for all.

In fact, this right has often been invoked in political debates in India. The electoral politics of India does indeed give particular scope for such use of what are seen as background rights. It is, of course, not altogether clear whether the reference to this right in the Indian constitution has in fact materially influenced the political debates. The constitutional statement is often cited, but very likely this issue would have figured in any case in these debates, given the nature of the moral and political concern. But whatever the constitutional contribution, it is interesting to ask whether the implicit acceptance of the value of the right to freedom from hunger makes any difference to actual policy.

It can be argued that the general acceptance of the right of freedom from acute hunger as a major goal has played quite a substantial role in preventing famines in India. The last real famine in India was in 1943, and while food availability per head in India has risen only rather slowly (even now the food availability per head is no higher than in many sub-Saharan countries stricken by recurrent famines), the country has not experienced any famine since independence in 1947. The main cause of that success is a policy of public intervention. Whenever a famine has threatened, a public policy of intervention and relief has offered minimum entitlements to the potential famine victims, and thus have the threatening famines been averted. It can be argued that the quickness of the response of the respective governments (both state and central) reflects a political necessity, given the Indian electoral system and the importance attached by the public to the prevention of starvation. Political pressures from opposition groups and the news media have kept the respective governments on their toes, and the right to be free from acute hunger and starvation has been achieved largely because it has been seen as a valuable right. Thus the recognition of the intrinsic moral importance of this right, which has been widely invoked in public discussions, has served as a powerful political instrument as well.

On the other hand, this process has been far from effective in tackling pervasive and persistent undernourishment in India. There has been no famine in post-independence India, but perhaps a third of India's rural population is perennially undernourished. So long as hunger remains non-acute and starvation deaths are avoided (even though morbidity and mortality rates are enhanced by undernourishment), the need for a policy response is neither much discussed by the news media, nor forcefully demanded even by opposition parties. The elimination of famines coexists with the survival of widespread "regular hunger." The right to "adequate means" of *nourishment* does not at all seem to arouse political concern in a way that the right to "adequate means" to *avoid starvation* does.

The contrast can be due to one of several different reasons. It could, of course, simply be that the ability to avoid undernourishment is not socially accepted as very important. This could be so, though what is socially accepted and what is not is also partly a matter of how clearly the questions are posed. It is, in fact, quite possible that the freedom in question would be regarded as a morally important right if the question were posed in a transparent way, but this does not happen because of the nature of Indian electoral politics and that of news coverage. The issue is certainly not "dramatic" in the way in which starvation deaths and threatening famines are.

Continued low-key misery may be too familiar a phenomenon to make it worthwhile for political leaders to get some mileage out of it in practical politics. The news media may also find little profit in emphasizing a non-spectacular phenomenon—the quiet survival of disciplined, non-acute hunger.

If this is indeed the case, then the implications for action of the goal of eliminating hunger, or guaranteeing to all the means for achieving this, may be quite complex. The political case for making the quiet hunger less quiet and more troublesome for governments in power is certainly relevant. Aggressive political journalism might prove to have an instrumental moral value if it were able to go beyond reporting the horrors of visible starvation and to portray the pervasive, non-acute hunger in a more dramatic and telling way. This is obviously not the place to discuss the instrumentalities of practical politics, but the endorsement of the moral right to be free from hunger—both acute and non-acute—would in fact raise pointed questions about the means which might be used to pursue such a goal. . . .

NOTES

1 This is presented as a "Directive Principle of State Policy." It does not have a direct operational role in the working of the Indian legal system, but it has considerable political force.
2 Robert Nozick, *Anarchy, State, and Utopia* (New York: Basic, 1974), pp. ix, 166.
3 Ronald Dworkin, *Taking Rights Seriously* (Cambridge, Mass.: Harvard University Press, 1977), p. 93.

QUESTIONS

1 Sen maintains that property rights may be overriden in order to prevent hunger, malnutrition, and poverty. Does he provide adequate supporting reasons for his claim?
2 Should the right not to be hungry be institutionalized in any society that purports to be a just society?

Two Reflections on the First United Nations Millennium Development Goal

Thomas Pogge

The first and most prominent development goal stated in the *United Nations* (UN) *Millennium Development Declaration* (2000) was "to halve, by the year 2015, the proportion of the world's people whose income is less than one dollar a day and

Reprinted with permission of the author and Taylor & Francis Ltd. from *Journal of Human Development* (www.tandf.co.uk/journals), vol. 5, no. 3 (November 2004), pp. 385–392.

the proportion of people who suffer from hunger." On Pogge's analysis of this goal, as discussed in the introduction to this chapter, the actual goal is to reduce the number of those living in extreme poverty (below one dollar per day) by 19 percent by 2015, from 1,094 million in 2000 to 883.5 million. Pogge sees this goal as grossly inadequate and morally reprehensible, given the magnitude of the problem and the resources possessed by affluent countries. In his first reflection, Pogge presents information about the catastrophic extent of world poverty before addressing and rebutting the claims of those who maintain that the cost of any more ambitious program would be too high. In his second reflection, Pogge makes two claims regarding affluent nations' responsibility for world poverty: (1) Both the great privileges of those in affluent nations and the extreme poverty of others arose through a historical process that was pervaded by unimaginable crimes. (2) Affluent nations use their economic, technological, and military advantages to impose a global institutional order that is manifestly and grievously unjust. In conclusion, Pogge responds to two objections raised by those who reject these two claims.

REFLECTION [ONE]—ON THE SPEED AND COST OF ALLEVIATING POVERTY

However little may be known about income poverty trends, we certainly know that the problem of world poverty is catastrophic. According to the official statistics, about:

- 799 million are undernourished (UNDP, 2003, p. 87);
- 1000 million lack access to safe drinking water (*ibid.,* p. 9);
- 2400 million lack basic sanitation (*ibid.*);
- 880 million have no access to basic medical care (UNDP, 1999, p. 22);
- 1000 million lack adequate shelter (UNDP, 1998, p. 49);
- 2000 million have no electricity (*ibid.*);
- 876 million adults are illiterate (UNDP, 2003, p. 6);
- 250 million children (aged 5–14 years) do wage work outside their family, at least 8.4 million of them in the "unconditionally worst" forms of child labor, which involve slavery, forced or bonded labor, forced recruitment for use in armed conflict, forced prostitution or pornography, or the production or trafficking of illegal drugs (International Labour Organisation, 2002, pp. 9, 11, 17, 18); and
- "Worldwide 34,000 children under age five die daily from hunger and preventable diseases" (USDA, 1999a, iii). Nearly one-third of all human deaths—some 18 million per year or 50,000 daily—are due to poverty-related causes (such as starvation, diarrhea, pneumonia, tuberculosis, measles, malaria, perinatal and maternal conditions) that could be prevented or cured cheaply through food, safe drinking water, vaccinations, rehydration packs, medicines, or better sanitation and hygiene (World Health Organisation, 2004, Annex Table 2). Women and girls are substantially over-represented among those suffering these deprivations (UNDP, 2003, pp. 310–330).

At 18 million per year, the global poverty death toll over the 15 years since the end of the Cold War was around 270 million, roughly the population of the United States. If the magnitude of the world poverty problem remains constant, the poverty death toll for the period from the *Millennium Declaration* [2000] to 2015 will likewise be about 270 million. Of course, this UN *Declaration* is a commitment to reduce the number of extremely poor, and hence presumably also the number of poverty deaths, by 19%. If all goes according to plan, we may then gradually reach an annual poverty death toll of 14 million in 2015, with 'only' 240 million deaths from poverty-related causes in the 2000–2015 period. Is this really a morally acceptable plan? A plan to be celebrated?

Consider some of the other catastrophes of the past century. The genocide in Rwanda, for example, when the UN and the rest of the world stood idly by while some 800,000 people were hacked to death. . . . Suppose some US politician had said, in April 1994, that the genocide in Rwanda is really terrible and that the world's governments should commit themselves to reducing the slaughter by 19% by the year 2009. How would this have been received? Or suppose a US politician had said, in 1942, that the German concentration camps are morally intolerable and that the world's governments should aim to achieve a 19% reduction in the population of these camps by the year 1957. . . . People would have been absolutely horrified by such a proposal.

So why were we not similarly horrified when the world's politicians proposed, in 2000, to reduce extreme poverty so that, 15 years later, the number it affects will have declined from 1094 million to 883.5 million and the annual death toll from 18 million to 14 million? Why do we greet such a proposal with celebration and self-congratulations?

Some would respond that the reason is cost. We simply cannot solve the problem any faster without huge costs to the cultures and economies of the advanced industrialized countries. They will admit that fighting the Nazis was quite costly too, and that decent people, even ones not themselves under threat, were nonetheless convinced that the Nazis simply had to be stopped, with all deliberate speed. But the cost of fighting world poverty, they may say, is much greater still. As Richard Rorty puts it, "the rich parts of the world may be in the position of somebody proposing to share her one loaf of bread with a hundred starving people. Even if she does share, everybody, including herself, will starve anyway" (1996, p. 10). How could it be wrong to refuse such a pointless course of self-sacrifice?

This response rests on a misconception. However immense the world poverty problem is in human terms, it is amazingly tiny in economic terms. Using the World Bank's poverty estimates, we can get a very rough sense of what the aggregate income is of all the people the Bank considers extremely poor. Assessed at market exchange rates, these 1092.7 million people together live on about $100 billion annually and would need some $40 billion more per year to reach the Bank's $ 1/day benchmark.[1]

To be sure, the Bank's IPL [the WTO's international poverty line of one dollar per day] is too low. So let us look at the Bank's statistics about those living on less than twice its IPL. Assessed at market exchange rates, these 2735.6 million people (nearly one-half of humankind) together live on about $406 billion annually and would need some $294 billion more per year to reach the $2/day benchmark.[2] How large are these amounts?

Start with the former: the collective income of the $2/day-poor. These $406 billion constitute about 1.3% of the annual global social product of ca. $31,500 billion. With only one-third as many people, the rich countries, by contrast, have over 60 times as much income: 81% of the global social product (World Bank, 2003, p. 235).

Consider the second amount, the additional annual income of $294 billion that the presently poor would need in order to reach the $2/day benchmark. This is 1.15% (l/87th) of the $25,506 billion annual aggregate national incomes of the rich countries *(ibid.).*

This $294 billion also is only about 40% of what the world is spending this year just on crude oil. It is well below the military budget of the United States alone. And it is far less also than the so-called peace dividend, which the rich countries reaped when they reduced their military spending after the end of the Cold War. Rorty's idea that universal starvation would result from an all-out effort to eradicate world poverty completely is simply preposterous.

While the $294 billion is quite small relative to our means, it is also four times larger than what the rich countries are actually spending on official development assistance (ODA). Initially meant to reach 1%, later 0.7%, of the rich countries' Gross National Product, actual ODA has steadily fallen throughout the prosperous 1990s, from 0.33% to 0.22% of the rich countries' aggregate Gross National Product—mainly through a drop from 0.21% to 0.10% in the United States, which has nearly one-third of the entire global social product (UNDP, 2002, p. 202). Moreover, most ODA is spent for the benefit of agents capable of reciprocation: only 23% goes to the 49 least developed countries. While India receives about $1.50 annually per citizen, high-income countries like the Czech Republic, Malta, Cyprus, Bahrain, and Israel receive between $40 and $132 per citizen annually (UNDP, 2002, pp. 203–205). A large part of ODA is allocated to support exporters at home or small affluent elites abroad, and only a tiny fraction, $4.31 billion, goes for 'basic social services' targeted on the poor. . . .

To be sure, some affluent countries do much better than the average, and five small ones—Norway, Sweden, Denmark, Luxembourg, and the Netherlands—come close to fulfilling their obligations (UNDP, 2003, p. 290). If the other affluent countries spent as much on ODA as these five and focused their ODA sharply on poverty eradication (notably including basic health care and education), then severe poverty worldwide could be essentially eliminated by 2015, if not before.

Many human beings live in severe poverty, lacking secure access to basic necessities. This is nothing new. What is new is that global inequality has increased to such an extent that such poverty is now completely avoidable at a cost that would barely be felt in the affluent countries.

REFLECTION [TWO]—ON POSITIVE AND NEGATIVE RESPONSIBILITY, BENEFITING VERSUS NOT HARMING

The hypothetical of US politicians proposing a planned 19% reduction over 15 years in response to the mass deaths in Germany or Rwanda suggested that the go-slow approach adopted and celebrated by the world's privileged today is morally no better than such a hypothetical go-slow approach would have been in 1942 or 1994.

The fact that a real effort toward eradicating severe poverty worldwide would be much less costly than the defeat of Nazi Germany suggests that the present go-slow approach against world poverty may actually be morally worse than the hypothetical go-slow approach against the Nazi concentration camps: it is for the sake of *small* gains that the world's affluent elites are refusing to undertake a much more substantial push against world poverty.

My [second] . . . reflection will highlight an additional asymmetry. The US bore no significant responsibility for the existence of the Nazi death camps; and the (hypothetical) commitment to reduce them by 19% over 15 years was then responsive to a merely positive duty to assist innocent persons at risk. The governments and citizens of today's affluent countries conceive of their relation to world poverty analogously: we tend to believe that we bear no significant responsibility for the existence of this problem and that our only moral reason to help alleviate it is our merely positive duty to assist innocent persons caught in a life-threatening emergency. This belief, however, is highly questionable.

Our world is marked by enormous inequalities in economic starting places. Some are born into abject poverty with a 30% chance of dying before their fifth birthday. Others are born into the civilized luxury of the Western middle class. These huge inequalities have evolved in the course of *one* historical process that was pervaded by monumental crimes of slavery, colonialism, and genocide—crimes that have devastated the populations, cultures, and social institutions of four continents.

The privileged of today are quick to point out that they had nothing to do with these crimes and that they should not be held to account for the sins of their forefathers. And right they are! But if they cannot inherit their ancestors' sins, then why can they inherit the *fruits* of those sins, the huge economic superiority prevailing at the end of the colonial period? In 1960, when most former colonies gained their independence, the inequality in per-capita income between Europe and Africa, for example, was 30:1. Foreign rule was removed. But the great inequality built up in the colonial period was left intact, making for a very unequal start into the post-colonial era.

One may think that the situation in 1960 is too long ago to contribute much to the explanation of severe poverty today. But consider what a 30:1 inequality means. Even if Africa had consistently achieved growth in per-capita income one full percentage point higher than Europe, this inequality ratio would still be nearly 20:1 today. At that rate, Africa would be catching up with Europe at the beginning of the twenty-fourth century.

Consider also the impact such huge inequalities have in negotiations about the terms of trade. With the exception of a few giants, such as China and India, poor countries have little bargaining power in international negotiations and also cannot afford the expertise needed to represent their interests effectively. (Such expertise can be quite costly. . . . [T]he initial World Trade Organisation [WTO] Treaty weighed in at 400 lbs or 26,000 pages.) As a result, they typically end up with a lousy deal. They opened their markets widely to foreign companies, paid royalties to foreign firms for films, music, drugs, and even seeds—and still found their own exports severely hampered by rich-country quotas, tariffs, anti-dumping duties as well as subsidies and export credits to domestic producers, all of which were somehow exempted from the supposed Big Move to free and open markets. Such asymmetries in the terms of trade surely play a role in explaining why the inequality in per-capita income between Europe and Africa has not declined, but has rather increased considerably since the end of the colonial period, standing today at roughly 40:1.

When they influence the design of common rules, pre-existing inequalities tend to be preserved and often aggravated. This phenomenon is evident within national societies, in which economic inequality tends to be quite stable over time. High inequality in Latin America and the United States persists over time, just as low inequality does in Scandinavia and Japan. Such stable diversity suggests that inequality is path dependent—that high inequality tends to reproduce itself because it gives the rich much greater power and also much stronger incentives to shape the common rules in their favor. Within national societies, one-person–one-vote democracy may mitigate the tendency for large inequalities to expand more and more. But there are no democratic practices the global poor might use to affect the economic rules beyond their own society. Even 85% of humankind, united, could not amend the WTO system.

The affluent countries and their citizens are then implicated in world poverty in two ways. We are implicated, first, because *our* great privileges and advantage as well as *their* extreme poverty and disadvantage have emerged through *one* historical process that was pervaded by unimaginable crimes. To be sure, we bear absolutely no moral responsibility for these crimes, even if we are direct descendants of people who do. Still, we are at fault for continuing to enforce the extreme inequalities that emerged in the course of that deeply unjust historical process.

Second, and independently, we are implicated because we are using our economic, technological, and military advantages to impose a global institutional order that is manifestly and grievously unjust. How do I know this order is unjust? Simply by the fact that an alternative global order would avoid most of the suffering that foreseeably persists under the present order: one-half of humankind living in abject poverty and 18 million dying annually from poverty-related causes. By imposing this grievously unjust global order upon the rest of the world, the affluent countries, in collaboration with the so-called elites of the developing countries, are harming the global poor—to put it mildly. To put it less mildly, the imposition of this global order constitutes the largest (although not the gravest) crime against humanity ever committed.

Most of those who reject this view are misled by either of two thoughts, which I will briefly address in conclusion. One thought is that our global institutional order cannot possibly be harming the global poor when severe poverty worldwide is in decline. This thought is powerfully reinforced by the lively debate about globalization in which statements about the global poverty trend, about being 'on track' toward the first UN MDG, have come to play a pivotal role.

. . . [I]t is by no means clear that severe poverty is in decline globally. But assume that it is. It does not follow that the existing global order is not harming the poor. After all, severe poverty may be going down not *because of,* but *despite* this order. Just as a boat may make progress even against a strong current or headwind, so the global poor may be making progress even against global rule-making processes that are slanted against them.

Moreover, even if the global institutional order were having a poverty-reducing effect, it might still be harming the global poor severely. Think of a slave-holding society, like the United States in its first 90 years. Suppose its institutional order, by raising overall prosperity, was gradually improving the slaves' condition. Does it follow that this order was not harmful to those whose enslavement it authorized and enforced? Or does a gradual improvement in the condition of those condemned to serfdom or corvée labor in feudal Russia or France really show that they were not harmed by this imposition? Obviously not! Obviously, whether an institutional order is harming people in the morally relevant sense depends not on a diachronic comparison with an earlier time, but on a counterfactual comparison with its feasible institutional alternatives. Most citizens of the affluent countries take comfort in the asserted decline of global poverty, thinking of themselves as benefactors of the global poor in the belief that the global institutional order they impose kills and scars fewer people each year. They should instead take intense discomfort in the fact that a feasible alternative global order could have avoided most life-threatening poverty and its associated evils.

The other misleading thought is that severe poverty today must be traced back to causal factors that are domestic to the countries in which it persists. This seems self-evident from the fact that severe poverty has evolved very differently in different countries–rapidly melting away in Japan, the Asian Tigers, and more recently China, while greatly worsening in Africa. Since all these countries were developing under the same global institutional order, this order cannot be at fault for the persistence of massive severe poverty in some of them.

Now it is true that there are great international variations in the evolution of severe poverty. And it is true that these variations must be caused by local (typically country-specific) factors. But it does not follow that these must be the only causally relevant factors, that global factors are irrelevant.

To see the fallacy, consider this parallel: there are great variations in the performance of my students. These variations must be caused by local (student-specific) factors. These factors, together, fully explain the overall performance of my class. Clearly, this parallel reasoning results in a falsehood: the overall performance of my class also crucially depends on the quality of my teaching and on various other 'global' factors besides. This shows that the inference is invalid.

To see this more precisely, one must distinguish two questions about the evolution of severe poverty. One concerns the observed variation in national trajectories. In the answer to this question, local factors must play a central role. Yet, however full and correct, this answer may not suffice to answer the other question, which concerns the overall evolution of poverty worldwide: even if student-specific factors explain observed variations in the performance of my students, the quality of my teaching may still play a major role in explaining why they did not on the whole do much better or worse than they actually did. Likewise, even if country-specific factors fully explain the observed variations in the economic performance of developing countries, global factors may still play a major role in explaining why they did not on the whole do much better or worse than they in fact did.

Many aspects of the global institutional order have such causal relevance. I have already mentioned the protectionist quotas, tariffs, anti-dumping duties, subsidies and export credits that the rich countries allowed themselves under WTO rules. Likewise, the absence of a global minimum wage and minimal global constraints on working hours and working conditions fosters a 'race to the bottom' where the ruling elites of poor countries, competing for foreign investment, are outbidding one another by offering ever more exploitable and mistreatable workforces.

Another important example is the global pharmaceutical regime, which rewards the inventors of new drugs by allowing them to charge monopoly prices for 20 years. These rules price most existing drugs out of the reach of the global poor. And they also skew medical research toward the affluent: medical conditions accounting for 90% of the global disease burden receive only 10% of all medical research world-wide. Of the 1393 new drugs approved between 1975 and 1999, only 13 were specifically indicated for tropical diseases (Médecins Sans Frontières, 2001, pp. 10–11). Millions of annual deaths could be avoided if rewards for medical research were based instead on its impact on the global disease burden. Such incentives could be funded, for instance, through a global 'Polluter Pays' regime that raises funds from countries in proportion to their citizens' and corporations' contributions to transnational environmental pollution. This would replace the current rules under which the more industrialized countries can pollute the oceans and atmosphere at will, thereby imposing much of the cost of their prosperity on the rest of the world, with the global poor generally benefiting least and being least able to protect themselves from the effects of pollution.

Global institutional factors also play an important role in sustaining many of the country-specific factors commonly adduced to explain the persistence of poverty. Thus, Rawls is quite right that when societies fail to thrive, "the problem is commonly the nature of the public political culture and the religious and philosophical traditions that underlie its institutions. The great social evils in poorer societies are likely to be oppressive government and corrupt elites" (1993, p. 77). But Rawls completely fails to note that such oppression and corruption are very substantially encouraged and sustained by global factors such as the international resource and borrowing privileges (Pogge, 2002, chapters 4 and 6), the still poorly policed bribe-paying practices of multinational corporations and the international arms trade.

This point also puts into perspective the popular cliché that membership in the WTO (and other international organizations) is voluntary. Yes, voluntary for a country's rulers. But not for the ruled. Nigeria's accession to the WTO was effected by its brutal dictator Sani Abacha, Myanmar's by the notorious SLORC (State Law and Order Restoration Council) junta, Indonesia's by kleptocrat Suharto, Zimbabwe's by Robert Mugabe, the Congo's (then named Zaire) by Mobutu Sese Seko, and so on.

Reflection two . . . supports the conclusion that the affluent countries, partly through the global institutional order they impose, bear a great causal and moral responsibility for the massive global persistence of severe poverty. Citizens of these countries thus have not merely a positive duty to assist innocent persons mired in life-threatening poverty, but also a more stringent negative duty to work politically and personally toward ceasing, or compensating for, their contribution to this ongoing catastrophe. . . .

NOTES

1 These figures are rough estimates derived as follows. If all people with incomes below $1/day were exactly at this benchmark, then the purchasing power of their collective annual income would be that of $430 billion in the US in 1993 ($32.74 × 12 months × 1092.7 million), which corresponds to the purchasing power of $560 billion in 2004 (www.bls.gov/cpi/home.htm). Yet, those who are extremely poor in this sense live, on average 28.4% below the $1/day benchmark (Chen and Ravallion, 2004, Tables 3 and 6; dividing the poverty gap index by the headcount index). So they have collective annual income with aggregate purchasing power of about $400 billion and would need additional annual income with aggregate purchasing power of about $160 billion annually for all of them to reach the Bank's $l/day benchmark. I divide these two figures by 4 to adjust for the fact that the purchasing power the Bank ascribes to the incomes of very poor people is, on average, at least four times greater than their value at market exchange rates. Thus the World Bank equates India's per-capita gross national income of $460 to $2450 PPP, China's $890 to $4260 PPP, Nigeria's $290 to $830 PPP, Pakistan's $420 to $1920 PPP, Bangladesh's $370 to $1680 PPP, Ethiopia's $100 to $710 PPP, Vietnam's $410 to $2130 PPP, and so on (World Bank, 2003, pp. 234–235).

2 These estimates are derived analogously. If all people with incomes below '2/day' were exactly at this benchmark, then the purchasing power of their collective annual income would be that of $2150 billion in the United States in 1993 ($65.48 × 12 months × 2735.6 million), which corresponds to the purchasing power of $2800 billion in 2004 (www.bls.gov/cpi/home.htm). Those who are poor in this sense live, on average, 42% below the $2/day benchmark (Chen and Ravallion, 2004, Tables 3 and 6; again dividing the poverty gap index by the headcount index). So they have collective annual income with aggregate purchasing power of about $1624 billion and would need additional annual income with aggregate purchasing power of about $1176 billion annually for all of them to reach the Bank's $2/day benchmark. I again divide both figures by 4 to estimate what these amounts come to at market exchange rates.

REFERENCES

International Labour Organisation (2002) *A Future without Child Labour,* International Labour Office, Geneva (also available through www.ilo.org).

Médecins Sans Frontiéres (2001) *Fatal Imbalance: The Crisis in Research and Development for Drugs for Neglected Diseases,* Médecins Sans Frontiéres, Geneva.

Pogge, T. (2002) *World Poverty and Human Rights,* Polity Press, Cambridge.

Rawls, J. (1993) 'The law of peoples', in S. Shute and S. Hurley (Eds.), *On Human Rights,* Basic Books, New York.

Rorty, R. (1996) 'Who are we? Moral universalism and economic triage', *Diogenes,* 173, pp. 5–15.

United Nations Development Programme (UNDP) (1998) *Human Development Report 1998,* Oxford University Press, New York.

UNDP (1999) *Human Development Report 1999,* Oxford University Press, New York.

UNDP (2002) *Human Development Report 2002,* Oxford University Press, New York.

UNDP (2003) *Human Development Report 2003,* Oxford University Press, New York.

United States Department of Agriculture (USDA)(1999a) *U.S. Action Plan on Food Security,* USDA, Washington, DC (www.fas.usda.gov/icd/summit/usactplan.pdf).

World Health Organisation (2004) *The World Health Report 2004,* WHO Publications, Geneva (www.who.int/whr/2004).

World Bank (2003) *World Development Report 2003,* Oxford University Press, New York.

QUESTIONS

1 Mindful of Pogge's analysis, what criticisms can you develop of Hardin's arguments in general and his lifeboat metaphor in particular?

2 What should be the UN's goal regarding the alleviation of extreme poverty by the year 2015?

Western Ethical Imperialism?

Max Borders

Borders raises a number of questions about first-world criticisms of the working conditions in foreign-owned factories in developing countries. He argues that we need to look at the situation from the perspective of people in the developing nations rather than simply applying first-world standards.

Almost daily, we are treated to stories about ghastly working conditions in the developing world. No minimum wage. No labor laws. No safety regulations. It's hot. It's cramped. Days are long. Breaks are short. It must be awful.

Some say globalization is the problem because it spreads without regard for the plight of those laborers who enable it to spread. In the parlance of the Marxist, people are being exploited by corporations in search of profit—and third world governments either can't keep up or are receiving kickbacks from the companies doing the exploiting.

It's true. Many of these conditions may truly be horrible by our western lights. Those of us who have benefited from air conditioning and indoor plumbing our entire lives can't imagine working more than twelve hours in a place where literally everyone is sweating. But have you talked to your grandparents about what life was like for them? Maybe your great grandparents? They may have a different story to tell about sweat and toil in a time when America and Europe were still developing.

In any case, we are seldom treated to the other side of the globalization story, especially the story about the indigenous people who actually want to work in these places. For example, consider:

- A 2004 story from a Hong Kong newspaper *Ming Pao,*[1] (via this Asian Labor blog,[2]) tells of riots by laborers in a Nike factory demanding more working hours. (Nike, due to pressure by western labor groups seeking "social justice," had begun limiting working hours.) Were these Taiwanese workers having their livelihoods undermined by a Western activist ethos? Sadly, it appears this story never made the English-speaking press.

Reprinted with permission of the author from the website of AWorldConnected, Institute for Humane Studies, George Mason University (www.aworldconnected.org), 2005.

- A story from Tomas Larrson's *A Race to the Top*,[3] demonstrates how child labor laws resulted in terrible unintended consequences: "The celebrated French ban on soccer balls sewn in Pakistan for the World Cup in 1998 resulted in significant dislocation of children from employment. Those who tracked them found that a large proportion ended up begging and/or in prostitution."[4] Begging? Prostitution? Surely factory work is better for families in countries struggling to achieve universal secondary education.
- Glenn Garvin's work for the *Miami Herald* detailed conditions in a Nicaraguan free trade zone, where Nicaraguans insisted "we need these jobs" after activists tried to pressure companies to close down due to "deplorable" conditions. "These may not be very good jobs in the United States," said Nicaraguan trade official Gilberto Wong, "but they're great jobs for Nicaragua. If we lose them, it will be a terrible blow." Working conditions are deplorable everywhere in Nicaragua, not just in the foreign-owned factories.[5]

People want to belong to noble causes. . . . But many college students, for example, believe they are doing good when they insist that their university sweatshirts and memorabilia come from non-sweatshop labor. Consider this excerpt from the USAS:

> United Students Against Sweatshops is an international student movement of campuses and individual students fighting for sweatshop free labor conditions and workers' rights. We define "sweatshop" broadly and recognize that it is not limited to the apparel industry, but everywhere among us. We believe that university standards should be brought in line with those of its students who demand that their school's logo is emblazoned on clothing made in decent working conditions.[6]

Might one reasonably ask: what are "decent" working conditions to an American college student who has not likely had to work much beyond a summer at Chili's? Do such students realize what sorts of alternatives are available to the poorest people of the world?

The problem lies in what we may think of as "ethical" here in the comfortable West. But people in the developing world live very different lives, and we have to try and look at things from their perspective. If Jose works for $0.45 per hour, that sounds terrible to us. But what are his peers earning on average? In the Glenn Garvin series cited above, factory workers made as much or more than the police. $0.45 per hour has a lot more purchasing power in Nicaragua than in Nantucket, so figures like that don't really make much sense until we understand the context. In other words, we have to consider the costs of living relative to a country—along with a number of other factors.[7]

Suppose more "socially responsible" companies were to offer more money and US-style working standards to their employees. Would the companies be able to give as many people the opportunity to work? After all, the labor (not to mention the regulatory costs) would be more expensive, so it would be more difficult for the company to grow. Furthermore, might local people wonder why factory employees now get, say, $0.50 per hour instead of $0.45—(which is already five cents more per hour than the police make!)

As the developing world continues to grow, laborers will have more bargaining power—both in terms of hours, pay, and working conditions. But they will not be able to get such power until they develop further economically. If we expect them to go from nothing to Western working conditions and pay immediately, we are only hurting them with our naïveté. (We may also be hurting poor people here at home who benefit from cheaper goods.)

These are difficult issues. When we think about the lives of people in poor countries, it can be disturbing. Maybe the best thing we can do in the rich, developed world is to try and understand the realities of our developing world counterparts. Maybe we should believe them when they tell us "we want these jobs." And while we might bristle at the idea of having to work in sweatshop conditions ourselves, we might also consider what an opportunity looks like for someone with very limited options living in one of the poorest parts of the world.

NOTES

1 http://www.mingpaonews.com.
2 Stephen Frost, "China Workers Riot for the Right to Work Overtime." http://www.asianlabour.org).
3 Tomas Larrson, *A Race to the Top* (Washington, D.C.: Cato Institute, 2001), p. 48.
4. Thomas DeGregori, "Child Labor or Prostitution?" (http://www.aworldconnected.com), October 8, 2002.
5 Glenn Garvin, "We Need These Jobs, *The Miami Herald,* November 30, 1997.
6 http://www.studentsagainstsweatshops.org.
7 Richard M. Ebeling, "Titled Real Estate" (http://www.aworldconnected.org).

QUESTIONS

1 What moral standards should be applied in our evaluations of working conditions in third-world countries?
2 Should we refuse to purchase goods made by workers who are subjected to inhumane working conditions?

A Consensus Statement on Sweatshop Abuse

United Trauma Relief

This document focuses on an assumption made by those who object to antisweatshop actions: International sweatshops are currently an economic necessity that, given economic development, will cease to exist. Several arguments defending international sweatshops are examined and rebutted.

http://web.mit.edu/utr/www/consensus.doc, August 2001. Reprinted with permission of the principal author, Sanjay Basu.

The term "sweatshop" refers to those factories relying on the exploitation and abuse of workers. Often (although not always) located in developing countries, these factories have been frequented by independent university researchers, who have published numerous accounts of worker imprisonment and physical abuse, as well as economic evidence revealing that many of these factories pay wages so small that their workers cannot live outside poverty. Several factories use horrific labor practices, and many factory workers have also been severely burned or mutilated in the workplace, while women among the labor population have often been forced to take birth control or abort their pregnancies (Given, 1997; Fernandez, 1997). The health burdens placed upon sweatshop workers have been extensively documented, and include exposure to noxious fumes, organophosphate compounds, and silica dust, resulting in record high cancer, asthma, bronchitis, pneumoconiosis, and leukemia rates in many regions because workers aren't provided with masks and gloves (Kim *et al.,* 2000).

These abuses are neither just nor irremediable, but many people believe that sweatshops are an economic necessity and will come to pass on their own with economic development. Closer examination of both the social and economic dimensions of sweatshop labor, however, reveals this presumption to be far from the truth.

Most objections to anti-sweatshop action stem from the idea that sweatshop jobs are the best opportunities available to people living in poor conditions. "They keep coming back day after day, so they must want these jobs." Trying to make the jobs better will simply mean that fewer jobs will be available, and people dependent on them will suffer. But those who have advanced this "economic" syllogism have ignored much of the evidence to the contrary. Although this idea may appear "intuitive," the reality surrounding the improvement of sweatshop conditions is quite contrary to intuition. Nevertheless, these "intuitive" arguments in support of sweatshops proliferate. Among them:

- "Any job is better than no job. These people would rather work in a sweatshop than starve."

Slavery might also be better than starvation, yet nobody advocates a return to slavery. Just because a bad job may be better than starvation doesn't justify labor abuses such as the beating and raping of workers or the threatening of worker's families—all abuses that have been regularly documented by independent researchers visiting sweatshop factories (Breslow, 1995; Foek, 1997). While accepting that a bad job might be better than nothing, we should continue to fight the abuse of human lives, and even a basic study of history reveals that most human progress as a society has occurred through such struggles for progress, not through maintenance of the status quo. If we justify abuse under the premise that is better than the worst alternative, we create a slippery slope leading down to the complete devaluation of human life. As *New York Times* columnist Bob Herbert, a vocal critic of sweatshop abuse, writes, "What's next, employees who'll work for a bowl of gruel?" (Herbert, 1996).

- "If companies are forced to increase wages or improve conditions, they won't simply pay the same number of workers more. They will relocate to somewhere with fewer restrictions."

The idea that companies will "not like" the improvement of conditions is indeed correct. But, obviously, if corporations were allowed to do whatever they wanted, our world would go to hell. That's precisely the reason we have regulations to mandate what is permissible and what isn't—it's the very reason we have seatbelts in our cars and arsenic limits for our water. The idea that corporations "won't simply pay" is ignorant of the basic idea of a corporate charter. Corporations, in becoming incorporated, are granted a charter by the state under the edict that they are responsible to the state, just like any citizen. The state sets a minimum wage, but one could say that corporations wouldn't "simply pay" that either. Because every corporation is ultimately required to be responsive to the state according to its charter, every corporation is required to pay a minimum wage anyway. Common sense and history argue against the idea that it would be best for corporations to act without any guidelines and have free reign over society. Therefore it's society's responsibility to determine what we allow and what we require of corporations, and corporations, because of the charter they have received, are just as responsible as regular citizens in having to follow law.

Can corporations afford to pay? The statistics speak for themselves: in 1965 the average CEO made 44 times the average factory worker; today, the average CEO makes 212 times the factory worker salary. Michael Eisner of Disney could pay every worker in his Haitian toy factories enough to feed and clothe themselves and their families annually if he would devote just 1% of his advertising budget to worker's salaries (Given, 1997).

As members of society, we should also ask ourselves: should corporations really be allowed to shop around the world for the most easily abused workforce, or should measures be put into place to prevent this abuse altogether? Indeed, such measures are starting to be put in place, and rather than engaging in a "race to the bottom"—a race for corporations to find the most abused workforce to manipulate— international response to the problem is calling for the construction of rules to put the rights of persons before the rights of exploiters (Cholewinski, 1997; Human Rights Watch, 1997; Rosen, Maurren, & Perez-Lopez, 1997). Such is the very nature of human progress through history, and only those who favor exploitation over human well-being are arguing that these rules should not be put into place.

- "Most companies that use sweatshops are actually just contracting through local producers, so they don't have a say in the conditions of factories."

This idea rests on a fundamental fallacy: that large multinational companies (e.g., NIKE, adidas, Jansport) contracting with local producers are helpless entities unable to have an effect on conditions in local factories. Modern evidence, however, disproves such a contention (Ross, 1997). Independent academics have learned that corporations often "squeeze their contractors into paying sub-minimum wages. Large retailers and retail chains pressure contract manufacturers by refusing to pay more than a rock-bottom price for manufacturing orders" (Given, 1997).

Public pressure, history shows, causes many multinationals to pressure local owners to improve working conditions in order to improve their reputations. As Iowa Senator Tom Harkin suggested, in rallying to produce a list of abusers and generate American consumer pressure against them, "Just as human rights organizations such as Amnesty International are able to document cases of human rights abuses and torture around the world, so can the identities of those industries and their host countries that are violating international labor standards . . . be identified" (Harkin, 1996). In fact, agencies have been created to monitor the conditions of such factories, and monitoring combined with public pressure can result in the improvement of such facilities. For example, reacting to public outrage in 1996, Liz Claiborne, NIKE, Phillips-Van Heusen, and L.L. Bean joined into an "Apparel Industry Partnership" to take steps to end sweatshop abuses (Salomon, 1996). Continued pressure will force the compliance of other companies as well.

- "Demands for a living wage will result in fewer workers as tasks will become automated. While those who remain employed will probably be better off, those who lose their jobs will not."

The cost of paying a fair, living wage in many countries is still far lower than the cost of automation. If automation did provide such an advantage, companies would have simply automated American plants, and reaped the many advantages of manufacturing close to home. Instead, they chose not to automate any further, and took advantage of lower wages and a more willing work force abroad. For the most part, the clothing industry is about as automated as is effective, and further automation is not very likely to occur. As a result, paying a living wage is highly unlikely to result in the "economic elite" scenario presented above. As evidenced by interviews with sweatshop workers, laborers are not seeking U.S. or European-level wages; workers in poorer countries want decent workplaces, ones in which they are not constantly threatened by torture or death (Mort, 1996).

- "You are trying to restrict global free trade. This type of trade is the only way to raise people out of poverty, and cause economies to develop. Once economies do develop, sweatshops will cease to exist. In a developed economy, companies will stop abusing their workers and will treat them well."

Those opposed to sweatshops are not trying to prevent trade, but are trying to prevent the abuse that has been justified under the premise of global trade. Protection for workers, and indeed respect for human rights, has never been mutually exclusive with trade (Richburg & Swardson, 1996). Companies should not be permitted to benefit by violating the rights of human beings, and "free trade" has never implied the blacklisting and killing of workers by death squads in Central America, the prevention of union building in Mexico, or the raping and beating of women in Sri Lanka (Human Rights Watch/Asia, 1995). As *New York Times* columnist Karl Meyer wrote, "We can no longer believe that anything goes in the global marketplace, regardless of social consequences. It is precisely this conviction that underlies efforts to attach human rights conditions to trading relations—to temper the amorality of the market" (Meyer, 1997).

Indeed, evidence against the idea that development necessarily results in improved conditions is abundant in American history. Not only do sweatshops continue to exist (mostly in Los Angeles and New York), but even places of employment that are not considered sweatshops are often far from optimal (Lee & Mitchell, 1998). Many employers, including even Harvard University, still fail to pay a living wage. Workers will continue to be exploited on a global scale until adequate protections are put into place through public pressure. Public pressure resulted in the improvement of sweatshop labor conditions within the American northeast after the industrial revolution; those sweatshops of the late 19th and early 20th centuries virtually disappeared after World War II because of increased public pressure (through programs like the National Consumers League's "White Label" inspections) resulting in government regulation of monopolies and the rise of trade unions (Golodner, 1997). Public pressure is the only insurance that conditions will improve elsewhere. Conditions do not simply improve as a result of economic growth. In El Salvador, for example, 50,000 new sweatshop jobs have been created in the last 10 years, with the country's exports jumping 4,000 percent. But real wages have been halved. "Its women can't afford to buy the clothes they make," says Neil Kearney, president of the International Textile, Garment and Leather Workers Union. "And people who protest are subject to rape and murder" (Clark, 1996).

As Lance Compa, an international labor law professor at Cornell University's School of Industrial and Labor Relations, recently wrote in *The Washington Post:* "After wealth has been created, respecting workers' rights and paying them fairly is still a choice, one that doesn't always depend on economics. Instead, choosing justice for workers is driven by organizing, bargaining and political action, increasingly on an international scale. . . . With a human rights dimension, more trade and investment are a potential source of great good for working people. Genuine comparative advantage for lower-wage countries is something the international community can accept, if it helps poorer nations develop, if wages and conditions can rise and if workers have a voice in society. But artificial advantage based on human rights violations is something else that the international community should stop" (Compa, 2001).

REFERENCES

Breslow, Marc. (1995, November/December). Crimes of Fashion: Those Who Suffer to Bring You Gap T-Shirts. *Dollars and Sense.*

Cholewinski, Ryszard. (1997). *Migrant Workers in International Human Rights Law: Their Protection in Countries of Employment.* New York: Oxford University Press.

Clark, Charles S. (1996). Child Labor and Sweatshops: The Issues. *Congressional Quarterly Researcher.*

Compa, Lance. (2001 July 31). Ensuring a Decent Global Workplace. *The Washington Post.*

Fernandez, Mary Rose. (1997, September). Commodified Women. *Peace Review.*

Foek, Anton. (1997, January/February). Sweatshop Barbie: Exploitation of Third World Labor. *Humanist.*

Given, Olivia. (1997). An Indictment of Sweatshops. In M. E. Williams (Ed.), *Child Labor and Sweatshops* (pp. 21–25). San Diego: Greenhaven.

Golodner, Linda. (1997, October 6). [Lecture] Apparel Industry Code of Conduct: A Consumer Perspective on Responsibility. *Notre Dame Center for Ethics and Religious Values in Business.*

Harkin, Tom. (1996, January). Put an End to the Exploitation of Child Labor. *USA Today Magazine.*

Herbert, Bob. (1996, June 10). Nike's Pyramid Scheme. *The New York Times.*

Human Rights Watch. (1997). *Corporations and Human Rights: Freedom of Association in a Maquila in Guatemala.* New York: Human Rights Watch.

Human Rights Watch/Asia. (1995). *Rape for Profit: Trafficking of Nepali Girls and Women to India's Brothels.* New York: Human Rights Watch, 1995.

Kim, Jim Yong *et al.* (2000). *Dying for Growth: Global Inequality and the Health of the Poor.* Cambridge: Common Courage Press.

Lee, Siu Hin & Mitchell, Celeste. (1998, February). Sweat Shop Workers Struggle in New York's Chinatown. *Z Magazine.*

Meyer, Karl. (1997, June 28). Editorial Notebook. *The New York Times.*

Mort, Jo-Ann. (1996, Fall). Immigrant Dreams: Sweatshop Workers Speak. *Dissent.*

Richburg, Keith B. & Swardson, Anne. (1996, August 5–11). Sweatshops or Economic Development? *Washington Post National Weekly Edition.*

Rosen, Sonia A., Jaffe, Maurren, & Perez-Lopez, Jorge. (1997). *The Apparel Industry and Codes of Conduct: A Solution to the International Child Labor Problems.* Upland, PA: Diane.

Ross, Andrew. (1997). *No Sweat: Fashion, Free Trade, and the Rights of Garment Workers.* New York: Verso.

Salomon, Larry. (1996, September/October). Sweatshops in the Spotlight. *Third Force.*

QUESTIONS

1 Do university students have an obligation to determine whether clothing sold in that university's shops is produced by workers in international sweatshops?
2 Does this consensus statement succeed in countering the various arguments that are often advanced in defense of international sweatshops?

Sweatshops

Matt Zwolinski

Zwolinski first looks at definitions of sweatshops. He holds that in the context of social criticism in which the term arose, the description of a place of employment as a "sweatshop" is best understood as reflecting a judgment regarding the producer's morally unacceptable treatment of employees. Zwolinski next examines the moral questions raised by international sweatshops. Like Borders, he asks whether it is appropriate to apply first-world standards to industries in third-world countries. Zwolinski's discussion focuses on two questions: (1) Are companies who contract with sweatshop manufacturers doing anything wrong? (2) Regardless of whether these companies are acting wrongly, what should we do about the situation of sweatshops? Zwolinski's response to each question is a cautious one. With respect to the first question, he discusses some of the prosweatshop arguments and holds that they are not decisive. With respect to the second question, Zwolinski stresses the need to do careful empirical research before engaging in specific antisweatshop actions to ensure that we adopt the best measures available to help those employed in sweatshops.

INTRODUCTION

The term 'sweatshop' is heavy with emotional, historical, and moral significance. It calls to mind images of women and children working long days in cramped, rat-infested quarters, abused by their supervisors and paid barely enough to survive and work another day. To others it will suggest the horrors of Mexican *maquiladoras*, where young female apparel workers are often subject to sexual harassment from the local supervisors, and punished severely for any attempt to organize.

Perhaps most frighteningly of all, the term suggests that the *responsibility* for these situations falls squarely on the shoulders of the average consumer. By as simple an act as buying a dress for oneself or running shoes for one's children, the story goes, one is providing economic support to the system which leads to the sorts of oppression described above. The only difference between the consumer who buys sweatshop-made products and the supervisor who runs the sweatshop his or her self is physical proximity to the offense. Morally speaking, we are all guilty.

But guilty of what, exactly? The term 'sweatshop' undoubtedly connotes something objectionable. But what precisely are the conditions which have to be met by a business before this term is appropriately applied? What makes a sweatshop a sweatshop?

DEFINITIONS

Unfortunately, the issues surrounding sweatshops and their economic context are so contentious that not even the definition of the term is free from controversy. . . . [T]he term has a historical reference, which picks out a particular method of production in the apparel industry in the early part of the 1900s. But we do not want our definition to rule out the possibility that sweatshops might exist *today*, in *other* industrial contexts. To tie the term 'sweatshop' to a particular industry in a particular historical era is to put too strict a limit on the broader social criticism that term was intended to invoke.

The term also has a legal meaning. The U.S. General Accounting Office defines a sweatshop as "an employer that violates more than one federal or state law governing minimum wage and overtime, child labor, industrial homework, occupational safety and health, workers compensation, or industry regulation." The advantage of this definition is that it provides a clear, quantifiable standard with which to assess the status of sweatshops within the United States, and a basis for pursuing legal action against them. In certain contexts, this definition may be entirely appropriate. Its disadvantage is much the same as that found in the historical definition discussed above—it seems too narrow to serve as a *general* definition. In the history of the United States, many sweatshops existed *prior* to the enactment of many of the worker-protection laws referenced in the GAO's definition.

Does this mean they were not really sweatshops? Similarly, many of today's sweatshops exist outside of the United States, in countries where legal protection for labor is minimal at best. Often, these companies operate without breaking any of the laws of their home country at all. If we wish to condemn these operations as 'sweatshops,' the legal definition will be inadequate.

Ultimately, then, the precise meaning of the term 'sweatshop' will vary depending on context. Historical and legal definitions have their place, but usually our description of a certain producer as a sweatshop will reflect a *moral* judgment. In other words, it will reflect our judgment that the producer is treating its employees inhumanely, or that it is violating their basic human rights or simple standards of decency. This definition, too, is not without its problems, for it raises a whole host of complicated moral questions such as what moral obligations employers have toward their employees, or what constitutes a fair wage for a day's work. Furthermore, by building moral wrongness into the definition, this approach rules out from the start the question of whether sweatshops might ever be morally permissible. Nevertheless, understanding 'sweatshop' as a moral term seems to best fit the way in which the term has been used in the context of social criticism in which it arose.

MORAL QUESTIONS

For all the controversy that surrounds the issue of sweatshops, one thing is perfectly clear: conditions in sweatshops are usually horrible. There may be debate about *how* horrible conditions are: whether wages are enough to maintain an adequate diet, whether physical abuse takes place in a particular factory, whether manufacturers are living up to their contractual and legal agreements, and so on. But no matter how significant these details may be, they are dwarfed by the broader conclusion: by any first-world standard of decency, sweatshop conditions are atrocious.

But are first-world standards of decency the appropriate standard to apply to industries in third-world countries? Even if we agree that conditions in sweatshops are horrible, we still must answer two important questions in order to reach any settled moral conclusion. First, are companies who contract with sweatshop manufacturers doing anything *wrong*? And second, whether they are wrong or not, what should we *do* about the situation of sweatshops?

Let us begin by considering the first question. Certain individuals, especially economists, have defended sweatshops on the grounds that they currently constitute the best available alternative for people living in developing countries. The wages paid by Nike's firm in Jakarta, they point out, might seem low by U.S. standards, but they are actually fairly high by the standards of the local economy. People freely choose to work at these factories because they can make more money there than they can anywhere else. If Nike were to close down the factory and begin producing exclusively in the United States, the situation of the workers it would have to lay off would not be improved—it would be worsened. They would either need to seek lower-paying employment elsewhere in the legitimate economy, or try to make money by illicit means, often by prostitution or theft.

This argument draws its support from the claim that individuals *choose* to work at sweatshops. If those individuals had a better alternative, they would have taken it.

Of course, this argument only holds where workers are not physically coerced into working at a particular plant. Cases of sweatshops hiring armed guards to ensure that their workforce does not leave exist but they are rare. For the rest, the argument runs, the fact that employees chose to work at sweatshops shows that they view sweatshops as the best employment available. Taking that option away by forcing sweatshops to shut down would end up harming precisely the people the anti-sweatshop activists are trying to help.

Not only would shutting down factories harm the individuals who would lose their jobs as a result, the argument continues, it would also slow down the development of the economy as a whole, and thus prevent the development of better options for future generations. Sweatshops, economists are quick to point out, tend not to dominate an economy for very long. Often, they are the first step in a long path of economic development, injecting capital and management training into an economy where it can serve as the basis for the creation of new domestic industries. In Korea and Taiwan, for instance, Nike is no longer able to maintain manufacturing operations because, as one source reports, "workers in these quickly developing economies are no longer interested in working in low-paying shoe and textile factories." Sweatshops, according to this argument, are a *symptom* of poverty, not a *cause* of poverty. But moreover, they are a *hopeful* symptom: for they signal the beginning of an economic development which will eventually bring that poverty to an end.

These arguments are powerful, and caution those opposed to sweatshops to think carefully about the results of the policy they advocate. But it is not clear that they are decisive. We began this section with two questions, and the sorts of arguments described above might give us reason to suppose that we have arrived at an answer to the first. If companies who contract with sweatshops thereby provide individuals in developing countries with better opportunities than they would otherwise have had, then maybe they are not acting wrongly, or at least, not as wrongly as some have supposed them to be.

But this still leaves us without an answer to the second question: what should we *do* about sweatshops? The arguments given above seem to leave this question largely unaddressed. After all, by and large, anti-sweatshop activists are not calling for U.S. companies to pull out of third-world countries altogether. They do not want sweatshops to be shut down, they want them to be *improved*. Students who agitate for code of conduct programs want U.S. companies to ensure that their subcontractors pay a living wage, that they provide safe and sanitary working conditions for employees, and that they respect workers' basic human rights. Sophisticated anti-sweatshop activists recognize that companies are making employees better off by their providing individuals with jobs. They simply demand that companies ensure that those jobs be provided in a way which meets some basic ethical guidelines.

Still, the issue of what guidelines companies, consumers, or international organizations should impose on sweatshops is a complicated matter. Many of the proposals to regulate sweatshops suffer from the same sort of problem as proposals to abolish them. In 1992, for instance, the U.S. Congress considered a bill known as the Child Labor Deterrence Act, which sought to prohibit the importation of any product made in whole or in part by individuals under the age of

15 who are employed in industry or mining. Proposals such as this seem not to recognize that in a developing economy, child labor can play a vital role. For families living in such conditions, almost all income is directed toward the basic necessities of life: food, medicine, shelter, clothing. When parents grow too old or sick to work, children often become the main breadwinners of the family. An effective ban on products made by child labor would mean that these children would lose their jobs. Because developing countries generally have little in the way of social welfare programs for families to fall back on, the effect of this loss can be devastating.

In dealing with sweatshops, then, good intentions are simply not enough. Well-intentioned proposals to provide workers with a living wage, or health or maternity benefits, can raise [the] amount of money companies are forced to spend on each worker, and in so doing create a pressure to lay off all but the most essential.

But these considerations do not settle the matter in favor of sweatshops; they simply caution that close empirical research is necessary before drawing any conclusion. Sweatshop critics Edna Bonacich and Richard Appelbaum are quick to respond to the above arguments, for instance, by pointing out that in the case of a typical $100 dress sold and made in the United States, only 6% of the purchase price goes to the individual who actually made the garment. 25% goes to profit and overhead for the manufacturer, 50% goes to the retailer, and the remaining is spent on raw materials. Using similar reasoning, the National Labor Committee pointed out to Disney Chairman Michael Eisner in 1996 that the effect of raising the pay of workers at the Classic Apparel facility in Haiti from their then-current 35 cents per hour wage to 58 cents an hour would be a mere 3 cent raise in price for an $11.99 garment. And if certain economists are right, raising wages in many circumstances might actually *lower* costs, or at least have no negative effect. Workers who are not paid enough to provide for their nutritional needs might not be as productive as those who are able to afford a steady and reliable diet.

It is difficult, then, to come to any generally applicable conclusions about the wrongness of sweatshops or the desirability of any sort of regulatory or consumer-driven alternative. By way of general principle, we can only say that any reasonable policy will need to pay careful attention to the way in which alternative stances towards sweatshops actually affect the persons they are intended to help. Discovering what helps and what doesn't is less a matter of applying a pre-packaged ideology (free-market or anti-sweatshop) than it is of doing careful research into the unique local conditions of particular sweatshops and their political and economic contexts. . . .

QUESTIONS

1 Corporations in the United States frequently move jobs from the United States to third-world countries, paying much lower wages and benefits. Are their actions morally defensible?

2 Should there be some international body charged with the responsibility of setting working standards and minimum wages globally?

SUGGESTED ADDITIONAL READINGS FOR CHAPTER 9

AIKEN, WILLIAM and HUGH LAFOLLETTE. eds.: *World Hunger and Morality,* 2d ed. Englewood Cliffs, N.J.: Prentice-Hall, 1995. Many of the essays in this book were written especially for this volume. The anthology is divided into five parts: (1) Lifeboat Ethics; (2) A Responsibility to Aid; (3) Rights and Justice; (4) Justice and Development; and (5) Hunger and the Environment.

BELSEY, ANDREW: "World Poverty, Justice and Equality." In Robin Attfield, ed., *International Justice and the Third World.* New York: Routledge, 1992. Belsey argues against the claim that the special obligations that inhabitants of affluent countries have to people who are geographically or genetically closer to them override the interests of people in the third world.

CHATTERJEE, DEEN K., ed.: *The Ethics of Assistance and the Distant Needy.* New York: Cambridge University Press, 2004. Several of the articles in this volume deal with the question of the moral significance of distance in determining our duties to those in need. The articles by Thomas Pogge, Henry Shue, Onora O'Neill, and Charles R. Beitz are especially useful in illustrating how philosopohical discussions of the justification of international actions with respect to world poverty should be informed by the reality of international politics.

MAITLAND, IAN: "The Great Non-Debate Over International Sweatshops." In Thomas L. Beauchamp and Norman E. Bowie, eds., *Ethical Theory and Business.* Upper Saddle River, N.J.: Prentice-Hall, 2001. Maitland, a defender of international sweatshops, advances arguments, based on both factual and ethical grounds, against the critics of sweatshops.

MURDOCH, WILLIAM W., and ALLAN OATEN: "Population and Food: Metaphors and the Reality." *Bioscience,* September 9, 1975, pp. 561–567. Murdoch and Oaten criticize Garrett Hardin's lifeboat, commons, and ratchet metaphors and bring out various factors, other than food supply, that affect population growth.

NUSSBAUM, MARTHA: *Women and Human Development: The Capabilities Approach.* New York: Cambridge University Press, 2000. Nussbaum wants to alter the theoretical grounds on which international development policy is based. She argues that international political and economic thought should be feminist in orientation and grounded in a cross-cultural normative account of central human capabilities.

O'NEILL, ONORA: "Justice, Gender, and International Boundaries." In Martha Nussbaum, ed., *The Quality of Life.* New York: Oxford University Press, 1993. O'Neill argues that an account of justice can combine abstract principles with a consideration of differences in their application. She illustrates her claim by an account of the case of poor women in impoverished economies.

RACHELS, JAMES: "Killing and Starving to Death." *Philosophy,* vol. 54, April 1979, pp. 159–171. Rachels, attacking the view that killing is worse than letting die, argues that letting die is just as bad as killing. For Rachels our duty not to let people die from starvation is as strong as our duty not to kill them.

VISVANATHAN, NALINI, LYNN DUGGAN, LAURIE NISONOFF, and NAN WIEGERSMA, eds.: *The Women, Gender and Development Reader.* London: Zed, 1997. This reader features landmark articles and essays on the impact of development on women's lives. The book is divided into five parts: (1) Theories of Women, Gender and Development; (2) Households and Families; (3) Women in the Global Economy; (4) International Women in Social Transformations; and (5) Women Organizing Themselves for Change.

CHAPTER 10

Animals

Human beings are responsible for a great deal of animal suffering. We use animals in experiments, raise and slaughter animals for food, and hunt and kill animals, sometimes merely for sport. Our treatment of animals raises numerous moral questions, some of which are discussed in this chapter.

SPECIESISM AND THE MORAL STATUS OF ANIMALS

In a now well-known book, *Animal Liberation,* Peter Singer, a utilitarian, forcefully calls attention to the suffering that human beings routinely inflict on nonhuman animals. (Utilitarianism holds that an action or practice is morally correct only if it is likely to produce the greatest balance of good over evil, everyone considered.) In order to satisfy human desires for meat, we raise animals in such a way that their short lives are dominated by pain and suffering. In order to obtain information, purportedly for the benefit of humans, we devise experimental projects that involve the infliction of intense pain on animals. Our experimentation on animals and our meat-eating habits are paradigm examples, for Singer, of morally unacceptable practices in regard to animals. Because Singer finds human beings so willing to subordinate important animal interests (e.g., an interest in avoiding suffering) to much less important human interests, he charges the human community with *speciesism.* In an excerpt from *Animal Liberation* reprinted in this chapter, Singer defines speciesism as a "prejudice or attitude of bias toward the interests of members of one's own species and against those of members of other species." Singer uses the term *speciesism* in order to emphasize the similarities between sexist and racist practices, on the one hand, and our treatment of animals, on the other. In Singer's view, it is just as wrong to discriminate against animals because of their species as it is to discriminate against women because of their sex and blacks because of their race.

Singer's arguments, in effect, attribute moral status to animals. An entity has moral status if it is due moral consideration in its own right and not simply because of its relations to other beings. Some philosophers have argued that animals have no moral status. In their view, any obligations we have regarding animals are based on the interests or rights of human beings. If we have an obligation not to mistreat dogs, for example, it may be because the mistreatment of dogs causes suffering to human beings, many of whom sympathetically identify with the suffering of animals. Singer, in contrast, appeals directly to animal interests in condemning much of our current use of animals. He holds, in effect, that sentience is the relevant criterion in determining whether an entity has moral status. Sentience can be described as the capacity to have conscious experiences, such as pleasure and pain. *All* sentient beings, Singer maintains, have interests, including an interest in avoiding pain and suffering. A fundamental principle of morality—*the principle of equal consideration of interests*—requires us to give equal consideration to the interests of all beings affected by our decisions. Animals, like human beings, are sentient beings with an interest in avoiding pain and suffering. Hence, we violate a fundamental principle of morality when we make decisions about the use of animals in experiments if we consider only human interests and fail to give equal consideration to the interests that animals have in avoiding suffering.

Whereas Singer focuses on animal *interests* as he advances a utilitarian line of reasoning, Tom Regan in this chapter focuses on animal *rights* as he advances his attack on speciesism. On Regan's analysis, animals, like humans, are bearers of rights because animals, like humans, have inherent value. To have inherent value, Regan maintains, an entity must be a conscious creature whose welfare is valuable or important to it, so that its having value is not dependent on its usefulness to others. Since animals are creatures of this sort, they have rights, which must be respected. Regan rejects the view that animals, while having some inherent value, have less inherent value than human beings. In his view, all entities that have inherent value have it equally and have an equal right to be treated with respect. Any attempt to specify a difference (e.g., rationality) between human beings and animals, which would purport to justify the attribution of lesser inherent value to the latter, would require us to attribute a lesser degree of inherent value to some "nonparadigm" human beings (e.g., the severely brain-damaged) if we were to be consistent in our moral reasoning. The same problem is faced, Regan maintains, by those who attempt to specify a criterion that rights holders must possess (e.g., the capacity for autonomy) that would exclude animals from the class of entities having rights.

Regan's claim that animals have rights is attacked by Carl Cohen in this chapter. Cohen's position rests on his conception of rights as claims or potential claims within a community of moral agents. Moral agency presupposes a capacity for free moral judgment and for exercising and responding to moral claims. To be a moral agent, one must have a capacity to understand the rules of duty that govern all members of the human community and to act in accordance with these rules. Only human beings have the relevant capacities. Hence, for Cohen, only human beings have moral rights. Cohen rejects Regan's contention that any criterion that might be used to exclude all animals from the class of entities having rights would also require us to exclude nonparadigm humans. In Cohen's view, although animals cannot have rights because they lack the relevant capacities, nonparadigm humans who also lack the relevant capacities (e.g., the severely mentally retarded) do have rights. In his view, such nonparadigmatic humans are still the bearers of rights because they belong to a species whose members are normally capable of moral agency. Cohen does not deny that animals have some sort of moral status. He grants that we do have some obligations to animals, including an obligation not to cause them needless suffering. In contrast to Singer, however, Cohen maintains that it is wrong to give animal and human interests equal consideration. Whatever moral status animals have because of their sentience, it is significantly less than that of human beings.

The question of possible differences in the moral status of human beings and animals is addressed by Mary Anne Warren in this chapter's final reading. A distinction made in the introduction to Chapter 1 between full moral status and partial moral status is useful here. Entities have full moral status if they have the same rights as paradigmatic (i.e., normal adult) human beings. They have partial moral status if their rights are lesser in some sense than those of paradigmatic humans. In comparing and contrasting human and animal rights, Warren effectively ascribes partial moral status to animals. According to her analysis, animal and human rights differ in respect to both their content and their strength (i.e., in the strength of the reasons required to override them). Warren holds that sentience is the basis for at least some rights. Thus, she rejects Cohen's conception of rights. Warren argues, however, that moral agency (moral autonomy), as well as other differences between humans and animals, may be a basis for attributing stronger rights to human beings than to animals. In respect to nonparadigmatic humans, Warren advances reasons to support her claim that we can consistently grant them the same rights as those of paradigmatic humans while attributing only lesser rights to animals.

VEGETARIANISM

Is the human interest in eating meat sufficiently important to justify our practice of raising and slaughtering animals? Intertwined with this question is the issue of a vegetarian diet. Advocates of vegetarianism offer diverse arguments to support their position. Some advocate a vegetarian diet simply because they believe it to be superior in terms of health benefits. If a vegetarian diet does offer special health advantages (a controversial claim), then each individual, as a matter of personal prudence, would be well advised to adopt it. Apart from this *prudential argument,* many vegetarians advance *moral arguments* in defense of their diet. One common moral argument, closely related to the considerations developed in Chapter 9, is based on the fact that hunger, malnutrition, and starvation seriously threaten many people in our world. It is morally indefensible, the argument goes, to waste desperately needed protein by feeding our grain to animals, which we then eat. Eight pounds of protein in the form of grain are necessary, on the average, to produce one pound of protein in the form of meat. Since this process is so inefficient, we are morally obliged to adopt a vegetarian diet so that our protein resources in the form of grain can be shared with those who desperately need help. Though this particular moral argument is not without force, it would not seem to establish a need for a completely vegetarian diet. It may well be that world hunger could effectively be alleviated if people in affluent countries were simply to consume *less meat.*

Probably the most important moral arguments advanced in defense of a vegetarian diet are those that take account of the impact of meat production on the animals themselves. Two lines of argument in this category can be distinguished: (1) Although it is not necessarily wrong to kill animals for food (assuming the killing is relatively painless), it is morally indefensible to subject them to the cruelty of "factory farming." Since the meat available in our society is produced in just this way, we are morally obliged not to eat it. R. G. Frey, in a reading in this chapter, labels this *the argument from pain and suffering*. (2) It is morally wrong to kill animals for food, however painless the killing; animals, like human beings, have a right to life. Regan's approach in this chapter exemplifies this second line of reasoning, which Frey labels *the argument from moral rights*. A different approach to vegetarianism, also discussed by Frey, is related to material in Chapter 11. According to this approach, what is required is a fundamental shift in our attitudes toward animals and the rest of the natural world, such that any eating of animal flesh is morally unacceptable, regardless of how animals are raised or killed.

ANIMAL EXPERIMENTATION

The use of animals in scientific experimentation intended to benefit human beings raises its own set of troubling questions. Is there any need to use animals in experimentation intended to benefit human beings? If there is a genuine need, can this provide a moral justification for the resulting pain, or even death, of animals? It is possible to distinguish four major lines of reasoning on the morality of animal experimentation: (1) Animal experimentation is never justified because using animals in this way is inconsistent with treating them with the respect due to entities having inherent worth. Entities of this sort cannot be used merely as things for others' benefit. Just as the use of human beings in experiments without their informed consent violates their right to be treated with the respect due those with inherent value, so, too, does the use of animals in experiments conducted in order to benefit humans. This first line of reasoning is in keeping with Regan's position. (2) Animal experimentation is justified only in those cases where we would be willing to conduct the same experiments on brain-damaged human subjects. This is Singer's claim. The underlying reasoning here can be expressed as follows: There may be relevant differences between "normal, adult" humans and animals that would justify our using the latter but not the former in some experiments—those that might be essential to save human lives or prevent great suffering. However, animals and certain nonparadigm humans do not differ in relevant respects. Hence, we are justified in using the former in experiments only where we are justified in using the latter. (3) Given sufficiently important human interests, the presumption against using animals as experimental subjects may be overridden. Although animals, because of their sentience, have rights, which must be taken into account, serious human interests can override them. The rights of nonparadigm humans cannot be overridden on the same grounds, however, since their rights are grounded not only in sentience but in other considerations. Warren's article exemplifies this third line of argument. (4) Animal experimentation for the benefit of humans is justifiable simply by appeal to human rights and interests. However, although animals do not have rights, not every experiment using animals is morally acceptable. If the same results could be achieved by using alternative methods (e.g., computer simulation), for example, then it would be morally wrong to conduct an experiment that inflicts needless suffering on animals. Cohen accepts this fourth position. He states, however, that it would be a mistake to think that alternative techniques could shortly replace most of the present experimentation using live animals as subjects.

Jane S. Zembaty

All Animals Are Equal

Peter Singer

Singer rejects speciesism, which he defines as a prejudice or an attitude of bias in favor of the interests of members of one's own species and against those of members of other species. In his view, speciesism is analogous to racism and sexism. Just as we have a moral obligation to give equal consideration to the interests of all human beings, regardless of sex or skin color, so, too, we have a moral obligation to give equal consideration to the interests of animals. Insofar as animals, like humans, have the capacity to suffer, they have an interest in not suffering. Not to take that interest into account is speciesist and immoral. Singer attacks our current practice of using animals in experiments that frequently inflict tremendous suffering, often for very trivial reasons. As a guiding principle for determining when an experiment using animals might be morally justifiable, Singer suggests that an experiment is justifiable only if it is so important that the use of brain-damaged humans would also be justifiable.

"Animal Liberation" may sound more like a parody of other liberation movements than a serious objective. The idea of "The Rights of Animals" actually was once used to parody the case for women's rights. When Mary Wollstonecraft, a forerunner of today's feminists, published her *Vindication of the Rights of Woman* in 1792, her views were widely regarded as absurd, and before long an anonymous publication appeared entitled *A Vindication of the Rights of Brutes*. The author of this satirical work (now known to have been Thomas Taylor, a distinguished Cambridge philosopher) tried to refute Mary Wollstonecraft's arguments by showing that they could be carried one stage further. If the argument for equality was sound when applied to women, why should it not be applied to dogs, cats, and horses? The reasoning seemed to hold for these "brutes" too; yet to hold that brutes had rights was manifestly absurd. Therefore the reasoning by which this conclusion had been reached must be unsound, and if unsound when applied to brutes, it must also be unsound when applied to women, since the very same arguments had been used in each case.

Reprinted with permission of the author from *Animal Liberation,* New York Review, second edition (1990), pp. 1–9, 36–37, 40, 81–83, 85–86.

In order to explain the basis of the case for the equality of animals, it will be helpful to start with an examination of the case for the equality of women. Let us assume that we wish to defend the case for women's rights against the attack by Thomas Taylor. How should we reply?

One way in which we might reply is by saying that the case for equality between men and women cannot validly be extended to nonhuman animals. Women have a right to vote, for instance, because they are just as capable of making rational decisions about the future as men are; dogs, on the other hand, are incapable of understanding the significance of voting, so they cannot have the right to vote. There are many other obvious ways in which men and women resemble each other closely, while humans and animals differ greatly. So, it might be said, men and women are similar beings and should have similar rights, while humans and nonhumans are different and should not have equal rights.

The reasoning behind this reply to Taylor's analogy is correct up to a point, but it does not go far enough. There are obviously important differences between humans and other animals, and these differences must give rise to some differences in the rights that each have. Recognizing this evident fact, however, is no barrier to the case for extending the basic principle of equality to nonhuman animals. The differences that exist between men and women are equally undeniable, and the supporters of Women's Liberation are aware that these differences may give rise to different rights. Many feminists hold that women have the right to an abortion on request. It does not follow that since these same feminists are campaigning for equality between men and women they must support the right of men to have abortions too. Since a man cannot have an abortion, it is meaningless to talk of his right to have one. Since dogs can't vote, it is meaningless to talk of their right to vote. There is no reason why either Women's Liberation or Animal Liberation should get involved in such nonsense. The extension of the basic principle of equality from one group to another does not imply that we must treat both groups in exactly the same way, or grant exactly the same rights to both groups. Whether we should do so will depend on the nature of the members of the two groups. The basic principle of equality does not require equal or identical *treatment;* it requires equal consideration. Equal consideration for different beings may lead to different treatment and different rights.

So there is a different way of replying to Taylor's attempt to parody the case for women's rights, a way that does not deny the obvious differences between human beings and nonhumans but goes more deeply into the question of equality and concludes by finding nothing absurd in the idea that the basic principle of equality applies to so-called brutes. At this point such a conclusion may appear odd; but if we examine more deeply the basis on which our opposition to discrimination on grounds of race or sex ultimately rests, we will see that we would be on shaky ground if we were to demand equality for blacks, women, and other groups of oppressed humans while denying equal consideration to nonhumans. To make this clear we need to see, first, exactly why racism and sexism are wrong. When we say that all human beings, whatever their race, creed, or sex, are equal, what is it that we are asserting? Those who wish to defend hierarchical, inegalitarian societies have often pointed out that by whatever test we choose it simply is not true that all

humans are equal. Like it or not we must face the fact that humans come in different shapes and sizes; they come with different moral capacities, different intellectual
abilities, different amounts of benevolent feeling and sensitivity to the needs of others, different abilities to communicate effectively, and different capacities to experience pleasure and pain. In short, if the demand for equality were based on the actual
equality of all human beings, we would have to stop demanding equality.

Still, one might cling to the view that the demand for equality among human
beings is based on the actual equality of the different races and sexes. Although, it
may be said, humans differ as individuals, there are no differences between the races
and sexes as such. From the mere fact that a person is black or a woman we cannot
infer anything about that person's intellectual or moral capacities. This, it may be
said, is why racism and sexism are wrong. The white racist claims that whites are
superior to blacks, but this is false; although there are differences among individuals, some blacks are superior to some whites in all of the capacities and abilities that
could conceivably be relevant. The opponent of sexism would say the same: a person's sex is no guide to his or her abilities, and this is why it is unjustifiable to discriminate on the basis of sex.

The existence of individual variations that cut across the lines of race or sex, however, provides us with no defense at all against a more sophisticated opponent of
equality, one who proposes that, say, the interests of all those with IQ scores below
100 be given less consideration than the interests of those with ratings over 100.
Perhaps those scoring below the mark would, in this society, be made the slaves of
those scoring higher. Would a hierarchical society of this sort really be so much better than one based on race or sex? I think not. But if we tie the moral principle of
equality to the factual equality of the different races or sexes, taken as a whole, our
opposition to racism and sexism does not provide us with any basis for objecting to
this kind of inegalitarianism.

There is a second important reason why we ought not to base our opposition to
racism and sexism on any kind of factual equality, even the limited kind that asserts
that variations in capacities and abilities are spread evenly among the different
races and between the sexes: we can have no absolute guarantee that these capacities and abilities really are distributed evenly, without regard to race or sex, among
human beings. So far as actual abilities are concerned there do seem to be certain
measurable differences both among races and between sexes. These differences do
not, of course, appear in every case, but only when averages are taken. More important still, we do not yet know how many of these differences are really due to the
different genetic endowments of the different races and sexes, and how many are
due to poor schools, poor housing, and other factors that are the result of past and
continuing discrimination. Perhaps all of the important differences will eventually
prove to be environmental rather than genetic. Anyone opposed to racism and sexism will certainly hope that this will be so, for it will make the task of ending discrimination a lot easier; nevertheless, it would be dangerous to rest the case against
racism and sexism on the belief that all significant differences are environmental in
origin. The opponent of, say, racism who takes this line will be unable to avoid
conceding that if differences in ability did after all prove to have some genetic connection with race, racism would in some way be defensible.

Fortunately there is no need to pin the case for equality to one particular outcome of a scientific investigation. The appropriate response to those who claim to have found evidence of genetically based differences in ability among the races or between the sexes is not to stick to the belief that the genetic explanation must be wrong, whatever evidence to the contrary may turn up; instead we should make it quite clear that the claim to equality does not depend on intelligence, moral capacity, physical strength, or similar matters of fact. Equality is a moral idea, not an assertion of fact. There is no logically compelling reason for assuming that a factual difference in ability between two people justifies any difference in the amount of consideration we give to their needs and interests. *The principle of the equality of human beings is not a description of an alleged actual equality among humans: it is a prescription of how we should treat human beings.*

Jeremy Bentham, the founder of the reforming utilitarian school of moral philosophy, incorporated the essential basis of moral equality into his system of ethics by means of the formula: "Each to count for one and none for more than one." In other words, the interests of every being affected by an action are to be taken into account and given the same weight as the like interests of any other being. A later utilitarian, Henry Sidgwick, put the point in this way: "The good of any one individual is of no more importance, from the point of view (if I may say so) of the Universe, than the good of any other." More recently the leading figures in contemporary moral philosophy have shown a great deal of agreement in specifying as a fundamental presupposition of their moral theories some similar requirement that works to give everyone's interests equal consideration—although these writers generally cannot agree on how this requirement is best formulated.[1]

It is an implication of this principle of equality that our concern for others and our readiness to consider their interests ought not to depend on what they are like or on what abilities they may possess. Precisely what our concern or consideration requires us to do may vary according to the characteristics of those affected by what we do: concern for the well-being of children growing up in America would require that we teach them to read; concern for the well-being of pigs may require no more than that we leave them with other pigs in a place where there is adequate food and room to run freely. But the basic element—the taking into account of the interests of the being, whatever those interests may be—must, according to the principle of equality, be extended to all beings, black or white, masculine or feminine, human or nonhuman.

Thomas Jefferson, who was responsible for writing the principle of the equality of men into the American Declaration of Independence, saw this point. It led him to oppose slavery even though he was unable to free himself fully from his slaveholding background. He wrote in a letter to the author of a book that emphasized the notable intellectual achievements of Negroes in order to refute the then common view that they had limited intellectual capacities:

> Be assured that no person living wishes more sincerely than I do, to see a complete refutation of the doubts I myself have entertained and expressed on the grade of understanding allotted to them by nature, and to find that they are on a par with ourselves . . . but whatever be their degree of talent it is no measure of their rights. Because Sir Isaac Newton was superior to others in understanding, he was not therefore lord of the property or persons of others.[2]

Similarly, when in the 1850s the call for women's rights was raised in the United States, a remarkable black feminist named Sojourner Truth made the same point in more robust terms at a feminist convention:

> They talk about this thing in the head; what do they call it? ["Intellect," whispered someone nearby.] That's it. What's that got to do with women's rights or Negroes' rights? If my cup won't hold but a pint and yours holds a quart, wouldn't you be mean not to let me have my little half-measure full?[3]

It is on this basis that the case against racism and the case against sexism must both ultimately rest; and it is in accordance with this principle that the attitude that we may call "speciesism," by analogy with racism, must also be condemned. Speciesism—the word is not an attractive one, but I can think of no better term—is a prejudice or attitude of bias in favor of the interests of members of one's own species and against those of members of other species. It should be obvious that the fundamental objections to racism and sexism made by Thomas Jefferson and Sojourner Truth apply equally to speciesism. If possessing a higher degree of intelligence does not entitle one human to use another for his or her own ends, how can it entitle humans to exploit nonhumans for the same purpose?[4]

Many philosophers and other writers have proposed the principle of equal consideration of interests, in some form or other, as a basic moral principle; but not many of them have recognized that this principle applies to members of other species as well as to our own. Jeremy Bentham was one of the few who did realize this. In a forward-looking passage written at a time when black slaves had been freed by the French but in the British dominions were still being treated in the way we now treat animals, Bentham wrote:

> The day *may* come when the rest of the animal creation may acquire those rights which never could have been withholden from them but by the hand of tyranny. The French have already discovered that the blackness of the skin is no reason why a human being should be abandoned without redress to the caprice of a tormentor. It may one day come to be recognized that the number of the legs, the villosity of the skin, or the termination of the *os sacrum* are reasons equally insufficient for abandoning a sensitive being to the same fate. What else is it that should trace the insuperable line? Is it the faculty of reason, or perhaps the faculty of discourse? But a full-grown horse or dog is beyond comparison a more rational, as well as a more conversable animal, than an infant of a day or a week or even a month, old. But suppose they were otherwise, what would it avail? The question is not, Can they *reason*? nor Can they *talk*? but, Can they *suffer*?[5]

In this passage Bentham points to the capacity for suffering as the vital characteristic that gives a being the right to equal consideration. The capacity for suffering—or more strictly, for suffering and/or enjoyment or happiness—is not just another characteristic like the capacity for language or higher mathematics. Bentham is not saying that those who try to mark "the insuperable line" that determines whether the interests of a being should be considered happen to have chosen the wrong characteristic. By saying that we must consider the interests of all beings with the capacity for suffering or enjoyment Bentham does not arbitrarily exclude from consideration any interests at all—as those who draw the line with reference to the possession of reason or language do. The capacity for suffering and enjoyment is *a prerequisite for having interests at all,* a condition that must be satisfied before we can speak of interests in a meaningful way. It would be nonsense to say that it was not in the interests of a stone to be kicked along the road by a schoolboy. A stone does not have interests because it cannot suffer. Nothing that we can do to it could possibly make any difference to its welfare. The capacity for suffering and enjoyment is, however, not only necessary, but also sufficient for us to say that a being has interests—at an absolute minimum, an interest in not suffering. A mouse, for example, does have an interest in not being kicked along the road, because it will suffer if it is.

Although Bentham speaks of "rights" in the passage I have quoted, the argument is really about equality rather than about rights. Indeed, in a different passage, Bentham famously described "natural rights" as "nonsense" and "natural and imprescriptable rights" as "nonsense upon stilts." He talked of moral rights as a shorthand way of referring to protections that people and animals morally ought to have; but the real weight of the moral argument does not rest on the assertion of the existence of the right, for this in turn has to be justified on the basis of the possibilities for suffering and happiness. In this way we can argue for equality for animals without getting embroiled in philosophical controversies about the ultimate nature of rights.

In misguided attempts to refute the arguments of this book, some philosophers have gone to much trouble developing arguments to show that animals do not have rights.[6] They have claimed that to have rights a being must be autonomous, or must be a member of a community, or must have the ability to respect the rights of others, or must possess a sense of justice. These claims are irrelevant to the case for Animal Liberation. The language of rights is a convenient political shorthand. It is even more valuable in the era of thirty-second TV news clips than it was in Bentham's day; but in the argument for a radical change in our attitude to animals, it is in no way necessary.

If a being suffers there can be no moral justification for refusing to take that suffering into consideration. No matter what the nature of the being, the principle of equality requires that its suffering be counted equally with the like suffering— insofar as rough comparisons can be made—of any other being. If a being is not capable of suffering, or of experiencing enjoyment or happiness, there is nothing to be taken into account. So the limit of sentience (using the term as a convenient if not strictly accurate shorthand for the capacity to suffer and/or experience enjoyment) is the only defensible boundary of concern for the interests of others. To mark this boundary by some other characteristic like intelligence or rationality would be to mark it in an arbitrary manner. Why not choose some other characteristic, like skin color?

Racists violate the principle of equality by giving greater weight to the interests of members of their own race when there is a clash between their interests and the interests of those of another race. Sexists violate the principle of equality by favoring the interests of their own sex. Similarly, speciesists allow the interests of their own species to override the greater interests of members of other species. The pattern is identical in each case.

ANIMALS AND RESEARCH

Most human beings are speciesists. . . . Ordinary human beings—not a few exceptionally cruel or heartless humans, but the overwhelming majority of humans—take an active part in, acquiesce in, and allow their taxes to pay for practices that require the sacrifice of the most important interests of members of other species in order to promote the most trivial interests of our own species. . . .

The practice of experimenting on nonhuman animals as it exists today throughout the world reveals the consequences of speciesism. Many experiments inflict severe pain without the remotest prospect of significant benefits for human beings or any other animals. Such experiments are not isolated instances, but part of a major industry. In Britain, where experimenters are required to report the number of "scientific procedures" performed on animals, official government figures show that 3.5 million scientific procedures were performed on animals in 1988.[7] In the United States there are no figures of comparable accuracy. Under the Animal Welfare Act, the U.S. secretary of agriculture publishes a report listing the number of animals used by facilities registered with it, but this is incomplete in many ways. It does not include rats, mice, birds, reptiles, frogs, or domestic farm animals used for experimental purposes; it does not include animals used in secondary schools; and it does not include experiments performed by facilities that do not transport animals interstate or receive grants or contracts from the federal government.

In 1986 the U.S. Congress Office of Technology Assessment (OTA) published a report entitled "Alternatives to Animal Use in Research, Testing and Education." The OTA researchers attempted to determine the number of animals used in experimentation in the U.S. and reported that "estimates of the animals used in the United States each year range from 10 million to upwards of 100 million." They concluded that the estimates were unreliable but their best guess was "at least 17 million to 22 million."[8]

This is an extremely conservative estimate. In testimony before Congress in 1966, the Laboratory Animal Breeders Association estimated that the number of mice, rats, guinea pigs, hamsters, and rabbits used for experimental purposes in 1965 was around 60 million.[9] In 1984 Dr. Andrew Rowan of Tufts University School of Veterinary Medicine estimated that approximately 71 million animals are used each year. In 1985 Rowan revised his estimates to distinguish between the number of animals produced, acquired, and actually used. This yielded an estimate of between 25 and 35 million animals used in experiments each year.[10] (This figure omits animals who die in shipping or are killed before the experiment begins.) A stock market analysis of just one major supplier of animals to laboratories, the Charles River Breeding Laboratory, stated that this company alone produced 22 million laboratory animals annually.[11]

The 1988 report issued by the Department of Agriculture listed 140,471 dogs, 42,271 cats, 51,641 primates, 431,457 guinea pigs, 331,945 hamsters, 459,254 rabbits, and 178,249 "wild animals": a total of 1,635,288 used in experimentation.

Remember that this report does not bother to count rats and mice, and covers at most an estimated 10 percent of the total number of animals used. Of the nearly 1.6 million animals reported by the Department of Agriculture to have been used for experimental purposes, over 90,000 are reported to have experienced "unrelieved pain or distress." Again, this is probably at most 10 percent of the total number of animals suffering unrelieved pain and distress—and if experimenters are less concerned about causing unrelieved pain to rats and mice than they are to dogs, cats, and primates, it could be an even smaller proportion.

Other developed nations all use large numbers of animals. In Japan, for example, a very incomplete survey published in 1988 produced a total in excess of eight million.[12] . . .

Among the tens of millions of experiments performed, only a few can possibly be regarded as contributing to important medical research. Huge numbers of animals are used in university departments such as forestry and psychology; many more are used for commercial purposes, to test new cosmetics, shampoos, food coloring agents, and other inessential items. All this can happen only because of our prejudice against taking seriously the suffering of a being who is not a member of our own species. Typically, defenders of experiments on animals do not deny that animals suffer. They cannot deny the animals' suffering, because they need to stress the similarities between humans and other animals in order to claim that their experiments may have some relevance for human purposes. The experimenter who forces rats to choose between starvation and electric shock to see if they develop ulcers (which they do) does so because the rat has a nervous system very similar to a human being's, and presumably feels an electric shock in a similar way.

There has been opposition to experimenting on animals for a long time. This opposition has made little headway because experimenters, backed by commercial firms that profit by supplying laboratory animals and equipment, have been able to convince legislators and the public that opposition comes from uninformed fanatics who consider the interests of animals more important than the interests of human beings. But to be opposed to what is going on now it is not necessary to insist that all animal experiments stop immediately. All we need to say is that experiments serving no direct and urgent purpose should stop immediately, and in the remaining fields of research, we should whenever possible, seek to replace experiments that involve animals with alternative methods that do not. . . .

When are experiments on animals justifiable? Upon learning of the nature of many of the experiments carried out, some people react by saying that all experiments on animals should be prohibited immediately. But if we make our demands as absolute as this, the experimenters have a ready reply: Would we be prepared to let thousands of humans die if they could be saved by a single experiment on a single animal?

This question is, of course, purely hypothetical. There has never been and never could be a single experiment that saved thousands of lives. The way to reply to this hypothetical question is to pose another: Would the experimenters be prepared to carry out their experiment on a human orphan under six months old if that were the only way to save thousands of lives?

If the experimenters would not be prepared to use a human infant then their readiness to use nonhuman animals reveals an unjustifiable form of discrimination on the basis of species, since adult apes, monkeys, dogs, cats, rats, and other animals are more aware of what is happening to them, more self-directing, and, so far as we can tell, at least as sensitive to pain as a human infant. (I have specified that the human infant be an orphan, to avoid the complications of the feelings of parents. Specifying the case in this way is, if anything, overgenerous to those defending the use of nonhuman animals in experiments, since mammals intended for experimental use are usually separated from their mothers at an early age, when the separation causes distress for both mother and young.)

So far as we know, human infants possess no morally relevant characteristic to a higher degree than adult nonhuman animals, unless we are to count the infants' potential as a characteristic that makes it wrong to experiment on them. Whether this characteristic should count is controversial—if we count it, we shall have to condemn abortion along with experiments on infants, since the potential of the infant and the fetus is the same. To avoid the complexities of this issue, however, we can alter our original question a little and assume that the infant is one with irreversible brain damage so severe as to rule out any mental development beyond the level of a six-month-old infant. There are, unfortunately, many such human beings, locked away in special wards throughout the country, some of them long since abandoned by their parents and other relatives, and, sadly, sometimes unloved by anyone else. Despite their mental deficiencies, the anatomy and physiology of these infants are in nearly all respects identical with those of normal humans. If, therefore, we were to force-feed them with large quantities of floor polish or drip concentrated solutions of cosmetics into their eyes [as has been done in experiments using animals], we would have a much more reliable indication of the safety of these products for humans than we now get by attempting to extrapolate the results of tests on a variety of other species. . . .

So whenever experimenters claim that their experiments are important enough to justify the use of animals, we should ask them whether they would be prepared to use a brain-damaged human being at a similar mental level to the animals they are planning to use. I cannot imagine that anyone would seriously propose carrying out the experiments described in this chapter on brain-damaged human beings. Occasionally it has become known that medical experiments have been performed on human beings without their consent; one case did concern institutionalized intellectually disabled children, who were given hepatitis. When such harmful experiments on human beings become known, they usually lead to an outcry against the experimenters, and rightly so. They are, very often, a further example of the arrogance of the research worker who justifies everything on the grounds of increasing knowledge. But if the experimenter claims that the experiment is important enough to justify inflicting suffering on animals, why is it not important enough to justify inflicting suffering on humans at the same mental level? What difference is there between the two? Only that one is a member of our species and the other is not? But to appeal to that difference is to reveal a bias no more defensible than racism or any other form of arbitrary discrimination. . . .

We have still not answered the question of when an experiment might be justifiable. It will not do to say "Never!" Putting morality in such black-and-white terms is appealing, because it eliminates the need to think about particular cases; but in extreme circumstances, such absolutist answers always break down. Torturing a human being is almost always wrong, but it is not absolutely wrong. If torture were the only way in which we could discover the location of a nuclear bomb hidden in a New York City basement and timed to go off within the hour, then torture would be justifiable. Similarly, if a single experiment could cure a disease like leukemia, that experiment would be justifiable. But in actual life the benefits are always more remote, and more often than not they are nonexistent. So how do we decide when an experiment is justifiable?

We have seen that experimenters reveal a bias in favor of their own species whenever they carry out experiments on nonhumans for purposes that they would not think justified them in using human beings, even brain-damaged ones. This principle gives us a guide toward an answer to our question. Since a speciesist bias, like a racist bias, is unjustifiable, an experiment cannot be justifiable unless the experiment is so important that the use of a brain-damaged human would also be justifiable.

This is not an absolutist principle. I do not believe that it could never be justifiable to experiment on a brain-damaged human. If it really were possible to save several lives by an experiment that would take just one life, and there were no other way those lives could be saved, it would be right to do the experiment. But this would be an extremely rare case. Admittedly, as with any dividing line, there would be a gray area where it was difficult to decide if an experiment could be justified. But we need not get distracted by such considerations now. . . . We are in the midst of an emergency in which appalling suffering is being inflicted on millions of animals for purposes that on any impartial view are obviously inadequate to justify the suffering. When we have ceased to carry out all those experiments, then there will be time enough to discuss what to do about the remaining ones which are claimed to be essential to save lives or prevent greater suffering. . . .

NOTES

1 For Bentham's moral philosophy, see his *Introduction to the Principles of Morals and Legislation,* and for Sidgwick's see *The Methods of Ethics,* 1907 (the passage is quoted from the seventh edition; reprint, London: Macmillan, 1963), p. 382. As examples of leading contemporary moral philosophers who incorporate a requirement of equal consideration of interests, see R. M. Hare, *Freedom and Reason* (New York: Oxford University Press, 1963), and John Rawls, *A Theory of Justice* (Cambridge: Harvard University Press, Belknap Press, 1972). For a brief account of the essential agreement on this issue between these and other positions, see R. M. Hare, "Rules of War and Moral Reasoning," *Philosophy and Public Affairs* 1 (2) (1972).

2 Letter to Henry Gregoire, February 25, 1809.

3 Reminiscences by Francis D. Gage, from Susan B. Anthony, *The History of Woman Suffrage,* vol. 1; the passage is to be found in the extract in Leslie Tanner, ed., *Voices from Women's Liberation* (New York: Signet, 1970).

4 I owe the term "speciesism" to Richard Ryder. It has become accepted in general use since the first edition of this book, and now appears in *The Oxford English Dictionary,* second edition (Oxford: Clarendon Press, 1989).

5 *Introduction to the Principles of Morals and Legislation,* chapter 17.

6 See M. Levin, "Animal Rights Evaluated," *Humanist* 37:14–15 (July/August 1977); M. A. Fox, "Animal Liberation: A Critique," *Ethics* 88: 134–138 (1978); C. Perry and G. E. Jones, "On Animal Rights," *International Journal of Applied Philosophy* 1: 39–57 (1982).

7 *Statistics of Scientific Procedures on Living Animals, Great Britain, 1988,* Command Paper 743 (London: Her Majesty's Stationery Office, 1989).

8 U.S. Congress Office of Technology Assessment, *Alternatives to Animal Use in Research, Testing and Education* (Washington, D.C.: Government Printing Office, 1986), p. 64.

9 Hearings before the Subcommittee on Livestock and Feed Grains of the Committee on Agriculture, U.S. House of Representatives, 1966, p. 63.

10 See A. Rowan, *Of Mice, Models and Men* (Albany: State University of New York Press, 1984), p. 71; his later revision is in a personal communication to the Office of Technology Assessment; see *Alternatives to Animal Use in Research, Testing and Education,* p. 56.

11 OTA, *Alternatives to Animal Use in Research, Testing and Education,* p. 56.

12 *Experimental Animals* 37: 105 (1988).

QUESTIONS

1 Is speciesism analogous to sexism and racism? Why or why not?

2 Has Singer advanced convincing reasons in support of the claim that an experiment using animals cannot be justifiable unless the experiment is so important that the use of a brain-damaged human would also be justifiable?

The Case for Animal Rights

Tom Regan

Like Singer, Regan attacks speciesism. In his view, animals, like humans, have rights, which are violated when they are not treated with the respect due to beings who have inherent value. Regan maintains not only that animals, like humans, have inherent value but also that all beings that have inherent value have it equally. In his view, any attempt to specify a characteristic, such as intelligence, as a basis for attributing a lesser degree of inherent value to animals must be rejected, since consistency in our moral reasoning would require us to attribute a lesser degree of inherent value to some human beings. Regan concludes by calling for the abolition of all scientific experiments using animals and the dissolution of all commercial animal agriculture.

Reprinted with permission of Basil Blackwell, Inc. from *In Defense of Animals* (1985), edited by Peter Singer, pp. 13–15, 21–25.

I regard myself as an advocate of animal rights—as a part of the animal rights movement. That movement, as I conceive it, is committed to a number of goals, including:

- the total abolition of the use of animals in science;
- the total dissolution of commercial animal agriculture;
- the total elimination of commercial and sport hunting and trapping.

There are, I know, people who profess to believe in animal rights but do not avow these goals. Factory farming, they say, is wrong—it violates animals' rights—but traditional animal agriculture is all right. Toxicity tests of cosmetics on animals violate their rights, but important medical research—cancer research, for example—does not. The clubbing of baby seals is abhorrent, but not the harvesting of adult seals. I used to think I understood this reasoning. Not any more. You don't change unjust institutions by tidying them up.

What's wrong—fundamentally wrong—with the way animals are treated isn't the details that vary from case to case. It's the whole system. The forlornness of the veal calf is pathetic, heart wrenching; the pulsing pain of the chimp with electrodes planted deep in her brain is repulsive; the slow, tortuous death of the racoon caught in the leg-hold trap is agonizing. But what is wrong isn't the pain, isn't the suffering, isn't the deprivation. These compound what's wrong. Sometimes—often—they make it much, much worse. But they are not the fundamental wrong.

The fundamental wrong is the system that allows us to view animals as *our resources,* here for *us*—to be eaten, or surgically manipulated, or exploited for sport or money. Once we accept this view of animals—as our resources—the rest is as predictable as it is regrettable. Why worry about their loneliness, their pain, their death? Since animals exist for us, to benefit us in one way or another, what harms them really doesn't matter—or matters only if it starts to bother us, makes us feel a trifle uneasy when we eat our veal escalope, for example. So, yes, let us get veal calves out of solitary confinement, give them more space, a little straw, a few companions. But let us keep our veal escalope.

But a little straw, more space and a few companions won't eliminate—won't even touch—the basic wrong that attaches to our viewing and treating these animals as our resources. A veal calf killed to be eaten after living in close confinement is viewed and treated in this way: but so, too, is another who is raised (as they say) 'more humanely'. To right the wrong of our treatment of farm animals requires more than making rearing methods 'more humane'; it requires the total dissolution of commercial animal agriculture.

How we do this, whether we do it or, as in the case of animals in science, whether and how we abolish their use—these are to a large extent political questions. People must change their beliefs before they change their habits. Enough people, especially those elected to public office, must believe in change—must want it—before we will have laws that protect the rights of animals. This process of change is very complicated, very demanding, very exhausting, calling for the efforts of many hands in education, publicity, political organization and activity, down to the licking of envelopes and stamps. As a trained and practising philosopher, the sort of contribution I can make is limited but, I like to think, important. The currency of philosophy is ideas—their meaning and rational foundation—not the nuts and bolts of the legislative process, say, or the mechanics of community organization. That's what I have been exploring over the past ten years or so in my essays and talks and, most recently, in my book, *The Case for Animal Rights*. I believe the major conclusions I reach in the book are true because they are supported by the weight of the best arguments. I believe the idea of animal rights has reason, not just emotion, on its side.

In the space I have at my disposal here I can only sketch, in the barest outline, some of the main features of the book. Its main themes—and we should not be surprised by this—involve asking and answering deep, foundational moral questions about what morality is, how it should be understood and what is the best moral theory, all considered. I hope I can convey something of the shape I think this theory takes. . . .

What to do? Where to begin? . . . Suppose we consider that you and I, for example, do have value as individuals—what we'll call *inherent value*. To say we have such value is to say that we are something more than, something different from, mere receptacles. Moreover, to ensure that we do not pave the way for such injustices as slavery or sexual discrimination, we must believe that all who have inherent value have it equally, regardless of their sex, race, religion, birthplace and so on. Similarly to be discarded as irrelevant are one's talents or skills, intelligence and wealth, personality or pathology, whether one is loved and admired or despised and loathed. The genius and the retarded child, the prince and the pauper, the brain surgeon and the fruit vendor, Mother Teresa and the most unscrupulous used-car salesman—all have inherent value, all possess it equally, and all have an equal right to be treated with respect, to be treated in ways that do not reduce them to the status of things, as if they existed as resources for others. My value as an individual is independent of my usefulness to you. Yours is not dependent on your usefulness to me. For either of us to treat the other in ways that fail to show respect for the other's independent value is to act immorally, to violate the individual's rights.

Some of the rational virtues of this view—what I call the rights view—should be evident. . . . For example, the rights view *in principle* denies the moral tolerability of any and all forms of racial, sexual or social discrimination; and . . . this view *in principle* denies that we can justify good results by using evil means that violate an individual's rights—denies, for example, that it could be moral to kill my Aunt Bea to harvest beneficial consequences for others. That would be to sanction the disrespectful treatment of the individual in the name of the social good, something the rights view will not—categorically will not—ever allow.

The rights view, I believe, is rationally the most satisfactory moral theory. It surpasses all other theories in the degree to which it illuminates and explains the foundation of our duties to one another—the domain of human morality. On this score it has the best reasons, the best arguments, on its side. Of course, if it were possible to show that only human beings are included within its scope, then a person like myself, who believes in animal rights, would be obliged to look elsewhere.

But attempts to limit its scope to humans only can be shown to be rationally defective. Animals, it is true, lack many of the abilities humans possess. They can't read, do higher mathematics, build a bookcase or make *baba ghanoush*.

Neither can many human beings, however, and yet we don't (and shouldn't) say that they (these humans) therefore have less inherent value, less of a right to be treated with respect, than do others. It is the *similarities* between those human beings who most clearly, most non-controversially have such value (the people reading this, for example), not our differences, that matter most. And the really crucial, the basic similarity is simply this: we are each of us the experiencing subject of a life, a conscious creature having an individual welfare that has importance to us whatever our usefulness to others. We want and prefer things, believe and feel things, recall and expect things. And all these dimensions of our life, including our pleasure and pain, our enjoyment and suffering, our satisfaction and frustration, our continued existence or our untimely death—all make a difference to the quality of our life as lived, as experienced, by us as individuals. As the same is true of those animals that concern us (the ones that are eaten and trapped, for example), they too must be viewed as the experiencing subjects of a life, with inherent value of their own.

Some there are who resist the idea that animals have inherent value. 'Only humans have such value,' they profess. How might this narrow view be defended? Shall we say that only humans have the requisite intelligence, or autonomy, or reason? But there are many, many humans who fail to meet these standards and yet are reasonably viewed as having value above and beyond their usefulness to others. Shall we claim that only humans belong to the right species, the species *Homo sapiens*? But this is blatant speciesism. Will it be said, then, that all—and only—humans have immortal souls? Then our opponents have their work cut out for them. I am myself not ill-disposed to the proposition that there are immortal souls. Personally, I profoundly hope I have one. But I would not want to rest my position on a controversial ethical issue on the even more controversial question about who or what has an immortal soul. That is to dig one's hole deeper, not to climb out. Rationally, it is better to resolve moral issues without making more controversial assumptions than are needed. The question of who has inherent value is such a question, one that is resolved more rationally without the introduction of the idea of immortal souls than by its use.

Well, perhaps some will say that animals have some inherent value, only less than we have. Once again, however, attempts to defend this view can be shown to lack rational justification. What could be the basis of our having more inherent value than animals? Their lack of reason, or autonomy, or intellect? Only if we are willing to make the same judgement in the case of humans who are similarly deficient. But it is not true that such humans—the retarded child, for example, or the mentally deranged—have less inherent value than you or I. Neither, then, can we rationally sustain the view that animals like them in being the experiencing subjects of a life have less inherent value. *All* who have inherent value have it *equally,* whether they be human animals or not.

Inherent value, then, belongs equally to those who are the experiencing subjects of a life. Whether it belongs to others—to rocks and rivers, trees and glaciers, for example—we do not know and may never know. But neither do we need to know, if we are to make the case for animal rights. We do not need to know, for example, how many people are eligible to vote in the next presidential election before we can know whether I am. Similarly, we do not need to know how many individuals have inherent value before we can know that some do. When it comes to the case for animal rights, then, what we need to know is whether the animals that, in our culture, are routinely eaten, hunted and used in our laboratories, for example, are like us in being subjects of a life. And we do know this. We do know that many—literally, billions and billions—of these animals are the subjects of a life in the sense explained and so have inherent value if we do. And since, in order to arrive at the best theory of our duties to one another, we must recognize our equal inherent value as individuals, reason—not sentiment, not emotion—reason compels us to recognize the equal inherent value of these animals and, with this, their equal right to be treated with respect.

That, *very* roughly, is the shape and feel of the case for animal rights. Most of the details of the supporting argument are missing. They are to be found in the book to which I alluded earlier. Here, the details go begging, and I must, in closing, limit myself to [one] final point. . . .

Having set out the broad outlines of the rights view, I can now say why its implications for farming and science, among other fields, are both clear and uncompromising. In the case of the use of animals in science, the rights view is categorically abolitionist. Lab animals are not our tasters; we are not their kings. Because these animals are treated routinely, systematically as if their value were reducible to their usefulness to others, they are routinely, systematically treated with a lack of respect, and thus are their rights routinely, systematically violated. This is just as true when they are used in trivial, duplicative, unnecessary or unwise research as it is when they are used in studies that hold out real promise of human benefits. We can't justify harming or killing a human being (my Aunt Bea, for example) just for these sorts of reason. Neither can we do so even in the case of so lowly a creature as a laboratory rat. It is not just refinement or reduction that is called for, not just larger, cleaner cages, not just more generous use of anaesthetic or the elimination of multiple surgery, not just tidying up the system. It is complete replacement. The best we can do when it comes to using animals in science is—not to use them. That is where our duty lies, according to the rights view.

As for commercial animal agriculture, the rights view takes a similar abolitionist position. The fundamental moral wrong here is not that animals are kept in stressful close confinement or in isolation, or that their pain and suffering, their needs and preferences are ignored or discounted. All these *are* wrong, of course, but they are not the fundamental wrong. They are symptoms and effects of the deeper, systematic wrong that allows these animals to be viewed and treated as lacking independent value, as resources for us—as, indeed, a renewable resource. Giving farm animals more space, more natural environments, more companions does not right the fundamental wrong, any more than giving lab animals more anaesthesia or bigger, cleaner cages would right the fundamental wrong in their case. Nothing less than the total dissolution of commercial animal agriculture will do this, just as, for similar reasons I won't develop at length here, morality requires nothing less than the total elimination of hunting and trapping for commercial and sporting ends. The rights view's implications, then, as I have said, are clear and uncompromising. . . .

QUESTIONS

1 Do all sentient beings have the same inherent value? Why or why not?
2 Is it always wrong to use animals in experiments intended to benefit human beings?

Moral Vegetarianism and the Argument from Pain and Suffering

R. G. Frey

Frey identifies three arguments advanced by proponents of moral vegetarianism: the argument from moral rights, the argument from killing, and the argument from pain and suffering. Frey argues that Singer and others who advance these kinds of arguments are committed only to conditional vegetarianism. That is, they are committed to the view that the wrongness of using animals for food is conditional on whether our treatment of animals in converting them into food violates their moral right to life and/or freedom from unnecessary suffering. The argument from pain and suffering, in particular, would have no force if animal raising and slaughtering practices were changed so as to eliminate both. In contrast, according to unconditional vegetarianism, it is always wrong to eat animals, irrespective of how they are raised or killed. This type of vegetarianism is rooted in a way of life—one that involves an attempt to live in harmony with everything else in the world, encroaching as little as possible on other creatures and things.

By moral vegetarianism, then, I have in mind those cases for vegetarianism which locate the moral basis for boycotting meat in our treatment of animals in rearing and converting them into food.

Modern proponents of vegetarianism on this basis have relied principally upon three arguments to show that eating meat is wrong.

The Argument from Moral Rights   This is the view that our present treatment of animals in converting them into food violates their moral right to life and/or freedom from unnecessary suffering. It is wrong to eat meat, then, because animals' moral rights have been violated in the course of their reaching our tables.

The Argument from Killing   This is the view that it is wrong to kill animals or to kill them for food, except, if at all, under conditions which few of us can pretend to be in.[1] It is wrong to eat meat because animals have undergone the irretrievable wrong of being killed, in the course of becoming food for human consumption.

Reprinted with permission of Blackwell Publishers from R. G. Frey, *Rights, Killing, and Suffering* (1983), pp. 21–23, 27, 30–35.

The Argument from Pain and Suffering   This is the view . . . that it is wrong to eat meat, because factory-farmed (and perhaps even some traditionally-farmed) animals have suffered a good deal and, thus, been wrongly treated, in the course of being turned into food. . . .

THE ARGUMENT FROM PAIN AND SUFFERING

This argument, championed by Peter Singer in *Animal Liberation*[2] and *Practical Ethics*,[3] by Stephen Clark in *The Moral Status of Animals*,[4] and by many others, moves either directly or indirectly to moral vegetarianism from the pain and suffering which animals undergo in being bred, raised, and slaughtered for food. . . .

The argument from pain and suffering, of course, has a past; its use by Singer and others is but the most recent among several. The significance it has come to have, especially under the stimulus of *Animal Liberation,* stems from its application to intensive methods of food production, to factory or commercial farming. What Singer, amongst others, has done is to give the argument new and important life, by describing how some aspects of intensive farming involve animal suffering and then using the argument to combat these farming practices.

I do not believe it betrays undue sensitivity to find certain practices employed on factory farms profoundly disturbing. To put no finer point on the matter, there are practices afoot on them, pre-eminently in the cases of laying hens and veal calves, of which we cannot be proud. Even if such practices are necessary to sustain the level of profits by which farmers, their families, the meat industry as a whole, and, through it, a very great many others prosper, we still do well not to be proud of having to resort to them. Some might suggest that the great pleasure human beings receive from consuming veal more than outweighs the suffering (no grain, no straw-bedding, no exercise, perpetual confinement in tiny slatted stalls, little muscle-growth, induced iron-deficiency and anemia, almost no daylight, tethered to prevent seeking iron and exercise)[5] which these calves undergo in reaching the table. Even so, treatment such as this is not the sort of thing in which, morally, we take pride; and if it is something required in order to sustain a level or style of life to which we have become accustomed, we still do well to be disturbed that this is so.

As information about the treatment of, for example, veal calves has been more widely disseminated, more people have come to see this treatment as wrong. But this is by no means the end or even the essence of the matter for Singer; for it is central to his position—in fact, it seems the main feature of his position—that moral vegetarianism is *the means by which each of us* can move directly to eliminate the pains of food animals. Once we come to see our treatment of veal calves as wrong, vegetarianism is seen by Singer as the means by which each of us can do something about this treatment. This emerges very clearly from the central argument of *Animal Liberation.*

Animals can suffer, and since they can suffer, they have interests. In view of this fact, the moral principle of the equal consideration of interests applies to them, and this means that we are not morally justified in setting aside, ignoring, or otherwise devaluing their interests. This, however, is precisely what some factory farming practices, with their accompaniment of animal suffering, appear to involve, and the immorality which this represents is, if anything, accentuated by the fact that we do not need meat in order to survive and to lead healthy lives.

We can, on the other hand, do something about this situation: by boycotting meat, we can draw down market forces upon the head of the factory farmer and so reduce or eliminate the suffering of food animals. When demand slackens, prices fall; when prices fall, profits diminish; and when profits diminish, the factory farmer has less capital to re-invest in food stock. (The same is true for farmers who employ traditional methods of farming.) By becoming a vegetarian, then, each of us hits directly and immediately at factory farming; for in giving up meat, we reduce the number of food animals bred and raised for market and thereby total animal suffering. Accordingly, a genuine concern for the interests of animals and so with a diminution in their suffering requires that we cease rearing animals for food and cease eating them.

The picture one carries away from Singer's book, then, is that becoming a moral vegetarian is the means by which each of us can reduce animal suffering and so help in the effort to right a wrong. Once we have identified certain farming practices as wrong, we can use vegetarianism as the tool, as the direct and immediate means for eliminating or mitigating those practices. What is more, this means is relatively painless on us, given that there are wholesome and nutritious alternatives to meat readily available. . . .

TWO CONCEPTIONS OF THE STATUS OF VEGETARIANISM

There is a curious feature of the arguments from moral rights, killing, and pain and suffering that I am sure many readers have noticed. It consists in the fact that, even if we were to regard the arguments as completely successful, they would by no means bar or eliminate all meat-eating. In this can be found the basis for distinguishing two very different conceptions of the status of vegetarianism.

Partial and Absolute Exclusions

When I first arrived at Oxford from Virginia, I became friendly with a mathematician from Calcutta. He was a vegetarian and abstained from all meat. Meals in college were very unpleasant for him, since they invariably featured meat dishes, and what vegetables there were were unappetizing, always the same, and—the great English gastronomic failure—overcooked. He regarded eating meat as an abomination; there were no circumstances—apart, perhaps from direst necessity, and even this was uncertain—in which he would allow it to be right. Eating meat was simply excluded from consideration, and there was an end to it.

The arguments from moral rights, killing, and pain and suffering do not have the same absolutely dismissive effect. The reason is that the objections which they severally pose are not actually to eating animals but to the treatment animals receive in the course of being converted into food. The result is obvious: to animals which have not undergone the treatment in question, the arguments do not apply. Thus, since the argument from moral rights makes the wrongness of violating animals' moral rights crucial, it places no objection in the way of eating meat from animals whose rights have not been violated. Someone who is a vegetarian solely on the basis of this argument, then, has no reason *per se* to abstain from such meat, any more than someone who is a vegetarian on the basis of the argument from pain and suffering has any reason *per se* to abstain from eating the flesh of animals who have not been cruelly treated in being turned into food. This does not mean, of course, that these individuals will eat the meat in question, only that they must have one more shot in their lockers, if they are going to abstain on principle from this meat as well.

To my Indian friend, this situation would appear very strange indeed. For here are purported vegetarians who, *prima facie,* have no reason not to eat this meat. *He* does not eat meat at all; eating meat is quite excluded from consideration, whether the animal has had its rights violated or been killed or been made to suffer, or whether it has simply fallen from the heavens at one's feet or miraculously appeared in one's cooking pot. To him, it would be exceedingly peculiar to think that his vegetarianism required him to look carefully into the question of whether this chicken has had its rights violated, or had dropped dead from heart seizure, or had not suffered at some point in the past, as if one as opposed to some other answer would make it right for him to eat meat. The plain fact is that, so far as *his* vegetarianism is concerned, such questions are beside the point. Conversely, to the proponents of the three arguments, these questions are very much to the point, and their vegetarianism is conditioned by the responses given in their respective cases.

To this Indian, then, proponents of the three arguments appear more exercised by rights, killing, and suffering than by eating animals. What the arguments make out to be morally wrong is not actually eating animals but violating their alleged moral rights or killing them or making them suffer. Do none of these things, and the wrongness of eating meat vanishes. Here, then, are vegetarians of whom vegetarianism is only demanded if animals are treated one way rather than another. In the case of the argument from pain and suffering, this result gives rise to a view which *prima facie* seems very strange. For there seems something odd indeed about a view which says in effect that when animals are (treated in such a way as to be) miserable they may not be eaten but when they are (treated in such a way as to be) happy and content they may be eaten. One's natural inclination would be to say the opposite, that when animals are contented, their lives are a benefit to them and that then, if ever, vegetarianism is demanded of us. . . .

Conditional and Unconditional Conceptions

If we think of the position of this Indian mathematician as unconditional vegetarianism and that of the proponents of the three arguments as conditional vegetarianism, then how might we characterize the essential difference between these two conceptions of vegetarianism?

In his paper 'Utilitarianism and vegetarianism',[6] Peter Singer objects to Cora Diamond's claim[7] that his position yields the curious result that it is perfectly permissible to eat animals which are accident victims:

> Why is this curious? It is only curious on the assumption that vegetarians must think it *always* wrong to eat meat. No doubt some vegetarians are moral absolutists, just as there are absolute pacifists, absolute anti-abortionists and absolute truth-tellers who would never tell a lie. I reject all these forms of moral absolutism.[8]

Doubtless Singer would regard unconditional vegetarians as absolutists, and doubtless there is a significant difference between my Indian friend and Singer on this score. But the suggestion of the above passage—that some people think it always wrong to eat meat, whereas others, including Singer, think it only sometimes wrong—is not quite explicit as to the full difference between them.

If we think in terms of a distinction between unconditional and conditional vegetarianism, then the point I was making earlier can be put this way: when conditions of food animal treatment are one way rather than another, conditional vegetarianism ceases to have a ground, the result of which is, in the circumstances, to remove from conditional vegetarians their reason for abstaining from meat. When conditions are one way rather than another, vegetarianism is pointless; for the whole point of conditional vegetarianism is to improve the conditions in which animals are bred, raised, and slaughtered for food, and if conditions are already of the appropriate sort, then there is no point in adopting vegetarianism as the tactic by which to make them of that sort. Here, it seems to me, is encapsulated the essence of conditional vegetarianism: it is a tactic by means of which one hopes to improve the treatment of food animals. This is especially clear in the case of Singer, who . . . regards vegetarianism based upon the argument from pain and suffering as the means by which to combat the pains of factory-farmed animals.

At the core of conditional vegetarianism, then, is a conception of vegetarianism as a tactic for combating the treatment or pains of food animals. But tactics are appropriate to circumstances, and a change in circumstances can, as we have seen, render one's tactics pointless. In the case of a conditional vegetarian, to persist in abstaining from meat, even when circumstances are of the desired sort, becomes a needless gesture.

Accordingly, to say merely that what separates my Indian friend from Singer is a form of absolutism, to say merely that conditional vegetarianism is limited (or applies only in respect of some animals) whereas unconditional vegetarianism is unlimited, leaves out any mention of the tactical conception of vegetarianism, which essentially defines the conditional position. This omission is of the utmost importance; for no one even remotely in sympathy with the views of my Indian friend could accept such a conception of vegetarianism. To this Indian, vegetarianism is something quite different: it represents a decision about how he will live in the world, a decision tantamount in part to the adoption of a way of life, for a world which contains a multiplicity of creatures and things, each as much a part of the whole as he is. It represents an attempt to live in harmony with the creatures and things he finds around him and to encroach on them as little as they on the whole encroach on him. It represents an effort to see himself as part of the world, and not a world—and law—unto himself. So far as I can see, nothing could be further from a tactical conception of vegetarianism than this conception of how we shall live in a world where we are but part of the whole, of which conception of vegetarianism is a constituent.

(Someone armed with such a conception of vegetarianism is very likely to find Singer's emphasis upon pain rather puzzling. For though my Indian friend is not indifferent to the pains of animals, it is not by virtue of the fact that they can feel pain that he thinks they warrant and obtain his respect. If asked whether it was because animals can feel pain that he tries to live in harmony with them, as one part of nature with another, he would, I think, view both the question and the questioner with deep puzzlement, not least because many portions of the whole of which he sees himself as a part *cannot* feel pain. In time, I believe he would come to think that only someone with a particular theory would seize upon pain in this way and elevate it or its avoidance to supreme importance in ethics.)

I myself am as much opposed to moral absolutisms as is Singer and, I suspect, for many of the same reasons. I have used the example of this Indian mathematician simply in order to bring out the tactical conception of vegetarianism, which lies at the heart of conditional vegetarianism, especially that of Singer.

Counter-Argument and Competing Tactics

Apart from the fact that, as we have seen, some vegetarians reject the tactical conception of vegetarianism, this conception is exposed to counter-arguments of a specific type. If we stick with Singer as our example, then these counter-arguments stem directly from the literature on utilitarianism.

The specific type of counter-argument is this: if vegetarianism is a tactic for combating the pains of food animals, then this tactic ceases to have any point whatever, if we develop ways of breeding, raising, and slaughtering animals painlessly. In this eventuality, we could eat all the meat we liked, and Singer would have no ground for complaint.

It will be claimed, however, that there is no meat available from animals which have not, in particular, been reared by painful methods. To this, there are three responses.

First, it is factually false; there are millions upon millions of animals presently being farmed but not factory-farmed. It is both tempting to argue and not obviously wrong to suggest that because traditional farming methods are held, even by vegetarians, to be vastly less painful than intensive ones, the argument from pain and suffering does not provide a reason for abstaining from the flesh of traditionally-farmed animals. . . .

Second, not all intensively farmed animals suffer to anything like the degree of veal calves, or have the same methods of production used upon them. To give but a single example, in the United States, dairy cows are commercially farmed, and when their days as milk-producers come to an end, they are sent to slaughter. However, their lives are by no means as miserable as those of veal calves.

Third, if we focus solely upon factory-farmed animals, then we can see clearly to what the tactical conception of vegetarianism finally exposes Singer. For just as not eating meat is a tactic for dealing with the pains of food animals, so, too, is the package involving, among other things, maintaining and expanding traditional farming techniques, progressivly eliminating painful practices in intensive farming, and funding research into and developing pain-killing drugs. As tactics, both are on all fours; one is not *per se* more morally correct than the other. Moreover, the latter tactic has two further attractions: first, it enables us not only to deal with animal pain but also to retain our present, meat-based diet intact, and second, it enables us to meet the claim that the heavy demand for meat today can only be satisfied by intensive methods of production.

In this way, vegetarianism, Singer's tactic, is confronted with competition. That is, we are confronted with different tactics for combating the pains of food animals, and the central issue between them becomes simply the degree of effectiveness in achieving this end. The determination of which of two tactics is more effective in lessening animal pain is not a piece of theory but a matter of fact. If technological developments succeed in the encompassing way the one tactic envisages, then it may well be, on grounds of effectiveness, the preferred one, as new and better pain-killers, administered painlessly, reach more and more animals. This very real possibility cannot be eliminated *a priori* through any theoretical considerations. This is especially true for utilitarians such as Singer, for whom it must always remain a contingent affair whether the implementation of one policy has consequences which, in comparison with those of the implementation of another, make it the preferred or right policy. Effectiveness, then, is everything, and vegetarianism must confront and defeat (or at least not be defeated by) one after another competitor on this score; it by no means is *obviously* the most effective tactic for reducing the pains of food animals, so that all potential competitors can be ignored *ab initio*. . . .

To my Indian friend, of course, all this squabbling over effectiveness is beside the point; for whether it is Singer or his opponent who has the more effective means for coming to grips with animal pain, eating meat remains an abomination, and that is that.

NOTES

1 I have in mind conditions of necessity, where the killing and eating of animals is necessary for our survival.
2 Peter Singer, *Animal Liberation,* London, Jonathan Cape, 1976.
3 Peter Singer, *Practical Ethics,* Cambridge, Cambridge University Press, 1980.
4 Stephen Clark, *The Moral Status of Animals,* Oxford, Clarendon Press, 1977.
5 Slaughter normally occurs anywhere from 12 to 15 weeks of this treatment.
6 Peter Singer, 'Utilitarianism and vegetarianism,' *Philosophy and Public Affairs,* vol. 9, 1980, pp. 325–37.
7 Cora Diamond, 'Eating meat and eating people,' *Philosophy,* vol. 53, 1978, pp. 465–79.
8 Singer, 'Utilitarianism and vegetarianism,' pp. 327–28; italics in original.

QUESTIONS

1 Is Frey correct in his claim that Singer is committed only to conditional vegetarianism?
2 Would Regan agree with Frey's understanding of the argument from moral rights?
3 Are we morally obliged to become vegetarians?

The Case for the Use of Animals
in Biomedical Research

Carl Cohen

Cohen, identifying himself as a speciesist, attacks both Singer and Regan and
defends the use of animals in biomedical research. Against Regan, Cohen argues
that animals have no rights, since they lack the capacities for free moral judgment
and for exercising or responding to moral claims. Against Singer, he maintains
that speciesism is not analogous to racism and sexism and that not all sentient
beings have equal moral standing. Furthermore, Cohen argues, we have an
obligation to enlarge the use of animals in research in the interest of protecting
potential human subjects. In his view, although we do have obligations to
animals, they have no rights against us on which research can infringe.

Using animals as research subjects in medical investigations is widely condemned
on two grounds: first, because it wrongly violates the *rights* of animals,[1] and second,
because it wrongly imposes on sentient creatures much avoidable *suffering*.[2]
Neither of these arguments is sound. The first relies on a mistaken understanding of
rights; the second relies on a mistaken calculation of consequences. Both deserve
definitive dismissal.

WHY ANIMALS HAVE NO RIGHTS

A right, properly understood, is a claim, or potential claim, that one party may exercise against another. The target against whom such a claim may be registered can be a
single person, a group, a community, or (perhaps) all humankind. The content of rights
claims also varies greatly: repayment of loans, nondiscrimination by employers, non-
interference by the state, and so on. To comprehend any genuine right fully, therefore,
we must know *who* holds the right, *against whom* it is held, and *to what* it is a right.

Alternative sources of rights add complexity. Some rights are grounded in constitution and law (e.g., the right of an accused to trial by jury); some rights are moral
but give no legal claims (e.g., my right to your keeping the promise you gave me);
and some rights (e.g., against theft or assault) are rooted both in morals and in law.

The differing targets, contents, and sources of rights, and their inevitable conflict, together weave a tangled web. Notwithstanding all such complications, this
much is clear about rights in general: they are in every case claims, or potential
claims, within a community of moral agents. Rights arise, and can be intelligibly
defended, only among beings who actually do, or can, make moral claims against
one another. Whatever else rights may be, therefore, they are necessarily human;
their possessors are persons, human beings.

Reprinted with permission from *The New England Journal of Medicine,* vol. 315 (October 2, 1986),
pp. 865–870.

The attributes of human beings from which this moral capability arises have been described variously by philosophers, both ancient and modern: the inner consciousness of a free will (Saint Augustine[3]); the grasp, by human reason, of the binding character of moral law (Saint Thomas[4]); the self-conscious participation of human beings in an objective ethical order (Hegel[5]); human membership in an organic moral community (Bradley[6]); the development of the human self through the consciousness of other moral selves (Mead[7]); and the underivative, intuitive cognition of the rightness of an action (Prichard[8]). Most influential has been Immanuel Kant's emphasis on the universal human possession of a uniquely moral will and the autonomy its use entails.[9] Humans confront choices that are purely moral; humans—but certainly not dogs or mice—lay down moral laws, for others and for themselves. Human beings are self-legislative, morally *auto-nomous.*

Animals (that is, nonhuman animals, the ordinary sense of that word) lack this capacity for free moral judgment. They are not beings of a kind capable of exercising or responding to moral claims. Animals therefore have no rights, and they can have none. This is the core of the argument about the alleged rights of animals. The holders of rights must have the capacity to comprehend rules of duty, governing all including themselves. In applying such rules, the holders of rights must recognize possible conflicts between what is in their own interest and what is just. Only in a community of beings capable of self-restricting moral judgments can the concept of a right be correctly invoked.

Humans have such moral capacities. They are in this sense self-legislative, are members of communities governed by moral rules, and do possess rights. Animals do not have such moral capacities. They are not morally self-legislative, cannot possibly be members of a truly moral community, and therefore cannot possess rights. In conducting research on animal subjects, therefore, we do not violate their rights, because they have none to violate.

To animate life, even in its simplest forms, we give a certain natural reverence. But the possession of rights presupposes a moral status not attained by the vast majority of living things. We must not infer, therefore, that a live being has, simply in being alive, a "right" to its life. The assertion that all animals, only because they are alive and have interests, also possess the "right to life"[10] is an abuse of that phrase, and wholly without warrant.

It does not follow from this, however, that we are morally free to do anything we please to animals. Certainly not. In our dealings with animals, as in our dealings with other human beings, we have obligations that do not arise from claims against us based on rights. Rights entail obligations, but many of the things one ought to do are in no way tied to another's entitlement. Rights and obligations are not reciprocals of one another, and it is a serious mistake to suppose that they are.

Illustrations are helpful. Obligations may arise from internal commitments made: physicians have obligations to their patients not grounded merely in their patients' rights. Teachers have such obligations to their students, shepherds to their dogs, and cowboys to their horses. Obligations may arise from differences of status: adults owe special care when playing with young children, and children owe special care when playing with young pets. Obligations may arise from special relationships: the payment of my son's college tuition is something to which he may have no right, although it may be my obligation to bear the burden if I reasonably can; my dog has no right to daily exercise and veterinary care, but I do have the obligation to provide these things for her. Obligations may arise from particular acts or circumstances: one may be obliged to another for a special kindness done, or obliged to put an animal out of its misery in view of its condition—although neither the human benefactor nor the dying animal may have had a claim of right.

Plainly, the grounds of our obligations to humans and to animals are manifold and cannot be formulated simply. Some hold that there is a general obligation to do no gratuitous harm to sentient creatures (the principle of nonmaleficence); some hold that there is a general obligation to do good to sentient creatures when that is reasonably within one's power (the principle of beneficence). In our dealings with animals, few will deny that we are at least obliged to act humanely—that is, to treat them with the decency and concern that we owe, as sensitive human beings, to other sentient creatures. To treat animals humanely, however, is not to treat them as humans or as the holders of rights.

A common objection, which deserves a response, may be paraphrased as follows:

> If having rights requires being able to make moral claims, to grasp and apply moral laws, then many humans—the brain-damaged, the comatose, the senile—who plainly lack those capacities must be without rights. But that is absurd. This proves [the critic concludes] that rights do not depend on the presence of moral capacities.[1,10]

This objection fails; it mistakenly treats an essential feature of humanity as though it were a screen for sorting humans. The capacity for moral judgment that distinguishes humans from animals is not a test to be administered to human beings one by one. Persons who are unable, because of some disability, to perform the full moral functions natural to human beings are certainly not for that reason ejected from the moral community. The issue is one of kind. Humans are of such a kind that they may be the subject of experiments only with their voluntary consent. The choices they make freely must be respected. Animals are of such a kind that it is impossible for them, in principle, to give or withhold voluntary consent or to make a moral choice. What humans retain when disabled, animals have never had.

A second objection, also often made, may be paraphrased as follows:

> Capacities will not succeed in distinguishing humans from the other animals. Animals also reason; animals also communicate with one another; animals also care passionately for their young; animals also exhibit desires and preferences.[11,12] Features of moral relevance—rationality, interdependence, and love—are not exhibited uniquely by human beings. Therefore [this critic concludes], there can be no solid moral distinction between humans and other animals.[10]

This criticism misses the central point. It is not the ability to communicate or to reason, or dependence on one another, or care for the young, or the exhibition of preference, or any such behavior that marks the critical divide. Analogies between human families and those of monkeys, or between human communities and those of wolves, and the like, are entirely beside the point. Patterns of conduct are not at issue. Animals do indeed exhibit remarkable behavior at times. Conditioning, fear, instinct, and intelligence all contribute to species survival. Membership in a community of moral agents nevertheless remains impossible for them. Actors subject to moral judgment must be capable of grasping the generality of an ethical premise in a practical syllogism. Humans act immorally often enough, but only they—never wolves or monkeys—can discern, by applying some moral rule to the facts of a case, that a given act ought or ought not to be performed. The moral restraints imposed by humans on themselves are thus highly abstract and are often in conflict with the self-interest of the agent. Communal behavior among animals, even when most intelligent and most endearing, does not approach autonomous morality in this fundamental sense.

Genuinely moral acts have an internal as well as an external dimension. Thus, in law, an act can be criminal only when the guilty deed, the *actus reus,* is done with a guilty mind, *mens rea.* No animal can ever commit a crime; bringing animals to criminal trial is the mark of primitive ignorance. The claims of moral right are similarly inapplicable to them. Does a lion have a right to eat a baby zebra? Does a baby zebra have a right not to be eaten? Such questions, mistakenly invoking the concept of right where it does not belong, do not make good sense. Those who condemn biomedical research because it violates "animal rights" commit the same blunder.

IN DEFENSE OF "SPECIESISM"

Abandoning reliance on animal rights, some critics resort instead to animal sentience—their feelings of pain and distress. We ought to desist from the imposition of pain insofar as we can. Since all or nearly all experimentation on animals does impose pain and could be readily forgone, say these critics, it should be stopped. The ends sought may be worthy, but those ends do not justify imposing agonies on humans, and by animals the agonies are felt no less. The laboratory use of animals (these critics conclude) must therefore be ended—or at least very sharply curtailed.

Argument of this variety is essentially utilitarian, often expressly so[13]; it is based on the calculation of the net product, in pains and pleasures, resulting from experiments on animals. Jeremy Bentham, comparing horses and dogs with other sentient creatures, is thus commonly quoted: "The question is not, Can they reason? nor Can they talk? but, Can they suffer?"[14]

Animals certainly can suffer and surely ought not to be made to suffer needlessly. But in inferring, from these uncontroversial premises, that biomedical research causing animal distress is largely (or wholly) wrong, the critic commits two serious errors.

The first error is the assumption, often explicitly defended, that all sentient animals have equal moral standing. Between a dog and a human being, according to this view, there is no moral difference; hence the pains suffered by dogs must be weighed no differently from the pains suffered by humans. To deny such equality, according to this critic, is to give unjust preference to one species over another; it is "speciesism." The most influential statement of this moral equality of species was made by Peter Singer:

The racist violates the principle of equality by giving greater weight to the interests of members of his own race when there is a clash between their interests and the interests of those of another race. The sexist violates the principle of equality by favoring the interests of his own sex. Similarly the speciesist allows the interests of his own species to override the greater interests of members of other species. The pattern is identical in each case.[2]

This argument is worse than unsound; it is atrocious. It draws an offensive moral conclusion from a deliberately devised verbal parallelism that is utterly specious. Racism has no rational ground whatever. Differing degrees of respect or concern for humans for no other reason than that they are members of different races is an injustice totally without foundation in the nature of the races themselves. Racists, even if acting on the basis of mistaken factual beliefs, do grave moral wrong precisely because there is no morally relevant distinction among the races. The supposition of such differences has led to outright horror. The same is true of the sexes, neither sex being entitled by right to greater respect or concern than the other. No dispute here.

Between species of animate life, however—between (for example) humans on the one hand and cats or rats on the other—the morally relevant differences are enormous, and almost universally appreciated. Humans engage in moral reflection; humans are morally autonomous; humans are members of moral communities, recognizing just claims against their own interest. Human beings do have rights; theirs is a moral status very different from that of cats or rats.

I am a speciesist. Speciesism is not merely plausible; it is essential for right conduct, because those who will not make the morally relevant distinctions among species are almost certain, in consequence, to misapprehend their true obligations. The analogy between speciesism and racism is insidious. Every sensitive moral judgment requires that the differing natures of the beings to whom obligations are owed be considered. If all forms of animate life—or vertebrate animal life?—must be treated equally, and if therefore in evaluating a research program the pains of a rodent count equally with the pains of a human, we are forced to conclude (1) that neither humans nor rodents possess rights, or (2) that rodents possess all the rights that humans possess. Both alternatives are absurd. Yet one or the other must be swallowed if the moral equality of all species is to be defended.

Humans owe to other humans a degree of moral regard that cannot be owed to animals. Some humans take on the obligation to support and heal others, both humans and animals, as a principal duty in their lives; the fulfillment of that duty may require the sacrifice of many animals. If biomedical investigators abandon the effective pursuit of their professional objectives because they are convinced that they may not do to animals what the service of humans requires, they will fail, objectively, to do their duty. Refusing to recognize the moral differences among species is a sure path to calamity. (The largest animal rights group in the country is People for the Ethical Treatment of Animals; its codirector, Ingrid Newkirk, calls research using animal subjects "fascism" and "supremacism." "Animal liberationists do not separate out the *human* animal," she says, "so there is no rational basis for saying that a human being has special rights. A rat is a pig is a dog is a boy. They're all mammals."[15])

Those who claim to base their objection to the use of animals in biomedical research on their reckoning of the net pleasures and pains produced make a second error, equally grave. Even if it were true—as it is surely not—that the pains of all animate beings must be counted equally, a cogent utilitarian calculation requires that we weigh all the consequences of the use, and of the nonuse, of animals in laboratory research. Critics relying (however mistakenly) on animal rights may claim to ignore the beneficial results of such research, rights being trump cards to which interest and advantage must give way. But an argument that is explicitly framed in terms of interest and benefit for all over the long run must attend also to the disadvantageous consequences of not using animals in research, and to all the achievements attained and attainable only through their use. The sum of the benefits of their use is utterly beyond quantification. The elimination of horrible disease, the increase of longevity, the avoidance of great pain, the saving of lives, and the improvement of the quality of lives (for humans and for animals) achieved through research using animals is so incalculably great that the argument of these critics, systematically pursued, establishes not their conclusion but its reverse: to refrain from using animals in biomedical research is, on utilitarian grounds, morally wrong.

When balancing the pleasures and pains resulting from the use of animals in research, we must not fail to place on the scales the terrible pains that would have resulted, would be suffered now, and would long continue had animals not been used. Every disease eliminated, every vaccine developed, every method of pain relief devised, every surgical procedure invented, every prosthetic device implanted—indeed, virtually every modern medical therapy is due, in part or in whole, to experimentation using animals. Nor may we ignore, in the balancing process, the predictable gains in human (and animal) well-being that are probably achievable in the future but that will not be achieved if the decision is made now to desist from such research or to curtail it.

Medical investigators are seldom insensitive to the distress their work may cause animal subjects. Opponents of research using animals are frequently insensitive to the cruelty of the results of the restrictions they would impose.[2] Untold numbers of human beings—real persons, although not now identifiable—would suffer grievously as the consequence of this well-meaning but shortsighted tenderness. If the morally relevant differences between humans and animals are borne in mind, and if all relevant considerations are weighed, the calculation of long-term consequences must give overwhelming support for biomedical research using animals.

CONCLUDING REMARKS

Substitution

The humane treatment of animals requires that we desist from experimenting on them if we can accomplish the same result using alternative methods—in vitro experimentation, computer simulation, or others. Critics of some experiments using animals rightly make this point.

It would be a serious error to suppose, however, that alternative techniques could soon be used in most research now using live animal subjects. No other methods now on the horizon—or perhaps ever to be available—can fully replace the testing of a drug, a procedure, or a vaccine, in live organisms. The flood of new medical possibilities being opened by the successes of recombinant DNA technology will turn to a trickle if testing on live animals is forbidden. When initial trials entail great risks, there may be no forward movement whatever without the use of live animal subjects. In seeking knowledge that may prove critical in later clinical applications, the unavailability of animals for inquiry may spell complete stymie. In the United States, federal regulations require the testing of new drugs and other products on animals, for efficacy and safety, before human beings are exposed to them.[16,17] We would not want it otherwise.

Every advance in medicine—every new drug, new operation, new therapy of any kind—must sooner or later be tried on a living being for the first time. That trial, controlled or uncontrolled, will be an experiment. The subject of that experiment, if it is not an animal, will be a human being. Prohibiting the use of live animals in biomedical research, therefore, or sharply restricting it, must result either in the blockage of much valuable research or in the replacement of animal subjects with human subjects. These are the consequences—unacceptable to most reasonable persons—of not using animals in research.

Reduction

Should we not at least reduce the use of animals in biomedical research? No, we should increase it, to avoid when feasible the use of humans as experimental subjects. Medical investigations putting human subjects at some risk are numerous and greatly varied. The risks run in such experiments are usually unavoidable, and (thanks to earlier experiments on animals) most such risks are minimal or moderate. But some experimental risks are substantial.

When an experimental protocol that entails substantial risk to humans comes before an institutional review board, what response is appropriate? The investigation, we may suppose, is promising and deserves support, so long as its human subjects are protected against unnecessary dangers. May not the investigators be fairly asked, Have you done all that you can to eliminate risk to humans by the extensive testing of that drug, that procedure, or that device on animals? To achieve maximal safety for humans we are right to require thorough experimentation on animal subjects before humans are involved.

Opportunities to increase human safety in this way are commonly missed; trials in which risks may be shifted from humans to animals are often not devised, sometimes not even considered. Why? For the investigator, the use of animals as subjects is often more expensive, in money and time, than the use of human subjects. Access to suitable human subjects is often quick and convenient, whereas access to appropriate animal subjects may be awkward, costly, and burdened with red tape. Physician-investigators have often had more experience working with human beings and know precisely where the needed pool of subjects is to be found and how they may be enlisted. Animals, and the procedures for their use, are often less familiar to these investigators. Moreover, the use of animals in place of humans is now more likely to be the target of zealous protests from without. The upshot is that humans are sometimes subjected to risks that animals could have borne, and should have borne, in their place. To maximize the protection of human subjects, I conclude, the wide and imaginative use of live animal subjects should be encouraged rather than discouraged. This enlargement in the use of animals is our obligation.

Consistency

Finally, inconsistency between the profession and the practice of many who oppose research using animals deserves comment. This frankly ad hominem observation aims chiefly to show that a coherent position rejecting the use of animals in medical research imposes costs so high as to be intolerable even to the critics themselves.

One cannot coherently object to the killing of animals in biomedical investigations while continuing to eat them. Anesthetics and thoughtful animal husbandry render the level of actual animal distress in the laboratory generally lower than that in the abattoir. So long as death and discomfort do not substantially differ in the two contexts, the consistent objector must not only refrain from all eating of animals but also protest as vehemently against others eating them as against others experimenting on them. No less vigorously must the critic object to the wearing of animal hides in coats and shoes, to employment in any industrial enterprise that uses animal parts, and to any commercial development that will cause death or distress to animals.

Killing animals to meet human needs for food, clothing, and shelter is judged entirely reasonable by most persons. The ubiquity of these uses and the virtual universality of moral support for them confront the opponent of research using animals with an inescapable difficulty. How can the many common uses of animals be judged morally worthy, while their use in scientific investigation is judged unworthy?

The number of animals used in research is but the tiniest fraction of the total used to satisfy assorted human appetites. That these appetites, often base and satisfiable in other ways, morally justify the far larger consumption of animals, whereas the quest for improved human health and understanding cannot justify the far smaller, is wholly implausible. Aside from the numbers of animals involved, the distinction in terms of worthiness of use, drawn with regard to any single animal, is not defensible. A given sheep is surely not more justifiably used to put lamb chops on the supermarket counter than to serve in testing a new contraceptive or a new prosthetic device. The needless killing of animals is wrong; if the common killing of them for our food or convenience is right, the less common but more humane uses of animals in the service of medical science are certainly not less right.

Scrupulous vegetarianism, in matters of food, clothing, shelter, commerce, and recreation, and in all other spheres, is the only fully coherent position the critic may adopt. At great human cost, the lives of fish and crustaceans must also be protected, with equal vigor, if speciesism has been forsworn. A very few consistent critics adopt this position. It is the reductio ad absurdum of the rejection of moral distinctions between animals and human beings.

Opposition to the use of animals in research is based on arguments of two different kinds—those relying on the alleged rights of animals and those relying on the consequences for animals. I have argued that arguments of both kinds must fail. We surely do have obligations to animals, but they have, and can have, no rights against us on which research can infringe. In calculating the consequences of animal research, we must weigh all the long-term benefits of the results achieved—to animals and to humans—and in that calculation we must not assume the moral equality of all animate species.

NOTES

1 Regan T. The case for animal rights. Berkeley, Calif.: University of California Press, 1983.

2 Singer P. Animal liberation. New York: Avon Books, 1977.

3 St. Augustine. Confessions. Book Seven. 397 A.D. New York: Pocketbooks, 1957:104–26.

4 St. Thomas Aquinas. Summa theologica. 1273 A.D. Philosophic texts. New York: Oxford University Press, 1960:353–66.

5 Hegel GWF. Philosophy of right. 1821. London: Oxford University Press, 1952:105–10.

6 Bradley FH. Why should I be moral? 1876. In: Melden AI, ed. Ethical theories. New York: Prentice-Hall, 1950:345–59.

7 Mead GH. The genesis of the self and social control. 1925. In: Reck AJ, ed. Selected writings. Indianapolis: Bobbs-Merrill, 1964:264–93.

8 Prichard HA. Does moral philosophy rest on a mistake? 1912. In: Cellars W, Hospers J, eds. Readings in ethical theory. New York: Appleton-Century-Crofts, 1952:149–63.

9 Kant I. Fundamental principles of the metaphysic of morals. 1785. New York: Liberal Arts Press, 1949.

10 Rollin BE. Animal rights and human morality. New York: Prometheus Books, 1981.

11 Hoff C. Immoral and moral uses of animals. N Engl J Med 1980; 302:115–8.

12 Jamieson D. Killing persons and other beings. In: Miller HB, Williams WH, eds. Ethics and animals. Clifton, N.J.: Humana Press, 1983:135–46.

13 Singer P. Ten years of animal liberation. New York Review of Books. 1985; 31:46–52.

14 Bentham J. Introduction to the principles of morals and legislation. London: Athlone Press, 1970.

15 McCabe K. Who will live, who will die? Washingtonian Magazine. August 1986:115.

16 U.S. Code of Federal Regulations, Title 21, Sect. 505(i). Food, drug, and cosmetic regulations.

17 U.S. Code of Federal Regulations, Title 16, Sect. 1500.40–2. Consumer product regulations.

QUESTIONS

1   Is speciesism a morally defensible position?
2   Do animals have rights?

Human and Animal Rights Compared

Mary Anne Warren

Along with Singer and Regan, Warren ascribes moral status to animals. In her view, animals, as sentient beings, do have rights. Her major concern, however, is with bringing out the *differences* between the rights of animals and those of human beings and with providing a justification for those differences. On

Reprinted with permission of the author from *Environmental Philosophy: A Collection of Readings* (Penn State University Press, 1983), edited by Robert Elliot and Arran Gare, pp. 112, 115–123.

Warren's account, the rights of animals and humans differ in respect to both their content and their *strength*—that is, in the strength of the reasons that are necessary to override them. Two reasons support the view that these differences are not arbitrary: (1) Human desires and interests are more extensive than those of animals, calling for differences in both the extent and strength of human rights. (2) The human capacity for moral autonomy, although not a necessary condition for having rights, can provide a reason for according somewhat stronger rights to human beings than to animals. Warren concludes by discussing the case of nonparadigm humans, who may not have a capacity for moral autonomy yet, unlike animals, have the *same* basic moral rights as paradigm humans, according to her analysis. She does not assert that animals and nonparadigm humans differ in their intrinsic value. Rather, both have intrinsic value and possess certain rights by virtue of their sentience. However, Warren argues, there are additional reasons, such as the value that nonparadigm humans have for paradigm humans, for ascribing stronger rights to nonparadigm humans than to animals.

None of the animal liberationists have thus far provided a clear explanation of how and why the moral status of (most) animals differs from that of (most) human beings; and this is a point which must be clarified if their position is to be made fully persuasive. That there is such a difference seems to follow from some very strong moral intuitions which most of us share. A man who shoots squirrels for sport may or may not be acting reprehensibly; but it is difficult to believe that his actions should be placed in *exactly* the same moral category as those of a man who shoots women, or black children, for sport. So too it is doubtful that the Japanese fishermen who slaughtered dolphins because the latter were thought to be depleting the local fish populations were acting quite *as* wrongly as if they had slaughtered an equal number of their human neighbours for the same reason. . . . There are two dimensions in which we may find differences between the rights of human beings and those of animals. The first involves the *content* of those rights, while the second involves their strength; that is, the strength of the reasons which are required to override them.

Consider, for instance, the right to liberty. The *human* right to liberty precludes imprisonment without due process of law, even if the prison is spacious and the conditions of confinement cause no obvious physical suffering. But it is not so obviously wrong to imprison animals, especially when the area to which they are confined provides a fair approximation of the conditions of their natural habitat, and a reasonable opportunity to pursue the satisfactions natural to their kind. Such conditions, which often result in an increased lifespan, and which may exist in wildlife sanctuaries or even well-designed zoos, need not frustrate the needs or interests of animals in any significant way, and thus do not clearly violate their rights. Similarly treated human beings, on the other hand (e.g., native peoples confined to prison-like reservations), do tend to suffer from their loss of freedom. Human dignity and the fulfillment of the sorts of plans, hopes and desires which appear (thus far) to be uniquely human, require a more extensive freedom of movement than is the case with at least many nonhuman animals. Furthermore, there are aspects of human freedom, such as freedom of thought, freedom of speech and freedom of political association, which simply do not apply in the case of animals.

Thus, it seems that the human right to freedom is more extensive; that is, it precludes a wider range of specific ways of treating human beings than does the corresponding right on the part of animals. The argument cuts both ways, of course. *Some* animals, for example, great whales and migratory birds, may require at least as much physical freedom as do human beings if they are to pursue the satisfactions natural to their kind, and this fact provides a moral argument against keeping such creatures imprisoned. And even chickens may suffer from the extreme and unnatural confinement to which they are subjected on modern "factory farms." Yet it seems unnecessary to claim for *most* animals a right to a freedom quite as broad as that which we claim for ourselves.

Similar points may be made with respect to the right to life. Animals, it may be argued, lack the cognitive equipment to value their lives in the way that human beings do. Ruth Cigman argues that animals have *no* right to life because death is no misfortune for them.[1] In her view, the death of an animal is not a misfortune, because animals have no desires which are *categorical;* that is which do not "merely presuppose being alive (like the desire to eat when one is hungry), but rather answer the question whether one wants to remain alive."[2] In other words, animals appear to lack the sorts of long-range hopes, plans, ambitions and the like, which give human beings such a powerful interest in continued life. Animals, it seems, take life as it comes and do not specifically desire that it go on. True, squirrels store nuts for the winter and deer run from wolves; but these may be seen as instinctive or conditioned responses to present circumstances, rather than evidence that they value life as such.

These reflections probably help to explain why the death of a sparrow seems less tragic than that of a human being. Human lives, one might say, have greater intrinsic value, because they are worth more *to their possessors.* But this does not demonstrate that no nonhuman animal has *any* right to life. Premature death may be a less *severe* misfortune for sentient nonhuman animals than for human beings, but it is a misfortune nevertheless. In the first place, it is a misfortune in that it deprives them of whatever pleasures the future might have held for them, regardless of whether or not they ever *consciously anticipated* those pleasures. The fact that they are not here afterwards, to *experience* their loss, no more shows that they have not lost anything than it does in the case of humans. In the second place, it is (possibly) a misfortune in that it frustrates whatever future-oriented desires animals *may* have, unbeknownst to us. Even now, in an age in which apes have been taught to use simplified human languages and attempts have been made to communicate with dolphins and whales, we still know very little about the operation of nonhuman minds. We know much too little to assume that nonhuman animals never consciously pursue relatively distant future goals. To the extent that they do, the question of whether such desires provide them with *reasons for living* or merely *presuppose* continued life, has no satisfactory answer, since they cannot contemplate these alternatives—or, if they can, we have no way of knowing what their conclusions are. All we know is that the more intelligent and psychologically complex an animal is, the more *likely* it is that it possesses specifically future-oriented desires, which would be frustrated even by *painless* death.

For these reasons, it is premature to conclude from the apparent intellectual inferiority of nonhuman animals that they have no right to life. A more plausible conclusion is that animals do have a right to life but that it is generally somewhat weaker than that of human beings. It is, perhaps, weak enough to enable us to justify killing animals when we have no other ways of achieving such vital goals as feeding or clothing ourselves, or obtaining knowledge which is necessary to save human lives. Weakening their right to life in this way does not render meaningless the assertion that they have such a right. For the point remains that *some* serious justification for the killing of sentient nonhuman animals is always necessary; they may not be killed merely to provide amusement or minor gains in convenience.

If animals' rights to liberty and life are somewhat weaker than those of human beings, may we say the same about their right to *happiness;* that is, their right not to be made to suffer needlessly or to be deprived of the pleasures natural to their kind? If so, it is not immediately clear why. There is little reason to suppose that pain or suffering are any less unpleasant for the higher animals (at least) than they are for us. Our large brains *may* cause us to experience pain more intensely than do most animals, and *probably* cause us to suffer more from the anticipation or remembrance of pain. These facts might tend to suggest that pain is, on the whole, a worse experience for us than for them. But it may also be argued that pain may be *worse* in some respects for nonhuman animals, who are presumably less able to distract themselves from it by thinking of something else, or to comfort themselves with the knowledge that it is temporary. Brigid Brophy points out that "pain is likely to fill the sheep's whole capacity for experience in a way it seldom does in us, whose intellect and imagination can create breaks for us in the immediacy of our sensations."[3]

The net result of such contrasting considerations is that we cannot possibly claim to know whether pain is, on the whole, worse for us than for animals, or whether their pleasures are any more or any less intense than ours. Thus, while we may justify assigning them a somewhat weaker right to life or liberty, on the grounds that they desire these goods less intensely than we do, we cannot discount their rights to freedom from needlessly inflicted pain or unnatural frustration on the same basis. There may, however, be *other* reasons for regarding all of the moral rights of animals as somewhat less stringent than the corresponding human rights.

A number of philosophers who deny that animals have moral rights point to the fact that nonhuman animals evidently lack the capacity for moral autonomy. Moral autonomy is the ability to act as a moral agent; that is, to act on the basis of an understanding of, and adherence to, moral rules or principles. H.J. McCloskey, for example, holds that "it is the capacity for moral autonomy . . . that is basic to the possibility of possessing a right."[4] McCloskey argues that it is inappropriate to ascribe moral rights to any entity which is not a moral agent, or *potentially* a moral agent, because a right is essentially an entitlement granted to a moral agent, licensing him or her to *act* in certain ways and to *demand* that other moral agents refrain from interference. For this reason, he says, "Where there is no possibility of [morally autonomous] action, potentially or actually . . . and where the being is not a member of a kind which is normally capable of [such] action, we withhold talk of rights."[5]

If moral autonomy—or being *potentially* autonomous, or a member of a kind which is *normally* capable of autonomy—is a necessary condition for having moral rights, then probably no nonhuman animal can qualify. For moral autonomy requires such probably uniquely human traits as "the capacity to be critically self-aware, manipulate concepts, use a sophisticated language, reflect, plan, deliberate, choose, and accept responsibility for acting."[6]

But why, we must ask, should the capacity for autonomy be regarded as a pre-condition for possessing moral rights? Autonomy is clearly crucial for the *exercise* of many human moral or legal rights, such as the right to vote or to run for public office. It is less clearly relevant, however, to the more basic human rights, such as the right to life or to freedom from unnecessary suffering. The fact that animals, like many human beings, cannot *demand* their moral rights (at least not in the words of any conventional human language) seems irrelevant. For, as Joel Feinberg points out, the interests of non-morally autonomous human beings may be defended by others, for example, in legal proceedings; and it is not clear why the interests of animals might not be represented in a similar fashion.[7]

It is implausible, therefore, to conclude that because animals lack moral autonomy they should be accorded *no moral rights whatsoever*. Nevertheless, it may be argued that the moral autonomy of (most) human beings provides a second reason, in addition to their more extensive interests and desires, for according somewhat *stronger* moral rights to human beings. The fundamental insight behind contractualist theories of morality is that, for morally autonomous beings such as ourselves, there is enormous mutual advantage in the adoption of a moral system designed to protect each of us from the harms that might otherwise be visited upon us by others. Each of us ought to accept and promote such a system because, to the extent that others also accept it, we will all be safer from attack by our fellows, more likely to receive assistance when we need it, and freer to engage in individual as well as cooperative endeavours of all kinds.

Thus, it is the possibility of *reciprocity* which motivates moral agents to extend *full and equal* moral rights, in the first instance, only to other moral agents. I respect your rights to life, liberty and the pursuit of happiness in part because you are a sentient being, whose interests have intrinsic moral significance. But I respect them as *fully equal to my own* because I hope and expect that you will do the same for me. Animals, insofar as they lack the degree of rationality necessary for moral autonomy, cannot agree to respect our interests as equal in moral importance to their own, and neither do they expect or demand such respect from us. Of course, domestic animals may expect to be fed, etc. But they do not, and cannot, expect to be treated as moral equals, for they do not understand that moral concept or what it implies. Consequently, it is neither pragmatically feasible nor morally obligatory to extend to them the same *full and equal* rights which we extend to human beings.

Is this a speciesist conclusion? Defenders of a more extreme animal-rights position may point out that this argument, from the lack of moral autonomy, has exactly the same form as that which has been used for thousands of years to rationalize denying equal moral rights to women and members of "inferior" races. Aristotle, for example, argued that women and slaves are naturally subordinate beings, because they lack the capacity for moral autonomy and self-direction,[8] and contemporary versions of this argument, used to support racist or sexist conclusions, are easy to find. Are we simply repeating Aristotle's mistake, in a different context?

The reply to this objection is very simple: animals, unlike women and slaves, really *are* incapable of moral autonomy, at least to the best of our knowledge. Aristotle certainly *ought* to have known that women and slaves are capable of morally autonomous action; their capacity to use moral language alone ought to have alerted him to this likelihood. If comparable evidence exists that (some) nonhuman animals are moral agents we have not yet found it. The fact that some apes (and, possibly, some cetaceans) are capable of learning radically simplified human languages, the terms of which refer primarily to objects and events in their immediate environment, in no way demonstrates that they can understand abstract moral concepts, rules or principles, or use this understanding to regulate their own behaviour.

On the other hand, this argument implies that if we *do* discover that certain non-human animals are capable of moral autonomy (which is certainly not impossible), then we ought to extend full and equal moral rights to those animals. Furthermore, if we someday encounter extraterrestrial beings, or build robots, androids or super-computers which function as self-aware moral agents, then we must extend full and equal moral rights to these as well. Being a member of the human species is not a necessary condition for the possession of full "human" rights. Whether it is nevertheless a *sufficient* condition is the question to which we now turn.

THE MORAL RIGHTS OF NONPARADIGM HUMANS

If we are justified in ascribing somewhat different, and also somewhat stronger, moral rights to human beings than to sentient but non-morally autonomous animals, then what are we to say of the rights of human beings who happen not to be capable of moral autonomy, perhaps not even potentially? Both Singer and Regan have argued that if any of the superior intellectual capacities of normal and mature human beings are used to support a distinction between the moral status of *typical,* or paradigm, human beings, and that of animals, then consistency will require us to place certain "nonparadigm" humans, such as infants, small children and the severely retarded or incurably brain damaged, in the same inferior moral category.[9] Such a result is, of course, highly counterintuitive.

Fortunately, no such conclusion follows from the autonomy argument. There are many reasons for extending strong moral rights to nonparadigm humans; reasons which do not apply to most nonhuman animals. Infants and small children are granted strong moral rights in part because of their *potential* autonomy. But *potential* autonomy, as I have argued elsewhere,[10] is not in itself a sufficient reason for the ascription of full moral rights; if it were, then not only human foetuses (from conception onwards) but even ununited human sperm-egg pairs would have to be regarded as entities with a right to life the equivalent of our own—thus making not only abortion, but any intentional failure to procreate, the moral equivalent of murder. Those who do not find this extreme conclusion acceptable must appeal to reasons other than the *potential* moral autonomy of infants and small children to explain the strength of the latter's moral rights.

One reason for assigning strong moral rights to infants and children is that they possess not just *potential* but *partial* autonomy, and it is not clear how much of it they have at any given moment. The fact that, unlike baby chimpanzees, they are already learning the things which will enable them to *become* morally autonomous, makes it likely that their minds have more subtleties than their speech (or the lack of it) proclaims. Another reason is simply that most of us tend to place a very high value on the lives and well-being of infants. Perhaps we are to some degree "programmed" by nature to love and protect them; perhaps our reasons are somewhat egocentric; or perhaps we value them for their potential. Whatever the explanation, the fact that we do feel this way about them is in itself a valid reason for extending to them stronger moral and legal protections than we extend to nonhuman animals, even those which may have just as well or better-developed psychological capacities. A third, and perhaps the most important, reason is that if we did *not* extend strong moral rights to infants, far too few of them would ever *become* responsible, morally autonomous adults; too many would be treated "like animals" (i.e., in ways that it is generally wrong to treat even animals), and would consequently become socially crippled, antisocial or just very unhappy people. If any part of our moral code is to remain intact, it seems that infants and small children *must* be protected and cared for.

Analogous arguments explain why strong moral rights should also be accorded to other nonparadigm humans. The severely retarded or incurably senile, for instance, may have no potential for moral autonomy, but there are apt to be friends, relatives or other people who care what happens to them. Like children, such individuals may have more mental capacities than are readily apparent. Like children, they are more apt to achieve, or return to moral autonomy if they are valued and well cared for. Furthermore, any one of us may someday become mentally incapacitated to one degree or another, and we would all have reason to be anxious about our own futures if such incapacitation were made the basis for denying strong moral rights.

There are, then, sound reasons for assigning strong moral rights even to human beings who lack the mental capacities which justify the general distinction between human and animal rights. Their rights are based not only on the value which they themselves place upon their lives and well-being, but also on the value which other human beings place upon them.

But is this a valid basis for the assignment of moral rights? . . . Regan argues that we cannot justify the ascription of stronger rights to nonparadigm humans than to nonhuman animals in the way suggested, because "what underlies the ascription of rights to any given X is that X has value independently of anyone's valuing X."[11] After all, we do not speak of expensive paintings or gemstones as having rights, although many people value them and have good reasons for wanting them protected.

There is, however, a crucial difference between a rare painting and a severely retarded or senile human being; the latter not only has (or may have) value for other human beings but *also* has his or her own needs and interests. It may be this which leads us to say that such individuals have intrinsic value. The sentience of nonparadigm humans, like that of sentient nonhuman animals, gives them a place in the sphere of rights holders. So long as the moral rights of all sentient beings are given due recognition, there should be no objection to providing some of them with *additional* protections, on the basis of our interests as well as their own. Some philosophers speak of such additional protections, which are accorded to X on the basis of interests other than X's own, as *conferred* rights, in contrast to *natural* rights, which are entirely based upon the properties of X itself. But such "conferred" rights are not necessarily any weaker or less binding upon moral agents than are "natural" rights. Infants, and most other nonparadigm humans have the *same* basic moral rights that the rest of us do, even though the reasons for ascribing those rights are somewhat different in the two cases. . . .

NOTES

1 Ruth Cigman, "Death, Misfortune, and Species Inequality," *Philosophy and Public Affairs* 10, no. 1 (Winter 1981): p. 48.

2 Ibid., pp. 57–58. The concept of a categorical desire is introduced by Bernard Williams, "The Makropoulous Case," in his *Problems of the Self* (Cambridge: Cambridge University Press), 1973.

3 Brigid Brophy, "In Pursuit of a Fantasy," in *Animals, Men and Morals,* ed. Stanley and Rosalind Godlovitch (New York: Taplinger Publishing Co., 1972), p. 129.

4 H. J. McCloskey, "Moral Rights and Animals," *Inquiry* 22, nos. 1–2 (1979): 31.

5 Ibid., p. 29.

6 Michael Fox, "Animal Liberation: A Critique," *Ethics* 88, no. 2 (January 1978): 111.

7 Joel Feinberg, "The Rights of Animals and Unborn Generations," in *Philosophy and Environmental Crisis,* ed. William T. Blackstone (Athens, Ga.: University of Georgia Press), 1974, pp. 46–47.

8 Aristotle, *Politics* I. 1254, 1260, and 1264.

9 Peter Singer, *Animal Liberation: A New Ethics for Our Treatment of Animals* (New York: Avon, 1975), pp. 75–76; Tom Regan, "One Argument Concerning Animal Rights," *Inquiry* 22, nos. 1–2 (1979): 189–217.

10 Mary Anne Warren, "Do Potential People Have Moral Rights?" *Canadian Journal of Philosophy* 7, no. 2 (June 1977): 275–89.

11 Regan, "One Argument Concerning Animal Rights," p. 189.

QUESTIONS

1 Is Warren correct in making the following claim? If we someday encounter extraterrestrial beings, or build robots, androids, or supercomputers which function as self-aware moral agents, then we must extend full and equal moral rights to these.

2 What human needs, if any, are sufficiently important to warrant the infliction of pain and suffering on animals?

SUGGESTED ADDITIONAL READINGS FOR CHAPTER 10

ARMSTRONG, SUSAN J, and RICHARD G. BOTZLER, eds.: *The Animal Ethics Reader.* New York: Routledge, 2003. This ten-chapter anthology includes chapters on theories of animal ethics, animal capacities, primates and cetaceans, the use of animals for food, and animal experimentation.

DeGRAZIA, DAVID: *Animal Rights: A Very Short Introduction.* New York: Oxford University Press, 2002. DeGrazia engages the issue of the moral status of animals, arguing that sentient animals are entitled to equal consideration. He also discusses the mental lives of animals and the various ways in which animals can be harmed Finally, he considers the ethics of meat-eating, the ethics of keeping pets and zoo animals, and the ethics of animal research.

————: "The Ethics of Animal Research: What Are the Prospects for Agreement?" *Cambridge Quarterly of Healthcare Ethics,* vol. 8, Winter 1999, pp. 23–34. DeGrazia provides some background on the ethical and political debate over animal research and identifies significant points of potential agreement between the perspectives of biomedicine and animal advocates.

DOMBROWSKI, DANIEL A.: *The Philosophy of Vegetarianism.* Amherst: University of Massachusetts Press, 1984. This book provides an interesting historical background for contemporary philosophical discussions of vegetarianism. Its critical examination focuses primarily on ancient Greek sources, from the early poetic tradition of Hesiod and Homer down to the neoplatonists in the Christian era.

FOX, MICHAEL ALLEN: *Deep Vegetarianism.* Philadelphia: Temple University Press, 1999. Fox argues that an in-depth examination of the vegetarian outlook raises a broad spectrum of philosophical issues connected with the moral, social, and political spheres of our lives. Surveying and analyzing a variety of significant arguments for vegetarianism, he maintains that the spectrum of arguments should urge us toward a vegetarian commitment in both theory and practice.

FREY, R. G.: *Interests and Rights: The Case Against Animals.* Oxford: Clarendon, 1980. In Frey's view, animals do not have interests, and thus they do not have moral rights. Accordingly, he contends, arguments for vegetarianism that are based on the claim that animals have moral rights are unsound.

GEORGE, KATHRYN PAXTON: "Ethical Vegetarianism Is Unfair to Women and Children." In James P. Sterba, ed., *Earth Ethics,* 2d ed. Upper Saddle River, N.J.: Prentice-Hall, 2000. The author criticizes both Peter Singer's and Tom Regan's arguments for vegetarianism. In her view, the moral ideal presented in these arguments does not apply to the majority of people—women, children, and the elderly as well as many people in non-Western countries. Thus, it relegates members of these groups to a moral underclass of beings who, because of their physiological natures or cultures, are not capable of being fully moral.

REGAN, TOM: *The Case for Animal Rights.* Berkeley: University of California Press, 1983. Regan argues that animals have a basic moral right to respectful treatment. He derives the following conclusions: (1) Vegetarianism is obligatory; (2) hunting and trapping are wrong; (3) the use of animals in science is impermissible.

————, and PETER SINGER, eds.: *Animal Rights and Human Obligations,* 2d ed. Englewood Cliffs, N.J.: Prentice-Hall, 1989. This very useful anthology begins with a section on animals in the history of Western thought. Some of the other sections are "Animal Rights," "Killing and the Value of Life," "The Treatment of Farm Animals," and "The Treatment of Animals in Science."

ROLLIN, BERNARD E.: *The Unheeded Cry: Animal Consciousness, Animal Pain and Science.* Oxford: Oxford University Press, 1989. Rollin provides a study of American and European attitudes toward animal consciousness and their relation to scientific experimentation using animals, beginning with George Romanes in the nineteenth century. Also included is an extensive bibliography beginning with citations from 1879.

SINGER, PETER: *Animal Liberation,* 2d ed. New York: New York Review, 1990. Singer advances a vigorous critique of our present attitudes toward animals and our dealings with them. He also provides a wealth of relevant factual material.

CHAPTER 11

The Environment

Much of our traditional thinking about morality is *anthropocentric*—that is, it assumes that moral obligation is essentially a function of *human* interests. Increasingly, however, anthropocentric approaches to morality are being challenged. Many thinkers concerned with our moral obligations with respect to the environment, like many of those concerned with our obligations with respect to animals, question whether an anthropocentric ethic can provide an adequate basis for all our moral obligations, including environmental ones. This chapter focuses on our moral obligations with respect to the environment and the appropriate moral foundation for those obligations. It also deals with issues of justice associated with the location of polluting industries, garbage dumps, and hazardous waste sites.

THE BASIS FOR OUR MORAL OBLIGATIONS
REGARDING THE ENVIRONMENT

We are becoming increasingly aware of the extent to which human activities pollute and destroy the natural environment. This is perhaps most dramatically exemplified by the growing international concern with global warming, much of which is now believed to be the result of human activities that have resulted in the buildup of greenhouse gases—chiefly carbon dioxide, methane, and nitrous oxide. While scientists cannot predict as yet just what the impact of global warming will be in the future, they identify the following as being at risk—our health, agriculture, water resources, forests, wildlife, and coastal areas.[1] Most reflective people would agree that much of the ongoing pollution produced by human activities and the resultant environmental destruction is morally wrong. Philosophers and other writers who are concerned with environmental issues disagree, however, about *why* it is morally wrong, for example, to pollute the environment, destroy wilderness areas, or contribute to the destruction of species. What is the basis of our moral obligations regarding the natural environment? Three fundamentally different approaches can be distinguished in reference to this question: (1) anthropocentric approaches, (2) sentientist approaches, and (3) biocentric, or ecocentric, approaches.

[1] The U.S. Environmental Protection Agency (http://www.epa.gov). This website provides useful information about global warming.

Anthropocentric Approaches

On the anthropocentric approach, our obligations regarding the environment are to be determined solely on the basis of human interests. It seems clear, for example, that we can appeal to human interests in order to ground a prima facie duty not to pollute the environment—that is, a duty not to pollute unless there are overriding moral considerations. Human welfare—in fact, human life—crucially depends on such necessities as breathable air, drinkable water, and eatable food. Thus, in the absence of overriding moral considerations, pollution is morally unacceptable precisely because it is damaging to the public welfare. On an alternative construal, still using an anthropocentric approach, the prima facie duty not to pollute may be understood as based on a basic human right: the right to a livable environment. Thus, we can assert, with some confidence, that there is a prima facie duty not to pollute. We are left, however, with the problem of weighing the collective human interest in a nonpolluted environment against competing human interests, often economic ones.

The following schematic example illustrates some of the complexities that confront us when environmental and economic interests clash. An industrial plant, representing a (small, large, massive) financial investment, producing a product that is (unessential, very desirable, essential) to society and providing a (small, large, enormous) number of jobs, pollutes the environment in a (minor, substantial, major) way. In which of these several cases is the continued operation of the plant morally unacceptable? Certainly the general public interest in the quality of the environment must be recognized. But what about the economic interests of the owners, employees, and potential customers? In sum, how is the collective human interest in a nonpolluted environment to be equitably weighed against competing economic interests?

At this point, some ethicists tend to appeal to the kind of cost-benefit analyses that characterize utilitarian thinking. William F. Baxter, who defends an anthropocentric ethical stance in this chapter, adopts this cost-benefit approach in arguing for "optimal pollution"—pollution whose harms are outweighed by various human interests, including economic and aesthetic ones. Others, such as Jan Narveson in this chapter, adopt a free market approach to pollution in keeping with the libertarian position advanced by John Hospers in Chapter 8 and discussed in the introduction to that chapter. The following ideas characterize free market environmentalism: All lands and areas of nature are owned by private persons; there are no public lands; all "environmental problems" are to be worked out by negotiation among the affected parties; there is no environmental legislation. In keeping with this view, Narveson argues that the best solution to environmental problems is a hands-off government policy that allows marketplace transactions to determine the extent and distribution of pollution. Narveson's position is critically evaluated in this chapter by Tony Smith, who rejects free market environmentalism. In another of this chapter's readings, Peter S. Wenz rejects both the cost-benefit analysis and free market approaches. In his view, neither position will result in a just distribution of the burdens associated with waste and pollution. Focusing on toxic wastes, Wenz argues that the poor, who are often members of minority groups, bear a disproportionate share of the hazards associated with toxic wastes. He proposes the adoption of policies that would require those who benefit the most from the activities resulting in such hazards to bear a proportionate share of the resulting burdens. Although Wenz is not an anthropocentrist, his reasoning in this chapter is limited to the effects of the hazards associated with toxic wastes on human beings.

An anthropocentric moral approach can be taken to other environmental issues as well. For example, it can be argued that the preservation of wilderness serves numerous human interests, and these interests can be viewed as the basis for an obligation to preserve wilderness areas. In this vein, it is pointed out that many people find communing with nature in wilderness areas to be an important source of aesthetic experience and spiritual renewal, that wilderness areas provide significant recreational opportunities for human beings, that the biodiversity stockpiled in wilderness areas can be of great human benefit in connection with the search for substances that have medicinal value, and so on.

Those who believe that an anthropocentric approach is capable of providing an adequate foundation for our obligations with regard to the environment usually insist on the importance of considering a wide range of human interests, not just economic ones, and they also usually insist on taking seriously the interests of future generations of human beings, not just those of presently existing human beings. Since human well-being is so intimately intertwined with the well-being of the environment, they point out, we must resist forces of environmental degradation; otherwise, sooner or later, the possibility of human beings' leading healthy and happy lives will be severely compromised.

Sentientist Approaches

On a sentientist approach, the interests of sentient beings determine our obligations regarding the environment. All sentient beings (not just human beings) are seen as having inherent (intrinsic) value and not merely instrumental value. As the distinction between inherent and instrumental value is usually drawn, some things are valuable as a *means* to some valued end; thus, their value is instrumental. Other things are valuable in themselves and, thus, are said to have inherent or intrinsic value. (Singer in Chapter 10 takes a sentientist approach insofar as he uses sentience as the criterion for determining what sorts of things are entitled to an equal consideration of their interests.) Since sentient beings include human beings, it can be argued on a sentientist approach, just as on an anthropocentric one, that, for example, mountains, forests, and snail darters should be preserved because of their aesthetic value to human beings. But, insofar, as nonhuman animals are also sentient beings, a sentientist would insist that animal interests must also be considered when determining our environmental obligations. Bernard E. Rollin's reasoning in this chapter illustrates sentientist thinking. Rollin maintains that we might have a moral obligation to preserve some natural habitat that is of no value to human beings if its destruction would harm some nonhuman animals.

Biocentric (Ecocentric) Approaches

In recent years, various writers have argued for an even more radical revision of traditional approaches to morality than that proposed by sentientists. In fact, sentientism is sometimes criticized as analogous to both racism and speciesism insofar as all three can be viewed as giving unjustified preference to one's own "kind." John Rodman, who coined the term *sentientism,* criticizes the sentientist approach as follows:

> The rest of nature is left in a state of thinghood, having no intrinsic worth, acquiring instrumental value only as resources for the well-being of an elite of sentient beings. Homocentrist rationalism has widened out into a kind of zoocentrist sentientism. . . . If it would seem arbitrary to a visitor from Mars to find one species claiming a monopoly of intrinsic value by virtue of its allegedly exclusive possession of reason, free will, soul, or some other occult quality, would it not seem almost as arbitrary to find that same species claiming a monopoly of intrinsic value for itself and those species most resembling it . . . by virtue of their common and allegedly exclusive possession of sentience?[2]

Aldo Leopold (1887–1948), whose famous essay "The Land Ethic" is partially reprinted in this chapter, argues for a more revolutionary environmental ethic. Insisting that moral consideration must be extended to all of nature, he writes:

> The land ethic simply enlarges the boundaries of the community to include soils, waters, plants, and animals, or collectively the land. . . . In short, a land ethic changes the role of *Homo sapiens* from conqueror of the land-community to plain member and citizen of it. It implies respect for his fellow-members, and also respect for the community as such. . . . A thing is right when it tends to preserve the integrity, stability, and beauty of the biotic community. It is wrong when it tends otherwise.[3]

Leopold's approach to our moral obligations with regard to the environment is sometimes said to involve a biotic view (*biotic* means "relating to life") and is, therefore, called *biocentric.* Proponents of a biocentric ethic consider all life to be inherently valuable, and they often understand "life" in such a broad sense that it includes even things that are not themselves living organisms, such as rivers, landscapes, ecosystems, and "the living earth." To the extent that biocentric approaches attach moral standing to ecosystems, they may also be labeled *ecocentric.*[4] (An *ecosystem* can be defined as a unit made up of a community of living things taken in conjunction with the nonliving factors of its environment.)

Leopold's land ethic provides one important articulation of a biocentric point of view. Another well-known expression of a biocentric point of view can be located in a school of thought known as *deep ecology.* Deep ecology is principally defined

---

[2]John Rodman, "The Liberation of Nature?" *Inquiry,* vol. 20, 1977, p. 91.

[3]Aldo Leopold, "The Land Ethic," in *A Sand County Almanac* (New York: Oxford University Press, 1966), pp. 210, 220, 240.

[4]Although the biocentric approaches explicitly discussed in this chapter are correctly labeled *ecocentric,* there is no necessary connection between biocentrism and ecocentrism. Indeed, one position in environmental ethics is called *biocentric individualism.* On this view, moral consideration is to be extended to all *individual* living things, but is not to be extended (at least not directly extended) to ecosystems or the biosphere as a whole. See, for example, Paul W. Taylor, *Respect for Nature: A Theory of Environmental Ethics* (Princeton, N.J.: Princeton University Press, 1986).

in reference to the writings of Arne Naess, Bill Devall, and George Sessions. Naess is a Norwegian philosopher, and the other two writers are Americans. In one of this chapter's readings, Devall and Sessions present the worldview of deep ecology in contrast to the "dominant worldview."

Proponents of deep ecology often contrast their approach with what they call *shallow ecology,* and they identify shallow ecology with anthropocentric approaches, which are committed to constructing an account of environmental obligations solely in reference to human interests and concerns. At any rate, deep ecology firmly rejects both anthropocentric and sentientist approaches to environmental obligations. It calls for a radical, fundamental revision in our attitude toward the natural world. Naess and Sessions write:

> The well-being and flourishing of human and nonhuman Life on Earth have value in them-selves (synonyms: intrinsic value, inherent value). These values are independent of the usefulness of the nonhuman world for human purposes. . . . Richness and diversity of life forms contribute to the realization of these values and are also values in themselves. . . . Humans have no right to reduce this richness and diversity except to satisfy *vital* needs.[5]

CRITICISMS OF BIOCENTRIC APPROACHES

Two articles in this chapter incorporate criticisms of biocentric approaches. Rollin argues that moral consideration is appropriately extended to individual animals but not to other natural entities. Thus, he claims that neither nonsentient natural objects (e.g., plants and rivers) nor "quasi-abstract entities, such as species and ecosys-tems" possess intrinsic value. In his view, an adequate environmental ethic can be based solely on the instrumental value that other natural entities have for sentient creatures. Thus, the paradoxes and difficulties that arise when intrinsic value is attributed to nonsentient natural objects and quasi-abstract entities can be avoided.

Ramachandra Guha argues in this chapter from a third-world perspective. He presents a wide-ranging critique of what he calls the *American* deep ecology move-ment. Guha rejects the anthropocentric-biocentric distinction, which he identifies as a central tenet of American deep ecology. He maintains that the distinction is of little use in helping us understand the dynamics of environmental degradation. Guha argues for what he considers a much more radical approach to environmen-tal issues—an approach that he sees as exemplified in countries such as Germany and India. This approach emphasizes the need to change the sociopolitical basis of the consumerism and militarism that, in his view, are responsible for so much envi-ronmental destruction. Thus, Guha's approach is "radical" in a different way than are biocentric approaches. Biocentric approaches are radical insofar as they call for a revolutionary revision of our fundamental moral categories. Guha's approach is politically radical, however, insofar as it calls for a rethinking of some of our fun-damental sociopolitical institutions.

Jane S. Zembaty

---

[5]These statements are part of a platform of the deep ecology movement originally formulated by Naess and Sessions in 1984. The platform as a whole is included—under the heading "Basic Principles of Deep Ecology"—in the selection by Devall and Sessions in this chapter.

People or Penguins: The Case for Optimal Pollution

William F. Baxter

Baxter adopts an anthropocentric approach to environmental trade-offs. He states four general goals, which, in his view, should serve as criteria for evaluating solutions to environmental problems. Baxter defends his anthropocentric approach and briefly discusses the kinds of trade-offs involved when interests in controlling pollution must be weighed against competing interests, including economic ones.

I start with the modest proposition that, in dealing with pollution, or indeed with any problem, it is helpful to know what one is attempting to accomplish. Agreement on how and whether to pursue a particular objective, such as pollution control, is not possible unless some more general objective has been identified and stated with reasonable precision. We talk loosely of having clean air and clean water, of preserving our wilderness areas, and so forth. But none of these is a sufficiently general objective: each is more accurately viewed as a means rather than as an end.

With regard to clean air, for example, one may ask, "how clean?" and "what does clean mean?" It is even reasonable to ask, "why have clean air?" Each of these questions is an implicit demand that a more general community goal be stated—a goal sufficiently general in its scope and enjoying sufficiently general assent among the community of actors that such "why" questions no longer seem admissible with respect to that goal.

If, for example, one states as a goal the proposition that "every person should be free to do whatever he wishes in contexts where his actions do not interfere with the interests of other human beings," the speaker is unlikely to be met with a response of "why." The goal may be criticized as uncertain in its implications or difficult to implement, but it is so basic a tenet of our civilization—it reflects a cultural value so broadly shared, at least in the abstract—that the question "why" is seen as impertinent or imponderable or both.

I do not mean to suggest that everyone would agree with the "spheres of freedom" objective just stated. Still less do I mean to suggest that a society could subscribe to four or five such general objectives that would be adequate in their coverage to serve as testing criteria by which all other disagreements might be measured. One difficulty in the attempt to construct such a list is that each new goal added will conflict, in certain applications, with each prior goal listed; and thus each goal serves as a limited qualification on prior goals.

Without any expectation of obtaining unanimous consent to them, let me set forth four goals that I generally use as ultimate testing criteria in attempting to frame solutions to problems of human organization. My position regarding pollution stems from these four criteria. If the criteria appeal to you and any part of what appears

Reprinted with permission of Columbia University Press from William F. Baxter, *People or Penguins: The Case for Optimal Pollution* (1974), pp. 1–13.

hereafter does not, our disagreement will have a helpful focus: which of us is correct, analytically, in supposing that his position on pollution would better serve these general goals. If the criteria do not seem acceptable to you, then it is to be expected that our more particular judgments will differ, and the task will then be yours to identify the basic set of criteria upon which your particular judgments rest.

My criteria are as follows:

1 The spheres of freedom criterion stated above.

2 Waste is a bad thing. The dominant feature of human existence is scarcity—our available resources, our aggregate labors, and our skill in employing both have always been, and will continue for some time to be, inadequate to yield to every man all the tangible and intangible satisfactions he would like to have. Hence, none of those resources, or labors, or skills, should be wasted—that is, employed so as to yield less than they might yield in human satisfactions.

3 Every human being should be regarded as an end rather than as a means to be used for the betterment of another. Each should be afforded dignity and regarded as having an absolute claim to an evenhanded application of such rules as the community may adopt for its governance.

4 Both the incentive and the opportunity to improve his share of satisfactions should be preserved to every individual. Preservation of incentive is dictated by the "no-waste" criterion and enjoins against the continuous, totally egalitarian redistribution of satisfactions, or wealth; but subject to that constraint, everyone should receive, by continuous redistribution if necessary, some minimal share of aggregate wealth so as to avoid a level of privation from which the opportunity to improve his situation becomes illusory.

The relationship of these highly general goals to the more specific environmental issues at hand may not be readily apparent, and I am not yet ready to demonstrate their pervasive implications. But let me give one indication of their implications. Recently scientists have informed us that use of DDT in food production is causing damage to the penguin population. For the present purposes let us accept that assertion as an indisputable scientific fact. The scientific fact is often asserted as if the correct implication—that we must stop agricultural use of DDT—followed from the mere statement of the fact of penguin damage. But plainly it does not follow if my criteria are employed.

My criteria are oriented to people, not penguins. Damage to penguins, or sugar pines, or geological marvels is, without more, simply irrelevant. One must go further, by my criteria, and say: Penguins are important because people enjoy seeing them walk about rocks; and furthermore, the well-being of people would be less impaired by halting use of DDT than by giving up penguins. In short, my observations about environmental problems will be people-oriented, as are my criteria. I have no interest in preserving penguins for their own sake.

It may be said by way of objection to this position, that it is very selfish of people to act as if each person represented one unit of importance and nothing else was of any importance. It is undeniably selfish. Nevertheless I think it is the only tenable starting place for analysis for several reasons. First, no other position corresponds to the way most people really think and act—i.e., corresponds to reality.

Second, this attitude does not portend any massive destruction of nonhuman flora and fauna, for people depend on them in many obvious ways, and they will be preserved because and to the degree that humans do depend on them.

Third, what is good for humans is, in many respects, good for penguins and pine trees—clean air for example. So that humans are, in these respects, surrogates for plant and animal life.

Fourth, I do not know how we could administer any other system. Our decisions are either private or collective. Insofar as Mr. Jones is free to act privately, he may give such preferences as he wishes to other forms of life: he may feed birds in winter and do with less himself, and he may even decline to resist an advancing polar bear on the ground that the bear's appetite is more important than those portions of himself that the bear may choose to eat. In short my basic premise does not rule out private altruism to competing life-forms. It does rule out, however, Mr. Jones' inclination to feed Mr. Smith to the bear, however hungry the bear, however despicable Mr. Smith.

Insofar as we act collectively on the other hand, only humans can be afforded an opportunity to participate in the collective decisions. Penguins cannot vote now and are unlikely subjects for the franchise—pine trees more unlikely still. Again each individual is free to cast his vote so as to benefit sugar pines if that is his inclination. But many of the more extreme assertions that one hears from some conservationists amount to tacit assertions that they are specially appointed representatives of sugar pines, and hence that their preferences should be weighted more heavily than the preferences of other humans who do not enjoy equal rapport with "nature." The simplistic assertion that agricultural use of DDT must stop at once because it is harmful to penguins is of that type.

Fifth, if polar bears or pine trees or penguins, like men, are to be regarded as ends rather than means, if they are to count in our calculus of social organization, someone must tell me how much each one counts, and someone must tell me how these life-forms are to be permitted to express their preferences, for I do not know either answer. If the answer is that certain people are to hold their proxies, then I want to know how those proxy-holders are to be selected: self-appointment does not seem workable to me.

Sixth, and by way of summary of all the foregoing, let me point out that the set of environmental issues under discussion—although they raise very complex technical questions of how to achieve any objective—ultimately raise a normative question: what *ought* we to do? Questions of *ought* are unique to the human mind and world—they are meaningless as applied to a nonhuman situation.

I reject the proposition that we *ought* to respect the "balance of nature" or to "preserve the environment" unless the reason for doing so, express or implied, is the benefit of man.

I reject the idea that there is a "right" or "morally correct" state of nature to which we should return. The word "nature" has no normative connotation. Was it "right" or "wrong" for the earth's crust to heave in contortion and create mountains and seas? Was it "right" for the first amphibian to crawl up out of the primordial ooze? Was it "wrong" for plants to reproduce themselves and alter the atmospheric composition in favor of oxygen? For animals to alter the atmosphere in favor of carbon dioxide both by breathing oxygen and eating plants? No answers can be given to these questions because they are meaningless questions.

All this may seem obvious to the point of being tedious, but much of the present controversy over environment and pollution rests on tacit normative assumptions about just such nonnormative phenomena: that it is "wrong" to impair penguins with DDT, but not to slaughter cattle for prime rib roasts. That it is wrong to kill stands of sugar pines with industrial fumes, but not to cut sugar pines and build housing for the poor. Every man is entitled to his own preferred definition of Walden Pond, but there is no definition that has any moral superiority over another, except by reference to the selfish needs of the human race.

From the fact that there is no normative definition of the natural state, it follows that there is no normative definition of clean air or pure water—hence no definition of polluted air—or of pollution—except by reference to the needs of man. The "right" composition of the atmosphere is one which has some dust in it and some lead in it and some hydrogen sulfide in it—just those amounts that attend a sensibly organized society thoughtfully and knowledgeably pursuing the greatest possible satisfaction for its human members.

The first and most fundamental step toward solution of our environmental problems is a clear recognition that our objective is not pure air or water but rather some optimal state of pollution. That step immediately suggests the question: How do we define and attain the level of pollution that will yield the maximum possible amount of human satisfaction?

Low levels of pollution contribute to human satisfaction but so do food and shelter and education and music. To attain ever lower levels of pollution, we must pay the cost of having less of these other things. I contrast that view of the cost of pollution control with the more popular statement that pollution control will "cost" very large numbers of dollars. The popular statement is true in some senses, false in others; sorting out the true and false senses is of some importance. The first step in that sorting process is to achieve a clear understanding of the difference between dollars and resources. Resources are the wealth of our nation; dollars are merely claim checks upon those resources. Resources are of vital importance; dollars are comparatively trivial.

Four categories of resources are sufficient for our purposes: At any given time a nation, or a planet if you prefer, has a stock of labor, of technological skill, of capital goods, and of natural resources (such as mineral deposits, timber, water, land, etc.). These resources can be used in various combinations to yield goods and services of all kinds—in some limited quantity. The quantity will be larger if they are combined efficiently, smaller if combined inefficiently. But in either event the resource stock is limited, the goods and services that they can be made to yield are limited; even the most efficient use of them will yield less than our population, in the aggregate, would like to have.

If one considers building a new dam, it is appropriate to say that it will be costly in the sense that it will require x hours of labor, y tons of steel and concrete, and z amount of capital goods. If these resources are devoted to the dam, then they cannot be used to build hospitals, fishing rods, schools, or electric can openers. That is the meaningful sense in which the dam is costly.

Quite apart from the very important question of how wisely we can combine our resources to produce goods and services is the very different question of how they get distributed—who gets how many goods? Dollars constitute the claim checks which are distributed among people and which control their share of national output. Dollars are nearly valueless pieces of paper except to the extent that they do represent claim checks to some fraction of the output of goods and services. Viewed as claim checks, all the dollars outstanding during any period of time are worth, in the aggregate, the goods and services that are available to be claimed with them during that period—neither more nor less.

It is far easier to increase the supply of dollars than to increase the production of goods and services—printing dollars is easy. But printing more dollars doesn't help because each dollar then simply becomes a claim to fewer goods, i.e., becomes worth less.

The point is this: many people fall into error upon hearing the statement that the decision to build a dam, or to clean up a river, will cost $X million. It is regrettably easy to say: "It's only money. This is a wealthy country, and we have lots of money." But you cannot build a dam or clean a river with $X million—unless you also have a match, you can't even make a fire. One builds a dam or cleans a river by diverting labor and steel and trucks and factories from making one kind of goods to making another. The cost in dollars is merely a shorthand way of describing the extent of the diversion necessary. If we build a dam for $X million, then we must recognize that we will have $X million less housing and food and medical care and electric can openers as a result.

Similarly, the costs of controlling pollution are best expressed in terms of the other goods we will have to give up to do the job. This is not to say the job should not be done. Badly as we need more housing, more medical care, more can openers, and more symphony orchestras, we could do with somewhat less of them, in my judgment at least, in exchange for somewhat cleaner air and rivers. But that is the nature of the trade-off, and analysis of the problem is advanced if that unpleasant reality is kept in mind. Once the trade-off relationship is clearly perceived, it is possible to state in a very general way what the optimal level of pollution is. I would state it as follows:

People enjoy watching penguins. They enjoy relatively clean air and smog-free vistas. Their health is improved by relatively clean water and air. Each of these benefits is a type of good or service. As a society we would be well advised to give up one washing machine if the resources that would have gone into that washing machine can yield greater human satisfaction when diverted into pollution control. We should give up one hospital if the resources thereby freed would yield more human satisfaction when devoted to elimination of noise in our cities. And so on, trade-off by trade-off, we should divert our productive capacities from the production of existing goods and services to the production of a cleaner, quieter, more pastoral nation up to—and no further than—the point at which we value more highly the next washing machine or hospital that we would have to do without than we value the next unit of environmental improvement that the diverted resources would create.

Now this proposition seems to me unassailable but so general and abstract as to be unhelpful—at least unadministerable in the form stated. It assumes we can measure in some way the incremental units of human satisfaction yielded by very different types of goods. . . . But I insist that the proposition stated describes the result for which we should be striving—and again, that it is always useful to know what your target is even if your weapons are too crude to score a bull's eye.

QUESTIONS

1 Does the life of a penguin have value only if humans value it?

2 Is human benefit the only morally relevant criterion in determining our obligations in regard to the rest of the natural world?

For Free Market Environmentalism

Jan Narveson

Narveson argues that the rational way to solve environmental problems is to adopt a libertarian, free market approach. Rejecting all governmental attempts to control pollution, he maintains that such matters are best left to individuals who, acting in their own interests, will decide for themselves how much pollution they are willing to accept for what benefits.

In a free market, individuals own and may do what they want with things, without fear of interference by others. Free market society is *consensual* society: exchanges occur only when owners believe they would be better off from them, compared with any other use they could make of their resources. If everything were owned by individuals or voluntary groups such as companies, the only means of dealing with what are usually treated as political matters would be private means. Would that be a good thing? I think so, but discuss here only the environmental questions. The free market philosophy's proposed moral rule for everything is: "No force or fraud, except to protect or compensate victims of force or fraud." On environmental matters, then, it is: "Do not use force against persons's utilizations of the environment, except by way of this very rule." The agreement not to employ force against each other is a strategy for handling the major source of evil in human lives—other people's actions. Each refrains from worsening the situation of the other provided the other will return that favor.

This version of a "social contract" is, in my view, the best and perhaps the only rational solution. It is hard to see how the use of force against people who have followed the above rule could ever *help* matters. Forcing is inherently *antiproductive*. Freedom allows each to produce whatever they wish, given the available possibilities. Would-be aggressors can put their energy to better use. Confining us all to

Reprinted with permission from *The Ag Bioethics Forum,* vol. 6, no. 2 (November 1994), pp. 2–5.

activities agreed to by all affected persons is the better way; unlike any others, it is "win-win."

THE ENVIRONMENT

One's environment is the rest of the world outside of oneself—the nonhuman part, for present purposes. What do we do about nature? My answer is the classic one: anyone is free to take anything not already taken by anyone else. This is effected simply by commencing to use it—say, by working on it. This classic view is shared by ordinary people, but denied by many philosophers, who think that the environment is *everybody's,* and that central control over it is essential. Let's see why they're wrong.

Suppose we all have our plots, our houses, our businesses. Where do environmental problems come in? There are two popular ones: resource exhaustion and pollution. Putting resources into the hands of individual people wanting to do the best they can with them solves the first problem, insofar as it is one. . . . I'll address only the pollution question. Pollutions are side effects of otherwise voluntary interactions, on people who didn't ask for them and don't want them. Polluted air or water has stuff in it that the breather or drinker disvalues: it stinks or it makes him sick. Some impurities affect health, some affect taste; both are evils, of different kinds. And frequently there must be trade-offs: manure makes the crops grow better, but it stinks. Each individual farmer decides whether he'd rather have the crops than the smell. But suppose the manure makes the neighbors' air smell worse? What are the rights and wrongs of this? They own their lungs; you insert things they don't want into them, violating their property rights. In principle, then, the free market view says, they may sue. But will they in fact? That depends on two things: how much they dislike it; and how much benefit they get from it. (I omit litigation costs.) Lower food prices made possible by your greater production may provide all the compensation desired, until smellfree fertilizers come along.

Suppose that what the owner puts in his neighbor's lungs not only stinks but harms his health. Does this automatically make it unacceptable? No. It still depends on the same two things: how much it damages their health, and how much that amount of health is worth to them. Some people prefer a smoke-filled life to a long life—say, 70 years with smoke to 80 without. It's their choice. But if their smoke infects my lungs, that is not their choice—smoke is no pleasure to me. You should refrain from smoking in my presence whenever we both have the right to be in that place together, unless you make it worth my while. Which you might: the pleasure of your company may outweigh both the risk to my health and the aesthetic cost of your smoking. People differ, and it is impossible to get a uniform schedule of costs for all. So it is inherently wrong-headed to go about such problems in the usual way: to empower a public law-making body with the power to make laws requiring all to conform.

Further problems arise from today's techno-political climate. Have scientists "discovered" that a certain body of water is "contaminated with a deadly poison"? Sounds bad—until you realize that every body of water in the world contains plenty of deadly poisons, as does practically all the food you eat, especially if it is "naturally" grown. To the question, "Could it kill you?"—the answer is always, "Yes"—if you eat enough of it, combine it with the wrong things, and so on. Should we avoid carcinogens? If we did, we'd all starve. But most carcinogens give us cancer at the ripe old age of 120, which we don't reach anyway. Even if they give it to us at 80, that might still be a good risk, especially if one would die of something else at 79 anyway.

It would be nice if we could know that x will give you cancer at age y. But we don't. We know only that the incidence of such-and-such types of cancer in populations that frequently eat x is higher than in other populations that don't. If eating x gives the J's a longer life-expectancy than the K's, a higher incidence of cancer among J's may be due to that very fact, since cancer increases dramatically with age. That's why so many of us get it now: not because we produce carcinogenic food additives, but because before our time people didn't live long enough to develop most cancers. In the above example, the J's should do nothing—least of all, stop eating x! Especially if they smoke.

Most of the touted pollution risks of death are on the order of 0.00000005. Should we do anything about that? No. The probability of death from other causes is several hundred times that. Imagine a pack-a-day smoker taking great care not to eat some food whose probability of inducing cancer is about 1% that of the cigarettes he smokes. He's like the man about to be executed who refuses a last cigarette on the ground that smoking is bad for his health! Almost all "environmental legislation" is exactly like that.

Before any action is taken, risks must be *significant*. Would I be able to distinguish my risks given the proposed procedure from those I face without it? Once we get into significant levels, we may negotiate: continue the pollution, with continued or increased compensation? Or decrease pollution and pay the costs of the decrease? In principle this is a situation between you and me, which we can settle to mutual advantage. Thus the free-market, libertarian solution to such problems lies precisely in the fact that liberty is not, contrary to Tony Smith's claim, a "moral absolute." Just the opposite: that's the contemporary regulator's view of it, not ours.

Pollution problems exist, of course. But they are always confined to particular groups of people, and usually to relatively small groups. What matters, for any given person, is whether that person is affected, and how much, and whether there are benefits derived from the pollutions that he prefers to the costs of cleanup. In all the currently popular cases, the benefits win.

Consider garbage, which in almost all of North America is handled by public agencies, and the frequent subject of newspaper diatribes about how the planet will ere long succumb to garbage unless we do something, and so forth. On this basis, people are required to spend hours sorting their garbage into two or n distinct varieties, each handled separately, with compulsory recycling—at four times the cost of unsorted garbage, not counting time lost. There would be no talk of a general garbage problem if we allowed these things to be handled rationally, on the free market. There it would be a private business. Garbage companies would charge by the bag, giving people an incentive to minimize garbage production, would dump it on land somebody owns. If it's poor for other uses, using it for waste storage will look attractive, if the price is right. And neighbors of a land-fill would be compensated for any damage to their property caused by leakages and the like—which will induce the garbage dump owners to minimize such leakage.

Is garbage disposal a looming environmental disaster, as we are told? Not at all. The fact is that it is quite trivial on the global landscape. All of the garbage that will be produced in North America in the entire 21st century would fit in a square land-fill 9 miles on a side and 300 feet deep—1/40,000 of the land surface of the United States. Some "disaster"! And of course, within that century better technologies will emerge anyway. Extensive recycling now is a waste of time and money.

To which we should add that giving a lot of *power* to certain people to decide what should be done about the environment and then do it is not a good way to do anything: the assumption that somehow state officials—*especially* democratically elected ones—know what to do about such matters boggles the mind. . . . Note how Tony Smith is forced to suggest, lamely, that the effect of absurd regulations will be to motivate entrepreneurs to find better ways of doing these things.

Aristotle pointed out that people tend to take the best care of what they themselves own. By contrast, they are not nearly as good at looking after other people's property—or, especially, other people's money. That, and only that, is the story of The Environment now, as always. In sum: what we should do now is extend the market principle much farther than we have, get government out of the act—and live better lives as a result. That is the rational way with environmental problems.

QUESTIONS

1 Does justice require the enactment and enforcement of laws that require companies and individuals to clean up the pollution resulting from their activities?
2 Suppose a community, town, or city agrees to allow some of its land to be used for the storage of toxic wastes in exchange for an increase of tax revenues or a necessary hospital. Is this a morally just transaction?

Against Free Market Environmentalism
Tony Smith

Smith critically evaluates four arguments advanced by free market environmentalists: (1) the tragedy of the commons argument; (2) the argument that, if private property owners cannot pass on the costs of pollution to others, they will be motivated to reduce pollution; (3) the argument that free markets are necessary, since market prices provide an objective measure of environmental values; and (4) the argument that the only appropriate role of the state in environmental matters is that of enforcing property rights.

Reprinted with permission from *The Ag Bioethics Forum*, vol. 6, no. 2 (November 1994), pp. 2, 5–7.

Free market environmentalists believe that the extension of private property rights and market transactions is sufficient to address environmental difficulties. They rest their case on four arguments. The first is the "tragedy of the commons" argument: whenever something is subject to collective use, individuals will tend to use it up as fast as possible. If we wish to see pieces of land, bodies of water, or plant and animal species used in a sustainable way, private property rights to these entities ought to be created, for owners tend to preserve their property.

Second, if polluters are able to externalize the costs of pollution onto others, they have no motivation to reduce or eliminate that pollution. But if property rights are extended and strictly enforced, owners will be able to sue polluters for damages to their property. When these suits are successful, the polluters are forced to internalize the costs of pollution, leading them to reduce those costs in the future.

Third, a trade-off must be made between the benefits of providing environmental amenities and the costs of doing so. Market prices provide an "objective measure" of environmental values, and so the proper trade-offs cannot be made unless markets are established. If farmers cannot prevent fishermen and women from using streams bordering their farms, for instance, they have no incentive to incur the expenses necessary to ensure that these streams are well stocked with fish. But if these same farmers were given private rights to these streams, they could exclude all fishermen and women not willing to pay them a fee. The possibility of collecting these fees creates a powerful incentive for them to ensure an adequate habitat for fish populations. Or consider the relationship between environmental groups and land developers. If the former do not have to bear any of the costs of foregone development, then they are likely to ignore these costs. In contrast, in a market setting environmental groups wishing to keep lands in a pristine condition must purchase those lands from their owners. In this manner they are forced to consider seriously the opportunity costs of keeping the land out of development.

Finally, free market environmentalists argue that the state has no role to play in environmental matters beyond that of enforcing property rights. State bureaucrats have particular interests of their own, and they are also susceptible to the influence of special interest groups. And they are not in a position to weigh accurately the costs and benefits of their policies. Is it any surprise that the government's record of environmental management has been deeply flawed?

Do these four arguments for free market environmentalism hold up? 1. There is no invisible hand operating in markets that ensures that environmentally sound practices will be employed just because property rights are in private hands, especially if the dominant form of property is investment capital. Investment today is more mobile than ever before. Capital accumulated in one region need not be reinvested in that same area; if returns are greater elsewhere there is a great likelihood that it will not be reinvested there. Self-interested economic agents will calculate the costs of environmentally benign practices against the costs they will incur if they do not institute those practices. If they estimate the former to exceed the latter, environmentally sound practices will likely not be employed. The owners of capital generally make investments in order to attain a return within a given unit of time. The key question for them is not "What will the physical condition of my holdings be at the end of this time period?" but instead "How much capital will I have accumulated by then?" If considerable amounts of capital can be accumulated at the cost of harming their holdings, this is of little concern as long as attractive investment opportunities are available elsewhere. If considerable amounts of capital can be accumulated at the cost of harming the environment, the environment may well be harmed as long as the harm does not foreclose investment opportunities elsewhere.

2. Can we rely on liability laws and the court system to force polluters to internalize the social costs of pollution? Suppose that a firm with a vast army of well paid corporate lawyers engages in polluting activities that inflict damages on a poor household. What are the chances that the household will be able to afford lawyers with the resources of the corporate lawyers? One would have to be quite naive to believe that in these circumstances the legal system can always be relied upon to ensure that the firms in question internalize the costs of their damaging practices.

Another problem is that liability laws work best in cases where tracing the causal chain of events is a relatively simple matter. Unfortunately the world in which we live is not always so simple. In many cases there are a variety of individual firms engaging in a multiplicity of practices that may—or may not—have had a causal role in bringing about an environmental harm. The greater the number of plausible causal stories, the more difficult it is legally to establish the liability of any particular individual or firm.

There is also the problem that unsound environmental practices can inflict harm on future generations. Future generations cannot sue in court today. *No* corporation takes into account costs for which it may be liable in two or three generations. And so even if the liability system were to work flawlessly, it would still fail to force polluters to internalize all of the costs of their polluting activities.

3. We now come to the third claim, the idea that market prices provide an "objective measure" of environmental matters. If environmental regulations save or extend human lives, how can that benefit be assigned a market price? The value of lives is often measured as a function of the wage premium coal miners, police, and other workers receive in return for facing dangerous conditions. Is a life worth only the wages necessary to attract workers with few alternatives into dangerous conditions? Other methods of fixing the value of a human life in price terms are equally controversial. This means that cost/benefit analysis performed in market prices has an inherent bias. All of the costs of environmental safeguards can be easily put in price terms by corporations, but many of their most profound benefits are not easily measured in market prices.

Leaving environmental trade-offs up to the marketplace means leaving them up to those with the greatest market power. It is true that groups like the Nature Conservancy Fund have been able to purchase land in order to take it out of development; the major environmental groups in the U.S. together have $414,607,984 in funds that in principle could be used in this fashion. But the Irvine Company owns land in areas south of Los Angeles whose value has been estimated to be in excess of $10 billion. If all of the major environmental groups in the U.S. pooled their entire resources together in order to prevent the environmental problems besetting Los Angeles (traffic jams, smog, noise, soil erosion, water shortages, etc.) from spreading south, they would still be $9,585,392,016 short of being able to purchase the holdings of just a single landholder in Southern California. Only giant land developers have access to this sort of capital, developers who have all too often not made environmental issues a central concern.

4. Finally there is the question of the state. Free market environmentalists talk of the provision of "environmental amenities." This language is far too weak. Citizens have a right to a livable environment, and enforcing rights is part of the legitimate function of government. The thesis that responsibility for the environment should be left entirely in the hands of private economic agents is as ludicrous as the idea that rights to freedom of speech or freedom of religion should be left entirely to the market. This means that governmental policies regarding the environment are in principle legitimate, such as bans on chemicals that are toxic to humans or that destroy the ozone layer.

Also, whatever the fantasies of libertarians might be, the state plays a crucial role in the development of technology. Since World War II federal expenditures have financed between one-half and two-thirds of total R&D in the U.S., and over two-thirds of basic research. The aerospace, communications, and electronics industries have thrived as a direct result of these public subsidies. Breakthroughs in environmental technologies are no less crucial to the public good. Publicly funded R&D programs ought to be established to develop manufacturing processes that are non-toxic to workers and pollution-free, along with programs addressing solid waste disposal, alternative sources of energy, environmental clean-ups, etc. Regulations minimizing pollutants and cutting allowable emissions are also a crucial part of technology policy; such regulations guarantee a market for innovations that attain these ends, and thus act as a spur to innovative activity.

It is true enough that state officials have all too often been swayed by the influence of private interest groups when formulating environmental policies. But there are measures that could be taken to lessen the possibility of this occurring (restrictions on lobbying, elimination of PAC funding, public funding of campaigns, etc.). It would be far more preferable to explore this direction than to simply rule out any role for public authorities in environmental matters, as the defenders of free market environmentalism advocate.

QUESTIONS

1 Can Narveson's position be defended against Smith's critique?
2 If corporate activities will result in harmful long-term consequences that will have a negative impact on future generations, should those activities be prohibited by law?

Just Garbage

Peter S. Wenz

Wenz questions the justice of the current distribution of hazards associated with toxic wastes and other *locally undesirable land uses* (LULUs). His concern is especially with the disproportionate effects that such distribution has on the poor, many of

Reprinted with permission of Rowman & Littlefield Publishers from *Faces of Environmental Racism* (1995), edited by Laura Westra and Peter S. Wenz, pp. 57–62, 65–71.

whom are minorities. In criticizing what he calls "environmental racism," Wenz invokes a principle of distributive justice—the "Principle of Commensurate Burdens and Benefits." According to this principle, all other things being equal, those who derive benefits should receive commensurate burdens. In his view, policies based on either the free market approach or the cost-benefit analysis approach are unjust, since they violate this principle of justice. Wenz's solution is a system that would assign LULU points to communities in accordance with the principle. Wealthier communities, which benefit the most from the activities resulting in LULUs, would be required to earn more LULU points than poorer ones. In his view, this would result in a more just system of distribution. Furthermore, since points could not be traded or sold, those who are wealthy would not be able to buy their way out of exposure to toxic waste and other LULUs. One possible result of this could be a decrease in toxic hazards, as members of economically advantaged groups who have the power to bring about the necessary changes will be motivated to do so. In Wenz's view, the LULU point approach should be applied intranationally, within all countries, as well as internationally, among countries.

Environmental racism is evident in practices that expose racial minorities in the United States, and people of color around the world, to disproportionate shares of environmental hazards. These include toxic chemicals in factories, toxic herbicides and pesticides in agriculture, radiation from uranium mining, lead from paint on older buildings, toxic wastes illegally dumped, and toxic wastes legally stored. In this [reading,] which concentrates on issues of toxic waste, both illegally dumped and legally stored, I will examine the justness of current practices as well as the arguments commonly given in their defense. I will then propose an alternative practice that is consistent with prevailing principles of justice.

A DEFENSE OF CURRENT PRACTICES

Defenders often claim that because economic, not racial, considerations account for disproportionate impacts on nonwhites, current practices are neither racist nor morally objectionable. Their reasoning recalls the Doctrine of Double Effect. According to that doctrine, an effect whose production is usually blameworthy becomes blameless when it is incidental to, although predictably conjoined with, the production of another effect whose production is morally justified. The classic case concerns a pregnant woman with uterine cancer. A common, acceptable treatment for uterine cancer is hysterectomy. This will predictably end the pregnancy, as would an abortion. However, Roman Catholic scholars who usually consider abortion blameworthy consider it blameless in this context because it is merely incidental to hysterectomy, which is morally justified to treat uterine cancer. The hysterectomy would be performed in the absence of pregnancy, so the abortion effect is produced neither as an end-in-itself, nor as a means to reach the desired end, which is the cure of cancer.

Defenders of practices that disproportionately disadvantage nonwhites seem to claim, in keeping with the Doctrine of Double Effect, that racial effects are blameless because they are sought neither as ends-in-themselves nor as means to reach a desired goal. They are merely predictable side effects of economic and political practices that disproportionately expose poor people to toxic substances. The argument is that burial of toxic wastes, and other locally undesirable land uses (LULUs), lower property values. People who can afford to move elsewhere do so. They are replaced by buyers (or renters) who are predominately poor and cannot afford housing in more desirable areas. Law professor Vicki Been puts it this way: "As long as the market allows the existing distribution of wealth to allocate goods and services, it would be surprising indeed if, over the long run, LULUs did not impose a disproportionate burden upon the poor." People of color are disproportionately burdened due primarily to poverty, not racism.[1] This defense against charges of racism is important in the American context because racial discrimination is illegal in the United States in circumstances where economic discrimination is permitted. Thus, legal remedies to disproportionate exposure of nonwhites to toxic wastes are available if racism is the cause, but not if people of color are exposed merely because they are poor.

There is strong evidence against claims of racial neutrality. Professor Been acknowledges that even if there is no racism in the process of siting LULUs, racism plays at least some part in the disproportionate exposure of African Americans to them. She cites evidence that "racial discrimination in the sale and rental of housing relegates people of color (especially African Americans) to the least desirable neighborhoods, regardless of their income level."[2]

Without acknowledging for a moment, then, that racism plays no part in the disproportionate exposure of nonwhites to toxic waste, I will ignore this issue to display a weakness in the argument that justice is served when economic discrimination alone is influential. I claim that even if the only discrimination is economic, justice requires redress and significant alteration of current practices. Recourse to the Doctrine of Double Effect presupposes that the primary effect, with which a second effect is incidentally conjoined, is morally justifiable. In the classic case, abortion is justified only because hysterectomy is justified as treatment for uterine cancer. I argue that disproportionate impacts on poor people violate principles of distributive justice, and so are not morally justifiable in the first place. Thus, current practices disproportionately exposing nonwhites to toxic substances are not justifiable even if incidental to the exposure of poor people.

Alternate practices that comply with acceptable principles of distributive justice are suggested below. They would largely solve problems of environmental racism (disproportionate impacts on nonwhites) while ameliorating the injustice of disproportionately exposing poor people to toxic hazards. They would also discourage production of toxic substances, thereby reducing humanity's negative impact on the environment.

THE PRINCIPLE OF COMMENSURATE BURDENS AND BENEFITS

We usually assume that, other things being equal, those who derive benefits should sustain commensurate burdens. We typically associate the burden of work with the benefit of receiving money, and the burdens of monetary payment and tort liability with the benefits of ownership.

There are many exceptions. For example, people can inherit money without working, and be given ownership without purchase. Another exception, which dissociates the benefit of ownership from the burden of tort liability, is the use of tax money to protect the public from hazards associated with private property, as in Superfund legislation. Again, the benefit of money is dissociated from the burden of work when governments support people who are unemployed.

The fact that these exceptions require justification, however, indicates an abiding assumption that people who derive benefits should shoulder commensurate burdens. The ability to inherit without work is justified as a benefit owed to those who wish to bequeath their wealth (which someone in the line of inheritance is assumed to have shouldered burdens to acquire). The same reasoning applies to gifts.

Using tax money (public money) to protect the public from dangerous private property is justified as encouraging private industry and commerce, which are supposed to increase public wealth. The system also protects victims in case private owners become bankrupt as, for example, in Times Beach, Missouri, where the government bought homes made worthless due to dioxin pollution. The company responsible for the pollution was bankrupt.

Tax money is used to help people who are out of work to help them find a job, improve their credentials, or feed their children. This promotes economic growth and equal opportunity. These exceptions prove the rule by the fact that justification for any deviation from the commensuration of benefits and burdens is considered necessary.

Further indication of an abiding belief that benefits and burdens should be commensurate is grumbling that, for example, many professional athletes and corporate executives are overpaid. Although the athletes and executives shoulder the burden of work, the complaint is that their benefits are disproportionate to their burdens. People on welfare are sometimes criticized for receiving even modest amounts of taxpayer money without shouldering the burdens of work, hence recurrent calls for "welfare reform." Even though these calls are often justified as means to reducing government budget deficits, the moral issue is more basic than the economic. Welfare expenditures are minor compared to other programs, and alternatives that require poor people to work are often more expensive than welfare as we know it.

The principle of commensuration between benefits and burdens is not the only moral principle governing distributive justice, and may not be the most important, but it is basic. Practices can be justified by showing them to conform, all things considered, to this principle. Thus, there is no move to "reform" the receipt of moderate pay for ordinary work, because it exemplifies the principle. On the other hand, practices that do not conform are liable to attack and require alternate justification, as we have seen in the cases of inheritance, gifts, Superfund legislation, and welfare.

Applying the principle of commensuration between burdens and benefits to the issue at hand yields the following: In the absence of countervailing considerations, the burdens of ill health associated with toxic hazards should be related to benefits derived from processes and products that create these hazards.

TOXIC HAZARDS AND CONSUMERISM

In order to assess, in light of the principle of commensuration between benefits and burdens, the justice of current distributions of toxic hazards, the benefits of their generation must be considered. Toxic wastes result from many manufacturing processes, including those for a host of common items and materials, such as paint, solvents, plastics, and most petrochemical-based materials. These materials surround us in the paint on our homes, in our refrigerator containers, in our clothing, in our plumbing, in our garbage pails, and elsewhere.

Toxins are released into the environment in greater quantities now than ever before because we now have a consumer-oriented society where the acquisition, use, and disposal of individually owned items is greatly desired. We associate the numerical dollar value of the items at our disposal with our "standard of living," and assume that a higher standard is conducive to, if not identical with, a better life. So toxic wastes needing disposal are produced as by-products of the general pursuit of what our society defines as valuable, that is, the consumption of material goods.

Our economy requires increasing consumer demand to keep people working (to produce what is demanded). This is why there is concern each Christmas season, for example, that shoppers may not buy enough. If demand is insufficient, people may be put out of work. Demand must increase, not merely hold steady, because commercial competition improves labor efficiency in manufacture (and now in the service sector as well), so fewer workers can produce desired items. More items must be desired to forestall labor efficiency-induced unemployment, which is grave in a society where people depend primarily on wages to secure life's necessities.

Demand is kept high largely by convincing people that their lives require improvement, which consumer purchases will effect. When improvements are seen as needed, not merely desired, people purchase more readily. So our culture encourages economic expansion by blurring the distinction between wants and needs.

One way the distinction is blurred is through promotion of worry. If one feels insecure without the desired item or service, and so worries about life without it, then its provision is easily seen as a need. Commercials, and other shapers of social expectations, keep people worried by adjusting downward toward the trivial what people are expected to worry about. People worry about the provision of food, clothing, and housing without much inducement. When these basic needs are satisfied, however, attention shifts to indoor plumbing, for example, then to stylish indoor plumbing. The process continues with need for a second or third bathroom, a kitchen disposal, and a refrigerator attached to the plumbing so that ice is made automatically in the freezer, and cold water can be obtained without even opening the refrigerator door. The same kind of progression results in cars with CD players, cellular phones, and automatic readouts of average fuel consumption per mile.

Abraham Maslow was not accurately describing people in our society when he claimed that after physiological, safety, love, and (self-) esteem needs are met, people work toward self-actualization, becoming increasingly their own unique selves by fully developing their talents. Maslow's Hierarchy of Needs describes people in our society less than Wenz's Lowerarchy of Worry. When one source of worry is put to rest by an appropriate purchase, some matter less inherently or obviously worrisome takes its place as the focus of concern. Such worry-substitution must be amenable to indefinite repetition in order to motivate purchases needed to keep the economy growing without inherent limit. If commercial society is supported by consumer demand, it is worry all the way down. Toxic wastes are produced in this context.

People tend to worry about ill health and early death without much inducement. These concerns are heightened in a society dependent upon the production of worry, so expenditure on health care consumes an increasing percentage of the gross domestic product. As knowledge of health impairment due to toxic substances increases, people are decreasingly tolerant of risks associated with their proximity. Thus, the same mindset of worry that elicits production that generates toxic wastes, exacerbates reaction to their proximity. The result is a desire for their placement elsewhere, hence the NIMBY syndrome—Not In My Back Yard. On this account, NIMBYism is not aberrantly selfish behavior, but integral to the cultural value system required for great volumes of toxic waste to be generated in the first place.

Combined with the principle of Commensurate Burdens and Benefits, that value system indicates who should suffer the burden of proximity to toxic wastes. Other things being equal, those who benefit most from the production of waste should shoulder the greatest share of burdens associated with its disposal. In our society, consumption of goods is valued highly and constitutes the principal benefit associated with the generation of toxic wastes. Such consumption is generally correlated with income and wealth. So other things being equal, justice requires that people's proximity to toxic wastes be related positively to their income and wealth. This is exactly opposite to the predominant tendency in our society, where poor people are more proximate to toxic wastes dumped illegally and stored legally. . . .

FREE MARKET APPROACH

Toxic wastes, a burden, could be placed where residents accept them in return for monetary payment, a benefit. Since market transactions often satisfactorily [result in] commensurate burdens and benefits, this approach may seem to honor the principle of commensuration between burdens and benefits.

Unlike many market transactions, however, whole communities, acting as corporate bodies, would have to contract with those seeking to bury wastes. Otherwise, any single individual in the community could veto the transaction. . . . Communities could receive money to improve such public facilities as schools, parks, and hospitals, in addition to obtaining tax revenues and jobs that result ordinarily from business expansion.

The major problem with this free market approach is that it fails to accord equal consideration to everyone's interests. Where basic or vital goods and services are at issue, we usually think equal consideration of interests requires ameliorating inequalities of distribution that markets tend to produce. For example, one reason, although not the only reason, for public education is to provide every child with the basic intellectual tools necessary for success in our society. A purely free market approach, by contrast, would result in excellent education for children of wealthy parents and little or no education for children of the nation's poorest residents. Opportunities for children of poor parents would be so inferior that we would say the children's interests had not been given equal consideration.

The reasoning is similar where vital goods are concerned. The United States has the Medicaid program for poor people to supplement market transactions in health care precisely because equal consideration of interests requires that everyone be given access to health care. The 1994 health care debate in the United States was, ostensibly, about how to achieve universal coverage, not about whether or not justice required such coverage. With the exception of South Africa, every other industrialized country already has universal coverage for health care. Where vital needs are concerned, markets are supplemented or avoided in order to give equal consideration to everyone's interests.

Another example concerns military service in time of war. The United States employed conscription during the Civil War, both world wars, the Korean War, and the war in Vietnam. When the national interest requires placing many people in mortal danger, it is considered just that exposure be largely unrelated to income and market transactions.

The United States does not currently provide genuine equality in education or health care, nor did universal conscription (of males) put all men at equal risk in time of war. In all three areas, advantage accrues to those with greater income and wealth. (During the Civil War, paying for a substitute was legal in many cases.) Imperfection in practice, however, should not obscure general agreement in theory that justice requires equal consideration of interests, and that such equal consideration requires rejecting purely free market approaches where basic or vital needs are concerned.

Toxic substances affect basic and vital interests. Lead, arsenic, and cadmium in the vicinity of children's homes can result in mental retardation of the children. Navaho teens exposed to radiation from uranium mine tailings have seventeen times the national average of reproductive organ cancer. Environmental Protection Agency (EPA) officials estimate that toxic air pollution in areas of South Chicago increases cancer risks one hundred to one thousand times. Pollution from Otis Air Force base in Massachusetts is associated with alarming increases in cancer rates. Non-Hodgkin's Lymphoma is related to living near stone, clay, and glass industry facilities, and leukemia is related to living near chemical and petroleum plants. In general, cancer rates are higher in the United States near industries that use toxic substances and discard them nearby.

In sum, the placement of toxic wastes affects basic and vital interests just as do education, health care, and wartime military service. Exemption from market decisions is required to avoid unjust impositions on the poor, and to respect people's interests equally. A child dying of cancer receives little benefit from the community's new swimming pool.

COST-BENEFIT ANALYSIS (CBA)

CBA is an economist's version of utilitarianism, where the sum to be maximized is society's wealth, as measured in monetary units, instead of happiness or preference satisfaction. Society's wealth is computed by noting (and estimating where necessary) what people are willing to pay for goods and services. The more people are willing to pay for what exists in society, the better off society is, according to CBA.

CBA will characteristically require placement of toxic wastes near poor people. Such placement usually lowers land values (what people are willing to pay for property). Land that is already cheap, where poor people live, will not lose as much value as land that is currently expensive, where wealthier people live, so a smaller loss of social wealth attends placement of toxic wastes near poor people. This is just the opposite of what the Principle of Commensurate Burdens and Benefits requires.

The use of CBA also violates equal consideration of interests, operating much like free market approaches. Where a vital concern is at issue, equal consideration of interests requires that people be considered irrespective of income. The placement of toxic wastes affects vital interests. Yet CBA would have poor people exposed disproportionately to such wastes.

In sum, . . . free market distribution . . . and cost-benefit analysis are inadequate principles and methodologies to guide the just distribution of toxic wastes.

LULU POINTS

An approach that avoids these difficulties assigns points to different types of locally undesirable land uses (LULUs) and requires that all communities earn LULU points.[3] In keeping with the Principle of Commensurate Burdens and Benefits, wealthy communities would be required to earn more LULU points than poorer ones. Communities would be identified by currently existing political divisions, such as villages, towns, city wards, cities, and counties.

Toxic waste dumps are only one kind of LULU. Others include prisons, half-way houses, municipal waste sites, low-income housing, and power plants, whether nuclear or coal fired. A large deposit of extremely toxic waste, for example, may be assigned twenty points when properly buried but fifty points when illegally dumped. A much smaller deposit of properly buried toxic waste may be assigned only ten points, as may a coal-fired power plant. A nuclear power plant may be assigned twenty-five points, while municipal waste sites are only five points, and one hundred units of low-income housing are eight points.

These numbers are only speculations. Points would be assigned by considering probable effects of different LULUs on basic needs, and responses to questionnaires investigating people's levels of discomfort with LULUs of various sorts. Once numbers are assigned, the total number of LULU points to be distributed in a given time period could be calculated by considering planned development and needs for prisons, power plants, low-income housing, and so on. One could also calculate points for a community's already existing LULUs. Communities could then be required to host LULUs in proportion to their income or wealth, with new allocation of LULUs (and associated points) correcting for currently existing deviations from the rules of proportionality.

Wherever significant differences of wealth or income exist between two areas, these areas should be considered part of different communities if there is any political division between them. Thus, a county with rich and poor areas would not be considered a single community for purposes of locating LULUs. Instead, villages or towns may be so considered. A city with rich and poor areas may similarly be reduced to its wards. The purpose of segregating areas of different income or wealth from one another is to permit the imposition of greater LULU burdens on wealthier communities. When wealthy and poor areas are considered as one larger community, there is the danger that the community will earn its LULU points by placing hazardous waste near its poorer members. This possibility is reduced when only relatively wealthy people live in a smaller community that must earn LULU points.

PRACTICAL IMPLICATIONS

Political strategy is beyond the scope of this [essay,] so I will refrain from commenting on problems and prospects for securing passage and implementation of the foregoing proposal. I maintain that the proposal is just. In a society where injustice is common, it is no surprise that proposals for rectifications meet stiff resistance.

Were the LULU points proposal implemented, environmental racism would be reduced enormously. To the extent that poor people exposed to environmental hazards are members of racial minorities, relieving the poor of disproportionate exposure would also relieve people of color.

This is not to say that environmental racism would be ended completely. Implementation of the proposal requires judgment in particular cases. Until racism is itself ended, such judgment will predictably be exercised at times to the disadvantage of minority populations. However, because most people of color currently burdened by environmental racism are relatively poor, implementing the proposal would remove 80 to 90 percent of the effects of environmental racism. While efforts to end racism at all levels should continue, reducing the burdens of racism is generally advantageous to people of color. Such reductions are especially worthy when integral to policies that improve distributive justice generally.

Besides improving distributive justice and reducing the burdens of environmental racism, implementing the LULU points proposal would benefit life on earth generally by reducing the generation of toxic hazards. When people of wealth, who exercise control of manufacturing processes, marketing campaigns, and media coverage, are themselves threatened disproportionately by toxic hazards, the culture will evolve quickly to find their production largely unnecessary. It will be discovered, for example, that many plastic items can be made of wood, just as it was discovered in the late 1980s that the production of many ozone-destroying chemicals is unnecessary. Similarly, necessity being the mother of invention, it was discovered during World War II that many women could work in factories. When certain interests are threatened, the impossible does not even take longer.

The above approach to environmental injustice should, of course, be applied internationally and intranationally within all countries. The same considerations of justice condemn universally, all other things being equal, exposing poor people to vital dangers whose generation predominantly benefits the rich. This implies that rich countries should not ship their toxic wastes to poor countries. Since many poorer countries, such as those in Africa, are inhabited primarily by nonwhites, prohibiting shipments of toxic wastes to them would reduce significantly worldwide environmental racism. A prohibition on such shipments would also discourage production of dangerous wastes, as it would require people in rich countries to live with whatever dangers they create. If the principle of LULU points were applied in all countries, including poor ones, elites in those countries would lose interest in earning foreign currency credits through importation of waste, as they would be disproportionately exposed to imported toxins.

In sum, we could reduce environmental injustice considerably through a general program of distributive justice concerning environmental hazards. Pollution would not thereby be eliminated, since to live is to pollute. But such a program would motivate significant reduction in the generation of toxic wastes, and help the poor, especially people of color, as well as the environment.

NOTES

1 Vicki Been, "Market Forces, Not Racist Practices, May Affect the Siting of Locally Undesirable Land Uses," in *At Issue: Environmental Justice,* ed. by Jonathan Petrikin (San Diego, Calif.: Greenhaven Press, 1995), 41.
2 Been, 41.
3 The idea of LULU points comes to me from Frank J. Popper, "LULUs and Their Blockage," in *Confronting Regional Challenges: Approaches to LULUs, Growth, and Other Vexing Governance Problems,* ed. by Joseph DiMento and Le Roy Graymer (Los Angeles, Calif.: Lincoln Institute of Land Policy, 1991), 13–27, especially 24.

QUESTIONS

1 Does environmental racism, as Wenz describes it, exist in your community? Can you give specific examples to illustrate your position?
2 In a just society, what principles should guide policies dealing with the placement of locally undesirable land uses (LULUs)?

The Land Ethic

Aldo Leopold

Leopold articulates a biocentric point of view under the heading of a *land ethic.* His understanding of "land" is very broad, including "soils, waters, plants, and animals." He argues that we must stop thinking of land merely as property and start thinking of it as worthy of respect and moral consideration in its own right. In accordance with Leopold's land ethic, humankind is not the conqueror of the "land-community" but "plain member and citizen" of it; we must respect fellow members of the community and the community as a whole. Leopold explicitly argues against a system of environmental conservation based solely on economic considerations. He also illustrates some of the interconnected workings of the land-community by employing the image of a pyramid. Leopold's discussion culminates in his famous statement of a moral principle formulated in reference to the "integrity, stability, and beauty of the biotic community."

When god-like Odysseus returned from the wars in Troy, he hanged all on one rope a dozen slave-girls of his household whom he suspected of misbehavior during his absence.

This hanging involved no question of propriety. The girls were property. The disposal of property was then, as now, a matter of expediency, not of right and wrong.

Concepts of right and wrong were not lacking from Odysseus' Greece: witness the fidelity of his wife through the long years before at last his black-prowed galleys clove the wine-dark seas for home. The ethical structure of that day covered wives, but had not yet been extended to human chattels. During the three thousand years which have since elapsed, ethical criteria have been extended to many fields of conduct, with corresponding shrinkages in those judged by expediency only.

THE ETHICAL SEQUENCE

This extension of ethics, so far studied only by philosophers, is actually a process in ecological evolution. Its sequences may be described in ecological as well as in philosophical terms. An ethic, ecologically, is a limitation on freedom of action in the struggle for existence. An ethic, philosophically, is a differentiation of social from anti-social conduct. These are two definitions of one thing. The thing has its origin in the tendency of interdependent individuals or groups to evolve modes of co-operation. The ecologist calls these symbioses. Politics and economics are advanced symbioses in which the original free-for-all competition has been replaced, in part, by co-operative mechanisms with an ethical content.

The complexity of co-operative mechanisms has increased with population density, and with the efficiency of tools. It was simpler, for example, to define the anti-social uses of sticks and stones in the days of the mastodons than of bullets and billboards in the age of motors.

The first ethics dealt with the relation between individuals; the Mosaic Decalogue is an example. Later accretions dealt with the relation between the individual and society. The Golden Rule tries to integrate the individual to society; democracy to integrate social organization to the individual.

There is as yet no ethic dealing with man's relation to land and to the animals and plants which grow upon it. Land, like Odysseus' slave-girls, is still property. The land-relation is still strictly economic, entailing privileges but not obligations.

The extension of ethics to this third element in human environment is, if I read the evidence correctly, an evolutionary possibility and an ecological necessity. It is the third step in a sequence. The first two have already been taken. Individual thinkers since the days of Ezekiel and Isaiah have asserted that the despoliation of land is not only inexpedient but wrong. Society, however, has not yet affirmed their belief. I regard the present conservation movement as the embryo of such an affirmation.

An ethic may be regarded as a mode of guidance for meeting ecological situations so new or intricate, or involving such deferred reactions, that the path of social expediency is not discernible to the average individual. Animal instincts are modes of guidance for the individual in meeting such situations. Ethics are possibly a kind of community instinct in-the-making.

THE COMMUNITY CONCEPT

All ethics so far evolved rest upon a single premise: that the individual is a member of a community of interdependent parts. His instincts prompt him to compete for his place in that community, but his ethics prompt him also to co-operate (perhaps in order that there may be a place to compete for).

The land ethic simply enlarges the boundaries of the community to include soils, waters, plants, and animals, or collectively, the land.

This sounds simple: do we not already sing our love for and obligation to the land of the free and the home of the brave? Yes, but just what and whom do we love? Certainly not the soil, which we are sending helter-skelter downriver. Certainly not the waters, which we assume have no function except to turn turbines, float barges, and carry off sewage. Certainly not the plants, of which we exterminate whole communities without batting an eye. Certainly not the animals, of which we have already extirpated many of the largest and most beautiful species. A land ethic of course cannot prevent the alteration, management, and use of these 'resources,' but it does affirm their right to continued existence, and, at least in spots, their continued existence in a natural state.

In short, a land ethic changes the role of *Homo sapiens* from conqueror of the land-community to plain member and citizen of it. It implies respect for his fellow-members, and also respect for the community as such.

In human history, we have learned (I hope) that the conqueror role is eventually self-defeating. Why? Because it is implicit in such a role that the conqueror knows, *ex cathedra,* just what makes the community clock tick, and just what and who is valuable, and what and who is worthless, in community life. It always turns out that he knows neither, and this is why his conquests eventually defeat themselves.

In the biotic community, a parallel situation exists. Abraham knew exactly what the land was for: it was to drip milk and honey into Abraham's mouth. At the present moment, the assurance with which we regard this assumption is inverse to the degree of our education.

The ordinary citizen today assumes that science knows what makes the community clock tick; the scientist is equally sure that he does not. He knows that the biotic mechanism is so complex that its workings may never be fully understood. . . .

SUBSTITUTES FOR A LAND ETHIC

When the logic of history hungers for bread and we hand out a stone, we are at pains to explain how much the stone resembles bread. I now describe some of the stones which serve in lieu of a land ethic.

One basic weakness in a conservation system based wholly on economic motives is that most members of the land community have no economic value. Wildflowers and songbirds are examples. Of the 22,000 higher plants and animals native to Wisconsin, it is doubtful whether more than 5 per cent can be sold, fed, eaten, or otherwise put to economic use. Yet these creatures are members of the biotic community, and if (as I believe) its stability depends on its integrity, they are entitled to continuance.

When one of these non-economic categories is threatened, and if we happen to love it, we invent subterfuges to give it economic importance. At the beginning of the century songbirds were supposed to be disappearing. Ornithologists jumped to the rescue with some distinctly shaky evidence to the effect that insects would eat us up if birds failed to control them. The evidence had to be economic in order to be valid.

It is painful to read these circumlocutions today. We have no land ethic yet, but we have at least drawn nearer the point of admitting that birds should continue as a matter of biotic right, regardless of the presence or absence of economic advantage to us.

A parallel situation exists in respect of predatory mammals, raptorial birds, and fish-eating birds. Time was when biologists somewhat overworked the evidence that these creatures preserve the health of game by killing weaklings, or that they control rodents for the farmer, or that they prey only on 'worthless' species. Here again, the evidence had to be economic in order to be valid. It is only in recent years that we hear the more honest argument that predators are members of the community, and that no special interest has the right to exterminate them for the sake of a benefit, real or fancied, to itself. . . .

Some species of trees have been 'read out of the party' by economics-minded foresters because they grow too slowly, or have too low a sale value to pay as timber crops: white cedar, tamarack, cypress, beech, and hemlock are examples. In Europe, where forestry is ecologically more advanced, the non-commercial tree species are recognized as members of the native forest community, to be preserved as such, within reason. Moreover, some (like beech) have been found to have a valuable function in building up soil fertility. The interdependence of the forest and its constituent tree species, ground flora, and fauna is taken for granted.

Lack of economic value is sometimes a character not only of species or groups, but of entire biotic communities: marshes, bogs, dunes, and 'deserts' are examples. Our formula in such cases is to relegate their conservation to government as refuges, monuments, or parks. The difficulty is that these communities are usually interspersed with more valuable private lands; the government cannot possibly own or control such scattered parcels. The net effect is that we have relegated some of them to ultimate extinction over large areas. . . .

To sum up: a system of conservation based solely on economic self-interest is hopelessly lopsided. It tends to ignore, and thus eventually to eliminate, many elements in the land community that lack commercial value, but that are (as far as we know) essential to its healthy functioning. It assumes, falsely, I think, that the economic parts of the biotic clock will function without the uneconomic parts. . . .

THE LAND PYRAMID

An ethic to supplement and guide the economic relation to land presupposes the existence of some mental image of land as a biotic mechanism. We can be ethical only in relation to something we can see, feel, understand, love, or otherwise have faith in.

The image commonly employed in conservation education is 'the balance of nature.' For reasons too lengthy to detail here, this figure of speech fails to describe accurately what little we know about the land mechanism. A much truer image is the one employed in ecology: the biotic pyramid. I shall first sketch the pyramid as a symbol of land. . . .

Plants absorb energy from the sun. This energy flows through a circuit called the biota, which may be represented by a pyramid consisting of layers. The bottom layer is the soil. A plant layer rests on the soil, an insect layer on the plants, a bird and rodent layer on the insects, and so on up through various animal groups to the apex layer, which consists of the larger carnivores.

The species of a layer are alike not in where they came from, or in what they look like, but rather in what they eat. Each successive layer depends on those below it for food and often for other services, and each in turn furnishes food and services to those above. Proceeding upward, each successive layer decreases in numerical abundance. Thus, for every carnivore there are hundreds of his prey, thousands of their prey, millions of insects, uncountable plants. The pyramidal form of the system reflects this numerical progression from apex to base. Man shares an intermediate layer with the bears, raccoons, and squirrels which eat both meat and vegetables.

The lines of dependency for food and other services are called food chains. Thus soil-oak-deer-Indian is a chain that has now been largely converted to soil-corn-cow-farmer. Each species, including ourselves, is a link in many chains. The deer eats a hundred plants other than oak, and the cow a hundred plants other than corn. Both, then, are links in a hundred chains. The pyramid is a tangle of chains so complex as to seem disorderly, yet the stability of the system proves it to be a highly organized structure. Its functioning depends on the co-operation and competition of its diverse parts.

In the beginning, the pyramid of life was low and squat, the food chains short and simple. Evolution has added layer after layer, link after link. Man is one of thousands of accretions to the height and complexity of the pyramid. Science has given us many doubts, but it has given us at least one certainty: the trend of evolution is to elaborate and diversify the biota.

Land, then, is not merely soil; it is a fountain of energy flowing through a circuit of soils, plants, and animals. Food chains are the living channels which conduct energy upward; death and decay return it to the soil. The circuit is not closed; some energy is dissipated in decay, some is added by absorption from the air, some is stored in soils, peats, and long-lived forests; but it is a sustained circuit, like a slowly augmented revolving fund of life. There is always a net loss by downhill wash, but this is normally small and offset by the decay of rocks. It is deposited in the ocean and, in the course of geological time, raised to form new lands and new pyramids.

The velocity and character of the upward flow of energy depend on the complex structure of the plant and animal community, much as the upward flow of sap in a tree depends on its complex cellular organization. Without this complexity, normal circulation would presumably not occur. Structure means the characteristic numbers, as well as the characteristic kinds and functions, of the component species. This interdependence between the complex structure of the land and its smooth functioning as an energy unit is one of its basic attributes.

When a change occurs in one part of the circuit, many other parts must adjust themselves to it. Change does not necessarily obstruct or divert the flow of energy; evolution is a long series of self-induced changes, the net result of which has been to elaborate the flow mechanism and to lengthen the circuit. Evolutionary changes, however, are usually slow and local. Man's invention of tools has enabled him to make changes of unprecedented violence, rapidity, and scope. . . .

THE OUTLOOK

It is inconceivable to me that an ethical relation to land can exist without love, respect, and admiration for land, and a high regard for its value. By value, I of course mean something far broader than mere economic value; I mean value in the philosophical sense. . . .

The 'key-log' which must be moved to release the evolutionary process for an ethic is simply this: quit thinking about decent land-use as solely an economic problem. Examine each question in terms of what is ethically and esthetically right, as well as what is economically expedient. A thing is right when it tends to preserve the integrity, stability, and beauty of the biotic community. It is wrong when it tends otherwise.

It of course goes without saying that economic feasibility limits the tether of what can or cannot be done for land. It always has and it always will. The fallacy the economic determinists have tied around our collective neck, and which we now need to cast off, is the belief that economics determines *all* land-use. This is simply not true. An innumerable host of actions and attitudes, comprising perhaps the bulk of all land relations, is determined by the land-users' tastes and predilections, rather than by his purse. The bulk of all land relations hinges on investments of time, forethought, skill, and faith rather than on investments of cash. As a land-user thinketh, so is he.

I have purposely presented the land ethic as a product of social evolution because nothing so important as an ethic is ever 'written.' Only the most superficial student of history supposes that Moses 'wrote' the Decalogue; it evolved in the minds of a thinking community, and Moses wrote a tentative summary of it for a 'seminar.' I say tentative because evolution never stops.

The evolution of a land ethic is an intellectual as well as emotional process. Conservation is paved with good intentions which prove to be futile, or even dangerous, because they are devoid of critical understanding either of the land, or of economic land-use. I think it is a truism that as the ethical frontier advances from the individual to the community, its intellectual content increases.

The mechanism of operation is the same for any ethic: social approbation for right actions; social disapproval for wrong actions.

By and large, our present problem is one of attitudes and implements. We are remodeling the Alhambra with a steamshovel, and we are proud of our yardage. We shall hardly relinquish the shovel, which after all has many good points, but we are in need of gentler and more objective criteria for its successful use.

QUESTIONS

1 Do songbirds and wildflowers have a right to exist? Do cockroaches and weeds have a right to exist?

2 Leopold claims that "[a] thing is right when it tends to preserve the integrity, stability, and beauty of the biotic community" and "[i]t is wrong when it tends otherwise." What are the implications of this principle for our way of life?

3 To what extent would you endorse Leopold's land ethic?

Environmental Ethics

Bernard E. Rollin

In contrast to Baxter's anthropocentric approach and Leopold's biocentric approach, Rollin adopts a sentientist approach to environmental issues. He contends that because humans and other animals are sentient beings who can be harmed, they have intrinsic value and moral rights. Rivers, forests, species, and ecosystems, in contrast, have only instrumental value, since they are not sentient beings and thus cannot be harmed, except in a metaphorical sense. Nonetheless, Rollin maintains, once we recognize the intrinsic value of *all* sentient beings, we can develop a rich environmental ethic based on the interests of human beings and other animals.

The past two decades have witnessed a major revolutionary thrust in social moral awareness, one virtually unknown in mainstream Western ethical thinking, although not unrecognized in other cultural traditions; for example, the Navajo, whose descriptive language for nature and animals is suffused with ethical nuances; the Australian Aboriginal people; and the ancient Persians. This thrust is the recognition that nonhuman entities enjoy some moral status as objects of moral concern and deliberation. Although the investigation of the moral status of nonhuman entities has sometimes been subsumed under the global rubric of environmental ethics, such a blanket term does not do adequate justice to the substantial conceptual differences of its components.

THE MORAL STATUS OF NONHUMAN THINGS

As a bare minimum, environmental ethics comprises two fundamentally divergent concerns—namely, concern with individual nonhuman animals as direct objects of moral concern and concern with species, ecosystems, environments, wilderness areas, forests, the biosphere, and other nonsentient natural or even abstract objects as direct objects of moral concern. Usually, although with a number of major exceptions,[1] those who give primacy to animals have tended to deny the moral significance of environments and species as direct objects of moral concern, whereas

Reprinted with permission from *Problems of International Justice* (Westview, 1988), edited by Steven Luper-Foy, pp. 125–131.

those who give moral primacy to enviro-ecological concerns tend to deny or at least downplay the moral significance of individual animals.[2] Significant though these differences are, they should not cloud the dramatic nature of this common attempt to break out of a moral tradition that finds loci of value only in human beings and, derivatively, in human institutions.

Because of the revolutionary nature of these attempts, they also remain somewhat undeveloped and embryonic. . . .

The most plausible strategy in attempting to revise traditional moral theory and practice is to show that the seeds of the new moral notions or extensions of old moral notions are, in fact, already implicit in the old moral machinery developed to deal with other issues. Only when such avenues are exhausted will it make sense to recommend major rebuilding of the machinery, rather than putting it to new uses. The classic examples of such extensions are obviously found in the extension of the moral/legal machinery of Western democracies to cover traditionally disenfranchised groups such as women and minorities. The relatively smooth flow of such applications owes much of its smoothness to the plausibility of a simple argument of the form:

> Our extant moral principles ought to cover all humans.
> Women are humans.
> _____
> ∴ Our extant moral principles ought to cover women.

On the other hand, conceptually radical departures from tradition do not lend themselves to such simple rational reconstruction. Thus, for example, the principle of *favoring* members of traditionally disenfranchised groups at the expense of innocent members of nondisenfranchised groups for the sake of rectifying historically based injustice is viewed as much more morally problematic and ambivalent than simply according rights to these groups. Thus, it would be difficult to construct a simple syllogism in defense of this practice that would garner universal acquiescence with the ease of the one indicated previously.

Thus, one needs to distinguish between moral revolutionary thrusts that are ostensibly paradoxical to common sense and practice because they have been ignored in a wholesale fashion, yet are in fact logical extensions of common morality, and those revolutionary thrusts that are genuinely paradoxical to previous moral thinking and practice because they are not implicit therein. Being genuinely paradoxical does not invalidate a new moral thrust—it does, however, place upon its proponents a substantially greater burden of proof. Those philosophers, like myself, who have argued for a recognition of the moral status of individual animals and the rights and legal status that derive therefrom, have attempted to place ourselves in the first category. We recognize that a society that kills and eats billions of animals, kills millions more in research, and disposes of millions more for relatively frivolous reasons and that relies economically on animal exploitation as a mainstay of social wealth, considers talk of elevating the moral status of animals as impossible and paradoxical. But this does not mean that such an elevation does not follow unrecognized from moral principles we all hold. Indeed, the abolition of slavery or the liberation of women appeared similarly paradoxical and economically impossible, yet gradually both were perceived as morally necessary, in part because both were implicit, albeit unrecognized, in previously acknowledged assumptions.[3]

My own argument for elevating the status of animals has been a relatively straightforward deduction of unnoticed implications of traditional morality. I have tried to show that no morally relevant grounds for excluding animals from the full application of our moral machinery will stand up to rational scrutiny. Traditional claims that rely on notions such as animals have no souls, are inferior to humans in power or intelligence or evolutionary status, are not moral agents, are not rational, are not possessed of free will, are not capable of language, are not bound by social contract to humans, and so forth, do not serve as justifiable reasons for excluding animals and their interests from the moral arena.

By the same token, morally relevant similarities exist between us and them in the case of the "higher" animals. Animals can suffer, as Jeremy Bentham said; they have interests; what we do to them matters to them; they can feel pain, fear, anxiety, loneliness, pleasure, boredom, and so on. Indeed, the simplicity and power of the argument calling attention to such morally relevant similarities has led Cartesians from Descartes to modern physiologists with a vested interest against attributing moral status to animals to declare that animals are machines with no morally relevant modes of awareness, a point often addressed today against moral claims such as mine. In fact, such claims have become a mainstay of what I have elsewhere called the "common sense of science." Thus, one who argues for an augmented moral status for animals finds it necessary to establish philosophically and scientifically what common sense takes for granted—namely, that animals *are* conscious.[4] Most people whose common sense is intact are not Cartesians and can see that moral talk cannot be withheld from animals and our treatment of them.

In my own work, appealing again to common moral practice, I have stressed our society's quasi-moral, quasi-legal notion of rights as a reflection of our commitment to the moral primacy of the individual, rather than the state. Rights protect what are hypothesized as the fundamental interests of human beings from cavalier encroachment by the common good—such interests as speech, assembly, belief, property, privacy, freedom from torture, and so forth. But those animals who are conscious also have fundamental interests arising out of *their* biologically given natures (or *teloi*), the infringement upon which matters greatly to them, and the fulfillment of which is central to their lives. Hence, I deduce the notion of animal rights from our common moral theory and practice and attempt to show that conceptually, at least, it is a deduction from the moral framework of the status quo rather than a major revision therein. Moral concern for individual animals follows from the hitherto ignored presence of morally relevant characteristics, primarily sentience, in animals. As a result, I am comfortable in attributing what Immanuel Kant called "intrinsic value," not merely use value, to animals if we attribute it to people.[5]

The task is far more formidable for those who attempt to make nonsentient natural objects, such as rivers and mountains, or, worse, quasi-abstract entities, such as species and ecosystems, into direct objects of moral concern. Interestingly enough, in direct opposition to the case of animals, such moves appear prima facie plausible to common morality, which has long expressed concern for the value and preservation of some natural objects, while condoning wholesale exploitation of others. In the same way, common practice often showed extreme concern for certain favored kinds of animals, while systematically exploiting others. Thus, many people in the United States strongly oppose scientific research on dogs and cats, but are totally unconcerned about such use of rodents or swine. What is superficially plausible, however, quite unlike the case of animals, turns out to be deeply paradoxical given the machinery of traditional morality.

Many leading environmental ethicists have attempted to do for nonsentient natural objects and abstract objects the same sort of thing I have tried to do for animals—namely, attempted to elevate their status to direct objects of intrinsic value, ends in themselves, which are morally valuable not only because of their relations and utility to sentient beings, but in and of themselves.[6] To my knowledge, none of these theorists has attempted to claim, as I do for animals, that the locus of such value lies in the fact that what we do to these entities matters to them. No one has argued that we can harm rivers, species, or ecosystems in ways that matter to them.

Wherein, then, do these theorists locate the intrinsic value of these entities? This is not at all clear in the writings, but seems to come down to one of the following doubtful moves:

1 Going from the fact that environmental factors are absolutely essential to the well-being or survival of beings that are loci of intrinsic value to the conclusion that environmental factors therefore enjoy a similar or even higher moral status. Such a move is clearly fallacious. Just because I cannot survive without insulin, and I am an object of intrinsic value, it does not follow that insulin is, too. In fact, the insulin is a paradigmatic example of instrumental value.

2 Going from the fact that the environment "creates" all sentient creatures to the fact that its welfare is more important than theirs. This is really a variation on (1) and succumbs to the same sort of criticism, namely, that this reasoning represents a genetic fallacy. The cause of something valuable need not itself be valuable and certainly not necessarily more valuable than its effect—its value must be established independently of its result. The Holocaust may have caused the state of Israel; that does not make the Holocaust more valuable than the state of Israel.

3 Confusing aesthetic or instrumental value for sentient creatures, notably humans, with intrinsic value and underestimating aesthetic value as a category. We shall return to this shortly, for I suspect it is the root confusion in those attempting to give nonsentient nature intrinsic value.

4 Substituting rhetoric for logic at crucial points in the discussions and using a poetic rhetoric (descriptions of natural objects in terms such as "grandeur," "majesty," "novelty," "variety") as an unexplained basis for according them "intrinsic value."

5 Going from the metaphor that infringement on natural objects "matters" to them in the sense that disturbance evokes an adjustment by their self-regulating properties, to the erroneous conclusion that such self-regulation, being analogous to conscious coping in animals, entitles them to direct moral status.

In short, traditional morality and its theory do not offer a viable way to raise the moral status of nonsentient natural objects and abstract objects so that they are direct objects of moral concern on a par with or even higher than sentient creatures. Ordinary morality and moral concern take as their focus the effects of actions on beings who can be helped and harmed, in ways that matter to them, either directly or by implication. If it is immoral to wreck someone's property, it is because it is someone's; if it is immoral to promote the extinction of species, it is because such extinction causes aesthetic or practical harm to humans or to animals or because a species is, in the final analysis, a group of harmable individuals.

There is nothing, of course, to stop environmental ethicists from making a recommendation for a substantial revision of common and traditional morality. But such recommendations are likely to be dismissed or whittled away by a moral version of Occam's razor: Why grant animals rights and acknowledge in animals intrinsic value? Because they are conscious and what we do to them matters to them? Why grant rocks, or trees, or species, or ecosystems rights? Because these objects have great aesthetic value, or are essential to us, or are basic for survival? But these are paradigmatic examples of *instrumental* value. A conceptual confusion for a noble purpose is still a conceptual confusion.

There is nothing to be gained by attempting to elevate the moral status of nonsentient natural objects to that of sentient ones. One can develop a rich environmental ethic by locating the value of nonsentient natural objects in their relation to sentient ones. One can argue for the preservation of habitats because their destruction harms animals; one can argue for preserving ecosystems on the grounds of unforeseen pernicious consequences resulting from their destruction, a claim for which much empirical evidence exists. One can argue for the preservation of animal species as the sum of a group of individuals who would be harmed by its extinction. One can argue for preserving mountains, snail darters, streams, and cockroaches on aesthetic grounds. Too many philosophers forget the moral power of aesthetic claims and tend to see aesthetic reasons as a weak basis for preserving natural objects. Yet the moral imperative not to destroy unique aesthetic objects and even nonunique ones is an onerous one that is well ingrained into common practice—witness the worldwide establishment of national parks, preserves, forests, and wildlife areas.

Rather than attempting to transcend all views of natural objects as instrumental by grafting onto nature a mystical intrinsic value that can be buttressed only by poetic rhetoric, it would be far better to nurture public appreciation of subtle instrumental value, especially aesthetic value. People can learn to appreciate the unique beauty of a desert, or of a fragile ecosystem, or even of a noxious creature like a tick, when they understand the complexity and history therein and can read the story each life form contains. I am reminded of a colleague in parasitology who is loath to destroy worms he has studied upon completing his research because he has aesthetically learned to value their complexity of structure, function, and evolutionary history and role.

It is important to note that the attribution of value to nonsentient natural objects as a relational property arising out of their significance (recognized or not) for sentient beings does not denigrate the value of natural objects. Indeed, this attribution does not even imply that the interests or desires of individual sentient beings always trump concern for nonsentient ones. Our legal system has, for example, valuable and irreplaceable property laws that forbid owners of aesthetic objects, say a collection of Vincent Van Gogh paintings, to destroy them at will, say by adding them to one's funeral pyre. To be sure, this restriction on people's right to dispose of their own property arises out of a recognition of the value of these objects to other humans, but this is surely quite sensible. How else would one justify such a restriction? Nor, as we said earlier, need one limit the value of natural objects to their relationship to humans. Philosophically, one could, for example, sensibly (and commonsensically) argue for preservation of acreage from the golf-course developer because failure to do so would mean the destruction of thousands of sentient creatures' habitats—a major infringement of their interests—while building the golf course would fulfill the rarefied and inessential interests of a few.

Thus, in my view, one would accord moral concern to natural objects in a variety of ways, depending on the sort of object being considered. Moral status for individual animals would arise from their sentience. Moral status of species and their protection from humans would arise from the fact that a species is a collection of morally relevant individuals; moral status also would arise from the fact that humans have an aesthetic concern in not letting a unique and irreplaceable aesthetic object (or group of objects) disappear forever from our *Umwelt* (environment). Concern for wilderness areas, mountains, deserts, and so on would arise from their survival value for sentient animals as well as from their aesthetic value for humans. (Some writers have suggested that this aesthetic value is so great as to be essential to human mental/physical health, a point perfectly compatible with my position.[7])

Nothing in what I have said as yet tells us how to weigh conflicting interests, whether between humans and other sentient creatures or between human desires and environmental protection. How does one weigh the aesthetic concern of those who oppose blasting away part of a cliff against the pragmatic concern of those who wish to build on a cliffside? But the problem of weighing is equally thorny in traditional ethics—witness lifeboat questions or questions concerning the allocation of scarce medical resources. Nor does the intrinsic value approach help in adjudicating such issues. How does one weigh the alleged intrinsic value of a cliffside against the interests of the (intrinsic-value-bearing) homebuilders?

Furthermore, the intrinsic value view can lead to results that are repugnant to common sense and ordinary moral consciousness. Thus, for example, it follows from what has been suggested by one intrinsic value theorist that if a migratory herd of plentiful elk were passing through an area containing an endangered species of moss, it would be not only permissible but obligatory to kill the elk in order to protect the moss because in one case we would lose a species, in another "merely" individuals.[8] In my view, such a case has a less paradoxical resolution. Destruction of the moss does not matter to the moss, whereas elk presumably care about living or being injured. Therefore, one would give prima facie priority to the elk. This might presumably be trumped if, for example, the moss were a substratum from which was extracted an ingredient necessary to stop a raging, lethal epidemic in humans or animals. But such cases—and indeed most cases of conflicting interests—must be decided on the actual occasion. These cases are decided by a careful examination of the facts of the situation. Thus, our suggestion of a basis for environmental ethics does not qualitatively change the situation from that of current ethical deliberation, whereas granting intrinsic value to natural objects would leave us with a "whole new ball game"—and one where we do not know the rules.

In sum, then, the question of environmental ethics . . . must be analyzed into two discrete components. First are those questions that pertain to direct objects of moral concern—nonhuman animals whose sentience we have good reason to suspect—and that require the application of traditional moral notions to a hitherto ignored domain of moral objects. Second are those questions pertaining to natural objects or abstract natural objects. Although it is nonsensical to attribute intrinsic or direct moral value to these objects, they nonetheless must become (and are indeed becoming) central to our social moral deliberations. This centrality derives from our increasing recognition of the far-reaching and sometimes subtle instrumental value these objects have for humans and animals. Knowing that contamination of remote desert areas by pollutants can destroy unique panoplies of fragile beauty, or that dumping wastes into the ocean can destroy a potential source of antibiotics, or that building a pipeline can have undreamed-of harmful effects goes a long way toward making us think twice about these activities—a far longer way than endowing them with quasi-mystical rhetorical status subject to (and begging for) positivistic torpedoing. . . .

NOTES

1 See the chapters in Tom Regan, *All That Dwell Therein* (Berkeley: University of California Press, 1982).
2 See Aldo Leopold, *A Sand County Almanac* (Oxford: Oxford University Press, 1949); J. Baird Callicott, "Animal Liberation: A Triangular Affair," *Environmental Ethics* 2 (1980):311–338; Holmes Rolston III, *Philosophy Gone Wild* (Buffalo, N.Y.: Prometheus Books, 1986).
3 See the discussions of this point in Peter Singer, *Animal Liberation* (New York: New York Review of Books, 1975); and B. Rollin, *Animal Rights and Human Morality* (Buffalo, N.Y.: Prometheus Books, 1981).
4 See my "Animal Pain," in M. Fox and L. Mickley (eds.), *Advances in Animal Welfare Science 1985* (The Hague; Martinus Nijhoff, 1985); and my "Animal Consciousness and Scientific Change," *New Ideas in Psychology* 4, no. 2 (1986):141–152, as well as the replies to the latter by P. K. Feyerabend, H. Rachlin, and T. Leahey in the same issue, p. 153. See also my *The Unheeded Cry: Animal Consciousness, Animal Pain, and Science* (Oxford: Oxford University Press, 1989).
5 See my *Animal Rights*, Part I.
6 See the works mentioned in footnotes 1 and 2.
7 This point is made with great rhetorical force in Edward Abbey, *Desert Solitaire* (New York: Ballantine Books, 1971).
8 See Holmes Rolston, "Duties to Endangered Species," *Philosophy Gone Wild*.

QUESTIONS

1 Is Rollin correct in holding that only sentient beings have intrinsic value?
2 Do you agree that, once we recognize the subtle instrumental value of ecosystems, forests, and so on, we will have a very strong foundation for revising those human activities that damage or destroy nonsentient natural objects?

Deep Ecology

Bill Devall and George Sessions

Devall and Sessions present deep ecology as a systematic alternative to "the dominant worldview of technocratic-industrial societies." They identify *self-realization* and *biocentric equality* as the two basic norms or intuitions underlying deep ecology. The norm of self-realization challenges the ordinary (Western) understanding of the self and ultimately requires each of us to identify with the nonhuman world. The norm of biocentric equality attributes equal intrinsic worth to "all organisms and entities in the ecosphere." Devall and Sessions also identify a set of eight principles considered basic to deep ecology. A commentary is then provided to explain each of the eight principles.

The term *deep ecology* was coined by Arne Naess in his 1973 article, "The Shallow and the Deep, Long-Range Ecology Movements."[1] Naess was attempting to describe the deeper, more spiritual approach to Nature exemplified in the writings of Aldo Leopold and Rachel Carson. He thought that this deeper approach resulted from a more sensitive openness to ourselves and nonhuman life around us. The essence of deep ecology is to keep asking more searching questions about human life, society, and Nature as in the Western philosophical tradition of Socrates. As examples of this deep questioning, Naess points out "that we ask why and how, where others do not. For instance, ecology as a science does not ask what kind of a society would be the best for maintaining a particular ecosystem—that is consid-ered a question for value theory, for politics, for ethics." Thus deep ecology goes beyond the so-called factual scientific level to the level of self and Earth wisdom.

Deep ecology goes beyond a limited piecemeal shallow approach to environmental problems and attempts to articulate a comprehensive religious and philosophical worldview. The foundations of deep ecology are the basic intuitions and experiencing of ourselves and Nature which comprise ecological consciousness. Certain outlooks on politics and public policy flow naturally from this consciousness. And in the con-text of this book, we discuss the minority tradition as the type of community most con-ducive both to cultivating ecological consciousness and to asking the basic questions of values and ethics addressed in these pages.

Many of these questions are perennial philosophical and religious questions faced by humans in all cultures over the ages. What does it mean to be a unique human individual? How can the individual self maintain and increase its uniqueness while also being an inseparable aspect of the whole system wherein there are no sharp breaks between self and the *other*? An ecological perspective, in this deeper sense, results in what Theodore Roszak calls "an awakening of wholes greater than the sum of their parts. In spirit, the discipline is contemplative and therapeutic."[2]

Reprinted with permission of the publisher from Bill Devall and George Sessions, *Deep Ecology: Living as if Nature Mattered* (Salt Lake City: Gibbs M. Smith, Inc., Peregrine Smith Books, 1985), pp. 65–73.

Ecological consciousness and deep ecology are in sharp contrast with the dominant worldview of technocratic-industrial societies which regards humans as isolated and fundamentally separate from the rest of Nature, as superior to, and in charge of, the rest of creation. But the view of humans as separate and superior to the rest of Nature is only part of larger cultural patterns. For thousands of years, Western culture has become increasingly obsessed with the idea of *dominance:* with dominance of humans over nonhuman Nature, masculine over the feminine, wealthy and powerful over the poor, with the dominance of the West over non-Western cultures. Deep ecological consciousness allows us to see through these erroneous and dangerous illusions.

For deep ecology, the study of our place in the Earth household includes the study of ourselves as part of the organic whole. Going beyond a narrowly materialist scientific understanding of reality, the spiritual and the material aspects of reality fuse together. While the leading intellectuals of the dominant worldview have tended to view religion as "just superstition," and have looked upon ancient spiritual practice and enlightenment, such as found in Zen Buddhism, as essentially subjective, the search for deep ecological consciousness is the search for a more objective consciousness and state of being through an active deep questioning and meditative process and way of life.

Many people have asked these deeper questions and cultivated ecological consciousness within the context of different spiritual traditions—Christianity, Taoism, Buddhism, and Native American rituals, for example. While differing greatly in other regards, many in these traditions agree with the basic principles of deep ecology.

Warwick Fox, an Australian philosopher, has succinctly expressed the central intuition of deep ecology: "It is the idea that we can make no firm ontological divide in the field of existence: That there is no bifurcation in reality between the human and the non-human realms . . . to the extent that we perceive boundaries, we fall short of deep ecological consciousness."[3]

From this most basic insight or characteristic of deep ecological consciousness, Arne Naess has developed two *ultimate norms* or intuitions which are themselves not derivable from other principles or intuitions. They are arrived at by the deep questioning process and reveal the importance of moving to the philosophical and religious level of wisdom. They cannot be validated, of course, by the methodology of modern science based on its usual mechanistic assumptions and its very narrow definition of data. These ultimate norms are *self-realization* and *biocentric equality*.

I   SELF-REALIZATION

In keeping with the spiritual traditions of many of the world's religions, the deep ecology norm of self-realization goes beyond the modern Western *self* which is defined as an isolated ego striving primarily for hedonistic gratification or for a narrow sense of individual salvation in this life or the next. This socially programmed sense of the narrow self or social self dislocates us, and leaves us prey to whatever fad or fashion is prevalent in our society or social reference group. We are thus robbed of beginning the search for our unique spiritual/biological personhood. Spiritual growth, or unfolding, begins when we cease to understand or see ourselves as isolated and narrow competing egos and begin to identify with other humans from our family and friends to, eventually, our species. But the deep ecology sense of self requires a further maturity and growth, an identification which goes beyond humanity to include the nonhuman world. We must see beyond our narrow contemporary cultural assumptions and values, and the conventional wisdom of our time and place, and this is best achieved by the meditative deep questioning process. Only in this way can we hope to attain full mature personhood and uniqueness.

A nurturing nondominating society can help in the "real work" of becoming a whole person. The "real work" can be summarized symbolically as the realization of "self-in-Self" where "Self" stands for organic wholeness. This process of the full unfolding of the self can also be summarized by the phrase, "No one is saved until we are all saved," where the phrase "one" includes not only me, an individual human, but all humans, whales, grizzly bears, whole rain forest ecosystems, mountains and rivers, the tiniest microbes in the soil, and so on.

II BIOCENTRIC EQUALITY

The intuition of biocentric equality is that all things in the biosphere have an equal right to live and blossom and to reach their own individual forms of unfolding and self-realization within the larger Self-realization. This basic intuition is that all organisms and entities in the ecosphere, as parts of the interrelated whole, are equal in intrinsic worth. Naess suggests that biocentric equality as an intuition is true in principle, although in the process of living, all species use each other as food, shelter, etc. Mutual predation is a biological fact of life, and many of the world's religions have struggled with the spiritual implications of this. Some animal liberationists who attempt to side-step this problem by advocating vegetarianism are forced to say that the entire plant kingdom including rain forests have no right to their own existence. This evasion flies in the face of the basic intuition of equality.[4] Aldo Leopold expressed this intuition when he said humans are "plain citizens" of the biotic community, not lord and master over all other species.

Biocentric equality is intimately related to the all-inclusive Self-realization in the sense that if we harm the rest of Nature then we are harming ourselves. There are no boundaries and everything is interrelated. But insofar as we perceive things as individual organisms or entities, the insight draws us to respect all human and nonhuman individuals in their own right as parts of the whole without feeling the need to set up hierarchies of species with humans at the top.

The practical implications of this intuition or norm suggest that we should live with minimum rather than maximum impact on other species and on the Earth in general. Thus we see another aspect of our guiding principle: "simple in means, rich in ends." . . .

A fuller discussion of the biocentric norm as it unfolds itself in practice begins with the realization that we, as individual humans, and as communities of humans, have vital needs which go beyond such basics as food, water, and shelter to include love, play, creative expression, intimate relationships with a particular landscape (or Nature taken in its entirety) as well as intimate relationships with other humans, and the vital need for spiritual growth, for becoming a mature human being.

Fig. 1

Dominant Worldview	Deep Ecology
Dominance over Nature	Harmony with Nature
Natural environment as resource for humans	All nature has intrinsic worth/biospecies equality
Material/economic growth for growing human population	Elegantly simple material needs (material goals serving the larger goal of self-realization)
Belief in ample resource reserves	Earth "supplies" limited
High technological progress and solutions	Appropriate technology; nondominating science
Consumerism	Doing with enough/recycling
National/centralized community	Minority tradition/bioregion

Our vital material needs are probably more simple than many realize. In technocratic-industrial societies there is overwhelming propaganda and advertising which encourages false needs and destructive desires designed to foster increased production and consumption of goods. Most of this actually diverts us from facing reality in an objective way and from beginning the "real work" of spiritual growth and maturity.

Many people who do not see themselves as supporters of deep ecology nevertheless recognize an overriding vital human need for a healthy and high-quality natural environment for humans, if not for all life, with minimum intrusion of toxic waste, nuclear radiation from human enterprises, minimum acid rain and smog, and enough free flowing wilderness so humans can get in touch with their sources, the natural rhythms and the flow of time and place.

Drawing from the minority tradition and from the wisdom of many who have offered the insight of interconnectedness, we recognize that deep ecologists can offer suggestions for gaining maturity and encouraging the processes of harmony with Nature, but that there is no grand solution which is guaranteed to save us from ourselves.

The ultimate norms of deep ecology suggest a view of the nature of reality and our place as an individual (many in the one) in the larger scheme of things. They cannot be fully grasped intellectually but are ultimately experiential. . . .

As a brief summary of our position thus far, Figure 1 summarizes the contrast between the dominant worldview and deep ecology.

III   BASIC PRINCIPLES OF DEEP ECOLOGY

In April 1984, during the advent of spring and John Muir's birthday, George Sessions and Arne Naess summarized fifteen years of thinking on the principles of deep ecology while camping in Death Valley, California. In this great and special place, they articulated these principles in a literal, somewhat neutral way, hoping that they would be understood and accepted by persons coming from different philosophical and religious positions.

Readers are encouraged to elaborate their own versions of deep ecology, clarify key concepts and think through the consequences of acting from these principles.

Basic Principles

1 The well-being and flourishing of human and nonhuman Life on Earth have value in themselves (synonyms: intrinsic value, inherent value). These values are independent of the usefulness of the nonhuman world for human purposes.

2 Richness and diversity of life forms contribute to the realization of these values and are also values in themselves.

3 Humans have no right to reduce this richness and diversity except to satisfy *vital* needs.

4 The flourishing of human life and cultures is compatible with a substantial decrease of the human population. The flourishing of nonhuman life requires such a decrease.

5 Present human interference with the nonhuman world is excessive, and the situation is rapidly worsening.

6 Policies must therefore be changed. These policies affect basic economic, technological, and ideological structures. The resulting state of affairs will be deeply different from the present.

7 The ideological change is mainly that of appreciating *life quality* (dwelling in situations of inherent value) rather than adhering to an increasingly higher standard of living. There will be a profound awareness of the difference between big and great.

8 Those who subscribe to the foregoing points have an obligation directly or indirectly to try to implement the necessary changes.

Naess and Sessions Provide Comments on the Basic Principles

RE (1)   This formulation refers to the biosphere, or more accurately, to the ecosphere as a whole. This includes individuals, species, populations, habitat, as well as human and nonhuman cultures. From our current knowledge of all-pervasive intimate relationships, this implies a fundamental deep concern and respect. Ecological processes of the planet should, on the whole, remain intact. "The world environment should remain 'natural'" (Gary Snyder).

The term "life" is used here in a more comprehensive nontechnical way to refer also to what biologists classify as "nonliving"; rivers (watersheds), landscapes, ecosystems. For supporters of deep ecology, slogans such as "Let the river live" illustrate this broader usage so common in most cultures.

Inherent value as used in (1) is common in deep ecology literature ("The presence of inherent value in a natural object is independent of any awareness, interest, or appreciation of it by a conscious being.").[5]

RE (2)   More technically, this is a formulation concerning diversity and complexity. From an ecological standpoint, complexity and symbiosis are conditions for maximizing diversity. So-called simple, lower, or primitive species of plants and animals contribute essentially to the richness and diversity of life. They have value in themselves and are not merely steps toward the so-called higher or rational life forms. The second principle presupposes that life itself, as a process over evolutionary time, implies an increase of diversity and richness. The refusal to acknowledge that some life forms have greater or lesser intrinsic value than others (see points 1 and 2) runs counter to the formulations of some ecological philosophers and New Age writers.

Complexity, as referred to here, is different from complication. Urban life may be more complicated than life in a natural setting without being more complex in the sense of multifaceted quality.

RE (3)   The term "vital need" is left deliberately vague to allow for considerable latitude in judgment. Differences in climate and related factors, together with differences in the structures of societies as they now exist, need to be considered (for some Eskimos, snowmobiles are necessary today to satisfy vital needs).

People in the materially richest countries cannot be expected to reduce their excessive interference with the nonhuman world to a moderate level overnight. The stabilization and reduction of the human population will take time. Interim strategies need to be developed. But this in no way excuses the present complacency— the extreme seriousness of our current situation must first be realized. But the longer we wait the more drastic will be the measures needed. Until deep changes are made, substantial decreases in richness and diversity are liable to occur: the rate of extinction of species will be ten to one hundred times greater than [in] any other period of earth history.

RE (4)   The United Nations Fund for Population Activities in their State of World Population Report (1984) said that high human population growth rates (over 2.0 percent annum) in many developing countries "were diminishing the quality of life for many millions of people." During the decade 1974–1984, the world population grew by nearly 800 million—more than the size of India. "And we will be adding about one Bangladesh (population 93 million) per annum between now and the year 2000."

The report noted that "The growth rate of the human population has declined for the first time in human history. But at the same time, the number of people being added to the human population is bigger than at any time in history because the population base is larger."

Most of the nations in the developing world (including India and China) have as their official government policy the goal of reducing the rate of human population increase, but there are debates over the types of measures to take (contraception, abortion, etc.) consistent with human rights and feasibility.

The report concludes that if all governments set specific population targets as public policy to help alleviate poverty and advance the quality of life, the current situation could be improved.

As many ecologists have pointed out, it is also absolutely crucial to curb population growth in the so-called developed (i.e., overdeveloped) industrial societies. Given the tremendous rate of consumption and waste production of individuals in these societies, they represent a much greater threat and impact on the biosphere per capita than individuals in Second and Third World countries.

RE (5)   This formulation is mild. For a realistic assessment of the situation, see the unabbreviated version of the I.U.C.N.'s *World Conservation Strategy*. There are other works to be highly recommended, such as Gerald Barney's *Global 2000 Report to the President of the United States*.

The slogan of "noninterference" does not imply that humans should not modify some ecosystems as do other species. Humans have modified the earth and will probably continue to do so. At issue is the nature and extent of such interference.

The fight to preserve and extend areas of wilderness or near-wilderness should continue and should focus on the general ecological functions of these areas (one such function: large wilderness areas are required in the biosphere to allow for continued evolutionary speciation of animals and plants). Most present designated wilderness areas and game preserves are not large enough to allow for such speciation.

RE (6)   Economic growth as conceived and implemented today by the industrial states is incompatible with (1)–(5). There is only a faint resemblance between ideal sustainable forms of economic growth and present policies of the industrial societies. And "sustainable" still means "sustainable in relation to humans."

Present ideology tends to value things because they are scarce and because they have a commodity value. There is prestige in vast consumption and waste (to mention only several relevant factors).

Whereas "self-determination," "local community," and "think globally, act locally," will remain key terms in the ecology of human societies, nevertheless the implementation of deep changes requires increasingly global action—action across borders.

Governments in Third World countries (with the exception of Costa Rica and a few others) are uninterested in deep ecological issues. When the governments of industrial societies try to promote ecological measures through Third World governments, practically nothing is accomplished (e.g., with problems of desertification). Given this situation, support for global action through nongovernmental international organizations becomes increasingly important. Many of these organizations are able to act globally "from grassroots to grassroots," thus avoiding negative governmental interference.

Cultural diversity today requires advanced technology, that is, techniques that advance the basic goals of each culture. So-called soft, intermediate, and alternative technologies are steps in this direction.

RE (7)   Some economists criticize the term "quality of life" because it is supposed to be vague. But on closer inspection, what they consider to be vague is actually the nonquantitative nature of the term. One cannot quantify adequately what is important for the quality of life as discussed here, and there is no need to do so.

RE (8)   There is ample room for different opinions about priorities: what should be done first, what next? What is most urgent? What is clearly necessary as opposed to what is highly desirable but not absolutely pressing?

NOTES

1 Arne Naess, "The Shallow and the Deep, Long-Range Ecology Movements: A Summary," *Inquiry* 16 (Oslo, 1973), pp. 95–100.

2 Theodore Roszak, *Where the Wasteland Ends* (New York: Anchor, 1972).

3 Warwick Fox, "Deep Ecology: A New Philosophy of Our Time?" *The Ecologist*, v. 14, 5–6, 1984, pp. 194–200. Arne Naess replies, "Intuition, Intrinsic Value and Deep Ecology," *The Ecologist*, v. 14, 5–6, 1984, pp. 201–204.

4 Tom Regan, *The Case for Animal Rights* (New York: Random House, 1983). For excellent critiques of the animal rights movement, see John Rodman, "The Liberation of Nature?" *Inquiry* 20 (Oslo, 1977). J. Baird Callicott, "Animal Liberation," *Environmental Ethics* 2, 4 (1980); see also John Rodman, "Four Forms of Ecological Consciousness Reconsidered" in T. Attig and D. Scherer, eds., *Ethics and the Environment* (Englewood Cliffs, N.J.: Prentice-Hall, 1983).

5 Tom Regan, "The Nature and Possibility of an Environmental Ethic," *Environmental Ethics* 3 (1981), pp. 19–34.

QUESTIONS

1 To what extent would you endorse the two basic norms of deep ecology?

2 To what extent would you endorse the eight basic principles of deep ecology?

3 Critics sometimes complain that deep ecology is an "antihuman" philosophy. Is there any substance to this charge?

Radical American Environmentalism and Wilderness Preservation: A Third World Critique

Ramachandra Guha

Guha advances a critique of the American deep ecology movement from a third-world perspective. He states and criticizes three of the central tenets he identifies with American deep ecology: (1) its distinction between anthropocentric and biocentric approaches to environmental issues, (2) its focus on wilderness preservation, and (3) its conviction that the American version of deep ecology represents the most radical trend in environmentalism. In respect to (1), Guha argues that this distinction is of little use in helping us understand the dynamics of environmental degradation. In respect to (2), he maintains that the implementation of the wilderness agenda is causing serious deprivation in third-world countries. In respect to (3), Guha points out that American deep ecologists fail to seriously question the ecological and sociopolitical basis of the consumer society,

Reprinted with permission of the author and the publisher from *Environmental Ethics*, vol. 11 (Spring 1989), pp. 71–76, 78–83.

even though its consumerism is responsible for so much environmental degradation. He gives examples from other cultures (Germany and India) to illustrate what he considers a far more radical environmentalism—one that emphasizes equity and the integration of ecological concerns with livelihood and work.

I   INTRODUCTION

The respected radical journalist Kirkpatrick Sale recently celebrated "the passion of a new and growing movement that has become disenchanted with the environmental establishment and has in recent years mounted a serious and sweeping attack on it—style, substance, systems, sensibilities and all."[1] The vision of those whom Sale calls the "New Ecologists"—and what I refer to in this article as deep ecology—is a compelling one. Decrying the narrowly economic goals of mainstream environmentalism, this new movement aims at nothing less than a philosophical and cultural revolution in human attitudes toward nature. In contrast to the conventional lobbying efforts of environmental professionals based in Washington, it proposes a militant defence of "Mother Earth," an unflinching opposition to human attacks on undisturbed wilderness. With their goals ranging from the spiritual to the political, the adherents of deep ecology span a wide spectrum of the American environmental movement. As Sale correctly notes, this emerging strand has in a matter of a few years made its presence felt in a number of fields: from academic philosophy (as in the journal *Environmental Ethics*) to popular environmentalism (for example, the group Earth First!).

In this article I develop a critique of deep ecology from the perspective of a sympathetic outsider. . . . I speak admittedly as a partisan, but of the environmental movement in India, a country with an ecological diversity comparable to the U.S., but with a radically dissimilar cultural and social history.

My treatment of deep ecology is primarily historical and sociological, rather than philosophical, in nature. Specifically, I examine the cultural rootedness of a philosophy that likes to present itself in universalistic terms. I make two main arguments: first, that deep ecology is uniquely American, and despite superficial similarities in rhetorical style, the social and political goals of radical environmentalism in other cultural contexts (e.g., West Germany and India) are quite different; second, that the social consequences of putting deep ecology into practice on a worldwide basis (what its practitioners are aiming for) are very grave indeed.

II   THE TENETS OF DEEP ECOLOGY

While I am aware that the term *deep ecology* was coined by the Norwegian philosopher Arne Naess, this article refers specifically to the American variant.[2] Adherents of the deep ecological perspective in this country, while arguing intensely among themselves over its political and philosophical implications, share some fundamental premises about human-nature interactions. As I see it, [the following are three of] the defining characteristics of deep ecology:

First, deep ecology argues, that the environmental movement must shift from an "anthropocentric" to a "biocentric" perspective. In many respects, an acceptance of the primacy of this distinction constitutes the litmus test of deep ecology. A considerable effort is expended by deep ecologists in showing that the dominant motif in Western philosophy has been anthropocentric—i.e., the belief that man and his works are the center of the universe—and conversely, in identifying those lonely thinkers (Leopold, Thoreau, Muir, Aldous Huxley, Santayana, etc.) who, in assigning man a more humble place in the natural order, anticipated deep ecological thinking. In the political realm, meanwhile, establishment environmentalism (shallow ecology) is chided for casting its arguments in human-centered terms. Preserving nature, the deep ecologists say, has an intrinsic worth quite apart from any benefits preservation may convey to future human generations. The anthropocentric-biocentric distinction is accepted as axiomatic by deep ecologists, it structures their discourse, and much of the present discussion remains mired within it.

The second characteristic of deep ecology is its focus on the preservation of unspoilt wilderness—and the restoration of degraded areas to a more pristine condition—to the relative (and sometimes absolute) neglect of other issues on the environmental agenda. I later identify the cultural roots and portentous consequences of this obsession with wilderness. For the moment, let me indicate three distinct sources from which it springs. Historically, it represents a playing out of the preservationist (read *radical*) and utilitarian (read *reformist*) dichotomy that has plagued American environmentalism since the turn of the century. Morally, it is an imperative that follows from the biocentric perspective; other species of plants and animals, and nature itself, have an intrinsic right to exist. And finally, the preservation of wilderness also turns on a scientific argument—viz., the value of biological diversity in stabilizing ecological regimes and in retaining a gene pool for future generations. Truly radical policy proposals have been put forward by deep ecologists on the basis of these arguments. The influential poet Gary Snyder, for example, would like to see a 90 percent reduction in human populations to allow a restoration of pristine environments, while others have argued forcefully that a large portion of the globe must be immediately cordoned off from human beings.[3] . . .

Third, deep ecologists, whatever their internal differences, share the belief that they are the "leading edge" of the environmental movement. As the polarity of the shallow/deep and anthropocentric/biocentric distinctions makes clear, they see themselves as the spiritual, philosophical, and political vanguard of American and world environmentalism.

III TOWARD A CRITIQUE

Although I analyze each of these tenets independently, it is important to recognize, as deep ecologists are fond of remarking in reference to nature, the interconnectedness and unity of these individual themes.

1 Insofar as it has begun to act as a check on man's arrogance and ecological hubris, the transition from an anthropocentric (human-centered) to a biocentric (humans as only one element in the ecosystem) view in both religious and scientific traditions is only to be welcomed. What is unacceptable are the radical conclusions drawn by deep ecology, in particular, that intervention in nature should be guided primarily by the need to preserve biotic integrity rather than by the needs of humans. The latter for deep ecologists is anthropocentric, the former biocentric. This dichotomy is, however, of very little use in understanding the dynamics of environmental degradation. The two fundamental ecological problems facing the globe are (i) overconsumption by the industrialized world and by urban elites in the Third World and (ii) growing militarization, both in a short-term sense (i.e., ongoing regional wars) and in a long-term sense (i.e., the arms race and the prospect of nuclear annihilation). Neither of these problems has any tangible connection to the anthropocentric-biocentric distinction. Indeed, the agents of these processes would barely comprehend this philosophical dichotomy. The proximate causes of the ecologically wasteful characteristics of industrial society and of militarization are far more mundane: at an aggregate level, the dialectic of economic and political structures, and at a micro-level, the life style choices of individuals. These causes cannot be reduced, whatever the level of analysis, to a deeper anthropocentric attitude toward nature; on the contrary, by constituting a grave threat to human survival, the ecological degradation they cause does not even serve the best interests of human beings! If my identification of the major dangers to the integrity of the natural world is correct, invoking the bogy of anthropocentricism is at best irrelevant and at worst a dangerous obfuscation.

2 If the above dichotomy is irrelevant, the emphasis on wilderness is positively harmful when applied to the Third World. If in the U.S. the preservationist/utilitarian division is seen as mirroring the conflict between "people" and "interests," in countries such as India the situation is very nearly the reverse. Because India is a long settled and densely populated country in which agrarian populations have a finely balanced relationship with nature, the setting aside of wilderness areas has resulted in a direct transfer of resources from the poor to the rich. Thus, Project Tiger, a network of parks hailed by the international conservation community as an outstanding success, sharply posits the interests of the tiger against those of poor peasants living in and around the reserve. The designation of tiger reserves was made possible only by the physical displacement of existing villages and their inhabitants; their management requires the continuing exclusion of peasants and livestock. The initial impetus for setting up parks for the tiger and other large mammals such as the rhinoceros and elephant came from two social groups, first, a class of ex-hunters turned conservationists belonging mostly to the declining Indian feudal elite and second, representatives of international agencies, such as the World Wildlife Fund (WWF) and the International Union for the Conservation of Nature and Natural Resources (IUCN), seeking to transplant the American system of national parks onto Indian soil. In no case have the needs of the local population been taken into account, and as in many parts of Africa, the designated wildlands are managed primarily for the benefit of rich tourists. Until very recently, wildlands preservation has been identified with environmentalism by the state and the conservation elite; in consequence, environmental problems that impinge far more directly on the lives of the poor—e.g., fuel, fodder, water shortages, soil erosion, and air and water pollution—have not been adequately addressed.[4]

Deep ecology provides, perhaps unwittingly, a justification for the continuation of such narrow and inequitable conservation practices under a newly acquired radical guise. Increasingly, the international conservation elite is using the philosophical, moral, and scientific arguments used by deep ecologists in advancing their wilderness crusade. A striking but by no means atypical example is the recent plea by a prominent American biologist for the takeover of large portions of the globe by the author and his scientific colleagues. Writing in a prestigious scientific forum, the *Annual Review of Ecology and Systematics,* Daniel Janzen argues that only biologists have the competence to decide how the tropical landscape should be used. As "the representatives of the natural world," biologists are "in charge of the future of tropical ecology," and only they have the expertise and mandate to "determine whether the tropical agroscape is to be populated only by humans, their mutualists, commensals, and parasites, or whether it will also contain some islands of the greater nature—the nature that spawned humans, yet has been vanquished by them." Janzen exhorts his colleagues to advance their territorial claims on the tropical world more forcefully, warning that the very existence of these areas is at stake: "if biologists want a tropics in which to biologize, they are going to have to buy it with care, energy, effort, strategy, tactics, time, and cash."[5]

This frankly imperialist manifesto highlights the multiple dangers of the preoccupation with wilderness preservation that is characteristic of deep ecology. As I have suggested, it seriously compounds the neglect by the American movement of far more pressing environmental problems within the Third World. But perhaps more importantly, and in a more insidious fashion, it also provides an impetus to the imperialist yearning of Western biologists and their financial sponsors, organizations such as the WWF and IUCN. The wholesale transfer of a movement culturally rooted in American conservation history can only result in the social uprooting of human populations in other parts of the globe. . . .

How radical, finally, are the deep ecologists? Notwithstanding their self-image and strident rhetoric (in which the label "shallow ecology" has an opprobrium similar to that reserved for "social democratic" by Marxist-Leninists), even within the American context their radicalism is limited and it manifests itself quite differently elsewhere.

To my mind, deep ecology is best viewed as a radical trend within the wilderness preservation movement. Although advancing philosophical rather than aesthetic arguments and encouraging political militancy rather than negotiation, its practical emphasis—viz., preservation of unspoilt nature—is virtually identical. For the mainstream movement, the function of wilderness is to provide a temporary antidote to modern civilization. As a special institution within an industrialized society, the national park "provides an opportunity for respite, contrast, contemplation, and affirmation of values for those who live most of their lives in the workaday world."[6] Indeed, the rapid increase in visitations to the national parks in postwar America is a direct consequence of economic expansion. The emergence of a popular interest in wilderness sites, the historian Samuel Hays points out, was "not a throwback to the primitive, but an integral part of the modern standard of living as people sought to add new 'amenity' and 'aesthetic' goals and desires to their earlier preoccupation with necessities and conveniences."[7]

Here, the enjoyment of nature is an integral part of the consumer society. The private automobile (and the life style it has spawned) is in many respects the ultimate ecological villain, and an untouched wilderness the prototype of ecological harmony; yet, for most Americans it is perfectly consistent to drive a thousand miles to spend a holiday in a national park. They possess a vast, beautiful, and sparsely populated continent and are also able to draw upon the natural resources of large portions of the globe by virtue of their economic and political dominance. In consequence, America can simultaneously enjoy the material benefits of an expanding economy and the aesthetic benefits of unspoilt nature. The two poles of "wilderness" and "civilization" mutually coexist in an internally coherent whole, and philosophers of both poles are assigned a prominent place in this culture. Paradoxically as it may seem, it is no accident that Star Wars technology and deep ecology both find their fullest expression in that leading sector of Western civilization, California.

Deep ecology runs parallel to the consumer society without seriously questioning its ecological and socio-political basis. In its celebration of American wilderness, it also displays an uncomfortable convergence with the prevailing climate of nationalism in the American wilderness movement. For spokesmen such as the historian Roderick Nash, the national park system is America's distinctive cultural contribution to the world, reflective not merely of its economic but of its philosophical and ecological maturity as well. In what Walter Lippman called the American century, the "American invention of national parks" must be exported worldwide. Betraying an economic determinism that would make even a Marxist shudder, Nash believes that environmental preservation is a "full stomach" phenomenon that is confined to the rich, urban, and sophisticated. Nonetheless, he hopes that "the less developed nations may eventually evolve economically and intellectually to the point where nature preservation is more than a business."[8]

The error which Nash makes (and which deep ecology in some respects encourages) is to equate environmental protection with the protection of wilderness. This is a distinctively American notion, born out of a unique social and environmental history. The archetypal concerns of radical environmentalists in other cultural contexts are in fact quite different. The German Greens, for example, have elaborated a devastating critique of industrial society which turns on the acceptance of environmental limits to growth. Pointing to the intimate links between industrialization, militarization, and conquest, the Greens argue that economic growth in the West has historically rested on the economic and ecological exploitation of the Third World. Rudolf Bahro is characteristically blunt:

> The working class here [in the West] is the richest lower class in the world. And if I look at the problem from the point of view of the whole of humanity, not just from that of Europe, then I must say that the metropolitan working class is the worst exploiting class in history. . . . What made poverty bearable in eighteenth or nineteenth-century Europe was the prospect of escaping it through exploitation of the periphery. But this is no longer a possibility, and continued industrialism in the Third World will mean poverty for whole generations and hunger for millions.[9]

Here the roots of global ecological problems lie in the disproportionate share of resources consumed by the industrialized countries as a whole *and* the urban elite within the Third World. Since it is impossible to reproduce an industrial monoculture worldwide, the ecological movement in the West must begin by cleaning up its own act. The Greens advocate the creation of a "no growth" economy, to be achieved by scaling down current (and clearly unsustainable) consumption levels. This radical shift in consumption and production patterns requires the creation of alternate economic and political structures—smaller in scale and more amenable to social participation—but it rests equally on a shift in cultural values. The expansionist character of modern Western man will have to give way to an ethic of renunciation and self-limitation, in which spiritual and communal values play an increasing role in sustaining social life. This revolution in cultural values, however, has as its point of departure an understanding of environmental processes quite different from deep ecology.

Many elements of the Green program find a strong resonance in countries such as India, where a history of Western colonialism and industrial development has benefited only a tiny elite while exacting tremendous social and environmental costs. The ecological battles presently being fought in India have as their epicenter the conflict over nature between the subsistence and largely rural sector and the vastly more powerful commercial-industrial sector. Perhaps the most celebrated of these battles concerns the Chipko (Hug the Tree) movement, a peasant movement against deforestation in the Himalayan foothills. Chipko is only one of several movements that have sharply questioned the nonsustainable demand being placed on the land and vegetative base by urban centers and industry. These include opposition to large dams by displaced peasants, the conflict between small artisan fishing and large-scale trawler fishing for export, the countrywide movements against commercial forest operations, and opposition to industrial pollution among downstream agricultural and fishing communities.[10]

Two features distinguish these environmental movements from their Western counterparts. First, for the sections of society most critically affected by environmental degradation—poor and landless peasants, women, and tribals—it is a question of sheer survival, not of enhancing the quality of life. Second, and as a consequence, the environmental solutions they articulate deeply involve questions of equity as well as economic and political redistribution. Highlighting these differences, a leading Indian environmentalist stresses that "environmental protection per se is of least concern to most of these groups. Their main concern is about the use of the environment and who should benefit from it."[11] They seek to wrest control of nature away from the state and the industrial sector and place it in the hands of rural communities who live within that environment but are increasingly denied access to it. These communities have far more basic needs, their demands on the environment are far less intense, and they can draw upon a reservoir of cooperative social institutions and local ecological knowledge in managing the "commons"— forests, grasslands, and the waters—on a sustainable basis. If colonial and capitalist expansion has both accentuated social inequalities and signaled a precipitous fall in ecological wisdom, an alternate ecology must rest on an alternate society and polity as well.

This brief overview of German and Indian environmentalism has some major implications for deep ecology. Both German and Indian environmental traditions allow for a greater integration of ecological concerns with livelihood and work. They also place a greater emphasis on equity and social justice (both within individual countries and on a global scale) on the grounds that in the absence of social regeneration environmental regeneration has very little chance of succeeding. Finally, and perhaps most significantly, they have escaped the preoccupation with wilderness preservation so characteristic of American cultural and environmental history.

IV A HOMILY

In 1958, the economist J. K. Galbraith referred to overconsumption as the unasked question of the American conservation movement. There is a marked selectivity, he wrote, "in the conservationist's approach to materials consumption. If we are concerned about our great appetite for materials, it is plausible to seek to increase the supply, to decrease waste, to make better use of the stocks available, and to develop substitutes. But what of the appetite itself? Surely this is the ultimate source of the problem. If it continues its geometric course, will it not one day have to be restrained? Yet in the literature of the resource problem this is the forbidden question. Over it hangs a nearly total silence."[12]

The consumer economy and society have expanded tremendously in the three decades since Galbraith penned these words; yet his criticisms are nearly as valid today. I have said "nearly," for there are some hopeful signs. Within the environmental movement several dispersed groups are working to develop ecologically benign technologies and to encourage less wasteful life styles. Moreover, outside the self-defined boundaries of American environmentalism, opposition to the permanent war economy is being carried on by a peace movement that has a distinguished history and impeccable moral and political credentials.

It is precisely these (to my mind, most hopeful) components of the American social scene that are missing from deep ecology. In their widely noticed book, Bill Devall and George Sessions make no mention of militarization or the movements for peace, while activists whose practical focus is on developing ecologically responsible life styles (e.g., Wendell Berry) are derided as "falling short of deep ecological awareness."[13] A truly radical ecology in the American context ought to work toward a synthesis of the appropriate technology, alternate life style, and peace movements. By making the (largely spurious) anthropocentric-biocentric distinction central to the debate, deep ecologists may have appropriated the moral high ground, but they are at the same time doing a serious disservice to American and global environmentalism.

NOTES

1 Kirkpatrick Sale, "The Forest for the Trees: Can Today's Environmentalists Tell the Difference," *Mother Jones* 11, no. 8 (November 1986): 26.
2 One of the major criticisms I make in this essay concerns deep ecology's lack of concern with inequalities *within* human society. In the article in which he coined the term *deep ecology,* Naess himself expresses concerns about inequalities between and within nations. However, his concern with social cleavages and their impact on resource utilization patterns

and ecological destruction is not very visible in the later writings of deep ecologists. See Arne Naess, "The Shallow and the Deep, Long-Range Ecology Movement: A Summary," *Inquiry* 16 (1973): 96 (I am grateful to Tom Birch for this reference).

3 Gary Snyder, quoted in Sale, "The Forest for the Trees," p. 32. See also Dave Foreman, "A Modest Proposal for a Wilderness System," *Whole Earth Review*, no. 53 (Winter 1986–87): 42–45.

4 See Centre for Science and Environment, *India: The State of the Environment 1982: A Citizen's Report* (New Delhi: Centre for Science and Environment, 1982); R. Sukumar, "Elephant-Man Conflict in Karnataka," in Cecil Saldanha, ed., *The State of Karnataka's Environment* (Bangalore: Centre for Taxonomic Studies, 1985). For Africa, see the brilliant analysis by Helge Kjekshus, *Ecology Control and Economic Development in East African History* (Berkeley: University of California Press, 1977).

5 Daniel Janzen, "The Future of Tropical Ecology," *Annual Review of Ecology and Systematics* 17 (1986): 305–6; emphasis added.

6 Joseph Sax, *Mountains Without Handrails: Reflections on the National Parks* (Ann Arbor: University of Michigan Press, 1980), p. 42. Cf. also Peter Schmitt, *Back to Nature: The Arcadian Myth in Urban America* (New York: Oxford University Press, 1969), and Alfred Runte, *National Parks: The American Experience* (Lincoln: University of Nebraska Press, 1979).

7 Samuel Hays, "From Conservation to Environment: Environmental Politics in the United States Since World War Two," *Environmental Review* 6 (1982): 21. See also the same author's book entitled *Beauty, Health and Permanence: Environmental Politics in the United States, 1955–85* (New York: Cambridge University Press, 1987).

8 Roderick Nash, *Wilderness and the American Mind,* 3rd ed. (New Haven: Yale University Press, 1982).

9 Rudolf Bahro, *From Red to Green* (London: Verso Books, 1984).

10 For an excellent review, see Anil Agarwal and Sunita Narain, eds., *India: The State of the Environment, 1984–85: A Citizens Report* (New Delhi: Centre for Science and Environment, 1985). Cf. also Ramachandra Guha, *The Unquiet Woods: Ecological Change and Peasant Resistance in the Indian Himalaya* (Berkeley: University of California Press, 1990).

11 Anil Agarwal, "Human-Nature Interactions in a Third World Country," *The Environmentalist* 6, no. 3 (1986): 167.

12 John Kenneth Galbraith, "How Much Should a Country Consume?" in Henry Jarrett, ed., *Perspectives on Conservation* (Baltimore: Johns Hopkins Press, 1958), pp. 91–92.

13 Devall and Sessions, *Deep Ecology,* p. 122. For Wendell Berry's own assessment of deep ecology, see his "Amplications: Preserving Wildness," *Wilderness* 50 (Spring 1987): 39–40, 50–54.

QUESTIONS

1 Is overconsumption by the industrialized world and by urban elites in the third world one of the most serious ecological problems we face today? If yes, what changes would you be willing to make in your life to help solve the problem?

2 Should the overcoming of inequalities in a society have priority over concerns such as the preservation of wilderness areas?

SUGGESTED ADDITIONAL READINGS FOR CHAPTER 11

ATTFIELD, ROBIN: *Environmental Ethics: An Overview for the Twenty-First Century.* Oxford: Polity Press, in association with Blackwell Publishing Ltd., 2003. Writing for both students and scholars, Attfield presents and critiques some of the central positions in environmental ethics. He then discusses such topics as sustainable development, the global community, and global citizenship.

BECKERMAN, WILFRED, and JOANNA PASEK, eds.: *Justice, Posterity, and the Environment.* Oxford: Oxford University Press, 2001. Beckerman and Pasek address questions raised by conflicts of interest—between different generations, between rich and poor nations, and between different groups within the same nation—when environmental policy decisions have to be made. Their focus is on the ethical aspects of environmental policy decision making rather than simply on the economic ones.

Environmental Ethics. This journal, identifying itself as "An Interdisciplinary Journal Dedicated to the Philosophical Aspects of Environmental Problems," began publication in 1979. It is an invaluable source of material relevant to the issues under discussion in this chapter.

Hypatia: A Journal of Feminist Philosophy, vol. 6, Spring 1991. Karen J. Warren was guest editor for this special issue, which provides a collection of philosophical articles on ecological feminism.

LIST, PETER C., ed.: *Radical Environmentalism: Philosophy and Tactics.* Belmont, Calif.: Wadsworth, 1993. This collection of readings deals first with so-called radical environmental philosophies (e.g., deep ecology and ecofeminism) and then deals with the activism and tactics of radical environmentalists.

SESSIONS, GEORGE, ed.: *Deep Ecology for the 21st Century.* Boston: Shambhala, 1995. This collection of thirty-nine articles provides a wide range of perspectives on deep ecology. The writings of Arne Naess are especially featured.

SHIVA, VANDANA: "Ecological Balance in an Era of Globalization." In Nicholas Low, ed., *Global Ethics and Environment.* London and New York: Routledge, 1999. Shiva argues that globalization and liberalized trade and investment have created growth by destroying the environment and local, sustainable livelihoods as pollution-intensive industries are relocated in third-world countries. The result is an unjust distribution of good and bad local environment as the environmental costs are exported to the third world while the wealthier countries reap the benefits of globalization.

STONE, CHRISTOPHER D.: *Earth and Other Ethics: The Case for Moral Pluralism.* New York: Harper & Row, 1987. Arguing for a need to rethink some of the most basic assumptions of ethics, Stone says that no one ethical framework can provide answers to all our ethical dilemmas, including those centered on the environment.

WENZ, PETER S.: *Environmental Ethics Today.* New York and Oxford: Oxford University Press, 2001. In this wide-ranging introduction to environmental ethics, Wenz integrates current facts, real controversies, and individual stories into his discussion of abstract philosophical concepts and positions in environmental ethics. Topics include economic globalization, biodiversity, genetic engineering, and pollution permits for corporations.

About the Contributors

Andrew Altman is Professor of Philosophy at Georgia State University.

George J. Annas is Edward R. Utley Professor at the Boston University School of Public Health, where he is also Chair of the Department of Health Law, Bioethics, and Human Rights.

William F. Baxter was William Benjamin Scott and Luna M. Scott Professor of Law at Stanford University.

Max Borders is Managing Editor of TCSDaily.com and adjunct scholar with the National Center for Policy Analysis (NCPA).

Dan W. Brock is Professor of Medical Ethics and Director, Division of Medical Ethics and University Program in Ethics and Health, Department of Social Medicine, Harvard University.

Daniel Callahan is a cofounder of The Hastings Center (Garrison, New York), where he is presently Director of International Programs.

Carl Cohen is Professor of Philosophy at the University of Michigan, Ann Arbor.

John Corvino is Assistant Professor of Philosophy at Wayne State University (Michigan).

Bill Devall is Professor Emeritus of Sociology at Humboldt State University (California).

David Dolinko is Professor of Law at the UCLA School of Law.

Nancy Fraser is Henry A. and Louise Loeb Professor of Political and Social Science at the New School for Social Research (New York City).

R. G. Frey is Professor of Philosophy at Bowling Green State University (Ohio).

Maggie Gallagher is President of the Institute for Marriage and Public Policy (Washington, D.C.).

Robert E. Goodin is Professor of Philosophy at the Research School of Social Sciences, Australian National University.

Ramachandra Guha, formerly Professorial Fellow at the the Centre for Contemporary Studies, Nehru Memorial Museum and Library (New Delhi, India), is now a full-time author and columnist.

Garrett Hardin was Professor of Human Ecology at the University of California, Santa Barbara.

John Hospers is Emeritus Professor of Philosophy at the University of Southern California.

Timothy Howell is Associate Professor of Psychiatry at the University of Wisconsin, Madison.

Alison M. Jaggar is Professor of Philosophy and Women's Studies at the University of Colorado at Boulder.

Charles R. Lawrence III is Professor of Law at Georgetown University Law Center.

Aldo Leopold, a prominent conservationist, was a professional forester in his early years and later became Professor of Game Management at the University of Wisconsin.

Margaret Olivia Little is Associate Professor of Philosophy and Senior Research Scholar, Kennedy Institute of Ethics, Georgetown University.

Helen E. Longino is Professor of Philosophy at the University of Minnesota.

David Luban is Frederick J. Haas Professor of Law and Philosophy at Georgetown University Law Center.

Don Marquis is Professor of Philosophy at the University of Kansas.

Howard McGary is Professor of Philosophy at Rutgers, The State University of New Jersey.

Diane E. Meier is Professor in the Department of Geriatrics and Adult Development and also Catherine Gaisman Professor of Medical Ethics, Mount Sinai School of Medicine (New York).

Franklin G. Miller is Head, Unit on Clinical Research, Department of Clinical Bioethics, National Institutes of Health.

Ethan A. Nadelmann is Executive Director of the Drug Policy Alliance.

Jan Narveson is Professor of Philosophy at the University of Waterloo (Ontario, Canada).

Stephen Nathanson is Professor of Philosophy at Northeastern University.

Kai Nielsen is Professor Emeritus of Philosophy at the University of Calgary (Alberta, Canada) and Adjunct Professor of Philosophy at Concordia University (Montreal, Quebec).

Thomas Pogge is Professorial Research Fellow, Centre for Applied Philosophy and Public Ethics, Australian National University, and also Associate Professor of Philosophy at Columbia University.

Louis P. Pojman was Professor of Philosophy at the United States Military Academy.

Stephen G. Potts, a physician, is in the Department of Psychological Medicine, Royal Infirmary of Edinburgh (Scotland).

Igor Primoratz is Professor Emeritus of Philosophy at the Hebrew University, Jerusalem, and Principal Research Fellow at the Centre for Applied Philosophy and Public Ethics, University of Melbourne.

Vincent C. Punzo is Professor Emeritus of Philosophy at Saint Louis University.

James Rachels was Professor of Philosophy at the University of Alabama at Birmingham.

Jonathan Rauch is Writer in Residence at the Brookings Institution, a senior writer for *National Journal,* and a correspondent for *The Atlantic Monthly.*

Tom Regan is Professor Emeritus of Philosophy at North Carolina State University.

Jeffrey Reiman is William Fraser McDowell Professor of Philosophy at American University.

Bernard E. Rollin is University Distinguished Professor of Philosophy and University Bioethicist at Colorado State University.

Amartya Sen is Lamont University Professor and Professor of Economics and Philosophy at Harvard University and is also Fellow of Trinity College, Cambridge University.

George Sessions is Professor Emeritus of Philosophy at Sierra College (California).

Daniel Shapiro is Associate Professor of Philosophy at West Virginia University.

Peter Singer is Ira W. DeCamp Professor of Bioethics, Center for Human Values, Princeton University.

Tony Smith is Professor of Philosophy at Iowa State University.

Thomas S. Szasz is Professor Emeritus of Psychiatry at the SUNY Upstate Medical University (Syracuse).

Judith Jarvis Thomson is Professor of Philosophy at the Massachusetts Institute of Technology.

Jeremy Waldron is Maurice and Hilda Friedman Professor of Law at Columbia University School of Law, where he is also Director of the Center for Law and Philosophy.

Mary Anne Warren is Professor Emerita of Philosophy at San Francisco State University.

David T. Watts is Associate Professor of Medicine at the University of Wisconsin, Madison.

Peter S. Wenz is Professor Emeritus of Philosophy at the University of Illinois at Springfield.

Mark R. Wicclair is Professor of Philosophy and Adjunct Professor of Community Medicine at West Virginia University and is Adjunct Professor of Medicine and Center for Bioethics and Health Law faculty, University of Pittsburgh.

James Q. Wilson is Ronald Reagan Professor of Public Policy at Pepperdine University (California).

Iris M. Young is Professor of Political Science at the University of Chicago.

Matt Zwolinski is Assistant Professor of Philosophy at the University of San Diego, where he is also Affiliated Scholar at the Institute for Law and Philosophy.